# Foundations of
# MARKETING

# Foundations of MARKETING

## FIFTH CANADIAN EDITION

M. DALE BECKMAN

DAVID L. KURTZ

LOUIS E. BOONE

## DRYDEN

Dryden Canada
A Division of Holt, Rinehart and Winston of Canada, Limited

Toronto Montreal Orlando Fort Worth San Diego
Philadelphia London Sydney Tokyo

**Canadian Cataloguing in Publication Data**
Beckman, M. Dale, 1934–
    Foundations of marketing

5th Canadian ed.
Includes index.
ISBN 0-03-922784-7

1. Marketing.  I. Kurtz, David L.  II. Boone,
Louis E.  III. Title.

HF5415.B43 1992      658.8      C91-094413-X


Editorial Director: Scott Duncan
Acquisitions Editor: Donna Muirhead
Developmental Editor: Cheryl Teelucksingh
Editorial Assistant: Yolanta Cwik
Director of Publishing Services: Steve Lau
Editorial Manager: Liz Radojkovic
Editorial Co-ordinator: Marcel Chiera
Production Manager: Sue-Ann Becker
Production Assistant: Denise Wake
Copy Editor: Riça Night
Cover Design: Dave Peters
Interior Design: Robert Garbutt Productions
Technical Art: Louisa Schulz/Dave Peters
Photo Editor: Jane Affleck
Cover Photograph: Mercer/Focus/Tony Stone Worldwide
Typesetting and Assembly: Compeer Typographic Inc.
Printing and Binding: Arcata Graphics Company

1 2 3 4 5   96 95 94 93 92

*To Bobby, a full partner*

# Preface

This fifth Canadian edition of *Foundations of Marketing* brings a fresh approach to the exposition of the subject. It builds on the strengths of the past four editions, which have been acclaimed by students for the interesting and relevant way that the topic is described.

New research and contemporary thinking about marketing have changed the way we have approached a number of topics. For example, this edition reflects recent research that questions the traditional sales–production–marketing era historical approach. A new approach has been written to more realistically portray the issues of product and sales orientation. And, beyond simply describing marketing orientation, the book explains the limitations that have brought the concept into question and shows what is required to really make it work.

This edition also makes a special effort to address the topics of marketing strategy, marketing planning, and the marketing mix in a manner that is consistent, clear, and pedagogically appropriate. Too often the term *strategy* is used so loosely that there is a great deal of confusion as to what it really means. Similarly, marketing planning and the marketing mix are often interchanged with confusing effects. *Foundations of Marketing*, fifth edition avoids the use of these terms until they can be introduced and developed properly. Then the topics are developed in a clear and sequential fashion: the strategy of the firm, of which marketing strategy is an essential component, is shown to be paramount. A marketing plan is required to implement the marketing strategy, and the marketing mix is part of the marketing plan.

Special attention is also given to the idea of the marketing mix. This powerful concept is sometimes simplified to the extent that students miss its importance. The idea of synergy between the mix elements is examined along with the complexity brought about by various combinations of the mix. Recognizing that students can readily handle it, more meaningful terminology is utilized to identify the mix elements.

This spirit of contemporary realism has been applied throughout the book. In another example, as the marketing research chapter is developed, the unfolding of an actual research project is intertwined as an example. Also, in response to suggestions of previous users, the book has been shortened, and some chapters have been reduced, or combined. Many other chapters have been extensively revised, or completely rewritten.

In addition to coverage of the standard marketing topics *Foundations of Marketing* has special chapters devoted to the marketing of services, not-for-profit marketing, and international marketing. Furthermore, the book introduces and elaborates the concept of *total quality management in marketing*. The final chapter shows how this concept can serve as a basis for the control and direction of the marketing process. Such an approach is unique to this book.

In the text, there are a number of special features that will add interest and assist the student:

- **Applying the Concepts** boxes help to relate theory to business practices.
- **Issues in International Marketing** features bring the important topic of the global market to students' attention throughout the course. These are then reinforced by a rewritten international marketing chapter.
- **Profiles** appear at the end of each part to present the careers of former marketing students.
- A running glossary found in the margin area beside the text makes definitions of key terms easier to locate.
- The addition of colour throughout this edition sets in place a consistent pattern of reference allowing for features to be easily identified.
- Special attention has been paid to layout, which was designed to aid learning. The sequence of topics, from most important to subsidiary matters, are clearly delineated by typeface and colour. Photographs have been included to add interest for the reader. They are also captioned in order to tie in directly with the text. The captions sometimes pose questions that relate to photos and text.
- A range of comprehensive as well as shorter **cases** are included. The cases provide opportunities for extensive or brief case discussions, as well as complete written assignments.
- **The Foundations of Marketing** disk computer exercises provide students with the opportunity to practice working with the concepts.

*Foundations of Marketing* is available in a complete educational package designed for both instructor and students. The package includes:

- **Study Guide.** Clark Green's work has led to an outstanding and comprehensive aid for students. It includes review exercises to be done by the students as well as many study questions and cases that can be discussed in class. A special feature of the study guide is an extensive and comprehensive marketing project that unfolds with the textual materials. This provides a thread that requires students to tie theory and practice together. Experience has proven this to be a powerful learning aid.
- **Instructor's Manual.** Completely rewritten by Vivian Vaupshas of McGill University, this extensive manual includes lecture suggestions, a film guide, reference materials, and suggestions for using the transparency manuals and acetates.
- **Test Bank.** Two thousand items are organized into quiz-type and comprehensive exam-type questions. The test bank is available on floppy disk and in printed format.
- **Transparencies.** A complete colour transparency package is available to adopters.
- **Videos and Videos Cases.** A package of more than twenty first class videos tied specifically to the concepts of the textbook is available to adopters of this book. To enhance the learning process, matching cases are included at the end of chapters in the text so that students can read about the issues and undertake written or oral assignments before the video is shown.

*Foundations of Marketing*, fifth Canadian edition, provides a contemporary and thorough exposition of marketing in a highly readable and enjoyable format. The usefulness of the book is greatly enhanced by the associated teaching and learning materials.

## ACKNOWLEDGEMENTS

The authors gratefully acknowledge the contributions of the many people involved in this project. In particular, we wish to thank Dr. Ed Bruning for his contributions to the revision of the channels and physical distribution chapters. We also express our appreciation to Doug Strang for his research assistance. Thanks also to the authors and researchers of the cases included. A great amount of initiative and effort is represented in these fine cases.

Our thanks also go to many colleagues across Canada who have reviewed portions of the book:

| | |
|---|---|
| J. Brown | Georgian College of Applied Art and Technology |
| W. Carlson | Southern Alberta Institute of Technology |
| F. Crane | Dalhousie University |
| J. Dart | University of Saskatchewan |
| S. Edgett | Brock University |
| J.D. Forbes | University of British Columbia |
| D. Gardiner | University of British Columbia |
| J. Graham | University of Calgary |
| C. Greene | Lethbridge University |
| T. Goddard | Conestoga College |
| P. Larson | University of Alberta |
| G. Smith | Humber College |
| R. Tangri | Saint Mary's University |
| V. Vaupshas | McGill University |
| A. Walker | Ryerson Polytechnical Institute |
| P.P. Yannopoulos | Brock University |

...and marketing instructors at Centennial College.

Special thanks go to the excellent professionals at HBJ-Holt for their dedication to the book. In particular our thanks go to Cheryl Teelucksingh for her diligence and special efforts under difficult conditions, to Donna Muirhead, Marcel Chiera, and Sue-Ann Becker, and to Riça Night, who copy edited the book.

M. Dale Beckman
Professor and Head
International Business Program
School of Business
The University of Victoria
Victoria, B.C.

David L. Kurtz
Department Head and
R.A. and Vivian Young Chairholder
University of Arkansas
Fayetteville, Arkansas

Louis E. Boone
Professor of Business Administration
University of South Alabama
Mobile, Alabama

March 1992

## Publisher's Note to Students and Instructors

This textbook is a key component of your course. If you are the instructor of this course, you undoubtedly considered a number of texts carefully before choosing this as the one that would work best for your students and you. The authors and publishers spent considerable time and money to ensure its high quality, and we appreciate your recognition of this effort and accomplishment. Please note the copyright statement.

If you are a student, we are confident that this text will help you to meet the objectives of your course. It will also become a valuable addition to your personal library.

Since we want to hear what you think about this book, please be sure to send us the stamped reply card at the end of the text. Your input will help us to continue to publish high-quality books for your courses.

# Brief Contents

# Contents

Part One
**Marketing and Its Environment**

Part Two
**Foundations of the Marketing Plan**

Part Three
**Consumer
Behaviour**

Part Five
**Pricing**

**Cases**

# PART ONE

# Marketing and Its Environment

CHAPTER 1
## The Nature of Marketing

●

CHAPTER 2
## The Environment for Marketing Decisions

The fundamental philosophy of marketing is that an organization should orient itself to serve the customer's needs. Part One of *Foundations of Marketing* shows why marketing must identify and respond to these needs. These chapters also provide essential definitions and explain some of the basic concepts on which marketing is based. As well, the relationship of marketing to society at large is explored.

## CHAPTER 1

# The Nature of Marketing

## CHAPTER OBJECTIVES

1. To define marketing and describe its primary nature.
2. To explain the types of utility and the role played by marketing in their creation.
3. To show the scope of marketing.
4. To contrast activities in each of the three orientations of business in the marketing domain.
5. To position marketing as one of the basic business functions.

**A** RECENT advertisement about the merger of two large law firms has set the competitive world of lawyers on its ear. The ad was catchy — not the bland variety that one is used to seeing from legal firms. "On October 2nd, one of the most significant legal happenings in Canada was settled out of court," the heading reads. The copy then describes the advantages of this new larger firm for clients.

In the old days — two or three years ago — you wouldn't have seen such a flashy advertisement. There would have been little fanfare about the announcement. But this is a sign that law firms are slowly catching on to modern marketing methods.

After the relaxation of government regulations lawyers are cautiously moving toward more marketing of their services. And the fact that they are doing so seems to be having positive effects on the services offered to customers.

There is a more competitive spirit, which is supported by clients who are shopping around more, no longer blindly staying with one law firm. The firms, for their part, are branching out. Some are offering new services, such as a planner and consultants on free trade. One firm tried to offer a $25.00 voucher to new clients (vetoed by the law society).

Other activities are gaining speed. Eaton's ran a telephone campaign, soliciting its credit card members to sign up for its $10-a-month prepaid legal plan. Another firm

*Convenience stores are an example of time, place, and ownership utility. They offer a wide range of goods, from dairy products to automotive-care goods, and remain open when the specialized dealers for these items have closed for the day.*

offered a prepaid plan through employers — as an employee benefit — at special group rates.

Many of these beginning marketing efforts are not yet very sophisticated. However, it is a welcome sight for the paying public to be getting more information about the lawyers that serve us. And marketing competition is producing a greater variety of services that consumers may choose from. The impact of marketing on an industry can be profound. It increases competition, improves service to customers, and will help to ensure that the firm with better services and more customer orientation will prosper accordingly.[1]

# Introduction

All business organizations perform two basic operating functions — they produce a good or a service, and they market it. This is true of all firms — from large corporations such as Canadian Airlines and Bombardier to the students who run a College Pro Painters franchise. Production and marketing are the very essence of economic life in any society.

## Production and Marketing Create Utility for the Consumer

**utility**    The want-satisfying power of a product or service.

Through the production and marketing of desired goods and services, businesses fulfill the needs of society, their customers, and their owners. They create **utility**, which may be defined as *the want-satisfying power of a product or service*. There are four basic kinds of utility – form, time, place, and ownership.

*Form utility* is created when the firm converts raw materials and component inputs into finished products and services. Glass, steel, fabrics, rubber, and other components are combined to form a new Mazda RX–7 or Taurus. Cotton, thread, and buttons are converted into GWG jeans. Sheet music, musical instruments, musicians, a conductor, and the facilities of Roy Thomson Hall are converted into a performance by the Toronto Symphony Orchestra. Although marketing inputs may be important in specifying consumer and audience preferences, the actual creation of form utility is the responsibility of the production function of the organization.

*Time, place*, and *ownership*, the other utilities, are created by marketing. They are created when products and services are available to the consumer when the person wants to purchase them (time utility) and at a convenient location (place utility), and where facilities are available whereby title to the product or service may be transferred at the time of purchase (ownership utility).

## Consumers: The Focus in Creating Utility

If an organization does not create utility, it will not survive. The design and marketing of want-satisfying goods, services, and ideas is the foundation for the creation of utility. The necessary focus of the successful firm in the creation of utility has been well stated by Peter Drucker, an expert on business management:

> If we want to know what a business is we have to start with its purpose. And its purpose must lie outside the business itself. In fact, it must lie in society since a business enterprise is an organ of society. There is one valid definition of business purpose: to create a customer.[2]

How does an organization "create" a customer? Professors Guiltinan and Paul explain:

> Essentially, "creating" a customer means identifying needs in the marketplace, finding out which needs the organization can profitably serve, and developing an offering to convert potential buyers into customers. Marketing managers are responsible for most of the activities necessary to create the customers the organization wants. These activities include:

- identifying customer needs
- designing products and services that meet those needs
- communicating information about those products and services to prospective buyers
- making the products or services available at times and places that meet customer's needs
- pricing the products to reflect costs, competition, and customers' ability to buy
- providing for the necessary service and follow-up to ensure customer satisfaction after the purchase.[3]

## The Essence of Marketing

The essence of marketing is the **exchange process**. This is the process by which two or more parties give something of value to one another to satisfy felt needs.[4] In many cases, the item is a tangible good, such as a newspaper, a hand calculator, or a pair of shoes. In other cases, intangible services, such as a car wash, transportation, or a

**exchange process** The process by which two or more parties give something of value to one another to satisfy felt needs.

*The essence of the marketing function is exchange. The tomato vendor (right) and the urban mall (opposite) both share this function. The mall may have a more complex organization, with a series of interdependent systems that work together, but it still answers the basic need to exchange goods.*

concert performance, are exchanged for money. In still other instances, funds or time donations may be offered to political candidates, a Red Cross office, or a church or synagogue.

The marketing function is both simple and direct in subsistence-level economies. For example, assume that a primitive society consists solely of Person A and Person B. Assume also that the only elements of their standard of living are food, clothing, and shelter. The two live in adjoining caves on a mountainside. They weave their own clothes and tend their own fields independently. They are able to subsist even though their standard of living is minimal.

Person A is an excellent weaver but a poor farmer, while Person B is an excellent farmer but a poor weaver. In this situation, it would be wise for each to specialize in the line of work that he or she does best. The net result would then be a greater total production of both clothing and food. In other words, specialization and division of labour will lead to a production surplus. But neither A nor B is any better off until they *trade* the products of their individual labour, thereby creating the exchange process.

Exchange is the origin of marketing activity. In fact, marketing has been described as "the process of creating and resolving exchange relationships."[5] When there is a need to exchange goods, the natural result is marketing effort on the part of the people involved.

As Wroe Alderson, a leading marketing theorist, has said, "It seems altogether reasonable to describe the development of exchange as a great invention which helped to start primitive man on the road to civilization."[6]

While the cave-dweller example is simplistic, it does point up the essence of the marketing function. Today's complex society may have a more complicated

exchange process, but the basic concept is the same: production is not meaningful until a system of marketing has been established. Perhaps the adage "Nothing happens until somebody sells something"[7] sums it up best.

## Marketing Defined

Ask five persons to define marketing and you are likely to get five definitions. Because of the visibility of personal selling and advertising, many respondents will say that marketing is selling, or that marketing is advertising. But marketing is much more comprehensive. "*Marketing is the process of planning and executing the conception, pricing, promotion and distribution of ideas, goods, and services to create exchanges that satisfy individual and organizational objectives.*"[8]

This definition implies much more than you may at first realize. The rest of this book is required to elaborate it. Note, however, that it applies not only to business but also to nonprofit organizations. Note also that the definition is specific in pointing out that the exchanges created by marketing activities must satisfy individual (consumer) objectives, as well as organizational objectives. In fact, professional marketers have found that success comes about much more easily when planning starts with a thorough analysis of customers and their needs. This is such an important concept, with so many ramifications, that we will spend the next section elaborating it.

**marketing** The process of planning and executing the conception, pricing, promotion, and distribution of ideas, goods, and services to create exchanges that satisfy individual and organizational objectives.

## Three Types of Business Orientation

Not all companies have an orientation that fits the foregoing *market-oriented* definition. Some are *product-oriented*, and others are *sales-oriented*.[9]

**An example of product orientation**

Source: *Calgary Herald*, (September 6, 1989). Copyright © 1989 United Feature Syndicate, Inc.

## Product and/or production orientation

In a product-oriented firm, the emphasis is on the product itself rather than on the consumer's needs. For the production-oriented firm, the dominant considerations in product design are those of ease or cheapness of production. In either case, market considerations are ignored or de-emphasized. Firms stress production of goods or services,[10] then look for people to purchase them. The prevailing attitude of this type of firm is that a good product will sell itself. Such a strategy is very limiting, for it assumes that the producer's tastes and values are the same as those of the market. Often a firm does not consider changing from this narrow approach until it runs into trouble.

## Sales orientation

A sales orientation is an advance from a product orientation. The firm is still quite product-oriented, but it recognizes that the world will not " beat a path to [its] door" to purchase its products. Therefore, it focuses its marketing efforts on developing a strong sales force to convince consumers to buy. "Get the customer to fit the company's offerings" could be a motto of such a sales-oriented strategy. Thus, to be successful, what you really need is an aggressive, high-powered sales organization and advertising program. Clearly, good, persuasive communication is an important part of a marketing plan. However selling is only one component of marketing. As marketing expert Theodore Levitt has pointed out, "marketing is as different from selling as chemistry is from alchemy, astronomy from astrology, chess from checkers."[11]

## Market orientation

Many firms have discovered that the product and sales orientations are quite limiting. They have found that it makes a great deal of sense to *pay careful attention to understanding customer needs and objectives and then make the business serve the interests of the customer rather than trying to make the customer buy what the business wants to produce.* A primary task under a market orientation, then, is to develop ways to research and understand various aspects of the market.

A market-oriented strategy can produce any of the good effects of the other two orientations, but it avoids their drawbacks. In addition, it can identify new opportunities and avoid nasty surprises as changes occur in the market.

A·P·P·L·Y·I·N·G  T·H·E  C·O·N·C·E·P·T·S

## *Customer Calls the Tune in Financial Institutions*

Financial institutions have taken a giant step away from a production orientation toward a market orientation. Once upon a time, customers did their banking at the banks' convenience.

Not any more. Changes came when banks realized that survival is ultimately in customers' hands, says Terry Rapsey, assistant general manager, service quality, at the Canadian Imperial Bank of Commerce.

Financial institutions have tended to develop procedures that were operationally sound but sometimes with little regard for the customer. "It was fine for the short term, " Rapsey says. But that approach would not work if the bank wanted to keep its customers for the long term.

This recognition of the importance of understanding and serving customers instigated wholesale changes internally at CIBC, as policies, procedures, systems, and support were redefined to focus on customer satisfaction. "If a proposed change is thought to be good for the organization and bad for the customer, then we have to rethink [the proposal]" he says.

At the Bank of Montreal, giving customers better access to banking services has priority. Up to 450 branches are now open on Saturdays. New banking hours reflect the requirement in the branch's location.

Downtown sites are often open from 8:30 AM to 5:00 PM to accommodate office workers.

At a time when service charges work against small savings accounts, freezing out children and their piggy-bank savings, the bank has a Junior Plan. This provides no-fee banking for customers 18 years old or younger. The Senior Plan offers a similar package for those 60 and over, and their spouses. A number of other services (such as bill payments, travellers' cheques and Canadian money orders) are also free.

Giving financial advice is a major marketing thrust at Royal Trustco Ltd. of Toronto. "We sit down with customers and give advice. This is the ultimate form of friendliness," says Paul Starita, senior vice president of marketing, personal financial service.

Financial services are also available by appointment during off hours, he says. "Our mobile lending officers have beepers and will meet you anywhere, anytime," he says. When he needed a mortgage recently, Starita contacted a mortgage officer, who met him under an overpass along Ontario's Highway 401. The loan was approved in a nearby McDonald's restaurant.

Source: Excerpted from "Customer Calls the Tune in Financial Institutions," *Financial Post* (May 15, 1989), p. 44.

---

In a market-oriented firm, the marketing function is not something that is tagged on at the end of the process. It takes a primary role right from the beginning of the planning process. A marketing orientation represents a set of processes touching on all aspects of the company.[12] It involves much more than just understanding the customer. Three characteristics make a company market-driven:

1. Information on all important buying influences permeates every corporate function. This means that detailed market knowledge is not the domain of the marketing department alone. A company can be market-oriented only if it completely understands its markets and the people who decide whether to buy its products or services. Customer information must reach all aspects of the organization, including R & D, engineering, manufacturing, and accounting.

2. Strategic and tactical decisions are made interfunctionally and interdivisionally. Functions and divisions of an organization will inevitably have conflicting objectives that mirror distinctions in cultures and modes of operation. The customer-oriented company possesses mechanisms for discovering these differences, encouraging candid discussion, and finding trade-offs that reconcile the various points of view. A good understanding of market needs serves as the basis for final decisions.

*All aspects of an organization must be aware of the needs of its customer base. At the research and development department of De Havilland Aircraft, designers working on new models must be aware of customer requirements relayed by the marketing department. The marketing department, in turn, uses the new design and research initiatives to promote new product lines and inform customers of improvements on existing stock.*

3. Divisions and functions make well–co-ordinated decisions and execute them with a sense of commitment. Marketing should not send a set of specifications to R & D, which then sends finished blueprints and designs to manufacturing, and so on. Joint discussion between functions makes the final company strategy much more relevant to the needs of the market.

## The Marketing Concept: A Guiding Philosophy for Marketing

**marketing concept** An organization-wide focus on providing chosen groups of customers with products that bring optimal satisfaction so as to achieve long-run profits.

The foregoing discussion provides a guiding philosophy for the marketing aspects of organization strategy. This market orientation, commonly known as the **marketing concept**, may be succinctly defined as *an organization-wide focus on providing chosen groups of customers with products that bring optimal satisfaction so as to achieve long-run profits.*

The words "long-run profits" differentiate the marketing concept from policies aimed at short-run profit maximization. The marketing concept, as a philosophy, provides the best chance for success in today's environment. The authors contend that marketing efforts should reflect ethical business practices and be congruent with the needs of society. The focus on consumer needs and the longer-run perspective encourages this.

The marketing concept also requires careful analysis and monitoring of competitors' actions. A company practising the marketing concept holds basic assumptions in relation to its competitors. Management believes that the firm has the capability to compete, that it is not at the mercy of its competitors and is a force of its own. At the same time, it recognises that the firm has to be up to date on its competitors' actions to make sure that it does not lose its competitive edge. An organization that views itself as dominated by others is incapable of taking new initiatives even if it identifies major unsatisfied customer needs.[13]

## I·S·S·U·E·S  I·N  I·N·T·E·R·N·A·T·I·O·N·A·L  M·A·R·K·E·T·I·N·G

### *Procter & Gamble as a Global Competitor*

A major challenge facing marketers in the 1990s is to be successful in a globally competitive world. Procter & Gamble Company entered the decade as a global powerhouse. It has operations in 46 countries — up from 22 countries in 1981 — and markets 160 consumer brands in more than 140 countries. But P&G's success in the international marketplace didn't come easily. In the past, P&G marketed its products abroad in the same way as in their home market, and the strategy didn't always work. In some cases it produced disastrous results. Consider, for example, how P&G erred in marketing disposable diapers in Japan, where the company lost $200 million before realizing that it needed to adjust to local competition.

When P&G introduced Pampers disposable diapers to Japan in 1973, it quickly captured 90 percent of the market. In the early 1980s, though, Japanese competitors Kao and Unicharm introduced superabsorbent diapers. Japanese parents stopped buying Pampers in favour of the more absorbent products. By 1985 P&G's share of the diaper market dropped to 6 percent.

Anxious to turn around the money-losing venture, P&G conducted marketing research to gain a better understanding of Japanese consumers' needs and wants. P&G learned that Japanese parents do not change their babies' diapers as often as their American counterparts do. Japanese consumers also said that better fit and comfort and less bulkiness are important considerations in buying diapers.

Armed with this knowledge, Edwin Artzt, then president of P&G International and now chairman and CEO of the company, created a product development team based in Japan. The Japanese team developed Ultra Pampers Plus, a thinner and more absorbent diaper than the original version. With this product, P&G regained its leadership position in Japan's diaper market.

Whereas P&G once operated as an export-driven multinational — a U.S.–based firm that sold products in foreign markets — today it operates as a world marketer. It has globalized its sources of product innovation by establishing technology centres in Japan, Great Britain, Belgium, Mexico, and Germany. Artzt says P&G plans to continue its "world technology" strategy so that "products, wherever we develop them — whether we develop them in the United States, Japan, or Europe — can be sold throughout the world."

P&G entered the 1990s as a strong global competitor, with 40 percent of its business coming from international sales. By pursuing its new global thrust, it plans to become a stronger competitor, poised to enter the twenty-first century with international sales accounting for 60 percent of its business.

Sources: Alecia Swasy, "At Proctor & Gamble, Change Under Artzt Isn't Just Cosmetic," *Wall Street Journal* (March 5, 1991); Zachary Schiller, Ted Holden, and Mark Maremont, "P&G Goes Global by Acting Like a Local," *Business Week* (August 28, 1989), p. 58; Procter & Gamble, *1990 Annual Report*, pp. 1–7; Laurie Freeman, "Japan Rises to P&G's No. 3 Market," *Advertising Age* (December 10, 1990), p. 42; Laurie Freeman, "P&G Products Immigrate to U.S." *Advertising Age* (October 30, 1989), p. 24.

## Marketing Is for Nonprofit Organizations, Too

Nonbusiness organizations like art galleries, churches, and charities have also found that they can benefit from the application of marketing principles. For instance, the Canadian government is Canada's leading advertiser, spending approximately $91.3 million annually on advertising. The Canadian Forces have well-developed marketing programs for recruiting volunteers; the United Way and other charitable groups have developed considerable marketing expertise; some police departments have used marketing-inspired strategies to improve their image with the public; and we are all familiar with the marketing efforts employed in political campaigns. Most arts organizations now employ a director of marketing. Chapter 20 discusses marketing in nonprofit settings more fully.

# Introduction to the Marketing Process

We have seen that effective marketing starts with gathering information about the consumer. The marketer sets out to make profits by satisfying customer needs with the firm's products.

**marketing functions** Buying, selling, transporting, storing, grading, financing, risk taking, and information collection and dissemination.

Eight **marketing functions** occur in the marketing process: *buying, selling, transporting, storing, grading, financing, risk taking, and information collection and dissemination.* These are inherent to a greater or lesser degree in all marketing transactions. They may be shifted to various members of the channel, or to the customer, but they cannot be eliminated.

Figuratively speaking, management asks itself the following questions:

1. What problems do our customers or potential customers have that our products or services can solve better than those of other suppliers?

2. Who has these problems?

3. What are the particular circumstances, actual or potential, that would suggest modifications in our products, prices, distribution, or communication?

The idea of thinking in terms of providing *solutions to problems* is a very useful one in marketing. It helps considerably in identifying new markets, finding new products for existing customers, finding new customers for existing products, and, very importantly, discovering potential and possibly unsuspected competition.[14] These concepts provide the basis for marketing planning. The next chapter will continue this introduction to marketing by examining how it operates within, and is affected by, the general environment.

# The Study of Marketing

Marketing is a pervasive element in contemporary life. In one form or another, it is close to every person. Three of its most important concerns for students are the following:

1. Marketing costs may be the largest item in the personal budget. Numerous attempts have been made to determine these costs, and most estimates have ranged between 40 and 60 percent. Regardless of the exact cost, however, marketing is obviously a key item in any consumer's budget.

   Cost alone, however, does not indicate the value of marketing. If someone says that marketing costs are too high, that person should be asked, "Relative to what?" The standard of living in Canada is in large part a function of the country's efficient marketing system. When considered in this perspective, the costs of the system seem reasonable. For example, marketing expands sales, thereby spreading fixed production costs over more units of output and reducing total output costs. Reduced production costs offset many marketing costs.

2. Marketing-related occupations account for 25 to 33 percent of the nation's jobs, so it is likely that many students will become marketers. Indeed, marketing opportunities have remained quite strong even during recent periods when many college graduates could not find jobs. History has shown that the demand for effective marketers is relatively unaffected by cyclical economic fluctuations.

3. Marketing provides an opportunity to contribute to society as well as to an individual company. Marketing decisions affect everyone's welfare. Furthermore,

opportunities to advance to decision-making positions come sooner in marketing than in most occupations.

Why study marketing? There are several reasons: Marketing is one of the essential business functions. Marketing affects numerous facets of daily life as well as individuals' future careers and economic well-being. The study of marketing is important because it is relevant to students today and tomorrow. Furthermore, working in marketing requires considerable initiative and creativity. Many find great satisfaction in such work. It is little wonder that marketing is now one of the most popular fields of academic study.

## Summary

This overview of the marketing process has pointed out that the two primary functions of a business organization are production and marketing. Organizations may take one of three orientations toward the marketplace: a product orientation, a sales orientation, or a market orientation. A market orientation results in products and marketing planning that are more attuned toward the needs and objectives of consumers. It is necessary for a market orientation to permeate the entire organization, not just the marketing department, in order for it to significantly affect the marketplace.

Marketing is the process of planning and executing the conception, pricing, promotion, and distribution of ideas, goods, and services to create exchanges that satisfy individual and organizational objectives. The marketing process starts with the gathering of information about the consumer. It then sets out to serve the product-related needs thus identified.

Marketing is one of the essential business functions. The study of marketing is also important because of the pervasiveness of marketing in society. Many choose marketing careers because such work involves much initiative and creativity.

### ■ KEY TERMS

| | | |
|---|---|---|
| utility | product orientation | marketing concept |
| exchange process | sales orientation | marketing functions |
| marketing | market orientation | |

### ■ REVIEW QUESTIONS

**1.** What are the four types of utility? With which is marketing concerned?

**2.** What are the two basic operating functions performed by all business organizations?

**3.** Relate the definition of marketing to the concept of the exchange process.

**4.** Contrast a product orientation and a sales orientation.

**5.** How does a market orientation differ from a product orientation and a sales orientation?

**6.** What is meant by this statement: "The essence of marketing is the exchange process"?

7. Define marketing.
8. What is the underlying philosophy of the marketing concept?

9. How can a firm "create" a customer?
10. In the marketing process, what three key questions should management ask?

# ■ DISCUSSION QUESTIONS AND EXERCISES

1. What types of utility are being created in the following examples?
   a. One-hour cleaners
   b. 7-Eleven convenience food store
2. How would you explain marketing and its importance in the Canadian economy to someone not familiar with the subject?
3. Identify the product and the consumer market in each of the following:
   a. Local cable television firm
   b. Vancouver Canucks hockey team
   c. Planned Parenthood
   d. Milk Marketing Board
4. "Professional marketers have found that success

   c. Michelin Tire factory in Nova Scotia
   d. Annual boat and sports equipment show in local city auditorium
   e. Regional shopping mall
   comes about much more easily when planning starts with a thorough analysis of customers and their needs." Explain and discuss.
5. Give two examples of firms you feel have the following orientations:
   a. Production orientation
   b. Sales orientation
   c. Market orientation
   Defend your answer.

# McDonald's in Moscow

Some companies are fortunate in their ability to attract a target market in nation after nation. The combination of benefits offered satisfies needs and wants present in people regardless of their income, language, or geographic location. Such a firm is McDonald's. World travellers are comforted when they locate the familiar "Golden Arches," realizing that they are assured of receiving known quality levels when they order a Big Mac, fries, and Coke in Milan, London, Tokyo, or Toronto. But could McDonald's succeed in the Soviet Union? George Cohon, president and CEO of McDonald's Restaurants of Canada, has devoted part of his time during a 14-year period, despite his many other obligations and duties, to ensuring just such a success.

During the 1976 Summer Olympics in Montreal, McDonald's loaned one of its buses to help transport visitors and officials to and from the games. Cohon noticed a group of Soviet officials on the bus, struck up a conversation, and ended by inviting them to dinner at the McDonald's across from the Montreal Forum. At the time, it was the busiest McDonald's in the world and Cohon could see that the Soviets were impressed with the efficiency of the operation.

This was the beginning of negotiations for opening a McDonald's in Moscow. The prospect of entering a market with 290 million potential customers drove Cohon to pursue his dream. Cohon was persistent in overcoming the political barriers, until finally he was able to negotiate a joint venture with the Moscow City Council to build and operate 20 McDonald's restaurants in Moscow. On January 31, 1990, the largest McDonald's in the world opened in Pushkin Square, off Gorky Street. Opening-day sales set a new record for a single day's operation, with 30 000 meals served.

At first glance, the Soviet Union did not appear to be a very desirable location for a quick-service operation, since food quality there does not always come up to Western standards and McDonald's prides itself on quality ingredients in its products. Soviet tastes are also quite different from Western tastes, and McDonald's could not be sure the Soviets would savour burgers and fries. Another formidable obstacle was that worker attitudes differ greatly in the Soviet Union, a fact that could potentially slow the quick-service operation to a turtle's pace. Inefficient distribution systems also posed a potential problem, since ingredients and materials might not be available when needed. And probably the best-known problem for Western firms establishing such joint ventures was that doing so meant that large capital sums would have to be invested in the Soviet Union.

One remaining obstacle — and certainly the one of most concern — was the ruble. By law, the ruble cannot be taken out of the Soviet Union, and it is not traded on the world market. Foreign investors who sell their products for rubles cannot therefore get their profits out of the country. But if the products are sold for dollars, nobody except foreign tourists and members of the Soviet elite can afford to purchase them.

So how did McDonald's of Canada expect to ensure that its Soviet product offerings would conform to McDonald's internationally uniform standards and also derive a profit from the venture? Since Soviet food shortages often have less to do with production than with distribution, the McDonald's Soviet operation could succeed only by organizing its own distribution system through its Moscow plant and trucks. The venture would achieve profits by taking a long-run approach. After all, the Soviet joint venture agreement called for the opening of 20 restaurants to begin with in Moscow. McDonald's would pour dollars into the first outlet and into the vast production and distribution network necessary to support it, but the product would be sold for rubles. The rubles would be used to pay all current expenses, such as salaries and materials purchases, and to finance the next outlet. In the future, some of the restaurants would accept only dollars for purchases, and those dollars would be used to make any necessary foreign purchases and to help build McDonald's business in the Soviet Union. Remaining dollars would constitute a profit that could be used in long-term growth strategies in the Soviet Union.

This plan only made it *possible* to make a profit; it did not *guarantee* that a profit would be made. Cohon saw that what interested the Soviets was not only the food but also the know-how that made the operation efficient. McDonald's in Moscow would be an example of Western capitalism at its best, and Cohon knew that the Soviets wanted to experience this as well as taste Western food. While the meat-and-potatoes diet was familiar to them, its presentation and preparation differed considerably from anything the Soviets had ever experienced.

Even though operations in the Soviet Union would resemble other foreign ventures, in that each outlet would begin with a reduced line of foods (no chicken, no breakfasts, no salads), Cohon's task was formidable. McDonald's uses its own particular potato — the Russet Burbank, which has proven to be the best potato for McDonald's french fries. Since this type of potato is not indigenous to the USSR, McDonald's french-fry experts from Holland brought Russet Burbank seed potatoes to the Soviet Union and worked with farmers there to develop a new crop of potatoes for McDonald's fries. Also, since some of the garnishes that are an integral part of the American hamburger, such as mustard and ketchup, are not readily available in the Soviet Union (and, in fact, in some cases, had never been introduced there), McDonald's had to import them initially.

The lack of some ingredients, the distribution problems, and the processing facility requirements prompted McDonald's to build the McComplex, a 100 000-square-foot distribution centre and processing plant in a suburb of Moscow. The facility includes a meat plant, a bakery, a potato plant, a dairy, and quality-assurance labs, as well as other offices and facilities. The McComplex was the first such facility under one roof established by McDonald's to service its local operations.

When a single ad was placed for workers in Moscow, 27 000 people applied for the 630 available jobs. The applicants selected were able to give the public an unaccustomed extra with their service — a smile. McDonald's brought four Soviet managers to Toronto for nine months of extensive training and then took them to Hamburger University in Oak Brook, Illinois, for two weeks. Upon graduation, all four of the trainees were on the Dean's list; one was first in his graduating class. McDonald's strategy was to enable the venture to be Soviet-run and as self-sufficient as possible while operating to McDonald's standards.

The first 50 customers on opening day were children brought in by the Soviet Children's Fund, of which Cohon was made the first non-Soviet member (he was also named president of the Fund's North American chapter). The Children's Fund also received half that day's sales. Outside the restaurant, entertainers helped keep the waiting crowd happy, employees gave them McDonald's flags and pins, and brochures were passed out explaining the many services offered, including wheelchair facilities and diaper-changing areas, as well as how to order. There were also instructions on how to eat what was ordered, since Muscovites were totally unfamiliar with burgers and fries. The clean, brightly lit building was as much an attraction as the food. The eager Muscovites crowded in for a taste of the West's lifestyle — "food, folks, and fun."

Approximately 15 million customers were served in the first year of operation. Escalating raw-ingredient prices (for example, the 700 percent increase in beef prices, which forced McDonald's to raise its restaurant prices) failed to dent business; the Pushkin Square outlet continued to serve approximately 50 000 customers every day. On opening day, Muscovites paid approximately 6 rubles for a McDonald's meal consisting of a Big Mac, french fries, and a Coke. Although the cost was more than the prices charged in state-owned restaurants, McDonald's offered a unique, quality product at a good value for Soviet families.

SOURCES    Jeffrey M. Hertzfeld, "Joint Ventures: Saving the Soviets from *Perestroika*, " *Harvard Business Review* (January–February 1991), pp. 80–91; Paul Hofheinz, "McDonald's Beats Lenin 3 to 1," *Fortune* (December 17, 1990), p. 11; Scott Hume, "How Big Mac Made It to Moscow," *Advertising Age* (January 22, 1990), pp. 16, 51; and Richard A. Melcher, "From Gung-Ho to Uh-Oh," *Business Week* (February 11, 1991), pp. 43–46. Updated information provided by Rem Langan, Senior Director of Marketing and Communications, McDonald's Restaurants of Canada, May 1991.

## Questions

1. Relate McDonald's marketing efforts in the Soviet Union to the marketing process introduction described in Chapter 1.
2. Relate each of the universal functions of marketing to this case.

C H A P T E R   2

# The Environment for Marketing Decisions

## C H A P T E R   O B J E C T I V E S

1. To identify the environmental factors that affect marketing decisions.
2. To explain the major legislative framework that regulates marketing activities.
3. To introduce three categories of competition faced by marketers and outline the issues to consider in developing a competitive strategy.
4. To show how the economic environment has a bearing on marketing planning.
5. To illustrate the association between marketing plans and the technological environment.
6. To demonstrate how the socio-cultural environment influences marketing decisions.

FROM a 60-room motel that opened in 1978 in Belleville, Ontario, Journey's End Motels Corporation has grown to include 114 motels, hotels, and all-suite hotels in Canada and the US. Journey's End has historically enjoyed occupancy levels higher than the industry average.

Despite its remarkable growth, the company has remained true to its original concept: simple, inexpensive rooms in motels and hotels without dining facilities, swimming pools, or even meeting rooms. It was a blueprint that allowed the company to take advantage of the recession in the early 1980s. As travel budgets were slashed, economy hotels and motels threw their doors open to the cost-conscious.

Journey's End is equipped with an excellent antidote for another headache disturbing the hospitality industry: the labour shortage in the service sector. With no need for kitchen staff, a lifeguard, or a sales team to sell meeting rooms, Journey's End needs fewer employees. "Our payroll costs are approximately 15.5% to 17%," says Tom Landers, the firm's executive vice-president. "They would be at least double that in a full-service hotel."

By following this apparently fail-safe formula, the chain has yet to falter. It recently added two new brands to its roster: Journey's End Hotels — each essentially a Journey's End Motel turned on its end — were launched in 1988; and Journey's End Suites — no-frills, all-suite hotels — were introduced in 1989.

Journey's End succeeded initially because its product was designed to be appropriate for the economic circumstances of the time. It continues to flourish because the product strategy serves an ongoing demand in the environment for reasonably priced quality accommodation. Furthermore, the development of new products was based on a good understanding of the current circumstances surrounding consumers' purchase decisions.[1]

# Introduction

The changing environment is constantly creating and destroying business opportunities. Journey's End responded appropriately to environmental opportunity by correctly analyzing and reacting to economic conditions and competitive circumstances. These are two of the five environmental forces we will discuss in this chapter. Environmental forces cannot be controlled by the marketing decision-maker. However, it is essential that they be identified and analyzed, and that their bearing on marketing plans be carefully considered.

The environment for marketing decisions may be classified into five components: the *competitive* environment, the *political and legal* environment, the *economic* environment, the *technological* environment, and the *social and cultural* environment. This is the structure upon which marketing decisions are made, as well as the frame of reference for marketing planning. Skillful environmental analysis is one of the major criteria for success in marketing planning. Figure 2–1 portrays this relationship.

The dynamic nature of the environment means that management at every level must continually re-evaluate marketing decisions and prepare for change. Even modest shifts in one or more of the environmental elements can alter the results of marketing decisions. For example, political/legal changes are now permitting the mass marketing of Digital Audio Tape recorders, a relatively new technological advance. This situation could have profound effects on the marketing of compact disc players, as people will be able to play and record CD-quality music.

FIGURE 2 – 1

**Components of the Marketing Environment**

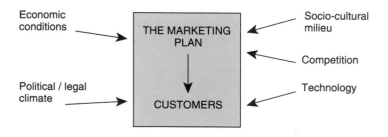

*Before marketing its new Digital Audio Tape (DAT) recorder, Sony carried out an environmental analysis. At present Sony is one of the primary manufacturers of this new technological innovation, but the company may be forced to re-evaluate its plan when it receives more competition from other manufacturers of the product. How will this affect Sony's marketing plan? How will it affect the other components of the marketing environment?*

# The Competitive Environment

*The interactive process that occurs in the marketplace as competing organizations seek to satisfy markets* is known as the **competitive environment.** Marketing decisions by an individual firm influence consumer responses in the marketplace; they also affect the marketing strategies of competitors. As a consequence, marketers must continually monitor the marketing activities of competitors — their products, channels of distribution, prices, and communication efforts.

In a few instances, organizations enjoy a monopoly position in the marketplace. Utilities, such as natural gas, electricity, water, and cable television service, accept considerable regulation from government in such marketing-related activities as rates, service levels, and geographic coverage in exchange for exclusive rights to serve a particular group of consumers. However, such instances are relatively rare. In addition, portions of such traditional monopoly industries as telephone service have been deregulated in recent years, and telephone companies currently face competition in such areas as the sale of telephone receivers, some long-distance services, and installation and maintenance of telephone systems in larger commercial and industrial firms.

In many industries the competition among firms is fierce. For example, consider the retail food industry. For supermarkets, the profit margin on most items is quite low. Therefore, to make an adequate return on investment a store must generate a high volume of sales. Supermarkets are thus very sensitive to fluctuations in sales caused by the actions of competitors. If one competitor advertises a sale on certain products, another will be inclined to match those sale prices. Or if a new store format (such as Loblaw's Superstores) is developed, it will be countered (as was done with Safeway's Food for Less outlets).

**competitive environment** The interactive process that occurs in the marketplace as competing organizations seek to satisfy markets.

## Types of Competition

Marketers face three types of competition. The most direct form of competition occurs among marketers of similar products. Xerox photocopiers compete with models offered by Canon, Sharp, and Olivetti. Estee Lauder cosmetics face competition from Helena Rubenstein and Revlon.

A second type of competition is competition among products that can be substituted for one another. In the construction industry and in manufacturing, steel products by Stelco may compete with similar products made of aluminum by Alcan. Cast-iron pipes compete with pipes made of such synthetic materials as polyvinyl chloride (PVC). In instances where a change such as a price increase or an improvement in the strength of a product occurs, demand for substitute products is directly affected.

The final type of competition involves all organizations that compete for the consumer's purchases. Traditional economic analysis views competition as a battle among companies in the same industry or among substitutable products and services. Marketers, however, accept the argument that *all* firms are competing for a limited amount of discretionary buying power. The Mazda 323 competes with a vacation in the Bahamas; the local live theatre centre competes with pay television and the Leafs, Blue Bombers, or Expos for the consumer's entertainment dollars.

Since the competitive environment often determines the success or failure of the product, marketers must continually assess the marketing strategies of competitors. New product offerings with technological advances, price reductions, special promotions, or other competitive actions must be monitored in order to adjust the firm's marketing program in the light of such changes. Among the first purchasers of any new product are the product's competitors. Careful analysis of the product — its physical components, performance attributes, packaging, retail price, service requirements, and estimated production and marketing costs — allows the market to forecast its likely competitive impact. If necessary, adjustments to current marketing procedures may take place as a result of the new market entry. The competitive environment is a fact of life for most marketers. They ignore it at their peril!

## Developing a Competitive Strategy

All marketers must develop an effective strategy for dealing with the competitive environment. Some will compete in a broad range of product markets in many areas of the world. Others prefer to specialize in particular market segments, such as those determined by geographic, age, or income factors. Essentially, determining a competitive strategy involves answering five questions:

1. Who are our competitors?
2. What is their strategy?
3. Should we compete?
4. If so, in what markets should we compete?
5. How should we compete?

The first question — who are our competitors? — focuses attention on the various potential challengers to be faced to gain a share of the market. Firms sometimes enter a market with an inadequate understanding of the extent of the competition.

I·S·S·U·E·S   I·N   I·N·T·E·R·N·A·T·I·O·N·A·L   M·A·R·K·E·T·I·N·G

## Time-Based Competition to Gain a Competitive Edge

Firms compete internationally on a variety of bases, including product quality, price, and customer service. With increased international competition and rapid changes in technology, a steadily growing number of firms are using time as a strategic competitive weapon. **Time-based competition** is a strategy of developing and distributing goods and services more quickly than competitors. Japanese firms, pioneers of time-based competition, have gained a competitive edge in industries such as automobiles and projection television by developing products in one-third to one-half the time taken by North American competitors. Toyota Motor Corporation reduced the time it takes to sell and distribute its cars from between four and six weeks to just eight days by developing a computerized order-entry system that links salespeople directly to production scheduling. Italian retailer Benetton has achieved global success by using a time-based strategy to respond quickly to marketplace demands. After spotting a new trend, Benetton uses computer technology to design, produce, and deliver new fashion items to its stores in less than one month. The flexibility and speedy responsiveness of time-based competitors enables them to improve product quality, reduce costs, offer a broader variety of products that cover more market segments, and enhance customer satisfaction.

Source: George Stalk, Jr., "Time: The Next Source of Competitive Advantage," *Harvard Business Review* (July–August 1988), pp. 41–51.

It is also important to develop an understanding of the strategies followed by one's competition. The marketer's strategy cannot be developed in a vacuum. It must be at least as good as, or more effective than, or different from that of competitors. Often a great deal of creativity is required to come up with a winning plan.

The third question — should we compete? — should be answered based on the resources and objectives of the firm and the expected profit potential for the firm. In some instances, potentially successful ventures are not considered due to a lack of a match between the venture and the overall organizational objectives. For example, a clothing manufacturer may reject an opportunity to diversify through the purchase of a profitable pump manufacturer. Or a producer of industrial chemicals might refrain from entering the consumer market and instead sell chemicals to another firm familiar with serving consumers at the retail level.

In other cases a critical issue is expected profit potential. If the expected profits are insufficient to pay an adequate return on the required investment, then the firm should consider other lines of business. Many organizations have switched from less profitable ventures quite efficiently. This decision should be subject to continual reevaluation so that the firm avoids being tied to traditional markets with declining profit margins. It is also important to anticipate competitive responses.

The fourth question concerns the markets in which to compete. This decision acknowledges that the firm has limited resources (engineering and productive capabilities, sales personnel, advertising budgets, research and development, and the like) and that these resources must be allocated to the areas of greatest opportunity. Too many firms have taken a "shotgun" approach to market selection and thus do an ineffective job in many markets rather than a good one in selected markets.

"How should we compete?" is the fifth question. It requires the firm's marketers to make the tactical decisions involved in setting up a comprehensive marketing strategy. Product, pricing, distribution, and communication decisions are the major elements of this strategy.

# The Political and Legal Climate

**political and legal climate**
The laws and interpretation of laws that require firms to operate under competitive conditions and to protect consumer rights.

Before you play the game, learn the rules! It would be absurd to start playing a new game without first understanding the rules, yet some businesspeople exhibit a remarkable lack of knowledge about marketing's **political and legal climate** — *the laws and interpretation of laws that require firms to operate under competitive conditions and to protect consumer rights.*[2] Ignorance of laws, ordinances, and regulations could result in fines, embarrassing negative publicity, and possibly civil damage suits.

It requires considerable diligence to develop an understanding of the legal framework of marketing. Numerous laws, often vague and legislated by a multitude of different authorities, characterize the legal environment for marketing decisions. Regulations affecting marketing have been enacted at the federal, provincial, and local levels as well as by independent regulatory agencies. Our existing legal framework was constructed on a piecemeal basis, often in response to a concern over current issues.

Canada has tended to follow a public policy of promoting a competitive marketing system. To maintain such a system, competitive practices within the system have been regulated. Traditionally, pricing and promotion have received the most legislative attention.

## Society's Expectations Create the Framework

We live in and desire a "free-enterprise society" — or do we? The concept of free enterprise is not clear, and has been gradually changing. At the turn of the century the prevalent attitude was to let business act quite freely. As a result, it was expected that new products and jobs would be created and the economy would develop and prosper.

This approach provided great freedom for the scrupulous and the unscrupulous. Although most businesses sought to serve their market targets in an equitable fashion, abuses did occur. Figure 2–2 shows an example of questionable marketing

FIGURE 2–2

**An Example of Questionable Advertising**

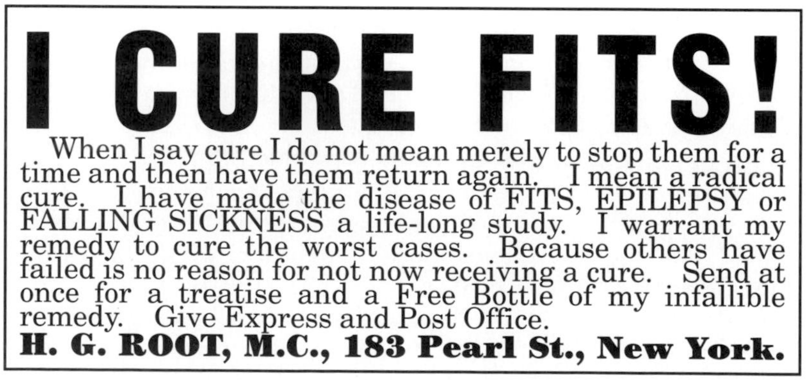

Source: S. Watson Dunn and Arnold M. Barban, *Advertising: Its Role in Modern Marketing* (Hinsdale, Dryden Press, 1986), p. 84. Reprinted by permission.

practices. Such advertisements were not unusual in the late 1800s and early 1900s. Advancing technology led to the creation of a multitude of products in many fields. Often the buying public did not have the expertise needed to choose among them.

With the increasing complexity of products, the growth of big, impersonal business, and the unfair or careless treatment of consumers by some firms, society's

FIGURE 2 – 3

## Legislation Administered by Consumer and Corporate Affairs Canada

1. **Fully Administered by CCA**
   - Bankruptcy Act and Bankruptcy Rules
   - Boards of Trade Act
   - Canada Business Corporations Act
   - Canada Cooperative Associations Act
   - Canada Corporations Act
   - Competition Act
   - Companies' Creditors Arrangement Act
   - Consumer Packaging and Labelling Act
   - Copyright Act
   - Department of Consumer and Corporate Affairs Act
   - Electricity and Gas Inspection Act
   - Government Corporations Operation Act
   - Hazardous Products Act
   - Industrial Design Act
   - National Trade Mark and True Labelling Act
   - Patent Act
   - Pension Fund Societies Act
   - Precious Metals Marking Act
   - Public Servants Invention Act
   - Tax Rebate Discounting Act
   - Textile Labelling Act
   - Timber Marking Act
   - Trade Marks Act
   - Weights and Measures Act

2. **Administered Jointly with Other Departments**
   - Bills of Exchange Act (with Finance)
   - Canada Agricultural Products Standards Act (with Agriculture)
   - Canada Dairy Products Act (with Agriculture)
   - Fish Inspection Act (with Fisheries and Oceans)
   - Food and Drugs Act (with Health and Welfare)
   - Maple Products Industry Act (with Agriculture)
   - Shipping Conferences Exemption Act (with Transport)
   - Winding-up Act (with Finance)

values changed. "Government should regulate business more closely," we said. Over time, governments at the federal and provincial levels have responded to this shift: many laws have been passed to protect consumers, and to attempt to maintain a competitive environment for business. Large bureaucracies have grown with this increase in market regulation.

A significant development in the legal environment at the federal level was the consolidation in 1967 of consumer and business regulation programs into Consumer and Corporate Affairs Canada, and the appointment of a cabinet minister to represent these interests at the highest level. Previously these functions had been scattered among several different government departments. Following the lead of the federal government, most provinces have established consumer and corporate affairs branches and have generally streamlined the regulation of these sectors. Figure 2–3 lists some of the significant federal legislation that affects business today. The list is quite comprehensive. The detailed study of provincial laws and regulations is beyond the scope of this text.

## The Competition Act Sets the Standards

Of all the legislation mentioned in Figure 2–3, the Competition Act (formerly the Combines Investigation Act) has the most significance in the legal environment for marketing decisions. The Act dates back to 1889, when it was enacted to protect the public interest in free competition.[3] Since then, various revisions have occurred in response to changes in social values and in business practices (see Figure 2–4).

The Act prohibits rather than regulates. That is, it does not spell out in detail the activities that industry may undertake, but greatly discourages certain activities through the threat of penal consequences.

The provisions of the Act fall into three main classes. Generally speaking, they prohibit the following:

1. Combinations that prevent, or lessen unduly, competition in the production, purchase, sale, storage, rental, transportation, or supply of commodities, or in the price of insurance.

2. Mergers, monopolies, or abuses of dominant market position that may operate to the detriment of the public.

3. Deceptive trade practices, including

   - price discrimination
   - predatory pricing
   - certain promotional allowances
   - false or misleading representations, by any means whatever, to promote the sale of a product or to promote a business
   - unsubstantiated claims of performance
   - misleading warranties or guarantees
   - misrepresentation as to the ordinary price
   - misleading testimonials for a product or service
   - double ticketing
   - pyramid sales
   - referral selling

- nonavailability of advertised specials
- sale above advertised price
- promotional contests

FIGURE 2 – 4

## Evolution of Major Combines Legislation

| Date | Legislation | Reason for Legislation |
|------|-------------|------------------------|
| 1888 | Combines Investigation Commission | To protect small businesses that suffered from monopolistic and collusive practices in restraint of trade by large manufacturers. |
| 1889 | Act for the Prevention and Suppression of Combinations Formed in Restraint of Trade | To declare illegal monopolies and combinations in restraint of trade. |
| 1892 | Above Act incorporated into the Criminal Code as Section 502 | To make the above a criminal offence. |
| 1900 | Above Act amended | To make the Act effective because as it stood, an individual would first have to commit an illegal act within the meaning of common law. Now, any undue restriction of competition became a criminal offence. |
| 1910 | Additional legislation passed to complement the Criminal Code and assist in the application of the Act | To stop a recent rush of mergers that had involved some 58 firms. |
| 1919 | The Combines and Fair Prices Act | To prohibit undue stockpiling of the "necessities of life" and prohibit the realization of exaggerated profits through "unreasonable prices." |
| 1923 | Combines Investigation Act | To consolidate combines legislation. |
| 1952, 1960 | Amendments to the above | |
| 1976 | Bill C-2; amendments | To include the service industry within the Act; to prohibit additional deceptive practices; to give persons the right to recover damages; to protect rights of small businesses. |
| 1986 | Competition Act replaces Combines Investigation Act | To facilitate prosecutions of illegal combinations, mergers, and monopolies. |

Despite the long history of the Combines Investigation Act, it proved remarkably powerless for prosecuting those who appeared to contravene either of the first two categories. The passage of the Competition Act to replace the Combines Investigation Act in June 1986 was an important change. Being classified as civil law, it corrected many problems in the strictly criminal, proof-beyond-a-reasonable-doubt approach of the old Combines Act. The new Competition Act also created a quasi-judicial body, known as the Competition Tribunal, to deal with matters via the civil route, and to make certain rules.

The first antimonopoly case after the new Competition Act was passed in 1986 was laid in 1989. NutraSweet Co., a subsidiary of U.S. chemical giant Monsanto, was charged with "abuse of dominance" (monopoly) in the Canadian market for aspartame, an artificial sweetener. The Bureau of Competition Policy said in a statement that NutraSweet, the sole supplier of aspartame in the United States, had captured more than 95 percent of the Canadian market. It claimed that NutraSweet demanded contracts with customers that precluded them from buying aspartame from anyone other than NutraSweet. Where exclusive contracts were not made, it claimed, NutraSweet insisted that customers give the company a chance to match the lowest prices charged by a competitor. The Bureau also charged NutraSweet with selling aspartame in Canada at a price below its acquisition cost or below its long-run average cost with the result of substantially lessening competition.

NutraSweet issued a statement disagreeing with the Bureau's charges and believed that the issue would be decided in its favour.[4] However, a few months later, in a precedent-setting decision, the Competition Tribunal ruled that NutraSweet had effectively maintained monopolistic powers over the $25-million domestic aspartame market at the expense of potential competitors.

NutraSweet invented aspartame in the 1960s but health testing delayed its introduction in many countries, including Canada, until the early 1980s. Soon afterward,

---

## A·P·P·L·Y·I·N·G  T·H·E  C·O·N·C·E·P·T·S

### *How One Company Keeps a Clean Slate*

Not many large advertisers can say they have never been caught under the misleading-advertising provisions of the Combines Investigation Act, but Canada Safeway Ltd. appears to have a clean record. A 1979 study carried out for the federal combines branch showed that practically every large supermarket chain in Canada — except Calgary-based Safeway — had been convicted for an offence of selling above advertised prices. The overcharging reportedly totalled a whopping $15 million to $20 million a year during the 1970s.

Safeway's spotless record stems, according to the company, from its strict adherence to policies that ensure that any claims made on price reduction or quality are completely accurate.

Safeway's 297 Canadian stores are split into six divisions, each with its own advertising manager, who is responsible for promotional strategy and claims in that division. The decentralized planning helps ensure greater control over claims made. In other companies, much of the advertising planning and co-ordination is carried out from head office. "By the time it gets out to a far-flung centre, if prices or products are substituted, the possibility of confusing or misleading results would be greater," says Jim Waters, Safeway's vice-president of public affairs.

The company also monitors charges and fines against competitors "and has expressed the strong desire [to senior operators] to see that Safeway would not become involved."

Source: *Financial Times of Canada* (July 18, 1983), p. 14.

NutraSweet's patents on the product began running out. In Canada that took place in 1987. But in preparation, NutraSweet tied up its customers in exclusive contracts. Under the Tribunal's order, NutraSweet can no longer enforce existing contracts or sign new ones that make it the exclusive aspartame supplier. Nor can NutraSweet sign contracts that give it the right to match, in the future, a competing bid from another aspartame producer. As well, it has been prohibited from giving financial inducements on the sale of aspartame to companies that display NutraSweet's swirl insignia on their products. The director of the Bureau of Competition Policy called the Tribunal's ruling a significant sign that anticompetitive behaviour by companies will not be tolerated.[5]

## Combines and Restraint of Trade

It is an offence to conspire, combine, agree, or arrange with another person to prevent or lessen competition unduly. The most common types of combination relate to price fixing, bid rigging, market sharing, and group boycotting of competitors, suppliers, or customers.

While this list covers much territory, it should be noted that in the following circumstances agreements between businesspersons are *not* unlawful.

1. Exchanging statistics.
2. Defining product standards.
3. Exchanging credit information.
4. Defining trade terms.
5. Co-operating in research and development.
6. Restricting advertising.

Consequently, it is permissible to report statistics centrally for the purpose of analyzing factors relating to industrial operation and marketing, as long as competition is not lessened unduly.

## Mergers

Until the passage of the Competition Act in 1986, the law regarding mergers was largely ineffective. Important provisions in the new Act changed the situation. The Competition Tribunal has the power to stop mergers that substantially lessen competition without offering offsetting efficiency gains. Furthermore, the Tribunal must be notified in advance of large mergers (transactions larger than $35 million in sales or assets, and/or companies with combined revenues or assets of more than $400 million). This enables the review and modification of large, complex mergers that are difficult to reverse once consummated.

The new Gemini air reservation system used by Air Canada and Canadian underwent close scrutiny by the Bureau of Competition Policy. The Bureau withdrew its demand for a breakup when the two airlines formally agreed not to use their joint operation as a means of discriminating against other airlines. Gemini is required to serve other airlines as well.

## Deceptive Trade Practices

This is an extremely important section for marketing decision-makers, as it contains a number of directly related provisions. There are real teeth in the legislation, which the marketer should be aware of. Many successful prosecutions have been made under this section.

### Misleading advertising

False statements of every kind (even in the picture on a package) made to the public about products or services are prohibited. For example, on November 15, 1986, First Choice Canadian Communications Corporation was convicted of making statements designed to mislead the public.[6] The company, in promoting the sale of subscriptions to its pay television service, claimed in newspaper advertisements that it would offer "all new movies every month." It was established that all new movies were provided only for the first three months of the service. The company was convicted and fined $15 000.

Often carelessness has been seen as responsible for the offence, and over the years, numerous advertisers have been prosecuted under the misleading-advertising provisions of the Combines Investigation Act. The fines meted out have been surprisingly small.

A greater level of determination to discourage deceptive advertising was signalled in 1983, when a fine levied against Simpsons-Sears sent shock waves through the

---

## A·P·P·L·Y·I·N·G  T·H·E  C·O·N·C·E·P·T·S

## *Unintended Effects of Competition Law*

In its charges against NutraSweet, the federal Bureau of Competition Policy obviously felt that NutraSweet was abusing its position in the aspartame market. The Bureau listed a range of alleged aggressive anticompetitive business practices that would have had the effect of lessening competition substantially in the aspartame market. NutraSweet denied the claims.

But the case against NutraSweet, as with many competition law matters, may not be that simple. It also raises questions about the principal purpose of competition legislation: is the objective to provide a market for a competitor — or the best prices and products to consumers?

Here is the problem. As part of its case against NutraSweet, the Bureau accused the company of maintaining low prices. Prices were set so low, it claimed, that prospective competitors found entering the market impractical. This was possible because there had effectively been a subsidization of the Canadian market from profits enjoyed by the company in other markets. Another allegation was that NutraSweet sold aspartame in Canada at a price "below its acquisition cost or below its long-run average cost."

Competitors, according to this logic, do not really have a chance of enter the market. If Tosoh, another supplier, could increase its share to 20 percent, with perhaps another 10 percent going to other companies,

then, presumably, one could conclude that the Canadian aspartame market is competitive.

But according to the Bureau's own allegations, the price of aspartame is already too low: below cost, and therefore below what any competitor can provide. Logic suggests that if NutraSweet were forced to change its alleged aggressive practices, and forced to concede more of the market to competitors, then the price of the product would have to go up.

Thus the question: What is the primary objective of competition policy? Is it to increase the number of companies, on the assumption that more companies with greater market shares provide greater benefits to society?

If the objective of a free market is ample product supply at the lowest possible prices, then it would appear that the market for aspartame is fulfilling that objective. The market, as described by the competition bureau, appears to be working perfectly. Faced with other companies trying to get into the aspartame market, NutraSweet is doing everything it possibly can to compete.

Source: Adapted from Terrence Corcoran, "NutraSweet Case Raises Question About Competition Law's Purpose," *Globe and Mail* (June 10, 1989).

entire advertising industry. Simpsons-Sears had been found guilty of advertising (through its catalogues and through newspapers, between 1975 and 1978) diamond rings that it claimed had been appraised at values significantly higher than those given by bona fide diamond appraisers consulted by Consumer and Corporate Affairs Canada. The fine imposed was a million dollars — the highest ever levied under the Act. This set a precedent for vigorous prosecution of violaters of the Act.[7]

It is an offence to make unsubstantiated claims. Therefore, claims for a product are expected to be based on an adequate and proper test. Significantly, the onus is on whoever is making the claim to prove its efficacy, rather than on someone else to prove that the product is not as claimed. This reverse onus has been challenged before the courts under the Charter of Rights as being unconstitutional because it purports to put the onus on the accused to prove innocence, but the section was upheld. One example, and there are many, concerns Professional Technology of Canada, which was convicted in Edmonton on May 27, 1986, for promoting a gas-saving device that purported to offer 10 to 35 percent better mileage for cars. The company was convicted and fined $12 500.[8]

Another important facet of the misleading-advertising legislation concerns pricing. Many businesses seem to be unaware that much care needs to be taken when advertising comparative prices. It is, for example, considered misleading for a retailer to advertise a television set as follows:

| | |
|---|---|
| Manufacturer's suggested list price | $680.00 |
| On sale for | $500.00 |

if the manufacturer's suggested list price is not normally followed in this area of activity, and the usual price is around $600. Although the retailer *is* offering a bargain, the magnitude of the saving is not indicated accurately.

Retailers may try to get around this provision by choosing different comparative expressions, such as "regular price," "ordinarily $...," "list price," "hundreds sold at," "compare with," "regular value," and the like. But such tactics may nevertheless be problematic. For example, in Moncton, Best for Less (a division of Dominion Stores Ltd.) compared its price to a "why pay up to" price on in-store signs, and depicted the savings. It was established that items were available from competitors at lower prices than the "why pay up to" prices, and the firm was convicted and fined $7650.[9]

The businessperson who genuinely seeks to comply with this provision should ask two questions:

1. Would a reasonable shopper draw the conclusion from the expression used that the figure named by way of comparison is a price at which goods have been, are, or will ordinarily be sold?

2. If the answer is yes, would such a representation be true?

## Pricing practices

It is an offence for a supplier to make a practice of discriminating in price among purchasers who are in competition with one another and who are purchasing like quantities of goods. Selling above the advertised price is also prohibited. Furthermore, the lowest of two or more prices must be used in the case of double-ticketed products. This latter provision has led to the development of easy-tear-off, two-price stickers, so that the sale price can readily be removed after a sale.

A·P·P·L·Y·I·N·G  T·H·E  C·O·N·C·E·P·T·S

## *The Cost of Resale Price Maintenance*

An Ontario waterbed manufacturer, Andico Manu-facturing Ltd., found that it couldn't make resale price maintenance work when it tried to pressure a Winnipeg dealer into raising the prices of its beds. The manufacturer was fined a total of $11 000 for cutting off supplies to its dealer, Burron Lumber of Winnipeg, when it refused to raise prices. Burron was charging considerably less for its waterbeds than other specialty waterbed stores in the city to which Andico also sold its products.

Andico was convicted of two offences under the Combines Investigation Act. A fine of $1000 was levied for attempting to influence Burron to raise prices, and another $10 000 fine was imposed for refusing to supply waterbeds and components to the lumber store.

According to trial evidence, Burron decided to enter the waterbed market in October 1981, and began buying waterbed kits and accessories from Andico. Burron president Ramond Burron testified that less than two weeks later, the company representative told him that other city waterbed retailers were pressuring him to stop selling to Burron because of its cut-rate

pricing policy. He was told that either he would have to raise his prices or his supplies would be cut off. He refused, and the supplier stopped filling his orders.

Andico's representative contended that he stopped selling products to Burron because he did not regard it as a "bona fide" waterbed retailer. He said he did not feel Burron had adequate waterbed display space at its lumber store, or qualified staff to sell and service waterbeds. He maintained that a manufacturer has a right to not sell products to an outlet that it feels is not a legitimate dealer.

The judge agreed that "there is nothing wrong with making sure the people [a firm] deals with have some financial stability." However, "in this case, the company did not have any such concerns. It exercised its decision solely on the basis that Burron should have been selling at higher prices than he was, and that if he didn't, he wouldn't get any more supplies."

Source: Adapted from Murray McNeill, "Waterbed Maker Fined $11 000," *Winnipeg Free Press* (November 23, 1983).

If you are a ski manufacturer and wish all ski shops to sell your skis at your suggested list price, can you force them to do so? No; it is an offence under the Act to deny supplies to an outlet that refuses to maintain the resale price. Thus, resale price maintenance is illegal, and a reseller is generally free to set whatever price is considered appropriate.

The Competition Act includes several other prohibitions, including ones against bait-and-switch selling, pyramid selling, and some types of referral selling and promotional contests.

## Other Provisions of the Competition Act

### Protection against foreign laws and directives

Foreign companies doing business in Canada have sometimes been constrained by laws or judgments in their home country to the detriment of competition in Canada, or of opportunities for Canadian international trade. For example, Canadian subsidiaries of American companies have felt constrained by American law against doing business with Cuba. This is theoretically no longer the case, because the Restrictive Trade Practices Commission (established under the anticombines provi-sions of the Competition Act) has been given power to rule against such interference in Canadian affairs.

### Civil damages

In some situations persons have the right to recover damages incurred as a result of a violation by others. This has profound implications. In some jurisdictions, not only

*Ogilvy's department store in Montreal had to change its name to Ogilvy to comply with Quebec government legislation requiring that all exterior signs be in French. There has been considerable debate over the effect of this legislation on the free-enterprise system. The debate continues. What is your opinion?*

can an individual sue for damages, but if the person wins, that judgment will apparently serve as evidence for anyone else who has experienced a similar loss. Would this mean that a company could face the possibility of virtually every purchaser of a product claiming damages? Consider the millions of dollars involved for an automobile manufacturer, for example. To our knowledge, there have been no such cases in Canada.

## Regulation, Regulation, and. . .More Regulation

So far, only some of the provisions from the most important federal Act have been cited. Figure 2–3 shows that the federal government has a virtual sea of regulations that marketers must be aware of. Provincial governments are also very active in this area. Fortunately, each marketer need not be aware of all provisions, for many are specific to situation, time, place, and products.

In addition, provincial and municipal governments have other laws and by-laws that must be considered when developing marketing plans. For example, regulations vary from province to province concerning the amount and nature of advertising directed at children. Some other significant laws or regulations relate to bilingual specifications for packaging and labelling; there are special language requirements in Quebec.

From a broad point of view, the legal framework for relations between business and consumers is designed to encourage a competitive marketing system employing fair business practices. In many respects various laws have resulted in more effective competition, although there are many who feel business is over-regulated and others who think that more regulations are needed. There is little doubt that consumers in Canada are protected as well as or better than consumers in any other country in their dealings with sellers, especially regarding truth in advertising. It is clear that governments will continue to act in response to society's expectations of a fair and honest marketplace.

# Economic Conditions

In addition to the competition and the political and legal climate, marketers must understand economic conditions and their impact on the organization. An economy with growing monetary resources, high employment, and productive power is likely to result in strong demand for goods and services.

In a deteriorating economic environment, on the other hand, many firms experience a decline. However, such conditions may represent good news for other companies. As inflation and unemployment go up and production declines, consumer buying patterns shift. Flour millers note that flour sales go up. Automobile repairs and home improvements also increase. Greeting card firms report that consumers buy fewer gifts, but more expensive cards. Hardware stores show higher sales. The economic environment will considerably affect the way marketers operate.

## Stages of the Business Cycle

Within the economic environment there are fluctuations that tend to follow a cyclical pattern comprising three or four stages:

1. recession (sometimes involves such factors as inflation and unemployment)
2. depression[10]
3. recovery
4. prosperity

### A·P·P·L·Y·I·N·G   T·H·E   C·O·N·C·E·P·T·S

## *Refusal-to-Deal Case Goes Against Chrysler*

A precedent-setting Competition Tribunal ruling appears to give new ammunition to small independent marketers in their dealings with major suppliers.

The Tribunal ordered Chrysler Canada Ltd. to resume supplying parts to a small Montreal-based exporter, Richard Brunet, who had been cut off by the auto company since 1986. Brunet operated an auto parts export business, selling primarily to South America and later to Europe.

He began dealing with Chrysler Canada in 1977. But he was informed in August 1986 that due to a change in corporate policy, Chrysler Canada would no longer sell parts to him. All overseas exports were now to be handled by the parent firm, Chrysler Corp. in the U.S.

Chrysler Canada claimed before the Tribunal that Brunet had agreed not to compete with Chrysler Corp.

in selling to franchised dealers overseas. In March 1986 Brunet told a Peruvian auto dealer he could supply certain parts cheaper than Chrysler. But Brunet said no such understanding existed and Chrysler's anger at his approach to the Peruvian dealer was the first indication he had that the company disapproved.

The Tribunal said Brunet "was shown little consideration" after his long association with Chrysler. "There was no warning that he might be cut off and there was no face-to-face meeting to discuss the situation."

Source: Excerpted from David Hatter, " 'Refusal-To-Deal' Case Goes Against Chrysler," *Financial Post* (October 14–16, 1989), p. 3.

No marketer can disregard the economic climate in which a business functions, for the type, direction, and intensity of a firm's marketing strategy depend on it. In addition, the marketer must be aware of the economy's relative position in the business cycle and how it will affect the position of the particular firm. This requires the marketer to study forecasts of future economic activity.

Of necessity, marketing activity differs with each stage of the business cycle. During prosperous times, consumers are usually more willing to buy than when they feel economically threatened. For example, during a recent recession, personal savings climbed to high levels as consumers (fearing possible layoffs and other workforce reductions) cut back their expenditures for many products they considered non-essential. Marketers must pay close attention to the consumer's relative willingness to buy. The aggressiveness of one's marketing strategy and tactics often depends on current buying intentions. More aggressive marketing may be called for in periods of lessened buying interest, as when auto makers use cash rebate schemes to move inventories. Such activities, however, are unlikely to fully counteract cyclical periods of low demand.

While sales figures may experience cyclical variations, the successful firm has a rising sales trend line. Achieving this depends on management's ability to foresee, correctly define, and reach new market opportunities. Effective forecasting and research is only a partial solution. Marketers must also develop an intuitive awareness of potential markets. This requires that one be able to correctly delineate opportunities.[11]

Besides recession, two other economic subjects have been of major concern to marketers in recent years: inflation and unemployment.

## Inflation

Another economic factor that critically influences marketing strategy is **inflation**, which can occur during any stage in the business cycle. Inflation is *a rising price level resulting in reduced purchasing power for the consumer.* A person's money is devalued (in terms of what it can buy). Traditionally, this circumstance has been more prevalent in countries outside North America. However, in the late 1970s and early 1980s Canada experienced "double-digit inflation" (an inflation rate higher than 10 percent a year). Although the rate of inflation has declined considerably since then, experiences of inflation's effects have led to widespread concern over political approaches to controlling interest rates and stabilizing price levels, and over ways in which the individual can adjust to such reductions in the spending power of the dollar.

**inflation**    A rising price level resulting in reduced purchasing power for the consumer.

**Stagflation** is a word that has been coined to describe a peculiar brand of inflation that Canada experienced in the 1970s. It applies to a situation where an economy has *high unemployment and a rising price level at the same time.* Formulating effective strategies is particularly difficult under these circumstances.

**stagflation**    High unemployment and a rising price level at the same time.

## Unemployment

Another significant economic problem that has affected the marketing environment in recent years is unemployment. The ranks of the unemployed — officially defined as people actively looking for work who do not have jobs — swelled to 12.4 percent of the Canadian labour force by January 1984. It then gradually declined, to 8.4 percent in 1989. By contrast, the unemployment rate was 4.4 percent in January 1966.

In the severe recession of the early 1980s, numerous businesses failed, production slowed, many factories ceased operation entirely, and thousands of workers found themselves out of work. The consequences of reduced income and uncertainty about future income were reflected in the marketplace in many ways.

### Government tools for combatting inflation and unemployment

The government can attempt to deal with the twin economic problems of inflation and unemployment by using two basic approaches: fiscal policy and monetary policy. **Fiscal policy** concerns *the receipts and expenditures of government*. To combat inflation, an economy could reduce government expenditures, raise its revenue (primarily taxes), or do a combination of both. It could also use direct controls such as wage and price controls. **Monetary policy** refers to *the manipulation of the money supply and market rates of interest*. In periods of rising prices, monetary policy may dictate that the government take actions to decrease the money supply and raise interest rates, thus restraining purchasing power.

Both fiscal and monetary policy have been used in our battles against inflation and unemployment. Their marketing implications are numerous and varied. Higher taxes mean less consumer purchasing power, which usually results in sales declines for nonessential goods and services. However, some taxes that have been collected may find their way into various job-creation programs. Income earned from these will tend to be spent on basic goods and services. Lower federal expenditure levels make the government a less attractive customer for many industries. A lowered money supply means that less liquidity is available for potential conversion to purchasing power. High interest rates often lead to a significant slump in the construction and housing industry.

Both unemployment and inflation affect marketing by modifying consumer behaviour. Unless unemployment insurance, personal savings, and union supplementary unemployment benefits are sufficient to offset lost earnings, the unemployed individual has less income to spend in the marketplace. Even if the individual is completely compensated for lost earnings, his or her buying behaviour is likely to be affected. As consumers become more conscious of inflation, they are likely to become more price-conscious in general. This can lead to three possible outcomes, all important to marketers. Consumers can (1) elect to buy now in the belief that prices will be higher later (automobile dealers have often used this argument in their commercial messages); (2) decide to alter their purchasing patterns; or (3) postpone certain purchases.

## Demarketing — Dealing with Shortages

Shortages — temporary or permanent — can be caused by several factors. A brisk demand may exceed manufacturing capacity or outpace the response time required to gear up a production line. Shortages may also be caused by a lack of raw materials, component parts, energy, or labour. Regardless of the cause, shortages require marketers to reorient their thinking.[12]

**Demarketing**, a term that has come into general use in recent years, refers to the process of *cutting consumer demand for a product, because the demand exceeds the level that can reasonably be supplied by the firm or because doing so will create a more favourable corporate image*. Some oil companies, for example, have publicized tips on how to cut gasoline consumption as a result of the gradual depletion of oil reserves. Utility companies have encouraged homeowners to install more insulation to lower heating

**fiscal policy**    The receipts and expenditures of government.

**monetary policy**    The manipulation of the money supply and market rates of interest.

**demarketing**    The process of cutting consumer demand for a product back to a level that can reasonably be supplied by the firm.

bills. And growing environmental concerns have resulted in companies' discouraging demand for plastic packaging for their products.

Shortages sometimes force marketers to be allocators of limited supplies. This is in sharp contrast to marketing's traditional objective of expanding sales volume. Shortages require marketers to decide whether to spread a limited supply over all customers so that none are satisfied, or to back-order some customers so that others may be completely supplied. Shortages certainly present marketers with a unique set of marketing problems.

## Technology

The **technological environment** consists of *the applications of knowledge based on scientific discoveries, inventions, and innovations*. It results in new products for consumers and improves existing products. It is a frequent source of price reductions through the development of new production methods or new materials. It also can make existing products obsolete virtually overnight — as slide rule manufacturers would attest.

**technological environment**
The applications of knowledge based on scientific discoveries, inventions, and innovations.

Marketing decision-makers must closely monitor the technological environment for a number of reasons. New technology may be the means by which they remain competitive in their industries. It may also be the vehicle for the creation of entirely new industries. For example, the development of the microchip and lasers has resulted in the development of major industries during the past 25 years.

In the case of high-technology products such as computers and related items, marketers face real challenges in keeping up with the pace of change. They not only must maintain an understanding of the industry, but also must somehow try to communicate totally new concepts and ways of solving problems to potential customers. As Francis McInerney, president of Northern Business Information, says,

"The time it takes to explain a product may be longer than the time it takes to introduce a whole new generation of products."[13] Laptop computer sales now comprise about 15 percent of personal computer sales. Toshiba expects them to replace desktop computers, and has set its strategy accordingly.

In addition, marketers must anticipate the effect such technological innovations are likely to have on the lifestyles of consumers, the products of competitors, the demands of industrial users, and the regulatory actions of government. The advent of videocassette recorders and of lower-cost satellite receiving stations may adversely affect concert attendance and movie ticket sales. A new process may result in reduction of pollution and produce changes in local ordinances.

## The Socio-Cultural Milieu

A probation officer and his wife have found a novel way of marrying people who do not belong to an organized religion or who prefer not to get married in a church. Edward and Ruth Simmons have formed a company called Weddings and have opened chapels in Hamilton and Burlington, Ontario. Weddings offers five different ceremonies: four religious and one secular. The rituals are open to change, at clients' request.

Edward Simmons says that he came up with the idea when he saw couples being married in the courts. "They would go in happy and come out with a stunned look on their faces. I don't think they realized the abruptness of the proceedings. That really bothered me," he said. "Religion doesn't always meet the needs of a secular society," he added. "In many cases, a place of worship won't marry couples who don't belong to it, people who have been divorced, couples that have been living together, and those who have crossed religious barriers."[14]

A few years ago, the success of the Simmonses' company would have been doubtful. However, changes in the socio-cultural fabric of Canada now make this type of business quite viable. This example illustrates the importance of understanding and assessing the relevant social and cultural components when making marketing decisions. The **socio-cultural environment** is *the mosaic of societal and cultural components that are relevant to the organization's business decisions.* Obviously, there are many different aspects of significance. One important category is the general readiness of society to accept a marketing idea; this aspect was important in the Simmonses' decision.

**socio-cultural environment**
The mosaic of societal and cultural components that are relevant to the business decisions of the organization.

Another important category is the trust and confidence of the public in business as a whole. Such relationships have been on the decline since the mid-1960s. Opinion polls suggest that people have lost confidence in major companies (although they maintain faith in the private-enterprise system). These declines should, however, be viewed in perspective. All institutions have lost public confidence to some degree. In fact, some would argue that governments and labour unions are even less popular than business.

The socio-cultural environment for marketing decisions has both expanded in scope and increased in importance. Today no marketer can initiate a strategy without taking the social environment into account. Marketers must develop an awareness of the manner in which it affects their decisions. The constant flux of social issues requires that marketing managers place more emphasis on solving these questions as part of the marketing decision process. Some firms have created a new position — manager of public policy research — to study the changing social environment's future impact on the company.

One question facing contemporary marketing is how to measure the accomplishment of socially oriented objectives. A firm that is attuned to its social environment must develop new ways of evaluating its performance. Traditional income statements and balance sheets are no longer adequate. This issue is one of the most important problems facing contemporary marketing.

Many marketers recognize societal differences between countries, but assume that a homogeneous social environment exists domestically. Nothing could be further from the truth! Canada is a mixed society composed of varied submarkets. These submarkets can be classified by age, place of residence, sex, ethnic background, and numerous other determinants.

For example, the Quebec market segment has historically been ignored by too many firms. In recent years, however, Quebec has been recognized as a distinct market within itself. The culture and values of this market require more careful treatment than merely translating English into French.

Sex is another increasingly important social factor. The feminist movement has had a decided effect on marketing, particularly promotion. Television commercials now feature women in less stereotyped roles than in previous years.

Since social variables change constantly, marketers must continually monitor their dynamic environment. What appears to be out-of-bounds today may be tomorrow's greatest market opportunity. Consider the way that previously taboo subjects such as feminine hygiene products are now commonly advertised.

The social variables must be recognized by modern business executives since they affect the way consumers react to different products and marketing practices. One of the most tragic — and avoidable — of all marketing mistakes is the failure to appreciate social differences within our own domestic market.

The rise of consumerism can be partly traced to the growing public concern with making business more responsible to its constituents. Consumerism is an evolving aspect of marketing's social environment. Certainly the advent of this movement has influenced the move toward more direct protection of consumer rights in such areas as product safety and false and misleading advertising. These concerns will undoubtedly be amplified and expanded in the years ahead.

## Summary

A consideration of several environmental factors is of paramount importance in making marketing decisions. Five specific variables should be considered: competitive, political and legal, economic, technological, and socio-cultural. These are important to the study of marketing because they provide the framework within which marketing strategies are formulated. The environmental factors discussed in this chapter are among the most dynamic aspects of contemporary business.

The competitive environment is the interactive process that occurs in the marketplace. Marketing decisions influence the market and are, in turn, affected by the counterstrategies of competition. The legal segment attempts to maintain a competitive environment as well as regulate specific marketing practices. The economic environment often influences the manner in which consumers will behave toward varying marketing appeals. Technology is very dynamic, producing new products and ways of doing business. Socio-cultural aspects, however, may become the most important to marketers. The matter of adapting to a changing social environment, both domestically and internationally, has advanced to the forefront of marketing thought.

# KEY TERMS

competitive environment
political and legal climate
economic environment
merger
misleading advertising
combine
restraint of trade

recession
inflation
stagflation
fiscal policy
monetary policy
technological environment
resale price maintenance

refusal to deal
business cycle
Competition Act
Combines Investigation Act
demarketing
socio-cultural environment

# REVIEW QUESTIONS

1. Identify and briefly describe the five components of the marketing environment.
2. Explain the types of competition faced by marketers.
3. What are the steps involved in developing a competitive strategy?
4. How does inflation affect marketing activity?
5. Discuss the legal constraints on pricing practices.
6. Trace the evolution of Consumer and Corporate Affairs Canada into an "activist watchdog" of marketing practices. Then evaluate the department's degree of success.
7. What are the major economic factors affecting marketing decisions?
8. Distinguish between inflation and stagflation. In what ways do they affect marketing?
9. Identify the ways in which the technological environment affects marketing activities.
10. Explain how the socio-cultural environment influences marketing.

# DISCUSSION QUESTIONS AND EXERCISES

1. Give an example of how each of the environmental variables discussed in this chapter might affect the following firms:
   a. McCain Foods
   b. Local aerobics exercise centre
   c. Swiss Chalet franchise
   d. Avon Products
   e. Sears catalogue department
   f. Local television station
2. Comment on the following statement: The legal framework for marketing decisions is basically a positive one.
3. Can the consumerism movement be viewed as a rejection of the competitive marketing system? Defend your answer.
4. As a consumer, do you favour laws permitting resale price maintenance agreements? Would your answer vary if you were the producer of Sony television sets? If you were the retailer of Sony television sets? Why or why not?
5. Would a gas station that sold gasoline to a city's police department for one cent a litre less than its price for other customers be in violation of the Competition Act? Why? Explain your answer.

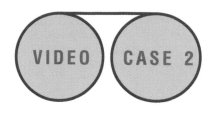

# VIDEO CASE 2

# Mitsubishi Motor Sales of America

What seemed to be an astute marketing decision back in 1970 proved to be one that strategists at Japan's Mitsubishi Heavy Industries would later regret. Mitsubishi is Japan's largest company, a giant conglomerate whose product lines range from ship-building to rocketry. Its subsidiary, Mitsubishi Motors Corporation (MMC), is the oldest and third largest Japanese auto maker, but its market share is far less than those of market leaders Toyota and Nissan.

In 1970, MMC marketers discovered a low-cost, low-risk way to enter the huge North American market, a market they had previously ignored to the benefit of Honda, Nissan, and Toyota. Chrysler Corporation executives, seeking to add small cars to their product line, agreed to purchase a 35 percent share in MMC in return for an exclusive franchise to distribute Mitsubishi models in North America under the Chrysler nameplate. As MMC spokesperson Tohei Takeuchi explains, the arrangement appeared to make sense in 1970, but proved less satisfactory after a few years: "It would have cost MMC a lot of money to expand into North America....Instead, we decided to use Chrysler's distribution network. But suddenly the North American consumer liked Japanese cars. The market changed, and we no longer needed help from an existing channel."

Even though one million Mitsubishi cars and small trucks were sold in North America between 1971 and 1981, they carried such nameplates as Dodge Colt, Challenger, and Plymouth Sapporos. North American car buyers were not being educated about the strengths of Mitsubishi models. In addition, MMC marketers were dissatisfied with Chrysler's marketing efforts and felt that the firm was emphasizing its own small cars over the Mitsubishi-built Colts and Sapporos because selling its own product was more profitable. They were all too aware of the fact that MMC's market share in Europe, where it controlled its own distribution, was double its North American market share.

The opportunity to end Chrysler's exclusive North American marketing rights came in 1980. Chrysler, in the midst of a financial crisis, was struggling to avoid bankruptcy when Japan's major banks refused to continue their previous practice of financing Mitsubishi shipments to Chrysler. Mitsubishi executives agreed to provide their own financing for Chrysler, but only if they would allow MMC to sell a minimum of 30 000 Mitsubishi cars in North America through its own dealer network. Chrysler executives had no viable alternative and agreed to the proposal in April 1981. A new subsidiary, Mitsubishi Motor Sales of America (MMSA), was created to direct the firm's marketing efforts.

The year 1982 was one of the worst times in automobile history to launch a new product line. The North American economy was in the midst of a severe recession further complicated by inflation. The high interest rates and economic uncertainty caused consumers to postpone major purchases, and the auto industry was in a major sales slump. In addition, the growing share of the North American auto market held by imports was prompting increasingly frequent demands for import quotas as a means of reducing the number of foreign car imports.

Japan's Ministry of International Trade and Industry responded by voluntarily limiting auto shipments to the U.S. to 1.68 million units annually. Each Japanese auto company's quota was based on average sales since 1976. While Mitsubishi was granted a quota of 112 500 cars annually, 82 500 of this total had to be shipped to Chrysler. MMSA faced the unenviable task of establishing a widespread distribution network with an annual nationwide sales ceiling of only 30 000 cars. While some auto industry representatives felt that the Voluntary Restraint Agreement would be lifted within a few years, no one knew for certain.

MMSA executives needed a marketing strategy that would produce sales and profit success in an environment filled with uncertainty. In addition to a low quota of cars and the need to create a strong dealership network, they also had to deal with such factors as well-known Japanese and North American competitors, low name recognition, and cultural differences that existed in this new market.

Richard Recchia, MMSA's executive vice-president, recognized that the first task facing his firm in the highly competitive import market was to convince consumers that Mitsubishi automobiles were special and unique. He decided to base his marketing strategy on the parent firm's demonstrated strengths.

*We didn't want our products to be perceived as just another Japanese car. So the product line we selected and the price lines within those product lines that we established were aimed at placing our products a step above other Japanese car lines in the same segment so people would perceive Mitsubishi as having more features, more technology, more innovation at a better price than the competition.*

Three models were selected: the two-door sport hatchback Cordia and the four-door Tredia sedan — both offered at approximately $10 000 — plus the sporty Starion turbo coupe, designed to compete with the Mazda RX7 and Nissan's bestselling ZX sports car. In addition, MMSA decided to market a line of small trucks, a product category not included under the Voluntary Restraint Agreement.

Crucial to MMSA's success was its dealer network. By limiting distribution of the Mitsubishi models to a quality network of a few dealerships, MMSA could assure each dealer sufficient inventory to be successful in the market. Moreover, the presence of high-volume, exclusive Mitsubishi dealers in carefully selected markets would serve as tangible evidence to auto buyers that the new cars represented substantial competition for Toyota, Honda, and other companies that consumers associate with Japanese imports.

The dealerships were strategically placed in geographic areas where concentrations of Japanese-car registrations were highest. Special computer programs were developed to create density maps that would pinpoint these locations for prospective dealerships. The first two years of operation saw Mitsubishi dealerships in only 22 metropolitan markets, but those markets accounted for 43 percent of total car sales in the entire nation.

MMSA marketers worked closely with these dealers to ensure marketplace success. Advertising expenditures were double the per-unit average of other Japanese auto makers. Some dealers began to report consumer requests for a fuel-efficient subcompact model; others asked for a more luxurious sedan to compete with the Cressida, Maxima, and Audi. MMSA responded by introducing the subcompact Mirage and the Galant sedan in 1985, enabling Mitsubishi dealers to offer car buyers a complete product line for the first time. Four new models were added in the 1991 model year, including the 3000 GT sports car, Mitsubishi's highest-image car to date. Advertising was expanded to include national TV coverage; the 1991 advertising budget was $120 million, up 20 percent from the 1990 budget. Recchia explained that it is essential to advertise a new model heavily for the first 90 days, followed by six months of advertising to enhance the model's image. "You have to live with [that image] for the life of the product," he said.

During the late 1980s, Mitsubishi benefited from changing consumer transportation preferences. In 1960, consumers bought one truck for every ten cars. In 1987, they bought one truck for every two cars. Compact trucks, such as Mitsubishi's Mighty Max and Montero, are not governed by the Voluntary Restraint Agreement, and they actually outsold the firm's car models in 1987.

To provide its dealers with additional models, Mitsubishi began importing the Hyundai Precis in 1987. Although the Precis (rhymes with "thesis") carries the Mitsubishi nameplate, its South Korean origin exempts it from the restraint quotas, thus permitting MMSA dealers to boost sales and profits without reducing imports of their own higher-priced and more profitable Japanese cars.

In the years since the creation of MMSA, Chrysler Corporation has continued to import and market Mitsubishi car and light-truck models under its own nameplate. During the 1980s,

Chrysler was more dependent on Japanese imports than the other U.S. auto makers. About 11 percent of its cars and 40 percent of its light trucks were built by Mitsubishi.

Relations between Chrysler and Mitsubishi changed during the late 1980s as Chrysler reduced its share of ownership in MMC to 12.8 percent. Meanwhile, the two firms formed a joint venture to build a giant production facility in Bloomington–Normal, Illinois. The new plant can produce up to 240 000 cars a year, and both firms share the output. Its benefits are enormous for Mitsubishi, since domestic production provides a means of avoiding the sales ceilings imposed by the Voluntary Restraint Agreement. Moreover, it allows MMSA to reduce the headaches resulting from the huge exchange-rate fluctuations between the Japanese yen and the U.S. dollar. North American sales of MMSA products were expected to approach 250 000 units in 1990, eight times the 1982 totals.

SOURCES    Takeuchi quotation from Lawrence Minard, "Just What Detroit Needs." Forbes (November 21, 1983), pp. 208, 210. See also "Mitsubishi Motors Corp.," *Advertising Age* (November 23, 1987), p. S–35: Andrew Tanzer, "Gentlemen, Start Your Engines," *Forbes* (April 8, 1985), p. 38: Doug Carroll, "Buyers Keep on Trucking," *USA Today* (February 8, 1988), p. 10E; Cleveland Horton, "Mitsubishi Maps Solo Success," *Advertising Age* (July 2, 1990), pp. 3, 33; Manning, Selvage & Lee.

## Questions

1. Relate the material in this case to each of the elements of the marketing environment.
2. Give specific examples of environmental factors that were truly uncontrollable. How did MMSA's marketing responses to these factors differ from those made in response to environmental variables that could be influenced by the firm?
3. What are the major differences between the MMSA marketing approach and the more typical approaches used by other marketers of imported automobiles? What modifications in the MMSA marketing approach do you expect to occur over the next five years?
4. Isuzu Motors is another relatively recent entry in the North American auto market, with an initial U.S. quota of 16 800 cars. Use the Mitsubishi experience to recommend a course of action for Isuzu.

## CAREER PROFILE

### Michele Burt-Archibald

Maritime Tel & Tel
Market Development

**Education:**

Bachelor of Commerce — Saint Mary's University
Major — Marketing/Management
Graduation — May 1989 (Magna Cum Laude)

Currently I am an Advertising and Promotional Manager in the Market Development Department at Maritime Tel & Tel. Working in a dynamic team environment, I develop and manage the implementation of communications programs for many of MT&T's products and services. As I design each program I work with the elements of the marketing communications mix (advertising, public relations, promotions) most appropriate to the marketing strategy for that product or service. As part of a team of researchers, product managers, and creative services, I get a close-up view of the whole marketing process — an invaluable foundation for future career development.

Outside of my responsibilities at MT&T, I also work as a marketing/advertising consultant for organizations as varied as a retirement village, an electronics sales firm, and a recreational vehicle rental company. Each of these contacts was originally made through class projects undertaken while studying toward my degree at Saint Mary's University.

The real strength of the marketing program at Saint Mary's was the way it combined the practical and theoretical aspects of marketing. I was given opportunities to connect theory and real-life situations through competitions, seminars, and guest speakers that related directly to my career interest. In one advertising course, every session featured a presenter from the business community who was working in an aspect of advertising. As a participant in the Manitoba Markstrat Competition — a two-month simulated marketing/strategic planning game — I got to match wits with marketing colleagues from all across North America. Finally, at business dinners and other events, I got to meet and talk personally with people working in my chosen field — many for companies in my own job market.

How did I get my marketing job? I started by researching companies in my chosen job market, then arranged to speak to the marketing department manager of each company on my short list. I introduced myself as a student looking to further my understanding of their company and its marketing department — and stressed that I was not there to apply for a job. After these first informational meetings, I formally applied to those

companies I felt offered relevant career opportunities for which I believed myself qualified.

In the formal job interview, I drew on discussions and information from the previous, informational interview. This foundation let me demonstrate how, in the context of each company's specific marketing needs, my skills and background were a natural fit. Then at follow-up interviews involving the marketing department, I could show more than just a general acquaintance with the company: I could demonstrate my deeper understanding of its particular role in the environment. Not only could I ask intelligent questions, I could actually offer appropriate suggestions. After each interview, I sent a letter expressing my continued interest, highlighting a fascinating point from the interview, and expressing my appreciation for the time.

In 10 years my goal is to become a Marketing Manager, with responsibilities for planning, directing, and controlling all the company's marketing functions. In addition, I will oversee all marketing decisions and personnel-related issues. To help ensure that I achieve my goal, I've met with various individuals who have helped me map out my best course of action, by identifying the skill set required for a Marketing Manager. My current position represents one facet of the required experience and expertise. My next strategic career move is planned to develop my skills in a product planning capacity, to give me a broader view of the marketing process. Further developmental moves will be designed to build on my marketing expertise and my overall company experience and understanding to prepare me for my 10-year goal.

# PART TWO

# Foundations of the Marketing Plan

CHAPTER 3
## Market Segmentation: Finding a Base to Start
●
CHAPTER 4
## The Market Segmentation Process
●
CHAPTER 5
## Obtaining Data for Marketing Decisions
●
APPENDIX A
## Locating Secondary Data
●
CHAPTER 6
## Marketing Strategy and the Marketing Plan

The focus of the four chapters in Part Two is planning —
*anticipating the future and determining the courses of
action designed to achieve organizational objectives.*
The chapters follow a logical sequence, commencing
with the establishment of a basis for the orientation of
the marketing plan through market segmentation. The
market segmentation process is then outlined, followed
by marketing research and sales forecasting. Part Two
culminates with a chapter on developing the marketing
plan.

## CHAPTER 3

# Market Segmentation: Finding a Base to Start

## CHAPTER OBJECTIVES

1. To introduce the concept of the marketing plan.
2. To identify the fundamental tasks in developing a marketing plan
3. To define market segmentation
4. To illustrate four types of market segmentation in consumer markets.
5. To discuss some aspects of the Canadian market in terms of the four types of consumer market segmentation.
6. To show the main types of segmentation in industrial markets

BEECHAM, Britain's second-largest pharmaceutical manufacturing company, needed new management and new plans; its profits had ceased to grow. The new manager, Robert Bauman, soon saw what was wrong: Beecham was fading because it had failed to adjust to changes that had taken place in its markets:

- Most drug companies owe their success to one or two blockbuster products protected by patents. Beecham's patents were running out, but it had done little to prepare itself for the inevitable decline in sales.

- The company was not paying enough attention to new market segments. Demand for medicines had changed. Beecham had originally built itself up by selling antibiotics, which are used to fight bacterial infections and which accounted for about two-thirds of its pharmaceutical sales. When antibiotics were new, bacterial infection was a major cause of sickness. But today's top-selling drugs are those used to treat chronic conditions, such as heart disease, ulcers, arthritis, or cancer.

- New technology has accelerated the pace of innovation; as a result, the profitable lifetime of a new drug has dropped from some 15 years to just a few. Drug companies need to be more inventive and have a continual flow of new medicines emerging from research laboratories. Beecham had little in the pipeline.

- Increased regulation had sharply raised the costs of developing new drugs, increasing the need to sell them globally to recover costs. Unlike its rivals, Beecham had not done much to expand abroad.

The company also lacked a common purpose. Its drug and consumer divisions were run separately, even at board level.

Bauman saw the drug industry as a maturing business that could benefit from some old-fashioned management discipline. First he gave Beecham a corporate strategy: to concentrate on high-margin pharmaceuticals and the more successful parts of its consumer business. Financial targets were set for the next five years, and new management was brought in to develop and implement new plans.

Within two years of Bauman's assuming leadership, Beecham's earnings per share rose 16 percent, compared with an annual increase of 6.5 percent during the previous two years. Bauman has shown that a hard look at a company, its products, and its markets can lead to plans that make a great deal of difference to that company's success. The company must plan constantly, and the plan must be based on an understanding of market trends and market segments.[1]

---

# Introduction

The marketing plan involves many factors, two of which are consumer and environmental analysis, the topics introduced in Chapters 1 and 2. They provide an important base for the rest of the book. Now we turn to the question of developing plans for marketing a product.

If you have a product to market, a decision must be made about the *target market* — that is, to whom will it be marketed? In most cases, greater success can by achieved by focusing on part of the entire market. Therefore, an analysis of appropriate target market segments is necessary. Other aspects of marketing planning include taking a careful look at what competitors are doing and at your own firm's situation and resources. Marketing research is also required. A marketing manager and his or her staff take all these elements into consideration in forecasting sales and developing a unique marketing plan that will enable the organization to compete successfully in the marketplace.

Figure 3–1 portrays a model of the marketing planning process. It will provide a preliminary perspective on the role each of Part Two's chapter topics plays in the marketing planning process. An expanded discussion of the model is included in Chapter 6. We will start the discussion of marketing planning with the topic of market segmentation.

## Fundamental Tasks in Developing a Marketing Plan

Although marketers may face hundreds of decisions in developing an effective plan for achieving organizational objectives, these decisions may be summarized as two fundamental tasks:

1. They must identify, evaluate, and ultimately select a target market.
2. Once the target market has been selected, they must develop and implement a marketing program designed to satisfy the chosen target group.

FIGURE 3–1

## The Marketing Planning Process

**I. Situation Analysis: Where Are We Now?**
  A. *Historical Background*
  B. *Consumer Analysis*

  • Who are the customers we are trying to serve?

  • What market segments exist?

  • How many consumers are there?

  • How much do they buy and why?

  C. *Competitive Analysis*

**II. Marketing Objectives: Where Do We Want to Go?**
  A. *Sales Objectives*
  B. *Profit Objectives*
  C. *Consumer Objectives*

**III. Strategy: How Can We Get There?**
  A. *Product/Service Decisions*
  B. *Pricing Decisions*
  C. *Distribution Decisions*
  D. *Communication Decisions*
  E. *Financial Considerations*
  F. *Control Aspects*

Source: Adapted from Stephen K. Keiser, Robert E. Stevens, and Lynn J. Loudenback, *Contemporary Marketing Study Guide* (Hinsdale, IL: Dryden Press, 1986), p. 482.

These two tasks reflect the philosophy of consumer orientation in action. The choice of a target market is based on recognizing differences among consumers and organizations within a heterogeneous market. The starting point is to understand what is meant by a *market*.

## What Is a Market?

A market is *people*. It is also business, nonprofit organizations, and government — local, provincial, and federal purchasing agents who buy for their "firms." But people alone do not make a market. The local dealer for foreign automobiles is unimpressed by news that 60 percent of the marketing class raise their hands in response to the question "Who wants to buy a new BMW?" The next question is, "How many of them are waving cheques in their outstretched hands?" A **market** *requires not only people and willingness to buy, but also purchasing power and the authority to buy.*

One of the first rules that the successful salesperson learns is to determine who in the organization or household has the authority to make particular purchasing decisions. Too much time has often been wasted convincing the wrong person that a product or service should be bought.

**market** Requires not only people and willingness to buy, but also purchasing power and the authority to buy.

## Types of Markets

Products may be classified as consumer or industrial goods. **Consumer goods** are *those products and services purchased by the ultimate consumer for personal use.* **Industrial goods** are *those products purchased to be used, either directly or indirectly, in the production of the other goods or for resale.* Most of the products you buy — books, clothes, milk — are consumer goods. Refined nickel is an industrial good for the mint; rubber is a raw material for Michelin.

Sometimes the same product is destined for different uses. The new set of tires when purchased by your neighbour are clearly consumer goods; yet when bought by Chrysler Corporation, they become part of a new Shadow and are classified as industrial goods, since they become part of another good destined for resale. The key to the proper classification of goods lies in the purchaser and in *the reasons for buying the good.*

## Market Segmentation

A country is too large and filled with too many diverse people and firms for any single marketing plan to satisfy everyone. Unless the product is an item such as an unbranded commodity, an attempt to satisfy everyone may doom the marketer to failure. Even a seemingly functional product like toothpaste is aimed at a specific market segment. Stripe was developed for children; Crest focuses on tooth-decay prevention; Ultra Brite hints at enhanced sex appeal; and Aqua Fresh promises both protection and teeth whiteners.

### A·P·P·L·Y·I·N·G  T·H·E  C·O·N·C·E·P·T·S

## *Is There a Women's Market Segment?*

Two out of three Canadian women believe they can live a satisfactory life without having children, yet a similar portion say children are the source of women's greatest satisfaction. By a two-thirds majority, Canadian women also reject the idea that a woman's place is in the home, and no less than 86 percent take the view that a single woman can lead a happy life.

These interesting if apparently conflicting findings come from a recent book by Rena Bartos, a recognized expert on marketing to women. In *Marketing to Women Around the World*, Bartos argues that such findings challenge conventional marketing wisdom and require marketers to re-examine their assumptions about marketing to women.

Bartos's basic thesis is that marketers in general have been so immersed in the specifics of their particular product categories that they have ignored the effect social change is having on consumer behaviour.

In a number of important categories, it seems, women's attitudes are changing faster in Canada than elsewhere in the world. For example, although

Canadian women rank second to U.S. women in workforce participation (52 percent versus 55 percent), Canada reported the highest proportion of career-oriented women working outside the home of any of the 10 countries Bartos studied. More working women in Canada feel their work is more than "just a job."

Bartos's book presents many facts about women that could be of interest to the marketer. The book does not argue that women deserve special marketing treatment, but rather that they should have *appropriate* treatment. Bartos writes: "If I had to use one word to describe the state of the women's market in the 10 countries studied, I would choose *diversity*. Women are not a monolithic group. In every country there is a diverse spectrum of segments representing a range of values and attitudes and a range of marketplace behaviour."

Source: Adapted from Wynne Thomas, "Canadian Women's Market," *Marketing* (September 11, 1989), p. 11.

The auto manufacturer who decides to produce and market a single automobile model to satisfy everyone will encounter seemingly endless decisions to be made about such variables as the number of doors, type of transmission, colour, styling, and engine size. In its attempt to satisfy everyone, the firm may be forced to compromise in each of these areas and, as a result, may discover that it does not satisfy anyone very well. Other firms appealing to particular segments — the youth market, the high–fuel-economy market, the large-family market, and so on — may capture most of the total market by satisfying the specific needs of these smaller, more homogeneous target markets. Although all people are different, we can group them together according to their similarity in one or more dimensions related to interests in a particular product category. This aggregation process is called **market segmentation**.

**market segmentation**
Grouping people according to their similarity in one or more dimensions related to interests in a particular product category.

Once a specific market segment has been identified, the marketer can design an appropriate marketing approach to match its needs, improving the chance of sales to that segment. Market segmentation can be used by both profit-oriented and nonprofit organizations.[2]

## Segmenting Consumer Markets

Market segmentation results from a determination of factors that distinguish a certain group of consumers from the overall market. These characteristics — such as

FIGURE 3 – 2

**Bases for Market Segmentation**

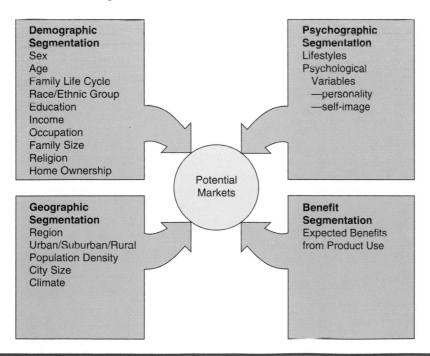

**Demographic Segmentation**
Sex
Age
Family Life Cycle
Race/Ethnic Group
Education
Income
Occupation
Family Size
Religion
Home Ownership

**Psychographic Segmentation**
Lifestyles
Psychological
  Variables
  —personality
  —self-image

Potential Markets

**Geographic Segmentation**
Region
Urban/Suburban/Rural
Population Density
City Size
Climate

**Benefit Segmentation**
Expected Benefits
from Product Use

*Toronto is Canada's largest city and the heart of Ontario's economic growth. Recent population influxes have stimulated growth and provided a market for restaurants, shopping malls, sidewalk vendors, public transit, and all the other goods and services required by a large urban centre.*

age, sex, geographic location, income and expenditure patterns, and population size and mobility, among others — are vital factors in the success of the overall marketing strategy. Toy manufacturers such as Fisher Price and Mattel study not only birthrate trends, but also shifts in income and expenditure patterns. Colleges and universities are affected by such factors as the number of high-school graduates, changing attitudes toward the value of college educations, and increasing enrolment of older adults. Figure 3–2 identifies four commonly used bases for segmenting consumer markets.

*Geographic segmentation*, the dividing of an overall market into homogeneous groups based on population location, has been used for hundreds of years. The second basis for segmenting markets is *demographic segmentation* — dividing an overall market on the basis of characteristics such as age, sex, and income level. Demographic segmentation is the most easily used method of subdividing total markets, and is therefore often implemented.

The third and fourth bases represent relatively recent developments in market segmentation. *Psychographic segmentation* uses behavioural profiles developed from analyses of the activities, opinions, interests, and lifestyles of consumers in identifying market segments. The final basis, *benefit segmentation*, focuses on benefits the consumer expects to derive from a product. These segmentation bases can be important to marketing strategies provided they are significantly related to differences in buying behaviour.

# Geographic Segmentation

A logical starting point in market segmentation is to find out where buyers are. It is not surprising, therefore, that one of the earliest bases for segmentation was geographic. Regional variations in consumer tastes often exist. Per capita consumption of seafood, for example, is higher in the Maritimes than in Alberta. Brick and stone construction, a mainstay in many homes in Ontario, is much less common in the West.

## Geographic Location of the Canadian Population

Canada's population has grown tremendously, from 3 million in 1867 to about 27 million in 1991. The Canadian population, like that of the rest of the world, is not distributed evenly. In fact, it is extremely uneven; large portions of this country are uninhabited.[3]

The term used to describe settled areas is *ecumene*, which literally means "inhabited space."[4] In Canada less than 8 percent of the land surface is occupied farmland. The ecumene in Canada is depicted in Figure 3–3. This map dramatically shows that a relatively small strip lying adjacent to the American border is the land area most heavily settled and utilized. Business and social activities therefore must operate in an east–west manner, over tremendous distances. It is thus not surprising to see the emergence of various distinct market segments, such as central Canada (Ontario and/or Quebec), the Maritimes, the Prairies, or British Columbia.

Not only do provinces vary widely in total population (see Figures 3–4 and 3–5), but pronounced shifts are also evident. People tend to move where work and opportunities exist. Thus, Ontario and British Columbia have been continuously attractive to those on the move. In the late 1970s Alberta experienced large population influxes because of the oil-induced prosperity there. Many left during the recession of the early 1980s.

Natural factors and immigration also influence population. Growth has occurred as a result of natural increase (births minus deaths) and net migration (immigration minus emigration). Overall, the rate of natural increase has been considerably higher than that of net migration. In fact, the Atlantic provinces and Saskatchewan depend on natural increase to restore population levels lost by emigration. On the other hand, Ontario, Alberta, and British Columbia have shown significant total population increases because they have received migration flows plus a natural increase. In recent years natural increases have been declining.

Immigration has had a tremendous impact on Canadian society. The injection of a steady stream of British immigrants and short bursts of central, eastern, and southern Europeans and southeast Asians into the Canadian population have created social pressures in assimilation and citizenship. Some areas have attracted much more immigration. In fact, Ontario contains 51.8 percent of Canada's living foreign-born people. The western provinces contain the greatest percentages of foreign-born "old-timers" (people who immigrated before 1946).

Postwar immigration tended to be from European urban centres to Canadian cities, whereas immigration before World War II was largely from European rural locations to Canadian rural areas.

A remarkable influence has been the immigration–emigration flow in Canada. Despite the fact that 8 million people entered the country through immigration

FIGURE 3–3

## The Canadian Ecumene, 1985

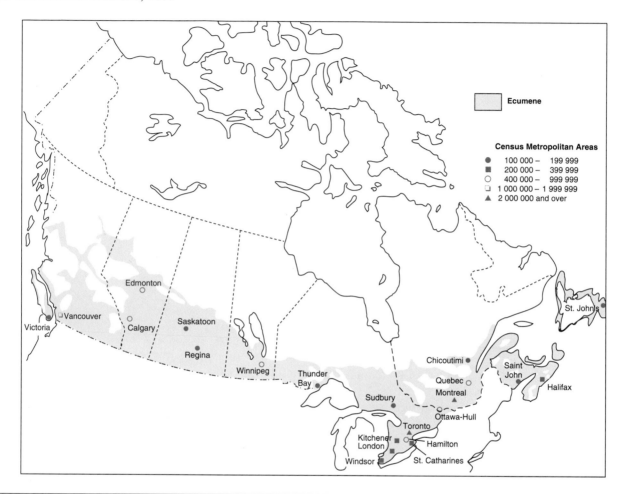

Source: Supply and Services, *Perspective Canada: A Compendium of Social Statistics* (Ottawa: Information Canada, 1974). Reproduced by permission. Updated.

between 1851 and 1961, it is estimated that more than 6 million *left*. From Confederation to 1967, Canada's growth was due largely to natural increase (14.5 million), whereas net migration produced only a 2.4-million increase.[5]

It is estimated that emigration has decreased in recent years. However, the tremendous immigration and emigration in proportion to the size of Canada's population has resulted in a somewhat unstable set of common goals and ends for Canadian society. The character of Canadian society has continually been pulled in various directions through the infusion of different ethnic groups at varying periods of history via immigration.

These factors have traditionally affected the political outlook of Canada's geographic regions. Marketers also recognize that they must take geographic market segments into account.

FIGURE 3-4

**Percentage Distribution of the Population of Canada by Province as of June 1990**

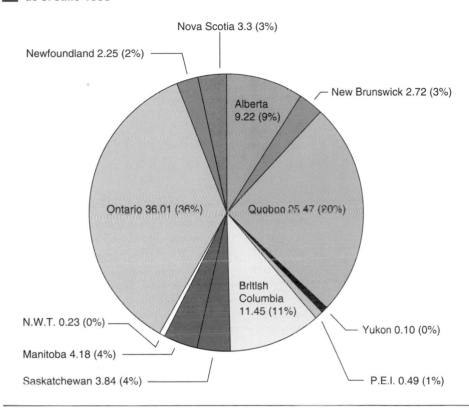

Source: Adapted from *Canadian Markets* (Financial Post Information Service, 1990), p. 7.

## People are in the cities

It is a myth that Canada's population is rural and agricultural. People have been migrating to the cities for many years. Figure 3–6 shows that by 1971, the percentage of rural dwellers had dropped to 24 percent, whereas 76 percent of the population was urban. Figure 3–7 shows populations and growth rates for Canada's 25 largest metropolitan areas. The three largest — Toronto, Montreal, and Vancouver — already contained approximately 30.5 percent of Canada's total population by 1990, and approximately 61 percent of Canada's population lived in cities of 100 000 and over.

The Canadian population, along with the American and the Australian, is one of the most mobile in the world. The average Canadian moves twelve times in a lifetime, as compared to eight times for the average English citizen and five for the typical Japanese.[6] However, this trend may be waning. The slowdown may be due to a number of factors: poor job prospects elsewhere; the tendency of wage earners in two-income families to refuse transfers; an aging population; and a heightened concern for the quality of one's life.

FIGURE 3 – 5

**Provincial and Territorial Populations, 1971, 1980, 1989 (in thousands)**

|  | *1971* | *1980* | *1989* |
|---|---|---|---|
| Newfoundland | 522 100 | 565 600 | 571 000 |
| Prince Edward Island | 111 600 | 122 800 | 130 000 |
| Nova Scotia | 789 000 | 845 100 | 885 900 |
| New Brunswick | 634 600 | 695 400 | 718 600 |
| Quebec | 6 027 800 | 6 386 100 | 6 692 100 |
| Ontario | 7 703 100 | 8 569 700 | 9 578 700 |
| Manitoba | 988 200 | 1 024 900 | 1 084 800 |
| Saskatchewan | 926 200 | 959 400 | 1 007 300 |
| Alberta | 1 627 900 | 2 140 600 | 2 423 000 |
| British Columbia | 2 184 600 | 2 666 000 | 3 053 300 |
| Yukon | 18 400 | 22 300 | 25 300 |
| Northwest Territories | 34 800 | 44 700 | 53 300 |
| TOTAL | 21 568 300 | 24 042 500 | 26 223 200 |

Source: Statistics Canada, *Canadian Post-Censal Estimates,* Catalogue No. 91-210, Volume 8, p. 29. By permission of Minister of Supply and Services Canada.

## Using Geographic Segmentation

There are many instances where markets for goods and services may be segmented on a geographic basis. Regional variations in taste often exist. Quebec has long been known for its interest in fine and varied foods.

Residence location within a geographic area is another important geographic variable. Urban dwellers may eat more meals in restaurants than their suburban and rural counterparts, while suburban dwellers spend proportionally more on lawn and garden care than do people in rural or urban areas. Both rural and suburban dwellers may spend more of their household income on gasoline and automobile needs than do urban households.

Climate is another important factor. Snow blowers, snowmobiles, and sleds are popular products in many parts of Canada. Residents of southwestern British Columbia may spend proportionately less of their total income on heating and heating equipment than other Canadians. Climate also affects patterns of clothing purchases.

Geographic segmentation is useful only when true differences in preference and purchase patterns for a product emerge along regional lines. Geographic subdivisions of the overall market tend to be rather large and often too heterogeneous for effective segmentation without careful consideration of additional factors. In such cases, it may be necessary to use several segmentation variables.

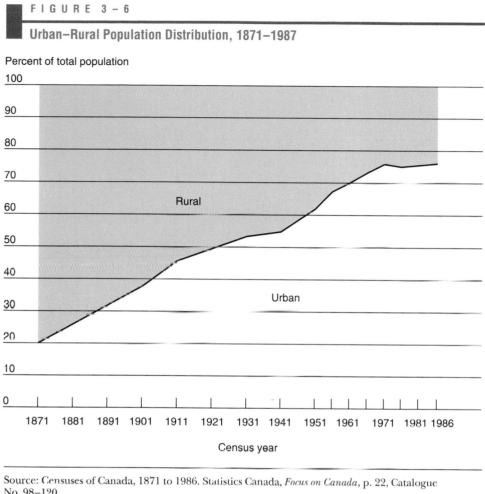

FIGURE 3 – 6

**Urban–Rural Population Distribution, 1871–1987**

Source: Censuses of Canada, 1871 to 1986. Statistics Canada, *Focus on Canada*, p. 22, Catalogue No. 98–120.

# Demographic Segmentation

The most common approach to market segmentation is to group consumers according to demographic variables. These variables — age, sex, income, occupation, education, household size, and others — are typically used to identify market segments and to develop appropriate market mixes. Demographic variables are often used in market segmentation for three reasons:

1. They are easy to identify and measure.
2. They are associated with the sale of many products and services.
3. They are typically referred to in describing the audiences of advertising media, so that media buyers and others can easily pinpoint the desired target market.[7]

Vast quantities of data are available to assist the marketing planner in segmenting potential markets on a demographic basis. Sex is an obvious variable for segmenting

FIGURE 3 – 7

## The 25 Largest Metropolitan Areas in 1990

| Rank | Area | 1990 Population (in thousands) | Ten-Year Growth Rate |
|------|------|-------------------------------|----------------------|
| 1 | Toronto | 3646 | 16.5% |
| 2 | Montreal | 2945 | 2.9% |
| 3 | Vancouver | 1471 | 16.0% |
| 4 | Ottawa–Hull | 867 | 16.6% |
| 5 | Edmonton | 783 | 5.7% |
| 6 | Calgary | 683 | 9.1% |
| 7 | Winnipeg | 639 | 7.8% |
| 8 | Quebec | 635 | 8.7% |
| 9 | Hamilton | 572 | 5.4% |
| 10 | London | 360 | 10.3% |
| 11 | St. Catharines–Niagara | 357 | 4.1% |
| 12 | Kitchener | 334 | 16.0% |
| 13 | Halifax | 302 | 8.7% |
| 14 | Victoria | 269 | 11.3% |
| 15 | Windsor | 265 | 5.8% |
| 16 | Oshawa | 222 | 19.0% |
| 17 | Saskatoon | 201 | 14.9% |
| 18 | Regina | 187 | 7.8% |
| 19 | St. John's | 168 | 8.5% |
| 20 | Chicoutimi–Jonquière | 159 | 0.4% |
| 21 | Sudbury | 157 | 0.3% |
| 22 | Sherbrooke | 138 | 10.2% |
| 23 | Kingston | 136 | 18.4% |
| 24 | Trois-Rivières | 133 | 5.9% |
| 25 | Thunder Bay | 123 | 0.5% |

Source: *Canadian Markets* (Financial Post Information Service, 1990), p. 22.

many markets, since many products are sex-specific. Electric-razor manufacturers have used sex as a variable in the successful marketing of such brands as Lady Remington. Diet soft drinks have often been aimed at female markets. Even deodorants are targeted at males or females.

Age, household size, stage in the family life cycle, and income and expenditure patterns are important factors in determining buying decisions. The often distinct differences in purchase patterns based on such demographic factors justify their frequent use as a basis for segmentation.

## Age — An Important Demographic Segmentation Variable

The population of Canada is expected to grow by 18 percent between 1991 and 2001, but this growth will be concentrated in persons aged 45 and older. This group represents two potentially profitable target markets.

The older and senior middle-aged adult segment (45–64) includes households where the children have grown up and most have left home. For many, housing costs are lower because mortgages are paid off. In general, this group finds itself with substantial disposable income because it is in a peak earning period, and many basic purchases for everyday living have been completed. This disposable income is often used for luxury goods, new furniture, and travel. While this segment currently represents 19.4 percent of the Canadian population, it will account for 65 percent of the growth in population between 1989 and 2001.

Not so many years ago, there was no such thing as a senior-citizen market, since few people reached old age. Now, however, some 11.3 percent of the total population is 65 or older. Not only is it comforting for this year's retiree to learn that at age 65 his or her average life expectancy is at least another 11.4 years, but the trend also creates a unique and potentially profitable segment for the marketing manager.[8] The manager of course will not ignore the youth segment, which will decline in proportion to the whole population, but remain large. Figure 3–8 shows the changing profile of the Canadian population.

Each of the age groups in Figure 3–8 represents different consumption patterns and each serves as the target market for particular firms. For instance, Gerber Products Company has been extremely successful in aiming at the parents-of-infants market, and prepackaged tours appeal to older consumers. Figure 3–9 lists some of the types of merchandise often purchased by the various age groups.

**A·P·P·L·Y·I·N·G  T·H·E  C·O·N·C·E·P·T·S**

### *The Over-50s*

Fifty-five percent of disposable income is in the hands of Canadians 50 and over. They have 80 percent of the savings-account dollars. They buy a third of all new cars, a third of the groceries sold. They switch brands, and try new products.

**What do Over-50s buy?**
New cars: They like them big and comfortable
Travel: 82 percent last year; 65 percent used a travel agent
Microwaves, dishwashers, computers, VCRs
Clothes: Over-50s women spend more that over-30s.

**What else do they do with their money?**
Canadian Over-50s control around 75 percent of all household financial holdings: stocks, bonds, savings. Sixty-four percent own their own homes, and don't plan to move. They don't pay mortgages, don't have to support kids. They're *loaded* and they want to enjoy that money. They eat out more than yuppies, buy creature comforts, pay extra for quality because they feel that means value.

This is obviously a market well worth considering. It could be segmented and marketing plans developed for each segment, with significant profit potential from each.

Source: Adapted from advertisement for *Today's Seniors* in *Marketing* (April 10, 1989), p.5.

FIGURE 3 – 8

## Population Projections by Age Group

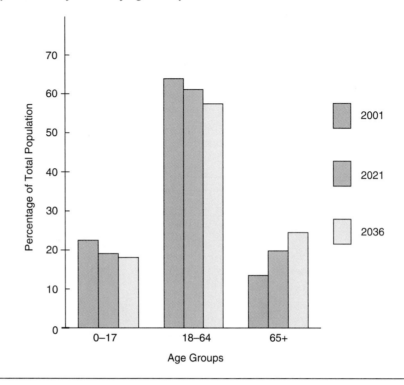

Source: Statistics Canada, *Population Projections for Canada, Provinces and Territories 1981–2036*.
Catalogue No. 91-520.

FIGURE 3 – 9

## Buying Patterns for Different Age Groups

| *Age* | *Name of Age Group* | *Merchandise* |
| --- | --- | --- |
| 0–5 | Young Children | Baby food, toys, nursery furniture, children's wear |
| 6–19 | School Children (including teenagers) | Clothing, sports equipment, records, school supplies, food, cosmetics, used cars |
| 20–34 | Young Adult | Cars, furniture, houses, clothing, recreational equipment, purchases for younger age groups |
| 35–49 | Younger Middle-aged | Larger homes, better cars, second cars, new furniture, recreational equipment |
| 50–64 | Older Middle-Aged | Recreational items, purchases for young marrieds and infants |
| 65+ | Senior Adults | Medical services, travel, drugs, purchases for younger age groups |

*The over-50 group has grown into a powerful marketing force in recent years. They travel more, spend more, and are generally more active than their parents were at the same age. Marketers will be challenged to find new ways of meeting the need of this dynamic age segment in the years to come.*

## Segmenting by Family Life Cycle

The **family life cycle** *is the process of family formation, development, and dissolution*. Using this concept the marketing planner combines the family characteristics of age, marital status, presence or absence of children, and ages of children in developing the marketing strategy. Patrick E. Murphy and William A. Staples have proposed a six-stage family life cycle with several subcategories. The stages of the family life cycle are shown in Figure 3–10.

The behavioural characteristics and buying patterns of persons in each life cycle stage often vary considerably. Young singles have relatively few financial burdens; tend to be early purchasers of new fashion items; are recreation-oriented; and make purchases of basic kitchen equipment, cars, and vacations. By contrast, young marrieds with young children tend to be heavy purchasers of baby products, homes, television sets, toys, and washers and dryers. Their liquid assets tend to be relatively low, and they are more likely to watch television than young singles or young marrieds without children. The empty-nest households in the middle-aged and older categories with no dependent children are more likely to have more disposable income; more time for recreation, self-education, and travel; and more than one member in the labour force than their full-nest counterparts with younger children.

**the family life cycle** The process of family formation, development, and dissolution.

███ FIGURE 3 – 1 0

███ **Family Life Cycle Stages**

1. Young Single
2. Young Married without Children
3. Other Young
   a. Young divorced without children
   b. Young married with children
   c. Young divorced with children
4. Middle-Aged
   a. Middle-aged married without children
   b. Middle-aged divorced without children
   c. Middle-aged married with children
   d. Middle-aged divorced with children
   e. Middle-aged married without dependent children
   f. Middle-aged divorced without dependent children
5. Older
   a. Older married
   b. Older unmarried (divorced, widowed)
6. Other
   All adults and children not accounted for by family life cycle stages.

Source: Adapted with permission from Patrick E. Murphy and William A. Staples, "A Modernized Family Life," *Journal of Consumer Research* (June 1979), p. 16.

Similar differences in behavioural and buying patterns are evident in the other stages of the family life cycle.[9]

Analysis of life cycle stages often gives better results than reliance on single variables, such as age. The buying patterns of a 25-year-old bachelor are very different from those of a father of the same age. The family of five headed by parents in their forties is a more likely prospect for the World Book Encyclopedia than the childless 40-year-old divorced person.

Marketing planners can use published data such as census reports to divide their markets into more homogeneous segments than would be possible if they were analyzing single variables. Such data are available for each classification of the family life cycle.

## The Changing Household

Half the households in Canada are composed of only one or two persons, and the average household size is 3.0 persons. This development is in marked contrast to households that averaged more than four persons before World War II. Married couples still form the largest segment of households, but in relative terms their numbers are decreasing.

There are several reasons for the trend toward smaller households. Among them are lower fertility rates; the tendency of young people to postpone marriage; the increasing desire among younger couples to limit the number of children; the ease and frequency of divorce; and the ability and desire of many young single adults and the elderly to live alone.

*Along with the move to smaller families, a parallel trend is developing toward parenting at an older age. More couples are starting families in their forties, and their needs are different from those of parents in their twenties and thirties. Marketing strategies must be revised to meet the needs of this new segment.*

Over 1.6 million people live alone today — approximately 20 percent of all households. The single-person household has emerged as an important market segment with a special title: **SSWD** (*single, separated, widowed, or divorced*). SSWDs buy approximately 25 percent of all passenger cars, but a much higher proportion of specialty cars. They are also customers for single-serving food products, such as Campbell's Soup-for-One and Green Giant's single-serving casseroles.

**SSWDs**  Single, separated, widowed, or divorced people.

## Segmenting Markets on the Basis of Income and Expenditure Patterns

Earlier, markets were defined as people and purchasing power. A very common method of segmenting consumer markets is on the basis of income. Fashionable specialty shops that stock designer-label clothing obtain most of their sales from high-income shoppers.

Income statistics can be analyzed by family structure. Families can be divided into two groups: husband–wife families and lone-parent families. The latter can be further subdivided by sex of the parent. Significant changes have occurred in the structure of families over time, as Figure 3–11 shows. Between 1980 and 1985, the number of husband–wife families increased by 4.8 percent, while that of male lone-parent families increased by 22 percent. However, the number of female lone-parent families increased by 19 percent. The three groups fared differently with respect to their incomes over the five-year period. Each group experienced a slight drop in real income. The average income in the husband–wife families remained twice that in female lone-parent families. And the average income in male lone-parent families was 63 percent higher than in female lone-parent families.[10]

FIGURE 3-11

**Percentage Distribution by 1980 and 1985 Family Income Groups of Families by Family Structure, Canada**

| Family Income Group (1985 dollars) | All Families | | Husband–Wife Families | | Male Lone-parent Families | | Female Lone-parent Families | |
|---|---|---|---|---|---|---|---|---|
| | 1980 | 1985 | 1980 | 1985 | 1980 | 1985 | 1980 | 1985 |
| Under $5 000 | 3.4 | 3.7 | 2.2 | 2.4 | 5.2 | 6.4 | 14.0 | 13.9 |
| $ 5 000–$ 9 999 | 4.3 | 4.7 | 2.6 | 2.8 | 5.8 | 8.9 | 15.4 | 19.7 |
| 10 000– 14 999 | 8.2 | 8.1 | 7.5 | 7.1 | 10.5 | 10.0 | 19.3 | 16.4 |
| 15 000– 19 999 | 8.1 | 9.1 | 7.6 | 8.7 | 8.9 | 9.9 | 12.3 | 11.9 |
| 20 000– 24 999 | 8.4 | 8.7 | 8.2 | 8.5 | 10.3 | 9.8 | 10.3 | 10.5 |
| 25 000– 34 999 | 19.3 | 18.5 | 19.8 | 19.0 | 21.9 | 20.4 | 13.9 | 14.0 |
| 35 000– 49 999 | 24.4 | 23.4 | 26.0 | 25.2 | 20.4 | 19.8 | 9.6 | 9.2 |
| 50 000 and over | 24.0 | 23.7 | 26.1 | 26.2 | 17.1 | 14.8 | 5.2 | 4.4 |
| Total | 100.0 | 100.0 | 100.0 | 100.0 | 100.0 | 100.0 | 100.0 | 100.0 |
| Number (in thousands) | 6 325 | 6 734 | 5 612 | 5 881 | 124 | 151 | 589 | 702 |
| Average income | $38 276 | 37 827 | 40 335 | 40 222 | 33 261 | 31 252 | 19 733 | 19 177 |
| Median Income | $34 143 | 33 434 | 36 038 | 35 758 | 29 155 | 27 405 | 15 505 | 15 005 |

Source: Statistics Canada, *Family Income: Census Families*, 1986 Census, Catalogue No. 93-117.

A household's expenditures may be divided into two categories: (1) basic purchases of essential household needs, and (2) other purchases that can be made at the discretion of the household members once the necessities have been purchased (disposable income). Total Canadian disposable income is estimated to have tripled in constant dollars since 1961.[11] This is a substantial increase.

## Engel's Laws

**Engel's Laws**   As family income increases, (1) a smaller percentage goes for food, (2) the percentage spent on housing and household operations and clothing will remain constant, and (3) the percentage spent on other items will increase.

How do expenditure patterns vary with increased income? More than a hundred years ago a German statistician named Ernst Engel published three general statements — **Engel's Laws** — based on his studies of spending behaviour. According to Engel, *as family income increases*:

1. A smaller *percentage* of expenditures goes for food.
2. The *percentage* spent on housing and household operations and clothing will remain constant.
3. The *percentage* spent on other items (such as recreation, education, etc.) will increase.

Are Engel's Laws still valid today? Figure 3-12 supplies the answers. A small decline in the percentage of total income spent for food occurs from low to high incomes. Note the emphasis on the word *percentage*. The high-income families will spend a greater absolute amount on food purchases, but their purchases will represent a smaller percentage of their total expenditures than will be true of low-income households.

FIGURE 3 – 1 2

## Percentage Annual Family Expenditures by Income Groups, 1986

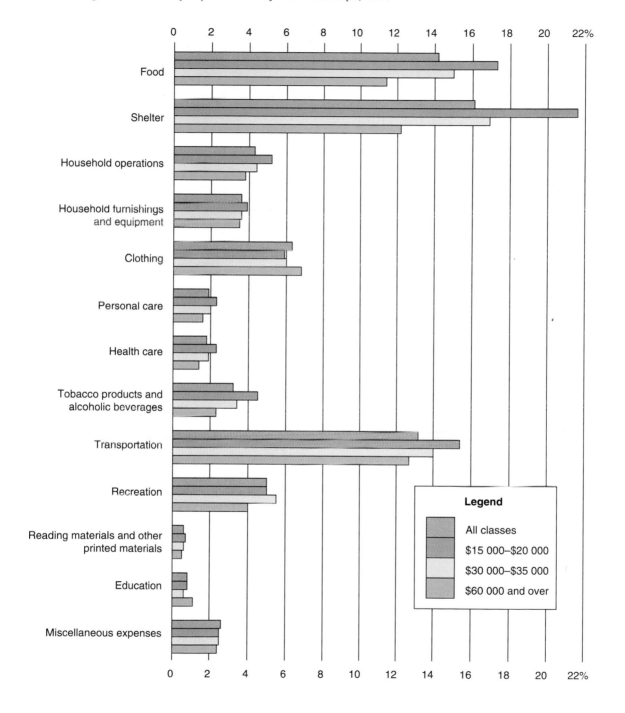

Legend

- All classes
- $15 000–$20 000
- $30 000–$35 000
- $60 000 and over

Source: *Family Expenditure in Canada*. Statistics Canada (1986), Catalogue No. 62-555, pp. 34–39.

With respect to Engel's second law, expenditures for shelter decline rather than remain constant. However, as predicted, there is relatively little change in the percentage of income spent on household operations and in household furnishings and equipment, as well as on clothing.

The third law is also true with respect to recreation and education. However, there are notable exceptions to the original generalization, such as transportation. It has become a much greater part of family expenditures than Engel might have dreamed.

Engel's Laws provide the marketing manager with useful generalizations about types of consumer demand that will evolve with increased income. They may also be useful when evaluating a foreign country as a potential target market.[12]

## Psychographic Segmentation

Although geographic and demographic segmentation traditionally have been the primary bases for grouping customers and industries into segments to serve as target markets, marketers have long recognized the need for fuller, more lifelike portraits of consumers for use in developing marketing programs. Even though traditionally used variables such as age, sex, family life cycle, income, and population size and location are important in segmentation, lifestyles of potential consumers may prove more important. Demographically, a truck driver and a college professor may be the same age and have the same income. Yet their purchasing behaviour will likely be very different.

**lifestyle**   The mode of living.

**Lifestyle** refers to *the mode of living* of consumers. Consumers' lifestyles are regarded as a composite of their individual behaviour patterns and psychological makeups — their needs, motives, perceptions, and attitudes. A lifestyle also bears the mark of many other influences — those of reference groups, culture, social class, and family members. A frequently used classification system for lifestyle variables is shown in Figure 3–13.

### FIGURE 3 – 1 3

### Lifestyle Dimensions

| *Activities* | *Interests* | *Opinions* | *Demographics* |
|---|---|---|---|
| Work | Family | Themselves | Age |
| Hobbies | Home | Social issues | Education |
| Social events | Job | Politics | Income |
| Vacation | Community | Business | Occupation |
| Entertainment | Recreation | Economics | Family size |
| Club membership | Fashion | Education | Dwelling |
| Community | Food | Products | Geography |
| Shopping | Media | Future | City size |
| Sports | Achievements | Culture | Stage in life cycle |

Source: Reprinted with permission from Joseph T. Plummer, "The Concept and Application of Lifestyle Segmentation," *Journal of Marketing* (January 1974), p. 34, published by the American Marketing Association.

# Psychographics

A technique that is sometimes used to develop more meaningful bases for segmentation is **psychographics**. Psychographics *is the use of psychological attributes, lifestyles, and attitudes in determining the behavioural profiles of different consumers*. These profiles are usually developed through market research that asks for agreement or disagreement with several hundred statements dealing with activities, interests, and opinions such as those listed in Figure 3–13. Because of the basis of the statements (*activities, interests* and *opinions*), they are sometimes referred to as **AIO statements**. Figure 3–14 contains a sample list of such statements. Market segments are identified on the basis of similar psychographic characteristics.

The Print Measurement Bureau, along with two market research organizations (Goldfarb, and Thompson Lightstone), jointly surveyed the Canadian market using

**psychographics** The use of psychological attributes, lifestyles, and attitudes in determining the behavioural profiles of different consumers.

**AIO statements** Statements about activities, interests, and opinions, used in developing psychographic profiles.

## FIGURE 3–14

### Lifestyle Profiles: Target Segment (TS) Compared with the Rest of the Population (ROP)

| | Percent Agreeing | | Significances of Differences by Dimension |
|---|---|---|---|
| | TS (%) | ROP (%) | |
| **Innovativeness** | | | |
| I often try new brands before my friends and neighbours do | 40* | 22 | (0.00) |
| I like to try new and different things | 95 | 69 | |
| When I see a new brand on the shelf I often buy it just to see what it is like | 40 | 20 | |
| **Opinion Leaders** | | | |
| My friends or neighbours often come to me for advice | 60 | 46 | (0.44) |
| I often seek out the advice of my friends regarding which brand to buy | 20 | 21 | |
| I sometimes influence what my friends buy | 30 | 32 | |
| I spend a lot of time talking to my friends about products and brands | 20 | 06 | |
| **Home Cleaners** | | | |
| I am uncomfortable when my home is not completely clean | 60 | 67 | (0.11) |
| I must admit I really don't like household chores | 15 | 51 | |
| My home is usually very neat and clean | 70 | 65 | |
| I don't like to see clothes lying about | 85 | 84 | |
| **Physical Fitness** | | | |
| Maintaining my physical fitness is important to me | 90 | 89 | (0.63) |
| I think that most people should try to stay physically fit | 100 | 94 | |

FIGURE 3 – 14 (CONTINUED)

### Lifestyle Profiles: Target Segment (TS) Compared with the Rest of the Population (ROP)

| | Percent Agreeing | | Significances of Differences by Dimension |
|---|---|---|---|
| | TS (%) | ROP (%) | |
| **Bargain Hunters** | | | |
| I shop a lot for specials | 70 | 63 | (0.27) |
| I usually watch for advertisements of announcements of sales | 75 | 65 | |
| I find myself checking the prices in the grocery store even for small items | 70 | 64 | |
| **Enjoy Outdoors** | | | |
| I enjoy hiking | 55 | 49 | (0.05) |
| I would rather see a movie than go camping | 20 | 38 | |
| I enjoy visiting state and national parks | 95 | 84 | |
| **Home Centred** | | | |
| I would rather spend a quiet evening at home than go out to a party | 80 | 67 | (0.13) |
| I am a homebody | 75 | 67 | |
| I like parties where there are lots of music and talk | 20 | 48 | |
| **Like Cooking** | | | |
| I love to cook | 70 | 57 | (0.15) |
| I am a good cook | 65 | 60 | |

*Forty percent of the target segment agreed that they often try new brands before their friends and neighbours do, compared with 22 percent in the rest of the population.

Source: T.K. Clarke, D.A. Schellinck, and Thomas L. Leonard, "Developing an Effective Communication Strategy to Modify Environment-Related Consumer Behaviour," *International Journal of Advertising* 4 (1985), p. 112.

the methodology outlined above.[13] Each research organization analyzed the data somewhat differently, and developed some interesting psychographic groupings.

## The Goldfarb Segments

There are six Goldfarb segments, divided neatly into *more* or *less* traditional, with 56 percent of the population falling into the *more* traditional segment. The Goldfarb segments are as follows:

*Day-to-Day Watchers* are quite satisfied with what life has to offer. They are early followers, rather than leaders, but they keep a close eye on the world around them.

*Old-Fashioned Puritans* are conservative to the point of being defensive, traditional to the point of inflexibility, and indifferent to the point of apathy. This is not the best group for new-product advertising.

*Responsible Survivors* are a cautious group; they are very brand-loyal and are heavy TV viewers.

## Psychographic Analysis

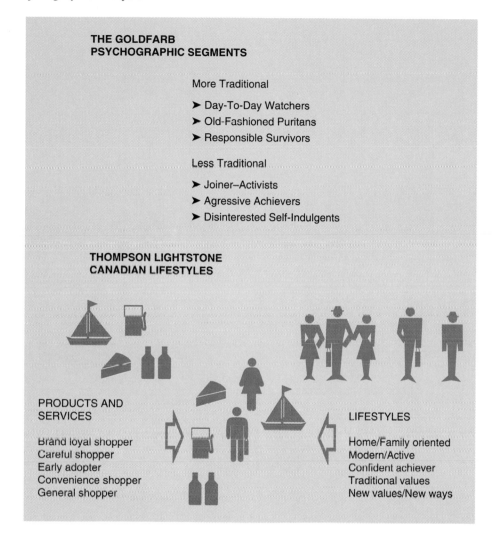

THE GOLDFARB
PSYCHOGRAPHIC SEGMENTS

More Traditional

➤ Day-To-Day Watchers
➤ Old-Fashioned Puritans
➤ Responsible Survivors

Less Traditional

➤ Joiner–Activists
➤ Agressive Achievers
➤ Disinterested Self-Indulgents

THOMPSON LIGHTSTONE
CANADIAN LIFESTYLES

PRODUCTS AND
SERVICES

Brand loyal shopper
Careful shopper
Early adopter
Convenience shopper
General shopper

LIFESTYLES

Home/Family oriented
Modern/Active
Confident achiever
Traditional values
New values/New ways

Source: Chaplin, "Pigeonholes," p. 1.

*Joiner–Activists* are leading-edge thinkers, but tend to be nonconformists.

*Aggressive Achievers* are confident, success-oriented people. They want to be leaders, love status-signalling goods, and need to have their psyches stroked regularly.
*Disinterested Self-Indulgents'* TV viewing is not dissimilar from the previous group. Their music tastes are a little more conservative, leaning to pop rock and oldies. They are also above average pay-TV viewers and VCR users.

## The Thompson Lightstone Segments

Thompson Lightstone isolated the traditional lifestyles' values based on needs, interests, and aspirations, and merged them with views toward pricing and advertising, buying behaviours, and preferences for products and services. Here are their market segments:

### Application of Psychographic Analysis

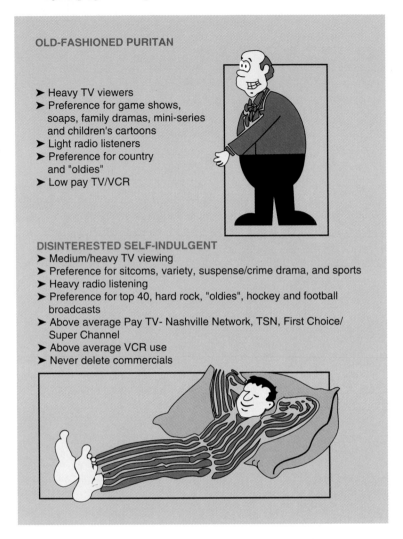

**OLD-FASHIONED PURITAN**

➤ Heavy TV viewers
➤ Preference for game shows,
  soaps, family dramas, mini-series
  and children's cartoons
➤ Light radio listeners
➤ Preference for country
  and "oldies"
➤ Low pay TV/VCR

**DISINTERESTED SELF-INDULGENT**

➤ Medium/heavy TV viewing
➤ Preference for sitcoms, variety, suspense/crime drama, and sports
➤ Heavy radio listening
➤ Preference for top 40, hard rock, "oldies", hockey and football
  broadcasts
➤ Above average Pay TV- Nashville Network, TSN, First Choice/
  Super Channel
➤ Above average VCR use
➤ Never delete commercials

Source: Chaplin, "Pigeonholes," p. 1.

*The Passive/Uncertain* segment exhibits low levels of involvement in the process of shopping, and a generally negative sentiment towards advertising.

*The Mature* market segment is a mix of secondary shoppers and empty-nesters. They tend to be older, with less financial clout. They buy a lot of lottery tickets.

*Home Economists* are the true bargain hunters. They include many homemakers. They spend a lot of time shopping.

*The Active/Convenience* segment is the typical "yuppie" (young upwardly mobile professional) in attitudes and purchase habits. They are the buyers of the premium products.

*Modern Shoppers* enjoy shopping for shopping's sake. They usually buy well, even if it is on impulse.

People in the *Traditional Home/Family-Oriented* segment tend to be very cautious in all their dealings and their attitudes. They shop for value, are brand-loyal, and preoccupied with family life and their children.

What can be done with such segment analyses? There are many possibilities. The Print Measurement Bureau cross-tabulated the two different sets of lifestyle clusters against questions they had asked about radio or TV listening/watching. Old-Fashioned Puritans were found to be heavy TV viewers and light radio listeners. They have a preference for game shows, soaps, family dramas, mini-series, and children's cartoons. In radio listening, they have a preference for country music and "oldies." They have low ownership of VCRs and low pay-TV usage. Such information is extremely useful to broadcasters and to advertisers. The procedure used for broadcasting could be applied to many other goods and services as well. The insights developed by such a process go far beyond demographic segmentation.

Psychographic segmentation often serves as a component of an overall segmentation strategy in which markets are also segmented on the basis of demographic/geographic variables. These more traditional bases provide the marketer with accessibility to consumer segments through orthodox communications channels such as newspapers, radio and television advertising, and other promotional outlets. Psychographic studies may then be implemented to develop lifelike, three-dimensional profiles of the lifestyles of the firm's target market. When combined with demographic/geographic characteristics, psychographics emerges as an important tool in understanding the behaviour of present and potential market targets.[14]

## Benefit Segmentation

Benefit segmentation is based on the attributes of products as seen by the customer. Segments are developed by asking consumers about the benefits they perceive in a good or service. Since many people perceive and use the same product differently, those who perceive benefits that are similar are clustered into groups. Each group then constitutes a market segment.

Many marketers now consider benefit segmentation one of the most useful method of classifying markets. One analysis of 34 segmentation studies indicated that benefit analysis provided the best predictor of brand use, level of consumption, and product type selected in 51 percent of the cases. In a pioneering benefit segmentation investigation, Daniel Yankelovich revealed that much of the watch industry operated with little understanding of the benefits watch buyers expect in their purchases. At the time of the study, most watch companies were marketing relatively expensive models through jewellery stores and using prestige appeals. However, Yankelovich's research revealed that less than one-third of the market was purchasing a watch as a symbol. In fact, 23 percent of his respondents reported they purchased the lowest-price watch and another 46 percent focused on durability and overall product quality. The Timex Company decided to focus its product benefits on those two categories and market its watches in drugstores, variety stores, and discount houses. Within a few years of adopting the new segmentation approach, it became the largest watch company in the world.[15]

FIGURE 3–15

## Benefit Segmentation of the Toothpaste Market

| | Segment Name | | | |
|---|---|---|---|---|
| | *The Sensory Segment* | *The Sociables* | *The Worriers* | *The Independent Segment* |
| Principal benefit sought | Flavour, product appearance | Brightness of teeth | Decay prevention | Price |
| Demographic strengths | Children | Teens, young people | Large families | Men |
| Special behavioural characteristics | Users of spearmint-flavoured toothpaste | Smokers | Heavy users | Heavy users |
| Brands disproportionately favoured | Colgate, Stripe | MacLean's, Plus White, Ultra Brite | Crest | Brands on sale |
| Personality characteristics | High self-involvement | High sociability | High hypochondriasis | High autonomy |
| Lifestyle characteristics | Hedonistic | Active | Conservative | Value-oriented |

Source: Reprinted by permission Russell I. Haley, "Benefit Segmentation: A Decision-Oriented Research Tool," *Journal of Marketing* (July 1968), p. 33, published by the American Marketing Association.

Figure 3–15 illustrates how benefit segmentation might be applied to the toothpaste market. The table reveals that some consumers are primarily concerned with price, some with preventing tooth decay, some with taste, and others with brightness "benefits". Also included are the demographic and other characteristics used in focusing on each subgrouping.[16]

## Segmenting Industrial Markets

While the bulk of market segmentation research has concentrated on consumer markets, the concept can also be applied to the industrial sector. The overall process is similar. Three industrial market segmentation approaches have been identified: geographic segmentation, product segmentation, and segmentation by end-use applications (see Figure 3–16).

### Geographic Segmentation

Geographic segmentation is useful in industries where the bulk of the customers are concentrated in specific geographical locations. This approach can be used in such instances as the automobile industry, concentrated in the central Ontario area, or the lumber industry, centred in British Columbia and Quebec. It might also be used in cases where the markets are limited to just a few locations. The oil-field equipment market, for example, is largely concentrated in cities like Calgary and Edmonton.

## Segmentation Bases for Industrial Markets

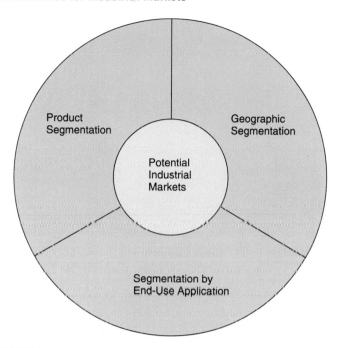

## Product Segmentation

It is possible to segment some industrial markets in terms of their need for specialized products. Industrial users tend to have much more precise product specifications than do ultimate consumers, and such products often fit very narrow market segments. For example, special rivets for bridge-building might be a market segment. Therefore, the design of an industrial good or service and the development of an associated marketing plan to meet specific buyer requirements is a form of market segmentation.

## Segmentation by End-Use Applications

A third segmentation base is end-use applications — that is, precisely how the industrial purchaser will use the product. (This is similar to benefit segmentation in consumer markets.) A manufacturer of, say, printing equipment may serve markets ranging from a local utility to a bicycle manufacturer to Agriculture Canada. Each end-use may dictate unique specifications of performance, design, and price. The market for desktop computers provides a good example: IBM has several computers for different market sizes. Caterpillar has equipment designed for road construction, as well as for other industrial applications. Regardless of how it is done, market segmentation is as vital to industrial marketing as it is in consumer markets.

# Summary

A market consists of people or organizations with the necessary purchasing power and willingness to buy. The authority to buy must also exist. Markets can be classified by the type of products they handle. Consumer goods are products purchased by the ultimate consumer for personal use. Industrial goods are products purchased for use either directly or indirectly in the production of other goods and services for resale. Products are typically directed toward specific market segments. The process of aggregating people or firms into relatively homogeneous groups is called market segmentation.

Consumer markets can be divided on the bases of geographic, demographic, psychographic, or benefit segmentation. Geographic segmentation is the process of aggregating into groups on the basis of population location. It is one of the oldest forms of segmentation. The most commonly used form is demographic segmentation, which classifies the overall market into groups based on such characteristics as age, sex, and income level. Psychographic segmentation uses behavioural and attitudinal profiles developed from analyses of the activities, opinions, interests, and lifestyles of consumers to identify market segments. The fourth approach, benefit segmentation, may be the most useful. It segments markets on the basis of the perceived benefits consumers expect to derive from a good or service.

There are three bases for industrial market segmentation: geographic segmentation, product segmentation, and segmentation by end-use applications. Geographic segmentation is commonly used, since many industries are concentrated in a few locations. A second industrial market segmentation base is by product. Industrial markets are characterized by precise product specifications, making this approach feasible. Segmentation by end-use applications is the final base. This approach is predicated on the use that the industrial purchasers will make of the good or service.

This chapter has examined the various bases for segmenting both consumer and industrial markets. Chapter 4 examines how these concepts may be applied to market segmentation strategies.

## ■ K E Y   T E R M S

| | | |
|---|---|---|
| market | psychographics | Engel's Laws |
| consumer goods | AIO statements | lifestyle |
| industrial goods | family life cycle | demographics |
| market segmentation | SSWD | benefit segmentation |

## ■ R E V I E W   Q U E S T I O N S

1. Explain why each of the four components of a market is needed for a market to exist.
2. Bicycles are consumer goods; iron ore is an industrial good. What about trucks — are they consumer goods or industrial goods? Defend your answer.
3. Identify and briefly explain the bases for segmenting consumer markets.

4. Identify the major population shifts that have occurred in recent years. How do you account for these shifts?
5. Explain and describe the use of AIO questions.
6. Why is demographic segmentation the most commonly used approach to marketing segmentation?
7. How can lifestyles be used in market segmentation?
8. Explain the use of product usage rates as a segmentation variable.
9. What market segmentation base would you recommend for the following:
   a. Professional soccer team
   b. Porsche sports car
   c. A CD, tape, and record publisher
   d. Scope mouthwash
10. Identify and briefly explain the bases of segmenting industrial markets.

# DISCUSSION QUESTIONS AND EXERCISES

1. Match the following bases for market segmentation with the items below:
   a. Geographic segmentation
   b. Demographic segmentation
   c. Psychographic segmentation
   d. Benefit segmentation
   _____ 1. A government-financed study divides households into five categories of eating patterns: meat eaters; healthy eaters; conscientious eaters; "in-a-dither" eaters; and on-the-go eaters.
   _____ 2. A department store chain decides to emphasize suburban rather than downtown outlets.
   _____ 3. "7-Up: clear, crisp, with no caffeine."
   _____ 4. A catalogue retailer targets its catalogues at 25- to 54-year-old women employed outside the home, with household incomes of $34 000.

2. Events such as the Olympics are extensively televised. What types of products would most likely benefit from advertising associated with the games? Would they appeal to more than one market segment?
3. Prepare a brief report on the future growth prospects of the geographic area in which you live.
4. How might a fast-food marketer such as Harvey's respond to the changing age mix projections shown in Figure 3.8?
5. Canadian census data reveal that a significant number of Canadians have a mother tongue other than English or French (mother tongue is defined as the language first learned and still understood). Some of the larger language groups are Italian (529 000 people), German (523 000), Ukrainian (292 000), and Chinese (224 000). How could a marketer use this demographic information?

# MICROCOMPUTER EXERCISE
## Engel's Laws

**Directions:** Use the Menu Item titled "Engel's Laws" on the *Foundations of Marketing* disk to solve the following problems.

1. The Martin family of Swift Current, Saskatchewan, uses a budget to monitor and control household expenditures. The family just prepared this year's budget to reflect the salary increases that both spouses expect at the beginning of the year. The general categories of expenditures and savings and the amounts allocated to each category are shown in Table A.

**TABLE A**

**Budget of the Martin Family**

| Budget Category | Last Year's Expenditures | This Year's Budgeted Amount |
|---|---|---|
| Food | $18 000 | $19 500 |
| Clothing and Housing | 24 000 | 29 250 |
| Other | 18 000 | 16 250 |
| Total | $60 000 | $65 000 |

Is the Martin budget for this year consistent with Engel's Laws? With which, if any, of the laws is the Martin budget in conflict?

**2.** Julia Wiley is a single, 26-year-old marketing-research analyst at a major consumer-goods company in Toronto. Last year, Wiley saved $3200 and spent the remainder of her salary as follows: food, $6400; housing and clothing, $12 800; and miscellaneous (including entertainment and vacations), $9600. But a recent promotion and salary increase have prompted Wiley to reevaluate her personal budget. She has decided to use a payroll-deduction program to increase her savings to $4200, cut her food expenditure to $5600, increase her housing and clothing outlays slightly to $14 000, and spend the rest of next year's $35 000 salary on miscellaneous items (including a vacation).

Does Wiley's budget conflict with Engel's Laws? If so, how?

**3.** The Jacobs family of Abbotsford, B.C., uses the budget shown in Table B.

Do the Jacobses' financial plans conflict with Engel's Laws? If so, how?

**TABLE B**

**Budget of the Jacobs Family**

| Budget Category | Last Year's Expenditures | This Year's Budgeted Amount |
|---|---|---|
| Food | $ 8 000 | $ 9 000 |
| Housing | 15 000 | 19 500 |
| Other | 4 000 | 3 500 |
| Total | $27 000 | $32 000 |

## VIDEO | CASE 3 | Lakeway

Services are the largest sector of the North American economy. In 1986 68 percent of Canadian workers were employed in the service sector. The shift toward services has been accompanied by increases in the proportions of single people, women working outside the home, and senior citizens in the population. At the same time, higher productivity and an increasing number of dual-income households has resulted in increased affluence.

Service providers must be sensitive to changing needs and desires if they are to remain competitive. In fact, this is much more true for service providers than for manufacturers. A defective radio can be replaced, but a spoiled vacation is lost forever.

Lakeway Resort in Austin, Texas, has taken this dictum to heart. When Lakeway opened almost 30 years ago, it quickly became a successful local-destination resort. But after 25 years its image and its occupancy rate had declined, and it was faced with increased competition. However, the resort industry in general was experiencing rapid expansion because discretionary spending had been increasing throughout this period. It was apparent that Lakeway's marketing approach needed to be changed.

In 1987 the Dolce company purchased Lakeway Resort as part of its strategy to develop a small network of high-grade conference facilities. Lakeway contained full conference facilities to meet the needs of its business customers, championship golf and tennis facilities to attract recreational customers, a wide assortment of lodgings, and the scenic beauty of the Texas hill country.

Dolce wanted to turn Lakeway into a "world-class resort" that would continue to attract its traditional local customers and add national conference customers and families. In other words, it planned to rebuild its existing markets and penetrate new markets. To do so, Lakeway would require investment to add new and maintain existing services, as well as commitment to outstanding service by the staff. Once these changes were implemented, Lakeway's target markets would have to be told about them.

The facilities were expanded and upgraded as planned. Ongoing addition of new services and expansion of existing services take a major place in the operational scheme at Lakeway. For instance, to attract families Lakeway began a "Kids under 12 eat free" program and a "summer camp" program. A recreation department was created to develop new activities for all market segments, and a recreation director hired to run it. Because management was aiming for a Mobil four-star rating, room service was introduced.

In the resort business it is essential to maintain a continuously high level of service. In employee–customer interactions, even brief lapses of service will discourage repeat patronage. Lakeway's staff has been trained in what Lakeway calls aggressive hospitality. Employees are encouraged to "go the extra mile" for their customers, and every month one employee is given an "aggressive hospitality award": the employee is given a lapel pin and a wall plaque, and his or her name is printed on all employees' paycheques for the following month.

At Lakeway, aggressive hospitality is not an empty phrase. Consider the actions of an employee in the Conference Services Department. One morning, while checking out a conference room with the customer just before the latter's presentation was to begin, he was told that the customer needed a TV and a VCR that had not been ordered with the other services in advance. The employee said there would be no problem, and when he found that only the TV was available, he drove to his parents' home nearby and borrowed their VCR for the presentation. Such initiative is indicative of the quality of the employees that Lakeway has been able to recruit. According to CEO Andrew J. Dolce, "Our real challenge is to continue to attract real quality people."

Once these changes had been made, Lakeway wanted to carry slightly different messages to each segment of its market: to former patrons, the message that new ownership, new management, and upgraded and expanded services made the Lakeway "experience" better than ever; to potential new patrons, an explanation of Lakeway's excellent facilities and superior hospitality.

Potential new clients comprise many diverse groups, including recreational clients throughout the nation, corporate clients, and the conference segment known as "smurf" — social, military, religious, and fraternal organizations. To promote its message to all these clients, Lakeway has relied on personal selling and direct mail, the latter achieving a response rate of over 8 percent, roughly three times the national average. Only 9 percent of Lakeway's marketing budget is spent on advertising, mostly in trade publications such as *Success Meeting Magazine*. Most of the business is generated by a force of highly talented salespeople who are keenly aware of each competitor's offerings, prices, and performance. Because of their skills, they have been successful at keeping prices and occupancy up in spite of poor economic times in Texas.

What has been the result of these changes? By 1989, occupancy was up and the mix had shifted from 87 percent to 65 percent Texas residents. By forming a realistic long-term plan for market development, and sensitively adjusting its services in response to market changes, Lakeway has achieved its goal and has reestablished its competitive position.

SOURCE     *Lakeway Resort* (Hinsdale, IL: Dryden Press, 1991).

## Questions

1. Relate the Lakeway decisions to the steps in the marketing planning process shown in Figure 3–1. Identify two examples in the cases that reflect tactical planning. Give an example of strategic planning by Lakeway marketers.

2. Which of the market segments illustrated on page 71 would be appropriate target markets for Lakeway?

3. If Lakeway had not existed as a resort before being purchased by the Dolce Company but had been a private club, how would Dolce's strategic plan for developing the resort have differed from the plan discussed in this case?

# The Market Segmentation Process

1. To explain the factors involved when choosing whether or not to design strategies for specific market segments.
2. To outline the stages in the market segmentation process.
3. To explain the concept of market positioning within market segments.
4. To show how target market decision analysis can be used in market segmentation.
5. To show how target market decision analysis can be used to assess the assortment of products offered to the market.

THE style of their headquarters reflects the two TV channels' personalities. Brash, youth-oriented, and devoted to popular music, MuchMusic is housed in a renovated historic building in the heart of downtown Toronto's trendy Queen Street West strip. Instead of a conventional studio, there are specially designed outlets that allow crews to shoot a live show practically anywhere in the building. By contrast, The Sports Network (TSN), dedicated to serving the most ardent armchair athletes, makes its home near a Toronto residential suburb, and has just opened a state-of-the-art broadcast facility right inside Toronto's SkyDome. Despite their differences, the two national 24-hour operations are success stories in the treacherous world of Canadian television. Both started as pay-TV channels, but have moved to basic cable, increasing their penetration to more than 5 million households. Besides proving that specialty TV works, the two services have made a big impact on domestic music and sport.

The success of both channels illustrates the value of intelligent market segmentation. MuchMusic has designed its product and marketing program to serve the 18-to-25 age group. The concept was the brainchild of Martin and Moses Znaimer,

*TSN, in its new $15-million studio at the SkyDome, projects an entirely different image from MuchMusic and appeals to a different group. By producing quality broadcasting that appeals to a specific market segment, it has taken a significant share of this market and made an important contribution to Canadian sports.*

president and executive producer of the channel. Since MuchMusic's launch in 1984, it has retained its staple of music videos while evolving to offer news, concerts, and special segments on country, heavy-metal, and soul music — as well as interviews with major rock stars. That formula of live shows — delivered by such hosts as Ziggy Lorenc, who look as if they have been plucked from a video themselves — has steadily increased the number of viewers.

MuchMusic's emphasis on Canadian artists has had a profound impact on the domestic pop-music industry. About 35 percent of the videos feature Canadian artists. The channel's early exposure of such Canadian performers as k.d. lang, Jane Siberry, and Bryan Adams boosted their careers. In this country, where a few people are spread out across a large geographic area, MuchMusic is one of the connecting factors for music fans. The channel has also stimulated the domestic video-production industry. In addition to playing Canadian videos, MuchMusic devotes 5 percent of its gross revenues ($500 000 in a recent fiscal year) to its VideoFACT foundation, which helps fledgling Canadian artists get videos produced.

Because it was supplied with relatively cheap programming — the record companies initially made videos available for free and now charge only a nominal fee — MuchMusic made a modest profit in the first year, and grew from there. TSN, in keeping with the expensive nature of sports coverage, achieved its projected break-even point in its third year and has made profits since then. The signs of its success are evident: it paid $5 million to become an official SkyDome partner and in May 1989 it opened Dome Productions, a $15-million studio at the dome site.

The channel itself has covered more than 72 professional and amateur sports. It sees itself as a complementary service to the major networks. Conventional networks have so many different constituencies to serve that they really cannot add to their sports coverage. TSN adds coverage that the networks cannot provide. It also lavishes attention on Canadian participants in international events. With more than 50 percent Canadian content, TSN has boosted the image of college-level sports and lesser-known but popular sports such as rowing.[1]

The success of these television networks illustrates how market segmentation can be used to develop a successful enterprise. Both began by identifying specific market groups; then, an analysis of those groups' needs resulted in the development of programs that have achieved a significant share of the market.

## Introduction

This chapter continues the discussion of market segmentation. Chapter 3 discussed the role of market segmentation in developing a marketing strategy and the bases for segmenting the consumer market (geographic, demographic, psychographic, and benefit segmentation). In this chapter, the emphasis shifts to the process of market segmentation.

We will consider the rationale for and process of matching product offerings to specific market segments. As we will see, selecting an appropriate strategy depends on a variety of internal and external variables facing the firm.

## Alternative Market Matching Strategies

Market segmentation may take many forms, theoretically ranging from treating the entire market as a single homogeneous entity to subdividing it into several segments and providing a separate marketing plan for each segment.

The very core of the firm's strategies is to match product offerings with the needs of particular market segments. To do so successfully the firm must take the following factors into consideration:

1. *Company Resources* must be adequate to cover product development and other marketing costs.
2. *Differentiability of products.* Some products can be easily differentiated from others. Some can be produced in versions designed specially for individual segments.
3. *Stage in the product life cycle.* As a product matures, different marketing emphases are required to fit market needs.
4. *Competitors' strategies.* Strategies and product offerings must be continually adjusted in order to be competitive.

Essentially, the firm makes a number of goods/service offerings to the market in view of these determinants. One firm may decide on a **single-offer strategy**. This defined as *the attempt to satisfy a large or a small market with one product and a single marketing program.* Such a strategy may be adopted for different reasons. A small manufacturer of wheelbarrows might concentrate on marketing one product to retailers in one city only because it does not have the resources to serve a mass

**single-offer strategy** The attempt to satisfy a large or a small market with one product and a single marketing program.

## A Single-Offer Strategy — Ford Motor Company in 1908

In 1908 Henry Ford introduced the Model T, and revolutionized the automobile business around the world. Until the late 1920s he sold only the Model T and Model T truck. Ford's strategy was based on the belief that if he could get the price of a serviceable, utilitarian automobile low enough, he could develop a large mass market. His competitors were several hundred manufacturers of automobiles who were producing vehicles that were virtually custom-built, with short production runs and high costs. Ford's strategy generated unprecedented sales. A dealership organization evolved, which carried spare parts and service facilities to users across North America and through much of Europe. The marketing program, including an excellent service network, quickly made Henry Ford a multimillionaire and contributed to economic development through improving the transportation system.

There are some dangers inherent in a single-offer strategy, however. A firm that attempts to satisfy a very wide market with a single product or service *fairly well* is vulnerable to competition from those who choose to develop more-specialized products that appeal to and serve segments of the larger market *very well*. Over time General Motors and Chrysler developed a wider variety of models, price ranges, styles, and colour options. What worked superbly in 1908 faltered in the 1920s, and Ford had to move to a multi-offer strategy. The firm developed the Model A and the Model B, offering them with various options. The company differentiated the product line further in the 1930s by introducing the first mass-produced V-8 engine, which was a company hallmark for years.

market. A large producer of drafting equipment might offer a single product line with a marketing program aimed at draftspersons because it believes that only this limited segment would be interested in the product. A single-offer strategy aimed at one segment is often called *concentrated marketing*; when aimed at mass markets it is often called *undifferentiated* or *mass marketing*. The marketing of Coca-Cola is an example of the latter.

On the other hand, another company with greater resources may recognize that there are several segments of the market that would respond well to specifically designed products and marketing programs. It adopts a **multi-offer strategy**. This is defined as *the attempt to satisfy several segments of the market very well with specialized products and unique marketing programs aimed at each segment*. A bank designs particular services to fit the unique needs of different consumer and commercial market segments. A multi-offer strategy is also called *differentiated marketing*.

When these determinants are combined with markets segmented on the dimensions discussed in Chapter 3, the firm is able to develop a market matching strategy.

## An Extensive Multi-Offer Strategy — Ford Motor Company in the Early 1990s

The market matching strategy of the Ford Motor Company in the 1990s is quite different from that of 1908. It has evolved with the changing environment that faces the automobile industry. Ford's product line is much expanded from the Model T days, but the company still does not produce products for *all* markets. Instead, it serves those markets where its resources, marketing skills, product strengths, and competitive offerings can be best exploited. Figure 4–1 compares the product lines then and now.

F I G U R E   4 – 1

## FIGURE 4-1

### Market Matching Strategies

| Market Segment | Product Offerings | | | |
| --- | --- | --- | --- | --- |
| | Ford Motor Company | | Audi/Volkswagen/Porsche | |
| | 1908 Single-Offer Strategy | Early 1990s Multi-Offer Strategy | 1955 Single-Offer Strategy | Early 1990s Multi-Offer Strategy |
| **General-purpose Cars** | | | | |
| Small | Model T | Escort Mercury Tracer | "Beetle" | Fox Golf |
| Medium | Model T | Tempo Topaz | | Jetta |
| Large | | Taurus Crown Victoria | | |
| **Sports Cars** | | | | |
| Low-priced | | EXP | | |
| Medium-priced | | Mustang Capri | | Scirocco |
| High-priced | | Thunderbird Cougar | | Porsche 911, 928,944 |
| **Luxury Cars** | | | | |
| Medium-priced | | Lincoln | | Audi Quattro Audi Avant |
| High-priced | | Continental | | Audi 5000 |
| **Vans** | | Aerostar | | Vanagon |
| **Trucks** | | | | |
| Small | Model T (truck) | Ford | | |
| Medium | | Ford | | |

## A·P·P·L·Y·I·N·G   T·H·E   C·O·N·C·E·P·T·S

### A Single-Offer Strategy for Different Reasons — Audi/Volkswagen/Porsche in 1955

When Volkswagen decided to enter the North American market, it chose to do so with only the "Beetle" for a variety of reasons. First, the company was strapped for funds and could not expand its production facilities, stretched to the limit in trying to supply automobile-short postwar Europe. It also recognized that a dealer-support system and spare-parts inventory had to be developed from scratch if it was to compete successfully in North America. With these constraints in mind Volkswagen marketers determined that the serviceable Beetle was the answer. The Beetle was relatively low-priced, was supported by an imaginative promotional campaign, and become an immediate success with those who wanted a small, relatively basic car. Volkswagen sold a much wider variety of products in Europe (and continued to introduce new products in that market much earlier than in North America). It deliberately chose to make a single offer to the North American market.

A·P·P·L·Y·I·N·G   T·H·E   C·O·N·C·E·P·T·S

## A Strategic Move to a Multi-Offer Strategy — Audi/Volkswagen/Porsche in the Early 1990s

Today, products under the Volkswagen parent company's control compete for a much broader number of market segments than did the Beetle. The changes are indicative of a major change in the segmentation strategies. The company has not only the products but also the resources and the marketing infrastructure to serve more segments.

A successful match of products to segments through the development of a marketing program with the appropriate product design, pricing strategy, distribution strategy, and communication strategy is vital to the market success of the firm.

Many firms, large and small, practise a multi-offer strategy in today's environment. Procter & Gamble markets Tide, Dash, Duz, Cheer, Bold, Gain, Oxydol, and Bonus, among other detergents, to meet the desires of specific groups of detergent buyers. IBM offers huge mainframe computers, mid-range sizes tailored for medium-sized organizations, and computers designed for the home market.

Generally speaking, the company with a multi-offer marketing strategy should produce more sales by providing higher satisfaction for each of several target markets than would be possible with only a single offer strategy. However, whether a firm should choose a single- or a multi-offer strategy depends on management's goals, as well as on the economics of the situation — whether the company has the resources, and whether greater profits can be expected from the additional expense of a multi-offer strategy.

A·P·P·L·Y·I·N·G   T·H·E   C·O·N·C·E·P·T·S

## Market Segmentation Works for the Arts

About three years ago the Vancouver Symphony Orchestra was in such poor financial condition that it could not pay its performers. Things have changed because of additional funding and because of market segmentation. In its 1989 season, the VSO offered an assortment of concerts designed to appeal to various target segments. There were choral concerts, eight "Lite Classics" concerts, 12 "Seagram Pops" concerts, and several smaller series — one for kids, one for seniors "(Tea & Trumpets")", and one cabaret series. All in all, there were 12 different groups of concerts, each aimed at different segments of the classical music market.

That is the way now for all symphony orchestras. As Tim Rendell, general manager of the Edmonton Symphony Orchestra, put it in the orchestra's annual report: "The Edmonton Symphony Orchestra has paid attention to the Edmonton marketplace....We have listened to our customers and have designed our programs accordingly."

Such marketing practices have resulted in the Edmonton Symphony's pulling out of its constant deficit, too. The 1989 subscription campaign "[broke] all previous renewal records."

Source: Adapted from Arnold Edinborough, "New Season Sees Orchestras Listening to The Marketplace," *Financial Post* (September 11, 1989), p. 16.

# The Stages of Market Segmentation

The marketer has a number of potential bases for determining the most appropriate market matching strategy. Geographic, demographic, and psychographic bases, as well as product attributes, are often used in converting heterogeneous markets into specific segments that serve as target markets for the consumer-oriented marketer. The industrial marketer segments geographically, by product, or by end-use application. In either case, a systematic five-stage decision process is followed. This framework for market segmentation is shown in Figure 4–2.

Since no single base for segmentation is necessarily the best, the analyst should segment the market in a way that most suits the situation. For example, demographic segmentation may be used in planning a print advertising campaign because magazines are normally aimed at specific demographic segments. The analyst thus often experiments with segmenting markets in several ways in the process of discovering which of the marketing elements can be changed for greatest effect. (Similarly, marketing opportunities are sometimes discovered by rating how well competitors have served segments differentiated on a particular dimension.) This is part of the interactive process of analysis. Figure 4–2 shows a systematic five-stage decision process that lends form to what are otherwise often complex and unstructured problems.[2]

## Stage I: Select Market Segmentation Bases

The decision process begins when a firm identifies characteristics of potential buyers as bases that will allow the marketer to classify them into market segments. For example, IBM might segment on the basis of computer usage (accounting firms) or by company size. Segmentation bases should be selected so that each segment contains customers who have similar needs, so that specific marketing programs can be designed to satisfy those needs. For example, before Procter & Gamble decides to market Crest to a segment made up of large families, management should be confident that most large families are interested in preventing tooth decay and thus receptive to the Crest marketing offer. In some cases, this objective is difficult to achieve. Consider the marketer seeking to reach the consumer segment that is over

FIGURE 4 – 2

## The Market Segmentation Decision Process

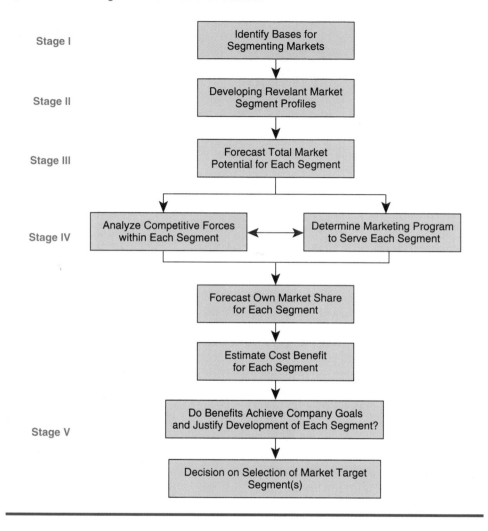

50 years of age. Saturday-evening television commercials can reach this group, but much of the expenditure may be wasted since the other major viewer group at that time consists of teenagers.[3]

## Stage II: Develop Relevant Profiles for Each Segment

Once segments have been identified, marketers should develop a profile of the relevant customer needs and behaviours in each segment.

Segmentation bases provide some insight into the nature of customers, but typically not enough for the kinds of decisions that marketing managers must make. Managers need precise descriptions of customers in order to match marketing offers to their needs. In other words, the task at this stage is to develop profiles of the typical customer in each segment with regard to lifestyle patterns, attitudes toward product attributes and brands, brand preferences, product-use habits, geographic location, demographic characteristics, and so on. For example, one regional retail chain surveyed female customers and identified the following profile: age 25–55; 147–160 cm tall; 38–55 kg; career-oriented; and having a household income of $20 000 or higher. The retailer used this profile to set up separate "petites" sections, one of the fastest-growing segments in the women's fashion industry.[4]

## Stage III: Forecast Market Potentials

In the third stage, market segmentation and market opportunity analysis are used together to produce a forecast of market potential within each segment. Market potential is the upper limit on the demand that can be expected from a segment and, combined with data on the firm's market share, sales potential.

This stage is management's preliminary go or no-go decision point as to whether the sales potential in a segment is sufficient to justify further analysis. Some segments will be screened out because they represent insufficient potential demand; others will be sufficiently attractive for the analysis to continue.

Consider the toothbrush part of the dental supply and mouthwash market — a multimillion-dollar annual market. Dentists say that people should buy three or four toothbrushes a year for efficient brushing, but the current annual replacement rate is only 1.3.[5] If a marketer could convince the public to replace their toothbrushes when they should, market potential should almost triple.

## Stage IV: Forecast Probable Market Share

Once market potential has been estimated, the share of that market that can be captured by the firm must be determined. This requires an analysis of competitors' positions in target segments. At the same time the specific marketing strategy and

### A·P·P·L·Y·I·N·G  T·H·E  C·O·N·C·E·P·T·S

## *A Market Niche for Western Star*

Western Star Trucks, Inc., of Kelowna, B.C., holds about 1.5 percent of the North American market for Class B heavy trucks. However, the company manages to make a profit, building about 3000 trucks a year in a market saturated with powerful and deep-pocket competitors, some of whom build more than 30 000 trucks a year.

It does so, says president and chief executive Joe Kalinowski, by being the only remaining custom truck builder in North America. It makes the Rolls-Royce of highway haulers for about the same price as the competition's standardized output.

It seems that labour and management both realize that they must overcome the disadvantages of distance from suppliers and customers, and put forth extra effort to succeed. But on top of this, management has developed a careful marketing plan that involves

appealing to a narrow segment of the heavy-truck market and serving that segment very well.

"We quite deliberately overbuild the trucks because we believe with what you pay for a truck you want to have a viable working vehicle for at least 10 years....At our volume, it is quite feasible to do *precisely* what the buyer wants, so we are able to customize that truck to absolutely maximize its legal loading," says Kalinowski.

Western Star's strategy of finding and serving a market niche once again proves the value of understanding the various components of the market, and matching a marketing program to serve a specific segment.

Source: Adapted from David Climenhaga, "Tiny B.C. Truck Manufacturer Succeeds in Taking on 'Cookie-cutter' Competition," *Globe and Mail* (June 29, 1989).

*Air Canada's marketing strategy for Executive Class seating emphasizes freedom and comfort. This approach was taken after an analysis of the needs of the senior executive segment. By targeting members of this group and providing services that satisfy their needs, the airline hopes to secure a greater market share.*

tactics should be designed for these segments. These two activities should lead to an analysis of the costs of tapping the potential demand in each segment.

Colgate once trailed Procter & Gamble nearly two to one in dishwashing liquids and also ran behind in heavy-duty detergents and soaps. A realistic assessment indicated that for most directly competitive products Colgate had little chance of overtaking P&G. So Colgate diversified its product line. Today, 75 percent of the firm's offerings do not face a directly competitive Procter & Gamble product, and those that do compete effectively.[6]

## Stage V: Select Specific Market Segments

Finally the accumulated information, analyses, and forecasts allow management to assess the potential for the achievement of company goals and justify the development of one or more market segments. Demand forecasts combined with cost projections are used to determine the profit and return on investment that can be expected from each segment. Analyses of marketing strategy and tactics will determine the degree of consistency with corporate image and reputation goals as well as with unique corporate capabilities that may be achieved by serving a segment. These assessments will, in turn, determine management's selection of specific segments as target markets.

At this point of the analysis the costs and benefits to be weighed are not just monetary, but include many difficult-to-measure but critical organizational and environmental factors. For example, the firm may not have enough experienced personnel to launch a successful attack on what clearly could be an almost certain monetary success. Similarly, a firm with 80 percent of the market may face legal problems with the federal Competition Tribunal if it increases its market concentration. A public utility may decide not to encourage higher electricity consumption because of environmental and political repercussions. The assessment of both financial and nonfinancial factors is a vital and final stage in the decision process.

There is not, and should not be, any simple answer to the market segmentation decision. The marketing concept's prescription to serve the customer's needs and to earn a profit while so doing implies that the marketer has to evaluate each possible marketing program on how it achieves this goal in the marketplace. By performing the detailed analysis outlined in Figure 4–2, the marketing manager can increase the probability of success in profitably serving consumers' needs.

# Target Market Decision Analysis

Identifying specific target markets is an important aspect of overall marketing strategy. Clearly delineated target markets allow management to effectively employ marketing efforts like product development, distribution, pricing, and advertising to serve these markets.

**Target market decision analysis**, *the evaluation of potential market segments*, is a useful tool in the market segmentation process. Targets are chosen by segmenting the total market on the basis of any given characteristics (as described in Chapter 3). The example that follows illustrates how target market decision analysis can be applied.[7]

**target market decision analysis**
The evaluation of potential market segments.

## A Useful Method of Identifying Target Markets

Sometimes marketers fail to take all potential market segments into consideration. One method of identifying target markets is simply to divide the total market into a number of boxes or cells. Each cell represents a potential target segment. The definition of the cells can be based on consumer benefits desired; on geographic, demographic, and psychographic characteristics; or on some combination of these. While this concept is simple, it can be extremely complex in practice, and creativity is often required.

Consider the decisions of an airline company's marketing manager who wishes to analyze the market potential for various levels of passenger service. The company wants to delineate all possible market targets and to assess the most profitable multi-offer strategy.

As a tool for outlining the scope of the market, the marketing manager devises a grid like the one in Figure 4–3. This enables the company to match the possible types of service offerings with various customer classifications. The process of developing the target market grid forces the decision-maker to consider the entire range of possible market matching strategies. New or previously underserved segments may be uncovered. The framework also encourages an assessment of the sales potential in each of the possible segments, and aids in the proper allocation of marketing efforts to areas of greatest potential.

Once the cells of the grid have been identified, the marketer can then evaluate the wants, needs, and motivations of each market segment. For example, it appears that senior executives would be the appropriate targets for the first-class service and extra-service categories. Further research could confirm or modify these evaluations and enable the marketer to determine whether the market segment's size makes it worth developing a special offering for. Apparently, airlines have analyzed the needs and motivations for this segment. They provide roomier seating, improved food, and check-in service to satisfy the needs thus identified. *Market segmentation thus enables appropriate marketing plan design.*

The cross-classification in Figure 4–4 shows that the matrix can be further subdivided to gather more specific data about the characteristics of the proposed target market and to accurately develop a suitable marketing mix. The potential bases for segmenting markets are virtually limitless. For example, the segments might have been based on psychographic data or on the benefits sought. In the latter

FIGURE 4 – 3

**Market for Airline Passenger Travel**

| Market | First-Class | Extra-Service Business Class | Regular Tourist Class | Seat-Sale Class | Age Specials | Charter |
|---|---|---|---|---|---|---|
| Senior Executives | X | X | ? | | | X |
| Employees of Large Firms | | X | X | ? | | X |
| Employees of Small Businesses | | X | X | X | | |
| Wealthy Individuals | X | X | | | | ? |
| Other Individuals | | | X | X | | X |
| Senior Citizens | | | ? | X | X | X |
| Youth | | | X | X | X | X |

X = Probable demand for service

? = Uncertain or limited demand

instance, prestige, comfort, and basic transportation might be some benefits that would assist in designing market offerings. Such divisions are sometimes made intuitively in the first place, but the final decisions are usually supported by concrete data.[8]

## Using Target Market Decision Analysis in Assessing a Product Mix

**product mix** The assortment of product lines and individual offerings available from a marketer.

**Product mix**, a concept we will take a detailed look at in Chapter 10, refers to *the assortment of product lines and individual offerings available from a marketer*. Target

FIGURE 4 – 4

**Employees of Large Firms, Extra-Service Class**

| Service Benefit Desired | Heavy-Traffic Regions | Southern Canada | Northern Canada |
|---|---|---|---|
| Schedules | X | | |
| Food | | | |
| Attendant Service | | | |
| Leg Room | | | |

FIGURE 4–5

## Using Target Market Decision Analysis to Evaluate a Product Mix

|  | Belongers | Achievers | Etc. |
|---|---|---|---|
| Romantic | Phone M<br>Phone A<br>Phone C |  |  |
| Character |  | Phone R<br>Phone Y |  |
| Contemporary |  |  |  |

Source: Reprinted from "Properly Applied Psychographics Add Marketing Luster," *Marketing News* (November 12, 1982), p. 10.

market decision analysis can be used to assess a firm's product mix and to point up needed modifications. For example, one telephone company has used the concept to evaluate its product offerings.[9] The company segments the total market by psychographic categories as shown in Figure 4–5. Two of these categories are "belongers" and "achievers." Belongers were defined in this instance as those who are motivated by emotional and group influences. Achievers were defined as those whose dominant characteristic is the need to get ahead.

A·P·P·L·Y·I·N·G    T·H·E    C·O·N·C·E·P·T·S

## Try Your Hand at Selecting Target Markets

For each of the following situations or products, pick the target market cells for which you would aim. The actual customer profiles are shown overleaf.

Source: Janet Guyon, "Gourmet-Food Market Grows as Affluent Shoppers Indulge," *Wall Street Journal* (May 6, 1982), p. 31; "Magazine Publisher Advertisers' Target Growing, 'Overlooked' Empty Nest Market," *Marketing News* (October 2, 1981), pp. 1, 10; and "Rolling Along," *Fortune* (December 14, 1981), p. 13.

**Exercise A: Gourmet Food Market:**   A type of store that features higher-priced, top-of-the-line gourmet foods.

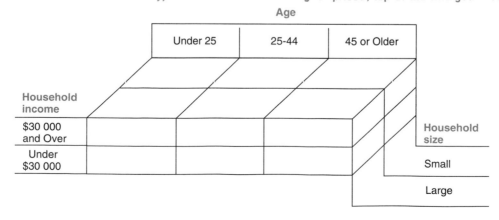

**Exercise B:** *Workbench*:   A magazine (circulation: 700 000) aimed at those who consider craftsmanship their hobby.

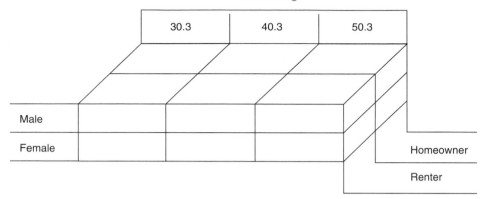

**Exercise C: Mercedes-Benz:**   Some models run in the $50 000 range. This exercise refers to North American buyers only.

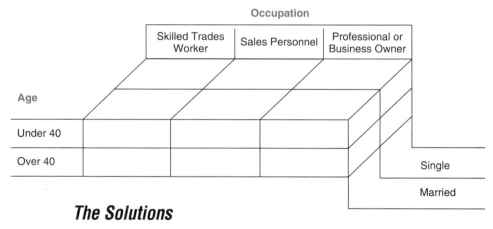

## The Solutions

The actual customer profiles for these items are as follows.

**Exercise A: Gourmet Food Market**

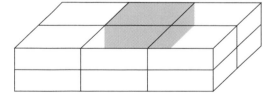

**Exercise B:** *Workbench* **Magazine**

**Exercise C: Mercedes-Benz**

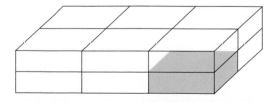

The telephone company's rule is to offer two and only two types of telephone sets in a given market segment in order not to have too complicated a market offering. The belonger segment was thus offered a regular phone and a romantic-type telephone to appeal to their sentiments. Achievers were offered the regular phone plus one designed to connote the idea of efficiency and character. This analysis helped to select a product from the assortment shown in Figure 4–5.

Target market decision analysis can go beyond merely identifying target markets. It can play a crucial role in actually developing marketing strategies such as product mixes.

## Product Positioning

After a target market has been selected your firm will naturally find others competing in that segment. The next task is to develop a marketing plan that will enable your product to compete effectively against them. It is unlikely that success will be achieved with a marketing program that is virtually identical to competitors', for they already have attained a place in the minds of individuals in the target market and have developed brand loyalty. Since people have a variety of needs and tastes, market acceptance is more easily achieved by **positioning** — *shaping the product and developing a marketing program in such a way that the product is perceived to be (and actually is) different from competitors' products.*

**positioning** Shaping the product and developing a marketing program in such a way that the product is perceived to be (and actually is) different from competitors' products.

This process requires a careful analysis of the features and strengths of competitive offerings, as well as a good understanding of the needs and wants of the target market. From comparing the two, the marketer tries to find a niche of significant size that is currently poorly served, and to develop an offering to fit that opportunity. Positioning generally goes beyond simply using promotion to differentiate a good or service in the mind of the customer, although this is often an important aspect.

7-Up used promotion as the sole element in positioning. The firm discovered that its product was missing the primary market for soft drinks — children, teenagers, and young adults — because 7-Up's image was as a mixer for older people's drinks. The firm used its now well-known "Uncola" campaign to first identify the product as a soft drink and then position it as an alternative to colas in the soft-drink market.

Another classic positioning campaign was that used by Avis to position itself against Hertz with the theme "Avis is only number two, so why go with us? Because we try harder." In this instance, the service was also adjusted to make the claim true.

An example of the use of a total marketing program in market positioning is the case of Digital Equipment Corporation (DEC). This firm successfully carved out a niche in the small-computer marketplace by identifying a competitive gap in IBM's domination of the computer market. IBM had concentrated on large mainframe applications, and had paid little attention to smaller business applications. The computer giant had easily fended off the efforts of many other major marketers — such as Xerox, General Electric, and Singer — to crack IBM's hold on computer sales. A major error made by these firms was their attempt to position their products in direct competition with IBM's mainframe computers. IBM's image as "the major computer producer" was too strongly entrenched in the minds of potential purchasers. They were unwilling to risk a major expenditure on a large computer from a newcomer.

All these new competitors eventually pulled out of the mainframe market. However, by designing a minicomputer to fit the market niche it had discovered, and supporting it with a complementary marketing program, DEC was able to capture a portion of the small computer market. Whether it can remain in that market over the long run remains to be seen. Still, using product positioning to evaluate and develop marketing strategies in the light of competitive offerings in the market is a valuable and basic concept. It should follow naturally from the market segmentation decision.

## Summary

This chapter continues the discussion of market segmentation introduced in Chapter 3. Various strategies associated with the market segmentation concept are considered here.

Correct strategy decisions depend on a host of situational variables. The basic determinants of market matching strategy are: (1) company resources, (2) degree of product homogeneity, (3) product newness, and (4) competitors' strategies.

After analyzing the market potential as well as these situational variables, the firm determines whether to adopt a single- or multi-offer strategy. It then proceeds to position its offering(s) in the market with a marketing program that will make it the most competitive.

The market segmentation process follows a sequential framework consisting of five stages. These stages can be outlined as follows:

- Stage 1. Determine the bases on which markets can be segmented.
- Stage 2. Develop consumer profiles for the appropriate market segments.
- Stage 3. Assess the overall market potential for the relevant market segments.
- Stage 4. Estimate market share and cost–benefit of each market segment given the existing competition and the marketing plan that is selected.
- Stage 5. Select the segments that will become the firm's target markets.

Target market decision analysis is a useful tool in the market segmentation process. A grid is developed that outlines the various market segments by their distinguishing characteristics. All bases for segmentation can be employed in target market decision analysis. In addition to selecting the actual target market segments, this type of analysis can also be used for assessing the firm's current and planned product mix.

In the next chapter, attention shifts to the research procedures and techniques used to acquire information for segmentation and for building effective marketing strategies. It covers marketing research and information systems.

## ■ KEY TERMS

| | | |
|---|---|---|
| single-offer strategy | positioning | market segmentation process |
| multi-offer strategy | target market decision | |
| product mix | analysis | |

## REVIEW QUESTIONS

1. Outline the basic features of a single-offer strategy.
2. Outline the basic features of a multi-offer strategy.
3. Outline the rationale of market matching strategies.
4. List and describe the five stages of the market segmentation process.
5. What is meant by target market decision analysis?
6. Show how target market decision analysis can help select market segments that the firm should attempt to reach.
7. Illustrate how the four consumer market segmentation bases can be used in target market decision analysis.
8. Illustrate how the three industrial market segmentation bases can be used in target market decision analysis.
9. How can target market decision analysis be used to assess a product mix?

## DISCUSSION QUESTIONS AND EXERCISES

1. What can be learned from the MuchMusic and TSN example at the beginning of the chapter? Discuss.
2. Prepare a term paper showing how an actual firm employs market segmentation in developing its marketing strategy.
3. Identify the conditions under which a single-offer market matching strategy would be appropriate and those under which a multi-offer would be appropriate.
4. Prepare a report that traces an actual company's experience as it moved through the various market segmentation stages.
5. Assess a firm's actual product mix using target market decision analysis.

# VIDEO CASE 4    Irvine Co.

The original 90 000 acres of the Irvine Ranch were purchased by James Irvine and his partners for 35 cents an acre in the 1860s. Running inland 22 miles from the Pacific Ocean, the ranch is located between Los Angeles and San Diego in what is now called Orange County. The tract includes the city of Irvine and sections of several other wealthy Los Angeles suburbs, such as Newport Beach.

For generations, the property was operated as a farm and ranch. In fact, nearly 60 000 acres of this highly fertile land are still used for agricultural pursuits. Major crops include tomatoes, avocados, asparagus, and Valencia oranges.

The area was virtually uninhabited until the 1950s. Then the Los Angeles megalopolis spread into the region, and Orange County quickly became one of the fastest-growing areas in the United States. As a result, the land soon became more valuable for housing development than for agricultural purposes. Thus the Irvine Co. set up a project to develop the property by creating planned communities. The Irvine plan was part of the so-called "New Town" concept that was popular at the time. Irvine's marketing plan involved setting up planned communities that included shopping, schools, churches, and recreational areas along with housing.

Today some 66 500 acres of the Irvine property — 15 percent of Orange County — remain undeveloped. As it is one of the largest undeveloped plots of land near a major U.S. city, its future worth is immeasurable.

Irvine's marketers planned to use a textbook approach to market segmentation. Since people have differing housing needs based on their life cycle stage, the firm should have made alternative housing available to cater to these varying needs. However, the traditional approach to building ignored these needs and treated the housing market as a monolith, recognizing different households' requirements only with variations in the number of bedrooms or overall square footage. The Irvine marketing approach involved an initial analysis of the housing market and the development of a product mix designed to appeal to different types of buyers. Families would live near families, adult households near other adult households, and so forth.

Market segmentation — the process of dividing a market into homogeneous target markets — provided the key to Irvine's planned-community concept. Irvine's management felt that market segmentation would allow the firm to meet both social and marketing goals by providing a structure for growth while allowing the development to proceed more rapidly. Market segmentation can be done on geographic, demographic, psychographic, or benefit bases. Irvine's management initially selected psychographic segmentation for characterizing its market. As noted in the chapter, psychographic segmentation is based on an analysis of consumer lifestyles. The company accumulated all sorts of information, about everything from the cars people drove to the wines they consumed. However, no one could relate these data to the types of housing people desired.

Irvine Co. soon turned to other means of segmenting its market. It began interviewing its home buyers, both to promote public relations and to obtain demographic data that would assist in future segmentation efforts. Builders were persuaded to design homes specifically targeted at given market segments. Thus, demographic segmentation enabled Irvine to build the homes people really wanted. In addition to standard one-, two-, and three-bedroom formats to match various household sizes, it offered such options as a triplex plan (which gave first-time buyers affordable but spacious housing) and nonrelated-adults dwellings with individual master bedrooms.

Irvine's market segmentation efforts hit a snag in the late 1970s. Inflation and substantial in-migration created an unprecedented housing boom in Southern California. Consumer demand soon exceeded product availability, forcing housing prices up 25 to 30 percent a year. Some houses were even being sold through lottery drawings. Also, some homes that had cost $80 000 in the 1950s had been sold with 25-year land leases rather than as deeded land. When the leases were reopened in the late 1970s, Irvine Co. sought increases as high as 3333 percent. It later backed away from this position, offering to sell the land or proposing new leases that were higher-priced but far less so than was originally proposed.

If the price hikes did not force buyers out of the housing market, mortgage rates did. A restrictive monetary policy designed to combat double-digit inflation produced interest rates of nearly 20 percent. As a result, new houses remained unsold. Irvine's market development strategy was blocked, as targeted groups could no longer afford the available housing. In fact, Orange Country's industrial growth was stymied as well, since people will not take jobs where they cannot afford to buy homes.

The housing boom began to subside in the early to middle 1980s, when home prices and mortgage rates came into closer balance with consumers' ability to purchase housing. Irvine Co. returned to its segmentation strategy. Once again, the challenge was to provide housing that would accommodate diverse needs and encourage families to remain in the community throughout their life cycles.

More recently, development has expanded to include office parks. Irvine sold 500 acres to the University of California at a cut rate to encourage high-tech commercial and industrial use, which Irvine hopes will attract corporate R & D facilities to adjacent properties. The stagnation of the housing market in 1990, however, put severe pressure on the company, and management is investigating alternative plans.

SOURCES    Julie Flynn and Mark Frons, "Owning Irvine, Calif., Isn't What It Used to Be," *Business Week* (March 9, 1987), pp. 80, 82; Gary Hector, "The Land Coup in Orange County," *Fortune* (November 14, 1963), pp. 91–92, 96, 100, 102; Gary Hector, "America's Richest Land Baron," *Fortune* (August 27, 1990), pp. 98–102; Harry Hurt III, "Donald Trump, Move Over," *Newsweek* (February 5, 1990), pp. 12–43.

## Questions

1. Discuss the importance of market segmentation for Irvine Co.
2. Why was demographic segmentation more effective than psychographic segmentation for Irvine Co.?
3. What specific aspects of demographic segmentation are evident in this case?

## CHAPTER 5

# Obtaining Data for Marketing Decisions

1. To describe the development and current status of the marketing research function.
2. To present the steps of the marketing research process.
3. To discuss the nature and sources of primary and secondary data.
4. To outline the methods of collecting survey data.
5. To discuss the nature of marketing information systems, and relate them to the marketing research function.

THERE'S nothing like a dash of competition to make businesses do some hard thinking about getting more information about the market. The manager of a prosperous community-sized shopping centre (Mall A) discovered that a competing developer was planning to construct a large upscale shopping centre (Mall B) within five kilometres of his site.

Before Mall B began construction, the manager of Mall A decided to do some marketing research to develop a better understanding of his existing customer base. A customer-origin study was undertaken. From this, a demographic profile of the existing shoppers was produced. This was done in order to identify the consumer segments and neighbourhoods in which the centre had a strong customer base.

Using postal codes collected from customers at the shopping centre, the manager was able to identify the exact size and shape of Mall A's trading area. Then Compusearch, a marketing research firm, applied its market segmentation system — called "Lifestyles" — to determine the profile of the mall's customers. The Lifestyles system classifies Canadians into one of 70 unique and identifiable consumer segments. Each segment contains its own demographic and consumer-expenditure characteristics.

From the results, the mall manager determined that the groups for whom this shopping centre had the strongest appeal were primarily the "Middle Class," as well as some "Working-Class" and "Empty-Nester" segments. It was these market segments that formed the mall's target group.

The manager then compared the findings with the existing tenant mix of the mall. He decided to replace several of the upper-end women's apparel stores, over the course of the next year, with shops that better reflected the needs of the significant "Middle-Class" customer base.

These strategies were implemented, monitored, and maintained until the new mall was established and operating. By using marketing research to profile its customers, Mall A was able to accurately identify which groups had the strongest affinity for the shopping centre. The marketing strategies that were developed and successfully implemented kept existing customers loyal to the mall. Mall A was able to maintain and actually increase its market share of target customers without suffering any appreciable loss from the opening of a new mall in the trade area.[1]

# Introduction

The quality of all marketing planning decisions depends on the quality of the information on which they are based. A variety of sources of marketing information are available to the marketing decision-maker. Some involve the regular information flow that occurs in a company — for example, sales-force reports, accounting data, and other internal statistics. Sophisticated firms are now applying the power of computers to analyze such internal data, and to simulate the effects of changes in strategy.

**marketing research** The systematic gathering, recording, and analyzing of data about problems relating to the marketing of goods and services.

Another important source of information is marketing research. **Marketing research** is "*the systematic gathering, recording, and analyzing of data about problems relating to the marketing of goods and services.*"[2]

The critical task of the marketing manager is decision-making. Managers earn their salaries by making effective decisions that enable their firms to solve problems as they arise, and by anticipating and preventing the occurrence of future problems. Many times, though, they must make decisions with limited information of uncertain accuracy. If the decision-maker undertakes some marketing research, much valuable additional information can be gained to help with the decision. Although the marketing research does not *make* the decision, it does makes it easier for the manager to do so.

Most of the market segmentation procedures outlined in Chapter 3 and 4 are based on information collected through marketing research. There is a growing use of marketing research for the development of marketing plans. Its regular use is now considered indispensable by most successful companies.

Marketing research in Canada may be said to have existed since there first were buyers and sellers. However, the day on which marketing research became a full-time profession was January 2, 1929. On that day, Henry King became the first full-time marketing researcher in Canada. His employer was an advertising agency, Cockfield Brown.[3]

In 1932, through the encouragement of Cockfield Brown, the first independent research company — Ethel Fulford and Associates — was founded in Toronto. In 1937, the Fulford company became known as Canadian Facts. Marketing research firms are now found in most major centres.

# Common Uses of Marketing Research

Marketing research studies generate data that may serve many purposes: for example, developing sales forecasts, determining market and sales potential, designing new products and packages, analyzing sales and marketing costs, evaluating the effectiveness of a firm's advertising, and determining consumer motives for buying products.

Some companies do not have their own marketing research departments: the function is often at least partly contracted out to specialists, because the research skill and activity levels are quite variable for different projects. Even large firms typically rely on outside agencies to conduct interviews. Such agencies have a large number of trained interviewers and have the appropriate systems in place to conduct the study.

There are two basic types of marketing research organizations that a firm may use. The first can be categorized as a *full- or partial-service research supplier*. Full-service firms will handle all aspects of the research and provide a final report to management, whereas those offering partial service specialize in some activity, such as conducting field interviews.

The second type of external research concern is known as a *syndicated service*. A syndicated service is an organization that offers to provide a standardized set of data on a regular basis to all who wish to buy it. Normally, such research firms specialize in providing information on a small number of industries. For example, the Consumer Panel of Canada regularly gathers information on consumer purchases of food and other household items from 3400 households. These data inform marketers about brand preferences, brand-switching, and the effects of various promotional activities. Since all major products in the category are reported, a purchaser of this information can see how competitors are doing as well.

Research is likely to be contracted to outside groups when:

1. Problem areas can be defined in terms of specific research projects that can easily be delegated.
2. There is a need for specialized know-how or equipment.
3. Intellectual detachment is important.[4]

## A·P·P·L·Y·I·N·G  T·H·E  C·O·N·C·E·P·T·S

### *Marketing Research in Action*

— Hershey Canada recently launched a line of milder-flavoured milk chocolate bars after surveys indicated that Canadians preferred a light, creamy chocolate. The company expects to pick up three extra market-share points within a year by developing a product and a marketing strategy based on continued marketing research.

— Canadian National Railways commissioned several research projects to find out what kind of new railway car might better serve the needs of CN customers. In one project, they hired students to count the number of tractor trailers travelling the

Toronto–Montreal corridor. As a result of their findings, CN introduced the Laser piggy-back service on the Toronto–Montreal run.

— Marketing research showed the Ontario government that it had the wrong theme in its "Rally Round Ontario" advertising program. Tourists felt that they were being asked to rally round a sinking ship. The findings led to the much more successful theme "Yours to Discover."

Source: Adapted from Frances Phillips, "Why It Pays To Be a Pollster," *Financial Post* (June 14, 1983), p. 2.

*An analysis of courseware use in Canadian schools would be the first step in evaluating the market potential of this product. Data from a number of different school situations would need to be collated before a final interpretation could be reached.*

## The Marketing Research Process

Infotech, a provincially based organization, was intrigued by the possibilities of stimulating in the province a computer software industry that would specialize in producing software for use in schools (known as "courseware"). Such an industry could be on the leading edge in the rapidly growing computer sector and thus could stimulate much economic growth in the province. In order to know whether such a strategy was worthwhile, Infotech commissioned a marketing research study. It wanted to know (a) the size of the courseware market in North America; (b) the trends in courseware for education usage; (c) what channels of distribution exist in the courseware industry and what it costs to use them; and (d) the marketing and financial aspects of courseware development.

Given the need for information, how is marketing research actually conducted? Normally, there are six steps involved in the marketing research process: (1) defining the problem; (2) exploratory research; (3) formulating a hypothesis; (4) research design; (5) collecting data; and (6) interpretation and presentation.

Figure 5–1 diagrams the marketing research process from information need to the research-based decision.

### Problem Definition

Problems are barriers that prevent the accomplishment of organizational goals. A clearly defined problem helps the researcher to focus the research process on securing the data necessary to solve the problem. Someone once remarked that well-defined problems are half solved.

FIGURE 5–1

**The Marketing Research Process**

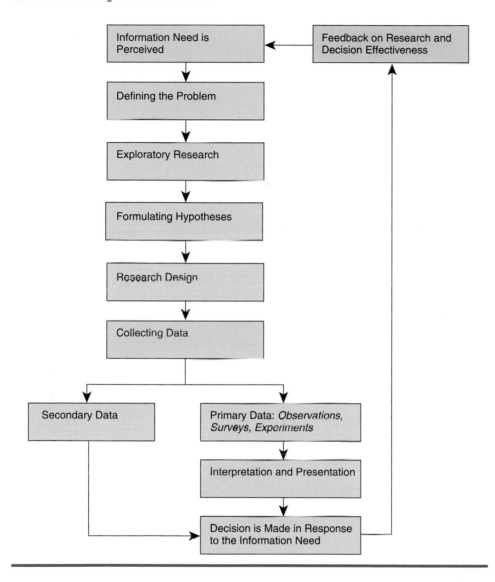

Problem definition is not always simple. Suppose a tennis player with a sore knee and other symptoms goes to the doctor for treatment. His "problem," he tells the doctor, is a sore knee. However, on further investigation, it is discovered that the knee pain is merely a symptom of the real problem: damage to an Achilles' tendon. Business problems are much the same. Sometimes it is easy to pinpoint the problem that requires research information to solve. However, it is often difficult to determine the specific problem since what the researcher is confronted with may be only symptoms of the real underlying problem. To focus research properly, the researcher must look *beyond* the symptoms. This is done through exploratory research.

F I G U R E  5 – 2

## Topics for the Exploratory Analysis

| | |
|---|---|
| **The Company and Industry** | 1. Company objectives |
| | 2. The companies in the industry (size, financial power) and industry trends |
| | 3. Geographic locations of the industry |
| | 4. The company's market share as compared with competitors' |
| | 5. Marketing policies of competitors |
| **The Market** | 1. Geographic location |
| | 2. Demographic characteristics of the market |
| | 3. Purchase motivations |
| | 4. Product-use patterns |
| | 5. Nature of demand |
| **Products** | 1. Physical characteristics |
| | 2. Consumer acceptance — strengths and weaknesses |
| | 3. Package as a container and as a promotional device |
| | 4. Manufacturing processes, production capacity |
| | 5. Closeness and availability of substitute products |
| **Marketing Channels** | 1. Channels employed and recent trends |
| | 2. Channel policy |
| | 3. Margins for resellers |
| **Sales Organization** | 1. Market coverage |
| | 2. Sales analysis by number of accounts per salesperson, size of accounts, type of account, etc. |
| | 3. Expense ratios for various territories, product types, account size, etc. |
| | 4. Control procedures |
| | 5. Compensation methods |
| **Pricing** | 1. Elasticity |
| | 2. Season or special promotional price cuts |
| | 3. Profit margins of resellers |
| | 4. Legal restrictions |
| | 5. Price lines |
| **Advertising and Sales Promotion** | 1. Media employed |
| | 2. Dollar expenditures as compared with competitors' |
| | 3. Timing of advertising |
| | 4. Sales promotional materials provided for resellers |
| | 5. Results from previous advertising and sales promotional campaigns |

## Exploratory Research

*In searching for the cause of a problem the researcher will learn about the problem area and begin to focus on specific areas for study.* This search, often called **exploratory research**, consists of discussing the problem with informed sources within the firm and with wholesalers, retailers, customers, and others outside the firm, and examining secondary sources of information. Marketing researchers often refer to internal data collection as the *situation analysis* and to exploratory interviews with informed persons outside the firm as the *informal investigation*. Exploratory research also involves evaluating company records, such as sales and profit analyses of its own and its competitors' products. Figure 5–2 provides a checklist of topics that might be considered in an exploratory analysis.

In the Infotech case, exploratory research was done through a review of the literature about courseware; then a series of in-person and telephone interviews was undertaken with knowledgeable people in departments of education and the school systems. Before a specific research plan could be designed, the researchers needed to know more about the subject and about the existing trends in the industry. Only then was it possible to begin planning a more complete research program. It was determined that the next steps should be (1) to systemically explore every current article written on the subject, and (2) to develop a plan to obtain information directly from different market groups. In some research projects, the next step might have been formulating hypotheses, but it did not seem appropriate in the Infotech situation.

**exploratory research** Learning about the problem area and beginning to focus on specific areas of study by discussing the problem with informed sources within the firm (a process often called *situation analysis*) and with knowledgeable others outside the firm (the *informal investigation*).

## Formulating Hypotheses

After the problem has been defined and an exploratory investigation conducted, the marketer should be able to formulate a **hypothesis**, *a tentative explanation about the relationship between variables as a starting point for further testing.* In effect, the hypothesis is an educated guess.

A marketer of industrial products might formulate the following hypothesis: "Failure to provide 36-hour delivery service will reduce our sales by 20 percent." Such a statement may prove correct or incorrect. Formulating a hypothesis does, however, provide a basis for investigation and an eventual determination of its accuracy. It also allows the researcher to move to the next step: developing the research design.

**hypothesis** A tentative explanation about the relationship between variables as a starting point for further testing.

## Research Design

The research design should be a comprehensive plan for testing the hypotheses formulated about the problem. **Research design** refers to *a series of advance decisions that, taken together, make up a master plan or model for conducting the investigation.* Developing such a plan allows the researcher to control each step of the research process. Figure 5–3 lists the steps involved in the research design.

The research design for Infotech was quite complicated. No fewer than five individual data collection procedures were planned. These included surveys of (1) departments of education across Canada and in selected American states, (2) principal textbook and software publishers, (3) key hardware and software manufacturers in Canada, and (4) a sampling of the teacher population.

**research design** A series of advance decisions that, taken together, make up a master plan or model for conducting the investigation.

FIGURE 5 – 3

## Sixteen Steps in the Research Design

| *Questions Faced* | *Steps to Take or Choices* |
|---|---|
| 1. What is needed to measure the outcome of the alternative solutions? | 1. Decide the subjects on which data are needed. |
| 2. What specific data are needed for that approach? | 2. Examine the time and cost considerations. |
| 3. From whom are such data available? | 3. Write exact statements of data to be sought. |
| 4. How should primary data be obtained? | 4. Search and examine relevant secondary data. |
| a. What are the types of data? | 5. Determine remaining data gaps. |
| b. What general collection methods shall be used? | 6. Define the population from which primary data may be sought. |
| c. How shall the sources be contacted? | 7. Determine the various needed facts, opinions, and motives. |
| d. How may their data be secured from the sources? | 8. Plan for obtaining data by survey, observational, or experimental methods. |
| e. Shall there be a complete count of the population or a sample drawn from it? How chosen? | 9. If using a survey, decide whether to contact respondents by telephone, by mail, or in person. |
| f. How will the fieldwork be conducted? | 10. Consider the questions and forms needed to elicit and record the data. |
| 5. How will the data be interpreted and presented? | 11. Decide on the coverage of the population: |
| | a. Choose between a complete enumeration and a sampling. |
| | b. If sampling, decide whether to select from the whole population or restricted portions of it. |
| | c. Decide how to select sample members. |
| | 12. Map and schedule the fieldwork. |
| | 13. Plan the personnel requirements for the field study. |
| | 14. Consider editing and tabulating requirements. |
| | 15. Anticipate possible interpretation of the data, and be sure it can answer the research questions that need answering. |
| | 16. Consider how the findings may be presented. |

Source: Adapted from David J. Luck, Hugh G. Wales, and Donald A. Taylor, *Marketing Research*, 3rd ed. (Englewood Cliffs, NJ: Prentice-Hall, 1970), p. 87. Reprinted by permission.

## Data Collection

After the research design has determined what data are needed, the data must then be collected. Data collection is a major part of the marketing research project. Two types of data are typically obtained: primary data and secondary data. **Primary data** refers to *data being collected for the first time* during a study. Primary data are normally the *last* to be collected.

**primary data**    Data being collected for the first time.

*As well as the Census of Canada, Statistics Canada conducts surveys on housing, manufacturing, agriculture, and mining. These findings provide valuable data on people's movements, likes and dislikes, economic status, and developing trends.*

**Secondary data** are *previously published matter*. They serve as an extremely important source of information for the marketing researcher.

**secondary data**   Previously published matter.

## Collecting Secondary Data

Not only are secondary data important, they are also abundant in many areas that the marketing researcher may need to investigate. In fact, the overwhelming quantity of secondary data available at little or no cost often challenges the researcher who wants to select only pertinent information.

**Secondary data** consist of two types: internal and external. *Internal secondary data* include records of sales, product performances, sales-force activities, and marketing costs. *External data* are obtained from a variety of sources. Governments — local, provincial, and federal — provide a wide variety of secondary data. Private sources also supply secondary data for the marketing decision-maker. An appendix at the end of this chapter describes a wide range of data sources.

### Government sources

The federal government provides the country's most important sources of marketing data, the most frequently used being census data. Although the government spends millions of dollars in conducting the various censuses of Canada, the information obtained thereby is available at no charge at local libraries and Statistics Canada offices, or it can be purchased at a nominal charge on computer tapes or in various other electronic forms for instant access. In fact, Statistics Canada produces several different censuses. Figure 5–4 briefly describes the main ones.

The current data are so detailed for large cities that breakdowns of population characteristics are available for areas comprising only a few city blocks (census tracts). Thus local retailers or shopping-centre developers can easily gather detailed information about the immediate neighbourhoods that will constitute their customer bases without spending time or money in conducting a comprehensive survey.

Part Two/Foundations of the Marketing Plan

FIGURE 5 – 4

## Census Data Collected by Statistics Canada

*Census of Canada.* Conducted once each decade, with certain categories checked every five years. It provides a count of all residents of Canada by province, city or town, county, or other suitable division, and, in large cities, by census tract. Particularly useful to marketers are the data provided by economic rather than political boundaries, such as greater metropolitan areas. Data are also gathered on age, sex, race, citizenship, education level, occupation, employment status, income, and family status of inhabitants. A less detailed census is conducted at the halfway point in the decade.

*Census of Housing.* Provides information regarding the housing conditions of Canadians, such as value of the dwelling, number of rooms, type of structure, ethnic origin of occupants, and year built.

*Census of Manufacturers.* Annual coverage of major industries revealing the value of products produced by industry, cost of materials and equipment, number of establishments, and wages paid.

*Census of Agriculture.* Conducted every five years. Data regarding the number of farms, number of persons residing on farms (by age and sex), value of farm products sold, area of each major crop, number of tractors, number of livestock, and presence of electricity and running water.

*Census of Minerals.* Data on employees, wages, quantities produced, cost of materials and supplies, types of equipment used, and hours worked.

FIGURE 5 – 5

## Family Expenditures on Food at Home and Away, 1986[a]

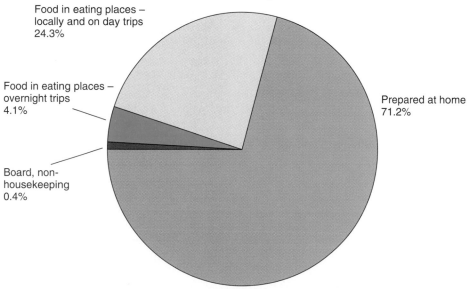

Food in eating places – locally and on day trips 24.3%

Food in eating places – overnight trips 4.1%

Board, non-housekeeping 0.4%

Prepared at home 71.2%

Note: Data are based on the 1986 17-city Survey of Urban Family Expenditure.
[a]Figures include all families and unattached individuals.
Source: *Handbook of Canadian Consumer Markets*, 4th ed. (Ottawa: Conference Board of Canada, 1989), p. D-23.

So much data is produced by the federal government that the marketing researcher often purchases summaries such as the *Canada Year Book* or *Market Research Handbook* or subscribes to *Statistics Canada Daily*. It is also possible to receive *Infomat Weekly*, which provides a listing of new releases by Statistics Canada. A further source of Statistics Canada data is the *Statistics Canada Catalogue*, which lists major data published by the agency. Furthermore, the researcher can gain access to unpublished data through on-line terminals at Statistics Canada User Local Reference Centres.

Provincial and city governments are other important sources of information on employment, production, and sales activities within a particular province.

## Private sources

Numerous private organizations provide information for the marketing executive. In the *Handbook of Canadian Consumer Markets*, published by the Conference Board of Canada, the marketer will find a wide range of illuminating and valuable data. Figures 5–5 and 5–6 illustrate the type of information collected therein for each of the provinces. Another excellent source is *Canadian Markets*, published by the *Financial Post*. Other good summary data can be found in the annual survey of buying power published by *Sales & Marketing Management* magazine. For activities in

## FIGURE 5–6

**Family Expenditures on Food at Home and Away** (average expenditures on food, urban families[a])

| Item | Expenditure (dollars) | | Percentage distribution | |
|---|---|---|---|---|
| | 1984 | 1986 | 1984 | 1986 |
| **Total food** | **4 773** | **5 314** | **100.0** | **100.0** |
| Prepared at home | 3 482 | 3 784 | 72.9 | 71.2 |
| Locally and on day trips | 3 424 | 3 718 | 72.9 | 70.0 |
| Overnight trips or longer | 58 | 66 | 1.2 | 1.2 |
| Board paid to private households | 16 | 19 | 0.3 | 0.4 |
| Food purchased in restaurants | 1 274 | 1 512 | 26.7 | 28.4 |
| Locally and on day trips | 1 084 | 1 293 | 22.7 | 24.3 |
| At work | 383 | 442 | 8.0 | 8.3 |
| At school | 37 | 48 | 0.8 | 0.9 |
| Other meals out | 549 | 661 | 11.5 | 12.4 |
| Between-meal food | 115 | 141 | 2.4 | 2.6 |
| On overnight trips or longer | 190 | 219 | 4.0 | 4.1 |
| On a job | 15 | 21 | 0.3 | 0.4 |
| At school and college | 8 | 13 | 0.2 | 0.2 |
| On vacation and other trips | 168 | 186 | 3.5 | 3.5 |

Note: The 1986 data are based on the Survey of Urban Family Expenditure carried out by Statistics Canada in 17 major cities across Canada. The 1984 data are based on a similar survey.
[a]Figures include all families and unattached individuals. Sources: Statistics Canada; The Conference Board of Canada.

Source: *Handbook of Canadian Consumer Markets*, 4th ed. (Ottawa: Conference Board of Canada, 1989), p. D-23.

a particular industry, trade associations are excellent resources. Advertising agencies continually collect information on the audiences reached by various media.

Several national firms offer information to businesses on a subscription basis. The largest of these, A.C. Nielsen Company, collects data every two months on product sales, retail prices, display space, inventories, and promotional activities of competing brands of food and drug products from a substantial sample of food stores and drugstores. The Consumer Panel of Canada (International Surveys), mentioned earlier, gathers information on consumer purchases.

## Advantages and Limitations of Secondary Data

The use of secondary data offers two important advantages over that of primary data:

1. Assembling previously collected data is almost always less expensive than collecting primary data.
2. Less time is involved in locating and using secondary data. Figure 5–7 shows the estimated time involved in completing a research study requiring primary data. The time involved will naturally vary considerably, depending on such factors as the research subject and the scope of the study.

The researcher must be aware of two potential limitations to the use of secondary data: (1) the data may be obsolete, and (2) the classifications of the secondary data may not be usable in the study. Published information has an unfortunate habit of

### FIGURE 5–7

#### Time Requirements for a Primary-Data Research Project

| *Step* | *Estimated Time Required for Completion* |
| --- | --- |
| Problem definition | Several days |
| Development of methodology | One week |
| Questionnaire design | One week |
| Questionnaire pretest and evaluation of pretest results | Two weeks |
| Field interviews | One to six weeks |
| Coding of returned questionnaires | One week |
| Data transfer to computer | One week |
| Data processing and statistical analysis | Seven to ten days |
| Interpretation of output | One week |
| Written report and presentation of findings | Two weeks |
| **Total elapsed time** | **Twelve to seventeen weeks** |

Source: Estimates by Alfred S. Boote, Corporate Director of Market Research, The Singer Company; quoted in "Everyone Benefits from Closer Planning, Research Ties," *Marketing News* (January 9, 1981), p. 30. Used by permission of the American Marketing Association.

*The "people meter" installed on top of this television monitors the family's TV viewing. By collating the data from many people meters, the A.C. Nielsen Company can analyze trends in TV viewing, and supply preliminary data to companies and other market researchers.*

rapidly going out of date. A marketing researcher analyzing the population of the Calgary metropolitan market in 1993 may well discover that much of the 1991 census data is already obsolete due to an upturn or downturn in the economy or new developments in the oil and gas industry.

Data may also have been collected previously on such bases as county or city boundaries, when the marketing manager requires it to be broken down by city blocks or census tracts. In such cases the marketing researcher may not be able to rearrange the secondary data in a usable form and must therefore collect primary data.

Secondary information proved very valuable in the Infotech study. A wide range of information sources were found. For example, relevant articles were found in such magazines as *Maclean's, Popular Computing*, and *Businessweek*. An especially valuable publication was *Electronic Learning*, which had no fewer than eight articles bearing on the topic.

In addition to such periodicals, the researchers found 11 different special reports on various aspects of the educational use of computers. Report titles included "School Uses of Computers" (from Johns Hopkins University, in the United States) and "Phase Two: A Periodical Reporting on Education Computing in Scotland."

Studying such secondary sources gave the researchers immense insight into the fundamental issues involved in using courseware in the educational system. But some important information was still needed before a decision could be made about proceeding with the courseware project. Thus, it was time to plan a primary-data collection process.

## Survey Design and Execution

Usually, secondary data are incomplete or do not fully relate to the problem at hand. The necessary information must then be obtained through one of several primary research methods. If hypotheses have been stated, facts should be gathered in such a way as to allow direct testing of the hypotheses.

The collection of primary data requires a considerable amount of technical expertise. Companies have found that they get the best information when specially-trained individuals handle the design and execution of the research.

## Collecting Primary Data

As Figure 5–3 indicated, the marketing researcher has three alternative methods for collecting primary data: observation, survey, or controlled experiment. No one method is best in all circumstances.

### The observation method

Observational studies are conducted by actually viewing (either directly or through mechanical means such as hidden cameras) the overt actions of the respondent. Examples of this approach include conducting traffic counts at a potential location for a fast-food franchise, checking licence plates at a shopping centre to determine the area from which shoppers are attracted, or using supermarket scanners to record sales of certain products.

The observation method has both advantages and drawbacks. Merits are that observation is often more accurate than questioning techniques like surveys and interviews, and that it may be the only way to get information about such things as actual shopping behaviour in a supermarket. It may also be the easiest way to get specific data. Limitations include observer subjectivity and errors in interpretation.

---

### A·P·P·L·Y·I·N·G   T·H·E   C·O·N·C·E·P·T·S

## *Garbology: Unobtrusive Marketing Research*

Sometimes it is better to use unobtrusive methods of marketing research than to ask people direct questions about their attitudes or behaviour. "Garbology" — a technique whereby the researcher monitors consumption behaviour by rummaging through selected garbage — is a good example of such a method.

The *Saturday Evening Post* used this technique during the early 1900s to convince Campbell Soup that working-class, not upper-class, families were the appropriate target market for canned soups. Empty soup cans were widely documented in trash found in working-class neighbourhoods but not upper-class neighbourhoods. The success of this project resulted in Campbell becoming a regular advertiser in the *Saturday Evening Post*.

Restaurant managers have used garbology for years to monitor customer satisfaction. Patrons throw away what they don't want to eat, or don't have room for. Thus, quality or quantity of food can be flagged by this method.

A marketing director for a large regional hospital was able to calculate the actual bed count of other area hospitals. Her unobtrusive measure involved the laundry. Her hospital happened to wash the bed sheets for all the other hospitals. A simple tally gave her daily bed counts for each competing community hospital.

Sources: William T. Neese, "Don't Be So Direct When Assessing Customer Satisfaction," *Marketing News* (February 4, 1991), p. 8; Leonard M. Fuld, "Did You Hear the One About the Oil Spots?" *Marketing News* (September 3, 1990), p. 30.

For instance, researchers might incorrectly classify people's economic status because of the way they were dressed at the time of observation.[5]

Sometimes firms use the observation method in evaluating advertisements. A specialist research service is hired to study patterns of viewer eye movements when looking at advertisements. This is done under laboratory conditions. The results from one such eye-tracking test led the advertiser to move the headline from the bottom of the ad to the top, since a majority of eye movements flowed to the top. Observation could also be used to determine the route shoppers take once inside a supermarket. From this information, positioning of items might be determined.

## The survey method

The amount and type of information that can be obtained through mere observation of overt consumer acts is limited; to obtain information on attitudes, motives, and opinions, the researcher must ask questions. The survey method is the most widely used approach to collecting primary data. There are three kinds of surveys: telephone interviews, mail surveys, and personal interviews.

*Telephone interviews* are inexpensive and fast ways to obtain limited quantities of relatively impersonal information. Many firms have leased WATS[b] services, which considerably reduce the cost of long-distance calls.

Telephone interviews account for the majority of all primary marketing research. They are limited to simple, clearly worded questions. Such interviews have two drawbacks: it is extremely difficult to obtain information about the personal characteristics of the respondent, and the survey may be prejudiced since two groups will be omitted — those households without telephones and those with unlisted numbers. One survey reported that alphabetical listings in telephone directories excluded one-fourth of large-city dwellers, and that they underrepresented service workers and separated and divorced persons. In addition, the mobility of the population creates problems in choosing names from telephone directories. As a result, a number of telephone interviewers have resorted to using digits selected at random and matched to telephone prefixes in the geographic area to be sampled. This technique is designed to correct the problem of sampling those with new telephone listings and those with unlisted numbers.

*Mail surveys* allow the marketing researcher to conduct national studies at a reasonable cost. While personal interviews with a national sample may be prohibitively expensive, by using the mail, the researcher can reach each potential respondent for the price of a postage stamp. Costs may be misleading, however, since *returned*

---

### A·P·P·L·Y·I·N·G  T·H·E  C·O·N·C·E·P·T·S

## *Unique Phone-Interview Method for Testing TV Ads*

A unique advertising and programming pretesting service that allows clients to study their advertisements and other concepts in a natural environment and context is now being used.

Videocassettes are mailed to respondents chosen from a demographic and lifestyle database of households with VCRs. Participants receive a 30-minute dummy videocassette featuring the clients' ads, along with requests for specific view dates and specific times for follow-up telephone interviews.

After respondents view the tapes, they are surveyed by telephone for their reactions.

Source: Adapted from "Home Video Test Pretests TV Ads," *Marketing News* (January 4, 1988), p. 31.

## *Telephone Interviewing with your Personal Computer*

It is now possible to design a questionnaire on a personal computer and then have the machine guide the researcher through each interview. This is done through the use of readily available software packages. After the questionnaire is developed, interviewers can sit at computers and start calling respondents. As questions are answered, a single keystroke records the response. Answers can easily be corrected, removed, or restored. The software program does the rest. It automatically pages to the next question and simultaneously tabulates answers.

When the survey is finished, the researcher can select how to analyze the data. If she wants to know the number of people between the ages of 25 and 45 who prefer Product X, the program will display the answer on the screen or on a printer. Various other tabulations are also available.

Systems like this expedite marketing research, and make it possible for even the smallest businesses and organizations to do the marketing research that is necessary for sound decision-making.

questionnaires for such a study range between 10 and 80 percent, depending on the length of the questionnaire and respondent interest (a 20 percent return is not uncommon). When returns are low, the question arises as to the opinions of the majority (who did not respond). Some surveys use a coin or other incentive to gain the reader's attention, an approach that can increase returns, but also increases costs. Unless additional information is obtained from nonrespondents, the results of the study are likely to be biased, since there may be important differences between the characteristics of these people and the characteristics of those who took the time to complete and return the questionnaire. For this reason a follow-up questionnaire is sometimes mailed to nonrespondents, or telephone interviews may be used to gather additional information. These extra steps naturally add to the survey's expense. In spite of these difficulties, mail surveys are widely used.

Mail questionnaires must be carefully worded and pretested to eliminate any potential misunderstanding by respondents. But misunderstandings can occur with even the most clearly worded questions. When a truck operated by a government agency accidentally killed a cow, an official responded with an apology and a form to be filled out. It included a space for "disposition of the dead cow." The farmer responded "kind and gentle."[7]

*Personal interviews* are typically the best means of obtaining more-detailed information, since the interviewer has the opportunity to establish rapport with the respondent. The interviewer can also explain questions that might be confusing or vague to the respondent.

Personal interviews are slow and are the most expensive method of collecting data. However, their flexibility — coupled with the detailed information that can be collected — often offsets these limitations. Recently, marketing research firms have rented locations in shopping centres, where they have greater access to potential buyers of the products in which they are interested. Downtown retail districts and airports are other on-site locations for marketing research.

A special type of personal interview is the **focus group interview.** *Focus group interviews* have been widely used in recent years as a means of gathering preliminary research information. In a focus group interview, eight to twelve people are brought together to discuss a subject of interest. Although the moderator typically explains the purpose of the meeting and suggests an opening discussion topic, he or she is interested in stimulating interaction among group members in order to develop the discussion of numerous points about the subject. Focus group sessions, which are often one to two hours long, are usually taped so that the moderator can devote full attention to the discussion.[8] This process gives the researcher an idea of how consumers view a problem. Often it uncovers points of view that the researcher had not thought of.

## The experimental method

The final and least-used method of collecting marketing information involves using *controlled experiments*. An experiment is a scientific investigation in which the researcher controls or manipulates a test group and observes this group as well as another group that did not receive the controls or manipulations. Such experiments can be conducted in the field or in a laboratory setting.

Although a number of marketing-related experiments have been conducted in the controlled environment of a laboratory, most have been conducted in the field. To date, the most common use of this method has been in *test marketing*.

### A·P·P·L·Y·I·N·G  T·H·E  C·O·N·C·E·P·T·S

## Two-Way Focus Groups Can Provide Startling Information

"Two-Way Focus" is the name of a research technique developed by Bozell, Jacobs, Kenyon & Eckhart. It allows one target group to listen to and learn from a related group.

Two-Way Focus emerged from work the agency was doing with physicians and patients related to the management of arthritis. The method gets at the inner workings of the relationship between providers of a good or service and customers.

There is often a huge gap between reality and perception. Often, what patients think they are accomplishing by taking a medicine is different from the actual result. And physicians often do not know what their patients are thinking, how they feel about the medicine they are taking, and what their emotional (as opposed to physiological) needs are.

To help close this gap, the agency first conducted a series of focus groups with arthritis patients. They heard over and over that physicians don't take the time to listen. Next, they held focus groups with physicians to learn how they managed their arthritis patients. These groups made it obvious that many physicians don't appreciate how much their patients really need to talk to them.

This more or less traditional focus group approach provided interesting insights into the physician–patient relationship. But it did not seem to be enough. Therefore, the researchers had physicians observe a

focus group of arthritis patients talking about their physicians and medications. They immediately followed the patient group with a focus group consisting of the physicians who had observed the patients.

The effect of the patient group on the physicians was startling. They emerged from behind the viewing room's one-way glass flushed and glassy-eyed. As they talked in their own group, with the researchers observing, it became apparent they had had little idea that patients would be taking as many as 10 to 15 medications at one time. Nor, it seems, had they really known the desperation their patients felt when their physicians did not take the time to really talk with them.

The company knew it had a breakthrough technique when, observing the physicians' group, researchers saw the transforming effect the patient group had on the physicians.

Two-Way Focus might also be used to help close other gaps — for example, those between financial consultants and investors, retail-store managers and shoppers, and franchisees and customers.

Source: Adapted from Michael Silverstein, "Two-Way Focus Groups Can Provide Startling Information," *Marketing News* (January 4, 1988), p. 31.

**test marketing** Introducing a new, untried product into a particular metropolitan area and then observing its degree of success.

Marketers face great risks in introducing new products. They often attempt to reduce this risk by **test marketing**: *introducing the new, untried product into a particular metropolitan area and then observing its degree of success*. Frequently used cities include Calgary, Lethbridge, and Winnipeg. Consumers in the test-market city view the product as they do any other new product since it is available in retail outlets and is advertised in the local media. The test-market city becomes a small replica of the total market. The marketing manager can then compare actual sales with expected sales and can project them on a nationwide basis. If the test results are favourable, the risks of a large-scale failure are reduced. Many products fail at the test-market stage: thus, consumers who live in these cities may purchase products that no one else will ever be able to buy.

The major problem with controlled experiments is the difficult task of controlling all variables in a real-life situation. The laboratory scientist can rigidly control temperature and humidity, but how can the marketing manager determine the effect of varying the retail price through refundable coupons when the competition decides to retaliate or deliberately confuse the experiment by issuing its own coupons?

In the future, experimentation will become more frequent as firms develop more sophisticated simulated competitive models requiring computer analysis. Simulation of market activities promises to be one of the great new developments in marketing.

In the Infotech market study, primary data were collected through four different research methods: (1) telephone surveys of departments of education across Canada and in selected American states: (2) personal and telephone interviews of principal Canadian textbook suppliers: (3) personal and telephone interviews of key hardware and software manufacturers and distributors: and (4) in-class surveys of teachers taking summer-school courses.

## The Data Collection Instrument

Most of the data collection methods depend on the use of a good questionnaire. Developing a good questionnaire requires considerable skill and attention. Referring to the objectives of that is needed to complete the study. With this list as a foundation, specific questions are written for the questionnaire. The questionnaire must then be pretested; a small sample of persons similar to those who will be surveyed are asked to complete it. Discussions with these sample respondents help uncover points that are unclear. The nature, style, and length of the questionnaire will vary depending on the type of data collection technique chosen. After pretesting and revising until the questionnaire works well, the researcher plans the necessary computer-coding setup on the questionnaire, to facilitate later data analysis.

The actual execution of the survey is beyond the scope of this book. Other important issues that need to be dealt with in planning the study are selecting, training, and controlling the field interviewers: editing, coding, tabulating, and interpreting the data; presenting the results; and following up on the survey. It is crucial that marketing researchers and research users co-operate at every stage in the research design. Too many studies go unused because marketing management views the results as not meaningful to them.

For the Infotech study, a team of four researchers worked almost full time for approximately three months to collect the secondary data, design and pretest questionnaires, and gather the primary data. The data were analyzed and presented in a 195-page report to the client.

*This researcher from Market Research Associates is conducting a traffic survey for the city of Halifax. The data collected from this survey will help city planners devise more-efficient traffic routes and patterns. Would this be classified as a probability or nonprobability sample?*

The report highlighted the size and growth of the market. It also showed that despite the favourable market size, the idea as originally conceived would be extremely difficult to implement. As a result of the study, the sponsor was able to make an informed decision about whether or not to go ahead. The marketing research presented information that could save the sponsor a great deal of time and money.

## Sampling Techniques

Sampling[9] is one of the most important aspects of marketing research. *The total group that the researcher wants to study* is called the **population** or **universe**. For a political campaign, the population would be all eligible voters. For a new cosmetic line, it might be all women in a certain age bracket. If this total group is contacted, the results are known as a **census**. Unless the group is small, the cost of such a survey will be overwhelming. Even the federal government attempts a full census only once every 10 years.

Information, therefore, is rarely gathered from the total population during a survey. Instead, researchers select a representative group called a sample. Samples can be classified either as probability samples or as nonprobability samples. A **probability sample** is *a sample in which every member of the population has a known chance of being selected*. Because **nonprobability samples** are *arbitrary*, standard statistical tests cannot be applied to them. Marketing researchers usually base their studies

**population** or **universe**  The total group that the researcher wants to study.

**census**  A collection of marketing data from all possible sources.

**probability sample**  A sample in which every member of the population has a known chance of being selected.

**nonprobability sample**  A sample chosen in an arbitrary fashion so that each member of the population does not have a representative chance of being selected.

on probability samples, but it is important to be able to identify all types of samples.[10] Some of the best-known sampling plans are outlined below.

**convenience sample**
A nonprobability sample based on the selection of readily available respondents.

A **convenience sample** is *a nonprobability sample based on the selection of readily available respondents.* Broadcasting's "on-the-street" interviews are a good example. Marketing researchers sometimes use such samples in exploratory research, but not in definitive studies.

**judgment sample**
A nonprobability sample of people with a specific attribute.

*Nonprobability samples of people with a specific attribute* are called **judgment samples**. Election-night predictions are usually based on polls of "swing voters" and are a type of judgment sample.

**quota sample**   A nonprobability sample that is divided so that different segments or groups are represented in the total sample.

A **quota sample** is *a nonprobability sample that is divided so that different segments or groups are represented in the total sample.* An example would be a survey of imported-auto owners that included 33 Nissan owners, 31 Toyota owners, 7 BMW owners, and so on.

**cluster sample**   A probability sample that is generated by randomly choosing one or more areas or population clusters and then surveying all members in the chosen cluster(s).

A **cluster sample** is *a probability sample that is generated by randomly choosing one or more areas or population clusters and then surveying all members in the chosen cluster(s).* This approach can be helpful in a situation where it is difficult to obtain a complete list of all members of the population, but where there is good information on certain *areas* (such as census tracts).

**simple random sample**   A probability sample in which every item in the relevant universe has an equal opportunity of being selected.

The basic type of probability sample is the **simple random sample**, *a sample in which every item in the relevant universe has an equal opportunity of being selected.* Provincial lotteries are an example. Each number that appears on a ticket has an equal opportunity of being selected and each ticket holder an equal opportunity of winning. Using a computer to select 200 respondents randomly from a mailing list of 1000 would give every name on the list an equal opportunity of being selected.

**systematic sample**   A probability sample that takes every nth item on a list, after a random start.

*A probability sample that takes every nth item on a list, after a random start,* is called a **systematic sample**. Sampling from a telephone directory is a common example.

---

## A·P·P·L·Y·I·N·G  T·H·E  C·O·N·C·E·P·T·S

### *Reducing the Cost of Marketing Research*

The developers of a computer-based system that seeks partners for cross-promotions have broadened its applications to include research. Changing markets have produced a need for more targeted, defined research. However, small marketers are often reluctant to invest in research due to the cost and lack of alternatives.

Until now the only alternative for small marketers has been omnibus studies. In such studies, a firm pays for the insertion of one or two questions, along with several others. However, because of their wide scope, these studies sometimes fail to provide the specialized information smaller marketers need to ensure effective marketing.

Now, clients can purchase a service called Match Marketing Research (MMR). This service helps find a partner for sharing the research project. When a client is seeking a research partner, its characteristics and needs are entered into a computer system, which searches through an existing databank for a compatible partner.

Once the partner is found, an associated firm, Consumer Contact, devises and executes the research program. MMR can reduce costs by 40 percent to 60 percent. This makes specialized research affordable for marketers who previously could not afford it.

Source: Adapted from "Computers Are Making Marketing Matches," *Marketing* (July 17, 1989), p. 13.

# Marketing Information Systems

For all companies, some market data flow in on a regular basis from sales and other marketing activities. And companies that undertake marketing research gain other periodic bursts of facts from such studies.

The value of such material can vary significantly. Data and information are not necessarily synonymous terms. *Data* refers to statistics, opinions, facts, or predictions categorized on some basis for storage and retrieval. *Information* is data relevant to the marketing manager in making decisions. Often, the right information does not seem to be available when a marketing decision has to be made. This can be because the company simply does not have it, or because it is not readily available in the firm's system.

The solution to the problem of obtaining relevant information appears simple — establish a systematic approach to information management by installing a planned marketing information system (MIS). Establishing an effective information system is, however, much easier said than done, as evidenced by the large number of firms that have attempted to develop an MIS and have succeeded only in increasing the amounts of irrelevant data available to them.

The ideal **marketing information system** should be *a designed set of procedures and methods for generating an orderly flow of pertinent information for use in making decisions, providing management with a picture of the current and future states of the market and with indications of market responses to company actions as well as to the actions of competitors.*[11]

Properly constructed, the MIS could serve as the nerve centre for the company, providing instantaneous information suitable for each level of management. It would act as a thermostat, monitoring the marketplace continuously so that management could adjust its actions as conditions change.

The analogy of an automatic heating system illustrates the role of marketing information in a firm's marketing system (see Figure 5–8). Once the objective of a temperature setting (perhaps 20°C) has been established, information about the actual temperature in the house is collected and compared with the objective, and a decision is made based on this comparison. If the temperature drops below an established figure, the decision is made to activate the furnace until the temperature reaches some established level. On the other hand, a high temperature may require a decision to turn off the furnace.

Deviation from the firm's goals of profitability, return on investment, or market share may necessitate changes in price structures, promotional expenditures, package design, or numerous marketing alternatives. The firm's MIS should be capable of revealing such deviations and possibly suggesting tactical changes that will result in attaining the established goals.

Many marketing executives feel that their company does not need a marketing information system, for various reasons. Two arguments are most often given: (1) the size of the company's operations does not warrant such a complete system, and (2) the information provided by an MIS is already being supplied by the marketing research department.

These contentions arise from a misconception regarding the services and functions performed by the marketing research department. Marketing research has already been described as typically focusing on a specific problem or project; the investigations involved have a definite beginning, middle, and end.

Marketing information systems, on the other hand, are much wider in scope and involve the continual collection and analysis of marketing information. Figure 5–9

**marketing information system**
A designed set of procedures and methods for generating an orderly flow of pertinent information for use in making decisions, providing management with a picture of the current and future states of the market and with indications of market responses to company actions as well as to the actions of competitors.

**The Decision — Turn the Furnace On or Off**

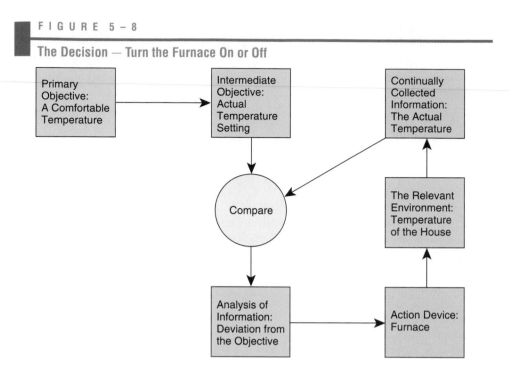

Source: Reprinted by permission from Bertram Schoner and Kenneth F. Uhl, *Marketing Research: Information Systems and Decision Making* (New York: Wiley, 1975), p. 10.

FIGURE 5 – 9

**Information Components of a Firm's MIS**

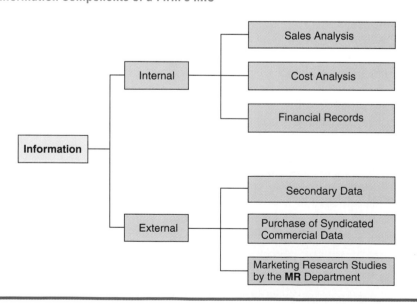

*Information collected by the Monsanto Information System is analyzed to determine consumer preferences and buying patterns. In this way, Monsanto can assemble data and predict future trends for its products without having to wade through government statistics or employ external resources. Many of the larger companies are expected to follow in Monsanto's footsteps in the near future.*

indicates the various information inputs — including marketing research studies — that serve as components of a firm's MIS.

Robert J. Williams, creator of the first and still one of the most notable marketing information systems in 1961 at the Mead Johnson division of Edward Dalton Company, explains the difference this way.

> The difference between marketing research and marketing intelligence is like the difference between a flash bulb and a candle. Let's say you are dancing in the dark. Every 90 seconds you're allowed to set off a flash bulb. You can use those brief intervals of intense light to chart a course, but remember everybody is moving, too. Hopefully, they'll accommodate themselves roughly to your predictions. You may get bumped and you may stumble every so often, but you can dance along.
>
> On the other hand, you can light a candle. It doesn't yield as much light, but it's a steady light. You are continually aware of the movements of the other bodies. You can adjust your own course to the courses of the others. The intelligence system is a kind of candle. It's no great flash on the immediate state of things, but it provides continuous light as situations shift and change.[12]

By focusing daily on the marketplace, the MIS provides a continuous, systematic, and comprehensive study of areas that indicate deviations from established goals. The up-to-the-minute data allow problems to be corrected before they adversely affect company operations. Figure 5–10 summarizes many of the applications and possible benefits of a sophisticated information system.

FIGURE 5-10

## Benefits Possible with an Information System

| Typical Applications | Benefits | Examples |
|---|---|---|
| *Control Systems* | | |
| 1. Control of marketing costs | 1. More timely computerized reports | 1. Undesirable cost trends are spotted more quickly so that corrective action may be taken sooner. |
| 2. Diagnosis of poor sales performance | 2. Flexible on-line retrieval of data | 2. Executives can ask supplementary questions of the computer to help pinpoint reasons for a sales decline and reach an action decision more quickly. |
| 3. Management of fashion goods | 3. Automatic spotting of problems and opportunities | 3. Fast-moving fashion items are reported daily for quick reorder, and slow-moving items are also reported for fast price reductions. |
| 4. Flexible promotion strategy | 4. Cheaper, more detailed, and more frequent reports | 4. Ongoing evaluation of a promotional campaign permits reallocation of funds to areas behind target. |
| *Planning Systems* | | |
| 1. Forecasting | 1. Automatic translation of terms and classifications between departments | 1. Survey-based forecasts of demands for complex industrial goods can be automatically translated into parts requirements and production schedules. |
| 2. Promotional planning and corporate long-range planning | 2. Systematic testing of alternative promotional plans and compatibility testing of various divisional plans | 2. Complex simulation models, developed and operated with the help of databank information, can be used for promotional planning by product managers and for strategic planning by top management. |
| 3. Credit manager | 3. Programmed executive decision rules can operate on databank information | 3. Credit decisions are automatically made as each order is processed. |
| 4. Purchasing | 4. Detailed sales reporting permits automation of management decisions | 4. Computer automatically repurchases standard items on the basis of correlation of sales data with programmed decision rules. |
| *Research Systems* | | |
| 1. Advertising strategy | 1. Additional manipulation of data is possible when stored for computers in an unaggregated file | 1. Sales analysis is possible by new market segment breakdowns. |
| 2. Pricing strategy | 2. Improved storage and retrieval capability allows new types of data to be collected and used. | 2. Systematic recording of information about past R & D contract bidding situations allows improved bidding strategies. |

FIGURE 5-10 (CONTINUED)

**Benefits Possible with an Information System**

| | | |
|---|---|---|
| 3. Evaluation of advertising expenditures | 3. Well-designed databanks permit integration and comparison of different sets of data. | 3. Advertising expenditures are compared to shipments by district to provide information about advertising effectiveness. |
| 4. Continuous experiments | 4. Comprehensive monitoring of input and performance variables yields information when changes are made. | 4. Changes in promotional strategy by type of customer are matched against sales results on a continuous basis. |

Source: Reprinted by permission of the *Harvard Business Review*. Exhibit from "How to Build a Marketing Information System," by Donald F. Cox and Robert E. Good, *Harvard Business Review* (May–June 1967), p. 146. Copyright © 1967 by the President and Fellows of Harvard College; all rights reserved.

## Successful Marketing Information Systems

Although only a few companies have sophisticated, computer-based marketing information systems, considerable attention is being focused on their contributions. By the end of the decade many of the larger companies will establish their own information systems. The Monsanto Company and General Mills Incorporated are examples of firms with a successful MIS in operation.

Monsanto has designed one of the most advanced marketing information systems in operation. The system provides detailed sales analyses by product, sales, district, type of mill, and end-use. Computer analyses are obtained from a continuing panel of households that represent a cross-section of the national market. Information is collected on purchase patterns by socio-economic group and is then analyzed to determine current buying trends.

Monsanto also collects survey data to record the actions of competitors. In addition the system generates short-, medium-, and long-range forecasts for the company and industry. Short-term forecasts are developed for each of 400 individual products.

The General Mills computer supplies each zone, regional, and district manager with a daily report on the previous day's orders by brand and a comparison of current projections of monthly sales with the monthly total projected the week before. Each of 1700 individual products is analyzed in terms of current profitability and projected annual profitability as compared with target projections made at the beginning of the year. The "problem" products requiring management attention are then printed out on the daily reports. A similar report looks for problem areas in each region and breaks down the nature of the problem according to cause (i.e., profit margins, over- or underspending on advertising and sales promotion.)[13]

As marketing research becomes increasingly scientific and is combined by a growing number of organizations into fully functional information systems, decision-makers benefit by making informed decisions about problems and opportunities. Sophisticated computer simulations make it possible to consider alternative courses of action by posing a number of "what if?" situations. These developments may convert the scenario we have imagined for 1999 into reality in a much shorter time.

A·P·P·L·Y·I·N·G  T·H·E  C·O·N·C·E·P·T·S

## A Peek at the Future of Information Systems

The year is 1999. The place is the office of the marketing manager of a medium-sized consumer products manufacturer. The participants in the following discussion are John, the marketing manager; Anne, the director of marketing science; Rod, Anne's assistant, who specializes in marketing research; and Scott, the sales manager for the company. The scene opens as Anne, Rod, and Scott enter John's office.

John: *Good morning. What's up for discussion this morning?*

Anne: *We want to take a look at the prospects for our new beef substitute.*

John: *What do we have on it?*

Rod: *We test marketed the product late in 1998 in four cities, so we have those data from last quarter.*

John: *Let's see how it did.*

(All four gather around the remote console video display unit. John activates the console and requests a display of the sales results from the most recent test market. The system retrieves the data and displays the information on the video device.)

John: *That looks good! How does it compare to the first test?*

(The console retrieves and displays the data from the first test in response to John's command.)

Rod: *Let me check the significance of the sales increase in the most recent test over last year's test.*

(Rod requests that the system test and display the likelihood that the sales increase could be a chance occurrence.)

Rod: *Looks like a solid sales increase.*

Anne: *Good! How did the market respond to our change in price?*

(Anne commands the system to display the graph of the price–quantity response based on the most recent test data.)

John: *Is that about what our other meat substitute products show?*

(John calls up past price–quantity response graphs for similar products.)

John: *Just as I suspected. This new product is a bit more responsive to price. What's the profit estimate?*

(John calls for a profit estimate for the product-planning model within the system.)

John: *Hmm. . .$5 500 000. Looks good. Is that based on the growth model I supplied to the model bank last week?*

Anne: *No. This is based on the market-share progress other food substitutes have shown in the past as well as the information we have on the beef substitute from our test markets.*

John: *Let's see what mine would do.*

(He reactivates the product-planning model, this time using his growth model. The profit implications are displayed on the console.)

John: *Well, my model predicts $5 million. That's close. Looks like my feelings are close to the statistical results.*

Anne: *Let's see if there's a better marketing strategy for this product. We must remember that these profit estimates are based on the preliminary plan we developed two weeks ago.*

(Anne calls for the marketing program generator to recommend a marketing program based on the data and judgmental inputs on file for this product.)

John: *I'm a little worried about our advertising appeals. Can we improve in this area?*

Anne: *Let's see what the response to advertising is.*

(The video unit shows a graph of the predicted sales–advertising response function.)

Anne: *If we changed from a taste appeal to a convenience appeal, what would the results be, John?*

John: *I think it would look like this.*

(John takes a light-pen and describes a new relationship on the video unit based on his judgment of the effectiveness of the new appeal.)

Rod: *Let me check something.*

(Rod calls for a sample of past sales–advertising response curves of similar products using the convenience appeal.)

Rod: *I think you're underestimating the response, on the basis of past data.*

John: *Well, this product is different. How much would it cost for a test of this appeal?*

(Rod calls a marketing research evaluation model from the console.)

Rod: *It looks like a meaningful test would cost about $5000.*

John: *I wonder what risk we'd run if we made a decision to go national with the product right now. What are the chances of a failure with this product as it stands if we include this morning's revisions to the marketing program?*

(A risk-analysis model is called up on the system.)

John: *Looks like a 35 percent chance of failure. Maybe we'd best run further tests in order to reduce the risk. What's next on the agenda this morning?*

Source: David B. Montgomery and Glen L. Urban, *Management Science in Marketing* (Englewood Cliffs, NJ: Prentice-Hall, 1969), pp. 1–3. Adapted by permission of Prentice-Hall, Inc., Englewood Cliffs, NJ.

# Summary

Information is vital for marketing decision-making. No firm can operate without detailed information on its market. Information may take several forms: one-time marketing research studies, secondary data, internal data, subscriptions to commercial information sources, and the output of a marketing information system.

Marketing research, an important source of information, deals with studies that collect and analyze data relevant to marketing decisions. It involves the specific delineation of problems, research design, collection of secondary and primary data, interpretation of research findings, and presentation of results for management action.

The most common market research activities are determining market potential, developing sales forecasts for the firm's products and services, competitive-product analysis, new-product estimates, studies related to marketing mix decisions and international trade, and social and cultural research. Outside suppliers are vital to the research function. Some outside research suppliers perform the complete research task, while others specialize in limited areas or provide syndicated data services.

The marketing research process can be divided into six specific steps: (1) defining the problem, (2) conducting exploratory research; (3) formulating hypotheses; (4) preparing a research design; (5) collecting data; and (6) interpreting and presenting the results. A clearly defined problem allows the researcher to obtain the relevant decision-oriented information. Exploratory research refers to information gained both outside and inside the firm. Hypotheses — tentative explanations of some specific event — allow the researcher to set out a specific research design, the series of decisions that, taken together, constitute a master plan or model for conducting the investigation. The data collection phase of the marketing research process can involve either primary data (original data) or secondary data (previously published data), or both. Primary data can be collected by three alternative methods: observation, survey, or experiment. Once the data are collected, it is important that researchers interpret and present them in a way that is meaningful to management.

Marketing decisions can be improved by developing a planned marketing information system. Properly designed, the MIS will generate an orderly flow of decision-oriented information as the marketing executive needs it. The number of firms with planned information systems is growing.

The first five chapters of this book have been designed to serve as building blocks for marketing planning. The next chapter will show how a marketing plan is developed.

## ■ K E Y   T E R M S

| | | |
|---|---|---|
| marketing research | secondary data | convenience sample |
| full-service research supplier | focus group interview | judgment sample |
| partial-service research supplier | test marketing | quota sample |
| syndicated service | population or universe | cluster sample |
| exploratory research | census | simple random sample |
| hypothesis | probability sample | systematic sample |
| research design | nonprobability sample | marketing information system |
| primary data | | |

# REVIEW QUESTIONS

1. Outline the development and current status of the marketing research function.
2. Explain the services offered by the different types of marketing research suppliers.
3. List and explain the various steps in the marketing research process.
4. Distinguish between primary and secondary data.
5. What advantages does the use of secondary data offer the marketing researcher? What potential limitations exist in using such data?
6. Distinguish among surveys, experiments, and observational methods of data collection.
7. Illustrate each of the three methods for gathering survey data. Under what circumstances should each be used?
8. Explain the differences between probability and nonprobability samples and the various types of each.
9. Distinguish between marketing research and marketing information systems.
10. What is the current status of marketing information systems?

# DISCUSSION QUESTIONS AND EXERCISES

1. Prepare a brief (two- to three-page) report on a syndicated marketing research service. Explain how the data the firm supplies are used by marketing decision-makers.
2. Collect from secondary-data sources the following information:
   a. retail sales in Victoria, British Columbia
   b. number of persons over 65 in Moncton, New Brunswick
   c. earnings per share for International Business Machines Corporation last year
   d. bituminous coal production in Canada
   e. consumer price index for last August
   f. number of households earning more than $35,000 annually in your home town or city
3. Look up the "Survey of Buying Power" data for your community or one nearby. What marketing implications can be drawn from this information?
4. James Roe, the vice-president of Gadget Electronics, a medium-to-large Canadian company, refuses to involve himself with the activities of his marketing research staff. He explains that he has hired competent professionals for the research department, and he does not plan to meddle in their operation. Critically evaluate Roe's position.
5. You have been asked to determine the effect on Gillette of Schick's introduction of a revolutionary new blade that is guaranteed to give a hundred nick-free shaves. Outline your approach to the study.
6. Many people fear the development of national databanks. What are the responsibilities of marketing researchers with regard to this issue?
7. The text presented a future scenario for marketing information systems. How realistic do you think this is? What are the personal requirements for managers who would be involved in using such a system?

# MICROCOMPUTER EXERCISE

## Sales Analysis

**Directions:** Use the Menu Item titled "Sales Analysis" on the *Foundations of Marketing* disk to solve each of the following problems.

1. A Saskatoon company organizes its sales force into three sales regions: A, B, and C. The average salaries in these regions are $32 000, $36 000, and $42 000, respectively. Region A sales personnel average $800 000 in sales; Region B sales

representatives, $740 000; and Region C personnel, $985 000. Selling expenses average $15 000 in all regions. Calculate the cost/sales ratios for each of the three regions.

**TABLE A**

**Morgenstern's Sales Analysis**

| Division | Average Sales per Salesperson | Average Sales Compensation | Average Selling Expenses |
|---|---|---|---|
| 1 | $651 000 | $31 650 | $14 175 |
| 2 | 778 000 | 30 500 | 27 700 |
| 3 | 664 000 | 28 100 | 9 375 |
| 4 | 602 000 | 33 650 | 7 300 |
| 5 | 518 000 | 29 500 | 7 100 |

2. One of the first assignments given to Gordon Morgenstern following his employment in the marketing department of a Halifax-based firm was to develop a sales analysis for the company's five sales divisions. Morgenstern's supervisor indicated a particular concern with Division 2's average selling expenses of $27 700. Morgenstern collected the data shown in Table A on sales, sales compensation, and selling expenses. What should Morgenstern tell his supervisor concerning the firm's cost/sales ratios?

3. The Alberta Division of a Montreal firm employs five sales representatives. All were assigned sales quotas of $750 000. The division's manager, Eleanor Tomlinson, is now preparing an analysis of how her people performed in 1987. The actual sales results were as follows.

| Salesperson | Actual Sales |
|---|---|
| Fulgoni | $734 000 |
| Watson | 825 000 |
| Hwong | 675 000 |
| O'Connell | 725 000 |
| Mitchell | 785 000 |

a. Calculate the performance-to-quota ratio for each of the sales representatives in the Alberta Division.

b. What is the overall performance-to-quota ratio for the Alberta Division?

VIDEO   CASE 5   The Disney Channel

In June 1985, the Walt Disney Company hired a new management team to revamp its then-fledgling pay-TV service, The Disney Channel. Having been launched in April 1983, The Disney Channel had gained just under 2 million cable subscribers in the intervening two years, less than had been budgeted under the Channel's original business plan. Under the new management, several strategies were devised to take advantage of the Channel's untapped growth potential.

First, the Channel's programming lineup was reconfigured to broaden the target audience beyond just children — that is, to appeal to adults as well. By 1986, a structured "daypart" programming schedule had been introduced that was designed to provide entertainment for different members of a subscribing household at different times of the day: preschoolers in the morning and early afternoon, older children in the late afternoon, families during the early evening, and adults after 10 PM. Programming from the Disney library, while remaining the centrepiece of the Channel's programming mix, was de-emphasized, and older Disney programs replaced with more-contemporary, original, made-for-The Disney Channel films and series.

Second, the Channel's marketing activities were streamlined, to focus on targeting the service's best subscription prospects. Free national previews, which allow basic-cable sub-scribers to sample The Disney Channel's programming for up to a week, became the centrepiece of the Channel's marketing program. Offered in conjunction with participating cable systems five times a year, each preview is preceded by national and local advertising as well as by targeted direct mailings to non–Disney Channel subscribers, encouraging them to tune in to The Disney Channel during the free preview period. Direct-response TV spots running on the Channel provide viewers with an 800 number to call if they are interested in having The Disney Channel installed in their homes. In this way, prospective new customers can be generated in a cost-effective manner for those cable systems that offer the preview to their subscribers. Marketing research is then used to monitor preview viewership and to assess the effectiveness of tune-in advertising so that improvements can be put into place for the subsequent national preview campaign.

Third, The Disney Channel developed a new wholesale rate card, which allowed those cable operators who offered the Channel for a low retail price to consumers to benefit by paying lower wholesale rates for the service. Research had proven that demand for The Disney Channel was relatively price-elastic, with cable systems that charged consumers lower retail prices for the Channel generating significantly higher sales than those cable systems that offered The Disney Channel at a higher price. As cable operators started to raise the retail price for basic cable to consumers, The Disney Channel's affiliate marketing staff was able to provide cable operators with a financial incentive to simultaneously reduce the price of The Disney Channel, thereby keeping the total price paid by the consumer for a subscription to basic cable *and* the Channel relatively unchanged.

These three major changes in strategy proved extremely effective in helping propel The Disney Channel's subscriber growth between 1985 and 1990, while the other major pay-television services, the Channel's primary competitors, were fighting to maintain their market share. As a basis of comparison, the Channel's subscribers grew 120 percent (to 5.6 million households) from December 1985 to December 1990, while the rest of the pay-TV industry combined grew by only 27 percent during that same period of time.

Competition remains intense within the maturing pay-television industry, and for The Disney Channel to continue to grow at a healthy rate, programming and marketing strategies must be continually reassessed. Anne Hotchkiss, director of marketing research for The Disney Channel from 1984 to 1991, was faced during her tenure with the task of using research to help identify new areas of opportunity for the Channel. In one instance, in planning her budget for the year ahead, she had arranged to meet with one of the several firms that The Disney Channel used to conduct its marketing and programming research projects. Specifically, she wanted information on: (1) how to increase market penetration; (2) the various market segments to which the Channel appealed and whether programming changes could capture new segments; and (3) the price thresholds for The Disney Channel.

SOURCES    Ronald Grover, Mark N. Vamos, and Todd Mason, "Disney's Magic," *Business Week* (March 9, 1987), pp. 62–65, 68–69; Myron Magnet, "Putting Magic Back Into the Magic Kingdom," *Fortune* (January 5, 1987), p. 65; "Marketing, Management Practices Separate Cable Winners, Losers," *Marketing News* (April 10, 1987), pp. 4, 35: "Ad Agencies Urged to Concentrate on Strategic Values of Cable TV," *Marketing News* (September 25, 1987), p. 5; Fannie Weinstein, "Disney, Nashville Nets Find Eager Product Tie-Ins," *Advertising Age* (December 7, 1987), p. S-6; Allan Dodds Frank, "Leisure and Recreation," *Forbes* (January 12, 1987), pp. 158–159; "Walt Disney Co.," *Advertising Age* (September 24, 1987), p. 86; David Ansen and Peter McAlevey, "The Mouse That Roared," *Newsweek* (March 3, 1986), pp. 62–65; Laura Landro, "Cable TV's New Freedom Promises Higher Prices — But Fewer Services," *Wall Street Journal* (December 12, 1986), p. 31; Pamela Ellis-Simons, "Hi Ho, Hi Ho," *Marketing and Media Decisions* (September 1986), pp. 52–54, 56–57, 60, 62, 64; update interview with Tom Wszalek, Disney Channel, April 1991; update interview with Dea Shandera, Disney Channel, May 1991.

## Questions

1. Chapter 5 describes the marketing research process. What steps in that process are evident in this case?
2. What type of information does The Disney Channel require for developing its future marketing strategy?
3. How should The Disney Channel gather the information needed for making a decision?

# Locating Secondary Data

The publications listed in this appendix refer mainly to the Canadian market. Some international marketing sources are covered briefly in the final section.

These are by no means all the sources of secondary data available for Canada or for international markets; however, it is hoped that they will serve as a starting point in a search for secondary sources of marketing data.[1]

## Canadian Government Publications

The federal government generates a vast array of publications through its various departments and agencies. Two publications are useful in keeping track of these materials. *The Weekly Checklist of Canadian Government Publications* lists departmental (including Statistics Canada) and parliamentary priced and nonpriced monographs and serials that have been released during the week. These materials are available free of charge to libraries that have negotiated a depository status agreement with the federal government. Check on the status of a library when using its federal government publications.

The second list, *Special List of Canadian Government Publications*, includes the reprints of publications that have already appeared in the above-mentioned *Weekly Checklist*, scientific and technical publications that are printed in limited quantities, and Crown Corporation publications.

Due to the diversity and quantity of these materials, library users are advised to consult with library staff when using federal government publications.

### Statistics Canada

Statistics Canada publishes extensive statistical information gathered through various sources. In addition to standard publications, data are disseminated on computer printouts, microfiche, microfilm, and magnetic tapes. Maps and other geographic reference materials are also available for some types of data. There are too

---

[1]This appendix was written with assistance from C. Dennis Felbel, Head of the University of Manitoba Management Library.

many publications and services to list and describe here, but detailed information can be obtained from Statistics Canada centres in the following locations:

- St. John's, Newfoundland
- Halifax, Nova Scotia
- Montreal, Quebec
- Ottawa, Ontario
- Toronto, Ontario
- Winnipeg, Manitoba
- Regina, Saskatchewan
- Edmonton, Alberta
- Calgary, Alberta
- Vancouver, British Columbia

Each centre has a collection of current Statistics Canada publications and reference documents that can be consulted or purchased. Copying facilities for printed materials and microform are also available, as is access to CANSIM (Statistics Canada's computerized database).

### Statistics Canada Catalogue

The *Catalogue* provides a description of Statistics Canada publications (both serial and occasional). Each description contains a brief summary of the publication as well as technical details and price.

Following the publication description section, the microdata files are explained. They consist of responses to surveys and are so constructed as to allow users to create their own tabulations.

The *Catalogue* also directs the user to other products and services available from Statistics Canada.

### CANSIM

CANSIM (Canadian Socio-economic Information Management System) is Statistics Canada's computerized database. It provides public access to current and historical statistics in various forms, as well as specialized data-analysis packages, graphics capabilities, and a bibliographic search service.

### Canadian Economic Observer

The most readily available Statistics Canada publication is likely to be the *Canadian Economic Observer* (titled the *Canadian Statistical Review* up to 1988). It is published monthly and provides information on the major changes in Canada's economy. It contains sections on current economic conditions in both written and statistical-table formats as well as sections on economic and statistical events, quarterly national accounts, and feature articles. The statistical summary portion of the *Observer* constitutes the remaining section; it provides detailed tables covering such categories as labour and financial markets, prices, trade, manufacturing, construction, agriculture, and transportation. Probably the most extensive Canadian source for economic indicators, population figures, national accounts, labour, prices, manufacturing, trade, mining, construction, agriculture, transportation, and financial markets.

# Provincial Government Publications

The provincial governments publish thousands of documents through their various departments and agencies. These publications cover a variety of topics, reflecting the many departments in which the documents originated: they range across the whole spectrum, from agriculture to urban affairs.

Because the available documents are too numerous to describe individually, we can only direct you to the major sources that list and describe the documents published by the provincial governments. As an illustration, here is the way to find documents in Manitoba. Information for other provincial governments can be obtained in a similar fashion.

## The Province of Manitoba

Like most provinces, Manitoba makes most of its publications available through a department or agency of the government. Publications are available through the following departments or agencies:

- agriculture
- ecology
- energy
- health
- industry
- mines
- Queen's Printer
- resources
- tourism

The Province of Manitoba also prepares a finding aid, *Manitoba Government Publications*, that lists its publications. It is issued as a monthly checklist with an annual cumulation by Manitoba Culture, Heritage and Recreation.

The guide is arranged alphabetically by issuing department or agency and provides brief bibliographical entries (with notes if required). The annual cumulation is indexed by name, title, branch, series, and keyword.

# Chambers of Commerce

Most major cities and towns have a Chamber of Commerce. A Chamber of Commerce is an association established to further the business interests of its community. The Chambers in most metropolitan cities publish information about their cities. These groups are often very useful sources of information. The type of information you can expect to find at most Chambers of Commerce includes economic facts, employment figures, government descriptions, demographic data, and quality-of-life statistics.

As an illustration, the Winnipeg Chamber of Commerce publishes an annual membership *Directory and Buyer's Guide*. It provides a description of Chamber services, a membership listing (both individual and corporate), and a buyer's guide by service or product.

# Market Reports, Surveys, Directories, Special Issues, and Newsletters

Many of the publications listed in the remainder of this appendix are available through university and public libraries. Because many of them can be fairly expensive, you may wish to locate them in a library before deciding whether you need to purchase them.

The publications are listed under major headings that describe the industry, trade, or sector to which they pertain. Some "special issues" may appear in libraries under the title of the magazine with which they are associated. Furthermore, some of the "annual" publications may not always be published.

## Advertising

*Canadian Advertising Rates and Data*
  Published monthly. Calls itself the media authority for all major Canadian broadcast and print media. Provides addresses, advertising rates, circulation, mechanical information, and personnel and branch-office information, in addition to a regular service section. (Maclean Hunter Business Publishing)

*National List of Advertisers*
  Published annually. Lists the names, addresses, brand names, personnel, and sales of more than 3000 national advertisers. Contains a cross-index of brand names, products, and manufacturers, as well as an advertising agency listing. (Maclean Hunter Business Publishing)

*Publication Profiles*
  Published annually. Describes the editorial profile of all major consumer, farm, and business publications in Canada. Does not duplicate *Canadian Advertising Rates and Data*, but serves as a companion volume. (Maclean Hunter Business Publishing)

## Automotive

*Automotive Marketer: Annual Buyer's Guide*
  Published as a special issue of the magazine; features a comprehensive listing of products and equipment and their suppliers. Intended for automotive retail operations. (Wadham Publications)

## Canadian Market, General

*Bank of Canada Review*
  Published monthly. Provides short articles and news items dealing with monetary policy. Contains extensive charts and tables on the major financial and economic indicators, payments, and external trade. (Bank of Canada)

*Canada Year Book*
  Published irregularly in recent years. Records developments in Canada's economic, social, and political life. Also useful for government department and agency information. The 1990 edition is the most recent. (Statistics Canada)

*Canadian Economic Observer*
  Described earlier under Statistics Canada heading. Published monthly. Formerly the *Canadian Statistical Review*. Contains current statistical information retrieved from CANSIM, Statistics Canada's computerized database. Also carries a feature article. (Statistics Canada)

*Canadian Markets*

Published annually. A very valuable source of demographic data for Canadian urban markets. Provides estimates and projections for population, households, retail sales, and personal income for markets nationwide. Buying-power indices are developed, allowing for market comparisons. Extensive provincial and municipal data are also provided in geographic sequence from east to west. (Financial Post Information Service)

*Canadian Outlook: Economic Forecast*

Published quarterly. Features forecasts on the major components of the Canadian economy, such as consumer expenditures, housing, government activity, trade, employment, financial markets, and costs and prices. These are followed by tables on the same topics. (Conference Board of Canada)

*Editor and Publisher Market Guide*

Published annually. A compilation of marketing data on all U.S. and Canadian markets where daily newspapers are published. Information includes geographic location (maps included), transportation features, demographics, and retailing and industrial features. (Editor and Publisher)

*Handbook of Canadian Consumer Markets*

Published biennially. Compiles consumer market data from government, trade, and Conference Board sources. In the form of tables and charts, detailed demographic and economic data are presented on six major subject areas: population, labour force and employment, income, expenditures, production and retail trade, and consumer and industry price indices. (Conference Board of Canada)

*Provincial Outlook: Economic Forecast*

Published quarterly. Similar format to *Canadian Outlook*, but with individual sections for each of the Canadian provinces. Tables are also by province for the key economic indicators. (Conference Board of Canada)

## Clothing

*Canadian Apparel Manufacturer: Buyer's Guide.*

Published annually as a special issue of *Canadian Apparel Manufacturer*. Covers apparel associations, apparel institutions, suppliers, manufacturers, and products (including trade names). (Canadian Textile Journal)

*Style: Buyer's Guide.*

Published annually as a special issue of *Style*. Valuable source of information on manufacturers, importers, and associations involved with women's clothing. (Style Communications)

## Construction, Public Works, Hardware

*Civic Public Works: Reference Manual And Buyer's Guides*

Published annually as individual issues of *Civic Public Works* in the fields of grounds maintenance/general operations, roads/streets/highways, solid-waste management/office equipment, and water and sewage. Provides information on suppliers and products. (Maclean Hunter Business Publishing)

*Construction Equipment Buyer's Guide*

Published annually as a special issue of *Heavy Construction News*. Lists manufacturers and distributors of products and accessories. (Maclean Hunter Business Publishing)

*Construction Record: Buyer's Guide*

Published annually as the April issue of *Construction Record*. Provides information on manufacturers, products, and distributors in the construction industry. (Southam Business Information)

*Construction Record: Top 200*

Published annually as the June issue of *Construction Record*. Provides ranking and activities of the top 200 construction firms in Canada. (Southam Business Information)

*Hardware Merchandising: Buyer's Guide And Annual Sources Directory*

Published annually as a special issue of *Hardware Merchandising*. Provides information on suppliers, agents, and products in the wide area of hardware. (Sentry Communications)

*Real Estate Development Annual*

Published annually as a special issue of *Canadian Building*. Provides information on Canadian real estate developers, the financial community supporting real estate development, and various development-related associations. (Maclean Hunter Business Publishing)

## Data Processing and Computers

*Canadian Computer Census*

Published annually. Provides information on computer installations in Canada. Organized by province, city, and manufacturer. (Canadian Information Processing Society)

*Canadian Datasystems: Reference Manual*

Published annually as the January issue of *Canadian Datasystems*. Provides information on suppliers and products for buyers and users of computer hardware, software, and services. Also contains an index for the previous year's feature articles in *Canadian Datasystems*. (Maclean Hunter Business Publishing)

*Directory Of EDP Management*

Published annually. Provides information on EDP executives and the companies that have major installations in Canada. (Canadian Information Processing Society)

## Drugs and Pharmaceuticals

*Directory Of Pharmaceutical Manufacturers, Drug Wholesalers And Major Retailers in Canada*

Published annually. Provides information on the manufacturing and distribution of pharmaceuticals across Canada. (Maclean Hunter Business Publishing)

*Drug Merchandising: Special Issues*

Published regularly: focus on special topics such as pharmacy computers, store design, and therapeutic advances. (Maclean Hunter Business Publishing)

## Electronics

*Canadian Electronics Engineering: Buyer's Guide*

Published annually as a special issue of *Canadian Electronics Engineering*. Provides information on electronics products, services, and domestic and foreign manufacturers. (Maclean Hunter Business Publishing)

*Canadian Electronics Engineering: Distribution Guide*

Published annually as a special issue of *Canadian Electronics Engineering*. Covers distributors of electronics engineering equipment. (Maclean Hunter Business Publishing)

*Electrical Bluebook*

Published annually. A directory that provides the names of the major products, companies, and players of the electrical industry. (Kerrwil Publications)

## Financial and Insurance

*Directory Of Benefits Consultants*

Published annually as a special section of *Benefits Canada*. Arranged by province, the directory lists name, address, telephone, contact names, and services provided for firms providing benefits consulting services. (Maclean Hunter Business Publishing)

*Directory Of Group Insurance*

Published annually as a special section of *Benefits Canada*. Contains information on companies providing group life, health, and annuity products. Branch offices are indicated. (Maclean Hunter Business Publishing)

*Directory Of Pension Fund Investment Consultants*

Published annually as a special section of *Benefits Canada*. Provides information on fund consultants, performance measurement firms, and firms offering database services. (Maclean Hunter Business Publishing)

*Directory Of Pension Fund Investment Services*

Published annually as a special section of *Benefits Canada*. Contains information on investment, insurance, and management companies that provide services to corporations and institutions. Each entry includes data on asset mix, clients, and size of pension funds managed. (Maclean Hunter Business Publishing)

## Food and Food Processing and Retailing

*Canadian Hotel And Restaurant: Equipment Sources Directory*

Published annually as a special issue of *Canadian Hotel and Restaurant*. Provides information on equipment and services for the restaurant and hospitality industry. (Maclean Hunter Business Publishing)

*Canadian Hotel And Restaurant: Food Sources Directory*

Published annually as a special issue of *Canadian Hotel and Restaurant*. Provides information on food processors, distributors, and suppliers for the restaurant and hospitality industry. (Maclean Hunter Business Publishing)

*Directory Of Restaurant And Fast Food Chains In Canada*

Published annually. Covers more than 600 companies, providing head- and regional-office information: personnel listings; and expansion, advertising, and financial data. (Maclean Hunter Business Publishing)

*Food In Canada: Buyer's Directory*

Published annually as a special issue of *Food in Canada*. Provides information on firms involved in processing, packaging, and supplying food equipment, ingredients, and additives. (Maclean Hunter Business Publishing)

*Food In Canada: Economic Review And Forecast*

Published annually as a special issue of *Food in Canada*. Provides a forecast for the components of the food and beverage industry. Reviews historical performance using statistics and tables. (Maclean Hunter Business Publishing)

## Forestry

*Canadian Forest Industries: Buyer's Guide*
Published annually as a special issue of *Canadian Forest Industries*. Provides information on companies that produce or supply products and services to the forest industry. Also lists trade names and associations. (Southam Business Information and Communications)

*Pulp And Paper Canada: Annual Directory*
Published annually as a special issue of *Pulp and Paper Canada*. Provides information on producers, suppliers, services, government departments, and trade and professional associations in the pulp and paper industry. (Southam Business Information and Communications)

## Furniture, Furnishings, and Appliances

*Canada's Furniture Magazine: Buyer's Guide*
Published annually as an issue of *Canada's Furniture Magazine*. Provides information on manufacturers and suppliers of home furnishings in Canada. (Victor Publishing)

*Hardware Merchandising: Buyer's Guide And Annual Sources Directory*
Described earlier under Construction, Public Works, Hardware heading.

*Home Goods Retailing: Buyer's Guide*
Published annually as a special issue of *Home Goods Retailing*. Covers manufacturers and distributors of furniture, accessories, and other interior-design products. (Maclean Hunter Business Publishing)

## Industrial

*Heating, Plumbing And Air Conditioning: Buyer's Guide*
Published annually as a special issue of *Heating, Plumbing and Air Conditioning*. Provides information on manufacturers, wholesalers, and distributors of products in the heating, plumbing, and air-conditioning industry. (Southam Business Information and Communications)

*Plant Engineering And Maintenance Sourcebook*
Published twice a year in conjunction with *Plant Engineering and Maintenance*. Provides information on individuals, companies, organizations, and associations dealing with plant and industrial problems. (Clifford/Elliott Ltd.)

## Materials Handling

*Materials Handling Handbook and Directory of Buying Sources*
Published annually as the directory issue of *Materials Management and Distribution*. Provides information on suppliers of warehouse equipment, such as computers, conveyors, dock equipment, and shelving. (Maclean Hunter Business Publishing)

## Metalworking

*Canadian Machinery and Metalworking: Census*
Published annually as a special issue of *Canadian Machinery and Metalworking*. Covers machine tools already installed, providing user name, location, and other specifics. Includes robotic installations. (Maclean Hunter Business Publishing)

*Canadian Machinery and Metalworking: Directory and Buyer's Guide*
Published annually as the directory issue of *Canadian Machinery and Metalworking*. Provides information on manufacturers, distributors, agents, services, associations, and engineers in the industry. (Maclean Hunter Business Publishing)

## Office Equipment and Supplies

*Office Equipment and Methods: Buyer's Guide and Directory*
Published annually as a special issue of *Office Equipment and Methods*. Provides information on office equipment products, suppliers, and industry associations. (Maclean Hunter Business Publishing)
*Office Management and Automation: Directory*
Published as the annual directory issue of *Office Management and Automation*. Provides information on computer and office automation companies, distributors, consultants, and services. (Plesman Publications)

## Packaging

*Canadian Packaging: Buyer's Guide*
Published annually as a special issue of *Canadian Packaging*. A directory of Canada's packaging industry, providing access to materials, equipment, and services. (Maclean Hunter Business Publishing)
*Canadian Packaging: Machinery Specifications Manual*
Published annually as a special issue of *Canadian Packaging*. Provides information on machinery manufacturers to the packaging industry. (Maclean Hunter Business Publishing)

## Petroleum and Mining

*Canadian Mines Handbook*
Published annually. Provides information on mining and exploration companies. Also includes stock-exchange data, maps of mining areas, industry associations, and statistical data for the industry. (Northern Miner Press)
*Canadian Mining Journal: Mining Sourcebook*
Published annually as a special issue of *Canadian Mining Journal*. Provides both operating and cost data for the industry, and lists sources of supply for materials, equipment, and services. (Southam Business Information and Communications)
*Canadian Oil and Gas Handbook*
Published annually. Provides information on oil and gas companies in Canada. Includes stock-exchange activity and statistical data for the industry. (Northern Miner Press)
*Canadian Oil Register*
Published annually. Covers the Canadian oil- and gas-related industries. Contains a "Who's Who" of management personnel, and individual sections listing companies, products, and services, respectively. (C.O. Nickle/Southam Business Information and Communications)
*Survey of Mines and Energy Resources*
Published annually. Provides a comprehensive review of mining and energy companies in Canada. Covers their operations, management, and financial status. (Financial Post Information Service)

## Photography

*Canadian Directory of Professional Photography*
 Published annually. Contains member listings as well as a buyer's guide to suppliers and manufacturers of photographic materials. (Professional Photographers of Canada)

## Printing, Publishing, Graphic Arts

*Canadian Printer: Buyer's Guide and Directory*
 Published annually as a special issue of *Canadian Printer*. Provides information on the industry including equipment specifications, forecasts, and statistics. (Maclean Hunter Business Publishing)

*Graphic Monthly: Estimators' and Buyers' Guide*
 Published annually. Designed to provide quick reference to the companies and services available in the graphic arts industry. (North Island Sound Ltd.)

## Product Design and Engineering

*Design Engineering: CAD/CAM Capabilities Guide*
 Published annually as a special issue of *Design Engineering*. Provides information on suppliers, systems, and products in the CAD/CAM industry. (Maclean Hunter Business Publishing)

*Design Engineering: Mechanical Power Transmission Buyer's Guide*
 Published annually as a special issue of *Design Engineering*. Provides information on products, suppliers, and manufacturers in the mechanical power transmission industry. (Maclean Hunter Business Publishing)

## Retailing

*Canadian Directory of Shopping Centres*
 Published annually. Provides information on more than 1300 major shopping centres, including tenants, managers/owners, and statistical data concerning rent costs, traffic, sales, and market population. (Maclean Hunter Business Publishing)

*Directory of Restaurant and Fast Food Chains in Canada*
 Published annually. Covers more than 600 companies, providing head- and regional-office information; personnel listings; and expansion, advertising, and financial data. (Maclean Hunter Business Publishing)

*Directory of Retail Chains in Canada*
 Published annually. Covers all major retail chains in Canada, providing information about personnel, merchandise range, financial status, location, and expansion status. (Maclean Hunter Business Publishing)

*Franchise Annual*
 Published annually. Covers more than 2500 American, 1100 Canadian, and 450 international business franchise opportunities. Specific information about each product or service is included. (Info Press)

*Monday Report on Retailers*
 Published weekly as a newsletter. Focuses on the expansion plans of the major chain retailers. Includes merchandising strategies, trends, and policy changes. (Maclean Hunter Business Publishing)

# Business Guides, Directories, and Indexes

*Blue Book of Canadian Business*

Published annually. Provides in-depth profiles of the leading Canadian companies, quick-reference information on a select group of companies, and rankings of the top companies by sales. (Canadian Newspaper Services International)

*Canadian Trade Index*

Published annually. Provides a classified list of products manufactured in Canada as well as a listing of manufacturers. Also included are sections on distributors, export companies, and trademarks. (Canadian Manufacturers' Association)

*Fraser's Canadian Trade Directory*

Published annually. A multivolume work that provides a classified list of manufacturers by product, as well as an alphabetical list. Also included are sections on trade names and on foreign manufacturers, with their Canadian agent or distributor. (Maclean Hunter Business Publishing)

*Moody's Industrial Manual*

Published annually with updates. One of seven Moody's manuals, this one covers companies listed on the major American stock exchanges. Provides corporate histories, business and product description, subsidiary and personnel listings, and financial statements. (Moody's Investors Service)

*Sales and Marketing Management*

Published monthly. An American journal that features articles on sales and marketing management. Of note are its annual issues of market survey data: Survey of Buying Power; Survey of Industrial and Commercial Buying Power; and Survey of Selling Costs. The reports can include Canadian data. (Bell Communications)

*Survey of Industrials*

Published annually. Covers all major Canadian public, listed, and unlisted industrial corporations. Provides details of operations, personnel and subsidiary listings, and financial data. (Financial Post Information Service)

# International Marketing Publications

*European Marketing Data and Statistics*

Published annually. Provides statistical information on 33 countries of Western and Eastern Europe. Data are presented in 24 sections in table form to allow for easy comparison, analysis, and planning. Covers a considerable number of 10-year trends. (Euromonitor)

*International Marketing Data and Statistics*

Published annually. Provides statistical information on all basic marketing parameters for 153 countries. Data are presented in 24 sections in table form for easy planning and analysis. Includes detailed consumer market information. (Euromonitor)

*Statistical Yearbook*

Published annually. Provides information on some 200 countries and territories that are members of the United Nations. Data are presented largely in table format. Covers education, science and technology, libraries, book production, cultural information, and radio and television broadcasting. (UNESCO)

*World Economic Survey*

Published annually. Provides access to current trends and policies in the world economy, allowing analysis of their implications for regions of the world and in particular their effect on the progress of developing countries. (United Nations, Department of International Economic and Social Affairs)

*World Tables*

Published annually. A collection of tables dealing with social and economic data from World Bank members. Specifically the tables show basic economic data for individual countries, indicators suitable for comparative purposes, and demographic/social data. (World Bank/Johns Hopkins University Press)

*Yearbook of International Trade Statistics*

Published annually. Provides basic information for United Nations member countries on external trade performances, including trends in current value, volume and price, trading partners, and the significance of imports and exports. Published in two volumes: Volume 1 contains detailed country-by-country data and Volume 2 gives prices, price indices, and commodity tables. (United Nations/Gower)

*Yearbook of Labour Statistics*

Published annually. Summarizes the principal labour statistics for some 180 countries, usually covering the most recent 10-year period. Data are drawn from national statistical services and are. presented in nine chapters on such topics as wages, unemployment, and hours of work. (International Labour Organization)

## CHAPTER 6

# Marketing Strategy and the Marketing Plan

## CHAPTER OBJECTIVES

1. To show that a strategic orientation is important for marketing.
2. To indicate how marketing strategy is related to the strategy that has been developed for the organization as a whole.
3. To relate the marketing plan to marketing strategy.
4. To show that the marketing plan should be developed in relation to the character of the marketing environment.
5. To discuss in detail the steps in the marketing planning process.
6. To describe the marketing mix and show its importance in the development of the marketing plan.
7. To show how the elements of the marketing mix can be combined to produce synergistic effects.

CHRYSLER Corp. has looked down the road and does not like what it sees. The company's two big profit-makers — the mini-van and the Jeep — are heading into a traffic jam of competition.

General Motors Corp., Ford Motor Co., and Japanese auto makers are all becoming involved in the production of mini-vans. And Jeep-like vehicles of all sizes, such as the Suzuki Sidekick and the Isuzu Trooper, are increasingly crowding the road.

With profits already skidding for several years because of expensive car-rebate and financing programs, the auto maker is facing its biggest challenge since coming back from the brink of bankruptcy in 1980.

While the stakes this time are not nearly as dramatic, Chrysler has put into high gear a risky strategy that refocuses on car design, a move that could well shape the company's fortunes through the end of the century.

The goal, says Robert Lutz, president of the company's Chrysler Motors subsidiary, is to sell more cars at higher profit margins by producing "home-run" vehicles that stand out in their class. At the same time, Lutz quickly adds, Chrysler cannot afford to turn its back on mini-vans and Jeeps.

Nonetheless, the change in strategy signals a bid by the company to recapture its glory days — the 1950s, 1960s, and early 1970s, when it won a reputation as an engineering powerhouse for cars with its racy Plymouth Road Runner, the stylish Chrysler Imperial, and the fabled Dodge 426-inch "hemi" engine, which powered many drivers to racetrack victories.

In the past decade, that reputation mainly disappeared. Buying time to recover its financial health, Chrysler made do with technologically outmoded and undistinguished passenger cars, turning its reliable but lacklustre k-body frame and powertrain, or close copies, into a workhorse for most of its car models. In lieu of pizazz Chrysler offered low prices and other financial incentives. The company simply did not have the money to develop new products. The mini-van, which Chrysler introduced in 1983, was the only truly breakthrough vehicle to emerge from that period.

Now, the company's 6000-member engineering staff has gotten ambitious marching orders: to make the Chrysler cars of the 1990s far more appealing to customers, especially the more affluent ones, in both design and performance. A key element of the plan is a radical restructuring of the engineering corps into "project" groups that will work on a specific model from inception to production. And they are consulting more often with marketing experts, to get feedback from consumers to guide them in fine-tuning design changes.

But whatever the risks of the reorganization, industry experts agree that it is time for Chrysler to do something big. The company's domestic market share in cars, which had been relatively steady, had begun to slip, along with profits. Clearly, a new comprehensive strategy and marketing plan seem to be in order.[1]

---

# Introduction

Success and excellence are temporary phenomena. Once achieved, they must be pursued continuously or they will erode.[2] The situation in which Chrysler found itself is commonplace. Firms often — suddenly or gradually — find that they need to reorient the direction of their efforts. A new strategy is called for.

On the basis of what we learned in the foregoing chapters, we can now consider the development of marketing strategy and the consequent marketing plan. In Chapter 1, we saw that marketing efforts will be more successful if a company has a market orientation. Chapter 2 showed that marketing activities are bounded by five components of the environment. Any strategy should explicitly take them into consideration.

As we discovered, in Chapters 3 and 4, markets are not homogeneous. There are normally several different segments to any market. In accordance with the marketing concept, marketing strategy must start with segmentation because it is almost impossible to plan effectively based on a diffuse set of customer needs.

Theodore Levitt has said that there are four simple requisites for the success of a business.[3]

1. The purpose of an enterprise is to create and keep a customer.

FIGURE 6–1

**An Overview of the Strategy and Marketing Planning Process**

2. To do that you have to produce and deliver goods and services that people want and value, at prices and under conditions that are reasonably attractive relative to those offered by others to a proportion of customers large enough to make those prices and conditions possible.

3. No enterprise, no matter how small, can do any of this by mere instinct or accident. It has to clarify its purposes, strategies, and plans, and the larger the enterprise the greater the necessity that these be clearly written down, clearly communicated, and frequently reviewed by the senior members of the enterprise.

4. And in all cases there must be an appropriate system of rewards, audits, and controls to assure that what's intended gets properly done, and when not, that it gets quickly rectified.

With respect to Levitt's third point, let us now consider how strategies are formulated. Two main aspects of strategy formulation will be discussed: strategy for the organization as a whole (corporate strategy), and marketing strategy. After marketing strategy has been established, the marketing plan can be developed (see Figure 6–1). You will find that discussing these concepts is relatively simple. But practitioners knows that implementing them is extremely difficult.

## Strategy for the Organization as a Whole

**Strategy** is *the overall purpose and direction of the organization that is established in the light of the challenges and opportunities found in the environment, as well as available organizational resources.* This is often referred to as **corporate strategy**. The process of developing a corporate strategy starts with an analysis of market and environmental

**corporate strategy**    The overall purpose and direction of the organization that is established in the light of the challenges and opportunities found in the environment, as well as available organizational resources.

---

**A·P·P·L·Y·I·N·G   T·H·E   C·O·N·C·E·P·T·S**

### *Mission Statement for MEDEC*

MEDEC, a key participant in the Canadian health-care delivery system, actively meets the needs and promotes the common interests of the industry which manufactures/distributes medical devices in the Canadian market. MEDEC is chief spokesman for the industry and undertakes:

• to assist the industry in delivering safe, effective,

best-technology medical devices to all Canadians; and

• to seek a business environment that encourages the growth of the industry and maximizes the value added to products and services in Canada.

Source: Medical Devices of Canada, *Annual Report*, 1988 [inside front cover; no page number].

FIGURE 6-2

## Stages in Formulating a Strategy for the Company as a Whole

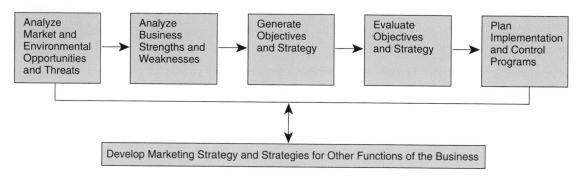

opportunities and threats facing the company as a whole. Simultaneously, the company undertakes an analysis of its own strengths and weaknesses. From this external and internal examination, the organization generates a list of *possible* alternative courses of action and objectives that could be followed. The next step involves evaluating and selecting the *most appropriate* alternative options for the organization. Finally, implementation and control programs must be planned for the strategy that has been developed. Figure 6–2 shows all five stages of the corporate strategy process.

The development of corporate strategy is the responsibility of the head of the organization, and requires inputs from all the functional areas of the company (for example, finance, production, and marketing).

The strategy chosen is often expressed in a *mission statement*. This formal statement channels all of the organization's activities. From the mission statement, all individuals can determine which activities are appropriate to engage in, and which are not. This keeps activities within a scope considered most suitable for the company. An example of a mission statement — this one from Medical Devices of Canada (MEDEC), an industry association — can be found in the accompanying box.

## Marketing Strategy

**marketing strategy**   A strategy that focuses on developing a unique long-run competitive position in the market by assessing consumer needs and the firm's potential for gaining competitive advantage.

**Marketing strategy**, which is based on the strategy set for the company as a whole, *focuses on developing a unique long-run competitive position in the market by assessing consumer needs and the firm's potential for gaining competitive advantage.*[4] Day and Wensley add that "[marketing] strategy is about seeking new edges in a market while slowing the erosion of present advantages."[5]

Knowing everything there is to know about the customer is not enough. To succeed, marketers must know the customer in a context that includes the competition; government policy and regulation; and the broader economic, social, and political macroforces that shape the evolution of markets. In other words, a strategic approach is necessary.

Figure 6–3 illustrates a marketing-oriented approach to strategy formulation and evaluation.[6] This model extends the corporate strategy model depicted in Figure 6–2 and shows the important components of marketing strategy. It incorporates three main interrelated sections: market opportunities/business strength analysis;

## FIGURE 6−3

### A Marketing-Oriented Approach to Strategy Formulation and Evaluation

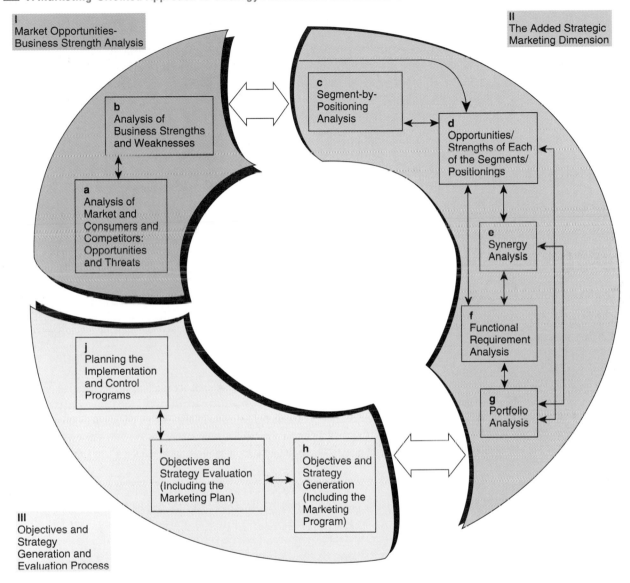

I
Market Opportunities-
Business Strength Analysis

II
The Added Strategic
Marketing Dimension

**b** Analysis of Business Strengths and Weaknesses

**a** Analysis of Market and Consumers and Competitors: Opportunities and Threats

**c** Segment-by-Positioning Analysis

**d** Opportunities/ Strengths of Each of the Segments/ Positionings

**e** Synergy Analysis

**f** Functional Requirement Analysis

**g** Portfolio Analysis

**j** Planning the Implementation and Control Programs

**i** Objectives and Strategy Evaluation (Including the Marketing Plan)

**h** Objectives and Strategy Generation (Including the Marketing Program)

III
Objectives and
Strategy
Generation and
Evaluation Process

Source: Adapted from Yoram Wind and Thomas S. Robertson, "Marketing Strategy: New Directions for Theory and Research," *Journal of Marketing* (Spring 1983), p. 12.

the strategic marketing dimension; and objectives and strategy generation and evaluation.

Marketing strategy is based on a thorough understanding of the company's strengths and weaknesses and of the opportunities and threats that it faces. Thus, Section I of Figure 6–3 shows the assessment of the firm from the perspectives of *market opportunities and business strength analysis*. As we have seen, planners also take this perspective when developing an overall corporate strategy. Marketing strategy analysis pays special attention to consumers and competitors.

The development of marketing strategy then turns to an examination of market segments, and the relative positionings within these segments. Five strategic marketing evaluations must be undertaken: (1) a segment-by-positioning analysis, (2) an examination of the opportunities and strengths of each of the segments/positions, (3) a synergy analysis, (4) a functional requirement analysis, and (5) a portfolio analysis. Together, they constitute the *strategic marketing dimension*, which is outlined in Section II of the model. Let's look at each of the five strategic marketing components in a little more detail.

*Segment-by-positioning analysis*    Each segment must first be subjected to an analysis by positioning. This means that the competing companies and brands in each segment are identified, and their positioning in the segment is indicated. For example, in the business microcomputer segment, IBM, Apple, and a number of "clone" manufacturers compete. IBM positions itself as the firm with leading-edge technology and high quality. Apple might be positioned as providing the most user-friendly and versatile quality computer. Several clones also compete in this segment, and will be positioned as providing various combinations of features at a low price.

The result of this step is the identification of certain segments and positions that are deemed worthy of further consideration. Many different reasons could lead to the decision to consider a segment further — for example, size, an opportunity to position a product where there is little competition, or evidence that existing competition can be overcome.

*Opportunities/strengths analysis*    Next, a more thorough analysis of the selected segments is undertaken. Management should carefully select the most desirable bases for segmentation and positioning to encompass all of the firm's current and potential offerings. In addition, the size and characteristics of each selected segment are identified as input into the next steps.

*Synergy analysis*    Synergy is the result of two or more variables working together so that their total effect is greater than normally would be expected by summing them (a sort of "2 + 2 = 5" effect). The development of a marketing plan should explicitly analyze synergistic effects. For example, advertising, distribution, and price could be combined in such a way as to result in positive *or* negative synergy.

*Functional requirement analysis*    Each segment/positioning must then be considered in terms of the requirements for success in each functional area. These requirements are compared with the company's strengths in each area. It may well be, for example, that the "heavy-user-satisfied/price" segment requires manufacturing expertise as the key to success, whereas the "heavy-user-satisfied/performance" segment requires technology (R & D) as the key to success. If the company's strengths lie in manufacturing rather than in R & D (or vice versa) there may be implications for segment/positioning selection.

*Portfolio analysis*    The final step in Section II is a portfolio analysis. Each organization normally has a range of goods or services. Some are new, with great potential,

*Canadian Tire started out by offering tires and automotive goods, but has expanded its product line to include everything from power tools and sports gear to housewares and electronic equipment. By crossing industry lines in this way, the retailer has sought to enlarge its market base and convince people that Canadian Tire is "more than tires."*

and the market for them is just being developed. Developing new markets often requires considerable resources. Other products are well established, and produce a strong positive cash flow. Still others are producing very little. This mix of products constitutes the product "portfolio." It is important to manage the portfolio in such a way that resources are allocated to the profitable and promising products. Decisions must be made about whether to delete those that are "over the hill."

Section III of the model in Figure 6–3 outlines the *objectives and strategy generation and evaluation process*, which is common to most strategic planning models. Its central focus is the generation of objectives and strategies, and the development of the *marketing plan* (which we will discuss next). The final stages are the necessary condition for all planning: evaluating objectives and strategies, and devising the necessary implementation and control programs.

## The Marketing Plan

The **marketing plan** — defined as *a program of activities that lead to the accomplishment of the marketing strategy* — is a tool of marketing strategy. Sometimes the marketing plan is referred to as the *marketing program*. In marketing planning, the first question to be addressed is "What should be included in the plan?" How can the planner have confidence that the marketing plan developed accomplishes the strategy that has been set out and includes the appropriate planning elements? The criterion for a marketing plan should be that it leads to organization effectiveness.

How does a manager know whether the plans made will be effective or not? Contingency theory, which originated in the organization behaviour literature, provides some excellent guidance. It argues that managerial decisions are not right or wrong *per se*. They must be made and assessed in the light of the circumstances surrounding the decisions. For example, if profits are falling because of declining sales, a decision to reduce or increase advertising might depend on whether the drop is caused by lack of awareness of the product, or adverse economic conditions (people know about the product but have no money). Therefore, a marketing plan

**marketing plan**    A program of activities that lead to the accomplishment of the marketing strategy.

should be based on a careful analysis of the key factors in the business environment. In a generic sense, most firms face the following conditions. Since the importance of each condition varies according to the individual firm's situation, it is impossible to present an exhaustive set.

*1. Increasing competition* The current environment is characterized by intense and increasing competitiveness. Some authors have argued that marketing strategy should be based on a competitive rather than a marketing orientation.[7] This is an extreme position. However, increased competition can be observed in several ways:

a. Intertype competition. Firms readily cross industry lines to compete if they think they can apply their technology to another field (for example, agricultural companies may begin producing recreational vehicles, or computer software firms may play a leading role in the production of machine tools and industrial robots).

b. International competition. A fundamental strategy of most countries today is to increase exports. Alert companies are responding. Consequently, domestic firms are finding aggressive new competitors facing them in traditional domestic markets.

c. More demanding economic conditions. As a result of the economic decline in the early 1980s, virtually all firms had to become more efficient and aggressive in order to survive. Many continued this posture as the economy turned around. The downturn of the early 1990s, combined with the above factors, thus portends a prolonged period of intense domestic and worldwide competition.

To take account of these conditions, a marketing plan should have a realistic assessment of the competitive domestic and worldwide industry environment. It should also include a statement of current market share, and a recognition of the shares and strategies of leading competitors. The plan should include an analysis of competitive strengths and weaknesses, and a forecast of market demand.

*2. Dynamic consumer society* Today's marketplace is characterized by fragmented, rapidly changing, sophisticated consumers. More products have emerged to more precisely meet tastes and higher consumer expectations. International travel and world communication have added to this sophistication. A marketing plan must include a thorough analysis of current customer motivations and trends.

*3. Hi-tech environment* Computers have revolutionized products and services. The inherent nature of many products, as well as their design and production, has changed. For example, the microchips now commonly built into such products as telephones and tools enable functions unheard of a few years ago. Many services are similarly affected.

*4. Social consciousness* An acute sensitivity to ecological issues continues to grow. The marketplace is showing evidence of the desire for a clean environment, as well as environmentally friendly products. In a related development, the requirements for socially responsible business behaviour continue to increase. If changes do not happen voluntarily, governmental regulation and legislation may be expected.

A comprehensive marketing plan should explicitly take such factors into consideration. Failing this, contingency theory suggests that it would be more difficult for the

*Loblaw's "Green Products" are one response to the growing public sensitivity to environmental issues. Many companies, from both the consumer and the industrial sectors, are incorporating recycling programs and energy-saving devices into their products and organizations. In this way, they help the environment, comply with government regulations, and improve their image in the eyes of potential customers.*

organization to be effective and competitive, and that the firm will sooner or later fall out of phase with its competitors and the environment.

*5. Other requirements for a marketing plan: Planning process requirements*   For every marketing plan statement, a system for expeditiously developing a complete plan is necessary. Possible elements of such a system include identifying problems and opportunities, conducting a postmortem of previous plans, stating alternative strategies considered, identifying risk factors, stating objectives, stating an action plan, and developing contingency plans.

*6. Other requirements for a marketing plan: Operational organizational requirements*
In order to make it operational, each plan should also include a statement of objectives, a budget statement, a section identifying those responsible for executing the plan, and specific timetables and controls for the new plan.

Figure 6–4 presents a model that demonstrates how these important environmental features might be identified. It also shows the corresponding marketing planning activities required to operate effectively in the environment. This can serve as a comprehensive guide for marketing planning.

When this model is used as a base for developing a marketing plan, decisions about whether to include a component of the plan are *contingent on the conditions found in the environment.* Following a contingency approach enables a firm to be more relevant in its planning. Because the process begins with a careful analysis of the environment, current conditions that are of direct significance as well as long-term trends can be identified and responded to. This process should also lead to a more comprehensive plan, as outlined in the right-hand column of the figure.

F I G U R E   6 – 4

## A Marketing Planning Model Based on Environmental Antecedents

| *Environmental Antecedents* | *Marketing Plan Requirements* |
|---|---|
| **1. Increasing Competition**<br>a. Intertype competition<br>b. Increasing complexity of economic conditions<br>c. International competition | • Statement of market share<br>• Recognition of shares and strengths of leading competitors<br>• Analysis of competitive strengths and weaknesses<br>• Forecast of market demand |
| **2. Dynamic Consumer/Buyer Society**<br>a. Rapid changes in tastes and behaviours<br>b. High customer expectations<br>c. Exposure to varied domestic and international mass media<br>d. Highly fragmented customer groups<br>e. Increasing customer sophistication | • Consideration of the changing needs of customers<br>• Product life cycle analysis<br>• Market segmentation analysis<br>• Product portfolio position analysis |
| **3. Hi-tech Environment**<br>a. Effect of technology on<br>  • product design<br>  • product performance<br>  • price<br>b. Automation of production | • Technological trends statement |
| **4. Social Consciousness**<br>a. Health and safety issues<br>b. Clean/pure environment issues<br>c. Increasing expectations for responsible business behaviour<br>d. Expectations for proactive governmental regulation/legislation | • Environmental issues statement<br>• Consideration of government regulatory issues |
| **5. Planning Process Requirements**<br>a. Existence of a system for expeditiously developing a complete plan | • Identification of problems and opportunities<br>• Postmortem of previous plans<br>• Statement of alternative strategies considered<br>• Identification of risk factors<br>• Statement of objectives<br>• Statement of action plan<br>• Development of contingency plans |

FIGURE 6–4 (CONTINUED)

## A Marketing Planning Model Based on Environmental Antecedents

| *Environmental Antecedents* | *Marketing Plan Requirements* |
| --- | --- |
| 6. *Operational Organizational Requirements*<br>  a. Guidance<br>  b. Control<br>  c. Financial responsibility<br>  d. Efficiency | • Statement of objectives<br>• Budget statement of proposed plan<br>• Responsibility for execution pinpointed<br>• Timetables and controls for the new plan specified |

I·S·S·U·E·S  I·N  I·N·T·E·R·N·A·T·I·O·N·A·L  M·A·R·K·E·T·I·N·G

## *Opel's Drive toward Number One*

Capitalizing on its strengths, alert to its weaknesses, and tuned in to opportunities in the wide-open European automobile market, Opel is mounting a serious challenge to Volkswagen's number-one position in Germany.

One of the obstacles the company must overcome is its past reputation. For years children chanted a derogatory rhyme that could be translated, "Every yokel drives an Opel." Recently Opel (a subsidiary of General Motors) revamped its product line and introduced more aerodynamic models that have helped improve its image. But Opel has benefited even more from some important strategic decisions.

While Volkswagen has made German customers wait as long as six months for new models, Opel has shifted supplies from sagging markets to satisfy German demand. In the first eight months of 1990 it captured 16.9 percent of the market in what was formerly West Germany, compared to Volkswagen's 20 percent. In fact, Opel now has a record 160 000 cars on order.

In an effort to cope with the increased demand, GM is building a new plant in what was formerly East Germany, where land is cheap, wages are low, and demand for cars is expected to triple by the end of the decade. Opel's existing European plants are already running at full capacity. "We're sold out," says a company executive.

Opel's success in Germany has stimulated GM to seek additional markets in Hungary and other European countries. In 1987 GM signed a five-year trade agreement with Hungary under which it buys components for Opels from a Hungarian manufacturer, Raba. In exchange, Hungary imports about 1000 Opels a year. GM is optimistic about its prospects in Eastern Europe. The short-term opportunities are good, and if the economies of these countries improve, the long-term prospects may be attractive as well.

Sources: Terence Roth and Bradley A. Steertz, "GM's Opel Is Closing in on Volkswagen as Top-Selling Brand in German Market," *Wall Street Journal* (October 4, 1990); Shawn Tully, "Doing Business in One Germany," *Fortune* (July 2, 1990), pp. 80–83; Allan T. Demaree, "The New Germany's Glowing Future," *Fortune* (December 3, 1990), pp. 146–154; and "Eastern Europe Beckons," *Advertising Age* (November 20, 1989), pp. 1, 45.

F I G U R E   6 – 5

## The Marketing Planning Process

### I. Situation Analysis: Where Are We Now?

**A. Historical Background**
- Nature of the firm, its sales and profit history, and current situation

**B. Consumer Analysis**
- Who are the customers we are trying to serve?
- What market segments exist?
- How many consumers are there?
- How much do they buy and why?

**C. Competitive Analysis**
- Given the nature of the markets — size, characteristics, competitive activities, and strategies — what marketing opportunities exist for this firm?

### II. Marketing Objectives: Where Do We Want to Go?

**A. Sales Objectives**
- What level of sales volume can we achieve during the next year?

**B. Profit Objectives**
- Given the sales level and the cost structure of the firm, what level of profits should be achieved?

**C. Consumer Objectives**
- How will we serve our target market customers?
- What do we want consumers to think about our firm?

### III. Developing A Marketing Mix: What Should We Do with Each of the Marketing Mix Elements?

**A. Product/Service Decisions**
- What products should we offer to meet consumers' needs?
- What is the exact nature of these products?

**B. Pricing Decisions**
- What level of prices should be used?
- What specific prices and price concessions are appropriate?

**C. Distribution Decisions**
- What channel(s) will be used in distributing our product offerings?
- Where should they be located?
- What should be their major characteristics?

**D. Communication Decisions**
- What mix of personal selling, advertising, and sales promotional activities is needed?
- How much should be spent, using what themes and what media?

**E. Financial Considerations**
- What will be the financial impact of this plan on a one-year pro-forma (projected) income statement?
- How does this income statement compare with our objectives?

**F. Control Aspects**

Source: Adapted from Stephen K. Keiser, Robert E. Stevens, and Lynn J. Loudenback, *Contemporary Marketing Study Guide* (Hinsdale, IL: Dryden Press, 1986), P. 482.

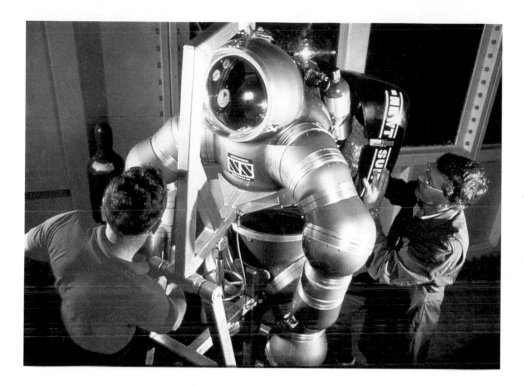

*International Hard Suits developed the "Newt suit" in response to a perceived need for a lightweight atmospheric diving suit designed to provide a practical and economical means of working at depths of up to 1000 feet. The firm is marketing the suit from Vancouver to a worldwide market with buyers from Japan, Canada, and the United States. If you were marketing this product, what sort of marketing mix would you suggest?*

What, then, should be included in a marketing plan? The answer can be determined from Figure 6–4. The left-hand column shows the environmental conditions that must be addressed. The marketing plan should meet these conditions. The right-hand column outlines the marketing plan components that are required to meet the conditions in the illustration. Obviously, as conditions change, different marketing plan components will be included, excluded, or emphasized.

Identifying key elements of the environment that must be responded to ensures that the marketing plan is focused on the right things. A further important advantage of this approach is that the marketing plan is not focused solely on current conditions. To properly understand the environment requires taking long-term trends into consideration. Providing that the organization's reward structure is not excessively focused on short-term results, a marketing plan based on current environmental conditions, as well as the forces behind them, will have a longer-term perspective. This should help to eliminate the excessively short and narrow vision that such critics as Hayes and Abernathy[8] decry. A more common description of a process for developing a marketing plan is shown in Figure 6–5. (It should in fact look familiar: we saw a less detailed version early in Chapter 3.)

## Implementing the Plan: The Marketing Mix

Marketing plans are implemented through four main elements: *products, pricing, distribution,* and *communication.* Each is an essential part of the marketing plan.

**Product management** includes *decisions about what kind of product is needed, its uses, package design, branding, trademarks, warranties, guarantees, product life cycles, and new-product development.* The marketer's concept of product involves much more than just the physical product. It takes into account the satisfaction of all consumer needs in relation to a good or service.

**product management**
Decisions about what kind of product is needed, its uses, package design, branding, trademarks, warranties, guarantees, product life cycles, and new-product development.

FIGURE 6-6

**The Marketing Mix**

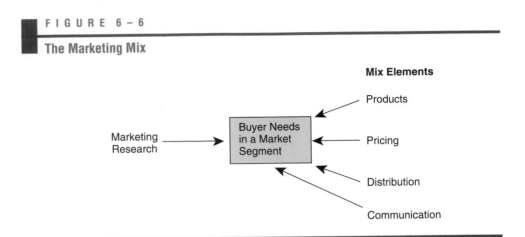

Mix Elements

Marketing Research → Buyer Needs in a Market Segment ← Products

← Pricing

← Distribution

← Communication

**pricing** The methods of setting competitive, profitable, and justified prices.

**distribution** The selection and management of marketing channels and the physical distribution of goods.

**marketing channels** The steps or handling organizations that a good or service goes through from producer to consumer.

**communication** Personal selling, advertising, sales promotion, and publicity.

**Pricing** involves decisions concerning *the methods of setting competitive, profitable, and justified prices.* Most prices are freely set in Canada. However, some prices, such as those for public utilities and housing rentals, are regulated to some degree, and are therefore subject to public scrutiny.

**Distribution** decisions involve *the selection and management of marketing channels and the physical distribution of goods.* **Marketing channels** are *the steps or handling organizations that a good or service goes through from producer to final consumer.* Channel decision-making entails selecting and working with the institutional structure that handles the firm's goods or services. This includes wholesalers, retailers, and other intermediaries.

**Communication** includes *personal selling, advertising, sales promotion, and publicity.* The marketing manager has many decisions to make concerning when, where, and how to use these elements of communication so that potential buyers will learn about and be persuaded to try the company's products.

The rest of this book will be devoted largely to explaining these four marketing elements. The elements of the marketing mix are shown in Figure 6–6.

Starting with a careful evaluation of the market — using market segmentation — every marketing plan must take into consideration the appropriate product for a

A·P·P·L·Y·I·N·G  T·H·E  C·O·N·C·E·P·T·S

## *One Management's View of What Can and Cannot Be Expected from Planning*

- Planning *will not* give you a "perfect crystal ball," nor will it enable you to predict the future with extreme accuracy.

- Planning *will not* necessarily prevent you from making mistakes.

- Planning *will* or should minimize the degree to which you are taken by surprise, and help you revise both programs and objectives whenever it is desirable to do so. In other words, planning *will* help you react creatively to change.

- Planning *will* result in the integration of all of the company's activities and maximize your efforts toward the attainment of corporate goals.

- Planning *does not* stifle creativity. Planning *enhances* creativity by creating orderly processes whereby viable objectives and plans can be reached.

Source: *Guide to Preparing Marketing Plans*, Publishing Group, Litton Industries, Inc.

*The marketing mix for a sidewalk café is different from that for a fast-food eatery or a fine restaurant. The target market would be younger than that of the fine restaurant but older than the fast-food customers. Distribution would be centred in tourist areas or the downtown core, and not so much in suburban areas. What other aspects would be different?*

particular segment, the price that should be charged for it, and the appropriate outlet in which it ought to be sold; and all of this information must be effectively communicated to the target market.

A quick examination of various companies' marketing programs shows that, even though they each have all the marketing variables, no two programs use them in exactly the same way. The *emphasis* and *use* of each can vary markedly. For example, the target market for McDonald's might be families with children. Its products are standardized and reliable, but not considered to match the same calibre as those of Dubrovnik's, a famous restaurant one might visit on an evening out. Dubrovnik's target market would be couples celebrating a special event or businesspeople entertaining their clients. Prices at McDonald's are low compared with those at the fine restaurant. In terms of distribution, it is important for McDonald's to have outlets at many locations, because consumers are not prepared to drive great distances to visit them. In contrast, people are fully prepared to drive downtown to the one Dubrovnik's location. McDonald's employs a communication program that involves extensive television advertising. Dubrovnik's counts on favourable word-of-mouth publicity, and purchases only a limited number of advertisements in local magazines and theatre guides.

The point is that each firm uses the elements of marketing differently — the marketing elements are *harmonized* in a unique way to form the main aspects of the marketing plan. This *blending of the four elements of marketing to satisfy chosen consumer segments* is known as the **marketing mix**. The marketing mix concept is one of the most powerful ever developed for marketers. It is now the main organizing concept for countless marketing plans. It gives executives a way to ensure that all elements of their program are considered in a simple yet disciplined fashion.[9]

The marketing planner must actually make wise decisions about *many* sub-elements of the marketing mix. This takes much skill and attention. While we

**marketing mix**   The blending of the four elements of marketing to satisfy chosen consumer segments.

A·P·P·L·Y·I·N·G   T·H·E   C·O·N·C·E·P·T·S

## *Interaction within the Mix*

The marketing mix concept emphasizes the fit of the various pieces and the quality and size of their interaction. There are three degrees of interaction. The least demanding is *consistency* — a logical and useful fit between two or more elements. It would seem generally inconsistent, for example, to sell a high-quality product through a low-quality retailer. It can be done, but the consumer must understand the reason for the inconsistency and respond favourably to it. Even more difficult is maintaining such an apparent inconsistency for a long time.

The second level of positive relationship among elements of the mix is *integration*. While consistency involves only a coherent fit, integration requires an active, harmonious interaction among the elements of the mix. For example, heavy advertising is sometimes harmonious with a high selling price because the added margin from the premium price pays for the advertising, and the heavy advertising creates the brand differentiation that justifies the high price. National brands of consumer package goods such as Tide laundry detergent, Campbell soup, and Colgate toothpaste use this approach. This does *not* mean, however, that heavy advertising and high product pricing are always harmonious.

The third — and most sophisticated — form of relationship is *synergy*, whereby each element is used to the best advantage in support of the total mix and results in effects greater than the sum of the parts.

Source: Adapted from Benson P. Shapiro, "Getting Things Done," *Harvard Business Review* (September–October 1985), p. 29.

normally talk of the four main categories of the mix,[10] it should be clearly understood that each of the mix elements can, and should be, divided into many subcategories when developing a marketing plan. For example, *communication* includes decisions about advertising, selling, and point-of-purchase promotion, to name a few. Neil Borden, who first coined the term "marketing mix," used to use a much more extensive list in his teaching and consulting. It is reproduced in the accompanying box.

## Analysis of Competitive Position

A major objective in strategy planning is to create and sustain a competitive advantage. There are two main approaches though which managers decide what advantages distinguish their business and how those advantages were gained.[11] One starts with the market and is customer-focused; the other is primarily competitor-centred. Competitor-centred assessments are based on direct management comparisons with a few target competitors. This approach is often seen in stalemated industries, where the emphasis is on "beating the competition." The key question here is, "How do our capabilities and offerings compare with those of competitors?" Businesses using this approach watch costs closely, quickly match the marketing initiatives of competitors, and look for a "sustainable edge" in technology.

Customer-focused assessments start with detailed analyses of customer benefits within end-use segments, working backward from the customer to the company to identify the actions needed to improve performance. This "market-back" orientation is found in service-intensive industries such as investment banking, where new services are easily imitated, cost of funds is the same, and entry is easy.[12] Less attention is given to competitors' capabilities and performance — the emphasis is on the quality of customer relationships. Evidence of continuing customer satisfaction and loyalty is more meaningful than market share in such circumstances.

A·P·P·L·Y·I·N·G  T·H·E  C·O·N·C·E·P·T·S

## Neil H. Borden's Marketing Mix

Elements of the Marketing Mix of Manufacturers

1. *Product Planning* — policies and procedures relating to:
   a. Product lines to be offered — qualities, design, etc.
   b. Markets to sell — whom, where, when, and in what quantity.
   c. New-product policy — R & D program.
2. *Pricing* — policies and procedures relating to:
   a. Price level to adopt.
   b. Specific prices to adopt — odd–even, etc.
   c. Price policy — one price or varying price, price maintenance, use of list prices, etc.
   d. Margins to adopt — for company, for the trade.
3. *Branding* — policies and procedures relating to:
   a. Selection of trademarks.
   b. Brand policy — individualized or family brand.
   c. Sale under private label or unbranded.
4. *Channels of Distribution* — policies and procedures relating to:
   a. Channels to use between plant and consumer.
   b. Degree of selectivity among wholesalers and retailers.
   c. Efforts to gain co-operation of the trade.
5. *Personal Selling* — policies and procedures relating to:
   a. Burden to be placed on personal selling and the methods to be employed in:
      1. Manufacturer's organization.
      2. Wholesale segment of the trade.
      3. Retail segment of the trade.
6. *Advertising* — policies and procedures relating to:
   a. Amount to spend — i.e., burden to be placed on advertising.
   b. Copy platform to adopt:
      1. Product image desired.
      2. Corporate image desired.
   c. Mix of advertising — to the trade, through the trade, to consumers.
7. *Promotions* — policies and procedures relating to:
   a. Burden to be placed on special selling plans or devices directed at or through the trade.
   b. Form of these devices for consumer promotions, for trade promotions.
8. *Packaging* — policies and procedures relating to:
   a. Formulation of package and label.
9. *Display* — policies and procedures relating to:
   a. Burden to be put on display to help effect sale.
   b. Methods to adopt to secure display.
10. *Servicing* — policies and procedures relating to:
    a. Providing service needed.
11. *Physical Handling* — policies and procedures relating to:
    a. Warehousing.
    b. Transportation.
    c. Inventories.
12. *Fact-Finding and Analysis* — policies and procedures relating to:
    a. Securing, analyzing and using facts in marketing operations.

Source: Neil H. Borden, "The Concept of the Marketing Mix," *Journal of Advertising Research* (June 1964), pp. 2–7.

## The Role of the Marketing Manager

To conclude our examination of marketing strategy and the marketing plan, Figure 6–7 illustrates some aspects of the role of the marketing manager. In the light of the opportunities and constraints perceived in the environmental framework, as well as the strategy, objectives, and resources of the firm, the manager develops a marketing plan. Products, pricing, distribution, and communication are blended together in a unique manner to make up the marketing mix. The result wins customers, sales, and profits for the firm. The rest of this text will elaborate on the many considerations involved in managing the elements of the mix.

FIGURE 6 – 7

## The Role of the Marketing Manager

**Components of the Marketing Environment**

1. The social environment and behaviour of consumers

2. The economic environment

3. The competitive environment

4. The legal environment

5. The technological environment

**External factors**

**Strategies, Objectives and Resources of the Organization**

**MARKETING MANAGER**

**Marketing Plan**

A unique blend of marketing elements related to each other and the forces bearing on the organization.

**Marketing Mix Elements**

1. Product decisions

2. Pricing decisions

3. Distribution decisions

4. Communication decisions

**Internal factors**

## Summary

*Strategy* is the overall purpose and direction of the organization; it is established in the light of the challenges and opportunities found in the environment, as well as the firm's resources. *Marketing strategy* is based on the strategy set for the company as a whole. It focuses on developing a unique long-run competitive position in the market by assessing consumer needs and the firm's potential for gaining competitive advantage.

The five strategic marketing components are segment-by-positioning analysis: opportunities–strengths analysis: synergy analysis: functional requirement analysis: and portfolio analysis.

The *marketing plan*, which is based on the marketing strategy, is a program of activities that lead to the accomplishment of the marketing strategy. It is sometimes known as the *marketing program*. The elements of a marketing plan should be contingent on the competitive situation and environment in which the firm finds itself. Thus, the elements that should be included in a marketing plan for one firm may differ from those required for another organization, which faces a different environment.

To implement the marketing plan, the marketer develops a marketing mix to serve the needs of buyers in defined market segments. The blending of the four elements of marketing (product, pricing, distribution, and communication) to satisfy chosen consumer segments is known as the *marketing mix*. Marketing research is sometimes also considered a part of the marketing mix.

A major objective in strategy planning is to create and sustain a competitive advantage. There are two main approaches through which managers decide what advantages distinguish their business and how these advantages are gained. One starts with the market and is customer-focused: the other is primarily competitor-centred.

## KEY TERMS

corporate strategy
mission statement
marketing strategy
marketing plan
contingency

marketing planning process
marketing mix
product
price

distribution
marketing channels
communication
analysis of competitive position

## REVIEW QUESTIONS

1. Distinguish between corporate strategy and marketing strategy.
2. Distinguish between marketing strategy and the marketing plan.
3. Identify the steps in the marketing planning process.
4. Outline the steps involved in developing a marketing strategy.
5. Explain why the marketing plan should be developed contingent on an environmental analysis.
6. Explain how two different companies could have different marketing mixes.
7. Explain why marketing strategy should take corporate strategy into consideration.
8. List Theodore Levitt's four requisites for success in business.

## DISCUSSION QUESTIONS AND EXERCISES

1. Use the marketing process format described in the chapter to develop a marketing plan for one of the following:
   a. Local retailer
   b. Local service provider
   c. Local shopping centre
   d. Nonprofit organization
   e. University or college athletic program (to generate fan support for intercollegiate sports events)
2. Outline the apparent marketing mix for Coca-Cola, and that for Perrier mineral water.
3. Explain the similarities and differences between the marketing mixes of the two products described in Question 2.
4. Contact a local firm and obtain a copy of its mission statement.
5. Contact a local firm and ask for an outline of the categories its managers use in preparing a marketing plan. How do these elements compare with those described in the text?

## CAREER PROFILE

### Norry L. Fitzpatrick

Statistics Canada, Pacific Region
Regional Manager, Communications and Marketing

**Education:**

University of British Columbia
Bachelor of Commerce and Business Administration
Graduation — 1978

UBC's Bachelor of Commerce degree provided me with a solid grounding in all areas of business. During my undergraduate year, I began developing skills involving the tangible elements of business such as plans, budgets, contracts, and performance. I also gained insight into the intangibles that help an organization meet its goals through its employees — for example, commitment, loyalty, and innovation. The Marketing Program introduced me to all facets of marketing, including sales, research, and advertising. With this foundation, I have been able to apply my knowledge and skills to several different areas of business, finally settling in marketing and public communications.

I chose sales as a starting point in my career. I had been advised that sales experience would serve me well in virtually anything else I might want to do. This was sound advice. The positions I held after that first sales job helped me develop my understanding of the marketing process and refine my management skills. It is not enough to get involved in just one aspect of marketing. It is critical to gain experience in unrelated areas, such as administration, in order to ultimately maximize your effectiveness as a manager in the field of marketing.

One study area that would prove to be significant in my career was market research. The UBC Marketing Program offered an introduction to methods used in research — for instance, survey taking and such secondary sources of data as customer lists and statistical analyses produced by outside sources. Sound research should be the basis for all business decisions. Knowing who your customers are and where to find them is the cornerstone to successfully marketing a product or service. An understanding of market research is critical to effective management, whether your responsibilities include actually carrying out the research or contracting with others to do it. Since Statistics Canada is the principal source of secondary data for most companies doing research, these courses have been invaluable to me in marketing the Department's products and services to corporations and consultants alike.

Weighing career and family, in the next 10 years I hope to move into a senior position in corporate communications with a large private-sector company.

The foundation of the marketing concept involves developing an understanding of the needs and desires of the customer, and then striving to serve those needs. Market segmentation provides a way to identify groupings of customers. After identification, a deeper understanding of the consumer helps establish successful marketing plans. Part Three discusses some of the many concepts that marketers bring to bear in analyzing customer behaviour. Both the internal factors and the external influences that affect decision-making in consumers and industrial buyers are explored.

LOOK YOUR DOG STRAIGHT IN THE EYES
AND TELL HIM HE DOESN'T DESERVE THIS DOG FOOD.

Go ahead, you tell him he doesn't deserve the shiniest coat, the whitest teeth, the healthiest skin, strongest muscles and the liveliest eyes.

However, you could feed him Pro Plan* from Ralston Purina,* and not have to say a thing.

Pro Plan is a carefully balanced blend of high quality ingredients like chicken, rice and wheat and not a hint of artificial colourings or flavourings.

Getting him to eat Pro Plan is easy. Telling him he doesn't deserve it, is a problem we're glad we don't have.

AVAILABLE IN FOUR FORMULAS ONLY AT SELECT PET FOOD OUTLETS.

*Reg. T.M. Ralston Purina Company. Ralston Purina Canada Inc., Registered User.

# Consumer Behaviour

## CHAPTER OBJECTIVES

1. To identify the personal and interpersonal influences on consumer behaviour.
2. To distinguish between needs and motives.
3. To explain perception.
4. To describe how attitudes influence behaviour.
5. To demonstrate how learning theory can be applied to marketing strategy.
6. To explain the role of culture in consumer behaviour.
7. To consider the effect of reference groups on consumer behaviour.
8. To differentiate among routinized response behaviour, limited problem-solving, and extended problem-solving.

IT would take a stone-faced, cold-hearted kind of person not to be affected by the print ad for Purina Pro Plan dog food.

There it is: A close-up shot of a golden retriever, his soft brown eyes just oozing love and devotion. The copy reads: "Look your dog straight in the eyes and tell him he doesn't deserve this dog food."

Go ahead. Try.

You can't do it. And the marketing people at Ralston Purina, Toronto, know you can't. They know, like the other major pet-food manufacturers, how loving and indulgent today's pet owners are toward their four-footed charges. And guilty.

Owners who are away at work all day believe that their pet deserves the best, the most luxurious, the most nutritionally complete food available.

"Some people see their pets as surrogate children," says Karen Kuwahara, Ralston's director of marketing, "but even those who don't still see it as a part of the family, so their concerns toward family members will also be projected onto their pet."

This has led to a premium or gourmet-product boom seen most prominently in the cat-food markets (feline owners tend to pamper their pets more than dog owners do). "There is a trend toward developing products that look like human food," says Michael Pearl, product manager of Starkist's pet-food line. "That was our strategy a few years back, when we introduced bite-sized morsels. Chances are if the owners think it looks good, they will project those values onto their cat."[1]

# Introduction

**consumer behaviour**  The acts of individuals in obtaining and using goods and services, including the decision processes that precede and determine these acts.

**Consumer behaviour** consists of *the acts of individuals in obtaining and using goods and services, including the decision processes that precede and determine these acts.*[2] This definition includes both the ultimate consumer and the purchaser of industrial products. A major difference in the purchasing behaviour of industrial consumers and ultimate consumers is that additional influences from within the organization may be exerted on the industrial purchasing agent.

# Classifying Behavioural Influences: Personal and Interpersonal

The field of consumer behaviour borrows extensively from other areas, like psychology and sociology.[3] The work of Kurt Lewin, for instance, provides an excellent classification of influences on buying behaviour. Lewin's proposition was that

$$B = f(P,E),$$

where behaviour ($B$) is a function ($f$) of the interactions of personal influences ($P$) and the pressures exerted on them by outside forces in the environment ($E$).[4]

This statement is usually rewritten for consumer behaviour as follows:

$$B = f(I,P),$$

where consumer behaviour ($B$) is a function ($f$) of the interaction of interpersonal influences ($I$), such as reference groups and culture, and personal determinants ($P$), such as attitudes, on the consumer. Understanding consumer behaviour, as Figure 7–1 illustrates, requires understanding both the individual's psychological makeup and the influences of others.

FIGURE 7 – 1

**Determinants of Consumer Behaviour**

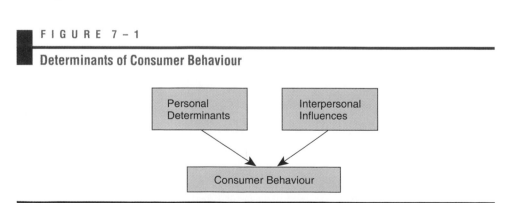

FIGURE 7–2

**Personal Determinants of Consumer Behaviour**

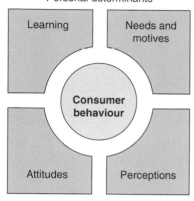

Personal determinants

Learning | Needs and motives

**Consumer behaviour**

Attitudes | Perceptions

Source: Adapted with permission from C. Glenn Walters and Gordon W. Paul, *Consumer Behavior: An Integrated Framework* (Homewood, IL: Irwin, 1970), p. 14. Copyright © 1970 by Richard D. Irwin, Inc.

# Personal Determinants of Consumer Behaviour

Consumer behaviour is a function of both interpersonal and personal influences. The personal determinants of consumer behaviour include the individual's needs, motives, perceptions, attitudes, and learning. Figure 7–2 shows how these determinants relate to one another.

## Needs and Motives

The starting point in the purchase decision process is the recognition of a felt need. A **need** is simply *the lack of something useful*. The consumer is typically confronted with numerous unsatisfied needs. It is important to note that a need must be sufficiently aroused before it may serve as a motive.

**need**   The lack of something useful.

**Motives** are *inner states that direct us toward the goal of satisfying a felt need*. The individual is *moved* (the root word of motive) to take action to reduce a state of tension and to return to a condition of equilibrium.

**motive**   An Inner state that directs us toward the goal of satisfying a felt need.

### Hierarchy of needs

Although psychologists disagree on specific classifications of needs, a useful theory that may apply to consumers in general was developed by A.H. Maslow.[5] He proposed a classification of needs (sometimes referred to as a hierarchy), as shown in Figure 7–3. It is important to recognize that Maslow's hierarchy *may not apply to each individual*, but seems to be true of groups in general. His list is based on two important assumptions:

1. People are wanting animals, whose needs depend on what they already possess. A satisfied need is not a motivator; only those needs that have not been satisfied can influence behaviour.

2. Once one need has been largely satisfied, another emerges and demands satisfaction.

FIGURE 7 – 3

**Need Classification Structure**

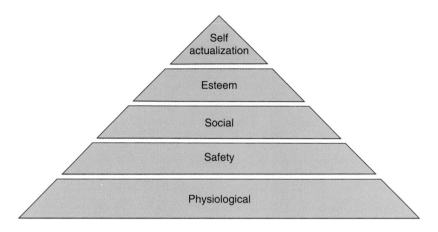

Source: Adapted from "A Theory of Human Motivation," in Abraham H. Maslow, *Motivation and Personality*, 2nd ed. Copyright © 1970 by Abraham H. Maslow. Reprinted by permission of Harper & Row, Publishers, Inc.

***Physiological needs***   The primary needs for food, shelter, and clothing normally must be satisfied before the higher-order needs are considered. A hungry person is possessed by the need to obtain food. Other needs are ignored. Once the physiological needs are at least partly satisfied, other needs come into the picture.

***Safety needs***   Safety needs include protection from physical harm, the need for security, and avoidance of the unexpected. Gratification of these needs may take the form of a savings account, life insurance, the purchase of radial tires, or membership in the local health club. Michelin Tire advertisements target this need.

***Social needs***   Satisfaction of physiological and safety needs may be followed by the desire to be accepted by members of the family and other individuals and groups — that is, the social needs. Individuals may be motivated to join various groups and to conform to their standards of dress, purchases, and behaviour, and may become interested in obtaining status as a means of fulfilling these social needs. Social needs seem to be becoming a more important cultural value. Many "lifestyle" advertisements, such as those often used by Coke and Pepsi, appeal to social needs.

***Esteem needs.***   The higher-order needs are prevalent in all societies. In developed countries with high per capita income, most families have been able to satisfy the basic needs. Therefore, one would expect such consumers to concentrate more on the desire for status, esteem, and self-actualization. These needs are more difficult to satisfy. At the esteem level is the need to feel a sense of accomplishment, achievement, and respect from others. The competitive need to excel — to better the performance of others and "stand out" from the crowd — is an almost universal human trait.

Esteem needs are closely related to social needs. At this level, however, the individual desires not just acceptance but also recognition and respect in some way.

### Self-Actualization — Need for Fulfillment

Source: ©1970 United Feature Syndicate, Inc.

***Self-actualization needs*** Self-actualization needs are the desire for fulfillment, for realizing one's own potential, for using one's talents and capabilities totally. Maslow defines self-actualization this way: "The healthy man is primarily motivated by his needs to develop and actualize his fullest potentialities and capacities. What man can be, he must be."[6] The author Robert Louis Stevenson was describing self-actualization when he wrote, "To be what we are, and to become what we are capable of becoming, is the only end of life."

As already noted, Maslow argues that a satisfied need is no longer a motivator. Once the physiological needs are satiated, the individual moves on to the higher-order needs. Consumers are periodically motivated by the need to relieve thirst or hunger, but their interests are most often directed toward the satisfaction of safety, social, and other needs.

Caution must be used in applying Maslow's theory. Empirical research shows little support for a universal hierarchical ordering of needs in *specific individuals*.[7] It would therefore be unsafe to use the theory to explain a particular purchase. The needs hierarchy and motive strength concept may be useful in considering the behaviour of consumers *in general*, however. It has been verified that in consumer buying, previously ignored desires often surface only after a purchase has satisfied a predominant (and *perhaps* lower-order) motive.[8]

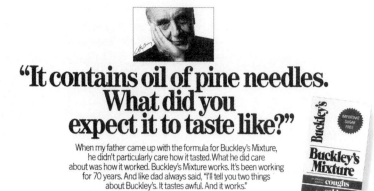

*Buckley's capitalized on a public perception in this famous ad campaign. The firm linked its product with the public perception that medicine must taste bad in order to be effective. Introducing Buckley senior completes the association with the sage wisdom one's parents would dispense along with the medicine.*

## Perceptions

Several years ago, a pharmaceutical firm developed Analoze, a cherry-flavoured combination painkiller and stomach sweetener that could be taken without water. The product failed because consumers associated the ritual of taking pills and a glass of water with pain relief.[9] Analoze was not perceived as an effective remedy because it violated their experience with other painkillers. Individual behaviour resulting from motivation is affected by how we perceive stimuli. **Perception** is *the meaning that each person attributes to incoming stimuli received through the five senses.*

Psychologists once assumed that perception was an objective phenomenon — that is, that the individual perceived what was there to be perceived. It is now recognized that what we perceive is as much a result of what we *want* to perceive as of what is actually there. This does not mean that people view dogs as pigeons. We can distinguish shopping centres from churches, and a retail store stocked with well-known brand names and staffed with helpful, knowledgeable sales personnel is perceived differently from a largely self-serve discount store. Woolco and Birks are both important retailers, but they carry quite different images.

Our perception of an object or event is the result of the interaction of two types of factors:

1. Stimulus factors, which are characteristics of the physical object such as size, colour, weight, or shape.
2. Individual factors, which are characteristics of the perceiver. These factors include not only sensory processes but also past experiences with similar items and basic motivations and expectations.

### Perceptual screens

The individual is continually bombarded with a myriad of stimuli, but most are ignored. In order to have time to function, each of us must respond selectively to stimuli. What stimuli we respond to, then, is the problem of all marketers. How can they gain the attention of the individual so that he or she will read the advertisement, listen to the sales representative, react to a point-of-purchase display?

Even though studies have shown that the average consumer is exposed to more than a thousand ads daily, most of them never break through our **perceptual screen**,

**perception** The meaning that each person attributes to incoming stimuli received through the five senses.

**perceptual screen** The filter through which messages must pass.

*the filter through which messages must pass*. Sometimes breakthroughs may be accomplished in the printed media through larger ads, since doubling the size of an ad increases its attention value by approximately 50 percent. Black-and-white TV ads with selective use of one colour, in contrast with the usual colour ads, are another device to break the reader's perceptual screen. Another method of using contrast in print advertising is to include a large amount of white space to draw attention to the ad, or to use white type on a black background. In general, the marketer seeks to make the message stand out, to make it sufficiently different from other messages that it gains the attention of the prospective customer. Piercing the perceptual screen is a difficult task.

With such selectivity at work, it is easy to see the importance of the marketer's efforts to develop brand loyalty to a product. Satisfied customers are less likely to seek or pay attention to information about competing products. They simply tune out information that is not in accord with their existing beliefs and expectations.

## Weber's Law

Our understanding of what it takes to get attention may be aided by considering Weber's Law. The relationship between the actual physical stimulus (such as size, loudness, or texture) and the corresponding sensation produced in the individual is known as *psychophysics*, which can be expressed as a mathematical equation:

$$\frac{\Delta I}{I} = k$$

where $\Delta I$ = the smallest increase in stimulus that will be noticeably different from the previous intensity

$I$ = the intensity of the stimulus at the point where the increase takes place

$k$ = a constant (that varies from one sense to the next)

In other words, *the higher the initial intensity of a stimulus, the greater the amount of the change in intensity that is necessary in order for a difference to be noticed.*

This relationship, known as **Weber's Law**, has some obvious implications in marketing. A price increase of $300 for a Firefly is readily apparent for prospective buyers; the same $300 increase on a $45 000 Mercedes seems insignificant. A large package requires a much greater increase in size to be noticeable than a smaller-sized package requires. People perceive *by exception*, and the change in a stimulus must be sufficiently great to gain the individual's attention.[10]

**Weber's Law** The higher the initial intensity of a stimulus, the greater the amount of the change in intensity that is necessary in order for a difference to be noticed.

## Subliminal perception

Is it possible to communicate with persons without their being aware of the communication? In other words, does **subliminal perception** — *a subconscious level of awareness* — really exist? In 1957 the phrases "Eat popcorn" and "Drink Coca-Cola" were flashed on the screen of a New Jersey movie theatre every five seconds for 1/300th of a second. Researchers then reported that these messages, although too short to be recognizable at the conscious level, resulted in a 58 percent increase in popcorn sales and an 18 percent increase in the sale of Coca-Cola. After the publication of these findings, advertising agencies and consumer protection groups became intensely interested in subliminal perception.[11] Subsequent attempts to duplicate these test findings have, however, invariably been unsuccessful.

Subliminal advertising is aimed at the subconscious level of awareness to avoid the perceptual screens of viewers. The goal of the original research was to induce consumers to purchase products without being aware of the source of the motivation. Although subliminal advertising has been universally condemned (and

**subliminal perception** A subconscious level of awareness.

declared illegal in Canada and California), experts believe that it is in fact unlikely that such advertising can induce purchases anyway. There are several reasons for this: (1) strong stimulus factors are typically required even to gain attention, as discussed earlier; (2) only a very short message can be transmitted subliminally; (3) individuals vary greatly in their thresholds of consciousness[12] (a message transmitted at the threshold of consciousness for one person will not be perceived at all by some people and will be all too apparent for others: when exposed subliminally, the message "Drink Coca Cola" might go unseen by some viewers, while others read it as "Drink Pepsi-Cola," "Drink Cocoa," or even "Drive Slowly");[13] (4) perceptual defences *also* work at the subconscious level.

Contrary to earlier fears, research has shown that subliminal messages cannot force the receiver to purchase goods that he or she would not consciously want.[14]

## Attitudes

Perception of incoming stimuli is greatly affected by attitudes regarding these stimuli. In fact, decisions to purchase products are based on currently held attitudes about the product, the store, or the salesperson.

**attitudes**   A person's enduring favourable or unfavourable evaluations, emotional feelings, or pro or con action tendencies toward some object or idea.

**Attitudes** may be defined as *a person's enduring favourable or unfavourable evaluations, emotional feelings, or pro or con action tendencies toward some object or idea.*[15] Attitudes are formed over a period of time through individual experiences and group contacts, and are highly resistant to change.

### Components of an attitude

Attitudes consist of three related components: cognitive, affective, and behavioural. The *cognitive* component is the information and knowledge one has about an object or concept. The *affective* component is one's feelings or emotional reactions. The *behavioural* component is the way one tends to act or to behave. In considering the decision to shop at a warehouse-type food store, a person obtains information from advertising, trial visits, and input from family, friends, and associates (cognitive). A consumer also receives inputs from others about their acceptance of shopping at this new type of store, as well as impressions about the type of people who shop there (affective). The shopper may ultimately decide to make some purchases of canned goods, cereal, and bakery products there, but continue to rely on a regular super-market for major food purchases (behavioural).

As Figure 7–4 illustrates, the three components exist in a relatively stable and balanced relationship to one another and combine to form an overall attitude about an object or idea.

### Producing attitude change

Given that a favourable consumer attitude is a prerequisite to market success, how can a firm lead prospective buyers to adopt a more favourable attitude toward its products? The marketer has two choices: either attempt to change attitudes to make them consonant with the product or determine consumer attitudes and then change the product to match them.[16]

If consumers view the product unfavourably, the firm may choose to redesign the product to better conform with their desires. To accommodate the consumer, the firm may make styling changes, variations in ingredients, changes in package size, and changes in retail stores handling the product. The other course of action — changing consumer attitudes toward the product without changing the product — is much more difficult.

FIGURE 7 – 4

## Three Components of an Attitude

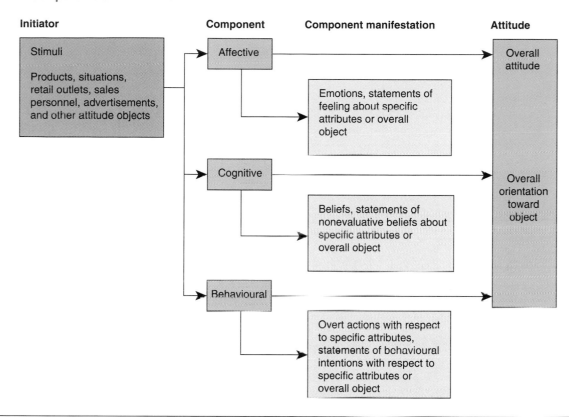

Source: Del I. Hawkins, Kenneth A. Concy, and Roger J. Best, *Consumer Behaviour: Implications for Marketing Strategy* (Dallas, TX: Business Publications, 1980), p. 334; the figure is adapted from M.J. Rosenberg and C.I. Hovland, *Attitude Organization and Change* (New Haven, CT: Yale University Press, 1960), p. 3. Reprinted by permission.

## Modifying an attitudinal component to affect attitude

Attitude change may occur when inconsistencies are introduced among the three attitudinal components. If one component can be influenced, the other two may be brought into congruence with the changed component, and the attitude will be modified.

One way to create an inconsistency in the cognitive component involves providing new information. In 1991, General Motors mounted a huge advertising program showing that its cars were more fuel-efficient and reliable than Japanese-produced cars. This information was expected to counteract "common knowledge" that Japanese-produced cars were superior on these characteristics. In another instance, beef producers first modified their product, then undertook comparative advertising to show the low amount of fat now contained in beef.

The affective component of attitude may be altered by relating the use of the product to desirable consequences for the user. This is a common appeal for health and beauty-aid products. Advertisements for a new perfume or cologne may imply that it will make one more attractive to the opposite sex.

The third alternative in attempting to change attitudes is to focus on the behavioural component, by inducing someone to engage in behaviour that is contradictory to the person's currently held attitudes. Attitude-discrepant behaviour of this type may occur if the consumer is given a free sample of a product. Such trials may lead to attitude change.

# Learning

Consumers *learn* about the values and uses of products. Since marketing is as concerned with the process by which consumer decisions change over time as with describing those decisions at one point in time, the study of how learning takes place is important. A useful definition of **learning** *is changes in behaviour, immediate or expected, as a result of experience.*[17]

**learning**   Changes in behaviour, immediate or expected, as a result of experience.

**drive**   Any strong stimulus that impels action.

**cue**   Any object existing in the environment that determines the nature of the response to a drive.

**response**   The individual's reaction to the cues and drives.

**reinforcement**   The reduction in drive that results from a proper response.

**shaping**   The process of applying a series of rewards and reinforcement so that more complex behaviour can evolve over time.

The learning process includes several components. The first component, **drive**, refers to *any strong stimulus that impels action*. Examples of drives include fear, pride, the desire for money, thirst, pain avoidance, and rivalry.

**Cues**, the second component of the learning process, are *any objects existing in the environment that determine the nature of the response to a drive*. Cues might include a newspaper advertisement for a new French restaurant, an in-store display, or a Petrocan sign on a major highway. For the hungry person, the shopper seeking a particular item, or the motorist needing gasoline, respectively, these cues may result in a specific response to satisfy a drive.

**A response** is *the individual's reaction to the cues and drives*, such as purchasing a bottle of Pert Plus shampoo, dining at a Harvey's, or deciding to enroll at a particular university or community college.

**Reinforcement** is *the reduction in drive that results from a proper response*. The more rewarding the response, the stronger the bond between the drive and the purchase of that particular item becomes. Should Pert Plus result in shiny, manageable hair through repeated use, the likelihood of its purchase in the future is increased.

## Applying learning theory to marketing decisions

Learning theory has some important implications for marketing strategists.[18] A desired outcome such as repeat purchase behaviour may have to be developed gradually. **Shaping** is *the process of applying a series of rewards and reinforcement so that more complex behaviour* (such as the development of a brand preference) *can evolve over time*. Both promotional strategy and the product itself play a role in the shaping process.

Figure 7–5 shows the application of learning theory and shaping procedures to a typical marketing scenario, in which marketers attempt to motivate consumers to become regular buyers of a certain product. An initial product trial is induced by a free sample package that includes a coupon offering a substantial discount on a subsequent purchase. This illustrates the use of a cue as a shaping procedure. The purchase response is reinforced by satisfactory product performance and a coupon for the next purchase.

The second stage is to entice the consumer to buy the product with little financial risk. The large discount coupon enclosed with the free sample prompts such an action. The package that is purchased has a smaller discount coupon enclosed. Again, the reinforcement is satisfactory product performance and the second coupon.

The third step would be to motivate the person to buy the item again at a moderate cost. The discount coupon accomplishes this objective, but this time there is no

FIGURE 7 – 5

**Application of Learning Theory and Shaping Procedure to Marketing**

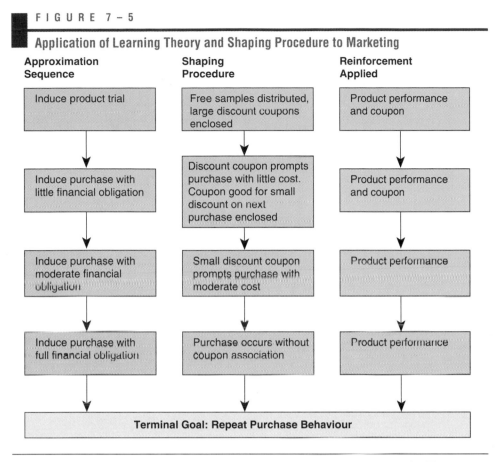

| Approximation Sequence | Shaping Procedure | Reinforcement Applied |
|---|---|---|
| Induce product trial | Free samples distributed, large discount coupons enclosed | Product performance and coupon |
| Induce purchase with little financial obligation | Discount coupon prompts purchase with little cost. Coupon good for small discount on next purchase enclosed | Product performance and coupon |
| Induce purchase with moderate financial obligation | Small discount coupon prompts purchase with moderate cost | Product performance |
| Induce purchase with full financial obligation | Purchase occurs without coupon association | Product performance |

**Terminal Goal: Repeat Purchase Behaviour**

Source: Adapted from Michael L. Rothschild and William C. Gaidis, "Behavioral Learning Theory: Its Relevance to Marketing and Promotion," *Journal of Marketing* (Spring 1981), p. 72.

additional coupon in the package. The only reinforcement is satisfactory product performance.

The final test comes when the consumer is asked to buy the product at its true price, without a discount coupon. Satisfaction with product performance is the only continuing reinforcement. Thus, repeat purchase behaviour has been literally shaped.

Kellogg used learning theory and shaping when it introduced its Nutri-Grain brand sugarless whole-grain cereal. Coupons worth 40 cents off — about a third of the product's cost — were distributed to elicit trial purchases by consumers. Inside boxes of the new cereal were additional cents-off coupons of lesser value.[19] Kellogg was clearly trying to shape future purchase behaviour by effective application of learning theory within a marketing strategy context.

## Interpersonal Determinants of Consumer Behaviour

People are social animals. They often buy products and services that will enable them to project a favourable image to others. The cultural environment, membership in reference groups, and family may influence such purchase decisions. A

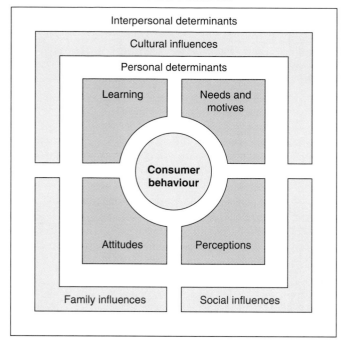

FIGURE 7–6

**Interpersonal Determinants of Consumer Behaviour**

Source: Adapted with permission from C. Glenn Walters and Gordon W. Paul, *Consumer Behavior: An Integrated Framework* (Homewood, IL: Irwin, 1970), p. 16. Copyright © 1970 by Richard D. Irwin, Inc.

general model of the interpersonal (or group) determinants of consumer behaviour is shown in Figure 7–6. It indicates that there are three categories of interpersonal determinants of consumer behaviour: cultural influences, social influences, and family influences. The figure also shows the involvement of personal determinants.

## Cultural Influences

Culture is the broadest environmental determinant of consumer behaviour. Sometimes it is a very elusive concept for marketers to handle. General Mills knew that few Japanese homes had ovens, so it designed a Betty Crocker cake mix that could be made in the electric rice-cookers widely used in that country. The product failed because of a cultural factor. Japanese homemakers regard the purity of their rice as very important, so they were afraid that a cake flavour might be left in their cookers.[20]

**culture** A learned way of life including values, ideas, and attitudes that influence consumer behaviour.

**Culture** can be defined as *the complex of values, ideas, attitudes, institutions, and other meaningful symbols created by people to shape human behaviour and the artifacts of that behaviour, transmitted from one generation to the next.*[21] It is the way of life learned and handed down through generations that gives each society its own peculiar characteristics and values.

### Core values in the Canadian culture

The list in Figure 7–7 provides a useful summary of characteristics significant to the Canadian culture today. There are trends and shifts in cultural values, yet tradition-

FIGURE 7-7

## Summary of Significant Canadian Characteristics

*As a function of being a part of the North American reality:*

Modern orientation

Openness to new ideas

Egalitarianism

A rich, developing society with many needs and high materialistic expectations

Growing, more diffuse "middle class"

*In relation to the United States:*

Conservative tendencies

Traditional bias

Greater confidence in bureaucratic institutions

Collectivity orientation — reliance on institutions such as state, big business, and the church as vs. personal risk-taking

Less achievement-oriented

Lower optimism — less willing to take risks

Greater acceptance of hierarchical order and stratification

Tolerance for diversity — acceptance of cultural mosaic

Family stability

Selective emulation of the United States — resistance to some American characteristics and dominance, yet willingness to emulate

Elitist and ascriptive tendencies

ally these changes have been gradual. Nevertheless, marketers must constantly assess cultural norms.[22] One of the most recent cultural trends is the search for more interpersonal relationships, rather than the self-centred orientation that characterized recent value structures. In other words, many people want greater friendship.[23] This trend has been noted by marketers, who now feature more family and friendship groups in their scenarios for commercials.

## Cultural influences: An international perspective

An awareness of cultural differences is particularly important for international marketers. Different attitudes, mores, and folkways all affect marketing strategy. Examples of cultural influences on marketing strategy are abundant in the international environment. Look at the marketing implications of the following situations:

- Because of inept translation, Schweppes Tonic Water was advertised in Italy as "bathroom water," and in South America, the Parker Pen Company unwittingly indicated that its product would prevent unwanted pregnancies.[24]
- The headline for a series of advertisements shown in Japan to introduce Seiko's new line of coloured-dial watches read as follows: "Like a Wind, I am the Colour of a Bird." To people in North America it was meaningless. But to Japanese consumers it meant something like: "This watch is light and delicate. It floats on your hand like a seedpod on the wind. Or a bird. A hummingbird with its jewel-like colours, the colours of the watch itself."[25]

- Feet are regarded as despicable in Thailand. Athlete's-foot remedies with packages featuring a picture of feet will not be well received there.[26]
- In Ethiopia the time required for a decision is directly proportional to its importance. This is so much the case that the low-level bureaucrats there attempt to elevate the prestige of their work by taking a long time to make decisions. North Americans there are innocently prone to downgrade their work in the local people's eyes by trying to speed things up.[27]

Often a marketing program that has been proven successful in Canada cannot be applied directly in international markets because of cultural differences. Real differences exist among different countries, and the differences must be known and evaluated by the international firm. When Helene Curtis introduced its Every Night shampoo line in Sweden, it renamed the product Every Day, since Swedes usually wash their hair in the morning.[28]

World marketers must become familiar with many aspects of the local population — including their cultural heritage. The local market segments in each country must be thoroughly analyzed prior to the development of a marketing plan, just as they are at home. The topic of cultural influences in international marketing is explored more fully in Chapter 19.

## Subcultures

**subculture**   A subgroup with its own distinguishing modes of behaviour.

Within each culture are numerous **subcultures** — *subgroups with their own distinguishing modes of behaviour.* Any culture as heterogeneous as that existing in Canada is composed of significant subcultures based on such factors as race, nationality, age, rural–urban location, religion, and geographic distribution. The size of such subculture groups can be very significant. For example, the Italian population in the Toronto area is about 500 000 — larger than the entire population of most Canadian cities.

Many people on the West Coast display a lifestyle emphasizing casual dress, outdoor entertaining, and water recreation. Mormons refrain from purchasing tobacco and liquor; orthodox Jews purchase kosher or other traditional foods; Chinese people may exhibit more interest in products and symbols that reflect their Chinese heritage.

*The French-Canadian market*   Although Canada has many subcultures, in fact, the two founding cultures — English and French — are the most influential, through sheer force of numbers. The francophone population is a significant market in Canada.[29] Twenty-five percent of the Canadian population identify French as their mother tongue. While most of this population resides in Quebec, there are significant French-speaking segments in other provinces. Proportionately, the largest is in New Brunswick, where 33.6 percent of the population (or 224 000) have French as their mother tongue.[30] Numerically, Ontario has the largest group, with 462 000.

The Quebec market is large enough and different enough to create an entire advertising industry of its own. Quebec constitutes about 27 percent of the total Canadian market for goods and services, and is the second-largest market in Canada.[31]

While there is no doubt that the Quebec market is substantially different from the rest of Canada, it is difficult to define those differences precisely. Considerable research over the years has pointed out many characteristics specific to the area — French-Canadians, for example, are said to be fonder of sweets than other Canadians are. However, other data can usually be found to contest any such finding, or at least to show that it is no longer true.

Such statements reflect measurement of traits in the Quebec culture at only one particular period. These measurements may be legitimate and necessary for a firm wishing to market a product in that segment at a particular point in time. However, similar differences can probably be detected between consumers in Nova Scotia and British Columbia, if you look for them.

Attention should not be concentrated on *specific* differences between the Quebec market and the rest of Canada, but rather on the fact that there is a basic cultural difference between the two markets. "Culture is a way of being, thinking and feeling. It is a driving force animating a significant group of individuals united by a common tongue, and sharing the same customs, habits and experiences."[32] Because of this cultural difference, some marketing programs may be distinctly different in Quebec than in the rest of Canada. In the French-Canadian market, it is not the products that are different, it is the state of mind.[33] For example, Renault achieved a Quebec market penetration 10 times greater than in the rest of Canada. Since the product and price were the same, the difference must have lain in the marketing program attuned to the Quebec market.

Michel Cloutier argues that many differences between the French- and English-Canadian cultures are the result of education and income.[34] As the gap between these factors narrows, and as cultures are affected by similar political and technological influences, so will the differences in values and consumption patterns narrow.

FIGURE 7-8

### Cultural Characteristics of English- and French-speaking Canadians

|  | *English-speaking* | *French-speaking* |
|---|---|---|
| Ethnic origin | Anglo-Saxon | Latin |
| Religion | Protestant | Catholic |
| Intellectual attitude | Pragmatic | Theoretical |
| Family | Matriarchy | Patriarchy |
| Leisure time | Professional class | Family circle |
| Individual vis-à-vis the environment | More social | More individualistic |
| Business management | Administrator | Innovator |
| Political tendencies | Conservative | Liberal |
| Consumption attitudes | Propensity to save; conformist; financier more than financed | Propensity to spend; innovator; financed more than financier |

Note: These cultural characteristics are very general, and there will be many variations within each culture.

Source: Georges Hénault, "Les conséquences du biculturalisme sur la consommation," *Commerce* (septembre 1971).

You've suffered in silence, the sub-comfort of their sub-compacts. Sacrificed performance in favour of the proverbial practical family sedan. In short, you've done your time. And now, you feel the need for a little good old-fashioned self-indulgence. We understand. All too well. Which is why, when it came time to totally-redesign the all new 1992 Crown Victoria, we kept one very important person in mind. You. Softer, smoother lines help shape an exterior that is positively modern. Without getting carried away. Flush-fit glass and concealed drip rails balance function and form for improved aerodynamics. And wind noise? What wind noise? Inside, a lavish interior goes out of its way to spoil not one, but six.

Speed-sensitive, variable-assist, power-steering makes handling more precise. More, responsive.

Add a standard driver's-side air-bag supplemental restraint system and available anti-lock brakes and safety goes without saying. But wait. We've saved the best for last. Under the hood, discover much to your delight, a more powerful, more fuel efficient 4.6L EFI overhead cam V-8. Alas, more power in the hands of the few. All things considered, the all new 1992 Crown Victoria can't help but leave one feeling somewhat guilty. But then again, isn't that the point?

**Consider it a reward for having survived 20 years of driving something else.**

**1992 Crown Victoria.**

*Ford* Quality is Job 1.

*Two ads for the same product: one for the Quebec market and one for the English-Canadian market. They're almost identical except for the endorsement of Jacques Duval in the French version. By including a Quebec personality in this ad, Ford hopes to appeal to the distinctive hopes and aspirations of French Canadians living in Quebec.*

Nevertheless, it appears that frames of reference and significant cues will continue to be different, requiring the marketer to be astute in dealing with these market segments. Figure 7–8 outlines some important cultural differences.

The key to success in this important Canadian market is having marketing specialists who understand people and who understand how to deal in that specific market. Sophisticated marketers now realize this. That is why there are so many Quebec advertising agencies.

## Social Influences

The earliest awareness of children confirms that they are members of a very important group — the family — from which they seek total satisfaction of their physiological and social needs. As they grow older, they join other groups — neighbourhood play groups, school groups, the Cub Scouts, Brownies, minor league hockey teams — as well as groups of friends. From these groups they acquire both status and role. **Status** refers to their *relative position in the group*. **Role** refers to the *rights and duties expected by other members of the group of the individual in a certain position in the group*. Some of these are formal groups (for example the Cub Scouts) and others are quite informal (friendship groups). But both types supply their members with status and roles and, in doing so, influence the activities, including the consumer behaviour, of each member.

**status** Relative position in a group.

**role** Rights and duties expected by other members of a group of the individual in a certain position in the group.

En récompense
pour avoir souffert
pendant 20 ans.

Vous avez souffert en silence dans le sous confort de leurs sous compactes. Sacrifié la performance en faveur du proverbial côté pratique du sedan familial. Bref, vous avez fait votre temps. Maintenant, vous sentez que vous avez besoin d'une véritable récompense. Nous vous comprenons. Voici précisément pourquoi, lorsqu'est venu le temps de redessiner la Crown Victoria 1992, nous n'avons pensé qu'à une personne. Vous. «*Silhouette élancée, lignes fluides, une carrosserie résolument moderne, sans aller trop loin. Glaces effleurantes et gouttières discrètes rallient formes et fonctions pour une meilleure aérodynamique*» — Jacques Duval, conseiller spécial. Le bruit du vent? Quel bruit de vent? L'intérieur généreux ne gâte pas qu'une personne mais six.

La direction à assistance variable suivant la vitesse rend la conduite encore plus précise, plus assidue.

Ajoutez à cela le coussin gonflable de sécurité pour le conducteur, de série, ainsi que le système de freinage antiblocage, offert en option, et le côté sécurité est complet. Mais ce n'est pas tout. Nous avons gardé le meilleur pour la fin. «*Sous le capot se cache votre élément préféré, un moteur V8 de 4,6L EFI à double arbre à came en tête plus puissant et plus économe en carburant*». Enfin, la puissance est l'apanage de certains élus. Tout bien considéré, vous vous sentirez peut-être un peu à part des autres en conduisant la nouvelle Crown Victoria 1992. Mais n'est-ce pas là le but recherché. **Crown Victoria 1992.**

**La qualité passe avant tout.**

## The Asch phenomenon: Group influence effects on conformity

Although most persons view themselves as individuals, groups are often highly influential in purchase decisions. In situations wherein individuals feel that a particular group or groups are important, they tend to adhere in varying degrees to the general expectations of that group.

The surprising *impact that groups and group norms can exhibit on individual behaviour* has been called the **Asch phenomenon**. The phenomenon was first documented in the following study conducted by the psychologist S.E. Asch:

> Eight subjects are brought into a room and asked to determine which of a set of three unequal lines is closest to the length of a fourth line shown some distance from the other three. The subjects are to announce their judgments publicly. Seven of the subjects are working for the experimenter, and they announce incorrect matches. The order of announcement is arranged such that the naive subject responds last. In a control situation, 37 naive subjects performed the task 18 times each without any information about others' choices. Two of the 37 subjects made a total of 3 mistakes. However, when another group of 50 naive subjects responded *after* hearing the unanimous but *incorrect* judgement of the other group members, 37 made a total of 194 errors, all of which were in agreement with the mistake made by the group.[35]

This widely replicated study illustrates the influence of groups on individual choice-making. Marketing applications range from the choice of automobile models

**Asch phenomenon** The impact that groups and group norms can exhibit on individual behaviour.

and residential locations to the decision to purchase at least one item at a Tupperware party.

### Reference groups

In order for groups to exert such influence on individuals, they must be categorized as **reference groups**, or groups whose *value structures and standards influence a person's behaviour*. Consumers usually try to keep their purchase behaviour in line with what they perceive to be the values of their reference group.

The status of the individual within the reference group produces three subcategories: **membership groups**, in which *the person actually belongs* (as is the case with, say, a country club); **aspirational groups**, a situation where *a person desires to associate with a group*; and **disassociative groups**, ones *with which the individual does not want to be identified by others*. For example, teenagers are unlikely to enjoy the middle-of-the-road music played on radio stations catering to their parents' generation.

It is obviously not essential that the individual be a member in order for the group to serve as a point of reference. This partly explains the use of athletes in advertisements. Even though few possess the skills necessary to pilot a racer, all racing fans can identify with the Mosport winner by injecting their engines with STP.

The extent of reference-group influence varies widely among purchases. For reference-group influence to be great, two factors must be present:

1. The item must be one that can be seen and identified by others.

2. The item must also be conspicuous in the sense that it stands out, is unusual, and is a brand or product that not everyone owns.

Figure 7–9 shows the influence of reference groups on both the basic decision to purchase a product and the decision to purchase a particular brand. The figure shows that reference groups had a significant impact on both the decision to

**reference group** A group whose value structures and standards influence a person's behaviour.

**membership group** A type of reference group to which individuals actually belong — as with, say, a country club.

**aspirational group** A type of reference group with which individuals desire to associate.

**disassociative group** A type of reference group, one with which an individual does not want to be identified by others.

---

## A·P·P·L·Y·I·N·G  T·H·E  C·O·N·C·E·P·T·S

### *The Right Words for the Right Market*

In advertising, language plays a key role. Misuse of language can be, and often is, a source of confusion and misunderstanding. Since language is more than just a sequence of words without reference to cultural context, the problem of translation is never as simple as the mere mechanical use of a dictionary. Occasionally, a literal translation may be acceptable. However, there are serious pitfalls. The following "gems" illustrate the point:

1. Car wash: Lavement d'auto (car enema).

2. Fresh milk used: Lait frais usagé (used fresh milk).

3. They are terrific: Elles sont terrifiantes (they are terrifying).

4. Big John: Gros Jos (large breast).

5. Chicken to take out: Poulet pour sortir (chicken to go out with).

The same observation applies to literal translations from French to English. Here are the literal English translations of a few extremely successful French-Canadian slogans:

1. He there knows that: Lui y connaît ça (he really knows what he's talking about)!

2. There is in it: Y en a dedans (there's a lot to it)!

3. That — that walks: Ça, ça marche (that really works)!

4. One chance out of thirteen: Une chance sur treize (thirteen to one)!

5. That's all a number: C'est tout un numéro (He's a [terrific] guy)!

Source: Eleine Saint-Jacques and Bruce Mallen, "The French Market Under the Microscope," *Marketing* (May 11, 1981), p. 14.

purchase an automobile and the type of brand that was actually selected. By contrast, reference groups had little impact on the decision to purchase canned peaches or the brand that was chosen.

## Social classes

Consumer behaviour is affected by **social class**, *the relatively permanent divisions in a society into which individuals or families are categorized based on prestige and community status.* Research by Lloyd Warner in the United States in the 1940s and by John Porter in Canada in the late 1950s identified a six-class system within the social structure of both small and large cities. Families were divided into two categories each of lower, middle, and upper classes on the basis of occupation, source of income (not amount), education, family background, and dwelling area. It was discovered that activities, interests, opinions, and buying behaviour were significantly affected by social class.

Income is not the main determinant of social-class behaviour, and the view that "a rich person is just a poor person with more money" is incorrect. Pipe-fitters paid at union scale will earn more money than many university professors, but their

**social class** The relatively permanent divisions in a society into which individuals or families are categorized based on prestige and community status.

FIGURE 7 - 9

## Extent of Reference-Group Influence on Product and Brand Decision

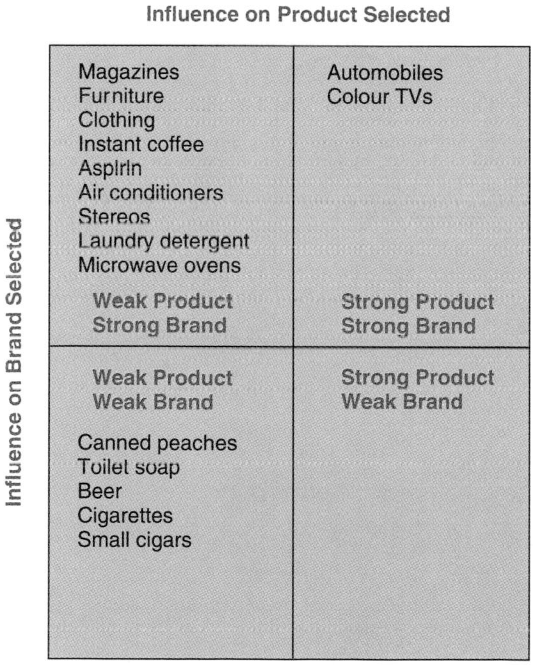

**Influence on Product Selected**

|  | | |
|---|---|---|
| *Influence on Brand Selected* | Magazines<br>Furniture<br>Clothing<br>Instant coffee<br>Aspirin<br>Air conditioners<br>Stereos<br>Laundry detergent<br>Microwave ovens<br><br>**Weak Product<br>Strong Brand** | Automobiles<br>Colour TVs<br><br><br><br><br><br><br><br>**Strong Product<br>Strong Brand** |
|  | **Weak Product<br>Weak Brand**<br><br>Canned peaches<br>Toilet soap<br>Beer<br>Cigarettes<br>Small cigars | **Strong Product<br>Weak Brand** |

Source: Reprinted from Donald W. Hendon, "A New and Empirical Look at the Influence of Reference Groups on Generic Product Category and Brand Choice: Evidence from Two Nations," *Proceedings of the Academy of International Business: Asia–Pacific Dimensions of International Business* (Honolulu: College of Business Administration, University of Hawaii, December 18–20, 1979), pp. 752–76; based on Francis S. Bourne, *Group Influence in Marketing and Public Relations* (Foundation for Research on Human Behavior, 1956), p. 8.

# A·P·P·L·Y·I·N·G  T·H·E  C·O·N·C·E·P·T·S

## Relating Social-Class Hierarchy and Lifestyles

Analysis of people's lifestyle can be a revealing thing. It can tell you where they live, how they live, where they travel, what motivates them. More important, it can tell you the kinds of things they purchase. Because it is lifestyle, not just income, that determines what a person buys!

Without knowledge of a person's lifestyle you cannot intelligently target a product or service. With that knowledge you have the means to accurately profile your consumer base. You will know where to market a new product, where to best locate a new store, where to promote with direct mail, where to spend your advertising budget wisely. In fact, you will have the answers to every important marketing question!

In order to meet marketers' needs for better information, Compusearch has developed a system that groups all the neighbourhoods in Canada into unique clusters. A total of 70 different lifestyles has been identified (48 in urban centres and 22 in rural or nonurban areas). Following is a description of the major categories and a sample target market profile. (See Figures 7–10 and 7–10a.)

Who can use these new insights?

- Direct-response advertisers can profile test mailings, target unaddressed mail, or boost name-list response.
- Publishers can profile their subscription lists, know who their readers are, and acquire more.
- Banks, credit card companies, retailers — anyone with a list of customers who buy more than one product or service — can attach the codes to each customer record, find their own areas of strength, and cross-sell products to those most likely to buy.
- Manufacturers can put their products in the right hands or test new products in the right place.
- Retailers can find the best areas to expand into, or they can better customize merchandise mix in existing locations.

Source: © "Lifestyles" is a trademark of Compusearch Market and Social Research Limited. Reprinted with the permission of Compusearch Market and Social Research Limited, 1987.

### FIGURE 7–10

**Major Categories — Lifestyles™**

| Code | Lifestyle Category | No. of Lifestyles | Percentage of All Households |
|---|---|---|---|
| | **Urban** | | |
| A | Affluent | 4 | 1.29% |
| U | Upscale | 4 | 6.95 |
| M | Middle and Upper-Middle Class | 7 | 17.68 |
| W | Working (Lower-Middle) Class | 6 | 15.34 |
| L | Lower Class | 5 | 7.01 |
| L | Young Singles | 5 | 4.25 |
| C | Young Couples | 3 | 3.46 |
| N | Empty Nesters | 5 | 8.58 |
| O | Old & Retired | 5 | 3.92 |
| E | Ethnic | 4 | 3.32 |
| | **Nonurban** | | |
| X | Upscale and Middle Class | 8 | 10.38 |
| Y | Working and Lower Class | 9 | 15.14 |
| Z | Farming | 5 | 2.70 |

purchase behaviour may be quite different. For example, the professor may be more interested in expenditures related to the arts and similar entertainment, whereas the pipe-fitter may have quite different tastes and interests in satisfying esthetic and entertainment needs.

Marketers have found that it is more meaningful to think about such differences in terms of variations in *lifestyle*. Market segmentation by lifestyle, as discussed in Chapter 4, is illustrated in the accompanying box.

## Opinion leaders

Each group usually contains a few members who can be considered **opinion leaders** or trend setters. These individuals are *more likely to purchase new products early and to serve as information sources for others in the group.*[36] Their opinions are respected, and they are often sought out for advice.

Generalized opinion leaders are rare. Individuals tend to be opinion leaders in specific areas. Their considerable knowledge about and interest in a particular product or service motivates them to seek out further information from mass media, manufacturers, and other supply sources; and, in turn, they transmit this information to their associates through interpersonal communications. Opinion leaders are found within all segments of the population.

**opinion leaders** Trend setters; individuals who are more likely to purchase new products early and to serve as information sources for others in a given group.

---

**FIGURE 7–10A**

**Elaboration of Two Lifestyle Categories in One Market Segment**

| | Lifestyle Descriptor | | # Clients | % Clients |
|---|---|---|---|---|
| **A F F L U E N T** | A1 | Wealthiest, highest education, large families in very expensive houses, age 45–54 | 2 539 | 1.03% |
| | A2 | Wealthy, well-educated families in expensive houses, age 45–64 | 6 732 | 2.73% |
| | A3 | Older, wealthy, well-educated couples and widow(er)s in apartments and condominiums | 1 388 | 0.56% |
| | A4 | Younger, wealthy, well-educated, larger families with young teenagers in high-value houses | 3 651 | 1.48% |
| | Total: | Affluent | 14 310 | 5.80% |
| **U P S C A L E** | U1 | High-income, older families with teenagers in higher-value houses; stable neighbourhoods | 12 665 | 5.13% |
| | U2 | High-income, very well-educated, small mixed and older households in old, expensive mixed housing | 7 648 | 3.10% |
| | U3 | Younger professional families with young children in new houses; both spouses work | 12 797 | 5.18% |
| | U4 | Middle-aged to older families with older children in modest housing | 11 741 | 4.76% |
| | Total: | Upscale | 44 851 | 18.17% |

### Applying the opinion leadership concept

Opinion leaders play a crucial role in interpersonal communication. The fact that they distribute information and advice to others indicates their potential importance to marketing strategy. Opinion leaders can be particularly useful in the launching of new products.

General Motors once provided a popular small car to college marketing classes as a basis for a course project. Rock stations have painted teenagers' cars for them. Of course, the paint job includes the stations' call letters and slogans. Politicians sometimes hold issues forums for community leaders. All these efforts are directed at the opinion leaders in a particular marketplace. These people play an important role in how successfully a new or established product, idea, or political candidacy is communicated to consumers.

## Family Influences

The family is an important interpersonal determinant of consumer behaviour. The close, continuing interactions among family members are the strongest group influences for the individual consumer.

Most people in our society are members of two families during their lifetime: the family into which they are born, and the family they eventually form as they marry and have children. With divorce an increasingly common phenomenon, many people become involved with three or more families.

The establishment of a new household upon marriage produces marketing opportunities. A new household means a new home and accompanying furniture. The need for refrigerators, vacuum cleaners, and an original oil painting for the living room depends not on the number of persons in each household but on the number of *households* themselves.

As children are added to the household, sizes of products purchased naturally increase. Two litres of milk will be purchased instead of one. Some larger families will purchase larger vehicles. Many other child-related purchases will be made over the period of time the youngsters remain in the home. Marketers find many opportunities in this market segment. For example, Chrysler achieved great success with its Magic Wagon, a vehicle with ample capacity for families that nevertheless handled as easily as a car.

Another market evolves as parents are left alone when the children move away from home. These parents may find themselves with a four-bedroom "empty nest" and a sizeable lawn to maintain each week. Lacking assistance from their children and no longer needing the extra space, they become customers for town houses, condominiums, and high-rise luxury apartments in the larger cities. This market segment also eventually purchases bifocals, and is a good target for organized tour packages.

### Marital roles in purchase decisions

Although an infinite variety of roles are played in household decision-making, four role categories are often used: (1) *autonomic* — situations in which an equal number of decisions is made by each partner, but each decision is made individually by one partner or the other; (2) *male-dominant*; (3) *female-dominant*; and (4) *syncratic* — situations in which decisions are made jointly by male and female.[37] Figure 7–11 shows the roles commonly played by household members in the purchase of a number of products.

*This Canadian Tire TV ad appeals to the family market. A father surprises his son with a brand new bicycle after the boy has longingly eyed it in a Canadian Tire store. By showing the happy resolution to a situation parents often find themselves in with their children, Canadian Tire implies that its products help bring families closer together.*

## Changing family roles

Two forces have changed the female's role as sole purchasing agent for most household items. First, a shorter work week provides each wage-earning household member with more time for shopping. Second, a large number of women are now in the work force. In 1950, only about a quarter of married women were also employed outside the home; by 1981 that figure had doubled. Currently, over half of all married women with school-age children hold jobs outside the home. Studies of family decision-making have shown that wives who work outside the home tend to exert more influence than wives who work in the home only. Households with two wage earners also exhibit a larger number of joint decisions and an increase in night and weekend shopping.

These changing roles of household members have led many marketers to adjust their marketing programs. Men's clothing stores, such as Stollery's in Toronto, now offer suits and accessories for the career woman. Although demand for men's suits has been sluggish in recent years, sales of women's suits increased 70 percent in 1980. Meanwhile a survey of 1000 married men revealed that 77 percent participate in grocery shopping and 70 percent cook. A Del Monte promotional campaign recognized these changes and de-emphasized women as the sole meal preparer. Its theme, "Good things happen when you bring Del Monte home," is applicable to both male and female food shoppers.[38]

### Children's roles in household purchasing

The role of the children evolves as they grow older. Their early influence is generally centred on toys to be recommended to Santa Claus and the choice of brands of cereals. Younger children are important to marketers of fast-food restaurants. Even

F I G U R E   7 – 1 1

**Marital Roles in 25 Decisions**

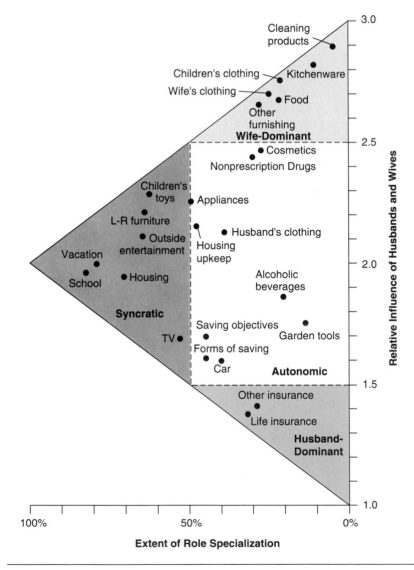

Source: Harry L. Davis and Benny P. Rigaux, "Perception of Marital Roles in Decision Processes," *Journal of Consumer Research* (June 1974), p. 57. Reprinted by permission from the *Journal of Consumer Research*, published by the Journal of Consumer Research, Inc.

*The influence of children should not be underestimated where clothing purchases are concerned. At a recent kids' fashion show in Toronto called "Dress the Dinosaur," three girls sport the latest fashions from "Peas in a Pod." Such events stimulate interest on the part of children as well as parents, and illustrate an increased awareness of children's role in purchasing decisions.*

though the parents may decide when to eat out, the children often select the restaurant.[39] As they gain maturity, they increasingly influence their clothing purchases.

One study revealed that thirteen- to fifteen-year-old teenage boys spend most of their money on food, snacks, movies, and entertainment. Girls in this same age group buy clothing, food and snacks, tickets for movies and entertainment, and cosmetics and fragrances. Sixteen- to nineteen-year-old boys spend most of their money on entertainment, dating, movies, automobiles and gasoline, clothing, food, and snacks, while girls of the same age buy clothing, cosmetics, fragrances, automobiles and gasoline, and movie and entertainment tickets.[40]

## The Consumer Decision Process

This chapter has shown that consumer behavior is the result of two main types of influences: personal determinants and interpersonal determinants. The purchase of all goods and services will be affected by some or all of the many variables discussed.

In the light of all this information, researchers have spent considerable effort trying to identify the process that a consumer goes through in making a purchase decision. One commonly accepted hypothesis suggests that the consumer decision process consists of six stages: problem recognition, search, evaluation of alternatives, the purchase decision, the purchase act, and postpurchase evaluation. Figure 7–12 illustrates a model of the process. Each step of the model is covered in the discussion that follows.

## Problem Recognition

This first stage in the decision process occurs when the consumer becomes aware of a discrepancy of sufficient magnitude between the existing state of affairs and a desired state of affairs. Once the problem has been recognized, it must be defined in order that the consumer may seek out methods for its solution. Having recognized the problem, the individual is motivated to achieve the desired state.

What sort of problems might a person recognize? Perhaps the most common is a routine depletion of the stock of products. A large number of consumer purchases involve the replenishment of items ranging from gasoline to groceries. In other instances, the consumer may possess an inadequate assortment of products. The individual whose hobby is gardening may make regular purchases of different kinds of fertilizers, seeds, or gardening tools as the size of the garden grows.

FIGURE 7–12

**Steps in the Consumer Decision Process**

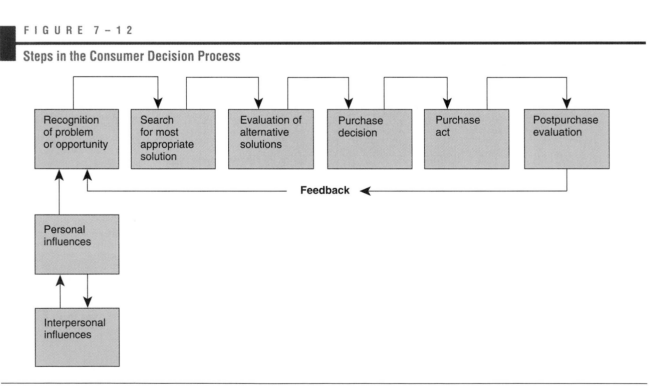

Source: Adapted from C. Glenn Walters and Gordon W. Paul, *Consumer Behavior: An Integrated Framework* (Homewood, IL: Irwin, 1970). p. 18 [© 1970 by Richard D. Irwin, Inc.] and John Dewey, *How We Think* (Boston: D.C. Heath, 1910), pp. 101–105; similar steps are also discussed in Del I. Hawkins, Roger J. Best, and Kenneth A. Coney, *Consumer Behavior: Implications for Marketing Strategy*, revised ed. (Plano, TX: Business Publications, 1983), pp. 447–606.

A consumer may also be dissatisfied with a present brand or product type. This situation is a common factor in the purchase of a new automobile, new furniture, or a new fall wardrobe. In many instances, boredom with current products and a desire for novelty may be the underlying rationale for the decision process leading to new-product purchases.

Another important factor is changed financial status. The infusion of added financial resources from such sources as a salary increase, a second job, or an inheritance may permit the consumer to recognize desires and make purchases that previously had been postponed due to their cost.[41]

## Search

Search, the second stage in the decision process, is the gathering of information related to the attainment of a desired state of affairs. This stage involves identifying alternative means of solving the problem.

*Internal search* is a mental review of the information that a person already knows relevant to the problem situation. This includes actual experiences and observations plus remembered reading or conversations and exposures to various persuasive marketing efforts.

*External search* is the gathering of information from outside sources. These may include family members, friends and associates, store displays, sales representatives, brochures, and such product-testing publications as *Canadian Consumer*.

In many instances, the consumer does not go beyond internal search but merely relies on stored information in making a purchase decision. Achieving a favourable experience flying with Canadian Airlines may sufficiently motivate a consumer to repurchase a ticket from Canadian rather than consider possible alternatives. Since external search involves both time and effort, the consumer will rely on it only in instances in which, for some reason, the information remembered is inadequate.

The search process will identify alternative brands for consideration and possible purchase. *The number of brands that a consumer actually considers in making a purchase decision* is known as the **evoked set**. In some instances, the consumer will already be aware of the brands worthy of further consideration; in others the external search process will permit the consumer to identify those brands. Not all brands will be included in the evoked set. The consumer may remain unaware of certain brands, and others will be rejected as too costly or as having been tried previously and considered unsatisfactory. In other instances, unfavourable word-of-mouth communication or negative reactions to advertising or other marketing efforts will lead to the elimination of some brands from the evoked set. While the number of brands in the evoked set will vary by product categories, research indicates that the number is likely to be as few as four or five brands.[42]

**evoked set**    The number of brands that a consumer actually considers in making a purchase decision.

## Evaluation of Alternatives

The third step in the consumer decision process involves the evaluation of alternatives identified during the search process. Actually, it is difficult to completely separate the second and third steps, since some evaluation takes place simultaneously with the search process as consumers accept, discount, distort, or reject some incoming information as they receive it.

Since the outcome of the evaluation stage is the choice of a brand or product in the evoked set (or, possibly, the search for additional alternatives, should all those identified during the search process prove unsatisfactory), the consumer must develop a set of **evaluative criteria**, *features the consumer considers in making a choice among alternatives*. These criteria can either be *objective* (federal government automobile fuel consumption tests in litres per 100 kilometres, or comparison of retail prices) or *subjective* (favourable image of Calvin Klein sportswear). Commonly used evaluative criteria include price, the reputation of the brand, perceived quality, packaging, size, performance, durability, and colour. Most research studies indicate that consumers seldom use more than six criteria in the evaluation process. Evaluative criteria for detergents include suds level and smell as indicators of cleaning power. High quality and potential for long wear were the underlying criteria in the choice of nylon stockings, according to one research study.[43]

## The Purchase Decision and the Purchase Act

When the consumer has evaluated each of the alternatives in the evoked set, using his or her personal set of evaluative criteria, and narrowed the alternatives to one, the result is the purchase decision and the act of making the purchase.

The consumer must decide not only to purchase a product but also where to buy it. Consumers tend to choose the purchase location by considering such factors as ease of access, prices, assortment, store personnel, store image, physical design, and services provided. The product category will also influence the store selected. Some consumers will choose the convenience of in-home shopping by telephone or mail order rather than complete the transaction in a retail store.[44]

## Postpurchase Evaluation

The purchase act results in the removal of the discrepancy between the existing state and the desired state. Logically, it should result in satisfaction to the buyer. However, even in many purchase decisions where the buyer is ultimately satisfied, it is common for that person to experience some initial postpurchase anxieties. He or she often wonders if the right decision has been made. Leon Festinger refers to this postpurchase doubt as **cognitive dissonance**.[45]

Cognitive dissonance is a psychologically unpleasant state that occurs after a purchase *when there exists a discrepancy among a person's knowledge and beliefs (cognitions)* about certain attributes of the final products under consideration. This occurs because several of the final product-choice candidates have desirable characteristics, making the final decision difficult. Consumers may, for example, experience dissonance after choosing a particular automobile over several alternative models, when one or more of the rejected models have some desired features that the purchased automobile lacks.

Dissonance is likely to increase (1) as the dollar value of the purchase increases, (2) when the rejected alternatives have desirable features not present in the chosen alternative, and (3) when the decision is a major one. The consumer may attempt to reduce dissonance in a variety of ways. He or she may seek out advertisements and other information supporting the chosen alternative or seek reassurance from acquaintances who are satisfied purchasers of the product. At the same time the individual will avoid information favouring unchosen alternatives. The Toyota purchaser is more likely to read Toyota advertisements and to avoid Honda and Ford ads. The cigarette smoker may ignore magazine articles reporting links between smoking and cancer.

Marketers should try to reduce cognitive dissonance by providing informational support for the chosen alternative. Automobile dealers recognize "buyer's remorse" and often follow up purchases with a warm letter from the president of the dealership, offering personal handling of any customer problems and including a description of the quality of the product and the availability of convenient, top-quality service.

The consumer may ultimately deal with cognitive dissonance by changing opinions, deciding that one of the rejected alternatives would have been the best choice, and forming the intention of purchasing it in the future.[46]

Should the purchase prove unsatisfactory, the consumer will revise purchase strategy to obtain need satisfaction. Feedback from the results of the decision process, whether satisfactory or not, will be called upon in the search and evaluation stages of similar buying situations.

## Classifying Consumer Problem-Solving Processes

The consumer decision process depends on the type of problem-solving effort required. Problem-solving behaviour has been divided into three categories: routinized response, limited problem-solving, and extended problem-solving.[47]

*Routinized response* Many purchases are made as a routine response to a need. The selection is a preferred brand or is made from a limited group of acceptable brands. The consumer has set the evaluative criteria and identified the available options. The routine purchase of a particular newspaper or regular brands of soft drinks or toilet soap would be examples.

*Limited problem-solving* Consider the situation in which the consumer has set evaluative criteria but encounters a new, unknown brand. The introduction of a new fragrance line might create a situation calling for limited problem-solving. The consumer knows the evaluative criteria but has not assessed the new brand on the basis of these criteria. A certain amount of time and external search will be required. Limited problem-solving is affected by the multitude of evaluative criteria and brands, the extent of external search, and the process by which preferences are determined. Some products — those with little significance, either materially or emotionally — a consumer may purchase first and evaluate later (while using them). These are known as **low-involvement products**.

*Extended problem-solving* Extended problem-solving occurs with important purchase decisions when evaluative criteria have not been established for a product category or when the individual wishes to review such criteria. Today many individuals are in the process of purchasing personal computers. Since most have never owned one before, they generally engage in an extensive search process. The main aspect of this process is the determination of appropriate evaluative criteria that are relevant to the needs of the decision-maker. How much computing power is required? Is portability important? What will be the machine's main uses? What special features are required? As the criteria are being set, an evoked set of brands is also established. Most extended problem-solving efforts are lengthy, involving considerable external search. *Products for which the purchaser is highly involved in making the purchase decision* are known as **high-involvement products**.

**low-involvement products**
Products with little significance, either materially or emotionally, which a consumer may purchase first and evaluate later (while using them).

**high-involvement products**
Products for which the purchaser is highly involved in making the purchase decision.

Regardless of the type of problem-solving, the steps in the basic model of the consumer decision process remain valid, except in the case of low-involvement products. The problem-solving categories described here relate only to the time and effort that is devoted to each step in the process.

# Summary

Consumer behaviour refers to the way people select, obtain, and use goods and services. Both personal and interpersonal factors determine patterns of consumer behaviour.

The personal determinants of consumer behaviour have been identified as needs, motives, perception, attitudes, and learning.

A need is the lack of something useful, while motives are the inner states that direct individuals to satisfy such needs. Maslow proposed a need classification structure that starts with basic physiological needs and proceeds to progressively higher levels of needs — safety, social, esteem, and self-actualization needs, respectively.

Perception is the meaning that people assign to incoming stimuli received through the five senses. Most stimuli are screened or filtered out; the marketer must break through these perceptual screens to present the message.

Attitudes are a person's evaluations and feelings toward an object or idea. An attitude has three components: cognitive (what the person knows), affective (what the person feels), and behavioural (how the person tends to act). Attitude change may be effected by changing one of the components of the attitude one wishes to influence.

Learning refers to changes in behaviour, immediate or expected, as a result of experience. The learning theory concept can be useful in building a consumer franchise before launching a particular brand.

There are three interpersonal determinants of consumer behaviour: cultural influences, social influences, and family influences. Culture — behavioural values that are created and inherited by a society — is the broadest of these three. Cultural norms can change over time, although traditionally the pace of change is slow.

Social influences are described as the nonfamily group influences on consumer behaviour. The role that groups play in individual decision-making can be very powerful. If a group's values or standards influence an individual's behaviour, the group may be called a reference group for that person. The importance of reference groups in specific product and brand decisions varies.

Social class and related lifestyles also influence consumer behaviour. Furthermore, the reaction of opinion leaders or trend setters to new products is highly influential in the future success of the good or service. Marketers can sometimes make special efforts to appeal to these bellwethers of consumer behaviour.

Family influences are the third major interpersonal determinant of consumer behaviour. Family purchasing patterns vary. In some cases, the female is dominant; in others, the male. Some purchase decisions are made jointly.

The consumer decision process consists of six stages: problem recognition, search, evaluation of alternatives, the purchase decision, the purchase act, and postpurchase evaluation. Various types of problem-solving effort may be involved in the decision process — routinized response, limited problem-solving, and extended problem-solving. In the case of low-involvement products, the prepurchase problem-solving process is skipped. Because the purchase is not very significant to the buyer, the product is evaluated after it is purchased.

## KEY TERMS

consumer behaviour
need
motive
perception
perceptual screen
Weber's Law
subliminal perception
attitudes
learning
drive

cue
response
reinforcement
shaping
culture
subculture
role
status
Asch phenomenon
reference group

membership group
aspirational group
disassociative group
social class
opinion leader
evoked set
evaluative criteria
cognitive dissonance
low-involvement product
high involvement product

## REVIEW QUESTIONS

1. What are the personal determinants of consumer behaviour?
2. Explain the concept of perception. Consider perceptual screens, selective perception, Weber's Law, and subliminal perception in your explanation.
3. How do attitudes influence consumer behaviour? How can negative attitudes be changed?
4. Explain the interpersonal determinants of consumer behaviour.
5. Describe the Asch phenomenon.

6. Why are reference groups important in the study of consumer behaviour?
7. Why are opinion leaders important to marketers?
8. Describe family influences on consumer behaviour and how they are changing.
9. List the steps in the consumer decision process.
10. Differentiate among routinized response behaviour, limited problem-solving, and extended problem-solving.

## DISCUSSION QUESTIONS AND EXERCISES

1. Using Maslow's classification system, state which needs are being referred to in the following advertising slogans:
   • No caffeine. Never had it. Never will. (7-Up)
   • Swedish engineering. Depend on it. (SAAB)
   • A blending of art and machine. (Jaguar)
   • The best bed a body can buy. (Simmons)
   • Don't leave home without it. (American Express Card)
2. For which of the following products is reference-group influence likely to be strong?
   a. Rolex watch
   b. Skis
   c. Shaving foam
   d. 10-speed bicycle

   e. Portable radio
   f. Personal computer
   g. Electric blanket
   h. Contact lenses
3. Find examples of shaping procedures being used in marketing applications.
4. Identify the opinion leaders in a group to which you belong. Why are these people the group's opinion leaders?
5. Relate a recent purchase you made to the consumer decision process shown in Figure 7–12.
6. For a recent shopping experience, analyze your attitudes as related to your consumer behaviour. Be sure your assessment considers all three components of an attitude.

# MICROCOMPUTER EXERCISE

## Evaluation of Alternatives

Consumers develop various methods for making purchase choices from alternative products or brands. For major purchases and cases where considerable risk is present, potential buyers may score or rank the brands that constitute their evoked set on the basis of various evaluative criteria. Then the question becomes how to best make the actual purchase decision. Approaches to this problem include (1) the overall-scoring method, (2) the weighted-scoring method, and (3) the minimum-score method.

- *Overall-Scoring Method.* This approach to ranking alternative purchase possibilities uses the highest total score to select a brand from among the evoked set. All the evaluative criteria are considered to be of equal importance, and the brand with the highest overall score is chosen.
- *Weighted-Scoring Method.* The second approach involves assigning different weights to the various evaluation criteria according to the consumer's perception of their relative importance. Once the variables are assigned their weighted scores, they are totalled, and the brand with the highest score is selected.
- *Minimum-Score Method.* This approach sets a floor for one or more of the evaluative criteria below which a brand will not be selected. For example, should the consumer decide that a brand must receive a ranking of 4 or more on "service availability," a brand ranked 3 for this criterion would be rejected, even though it might receive the highest overall score. The minimum-score method is frequently used in conjunction with either the overall-scoring method or the weighted-scoring method.

It should be noted that these methods are representative of quantitative approaches to a typically qualitatively oriented subject. Not all consumers behave in such a fashion. Moreover, those who do may differ significantly in their scoring evaluations. The problems that follow refer to a specific situation in which the individual has already determined the evaluative criteria and the evoked set.

**Directions:** Use the Menu Item titled "Evaluation of Alternatives" on the *Foundations of Marketing* disk to solve the following problems.

1. A Hamilton consumer is considering four brands of washing machine (the evoked set). The consumer has decided to evaluate the brands on the bases of price, quality, warranty, and service availability (the evaluative criteria). The consumer has also decided to give each model a score of 1 (poor) to 5 (best) on each of the evaluative criteria. These scores are shown in Table A.

   a. Which model would the consumer select if he or she were using the overall-scoring method?

   b. Suppose the consumer considers price 50 percent more important than any of the other evaluative criteria. Which model would be selected?

   c. Suppose the consumer, using the overall-scoring method, also decides that any model that scores lower than 3 on any variable is not acceptable. Which model would be selected?

   d. Would your response to Question C change if the consumer used the weighted-scoring method?

## TABLE A

## A Consumer Evaluation of Washing Machines

| Evoked Set | Evaluative Criteria: Decision Factors | | | |
|---|---|---|---|---|
| | *(A)* | *(B)* | *(C)* | *(D)* Service |
| *Alternatives* | *Price* | *Quality* | *Warranty* | *Availability* |
| 1. Washmaster | 4 | 3 | 4 | 4 |
| 2. Magic Washer | 4 | 4 | 4 | 4 |
| 3. Wonder Machine | 2 | 5 | 5 | 2 |
| 4. The Marvel | 5 | 5 | 4 | 2 |

2. Pierre Rousseau, of Saint John, N.B., is attempting to select a new car based on the following criteria: price, trade-in allowance, styling, riding comfort, and fuel economy. Rousseau had earlier narrowed his decision to four models: the Elegance, the Standard, the Speedo, and the Majestic. He then decided to rate each model on each of the specified evaluative criteria. Rousseau used a 3 to represent "excellent," 2 for "good," and 1 for "fair." His rankings are shown in Table B.

## TABLE B

## A Consumer Evaluation of Cars: Example 1

| Evoked Set | Evaluative Criteria: Decision Factors | | | | |
|---|---|---|---|---|---|
| | *(A)* | *(B)* Trade-in | *(C)* | *(D)* Riding | *(E)* Fuel |
| *Alternatives* | *Price* | *Allowance* | *Styling* | *Comfort* | *Economy* |
| 1. Elegance | 2 | 2 | 3 | 3 | 2 |
| 2. Standard | 2 | 2 | 2 | 2 | 3 |
| 3. Speedo | 3 | 3 | 3 | 3 | 1 |
| 4. Majestic | 3 | 3 | 1 | 1 | 3 |

a. Which model would Rousseau select if he were using the overall-scoring method?

b. Suppose Rousseau considered fuel economy, price, and trade-in allowance each 50 percent more important than the other two evaluative criteria. Which model would he select?

c. Suppose Rousseau, while using the overall-scoring method, also decided not to accept any model that he rated lower than "good" on fuel economy, price, and trade-in allowance. Which model would he prefer?

d. Would Rousseau's decision in Question C change if he decided to use the weighted-scoring method?

3. Like Pierre Rousseau in Problem 2, Judy Krantz is also contemplating the purchase of a new car. In fact, she and Rousseau conferred before assigning the ratings for the Elegance, Standard, Speedo, and Majestic. However, Krantz also

considers another auto model, the Olympic, to be a viable option. Her rankings are shown in Table C.

### TABLE C

**A Consumer Evaluation of Cars: Example 2**

| Evoked Set | Evaluative Criteria: Decision Factors | | | | |
|---|---|---|---|---|---|
| | *(A)* | *(B)* Trade-in | *(C)* | *(D)* Riding | *(E)* Fuel |
| *Alternatives* | *Price* | *Allowance* | *Styling* | *Comfort* | *Economy* |
| 1. Elegance | 2 | 2 | 3 | 3 | 2 |
| 2. Standard | 2 | 2 | 2 | 2 | 3 |
| 3. Speedo | 3 | 3 | 3 | 3 | 1 |
| 4. Majestic | 3 | 3 | 1 | 1 | 3 |
| 5. Olympic | 3 | 2 | 2 | 2 | 2 |

a. Which model would Krantz select if she were using the overall-scoring method?

b. Suppose Krantz considered riding comfort and fuel economy 100 percent more important than styling and price, and trade-in allowance 200 percent more important than styling. Which model would she select?

c. Suppose Krantz, while using the overall-scoring method, also decided not to accept a car that she rated lower than "good" on any variable. Which model would she select?

d. Would Krantz's decision in Question C change if she decided to use the weighted-scoring method?

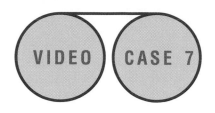

# Kawasaki Motors Corp.

Kawasaki Motors Corp., U.S.A., is a wholly owned subsidiary of Japan's Kawasaki Heavy Industries Ltd. and sells about $375 million worth of motorcycles annually in the United States. Kawasaki offers these consumers two types of motorcycles — sports models and custom models — each of which appeals to a different group of buyers.

Kawasaki asked its advertising agency, Kenyon & Eckhardt, to develop a print advertisement that would appeal to buyers of both sports and custom models without alienating either group. The firm needed an advertisement that would stand out from the 2400 ads that consumers are exposed to each week, and that would break through the clutter that characterizes contemporary advertising.

To accomplish these objectives, Peter Goodwin, the account supervisor for Kawasaki, asked Renee Fraser, a psychologist and the agency's research director, to gather information about motorcycle owners to find out why they buy what they do. The agency's creative people — artists and copywriters — needed this information to create an advertisement that satisfied the needs of motorcycle buyers. The advertisement had to influence the purchase decisions of new buyers and also reassure current owners that they had made the right choice. This latter goal is known as alleviating cognitive dissonance, the post-purchase doubt that accompanies any major purchase.

Fraser understood the importance of her task. She remarked, "To make persuasive advertising we have to really understand what motivates the consumer." Fraser began by checking some databases to learn about the people who buy motorcycles. This secondary research produced considerable demographic statistics such as income, age, and so forth. But Fraser realized that this information was useless because it did not tell her what really motivated people to buy motorcycles.

As a result, Fraser decided to gather some primary data by using focus groups, personal in-depth interviews, and field research. In speaking to motorcycle owners, Fraser learned that the motorcycle-buying audience comprises a wide range of people from many social classes — blue-collar workers, professionals (doctors, engineers, lawyers), and even movie stars. Owners are much more diverse than the stereotypical motorcycle rider.

The motorcycle owners interviewed shared many common traits: cycling gave them a sense of power, a sense of being in control, and a feeling of independence and freedom (which are core values discussed in the interpersonal determinants section of Chapter 7). They liked being outside, feeling the wind on their faces, and enjoyed the thrill and speed of riding, as well as being able to control the risk and dangers involved. Owning and riding a motorcycle was important in their self-concept and in satisfying esteem needs. One of the people that Fraser interviewed expressed the feeling this way: "I sort of feel like a pioneer." Fraser herself commented "it was almost as if there was a relationship between them and the bike; it was their thing."

In later meetings with other Kenyon & Eckhardt personnel, Fraser noted that motorcycle riders "want to demonstrate to other people what they really are....It's almost like they take off their clothes and they are Superman underneath." The research director continued, "One of the fantasies these men have about themselves on the bike is that they are the lone cowboy....They identify very strongly with that image of themselves."

The Kenyon & Eckhardt staff decided that motorcycle riders in general are not concerned so much with vehicle performance as with the way the motorcycle looks and the way it makes them look. The challenge was to come up with a print advertisement that would appeal to this image and break through the advertising clutter discussed earlier.

The agency's art department eventually designed a print advertisement showing a lone rider rounding a bend, with the bike leaning to the side and the rider's knee almost touching the ground. The rider's position had been suggested several times by the people Fraser interviewed. The Kawasaki advertisement captures the thrill of riding — the wind, the speed, the danger. It depicts the self-image of cyclists, projecting a positive relationship between the product and the buyer. Both types of cyclists — those who ride sports bikes and those who ride custom models — can see themselves in this ad.

## Questions

1. Which categories of the personal and interpersonal determinants of consumer behaviour influence a person's decision to purchase a motorcycle?
2. Use this video case to explain the relationship between marketing research and the study of consumer behaviour.
3. Discuss how you would respond to the Kawasaki print ad.

## CHAPTER 8

# Industrial Buyer Behaviour

1. To provide an overview of the industrial buying process.
2. To differentiate among the three types of industrial markets.
3. To identify the three distinctive features of industrial markets.
4. To explain the characteristics of industrial market demand.
5. To identify the basic categories of industrial products.
6. To show the nature and importance of government markets.

MICRONAV, a Cape Breton–based company, knows all the clients it could possibly sell to. Such a situation might seem surprising from the perspective of a firm selling to the consumer market, but it is not especially unusual for the industrial market.

Marketing to industrial buyers often requires a special understanding of how they buy and what motivates them. Micronav has been very successful in meeting the needs of its market. Founded in 1981, the firm has gone from installing a prototype unit at the Sydney (N.S.) airport to winning a 12-year contract, worth between $35 million and $50 million, that involves installing Micronav's state-of-the art landing systems at 40 airports across the country. Further contracts involving another 105 airports are expected to yield up to $300 million.

But that's just the tip of the iceberg. The International Civil Aviation Organization, the United Nations' aviation body, has said that the world's airports must convert to microwave airfield landing system (MLS) technology by 1998. "The potential for the export market is great," says David Underwood, the company's director of marketing; he estimates that Micronav stands a good chance of getting a share of the $6 billion market over the next decade.

In marketing its product, the company has spent a great deal of energy making sure that when transportation experts in this specialized market around the world think about microwave landing systems, their next thought is Micronav. Normal mass advertising is not considered necessary, because a few specialists in each country make the decisions about the systems their country's airports will use. It is possible to send a mailing to all the people who would be interested.

"We are dealing with a very closely knit world community," Underwood says. "A world body sets the standards for equipment, so our marketing is always directed toward the key people in the industry. We often speak to the one individual who is responsible for making decisions for every civil airport in a given country."

Keeping in touch with such a small group is not difficult, but the company ensures that all potential clients stay informed with new information releases about their programs. The selling that the staff does consists of demonstrating that Micronav's equipment is well designed and highly reliable and that it should be the equipment the clients select to fill their needs.

Because there are only three companies involved in MLS production worldwide, Micronav knows competitive products and marketing activities very well. Marketing Micronav's systems often means sending staff to aviation trade shows such as the Paris Air Show. Underwood believes that this provides a good chance to "come face to face with the individuals who make the decisions."

If Micronav has its way, it will be *the* international firm that civil airports around the world will call on to get planes out of the sky and onto the runway in any type of weather.[1]

## Introduction

The marketing activities of a company that, like Micronav, operates in the industrial market are obviously quite different from those of a consumer product company such as Levi Strauss. Many companies have found that marketing practices that have proven successful in one will not necessarily produce success in the other.

The consumer market consists of individuals who purchase goods and services for *personal* use. The **industrial market** consists of *individuals and organizations who acquire goods and services to be used, directly or indirectly, in the production of other goods and services or to be resold*.

**industrial market**  Individuals and organizations who acquire goods and services to be used, directly or indirectly, in the production of other goods and services or to be resold.

Although industrial marketers face decisions very similar to those of their consumer market counterparts, important differences exist in the characteristics of target markets and in the development of an appropriate marketing mix. As James D. Hlavacek has noted, "Overall, the strategic and tactical emphasis and elements in the industrial and consumer marketing mixes are as different as silicon chips and potato chips."[2]

## Types of Industrial Markets

The industrial market can be divided into three categories: producers, trade industries (wholesalers and retailers), and governments. **Producers** are *those who transform goods and services through production into other goods and services*. Producers include manufacturing firms, farmers and other resource industries, construction contractors, and providers of services (such as transportation, public utilities, and banks). In

**producers**  Those who transform goods and services through production into other goods and services.

*It is a common misconception that the industrial market is limited to factories and manufacturing firms. In fact, anyone who takes raw materials or services and transforms them into other goods or services is part of the industrial market. This apple farmer is part of the industrial market, since he takes apple seeds, fertilizer, and other materials and produces apples for resale and use in other products.*

the production process, some products aid in producing another product or service (for example, an airplane provides transportation); others are physically used up in the production of a product (wheat becomes part of cereal); and still others are routinely used in the day-to-day operations of a firm (light bulbs and cleaning materials are maintenance items).

**Trade industries** are *organizations, such as retailers and wholesalers, that purchase for resale to others*. In most instances, resale products (for example, clothing, appliances, sports equipment, and automobile parts) are finished goods that are marketed to customers. In other instances, some processing or repackaging may take place. Retail meat markets may make bulk purchases of sides of beef and convert them into individual cuts for their customers. Lumber dealers and carpet retailers may purchase in bulk, then provide quantities and sizes to meet customers' specifications. In addition to resale products, trade industries also buy cash registers, computers, display equipment, and other products required to operate their business. These products (as well as maintenance items and the purchase of such specialized services as marketing research studies, accounting services, and consulting) all represent industrial purchases. Retailing and wholesaling activities are discussed in separate chapters later in the text.

**trade industries**
Organizations, such as retailers and wholesalers, that purchase for resale to others.

**Governments** at the federal, provincial, and local level represent the final category of industrial purchasers. This important component of the industrial market purchases a wide variety of products, ranging from highways to education to F–16 fighter aircraft. The primary motivation of government purchasing is to provide some form of public benefit such as national defence, education, or health services. Buying behaviour in government markets is discussed separately in this chapter because of its immense size and importance.

## Scope of the Industrial Market

The industrial market is vast. As Figure 8–1 shows. In the manufacturing sector alone there are nearly 38 000 establishments, and they employ more than 1.8 million people. The significance of this market is dramatized in the amount of materials and supplies used in their operations — over $143 billion worth! In total, the industrial market accounts for some 50 percent of purchases of manufactured goods in Canada.

**value added**   The increase in value of input material when transformed into semi-finished or finished goods.

One measure of industrial output is the **value added** by manufacturing: *the increase in value of input material when transformed into semi-finished or finished goods.* For example, value is added to a tonne of iron ore when it is made into steel plate, and

FIGURE 8 – 1

**Summary of Manufacturers by Province, 1986**

| Province | Number of Establishments | Total Employees | Materials and Supplies Used | Total Value Added |
|---|---|---|---|---|
| | | | ($000s) | ($000s) |
| *All Canada | 38 380 | 1 808 716 | 143 366 148 | 107 581 862 |
| Newfoundland | 322 | 17 274 | 1 423 726 | 680 400 |
| Prince Edward Island | 141 | 3 418 | 208 867 | 116 540 |
| Nova Scotia | 815 | 35 686 | 2 573 371 | 1 951 311 |
| New Brunswick | 703 | 31 805 | 3 091 864 | 1 586 698 |
| Quebec | 11 603 | 503 403 | 32 776 805 | 27 054 822 |
| Ontario | 16 140 | 934 918 | 78 999 904 | 58 420 761 |
| Manitoba | 1 282 | 52 840 | 3 097 124 | 2 547 254 |
| Saskatchewan | 847 | 12 295 | 1 777 340 | 1 158 989 |
| Alberta | 2 747 | 76 347 | 9 551 392 | 5 130 565 |
| British Columbia | 4 282 | 133 391 | 10 600 622 | 8 917 763 |
| NWT & Yukon | 38 | 339 | 23 227 | 16 756 |

*Note: There may be a discrepancy between figures for Canada and the total of all provinces due to varying sources of information.

Source: *Canadian Markets* (Toronto: Financial Post, 1990), various pages.

*This drilling equipment was purchased by Imperial Oil for its Cold Lake, Alberta, oil well. Since much of the oil in Canada is located in Alberta, the market for this equipment is concentrated in this geographic area.*

more value is added when the plate is stamped into refrigerator bodies. As shown in Figure 8–1, the value added by manufacturing in Canada totalled approximately $107.5 billion in 1986.

## Distinctive Features of the Industrial Market

The industrial market has three distinctive features: geographic market concentration, a relatively small number of buyers, and systematic buying procedures.

### Geographic Market Concentration

The market for industrial goods in Canada is much more concentrated geographically than that for consumer goods. The largest markets are in Ontario and Quebec. However, industrial markets for specific items often do not follow the general pattern. As an example, the market for marine engines and fishing gear is concentrated on the Atlantic and Pacific coasts, while that for oil-drilling equipment centres on Alberta, British Columbia, and to a lesser extent Saskatchewan. The latter market is now expanding into Newfoundland.

### Small Number of Buyers

The industrial market is concentrated not only on a geographical basis, but also by a limited number of buyers. Although there are approximately 38 000 manufacturing firms in Canada, a small proportion of firms — those with 500 or more employees — are typically responsible for approximately half the total dollar value added by manufacturing.

The concentration of the industrial market greatly influences the strategy used in serving this market. The industrial marketer can usually make more profitable use of a sales force to provide regular personal contacts with a small, geographically concentrated market than consumer goods companies can provide with ultimate consumers. Wholesalers are less frequently used, and the marketing channel for industrial goods is typically much shorter than that for consumer goods. Advertising plays a much smaller role in the industrial-goods market, as funds may be more effectively spent on the sales force and other means of promotion than with consumer goods.

## Standard Industrial Classifications

The marketer focusing on the industrial market is aided by a wealth of information collected by the federal government, including data on the number of firms, their sales volumes, and the number of employees by category for firms in each industry. The data are broken down using a system known as **Standard Industrial Classifications** (SIC codes). The SIC codes begin with 18 divisions; under each division is a list of major groups into which all types of businesses are divided. The main divisions are listed below.

**Standard Industrial Classification (SIC) codes**   A series of industrial classifications developed by the federal government for use in collecting detailed statistics for each industry.

### Industrial Classifications

| Division | Industry | Groups | Number of Groups |
|---|---|---|---|
| A | Agriculture | 011–023 | 10 |
| B | Fishing and trapping | 031–033 | 3 |
| C | Logging and forestry | 041–051 | 2 |
| D | Mines, quarries, and oil wells | 061–092 | 8 |
| E | Manufacturing industries | 101–399 | 110 |
| F | Construction industries | 401–449 | 14 |
| G | Transportation and storage | 451–479 | 12 |
| H | Communications and other utilities | 481–499 | 8 |
| I | Wholesale trade industries | 501–599 | 30 |
| J | Retail trade industries | 601–692 | 29 |
| K | Finance and insurance industries | 701–749 | 18 |
| L | Real estate operator and insurance agent industies | 751–761 | 3 |
| M | Business service industries | 771–779 | 8 |
| N | Government service industries | 811–841 | 17 |
| O | Educational service industries | 851–859 | 6 |
| P | Health and social service industries | 861–869 | 9 |
| Q | Accommodation, food, and beverage service industries | 911–922 | 6 |
| R | Other service industries | 961–999 | 25 |

Source: Adapted from *Standard Industrial Classification*, 1980 Statistics Canada Catalogue 12–501, pp. 29–47.

Each major division within these broad groups is further divided into three subcategories (known as "major group," "group," and "class"). For example, Division A (the full name of which is Agricultural and Related Service Industries) is divided as follows:

> **DIVISION A — AGRICULTURAL AND RELATED SERVICE INDUSTRIES**
>   **Major Group 01 — Agricultural Industries**
>   *Group* — 011 Livestock Farms
>   Class — 0111 Dairy Farms
>   0112 Cattle Farms
>   0113 Hog Farms
>   etc.
>   *Group* — 012 Other Animal Specialty Farms
>   0121 Honey and Other Apiary Product Farms
>   0122 Horse and Other Equine Farms
>   etc.

For each of the subcategories, Statistics Canada collects statistics. The SIC code system can thus aid greatly in analyzing the industrial market.

Beyond the SIC data, trade associations and business publications provide additional information on the industrial market. Many such publications are listed in Appendix A (which follows Chapter 5). Such secondary sources often serve as useful starting points for analyzing industrial markets.

# Industrial Market Demand

Demand for goods and services is affected by many factors. Beyond the strength or weakness of the general economic environment, four primary characteristics distinguish industrial market demand: *derived demand*, *joint demand*, *inventory adjustments*, and *demand variability*.

## Derived Demand

The demand for an industrial product is typically **derived demand** — that is, *demand derived from (or linked to) demand for a consumer good*. The demand for cash registers (an industrial good) is partly derived from demand at the retail level (consumer products). Lower retail sales may ultimately result in lower demand for cash registers.

The "downsizing" of automobile engines by auto manufacturers in an attempt to develop smaller, fuel-efficient cars adversely affects spark-plug manufacturers like Champion. Since four-cylinder engines use half as many plugs as V-8s, Champion's total sales may decline drastically unless total auto sales increase dramatically, or unless Champion can increase its share of the total market.

**derived demand**   In the industrial market, demand for an industrial product that is linked to demand for a consumer good.

## Joint Demand

The demand for some industrial products is *related to the demand for other industrial goods*. There is a **joint demand** for coke and iron ore in the manufacture of pig iron. If the coke supply is reduced, there will be an accompanying reduction in the demand for iron ore.

**joint demand**   In the industrial market, demand for an industrial product that is related to the demand for another industrial good (because the latter item is necessary for the use of the first item).

A·P·P·L·Y·I·N·G  T·H·E  C·O·N·C·E·P·T·S

## Responding to Buyer Needs

It is not often a manufacturer drops almost half its product line and still expects its strength in that category to increase. But that is exactly what glue maker LePage's has done.

LePage's, Canada's largest adhesives maker, has revamped its glue lineup and merchandising, dropping 14 out of its 30 products and introducing a new display/consumer information system.

The program is called "carded relaunch." The company came to the realization that there were problems with the existing systems of marketing and displaying glue:

- Confusion and lost opportunity. After fruitlessly trying to determine what glue they should buy, too many potential customers walk away frustrated.
- Disappointment, and consumer dollars wasted, because the consumer buys the wrong product for the job.
- Poor merchandising, caused by restricted retail shelf space. For retailers, there is inefficient use of shelf space, and high handling and inventory costs.

LePage's realizes that glue is simply a low-interest consumer category. Consumers must educate themselves about gluing when they have a problem. On the other hand, the glue industry is research-driven. It is quite capable of putting out products faster than anybody can understand. Consequently, one executive said, "All we've managed to do is cover the shelves with stuff that's become extremely confusing and overwhelming."

To correct these problems, the company has reduced the number of products and introduced a new display/consumer information system. The firm's goals are to educate consumers, capture attention in-store, and build loyalty to Lepage's. It's confident that its new system will successfully respond to the needs of retailers as well as those of final consumers.

Source: Adapted from Ken Riddell, "Less Stock, More Loyalty," *Marketing* (September 18, 1989), p. B11.

## Inventory Adjustments

**inventory adjustments**
Changes in the amounts of materials a manufacturer keeps on hand.

*Changes in the amounts of materials a manufacturer keeps on hand* can have an impact on industrial demand. A two-month supply of raw materials is often considered the optimal inventory in some manufacturing industries.[3] But suppose economic conditions or other factors dictate that this level be increased to a 90-day supply. The raw materials supplier would then be bombarded with a tremendous increase in new orders. Thus, **inventory adjustments** can be a major determinant of industrial demand.

## Demand Variability

**demand variability**    In the industrial market, the impact of derived demand on the demand for interrelated products used in producing consumer goods.

**accelerator principle**    The disproportionate impact that changes in consumer demand have on industrial market demand.

Derived demand in the industrial market is related to and often creates immense variability in industrial demand. Assume the demand for industrial product A is derived from the demand for consumer product B — an item whose sales volume has been growing at an annual rate of 10 percent. Now suppose that the demand for product B slowed to a 5 percent annual increase. Management might decide to delay further purchases of product A, using existing inventory until the market conditions were clarified. Therefore, product A's **demand variability** becomes significantly affected by even modest shifts in the demand for product B. *The disproportionate impact that changes in consumer demand have on industrial market demand* is called the **accelerator principle**.

When it reduced its product line, Lepage's issued an information package to retailers outlining the benefits of the new system. Using the "Glues Brothers" and the simplicity and harmony of blues music as the campaign's central motif, the manufacturer hoped to convince retailers of the efficiency of the new plan. Sometimes a multi offer plan, with products blanketing the shelves, is not the best strategy.

## Basic Categories of Industrial Products

There are two general categories of industrial products: capital items and expense items. **Capital items** are *long-lived business assets that must be depreciated over time.* **Depreciation** is *the accounting concept of charging a portion of the cost of a capital item as a deduction against the company's annual revenue for purposes of determining its net income.* Examples of capital items include major installations like new plants and office buildings as well as equipment.

**Expense items**, by contrast, are *products and services that are used within a short period of time.* For the most part, they are charged against income in the year of purchase. Examples of expense items include the supplies that are used in operating the business, ranging from raw materials and fabricated parts to paper clips and machine lubricants.

Chapter 9 presents a comprehensive classification of industrial products. This initial breakdown into capital and expense items is useful because buying behaviour varies significantly depending on how a purchase is treated from an accounting viewpoint. Expense items may be bought routinely and with minimal delay, while capital items involve major fund commitments and are thus subject to considerable review by the purchaser's personnel. Differences in industrial purchasing behaviour are discussed in the sections that follow.

**capital items**    Long-lived business assets that must be depreciated over time.

**depreciation**    The accounting concept of charging a portion of the cost of a capital item against the company's annual revenue for purposes of determining its net income.

**expense items**    Products and services that are used within a short period of time.

# The Nature of the Industrial Purchase: Systematic and Complex

Industrial purchasing behaviour tends to be more complex than the consumer decision process described in Chapter 7. There are several reasons for this increased complexity:

1. Many persons may exert influence in industrial purchases, and considerable time may be spent obtaining the input and approval of various organizational members.

2. Organizational purchasing may be handled by committees with greater time requirements for majority or unanimous approval.

3. Many organizations attempt to use several sources of supply as a type of insurance against shortages.

Most industrial firms have attempted to systematize their purchases by employing a professional buyer — the industrial *purchasing manager* — who is responsible for handling most of the organization's purchases and for securing needed products at the best possible price. Unlike the ultimate consumer (who makes periodic purchase decisions), a firm's purchasing department devotes all its time and effort to determining needs, locating and evaluating alternative sources of supply, and making purchase decisions.

## The Complexity of Industrial Purchases

Where major purchases are involved, negotiations may take several weeks or months, and the buying decisions may rest with a number of persons in the organization. The choice of a supplier for industrial drill presses, for example, may be made jointly by the purchasing manager and the company's production, engineering, and maintenance departments. Each of these principals has a different point of view and they must all be reconciled in making a purchase decision. As a result, representatives of the selling firm must be well versed in all aspects of the product or service and be capable of interacting with the managers of the various departments involved. In the instruments industry, for instance, it takes an average of 5.3 face-to-face presentations to make a sale. The average cost of closing the sale — including salesperson compensation and travel and entertainment expenses — is $1315.46. Figure 8–2 shows the average number of sales calls required to complete a sale in several industries and the average cost of each sale.

Many industrial goods are purchased over long periods of time on a contractual basis. A manufacturing operation requires a continual supply of materials, and a one- or two-year contract with a supplier ensures a steady supply of raw materials as they are needed. Other industrial goods, such as conveyors, typewriters, and forklifts, generally last several years before replacement is necessary.

Purchase decisions are frequently made on the bases of service, certainty of supply, and the efficiency of the products. These factors may be even more important than the prices quoted for the products. Automobile manufacturers purchase steel, glass windows, spark plugs, and batteries as ingredients for their output. Since demand for these parts is derived entirely from the demand for consumer goods, price changes do not substantially affect their sale. Price increases for paint will have little effect on auto sales at General Motors, since paint represents a minute portion of the total costs of the automobile.

FIGURE 8 – 2

### Sales Call Statistics and Operating Expenses

| Industry Group | Cost Per Call | Number of Calls Needed to Close a Sale | Sales Force Cost as a Percentage of Total Sales |
|---|---|---|---|
| Business services | | 4.6 | 19.3% |
| Chemicals | 165.80 | 2.8 | 3.0 |
| Communications | 40.60 | 4.0 | 21.6 |
| Construction | 111.20 | 2.8 | 3.2 |
| Electronics | 133.30 | 3.9 | 12.0 |
| Fabricated metals | 80.80 | 3.3 | 6.4 |
| Food Products | 131.60 | 4.8 | 9.6 |
| Instruments | 226.00 | 5.3 | 10.3 |
| Insurance | 53.00 | 3.4 | 15.6 |
| Machinery | 68.50 | 3.0 | 13.0 |
| Misc. Manufacturing | 85.90 | 2.8 | 13.2 |
| Office equipment | 25.00 | 3.7 | 15.0 |
| Printing/Publishing | 70.10 | 4.5 | 8.3 |
| Retail | 25.00 | 3.3 | 23.5 |
| Rubber/Plastics | 248.20 | 4.7 | 2.8 |
| Utilities | 89.90 | 4.8 | 17.3 |
| Wholesale (Consumer) | 84.10 | 3.0 | 7.0 |
| Wholesale (Industrial) | 50.00 | 3.3 | 12.6 |
| Average | 96.39 | 3.8 | 11.9% |

Note: Industry groups reflect categories selected and reported by Dartnell Corporation. The overall average has been calculated based on data from the 18 industries listed.

Source: Dartnell Corporation, *25th Survey of Sales Force Compensation*, © 1989, Dartnell Corporation.

## Purchase of a Capital Item

A utility company that was considering buying a reinforced Fiberglas utility pole faced a complicated decision process. The sales representative dealt with the members of several departments of the utility company and went through months of negotiations before a purchase was made. The new pole had several advantages over the traditional steel, wood, or aluminum post: it was lightweight; had nonelectrical-conducting and noncorrosive properties; never needed painting; and met all strength requirements. Its major disadvantage, other than its unfamiliarity to the purchaser, was its high initial purchase price compared to the alternatives. The decision process began when the manager of the utility consulted the engineering head, who in turn brought in the purchasing manager. Purchasing then prepared a list of alternative suppliers and materials, which was approved by engineering, and the purchasing manager discussed the organization's needs in detail with the sales

F I G U R E   8 – 3

## The Decision to Purchase a New Type of Utility Pole

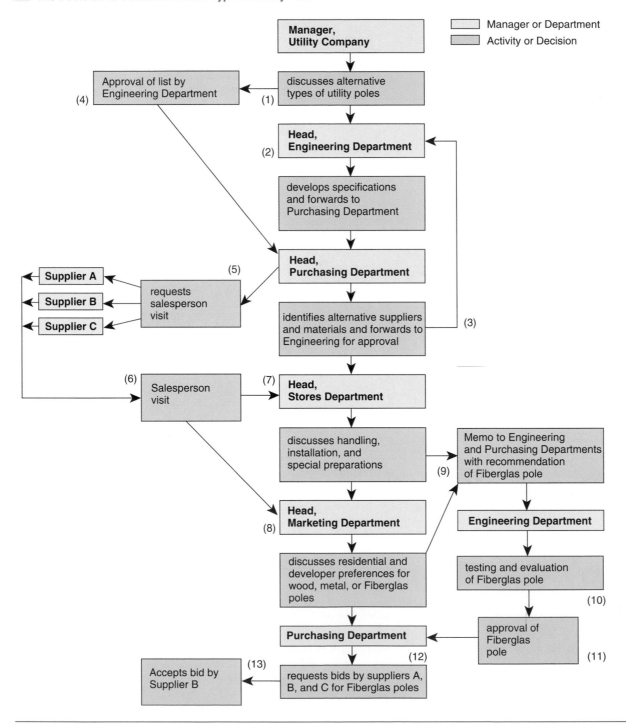

Source: Adapted from Arch G. Woodside, "Marketing Anatomy of Buying Process Can Help Improve Industrial Strategy," *Marketing News* (May 1, 1981), Section 2, p. 11. Used by permission of the American Marketing Association.

representatives of three suppliers. The salespeople met with the managers of the stores department, the marketing department, and the engineering department. After a series of meetings with the salespeople and numerous discussions among the utility's department heads, the utility decided to submit the new Fiberglas pole to a test conducted by the engineering department. The results of the test were reported to the various department heads, and bids were then requested from suppliers A, B, and C. These bids were reviewed by the department heads, who ultimately decided to select the Fiberglas pole offered by supplier B. This complex decision process is diagrammed in Figure 8–3.[4]

# Classifying Industrial Purchasing Situations

Industrial buying behaviour is affected by the degree of effort and involvement by different levels within the organization. There are three generally recognized industrial purchasing situations: straight rebuy, modified rebuy, and new task buying.[5]

## Straight Rebuy

A **straight rebuy** is *a recurring purchase decision involving an item that has performed satisfactorily and is therefore purchased again by a customer.* This industrial buying situation occurs when a purchaser is pleased with the good or service and the terms of sale are acceptable. Seeing little reason to assess other options, the purchaser follows some routine buying format.

Low-cost items like paper clips and HB pencils are typically rebought. If the purchaser is pleased with the products and their prices and terms, future purchases will probably be treated as a straight rebuy from the current vendor. Even expensive items especially designed for a customer's needs can be treated as a straight rebuy in some cases. For example, a manufacturer might be virtually committed to buying additional lathes from a certain company because it purchased them before and wants to keep a standardized production situation.

Marketers facing straight rebuy situations should concentrate on maintaining good relations with the buyer through prompt attention, adequate service, and the like. Competitors are faced with the difficult task of presenting a unique sales proposal that will break this chain of repurchases.

> **straight rebuy** A recurring purchase decision involving an item that has performed satisfactorily and is therefore purchased again by a customer.

## Modified Rebuy

A **modified rebuy** is *a situation where purchasers are willing to re-evaluate their available options.* The decision-makers feel that it is to their advantage to look at alternative product offerings using established purchasing guidelines. A modified rebuy situation may occur if a marketer allows a straight rebuy situation to deteriorate because of poor service or delivery or if quality, cost, and service differences are perceived.

Industrial marketers want to move purchasers into a straight rebuy position by responding to all their product and service needs. Competitors, on the other hand, try to move buyers into a modified rebuy situation by correctly assessing the factors that would make buyers reconsider their decisions.

> **modified rebuy** A situation in which purchasers are willing to re-evaluate their available options.

*Many people may be involved in an industrial buying action. An executive may discuss a product with the end user and on the "shop floor" to get a better idea of the user's needs and an evaluation of product performance. In this way, lines of communication are kept open between the various levels of decision-making, and the final purchase may reflect many different viewpoints. Marketers should be aware of this interactive process, even if they deal primarily with one person or department.*

## New Task Buying

**new task buying** First-time or unique purchase situations that require considerable effort on the part of the decision-makers.

**New task buying** refers to *first-time or unique purchase situations that require considerable effort on the part of the decision-makers*. Once such a need has been identified, evaluative criteria can be established and an extensive search launched. Alternative product and service offerings and vendors are considered. A new task buying situation may arise when a firm enters a new field and has to seek out suppliers of component parts that have not previously been purchased.

Industrial marketers should work closely with the purchaser in the case of new task buying situations. This will allow them to study the factors the purchaser considers important and to design their marketing proposal to match the needs of the purchaser.

## The Buying Centre Concept

**buying centre** Everyone who participates in some fashion in an industrial buying action.

The buying centre concept is an important key to understanding industrial purchase behaviour.[6] The **buying centre** simply refers to *everyone who participates in some fashion in an industrial buying action*. For example, a buying centre may include the architect who designs a new research laboratory; the scientist who will use the facility; the purchasing manager who screens contractor proposals; the chief executive officer who makes the final decision; and the vice-president for research who signs the formal contracts for the project.[7]

Buying centres are not part of a firm's formal organizational structure. They are informal groups whose composition will vary from one purchase situation to another and from one firm to the next. Buying centres typically include anywhere from four to twenty participants,[8] and tend to evolve as the purchasing process moves through its various stages.

Buying centre participants play the roles of users, gatekeepers, influencers, deciders, and buyers in the purchasing decision process. Each of these roles is described in Figure 8–4.

A critical task for the industrial marketer is to determine the specific role and the relative buying influence of each buying centre participant. Sales presentations and information can then be tailored to the role that the individual plays at each step in

FIGURE 8 – 4

## Definitions of Buying Centre Roles

| Role | Description |
| --- | --- |
| *Users* | As the role name implies, these are the personnel who will be using the product in question. Users may have anywhere from an inconsequential to an extremely important influence on the purchase decision. In some cases, the users initiate the purchase action by requesting the product. They may even develop the product specifications. |
| *Gatekeepers* | Gatekeepers control information to be reviewed by other members of the buying centre, either by the ways they disseminate printed information or advertisements or by controlling which salesperson will speak to which individuals in the buying centre. The purchasing manager might perform this screening role by opening the gate to the buying centre for some sales personnel and closing it to others. |
| *Influencers* | These individuals affect the purchasing decision by supplying information for the evaluation of alternatives or by setting buying specifications. Typically, technical personnel such as engineers, quality control personnel and research and development personnel are significant influences to the purchase decision. Sometimes individuals outside the buying organization can assume this role (e.g., an engineering consultant or an architect who writes very tight building specifications). |
| *Deciders* | Deciders are the individuals who actually make the buying decision, whether or not they have the formal authority to do so. The identity of the decider is the most difficult role to determine: buyers may have formal authority to buy, but the president of the firm may actually make the decision. A decider could be a design engineer who develops a set of specifications that only one vendor can meet. |
| *Buyers* | The buyer has *formal* authority for selecting a supplier and implementing all procedures connected with securing the product. The power of the buyer is often usurped by more powerful members of the organization. Often the buyer's role is assumed by the purchasing manager, who executes the clerical functions associated with a purchase order. |

Source: Adapted from Frederick E. Webster, Jr., and Yoram Wind, *Organizational Buying Behavior* (Englewood Cliffs, NJ: Prentice-Hall, 1972), pp. 77–80. This adaptation is reprinted form Michael D. Hutt and Thomas W. Speh, *Industrial Marketing Management* (Hinsdale, IL Dryden Press, 1981), p. 83.

the purchase process. Industrial marketers have also found that while their initial, and in many cases most extensive, contacts are with the purchasing department, the buying centre participants having the greatest influence are often elsewhere in the company.[9]

## The Process of Buying Industrial Goods and Services

The exact procedures that are used in buying industrial goods and services vary according to the buying situation confronted — straight rebuy, modified rebuy, or new task buying.[10] Most industrial purchases follow the same general process. Research by Agarwal, Burger, and Venkatesh suggested the model presented in Figure 8–5. While this model was formulated for industrial machinery purchases, it has general application to the industrial buying process.

FIGURE 8 – 5

### A Model of the Industrial Buying Process

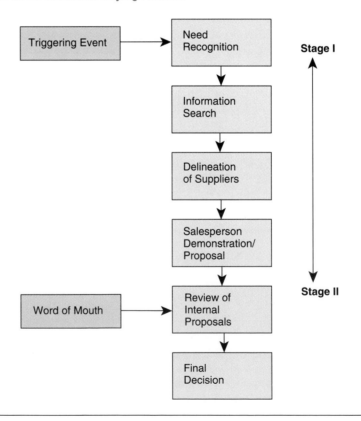

Source: Reprinted from Manoj K. Agarwal, Philip C. Burger, and Alladi Venkatesh, "Industrial Consumer Behavior: Toward an Improved Model," in *Developments in Marketing Science*, eds. Venkatakrishna V. Bellur et al. (Miami Beach: Academy of Marketing Science, 1981), p. 72.

## Dissecting the Model

The specific steps as shown in Figure 8–5 are outlined below.

*Need recognition*   A triggering event such as an equipment failure stimulates recognition of a perceived need for an industrial purchase.

*Information search*   Buying centre members begin to collect information on potential suppliers from sales personnel, advertisements, word of mouth, pamphlets, and other sources. The net result is to delineate the technical nature of the purchase.

*Delineation of suppliers*   Given the specifications established in the previous step, potential suppliers are then determined. Budget considerations may also be a factor in this step.

*Sales demonstration/proposal*   Vendor sales representatives are then invited to provide demonstrations and sales proposals. These proposals typically include technical and economic options as well as prices.

*Word of mouth*   Buying centre members may then contact current users of the product for their evaluation of its performance. Reliability, costs, and operational abilities are explored. Some vendors are eliminated because of negative information.

*Final decision*   Eventually a purchase decision is made. In many cases, this extensive process leads to a consensus decision, but some buying centre members have more influence than others in this final decision stage.

## Reciprocity

A controversial practice in a number of industrial purchasing situations is **reciprocity**, *the extension of purchasing preference to suppliers who are also customers*. For example, an office equipment manufacturer may favour a particular supplier of component parts if the supplier has recently made a major purchase of the manufacturer's office equipment. Reciprocal arrangements were traditionally used in industries with homogeneous products with similar prices, such as the chemical, paint, petroleum, rubber, and steel industries.

Two other forms of reciprocity have been used. *Reverse reciprocity* is the practice of supplying parts and raw materials that are in short supply to firms who can provide other needed supplies in return. In times of shortages, reverse reciprocity occasionally emerges as firms attempt to obtain raw materials and parts to continue operations. A more recent reciprocity spinoff is the *voluntary price roll-back*, where purchasers request vendors to agree to temporary price cuts or freezes. While no threats are made, it is difficult for a supplier to refuse a request from a major purchaser. This sometimes forces the vendor to ask for concessions from its own workforce and/or suppliers.[11] The various forms of reciprocity are evidence of the close links that exist between the different elements of the industrial marketplace.[12]

**reciprocity**   The extension of purchasing preference to suppliers who are also customers.

# Government Markets

The various levels of government make up a sizeable segment of the market for industrial products. There are many similarities between the government market and other industrial markets, for they seek to purchase many similar goods and services. However, the numerous regulations that affect government purchases create differences in the way items are procured.

Government expenditures represent nearly 52 percent of Canada's gross domestic product. More than 60 000 firms supply close to 20 000 items and services to the various levels of government, whose total spending in a recent year amounted to approximately $237 billion. The federal government accounted for about 42 percent of that total. Figure 8–6 indicates the major categories of government expenditures.

## How Governments Buy

**bids** Price quotations from potential suppliers.

**specifications** Specific descriptions of needed items for prospective bidders.

Since most government purchases must, by law, be made on the basis of **bids** (*price quotations from potential suppliers*), the government buyer must develop **specifications** — *specific descriptions of needed items* for prospective bidders (this is often done in the industrial market also). For the federal government most of the branded items, such as general-purpose supplies, are purchased by the Department of Supply and Services. Each province generally has a comparable office for such items.

FIGURE 8 – 6

### Gross General Expenditures, All Levels of Government

| Function | $(thousands) |
|---|---|
| General services | 15 832 089 |
| Protection of persons and property | 19 157 833 |
| Transportation and communications | 13 044 977 |
| Health | 30 277 303 |
| Social services | 56 956 816 |
| Education | 28 490 062 |
| Resource conservation and industrial development | 14 297 225 |
| Environment | 4 493 168 |
| Recreation and culture | 4 990 107 |
| Foreign affairs and international assistance | 2 793 000 |
| Regional planning and development | 1 095 600 |
| Debt charges | 35 514 521 |
| Other expenditures | 10 343 144 |
| TOTAL GROSS GENERAL EXPENDITURE | 237 285 845 |

Source: *Consolidated Government Finance, 1986* (Ottawa: Statistics Canada, 1988 Catalogue No.68-202, pp. 42–43. By permission of the Minister of Supply and Services Canada.

## Bidding on Government Contracts

All Canadian business and industrial operations are eligible to bid on federal government contracts.[13] The only requirement is that the firm must indicate interest and be prepared to provide evidence that it can supply needed goods or services in accordance with the specified time, cost, quality, performance, and other terms and conditions.

There are three ways of obtaining bids:

1. An *invitation to tender* is normally used for all purchases of more than $5000. Two or more bids are requested and the contract award is to be based on the lowest responsive bid. To ensure fairness, unclassified tenders are opened publicly.
2. *Requests for quotations* may be used for all purchases of less than $5000. They are not opened publicly.
3. *Requests for proposals* are used for all noncompetitive purchases valued at more than $5000, and for competitive purchases where the selection of the supplier cannot be made solely on the basis of the lowest-priced responsive bid. The evaluation of proposals is based on schedule, price, and the relevant technical, scientific, financial, managerial, and socio-economic factors identified in the solicitation. Requests for proposals are not opened publicly.

In addition to the head office (in Hull, Quebec), there are regional or district suboffices throughout the country that also purchase for the federal government. Although the details are not exactly the same, similar types of procedures are used by provincial and municipal governments.

## Source Lists

The Department of Supply and Services keeps extensive records of thousands of commodity groupings purchased. Matched against these are the names of companies that have indicated they want to be considered as suppliers, and that the department considers capable of carrying out a contract. These records are referred to when requirements arise. A firm wishing to be listed should write to the Executive Secretary for Supply Administration in Hull, or to the regional or district office in its area. Separate lists are maintained at head office and in each regional or district office.

## Selling to Government Markets

Sometimes it is difficult for government to obtain bidders, even for relatively large contracts. Despite its immense size, the government market is often viewed as too complex and unprofitable by many suppliers. A survey conducted by *Sales and Marketing Management* reported that industrial marketers registered a variety of complaints about government purchasing procedures. These included excessive paperwork, bureaucracy, needless regulations, emphasis on low bid prices, decision-making delays, frequent shifts in procurement personnel, and excessive policy changes.[14]

On the other hand, marketers generally credit the government with being a relatively stable market. Once an item is purchased from a firm by the government, the probability of more sales is good. Other marketers cite such advantages as the instant credibility established by sales to the federal government, timely payment, excise and sales tax exemptions, acceptance of new ideas, and reduced competition.

Only a few industrial firms maintain a separate government sales manager or sales force. But many firms have experienced success with specialized government marketing efforts. It is expected that a growing number of large companies will organize for dealing with government purchasers.

## Summary

The industrial-goods market consists of all entities that buy goods and services for use in producing other products for resale. The market has three distinctive characteristics: (1) geographic market concentration, (2) a relatively small number of buyers, and (3) systematic buying procedures.

The industrial market is heavily concentrated in Ontario and Quebec. A large portion of the value added by manufacturing is accounted for by these provinces. The number of buyers is quite small in the industrial market, as compared with the consumer market. Industrial marketers often find the Standard Industrial Classification (SIC) codes — which categorize all businesses into specifically defined groups — to be a useful tool in analyzing the industrial market.

Industrial market demand has four major characteristics. Derived demand means the demand for certain industrial goods is linked to the demand for consumer goods. Joint demand refers to demand for some industrial products that is related to the demand for other products used jointly with the first. Changes in inventory policy can also have a significant effect on industrial demand. The fourth characteristic of industrial market demand involves the accelerator principle, which indicates that even modest changes in consumer demand can have a disproportionate impact on industrial demand.

### A·P·P·L·Y·I·N·G   T·H·E   C·O·N·C·E·P·T·S

## Making It Simpler to Sell to Government

The federal government has made its multibillion-dollar procurement process easier and more open through a publication listing all goods it needs to buy. The weekly list is called *Government Business Opportunities*.

Prospective suppliers to government can buy the list and use it as a tool for getting contracts. The publication reflects the move to an open tendering system. Previously, the government kept lists of suppliers and invited them to bid when contracts came up.

But the Canada–U.S. Free Trade Agreement requires both Canada and the United States to open their tendering to suppliers from the other country.

Canada had to bring its tendering into line with the method used in the United States.

U.S. companies now will have access to $400 million worth of Canadian procurement a year, while about $3 billion of U.S. procurement will be accessible to Canadian companies.

The publication replaces information previously carried in the *Canada Gazette* and is the only source of information on about 5000 procurement opportunities that are affected by the free-trade agreement.

Source: Adapted from "Contract List Made Simpler for Bidders," *Globe and Mail* (April 13, 1987), B6.

There are two basic categories of industrial products: capital items and expense items. Capital items are long-lived business assets that must be depreciated for a period ranging from 3 to 15 years. Depreciation is the accounting concept of charging a portion of the cost of a capital item as a deduction against the company's annual revenue for purposes of determining its net income. Expense items, by contrast, are products and services that are used within a short period of time. For the most part, they are charged against income in the year of purchase.

Industrial buyer behaviour tends to be more complex than the behaviour of individual consumers. More people and time are involved, and buyers often seek several supply sources. There are three generally recognized industrial purchasing situations: straight rebuy, modified rebuy, and new task buying. A straight rebuy is a recurring purchase decision where an item that has performed satisfactorily is purchased again. A modified rebuy is a situation where purchasers are willing to re-evaluate their available options. New task buying refers to first-time or unique purchase situations that require considerable effort on the part of the decision-makers.

Industrial buying behaviour may also be illustrated by the concept of the buying centre. The buying centre simply refers to everyone who participates in some fashion in an industrial buying action. Buying centres include users, decision-makers, influencers, gatekeepers (who control information), and buyers (who actually consummate the transaction). The actual process of buying an industrial product or service consists of recognizing a need, searching for information, delineating vendors, soliciting sales proposals, reviewing proposals, and making the actual purchase decision. A controversial practice that comes into play for some industrial purchasing situations is reciprocity — the extension of purchasing preference to suppliers who are also customers.

Government markets are a sizeable segment of the economy. Government differs from other industrial markets because of the numerous regulations that bear on procurement practices. For instance, most government purchases are made on the basis of bids or written sales proposals from vendors. Industrial buying often is similar in this respect.

## ▪ K E Y   T E R M S

| | | |
|---|---|---|
| industrial market | joint demand | modified rebuy |
| producers | inventory adjustments | new task buying |
| trade industries | demand variability | buying centre |
| value added | accelerator principle | reciprocity |
| Standard Industrial Classification | capital item | bids |
| (SIC) Codes | expense item | specifications |
| derived demand | straight rebuy | |

## ▪ R E V I E W   Q U E S T I O N S

1. What are the three major types of industrial markets?
2. Describe the three distinctive features of industrial markets.
3. Explain the characteristics of industrial market demand.
4. Differentiate between capital items and expense items.

5. Why is industrial purchase behaviour so complex?
6. Differentiate among straight rebuy, modified rebuy, and new task buying.
7. Explain the concept of a buying centre.
8. Outline the general process for buying goods and services.

9. Discuss the issue of reciprocity.
10. Explain how government markets differ from other industrial markets.

# DISCUSSION QUESTIONS AND EXERCISES

1. Prepare a brief report on the market opportunity that exists in some specific industrial market. Be sure to consult all the standard reference sources on the industrial marketplace.
2. How could an industrial marketer use the SIC codes?
3. Find some actual examples in which derived demand, joint demand, inventory adjustments, and the accelerator principle have affected industrial market demand. Report your findings to the class.
4. Prepare a report on a recent purchase by a local organizational buyer. What can be learned from this exercise?
5. Prepare a brief report on the market opportunity that exists in a specific government market. Identify all the information sources that are available for such an assessment.

# MICROCOMPUTER EXERCISE
## Competitive Bidding

*Developing a Bidding Strategy*    Because many government and other organizational purchasers make buying decisions on the basis of competitive bids from alternative suppliers, determining the most appropriate bid is an important assignment for industrial marketers. One way to quantify this task is to use the concept of expected net profit (ENP). The formula for calculating ENP is as follows.

$$\text{Expected Net Profit} = P(\text{Bid} - \text{Cost})$$

where
P = the probability of the buyer accepting the bid
Bid = the bid price of the product or project
Cost = the estimated total cost of the product or project

**Directions:** Use the Menu Item titled "Competitive Bidding" on the *Foundations of Marketing* disk to solve each of the following problems.

1. Esta Morgenroth, marketing manager of Ottawa-based Electronic Industries, wants to submit a bid for a government project that she estimates will cost $23 000. She has prepared two preliminary proposals: (1) a bid for $60 000, and (2) a bid for $50 000. If Morgenroth estimates that there is a 40 percent chance of her first bid being accepted, and a 60 percent chance of her second bid being accepted, which of the two bids would yield the best expected net profit?

2. Product development engineers at Hamilton Industries have developed a new industrial scrubber. Marketing executives at the Ontario firm are actively working on a large sale to the leading firm in its target market, a firm whose purchase decisions are frequently imitated by other companies in the industry. One of

Hamilton's executives has proposed a price of $60 000 per unit, while another has suggested $70 000. Total costs of the scrubber average $45 000 per unit. Hamilton's marketing research department has assigned a 55 percent probability of the buyer accepting the lower price, and a 45 percent probability of purchase at the higher price. Use the ENP formula to recommend a bid price for the scrubber.

3. Eric Industries, Inc., has been supplying Milwaukee Manufacturing with a certain rivet for years. Milwaukee Manufacturing treats these purchases from Erie as what is referred to in this chapter as a straight rebuy. Erie's price of $400 per thousand rivets has remained unchanged for the past three years. But the cost of producing the rivet has recently risen from $300 to $325 per thousand. Erie's national sales manager would like to pass the $25 cost increase along to Milwaukee Manufacturing in the form of a price increase. However, Erie's president feels that a 20 percent chance exists that Milwaukee Manufacturing would locate a different supplier. At $400 per thousand, the president is 95 percent confident that the Milwaukee firm will continue to be an Erie Industries customer. What should Erie's management do in this case?

**VIDEO** **CASE 8**   **Skyfox Corp.**

A first-time visitor to the annual Paris Air Show would be amazed at the capabilities and technical sophistication of the military aircraft on exhibit. Government buyers and military officers from all over the world view the latest aircraft, listen to company sales representatives, and make purchase decisions. A General Dynamics representative points out that the 32-foot-long F-16 Fighting Falcon can fly at twice the speed of sound at a ceiling of 50 000 feet. Next to the General Dynamics display, another sales representative is extolling the virtues of the United Kingdom's Mach 2.2 Tornado fighter, with its two 27mm cannons and an assortment of Sidewinder and Sky Flash missiles.

But these high-tech military marvels carry a stratospheric price tag. It can easily cost a country over $1 billion to equip even the most modest air force. Additional millions are required for months of intensive training for the pilots who will fly these planes, spare-parts inventory for maintenance, and similar training for ground personnel needed for maintaining the aircraft.

While heading up United Nations food airlifts to several famine-plagued areas, Russell O'Quinn realized that many less developed countries did not require the technologically advanced planes of modern aviation. O'Quinn, a former test pilot, thought specifically of the venerable T-33, which had been the standard jet trainer for air forces around the world since the 1950s. In fact, some 1100 T-33s are still in service, and many more are in storage.

O'Quinn developed a plan for resurrecting the T-33. He envisioned a redesigned and upgraded aircraft that would be integrated with an original T-33 air frame, which is known for its virtually unlimited life. O'Quinn's configuration would offer potential buyers an aircraft that would be the match of today's sophisticated trainers at a considerably lower price. The new plane, dubbed Skyfox, would be fuel-efficient and would maintain the handling features of the old T-33. The target market for the Skyfox would be smaller nations with limited defence budgets.

Skyfox Corp. was set up in Mojave, California, to develop the prototype. The firm was financed with private capital. The resulting flight test plane differed markedly from the T-33 despite a 70 percent common structure. The T-33's single 4600-pound-thrust Allison T-33 centrifugal force turbojet engine was replaced by two externally mounted, 3700-pound-thrust Garett TFE-731-3 turbofan engines. This gave the Skyfox 60 percent more thrust while reducing its fuel consumption. The Skyfox also had the longest range of any plane in its category, because its external engine placement allowed extra fuel to be carried in the internal engine bay. The cockpit was also upgraded with a Stencil MK3 ejection seat, Canadian Marconi fibre optics instruments and display panels, and off-the-shelf Collins avionics.

Designing the Skyfox proved to be the easy part. Selling it was an entirely different matter. Securing consumer acceptance of a new product, particularly one in the $3-million-to-$3.5-million range, is always difficult. Buyers are wary of the risks associated with any new item. But in the case of Skyfox, 70 percent of the so-called new product was really an old product — the T-33.

After the testing of the Skyfox, O'Quinn's company benefited from considerable free publicity. The Skyfox project was described in several trade and popular publications. Still, Skyfox Corp. was unable to translate this publicity into actual orders; only Portugal expressed an interest.

O'Quinn began searching for a merger with a larger firm that would provide the needed financial and marketing clout. Eventually he concluded a licensary agreement with Boeing to produce and market the Skyfox. (A licensary agreement is an arrangement whereby a technology is transferred to another party in exchange for some specified type of payment.) Management at Boeing Military Aircraft Co. adopted a broader view of the Skyfox's potential role. It saw the Skyfox as a multipurpose aircraft that could conduct a variety of missions, such as reconnaissance, maritime patrol, electronic warfare simulation, and target towing, in addition to serving as a jet trainer.

While Boeing estimated that only 700 T-33s were still in service (compared to Skyfox Corp.'s estimate of 1100), it agreed with O'Quinn's original assessment of the product. The Skyfox appears to be a cost-effective way to extend an airplane's life by an additional 20 years. Boeing also broadened the target market for the Skyfox to include the U.S. Air Force/Air National Guard, Canada, South Korea, Greece, and Portugal.

After three years of efforts to market the Skyfox, Boeing withdrew from the venture. Skyfox Corp. continued to develop the airplane, substituting larger, more powerful engines and expanding its performance range. Although well over 100 orders have been received, the company still seeks funding and production capabilities. Potential buyers require assurances of long-term support, especially availability of parts, which Skyfox is unable to provide at present. Two major firms with operations on the scale of Boeing's have expressed interest, so there is hope that the Skyfox project will eventually get off the ground.

SOURCES    Brendon M. Greeley, Jr., "Boeing Markets Newly Acquired Skyfox Twin-Engine Jet Trainer," *Aviation Week and Space Technology* (August 11, 1986), pp. 54–55; "Skyfox Seeks Merger to Fund Production of Jet Trainer Aircraft," *Aviation Week and Space Technology* (January 21, 1985), p. 21; and Robert R. Ropelewski, "Skyfox Updates T-33 Trainer Effectively," *Aviation Week and Space Technology* (March 8, 1984), pp. 39, 42, 44, 46; updated by Boeing Military Aircraft Co. (February 1, 1988); update interview with Russell O'Quinn, Skyfox Corp. (April 1991). The information on the F-16 and Tornado is from Chris Bishop and David Donald, eds., *World Military Power* (New York: Military Press, 1986), p.33.

## Questions

1. Classify the organizational buying situation for the Skyfox. Why did you select this classification category?

2. Relate the buying centre concept to the potential purchase of Skyfox.

3. How should Skyfox be marketed?

4. Would Skyfox be an attractive investment for another aircraft manufacturer?

## David Kruschell

PHH Canada Inc.
Western Regional Manager

**Education:**

Northern Alberta Institute of Technology
Business Administration — Marketing/Management
NAIT Marketer of the Year, 1984
Graduation — 1984

The great benefit of the NAIT marketing program was its practicality. I found the courses intensive and challenging, and from the beginning the instructors made good on their expressed desire: to apply theory to real business situations that marketers would encounter. This hands-on approach helped me feel confident and well prepared when I was ready to enter the work force.

After graduating from NAIT, I worked for Procter & Gamble as a marketing representative for 18 months. I then received a promotion to unit manager, with responsibility for the sales activities of one division in Northern Alberta. Two months later I moved to PHH Canada Inc., taking on the duties of district sales manager for the Edmonton office. After serving two years in that position, I was transferred to PHH's Calgary office to act as a client services manager for a business unit. Finally, almost two years after the last promotion, I was approached to move to another division of PHH, where I am now the Western Regional Manager for PHH Home Equity Inc. I have profit-and-loss responsibility for the division within the four Western Provinces.

In retrospect, I can see how certain courses have benefited me in my present position. Many business students look upon the first-year courses as nonchallenging and wish to get on to more exciting topics, but it is just these courses that I have found the most beneficial. The basic courses in law and accounting provided me with what turned out to be invaluable information. For example, what I learned in my law course about contract law now helps me understand the legalities of the agreements that we enter into every day.

Another area of study I have found useful is Organizational Behaviour. I learned that knowing what motivates employees is crucial to being an efficient manager — and, more important, that money is not the basic goal that drives individuals. Realizing the complexities of human needs helps managers to empathize with employees' job-related problems and to build a better working relationship. I have found this skill to be such an integral part of the position that I encourage all my managers to take an Organizational Behaviour course. Overall, my marketing background has provided me with many exciting opportunities but at the same time has not in any way limited the potential direction I can take in the future.

My personal goal is to be in senior management with my current employer either in Canada, the United States, or Europe. The trend toward globalization in business is creating a wide array of choices for individuals who wish to pursue a career in marketing, and I hope to be able to take advantage of this exciting new option.

The concept of a product is more complex than it may seem at first. The chapters in this section point out the many important attributes that comprise a product. The development and management of products over time is also discussed. The last chapter is devoted to considering one important category of products known as services. A large and growing portion of economic activity is accounted for by services.

CHAPTER 9

# Product Strategy

## CHAPTER OBJECTIVES

1. To relate product strategy to the other variables of the marketing mix.
2. To explain the concept of the product life cycle, as well as its uses and limitations.
3. To identify the determinants of the speed of the adoption process.
4. To explain the methods for accelerating the speed of adoption.
5. To identify the classifications for consumer products and to briefly describe each category.
6. To classify the types of industrial products.

Two teams of students from the University of Toronto's master's program in business administration have each won $1,000 for developing the best marketing plans to stimulate the sales of tea and coffee.

The contest, which was sponsored by the Tea and Coffee Association of Canada, pitted the U of T students against similar teams of MBA students from McMaster University. Their assignment was to develop ideas for new retail brands of tea and coffee in order to counter recent inroads made in the marketplace by soft drinks and fruit juices.

In order to win, the students not only had to combine good research

data with creativity, but also to prepare complete marketing plans including recommendations on pricing, advertising, and promotion.

Kevin Greenwood, an MBA graduate and member of the "coffee" team, said the group decided to approach the problem "as if we were an advertising agency pitching for new business. In order to win, we had to sell the client on our ideas, and the key to doing that was to have the client's customers (i.e., the consumers) tell them how promising our ideas were."

To this end, the students "concept tested" their ideas in four major Canadian cities (Vancouver,

Winnipeg, Toronto and Montreal) before submitting them to the contest sponsors.

The winning ideas for tea included "SPLASH," an all-natural carbonated fruit and tea drink served cold as an alternative to pop or fruit seltzers, and "Vitali Tea," which combines tea with spring water, plus vitamins and minerals to make a healthy fluid replenisher for active individuals.

Coffee suggestions included "Cachet," a roast coffee product packed in a single-serving filter for in-cup brewing, and "Café Cool," a refreshing bottled coffee beverage served cold or on ice.

Although the contest was not designed to develop a specific product, the MBA students believe their ideas could set trends for the traditional beverage industries to follow.

"The shift towards cold beverages and products with 'natural' profiles is irreversible," says Julie Otto, a recent graduate and member of the winning "tea" team. "The tea and coffee industries can attempt to buck this trend or they can take heed of the old adage 'If you can't beat 'em, join 'em' ".[1]

THE new products proposed by the MBA students described in the above article are creative and appear promising. And the teams' preliminary testing of the acceptability of their "concepts" was no doubt a smart approach. But much more would have to be done by marketers to bring a product such as Splash successfully to the marketplace.

Marketing managers not only face many decisions about designing and positioning *new* products, but also must manage existing ones. Over the life of each product, they have to determine whether prices should be lowered or raised, whether money should be spent on redeveloping older products, and how such products should be promoted and distributed. Finding and introducing new products and managing older ones are major aspects of marketing management.

## Introduction

This is the first of three chapters dealing with the "product" component of the marketing mix. Here the basic concepts and definitions of this marketing element are laid out.

Marketing planning efforts begin with the choice of products to offer the target market. Pricing, marketing channels, and marketing communication (the other variables of the marketing mix) are all based on the nature of the product.

Everyone knows what a product is — or do they? We must first make sure we understand what a product really is.

## Products: A Definition

A narrow definition of the word *product* might focus on the physical or functional characteristics of a good offered to consumers. For example, a Sony videocassette recorder is a rectangular container of metal and plastic wires connecting it to a television set, accompanied by a series of special tapes for recording and viewing.

# FROM BAY STREET TO THE BEAUFORT SEA, CANADA COPIES ON CANON.

What makes Canon copiers so popular that they can be found everywhere from the head office to the last frontier?

For some, it's our wide range of models, which includes the NP-1020 – ideally suited to small business – and the NP-9800, our fastest, most productive copier, capable of cutting even the biggest jobs down to size.

Others like our spirit of innovation – reflected in the fact that we devote over 11% of sales to research and development. That investment pays off handsomely with innovative, technologically superior products; in recent years it has also resulted in Canon's registering a record number of patents in the U.S.A. alone.

There are even those who like the fact that buying from Canon means using the same brand of copier as over half of Canada's top five hundred businesses.

And not surprisingly, many people take comfort in the knowledge that we back our products with a service network that's second to none.

From Victoria to St. John's, there are over one hundred Canon dealers. These dealers, employing over 3000 men and women, including 1100 Canon trained technicians, are dedicated solely to the sales and service of Canon NP copiers. It's the largest copier dealer network in the country.

The obvious conclusion is that there are many valid reasons for owning a Canon copier, whether you do business in the city or on the sea.

Find out more about Canon copiers by calling toll-free 1-800-387-1241.

Canon
Canada copies on Canon.

This is the core product. But purchasers have a much broader view of the recorder. They have bought the convenience of viewing television programs at their leisure; the warranty and service that Sony, the manufacturer, provides; the prestige of owning this fine product; and the ability to rent or purchase recently released movies for home viewing. Thus, the brand image, warranty, and service are also all parts of the product as seen by the consumer.

Marketing decision-makers must have this broader concept in mind and realize that people purchase more than just the physical features of products. *They are buying want satisfaction.* Most drivers know very little about the gasoline they so regularly purchase. If they bother to analyze it, they discover that it is almost colourless and emits a peculiar odour. However, most of them do not think of gasoline as a product at all — to them, gasoline is a tax. It is a payment that they must periodically make for the privilege of driving their cars on the streets and highways. And the friendly service-station attendant is a tax collector. Petroleum retailers should be aware of this image in the minds of many customers before spending huge sums to promote dozens of secret ingredients designed to please the motorist.

The shopper's conception of a product may be altered by such features as packaging, labelling, or the retail outlets in which the product may be purchased. An image of high quality has been created for Maytag appliances, whose television commercials describe the Maytag repairer as "the loneliest person in town." More than 30 years ago, the firm's president set a standard of "10 years of trouble-free operation" for automatic clothes washers. The company's success in achieving a

*An image of reliability is created by this Canon advertisement; in addition, it exhibits the strength and reach of the firm's dealer network. A reputation for reliability and service will help change public perceptions about Canon's products.*

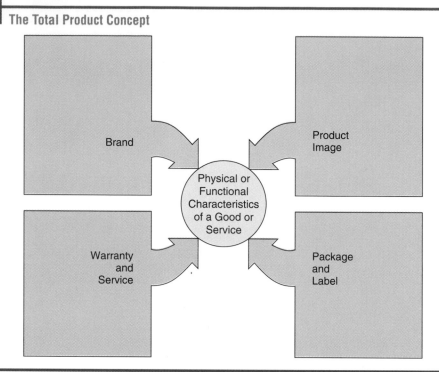

FIGURE 9–1

The Total Product Concept

Brand

Product Image

Physical or Functional Characteristics of a Good or Service

Warranty and Service

Package and Label

reputation for high product quality is evident in Maytag's continued sales growth record, even though the washer's retail price is about $70 higher than the nearest competitor's.

Some products have no physical ingredients. A haircut and blow-dry at the local hair stylist produces only well-groomed hair. A tax counsellor produces only advice. Thus, a broader view of product must also include services.

A **product**, then, may be defined *as a total bundle of physical, service, and symbolic characteristics designed to produce consumer want satisfaction.*[2] Figure 9–1 reflects this broader definition — known as the total product concept — by identifying the various components of the total product.

An important feature of many products is a product **warranty**. The warranty is *a guarantee to the buyer that the supplier will replace a defective product (or part of a product) or refund its purchase price during a specified period of time.* Such warranties serve to increase consumer purchase confidence and can prove to be an important means of stimulating demand. Zippo lighters used a warranty as one of the most important features of the firm's marketing strategy. The manufacturer agreed to a lifetime guarantee, promising to repair or replace any damaged or defective Zippo lighter regardless of age. Many retailers have a broad, unwritten but frequently honoured warranty of satisfaction or your money back.

**product** A total bundle of physical, service, and symbolic characteristics designed to produce consumer want satisfaction.

**warranty** A guarantee to the buyer that the supplier will replace a defective product (or part of a product) or refund its purchase price during a specified period of time.

## The Product Life Cycle

Product *types*, like individuals, pass through a series of stages. The lifecycle for humans is quite specific: infancy to childhood to adulthood to retirement to death. Products also progress through stages, although a product's progress through the stages is sometimes not very clear-cut. This progression of *introduction, growth,*

FIGURE 9-2

**Stages in the Product Life Cycle**

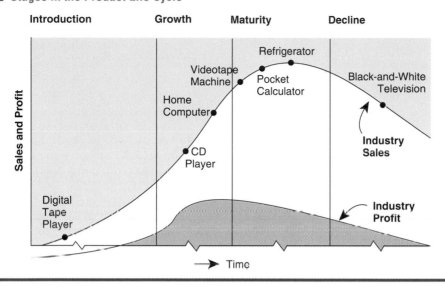

maturity, and decline is known as the **product life cycle**. An idealized model of the cycle is depicted in Figure 9–2, with examples of products currently at each stage of development.[3] In many situations, however, the model does not fit very well. For example, there is little evidence that refrigerators enter a decline or death stage.

**product life cycle**   The progression of a product through introduction, growth, maturity, and decline stages.

## Stages of the Cycle

### Introductory stage

The firm's objective in the early stages of the product life cycle is to stimulate demand for the new market entry. Since the product is not known to the public, promotional campaigns stress information about its features. Promotion may also be directed toward middlemen in the channel, to induce them to carry the product. In this initial phase the public is being acquainted with the merits of the new product and acceptance is being gained.

As Figure 9–2 indicates, losses are common during the introductory stage due to heavy promotion as well as extensive research and development expenditures. But the groundwork is being laid for future profits. Firms expect to recover their costs and to begin earning profits when the new product moves into the second phase of the cycle — the growth stage.

In the case of the videodisc, RCA Corporation and a joint team of the Netherlands-based Philips and MCA, Inc., spent more than $200 million on development prior to its introduction. But they projected that annual sales would hit $500 million.[4] Despite their efforts, however, the market turned its back on the videodisc, and the product never made it past the introductory stage in the home market.

### Growth stage

Sales volume rises rapidly during the growth stage as new customers make initial purchases and as repurchases are made by the early users of the product. Word-of-mouth and mass advertising induce hesitant buyers to make trial purchases. Home computers are now in this phase of the cycle.

## Some Trends and Products at Various Stages of the Product Life Cycle: Marketing Flops in the Hectic '80s — And Selling That Hit the Spot

The 1980s were a beat-the-clock decade. We hustled to microwave hamburgers, deposit cheques at automatic teller machines, and videotape television programs we had missed the first time around.

More women left the home and invaded corporate offices.

Our health and well-being emerged as a prime concern.

Marketers, observing it all from the sidelines, cashed in on some of the trends but missed out on others. Herewith is a glimpse of some of the marketing duds and delights of the decade.

The biggest flop was New Coke, a sweeter version of the soft drink that was introduced with fanfare in 1985 as Coca-Cola tried to stem the Pepsi Generation.

Consumers balked at the unfamiliar. Quick on the rebound, Coca-Cola resurrected the old Coke, renamed it Classic and lured back customers. New Coke became "a gold-plated Edsel," as one observer put it.

There were some delights that turned into duds. Cabbage Patch dolls were all the rage in 1983. But when the fad faded, the toy maker was left virtually empty-handed because it had put all its eggs in the Cabbage Patch basket.

Fax machines have altered our way of communicating, which makes them a delight to marketers. But the machines have also been inundated with junk mail and ads that annoy people and can ultimately dampen interest in the products.

There [were] other marketing blunders [in the 1980s].

- Bad service. [One main] reason retailers are sitting idly. People don't have time to browse; they need quick help in a store and often don't get it. Department stores are the worst, having cut back on sales staff.
- Commercials in movie theatres. The ads are booed more than ever these days. North American ads are not like those in Europe, where commercials in cinemas are an art form.
- Home banking and shopping, via computer, still aren't a tap of the keyboard away, as some had predicted.

- Sexism in ads. Stereotypes and the exploitative use of women's bodies are frowned on more. Unfortunately, they're still rampant.
- Tobacco advertising. Most of it has been rendered unlawful. The industry had glamorized smoking too much in its ads while refusing to shoulder responsibility for the health-related problems. Smoke-free flights and workplaces are also playing havoc with industry sales.
- Mass media advertising. The TV clicker, cable channels, and specialty magazines made advertisers realize that pitching products to a mass audience wasn't working the way it once did. Niche marketing — targeting choice customers — became a new buzzword.

There [were] also some clear triumphs:

- Environment pitches. Ethics and consciousness-raising are back in vogue. Companies are starting to capitalize on the view that the good corporation is one that helps preserve our planet, too.
- Non-name house brands. Loblaws was the trailblazer with its President's Choice and no-name labels.
- Bank machines. They're fast and handy. They're also helping to rid consumers of their fear of technology.
- The health craze. This includes non-cholesterol anything and "light" or "diet" food and drink. Less is best, unless it's for the occasional indulgence. Then the sky is the limit on the calorie count.
- Microwave ovens. They've changed the way we cook and brought a whole new meaning and market to convenience foods.
- Video games. They've transformed homes into video arcades. They've also stolen away sales from conventional toys.
- Car phones. For status alone, they couldn't be beat.
- VCRs, home videos, and compact discs. Our homes are becoming entertainment centres.

It was a decade for consumption, a continuation of the 1970s lust for acquisitions. That may wane in the coming years as the population ages and turns to more traditional values.

Still, marketers face new opportunities in the next

decade with the opening of the Iron Curtain for Western business.

Already, companies are in on the action. A U.S. fragrance firm, for example, shot a commercial at the graffiti-laden Berlin Wall, hiring East Berliners as extras. Back home, Canadian and U.S. entrepreneurs are selling certified souvenirs of rubble from the wall at about $12 to $20 a shot.

Will East-European-freedom marketing be among the list of hits or misses of the next decade? Read this space in 10 years.

Source: Marina Strauss, "Marketing Flops in the Hectic '80s — And Selling That Hit the Spot," *Globe and Mail* (December 21, 1989).

As the firm begins to realize substantial profits from its investment during the growth stage, it attracts competitors. Success breeds imitation, and firms rush into the market with competitive products in search of profit during the growth stage. As soon as the dramatic market acceptance of the CD player was realized, many manufacturers jumped into the market with their versions of the product.

## Maturity stage

Industry sales continue to grow during the early portion of the maturity stage, but eventually reach a plateau as the backlog of potential customers is exhausted. By this time a large number of competitors have entered the market, and profits decline as competition intensifies.

In the maturity stage, differences among competing products have diminished as competitors have discovered the product and promotional characteristics most desired by the market. Heavy promotional outlays emphasize subtle differences among competing products, and brand competition intensifies.

Available products now exceed demand. Companies attempting to increase sales and market share must do so at the expense of competitors. As competition intensifies, the tendency grows among competitors to cut prices in a bid to attract new buyers. Even though a price reduction may be the easiest method of inducing additional purchases, it is also one of the simplest moves for competitors to duplicate. Reduced prices will result in decreased revenues for all firms in the industry unless the price cuts produce enough increased purchases to offset the loss in revenue on each product sold.[5]

## A·P·P·L·Y·I·N·G  T·H·E  C·O·N·C·E·P·T·S

### *Example of Product Maturity*

Bill Loewen saw the tedious work that was involved in accounting for, and handling payrolls. Large firms had computer systems which could cope, but most small firms did not. So he established Comcheq to provide a centralized "quickpay" payroll service to smaller companies. Market response has been so great that Comcheq has grown into an outstandingly successful company, adding other products over time.

Comcheq's "quickpay" service now may have reached maturity. The days of such service being exclusive to Comcheq are gone. Now customers have the option of buying microcomputers along with relevant payroll software to process paycheques. Since Comcheq's customers must still invest many hours of labour to record and process a payroll they might as well do it in-house.

FIGURE 9–3

**Overlap of Life Cycle for Products A and B**

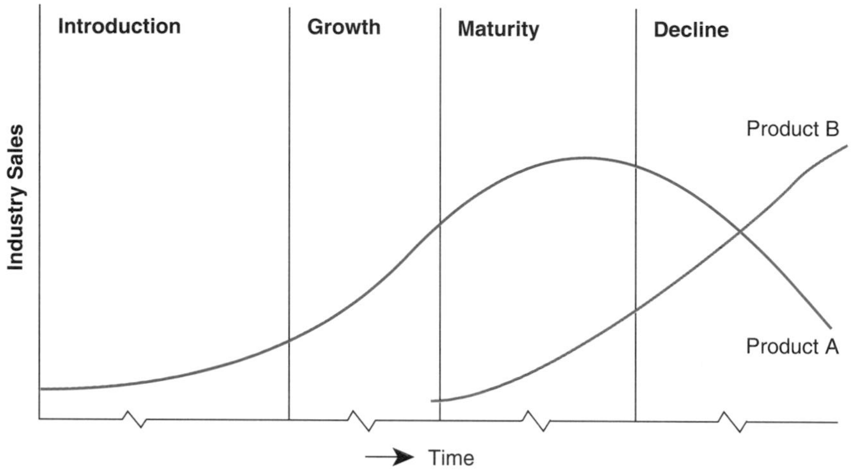


### Decline stage

In the final stage of the product's life, new innovations or shifting consumer preferences bring about an absolute decline in total industry sales. The safety razor and electric shavers replace the straight razor, a new Nintendo game replaces an earlier version as the latest fad, and the slower personal computer is replaced by a faster, more powerful model. As Figure 9–3 indicates, the decline stage of the old product is often also the growth stage for the new market entry.

Industry profits decline and in some cases actually become negative as sales fall and firms cut prices in a bid for the dwindling market. Manufacturers gradually begin to leave the industry in search of more profitable products.

## Departures from the Traditional Product Life-Cycle Model

The preceding discussion has examined what is considered the traditional product life cycle, with its four clearly delineated stages. Some marketing theorists divide the life cycle into additional stages, but these four, identified in Figure 9–2, are generally accepted within the marketing discipline.

Yet despite the vast body of material written on the subject, considerable controversy surrounds the format and usefulness of product life-cycle theory. On the one hand, the concept has an enduring appeal because of the intuitive logic of the birth-to-decline biological analogy.[6] As such, it has considerable descriptive value when used as a systematic framework for explaining market dynamics.

However, the simplicity of the concept has led to simplistic uses and expectations for the model, and this has called the concept itself into question. Part of the problem lies in failing to distinguish between the life cycle of a *product type* and that of an *individual brand* within that generic product category. Life-cycle theory is most applicable to product types. A truly new brand is obviously also the generic category for a while, but as competing brands are introduced, it becomes one of several brands within that category. The greatest misuse of product life-cycle theory is to consider it a *predictive* model for anticipating when changes will occur and to presume that one stage will always succeed another. Managers can make grave errors if they naively interpret a particular rise or fall in sales as a sign that a product has moved from one stage to another. Such an interpretation could lead to serious errors in strategy, such as concluding that a product is in decline and removing it from the market.

A second criticism involves the use of the life cycle as a *normative* model, which *prescribes* the alternative strategies that should be considered at each stage. As will be shown later, there are strategies that are generally appropriate at various stages of the life cycle of a product *category*. In the case of an individual brand *within* a product category, however, as Enis, LaGrace, and Prell argue, "the product life cycle [of a brand] is a *dependent* variable....That is, the brand's stage in the product life cycle depends primarily upon the marketing strategy implemented for that product at a particular time."[7]

A more realistic view is that life-cycle analysis serves several different roles in the formulation of strategy. In the case of both generic product type and individual brand, the life cycle serves as an *enabling condition* in the sense that the underlying forces that inhibit or facilitate growth create opportunities and threats with strategic implications. The stage of the life cycle also acts as a *moderating variable* through its influence on the value of market-share position and the profitability consequences of strategic decisions. In the case of an individual brand, a stage in the life cycle is partly a *consequence* of managerial decisions. Its position is not necessarily a *fait accompli*, which can only be reacted to, but instead is only one of several scenarios that are conditional on the life cycle of the product category, on competitive actions, and on managerial decisions.

## Other Life-Cycle Issues

Three other issues that modify the original life-cycle concept are (1) the length of each product life-cycle stage; (2) the existence of product life-cycle variants; and (3) the current role of product and service fashions and fads.

### Length of cycle stages

Professor John O. King has argued that product life-cycle models should reflect the reality that goods and services move through the cycle at varying speeds. He suggests that the model should be drawn to show a broken horizontal axis to reflect the fact that the stages may be of varying lengths, as we did in Figures 9–2 and 9–3. Research now suggests that product life cycles may be getting shorter, especially in the introductory and growth stages.[8] While definitive conclusions are not yet available, most marketers do accept the fact that product life cycles and their stages show considerable variation in length.

### Alternative product life cycles

In a study dealing with 100 categories of food, health, and personal-care products, the Marketing Science Institute reported that the traditional life-cycle model was applicable for only 17 percent of the general categories and 20 percent of the specific brands.[9] Variants to the traditional model are shown in Figure 9–4.

## Alternative Product Life Cycles

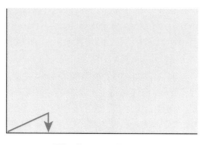

**The Instant Bust**

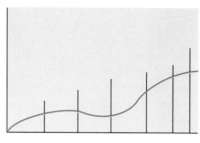

**The Aborted Introduction**

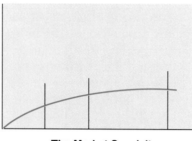

**The Market Specialty**

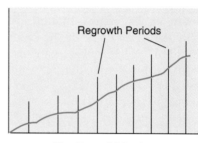

**The Pyramid Cycle**

Source: Reprinted from Chester R. Wasson, *Dynamic Competitive Strategy and Product Life Cycle*, 3rd ed. (Austin, TX: Austin Press, 1978), p. 13.

As shown in Figure 9-4, some products simply do not make it. These can be labelled the "instant busts"; a failure simply does not go through the four steps of the traditional model. Still other products are introduced but information derived from test-market situations indicates that changes will be necessary if the product launch is to be successful. (Test markets are described in Chapter 10.) The products then have to be modified in some way — such as in design, packaging, promotional strategy — before they are reintroduced. This type of start-up, start-again launch is labelled the "aborted introduction" in Figure 9–4.

Still other products become market specialty items (discussed later in this chapter) and provide long and stable maturity stages. A common variant is the "pyramided cycle", where the product is adapted through new technology or a revised marketing strategy. The pyramided cycle (also discussed later in the chapter) is characterized by a series of regrowth periods.

### Fashions and fads

**fashions** Currently popular products that tend to follow recurring life cycles.

Fashions and fads are also important to marketers. **Fashions** are *currently popular products that tend to follow recurring life cycles.*[10] Women's apparel fashions provide the

*The distinctive sound and style of Blue Rodeo has made them popular with teens and young adults. They speak a language that the younger generation can relate to. The marketer's challenge is to become conversant with this language without alienating any "outside" groups in the process.*

best examples. The miniskirt was reintroduced in 1982 after being out of fashion for over a decade. In 1990 it again appeared.

By contrast, **fads** are *fashions with abbreviated life cycles*. Consider the case of popular music for teenagers. Disco gave way to punk and new wave, which was replaced by the "new music," a take-off on rock and roll.[11] Rap music is another example of the many music fads that come and go. Most fads experience short-lived popularity and then fade quickly. However, some maintain a residual market among certain market segments. Both these fad cycles are shown in Figure 9–5.

**fads** Fashions with abbreviated life cycles.

---

**FIGURE 9 – 5**

**Fad Cycles**

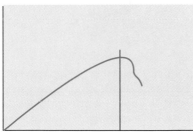

**The Fad**

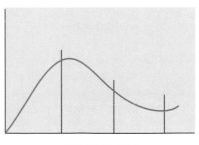

**The Fad with a Significant Residual Market**

---

Source: Reprinted from Chester R. Wasson, *Dynamic Competitive Strategy and Product Life Cycle*, 3rd ed. (Austin, TX: Austin Press, 1978), p. 13.

# Product Life-Cycle Considerations in Marketing Strategy

Marketing strategy related to the product life cycle is most useful when carried out on an individual *brand* basis rather than a generic product category basis.[12] There are too many uncontrollable variables at the generic level.

The product life cycle — with all its variants — is a useful tool in marketing strategy decision-making. The knowledge that profits assume a predictable pattern through the stages and that promotional emphasis must shift from product information in the early stages to brand promotion in the later ones allows the marketing decision-maker to take advantage of conditions that often exist in each stage of the product life cycle through appropriate marketing efforts.

A firm's marketing efforts should emphasize stimulating demand at the introductory stage. The emphasis shifts to cultivating selective demand in the growth period. Market segmentation should be used extensively in the maturity period. During the decline, the emphasis again shifts to increasing primary demand. Figure 9–6 suggests possibilities for appropriate pricing, distribution, product development, and service and warranty strategies for each life-cycle stage. The reader is again cautioned that the life cycle does not determine the strategy.

## Extending the Product Life Cycle

For a life cycle *brand* is often subject to managerial strategy. One example is the practice of extending the cycle as long as possible. Marketing managers can accomplish this objective if they take action early in the maturity stage. Product life cycles can sometimes be extended indefinitely by actions designed to accomplish one or more of the following:

1. Increase the frequency of use by present customers.
2. Add new users.
3. Find new uses for the product.
4. Change package sizes, labels, or product quality.[13]

Examples of such actions are cited below.

### Increase the frequency of use
Noxzema was originally intended as an occasional-use skin medicine, but it was repositioned as a routine-use beauty-care item. This substantially increased the rate of use — and amount purchased.

### Add new users
Cadillac introduced its Cimarron to attract non–Cadillac buyers who usually purchased cars like BMWs. New variations of Crest and Colgate were introduced as sweeter-tasting gels to appeal to younger consumers, further extending the life cycles of these well-known brands.[14] Finding new users is often difficult, however. Gerber, for example, failed in attempts to sell its products to the 15-to-22 age group as desserts and snacks. Many still regarded Gerber products as baby food.[15]

### Find new uses
Q-Tips cotton swabs were originally sold as a baby-care item, but Chesebrough-Pond's Inc.'s marketers found a new use for them as makeup applicators. Cow Brand

FIGURE 9-6

## Organizational Conditions, Marketing Efforts, and Environmental Conditions at Each Stage of the Product Life Cycle

| *Introduction* | *Growth* | Maturity | | *Decline* |
| --- | --- | --- | --- | --- |
| | | *Early Maturity* | *Late Maturity* | |
| **Organizational conditions** | | | | |
| High costs | Smoothing production | Efficient scale of operation | Low profits | |
| Inefficient production levels | Lowering costs | Product modification work | Standardized production | |
| Cash demands | Operation efficiencies | Decreasing profits | | |
| | Product improvement work | | | |
| **Environmental Conditions** | | | | |
| Few or no competitors | Expanding markets | Slowing growth | Faltering demand | Permanently declining demand |
| | | Strong competition | Fierce competition | |
| Limited product awareness and knowledge | Expanded distribution | Expanded market | Shrinking number of competitors | Reduction of competitors |
| Limited demand | Competition strengthens | Heightened competition | Established distribution patterns | Limited product offerings |
| | Prices soften a bit | | | Price stabilization |
| **Marketing Efforts** | | | | |
| Stimulate demand | Cultivate selective demand | Emphasize market segmentation | Ultimate in market segmentation | Increase primary demand |
| Establish high price | Product improvement | Improve service and warranty | Competitive pricing | Profit opportunity pricing |
| Offer limited product variety | Strengthen distribution | Reduce prices | Retain distribution | Prune and strengthen distribution |
| Increase distribution | Price flexibility | | | |

Source: Adapted from Burton H. Marcus and Edward M. Tauber, *Marketing Analysis and Decision Making* (Boston: Little, Brown, 1979), pp. 115–116. Copyright © 1979 by Burton H. Marcus and Edward M.Tauber. Reprinted by permission of Little, Brown and Company.

baking soda was used primarily in cooking until its product life cycle was extended by finding new uses as a denture cleaner, swimming-pool pH adjuster, cleaning agent, flame extinguisher, first-aid remedy, and refrigerator freshener.[16]

### Change the package size, label, or product quality

Levi Strauss Canada Inc. introduced a limited-edition jean called 555. The straight-leg jean uses details of the original jean that Levi Strauss made during the California

Gold Rush of 1849. Each pair carries a five-digit serial number. A postage-paid card is used to register each pair of the jeans.[17] One of the best examples of a product that has been managed well and has avoided the decline stage is Tide. This synthetic detergent, introduced in 1947, continues to sell well in the 1990s. But more than 50 modifications of packaging, cleaning performance, sudsing characteristics, esthetics, and physical properties have been made during its lifetime.[18]

## Consumer Adoption Process

**adoption process** A series of stages consumers go through, from learning of a new product to trying it and deciding to purchase it regularly or to reject it.

Once the product is launched, consumers begin a process of evaluating the new item. This evaluation is known as the **adoption process** — the process whereby potential consumers go through *a series of stages from learning of the new product to trying it and deciding to purchase it regularly or to reject it.* The process has some similarities to the consumer decision process discussed in Chapters 7 and 8. The stages in the consumer adoption process can be classified as follows:

1. *Awareness.* Individuals first learn of the new product but lack information about it.
2. *Interest.* They begin to seek out information about it.

---

### I·S·S·U·E·S  I·N  I·N·T·E·R·N·A·T·I·O·N·A·L  M·A·R·K·E·T·I·N·G

## *British Airways Focuses on the Customer*

BA = British Airways = Bloody Awful.

That's the way people used to think about British Airways. But not anymore. Now the airline is ranked among the top three in the world — along with Swissair and Singapore Airlines — in customer service. What happened?

BA's transformation began in 1983, when Sir Colin Marshall became CEO. Marshall immediately set to work to change the airline's focus from operations to customers. Market surveys showed that passengers place twice as much importance on friendly service as they do on operational factors like fast check-in. But BA was not a customer-oriented organization; even its managers had failed to recognize how highly passengers value sympathy and courtesy. Marshall's greatest challenge was to convince the airline's 35 000 employees that travellers need to be treated like people, not like units or components of a transportation system.

Marshall launched an extensive training program, called "Putting People First," that was designed to teach employees to put themselves in the passenger's shoes. A new motto — "To fly, to serve" — was created, and $80 million was spent upgrading business- and first-class accommodations. Marshall (who was once a steward on a cruise ship) also undertook to "deregiment" the airline: first-class passengers are

served meals at times of their choosing; the menu has been broadened; and on some aircraft, in-flight movies have been replaced by individual video screens showing a wide selection of classics and recent box-office hits. Business-class service has been expanded, and passengers may now enjoy such amenities as a separate check-in counter and a departure lounge with comfortable chairs and free refreshments.

Perhaps the most significant aspect of British Airways' experience is that management recognized that the entire organization had to improve its performance; simply telling service personnel to "smile" would not do the job. According to Marshall, BA's success is a result of careful setting of goals and an overall team effort. The airline as a whole set out "to be the best" — and succeeded.

Sources: John Marcom, Jr., "The Middle of the Bus," *Forbes* (July 9, 1990), pp. 96–97; Mark Maremont, "How British Airways Butters Up the Passenger," *Business Week* (March 20, 1990), p. 94; Lois Madison Reamy, "The World's Best Airlines," *Institutional Investor* (June 1989), pp. 195–198; Patricia Sellers, "How to Handle Customers' Gripes," *Fortune* (October 24, 1988); and Michael Thomas, "Coming to Terms with the Customer," *Personnel Management* [U.K.] (February 1987), pp. 24–28.

3. *Evaluation.* They consider whether the product is beneficial.

4. *Trial.* They make a trial purchase in order to determine its usefulness.

5. *Adoption/Rejection.* If the trial purchase is satisfactory, they decide to make regular use of the product.[19] Of course, rejection may take place at any stage of the process.

Marketing managers need to understand the adoption process so that they can move potential consumers to the adoption stage. Once the manager is aware of a large number of consumers at the interest stage, steps can be taken to stimulate sales. For example, when consumer interest in buying a combined shampoo/conditioner began to grow, Procter & Gamble introduced Pert Plus with samples sent to homes in addition to its regular advertising campaign. Sampling, if it is successful, is a technique that reduces the risk of evaluation and trial, moving the consumer quickly to the adoption stage.

## Adopter Categories

Some people will purchase a new product almost as soon as it is placed on the market. Others wait for additional information and rely on the experiences of the first purchasers before making trial purchases. **Consumer innovators** are the *first purchasers* at the beginning of a product's life cycle. Some families were first in the community to buy colour television sets.[20] Some doctors are the first to prescribe new drugs,[21] and some farmers will use new hybrid seeds much earlier than their neighbors do.[22] Some people are quick to adopt new fashions,[23] while some drivers are early users of automobile diagnostic centres.[24]

A number of investigations analyzing the adoption of new products have resulted in the identification of five categories of purchasers based on relative time of adoption, which are shown in Figure 9–7.

**consumer innovators**   The first purchasers — those who buy a product at the beginning of its life cycle.

**FIGURE 9 – 7**

**Categories of Adopters on the Basis of Relative Time of Adoption**

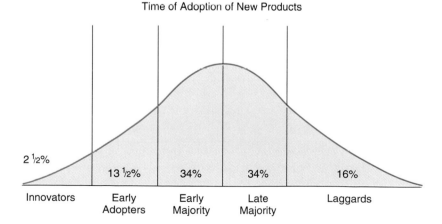

Time of Adoption of New Products

2 ½%   13 ½%   34%   34%   16%

Innovators   Early Adopters   Early Majority   Late Majority   Laggards

Source: Everett M. Rogers and F. Floyd Shoemaker, *Communication of Innovations* (New York: Free Press, 1971), p. 182. Copyright © 1971 by The Free Press of Glencoe. Reprinted by permission.

The **diffusion process** refers to this *gradual or quick acceptance of new products and services by the members of a community or social system.* Figure 9–7 shows this process as following a normal distribution. A few people adopt at first, and then the number of adopters increases rapidly as the value of the innovation becomes apparent. The rate finally diminishes as fewer potential consumers remain in the nonadopter category.

Since the categories are based on the normal distribution, standard deviations are used to partition each category. Innovators are defined as the first 2.5 percent of those individuals who adopt the new product; laggards are the final 16 percent to adopt. Excluded from the figure are the nonadopters — persons who never adopt the innovation.

## Identifying the First Adopters

Locating first buyers of new products represents a challenge for the marketing manager. If the right people can be reached early in the product's development or introduction, they may serve as a test market, evaluating the products and possibly making suggestions for modifications. Since early purchasers are frequently opinion leaders, from whom others seek advice, their attitudes towards new products are communicated in their neighborhood and in clubs and organizations. Acceptance or rejection of the innovation by these purchasers may serve as a kind of signal for the marketing manager, indicating the probable success or failure of the new product.[25]

Unfortunately, persons who are first adopters of one new product may not necessarily be innovators for other products or services. A large number of studies have, however, established some general characteristics possessed by most first adopters.

In general, first adopters tend to be younger, have a higher social status, be better educated, and enjoy a higher income. They are more mobile than later adopters, and change both their jobs and their home addresses more often. They are more likely to rely on impersonal information sources than are later adopters, who depend more on promotional information from the company and word-of-mouth communications.[26]

## What Determines the Rate of Adoption?

The electronic calculator replaced the slide rule as the engineering student's friend as soon as prices came within range of the student budget. On the other hand, it took 13 years to convince most corn farmers to use hybrid seed corn — an innovation capable of doubling corn yields — even though some progressive farmers adopted it at once. The adoption rate is influenced by five characteristics of the innovation.[27]

1. *Relative advantage:* the degree to which the innovation appears superior to previous ideas. The greater the relative advantage — whether manifested in lower price, physical improvements, or ease of use — the faster the adoption rate.
2. *Compatibility:* the degree to which the innovation is compatible with existing facilities or consistent with the values and experiences of potential adopters. The business student who purchases a personal computer will likely buy one that is compatible with those at the school he or she attends or with those of his or her friends.

---

### A·P·P·L·Y·I·N·G  T·H·E  C·O·N·C·E·P·T·S

## *Factors Affecting Product Development Considerations in the 1990s*

Where have all the "flower children" gone? They've grown up to become "green consumers." Every era has its own lingo. Some words and terms that were current only 20 years ago are now language relics, while many words and phrases in common usage today were unknown in 1970. Here is a lexicon that illustrates our changing times.

| YESTERDAY | TODAY |
|---|---|
| The Peace Movement | The Green Movement |
| Cold war | Global warming |
| "Make love, not war" | "Think globally, act locally" |
| Dropping out | Recycling |

| | |
|---|---|
| Acid rock | Acid rain |
| LSD | PCBs |
| Pet rocks | Endangered species |
| The Me generation | The Tree generation |
| "Shop till you drop" | "Living with less" |
| Conspicuous consumption | Sustainable development |

Five names we wish had never been in the news: **Love Canal, Bhopal, Chernobyl, the *Exxon Valdez*, Hagersville**

Source: "The Environmental Issue," *Royal Bank Reporter* (Spring 1990), p. 9.

---

3. *Complexity:* the more difficult to understand or use the new product is, the longer it will take to be generally accepted in most cases.

4. *Divisibility:* the degree to which the innovation may be used on a limited basis. First adopters face two types of risk — financial losses and the risk of ridicule by others — if the new product proves unsatisfactory. The option of sampling the innovation on a limited basis allows these risks to be reduced and, in general, should accelerate the rate of adoption.[28] Computers can be divisible; instead of buying a complete new system on the market, a consumer can try the basic components using a home TV set, and do without a printer.

5. *Communicability:* the degree to which the results of the product may be observable by or communicated to others. If the superiority of the innovation can be displayed in a tangible form, it will increase the adoption rate.

These five characteristics can be used, to some extent, by the marketing manager in accelerating the rate of adoption. First, will consumers perceive the product as complex, or will its use necessitate a significant change in typical behavioural patterns? Product complexity must be overcome by promotional messages of an informational nature. Products should be designed to emphasize their relative advantages and, whenever possible, be divisible for sample purchases. If divisibility is physically impossible, in-home demonstrations or trial placements in the home may be used. Positive attempts must also be made to ensure compatibility of the innovation with the adopters' value systems.

These actions are based on extensive research studies of innovators in agriculture, medicine, and consumer goods. They should pay off in increased sales by accelerating the rate of adoption in each of the adopter categories.

## Consumer Products and Industrial Products: A Definition

How a firm markets its products depends largely on the product itself. For example, a perfume manufacturer stresses subtle promotions in prestige media such as

*Chatelaine* and *Vogue* magazines, and markets the firm's products through exclusive department stores and specialty shops. Cadbury Schweppes Powell Ltd. markets its candy products through candy wholesalers to thousands of supermarkets, variety stores, discount houses, and vending machines. Its marketing objective is to saturate the market and to make its candy as convenient as possible for potential buyers. A firm manufacturing and marketing fork-lifts may use sales representatives to call on purchasing managers and ship its product either directly from the factory or from regional warehouses.

Marketing strategy differs for consumer products and industrial products. As defined earlier, consumer products are those destined for use by the ultimate consumer, and industrial products are those used directly or indirectly in producing other goods for resale. These two major categories can be broken down further.

## Characteristics of Consumer Products

The consumer assesses satisfaction by calculating benefits expected minus costs incurred. Costs involve *effort* and *risk*.[29] Effort is the amount of money, time, and energy the buyer is willing to expend to acquire a given product. In addition, there are risks that the product will not deliver the benefits sought. There are five types of such possible risk: financial, psychological, physical, functional, and social.

There are four categories of products — convenience, preference, shopping, and specialty. Each category can be defined according to the buyer's evaluation of the effort and risk required to obtain the product. Figure 9–8 illustrates the classification system. Two points shown in the figure should be especially noted. First, increasing risk and effort permits the marketer to broaden the scope of marketing strategy (shown by the widening arrow). That is, a wider variety of marketing-mix combinations can be used to gain a differential advantage for shopping and specialty products than can be used for convenience and preference products. Second, the concept of high and low product involvement is incorporated into this classification. The shaded area represents low involvement.

**convenience products** Products that are lowest in terms of both effort and risk.

*Convenience products* As shown in Figure 9–8, **convenience products** are defined as *lowest in terms of both effort and risk*. That is, the consumer will not spend much money or time in purchasing these products, nor does he or she perceive significant levels of risks in making a selection. These are the products the consumer wants to purchase frequently, immediately, and with a minimum of effort: common illustrations are commodities, "unsought" (emergency) items, and impulse products.

Examples of consumer goods that fall into the convenience category include fresh produce and grocery staples, umbrellas, gum, and batteries. Convenience services would include taxis and mass transit.

**preference products** Products that are slightly higher on the effort dimension and much higher on risk than convenience products.

*Preference products* The second category shown in Figure 9–8 is termed **preference products.** Such products are *slightly higher on the effort dimension and much higher on risk than convenience products*. In fact, the distinction between convenience and preference products is primarily one of buyer-perceived risk. Often the consumer perceives a higher level of risk chiefly due to the marketer's efforts, particularly in branding and advertising. Some companies, for example, have successfully convinced consumers that their brand of a low-priced product conveys greater benefits than competing ones — as, for example, with Bayer aspirin.

## FIGURE 9 – 8

### A Strategic Classification of Products

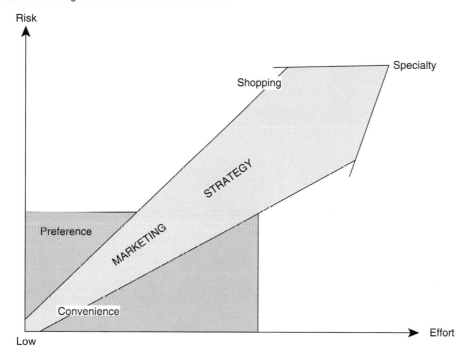

Widening arrow indicates broadened scope of marketing-mix differentiating factors

Shaded area indicates low buyer involvement with these types of products

Source: Patrick Murphy and Ben M. Enis, "Classifying Products Strategically," *Journal of Marketing* (July 1986), p. 25.

The most prominent examples of preference products are in the consumer packaged goods industry (for example, toothpaste and soft drinks). Consumers may "prefer" the taste and image of Diet Coke, based on advertising appeals or brand preference. However, they are likely to substitute Diet Pepsi or perhaps a low-calorie brand of iced tea if the monetary or time effort involved in acquiring the preferred product is too large.

Since the consumer is unwilling to expend much effort in purchasing convenience or preference goods, the manufacturer must strive to make obtaining them as convenient as possible. Newspapers, soft drinks, and candy are sold in almost every supermarket, variety store, service station, and restaurant. Where retail outlets are physically separated from a large number of consumers, the manufacturers may use vending machines for their customers' convenience. They must protect fragile brand loyalty by ensuring that their product is easily available.

Retailers usually carry several competing brands of preference products and are unlikely to promote any particular brand. The promotional burden therefore falls

*A pink Mercedes? The manufacturers of this product were certainly serving a specialty market when they designed this car. Everything about it, from the colour to the styling, makes it a high-risk item. But the customer who finally buys it would likely be willing to pay more for it because of its unconventional features. Can you think of any other products that fit into this category?*

on the manufacturer. Firms must advertise extensively to develop consumer acceptance for their products.

**shopping products** Products that are usually purchased only after the consumer has compared competing products.

*Shopping products*   In contrast with convenience goods, **shopping products** are usually purchased only *after the consumer has compared competing products* on such bases as price, quality, style, and colour in competing stores. The consumer is willing to forgo consumption for a period in order to evaluate product offerings because he or she anticipates gaining monetary savings and/or greater satisfaction of needs by evaluating alternatives.

The purchaser of shopping products lacks complete information prior to the actual purchase and gathers additional information during the shopping trip. A woman intent on adding a new dress to her wardrobe may visit many stores, try on perhaps 30 dresses, and spend days making the final decision. She may follow a regular route from store to store in surveying competing offerings and will ultimately select the dress that most appeals to her. New stores carrying assortments of shopping products must ensure that they are located near other shopping-product stores so that they will be included in shopping expeditions.

Shopping products are typically more expensive than convenience or preference products and are most often purchased by women. In addition to women's apparel, shopping products include such items as jewellery, furniture, appliances, shoes, and used automobiles.

Some shopping products, such as children's shoes, may be classified as *homogeneous* — that is, the consumer views them as essentially the same — while others, such as furniture and clothing, are *heterogeneous* — essentially different. Price is a more important factor in the purchase of homogeneous shopping products while quality and styling are more important in the purchase of heterogeneous products.[30]

Brands are often less important for shopping than for convenience products. Although some furniture brands may come to mind, they are typically less important than the physical attributes of the product, its price, styling, and even the retail store that handles the brand. And although apparel companies have spent large amounts of money in promoting their brands, the dress buyer knows that the brand is inside the dress, and is generally more impressed with how the dress looks on her and with its fit than with the hidden label.

Manufacturers of shopping products use fewer retail stores than is common for convenience or preference products since purchasers can be expected to expend some effort in finding what they want to buy and retailers will expend more effort on selling an exclusively distributed product. Thinness of the market may also affect the number of outlets. Retailers often purchase directly from the manufacturer or its representative rather than going through the wholesalers. Fashion merchandise buyers for department stores and specialty shops make regular visits to Toronto, Montreal, New York, and Winnipeg on buying trips. Manufacturers often visit regional centres such as Vancouver, Edmonton, or Moncton to meet retailers there. Buyers for furniture retailers often go directly to the factories of furniture manufacturers or visit major furniture trade shows.

*Specialty products* As the arrowhead in Figure 9–8 shows, marketing managers may attempt to move their shopping products into the specialty category. This means that consumers will no longer "shop" for alternatives but will accept only one brand. The major distinction between shopping products and specialty products revolves around effort, rather than risk. The specialty-products purchaser is well aware of what he or she wants and is willing to make a special effort to obtain it. The nearest Leica camera dealer may be 20 km away, but the camera enthusiast will go to that store to obtain what he or she may consider to be the ultimate in cameras. The Campbell River collector who longs for a $2500 *objet d'art* of Steuben glassware is willing to journey to Vancouver to find the nearest Steuben dealer.

**Specialty products** are the *highest in both effort and risk, due to some unique characteristics that cause the buyer to prize that particular brand*. The buyer possesses relatively complete information about the product prior to the shopping trip and is unwilling to accept substitutes.

Specialty products are typically high-priced and are frequently branded. Since consumers are willing to exert a considerable effort in obtaining the good, fewer retail outlets are needed. Mercury outboard motors and Porsche sports cars may be handled by only one or two retailers for each 100 000 population.

**specialty products** Products that are highest on both effort and risk, due to some unique characteristics that cause the buyer to prize that particular brand.

## Applying the Consumer Goods Classification System

The four-way classification system described above gives the marketing manager additional information for use in developing a marketing strategy. For example, if a new food product sells well in a test market as a preference good, this provides insights about marketing needs in branding, promotion, pricing, and distribution methods. The impact of the product classifications on their associated consumer factors and to marketing-mix variables is shown in Figure 9–9.

But the classification system also poses problems of which the marketing manager must be aware. One pitfall is that it suggests a neat, four-way series of demarcations into which all products can easily be fitted. Some products do fit neatly int one of the classifications, but others fall into grey areas between categories.

How, for instance should a new automobile be classified? It is expensive, is branded, and is handled by a few exclusive dealers in each city. But before it is

**Managerial Implications of Classifying Products Strategically**

| | Product Category | | | |
|---|---|---|---|---|
| *Managerial Focus* | *Convenience* | *Preference* | *Shopping* | *Specialty* |
| Buyer's perception of price | low effort, low risk | low effort, medium risk | high effort, medium risk | high effort, high risk |
| Buyer behaviour | impulse or habit (auto reorder) | routine (straight rebuy) | limited (modified rebuy) | extensive (new task) |
| Marketer's objective | move to preference or shopping category, or dominate via low cost | brand loyalty | source or store loyalty | absolute (source *and* brand) loyalty |
| Marketer's basic strategy | high volume, cost minimized, or move product | high volume, brand identify, differentiation | high volume or high margin, segmentation | high margin, limited volume, market "niche" |
| Product strategy | standard grades and quantities, quality control, innovations copied quickly | standard grades and quantities, quality control, some R&D | standard base, many options, much R&D, warranties | custom design, much R&D, warranties, personalized service |
| Price strategy | market | market | bundled or negotiated | negotiated |
| Monetary nonmonetary | minimize time and risk | minimize time, warrant risk | accommodate time, warrant risk | pamper for time and risk |
| Place strategy | saturation distribution | intensive distribution | selective distribution | exclusive distribution |
| Promotion | point-of-purchase, some sales promotion | mass advertising, sales promotion, some personal selling | personal selling, some advertising | publicity, personal selling, testimony |

Source: Murphy and Enis,"Classifying Products Strategically," p. 35

classified as a specialty good, other characteristics must be considered. Most new-car buyers shop extensively among competing models and auto dealers before deciding on the best "deal." A more effective method of using the classification system, therefore, is to consider it a continuum representing degrees of effort expended by the consumer.[31] The new-car purchase can then be located between the categories of shopping and specialty products, but nearer the specialty-products end of the continuum.

A second problem with the classification system is that consumers differ in their buying patterns. One person will make an unplanned purchase of a new Dodge Spirit, while others will shop extensively before purchasing a car. One buyer's impulse purchase does not make the Spirit a convenience product. Products are classified by the purchase patterns of the *majority* of buyers.

*The generator floor of the Mactaquac Hydro-Electric plant in New Brunswick. An industrial installation of this size — complete with the generators and pumps, the accessory equipment, and the component parts and materials required to ensure its operation — represents a major marketing and sales opportunity. A well-trained sales representative, after researching the plant's needs, could design a product package that would satisfy a specific requirement and win his or her company a lucrative contract.*

## Classifying Industrial Products

The foregoing classification system can also be used for industrial products. But a more common system categorizes industrial products into five categories: installations, accessory equipment, fabricated parts and material, raw materials, and industrial supplies. Industrial buyers are professional customers; their job is to make effective purchase decisions. Although details may vary, the purchase decision process involved in buying supplies of flour for General Mills, for example, is much the same as that used in buying the same commodity for Robin Hood. Thus this classification system for industrial goods is based on product uses rather than on consumer buying patterns.

*Installations* **Installations** are *major capital assets (like factories and heavy machinery) that are used to produce products and services.* Installations are the specialty products of the industrial market. New aircraft for Canadian Airlines International, locomotives for Canadian National, or a new pulp mill for MacMillan Bloedel, are examples of installations.

Since installations are relatively long-lived and involve large sums of money, their purchase represents a major decision for an organization. Sales negotiations often extend over a period of several months and involve the participation of numerous decision-makers. In many cases, the selling company must provide technical expertise. When custom-made equipment is involved, representatives of the selling firm work closely with the buyer's engineers and production personnel to design the most feasible product.

**installations** Major capital assets that are used to produce products and services.

Price is almost never the deciding factor in the purchase of installations. The purchasing firm is interested in the product's efficiency and performance over its useful life. The firm also wants a minimum of breakdowns. "Down time" is expensive because employees are nonproductive (but must still be paid) while the machinery is being repaired.

Since most of the factories of firms that purchase installations are geographically concentrated, the selling firm places its promotional emphasis on well-trained salespeople, who often have a technical background. Most installations are marketed directly on a manufacturer-to-user basis. Even though a sale may be a one-time transaction, contracts often call for regular product servicing. In the case of extremely expensive installations, such as computers and electronic equipment, some firms lease the installations rather than sell them outright and assign personnel directly to the lessee to operate or to maintain the equipment.

**accessory equipment**
Second-level capital items that are used in the production of products and services but are usually less expensive and shorter-lived than installations.

*Accessory equipment*    Fewer decision-makers are usually involved in purchasing **accessory equipment** — *second-level capital items that are used in the production of products and services but are usually less expensive and shorter-lived than installations.* Although quality and service remain important criteria in purchasing accessory equipment, the firm is likely to be much more price-conscious. Accessory equipment includes such products as desktop calculators, hand tools, portable drills, small lathes, and typewriters. Although these goods are considered capital items and are depreciated over several years, their useful life is generally much shorter than that of an installation.

**industrial distributor**    A wholesaler who operates in the industrial goods market and typically handles small accessory equipment and operating supplies.

Because of the need for continuous representation and the more widespread geographic dispersion of accessory equipment purchasers, a *wholesaler*, often called an **industrial distributor**, may be used to contact potential customers in each geographic area. Technical assistance is usually not necessary, and the manufacturer of accessory equipment can often use such wholesalers quite effectively in marketing the firm's products. Advertising is more important for accessory manufacturers than it is for installation producers.

**component parts and materials**
Finished industrial goods that actually become part of the final product.

*Component parts and materials*    While installations and accessory equipment are used in producing the final product, **component parts and materials** are the *finished industrial goods that actually become part of the final product.* Champion spark plugs make a new Chevrolet complete; nuts and bolts are part of a Peugeot bicycle; tires are included with a Dodge pickup truck. Some materials, such as flour, undergo further processing before producing a finished product.

Purchasers of component parts and materials need a regular, continuous supply of uniform-quality goods. These goods are generally purchased on contract for a period of one year or more. Direct sale is common, and satisfied customers often become permanent buyers. Wholesalers are sometimes used for fill-in purchases and in handling sales to smaller purchasers.

**raw materials**    Farm products (such as cattle, wool, eggs, milk, pigs, and canola) and natural products (such as coal, copper, iron ore, and lumber).

*Raw materials*    Farm products (such as cattle, wool, eggs, milk, pigs, and canola) and natural products (such as coal, copper, iron ore, and lumber) constitute **raw materials**. They are similar to component parts and materials in that they become part of the final products.

Since most raw materials are graded, the purchaser is assured of standardized products with uniform quality. As with component parts and materials, direct sale of raw materials is common, and sales are typically made on a contractual basis. Wholesalers are increasingly involved in the purchase of raw materials from foreign suppliers.

Price is seldom a controllable factor in the purchase of raw materials, since it is often quoted at a central market and is virtually identical among competing sellers. Purchasers buy raw materials from the firms they consider most able to deliver in the quantity and the quality required.

*Supplies*    If installations represent the specialty products of the industrial market, then operating supplies are the convenience products. **Supplies** are *regular expense items necessary in the daily operation of a firm, but not part of its final product.*

Supplies are sometimes called **MRO items**, because they can be divided into three categories: (1) *maintenance items,* such as brooms, floor-cleaning compounds, and light bulbs; (2) *repair items,* such as nuts and bolts used in repairing equipment; and (3) *operating supplies,* such as heating fuel, lubricating oil, and office stationery.

The regular purchase of operating supplies is a routine aspect of the purchasing manager's job. Wholesalers are very often used in the sale of supplies due to the items' low unit prices, small sales, and large number of potential buyers. Since supplies are relatively standardized, price competition is frequently heavy. However, the purchasing manager spends little time in making purchase decisions about such products. He or she frequently places telephone orders or mail orders, or makes regular purchases from the sales representative of the local office-supply wholesaler.

> **supplies**    Regular expense items necessary in the daily operation of a firm, but not part of its final product.
>
> **MRO items**    Industrial supplies, so called because they can be categorized as maintenance items, repair items, or operating supplies.

---

**A·P·P·L·Y·I·N·G  T·H·E  C·O·N·C·E·P·T·S**

## *The Ordeal of Becoming a McDonald's French Fry*

French fries are a big deal at McDonald's. They account for about one-fifth of total sales. Leaving out breakfast sales, 70 percent of McDonald's customers order them. As a result, McDonald's pays particular attention to the raw materials used in its popular product.

McDonald's uses only Russet Burbanks, which have a unique taste and make crispier french fries because of a high solid-to-water ratio. McDonald's has exacting standards for its fries. McDonald's fries are:

- Steamed, not blanched or quick-scalded
- Dried at higher than normal heat levels, and
- Sprayed with sugar, not dipped.

The company believes this process produces better fries. Even the length has to be just right. Only 20 percent of McDonald's fries can be less than 2 inches long; 40 percent have to be 2 to 3 inches long; and another 40 percent must exceed 3 inches.

McDonald's ran into some problems with its raw materials standards when it expanded overseas. Russet Burbanks are not grown in Europe, and potato imports are prohibited. McDonald's considers European-grown potatoes unacceptable, so it tried some unique approaches to getting Russet Burbanks into Europe. The Dutch agreed to admit five potatoes after an eight-month quarantine, but they were destroyed by a potato virus. McDonald's planted Russet Burbanks in Spain under the theory that they would be acceptable throughout Europe when Spain joined the Common Market in 1983, but this effort also failed. However, McDonald's did get its potatoes to grow in Tasmania, so they can now supply Australian outlets with the proper type of french fries. In any case, it is clear that McDonald's regards Russet Burbanks as an important raw material in its business.

Source: Meg Cox, "A French-Fry Diary: From the Idaho Furrow to Golden Arches," *Wall Street Journal* (February 8, 1982), pp. 1, 23.

# Summary

A critical variable in the firm's marketing mix is the product it plans to offer its target market. The best price, most efficient distribution channel, and most effective promotional campaign cannot maintain continuing purchases of an inferior product.

Consumers view products not only in physical terms but more often in terms of expected want satisfaction. The broad marketing conception of a product encompasses a bundle of physical, service, and symbolic attributes designed to produce this want satisfaction. The total product concept consists of the product image, brand, package and label, and warranty and service.

Most successful products pass through the four stages of the product life cycle: introduction, growth, maturity, and decline. The rate at which they pass through the cycle is affected partly by many external, uncontrollable factors. It can also be affected in many instances by managerial decisions. Therefore, marketers should not view the product life cycle simply as a deterministic phenomenon to which they can only react.

Several departures from the traditional product life cycle are noted. First, there is evidence that product life cycles may be getting shorter, particularly in the introductory and growth stages. Second, research shows that a number of products do not actually conform to the standard product life-cycle model, and several alternative product life cycles are outlined. Finally, there is the matter of fashions and fads. Fashions are currently popular products that tend to have recurring life cycles. By contrast, fads are fashions with abbreviated life cycles.

The product life-cycle concept provides significant opportunities to adjust marketing strategy. Pricing, distribution, and communication strategies, as well as product strategy, may affect the life-cycle stage, and should also be appropriate to it. Marketers often attempt to extend the life cycles of successful individual products. Of course, they generally have little control over the life cycle of a product *category*.

Consumers go through a series of stages in adopting new product offerings: initial product awareness, interest, evaluation, trial purchase, and adoption or rejection of the new product.

Although first adopters of new products vary among product classes, several common characteristics have been isolated. First adopters are often younger, better educated, and more mobile, and they have higher incomes and higher social status than later adopters.

The rate of adoption for new products depends on five characteristics: (1) relative advantage, the degree of superiority of the innovation over the previous product; (2) compatibility, the degree to which the new product or idea is consistent with existing operations or the value system of potential purchasers; (3) complexity of the new product; (4) divisibility, the degree to which trial purchases on a small scale are possible; and (5) communicability, the degree to which the superiority of the innovation can be transmitted to other potential buyers.

Goods and services are classified as either consumer or industrial products. Consumer products are used by the ultimate consumer and are not intended for resale or further use in producing other products. Industrial products are used either directly or indirectly in producing other products for resale.

Differences in consumer buying habits can be used to further classify consumer products into four categories: convenience products, preference products, shopping products, and specialty products. Industrial products are classified on the basis of product uses. The five categories in the industrial-goods classification are installations, accessory equipment, component parts and materials, raw materials, and industrial supplies.

## KEY TERMS

product
warranty
product life cycle
fashions
fads
adoption process
consumer innovator

diffusion process
convenicncc products
preference products
shopping products
specialty products
installations

accessory equipment
industrial distributor
component parts and materials
raw materials
supplies
MRO items

## REVIEW QUESTIONS

1. Describe the total product concept.
2. Draw and explain the product life-cycle concept.
3. Outline the various forms that the traditional product life cycle might take.
4. Suggest several means by which the life cycle of a product (such as Scotch Tape) can be extended.
5. Identify and briefly explain the stages in the consumer adoption process.
6. Describe each of the determinants of the rate of adoption.

7. Why is the basis used for categorizing industrial products different from that used for categorizing consumer products?
8. Compare a typical marketing mix for convenience products with a mix for specialty products.
9. Outline the typical marketing mix for a shopping product.
10. Discuss the marketing mix for the various types of industrial products.

## DISCUSSION QUESTIONS AND EXERCISES

1. Select a specific product in each stage of the product life cycle (other than those shown in the text). Explain how marketing strategies might vary by life-cycle stage for each product.
2. Trace the life cycle of a recent fad. What marketing strategy implications can you draw from your study?
3. Home burglar-alarm systems using microwaves are a fast-growing product in the home-security market. Such systcms operate by filling rooms with microwave beams, which set off alarms when an intruder intercepts one of them. What suggestions can you make to accelerate the rate of adoption for this product?
4. Classify the following consumer products:
   a. Furniture
   b. Puma running shoes

   c. Felt-tip pen
   d. Head of lettuce
   e. Nissan sports car
   f. Binaca breath freshener
   g. *Hockey News* magazine
   h. Original oil painting
5. Classify the following into the appropriate industrial products category. Briefly explain your choice for each.
   a. Calculators
   b. Land
   c. Light bulbs
   d. Marketing research consulting
   e. Paper towels
   f. Nylon
   g. Airplanes
   h. Tires

# MICROCOMPUTER EXERCISE

## Return on Investment

**Directions:** Use the Menu Item titled "Return on Investment" on the *Foundations of Marketing* disk to solve each of the following problems.

1. The management of Blue Grass Ind. of Vancouver is considering the development of a new product. Total development costs are estimated at $2 million, with forecasted sales of $12 million and profits of $1 million. Calculate the ROI for the new product.

2. Simpson Manufacturing Co. of Guelph, Ontario, has marketed an industrial grinder for years. Current sales are $10 million annually, but last year Simpson Manufacturing earned only $450 000 on the product due to the rapidly rising costs of component parts. A recent proposal for a new version of the grinder using less-expensive components would increase profits to $900 000 while maintaining sales at $14 million. However, this would require several plant-layout changes costing $2.8 million. What is the ROI of the proposed new product?

3. MotorSports of Penticton, B.C., has developed a new type of ski boat. Special placement tests at ski-instruction schools on Lake Okanagan proved highly successful. The firm's top management estimates that it would be able to generate $7 million in revenue from the sale of the boat at wholesale prices. However, development expenses for the boat are estimated at $3 million. Management believes that the new boat would add $800 000 to the firm's annual profits. What is the ROI of the proposed ski boat?

# Carushka

The bodywear industry has grown by leaps and bounds over the past decade. It began with dancewear, which later was picked up by millions of aerobics-class participants. The next step — from aerobics classes to fitness centres — was a logical extension of the product's sales curve. Today bodywear, alternatively called *dancewear* or *exercise wear*, has become acceptable street dress.

Ric Wanetik, a vice-president at Marshall Field's (a U.S. department-store chain), has assessed the reason for this evolution: "I happen to believe people buying this merchandise aren't necessarily doing it to run out and exercise in; they're buying it because it's fashion-smart." Designer Rebecca Moses echoes this view: "People like the way they look in workout clothes, so they incorporated elements of these designs into their everyday wardrobes."

But despite its rapid growth, designer bodywear is a highly volatile market. Designs, labels, and even manufacturers are continually emerging and disappearing as consumer tastes shift. In fact, the entire life cycle of designer bodywear is only about three months.

Firms that seek to compete in this marketplace must have a coherent product strategy. One designer, Carushka, has based her overall product and competitive strategy on innovation: "I am willing to take the step where no one else is. I am a pioneer." Carushka got the idea for her first leotard, a striped model, while watching a Gene Kelly movie. She was the first designer to do stripes, the first to do cottons, and the first to do prints. It is no wonder that the motto of Carushka's company became "Expect the unexpected."

When she began her business, Carushka would load her station wagon with her merchandise and deliver it personally to her first 100 accounts. The leotards were packaged in plastic bags with invoices attached, because Carushka operated on a cash-only basis at the time.

Then her line became popular with specialty boutiques that sold it to the consumer innovators in this marketplace. Since her firm was too small to advertise to such a large market, Carushka developed an alternative marketing strategy: she began sending her designs free to celebrities. The resulting media coverage brought her the broader audience she was seeking. Word-of-mouth promotion then took over, and Carushka became an overnight success. Later she tripled her sales by selling her line through department stores.

The innovative designer applied some unorthodox theories to her company and her lines. A believer in inner personality, numerology, and astrology, Carushka used astrology to pick people for the various functions within the company and numerology to number her garments, avoiding numbers she considered unlucky. But these tactics did not help Carushka when she tried to market a line of men's bodywear. She had teamed up with actor/dancer John Travolta, and the initial response to the line was quite positive, with $1 million worth of product shipped in the first four months. However, the men's bodywear segment of the industry did not hold up in the long run.

Despite this failure, Carushka remained true to her strategic emphasis on innovation. She refused to test-market her new lines, explaining, "This is my look. You either buy it or you don't." But Carushka also admitted that "you have to be crazy to be an entrepreneur."

Entrepreneurial enterprises like Carushka's face two types of risk. First, there is the constant danger that consumers will reject the product offering, as in the case of the Travolta line. Second, in a fashion-oriented industry such as bodywear even the most innovative ideas can quickly be copied. As a result, the pace of innovation becomes a key factor in the long-term success of a firm like Carushka's.

Carushka also believes that the bodywear market will go back to basics. In fact, this is exactly what happened to her own business. The designer was forced to take a few years off due to health reasons. When she reopened in January 1987, she again concentrated on her original customer base — specialty boutiques. She remarked, "They are more fun than selling to department stores." Carushka no longer uses sales reps; she now sells via consumer and retail mail orders and through wholesalers. An international sales effort has met with great success, particularly in Japan, where customers expect high quality and are prepared to pay well for it.

While wholesale sales remain the largest portion of the business, Carushka has been working with a catalogue retailer, to increase mail- and phone-order business. And in 1990 Carushka opened her own retail store on Ventura Boulevard in Sherman Oaks, California. Within a year the boutique, with its fantasy-world design, had become a magnet for celebrities and for the young and affluent.

Carushka still believes in the importance of innovation in the bodywear industry. Her company's slogan remains "Expect the unexpected."

SOURCES    Allison Kyle Leopold. "Workout Clothes: From the Gym to the Street," *New York Times Magazine* (September 28, 1986), pp. 67–68, 110; "Carushka Is Still Shipping, Says Company Won't Close," *Women's Wear Daily* (June 14, 1985), p. 10; and Jim Seale, "Exercise Wear," *Stores* (June 1987), pp. 13–19; update interview with Kim Spath, Carushka, April 1991.

## Questions

1. How would you classify Carushka with respect to product life-cycle stage?
2. Relate this case to the chapter's discussion of fashions and fads.
3. How did Carushka's product strategy facilitate the consumer adoption process?
4. What part of the consumer products classification would best match Carushka's product lines?
5. Assess Carushka's decision to increase mail- and phone-order business.

# Product Management

1. To explain the various product-mix decisions that must be made by marketers.
2. To explain why most firms develop a line of related products rather than a single product.
3. To outline alternative new-product strategies and the determinants of their success.
4. To identify and explain the various organizational arrangements for new-product development.
5. To list the stages in the product development process.
6. To discuss the role of brands, brand names, and trademarks.
7. To explain the package and its major functions.

IN California, police forces are using Canadian eggs to fight crime. The Japanese are using them to brush their teeth. And women everywhere are using them to find out whether they are pregnant.

All this has come about because Export Packers of Winnipeg decided that the product it was handling could be extended into a whole line of other products. The new line of products features valuable enzymes in egg white that the company has found are literally worth their weight in gold.

Export Packers Ltd., with $207 million in annual sales, has been processing eggs — mainly for large food manufacturers like Robin Hood, Catelli, and General Mills — since 1925. However, in 1982, the country's largest egg processor began a lucrative sideline using sophisticated technology imported from Italy.

Under a licence granted by a Milan company, which developed the process, Export Packers began extracting an enzyme called lysozyme from the whites of eggs. Lysozyme is an antibacterial agent that is used as a cheese preservative, among other things. The Japanese put it in toothpaste.

Export Packers now manufacture's 35 000 kilograms each year. And at $80 to $100 (U.S.) a kilogram, the returns are pretty good.

The company's success in commercially extracting lysozyme gave it incentive to examine other valuable products that could be extracted from eggs. It started its own research laboratory and began to develop technology to extract other egg white components.

One product is the enzyme avidin, used in pregnancy-test kits. Successfully removing this product on a commercial basis is no mean feat, since the enzyme makes up only 0.005 of the egg white. It took the company two years to perfect the process. At a selling price of $250 000 per kilogram, avidin is worth the trouble.

Next, Export Packers developed a process for extracting two other enzymes: riboflavin-binding protein and ovomucoid. The former is worth between $200 000 and $300 000 a kilogram, while the latter is worth about $10 000 a kilogram.

Both are used in drug tests. Ovomucoid is used by law enforcement agencies to detect cocaine in body fluids.

The technology for extracting these products was developed by local talent. "We are kind of proud of that fact," says Leslie Carvalho, Export's manager of technical services. "When somebody is going to pay you $200 000 a kilogram, it's got to be a very good product," he said.

The firm is currently doing research on commercial methods of reducing or removing the cholesterol that is found in the egg's yellow centre. That would allow food manufacturers to advertise their products as low-cholesterol for the health-conscious consumer. Export Packers is also looking at extracting other materials in the yolk for use in pharmaceuticals.

While Export Packers' main business is eggs — its 110 employees process some 1.5 million eggs each day — the company has successfully expanded its product line into other areas. This development is giving the company a mix of quite different products on which to base its current and future business. Thus, drastic downturns or fluctuations in one component of the business may be offset by other products.[1]

# Introduction

Product management requires continual diligence in assessing the changing needs of the market. Normally it is important to have products that provide a range of opportunities for the company. This range of products is described as a product mix. A **product mix** is the *assortment of product lines and individual offerings available from a marketer*. Its two components are the **product line,** *a series of related products, and the* **individual offerings** *or single products within those lines.*

**product mix**    The assortment of product lines and individual offerings available from a marketer.

**product line**    A series of related products.

**individual offerings**    Single products within a product line.

Product mixes are typically measured by width and depth of assortment. Width of assortment refers to the number of product lines that the firm offers, while depth of assortment refers to the extension of a particular product line.[2] Canada Packers offers an assortment of consumer product lines — meats, and several unrelated grocery items such as peanut butter (see Figure 10–1). These product lines would be considered the width of the Canada Packers product mix. The depth is determined by the number of individual offerings within each product line. For example, their meat line consists of fresh meats, smoked meats, and processed meats, while the grocery line is represented by York peanut butter and several types of canned vegetables. The company also sells a nonedible line of byproducts.

### FIGURE 10-1

### The Canada Packers Product Mix

| | Width of Assortment | | |
|---|---|---|---|
| | *Meats* | *Groceries* | *Nonedible* |
| **Depth of Assortment** | Fresh meats | Peanut butter | By Products |
| | Bacon | Mincemeat | Soap |
| | Pepperoni | Canned pumpkin | Hides |
| | Wieners | Cheese | Pharmaceutical raw materials |
| | Bologna | Lard | |
| | Canned ham | Shortening | |
| | Poultry | | |
| | Kolbassa | | |
| | Garlic sausage | | |

## The Existing Product Mix

The starting point in any product-planning effort is to assess the firm's current product mix. What product line does it now offer? How deep are the offerings within each of the product lines? The marketer normally looks for gaps in the assortment that can be filled by new products or by modified versions of existing products. Expansion or redevelopment of existing product lines is usually the easiest approach for a firm to take, since the market requirements for these lines are generally well known.

## Cannibalization

The firm wants to avoid a costly new-product introduction that will adversely affect sales of one of its existing products. A *product that takes sales from another offering in a product line* is said to be **cannibalizing** the line. Marketing research should ensure that cannibalization effects are minimized or at least anticipated. When Coca-Cola introduced Diet Coke, its marketers were resigned to the fact that sales of their existing diet brand, Tab, would be negatively affected.

**cannibalizing**  Situation involving one product taking sales from another offering in a product line.

## Line Extension

An important rationale for assessing the current product mix is to determine whether line extension is feasible. A **line extension** refers to *the development of individual offerings that appeal to different market segments but are closely related to the existing product line*. If cannibalization can be minimized, line extension provides a relatively cheap way of increasing sales revenues at minimal risk. Oh Henry chocolate bars can now be purchased in an ice-cream-bar format, in addition to their traditional form. This illustrates the line extension of an existing product.

**line extension**  The development of individual offerings that appeal to different market segments but are closely related to the existing product line.

Once the assessment of the existing product mix has been made and the appropriate line extensions considered, marketing decision-makers must turn their attention to product-line planning and the development of new products.

# The Importance of Product Lines

Firms that market only one product are rare today. Most offer their customers a product line — a series of related products. Polaroid Corporation, for example, began operations with a single product, a polarized screen for sunglasses and other products. Then, in 1948, it introduced the world's first instant camera. For the next 30 years, these products proved sufficient for annual sales and profit growth. By 1983, however, instant cameras accounted for only about two-thirds of Polaroid's sales. The company had added hundreds of products in both industrial and consumer markets, ranging from nearly 40 different types of instant films (for various industrial, medical, and other technical operations) to batteries, sonar devices, and machine tools.[3] Several factors account for the inclination of firms such as Polaroid to develop a complete line rather than concentrate on a single product.

## Desire to Grow

A company places definite limitations on its growth potential when it concentrates on a single product. In a single 12-month period, Lever Brothers once introduced 21 new products in its search for market growth and increased profits. A study by a group of management consultants revealed that firms expect newly developed products to account for 37 percent of their sales and 51 percent of their profits over the five years following the products' introduction.[4]

Firms often introduce new products to offset seasonal variations in the sales of their current products. Since the majority of soup purchases are made during the winter months, Campbell Soup Company has made attempts to tap the warm-weather soup market. A line of fruit soups to be served chilled was test-marketed, but results showed that consumers were not yet ready for fruit soups. The firm continued to search for warm-weather soups, however, and in some markets it has added gazpacho (and other varieties meant to be served chilled) to its product line.

## Making Optimal Use of Company Resources

By spreading the costs of operations over a series of products, a company may find it possible to reduce the average costs of all products. Texize Chemicals Company started with a single household cleaner and learned painful lessons about marketing costs when a firm has only one major product. Management rapidly added the products K2r and Fantastik to the line. The company's sales representatives can now call on middlemen with a series of products at little more than the cost for marketing a single product. In addition, Texize's advertising produces benefits for all products in the line. Similarly, production facilities can be used economically in producing related products. For example, auto companies regularly produce a range of products, from convertibles to vans to sports cars, from a basic car design. Finally, the expertise of all the firm's personnel can be applied more widely to a line of products than to a single one.

## Increasing Company Importance in the Market

Consumers and middlemen often expect a firm that manufactures and markets small appliances to also offer related products under its brand name. The Maytag Company offers not only washing machines but also dryers, since consumers often demand matching appliances. Gillette markets not only razors and blades but also a

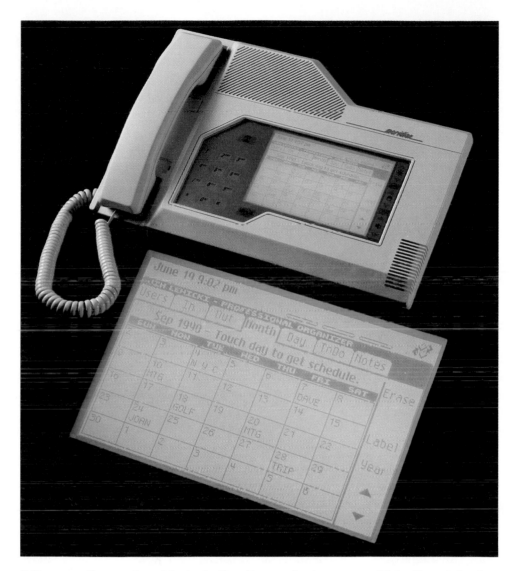

*Northern Telecom's new line of business telephones combines new features with a contemporary new design. New concepts and directions are constantly being followed by NorTel's research and development department. By adding new products to its regular line, the firm is able to meet the changing needs of the business telephone market.*

full range of grooming aids, including Foamy shaving cream, Right Guard deodorant, Gillette Dry Look hair spray, and Super Max hair dryers.

The company with a line of products is often more important to both the consumer and the retailer than is the company with only one product. Shoppers who purchase a tent often buy related items, such as tent heaters, sleeping bags and air mattresses, camping stoves, and special cookware. Recognizing this tendency, the Coleman Company now includes in its product line dozens of items associated with camping. The firm would be little known if its only product were lanterns. Similarly, new cameras from Eastman Kodak help the firm sell more film — a product that carries a 60 percent profit margin.[5]

## Exploiting the Product Life Cycle

As its output enters the maturity and decline stages of the life cycle of a product category, the firm must add new products if it is to prosper. The regular addition of new products to the firm's line helps ensure that it will not become a victim of product obsolescence. In the 1980s, Northern Telecom realized that the basic rotary-dial telephone was a very tired product, one that was in the decline stage of its life cycle. A new line of telephones had to be developed in order to retain a share of the residential telephone market.

# New-Product Planning

The product development effort requires considerable advance planning. New products are the lifeblood of many business firms, and a steady flow of new entries must be available if such firms are to survive. Some new products represent major technological breakthroughs: for instance, biotechnology, which permits the transfer of genes from any living organism to another, has the potential to spur the invention of many new pharmaceutical products. Other new products are simple product-line extensions — that is, the "new" product is new only to the company or to the customer. One survey found that for products introduced in one five-year period, about 85 percent were line extensions, and only 15 percent were truly new products.[6]

## The Product Decay Curve

New-product development is risky and expensive. In 1989, despite the continuing potential of biotechnology, only one of 400 North American start-ups, Geneutech, had made a sustained profit.[7] A Conference Board study of 148 medium and large North American manufacturing companies revealed that one out of three new industrial and consumer products introduced within the previous five years had failed. The leading cause of new-product failure was insufficient or poor marketing research.[8]

Dozens of new-product ideas are required to produce even one successful product. Figure 10–2 depicts the product decay curve from a 1968 survey of 51

**A·P·P·L·Y·I·N·G  T·H·E  C·O·N·C·E·P·T·S**

### *Factory of the Future May Be New Era for Marketing*

Substantial changes are taking place on the factory floor. Marketing is being radically affected, too, and is itself influencing the changes.

One of the changes is an accelerated movement toward the "factory of the future" — a completely automated factory capable of making high-quality products at great speed and low cost.

At the core of the changes in the factory is the new generation of flexible manufacturing systems, which lie between the extremes of assembly-line production (which depends on large throughput and standardization) and hand crafting (which allows individual customization, but with lower output).

The significance for marketing is the ability of such systems to make products in batches at a cost per unit, regardless of batch size, approximately equal to that associated with mass production. This will allow a

fracturing of mass markets into smaller segments, providing expanding ranges of options, models sizes, colours, and customizing.

For example, a saw manufacturer has developed a computer-driven laser-cutting system capable of producing specialized blades to suit the special needs of individual customers. The sales rep takes a terminal to the customer, discusses special needs, then punches a button to activate the laser in the home plant to cut the specialized blades.

Such possibilities will have great significance for the product mixes maintained by companies, as well as for the process of new product development.

Source: Adapted from Ron McTavish, "Factory of the Future May Be New Era for Marketing," *Marketing News* (October 9, 1989), p. 1 of reprint.

F I G U R E  1 0 – 2

**Decay Curve of New-Product Ideas**

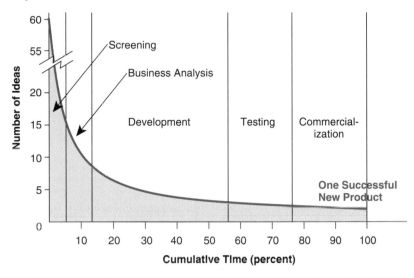

Source· Reprinted by permission from *New Products Management for the 1980s* (New York: Booz, Allen & Hamilton, 1982), p. 3.

companies. Of every 58 ideas produced in these firms, only 12 passed the preliminary screening test designed to determine whether they were compatible with company resources and objectives. Of these 12, only 7 showed sufficient profit potential in the business analysis phase. Three survived the development phase, two made it through the test-marketing stage, and only one, on the average, was commercially successful. Thus, less than 2 percent of new ideas resulted in a successful product.

A 1981 follow-up study reported that while the success rate had not improved, new-product development was becoming more cost-effective. According to the new data, some 54 percent of total new-product expenditures were made on products that became successes, compared with 30 percent in 1968. Capital investment in new products had fallen from 46 percent to 26 percent of total new-product spending.[9] These figures suggest that new-product development has become more efficient.

## Determinants of Success for New Products

What determines the success or failure of a new product? A research effort known as Project New Product suggests the following six categories as determinants of new-product outcomes.[10]

1. The relative strengths of the new product and its marketplace launch.
2. The nature and quality of the information available during the product development process.
3. The relative proficiency of new-product development efforts.
4. The characteristics of the marketplace at which the new product is aimed.
5. The fit or compatibility of the new product and the firm's resource base.
6. The specific characteristics of the new-product effort.

These hypothetical variables allowed Robert Cooper of McMaster University to classify various types of new products. Cooper contends that the most important key to new-product success lies in the product strategy itself. In his research he found that in the cases he studied, the best 20 percent of the products had an astounding success rate of 82 percent. In contrast, the 20 percent at the other end of the scale (the "me-too" products) suffered a *failure* rate of 78 percent.

## Characteristics of the Superior Product

What, then, *is* a superior product? Cooper found that a number of characteristics constituted the superior-product dimension. In descending order of importance, these critical characteristics are as follows:

1. A product that meets customers' needs better than competing products.
2. A product that offers features or attributes to the customer that competing products do not.
3. A product of higher quality than competitive products (one that has tighter specifications, is stronger, lasts longer, or is more reliable).
4. A product that does a special task or job for the customer — something that cannot be done with existing products.
5. A product that is highly innovative, totally new to the market.
6. A product that permits the customer to reduce costs.[11]

Products with these characteristics supported by creative marketing strategies will greatly contribute to a profitable product line.

### Product Development Strategies

The firm's strategy for new-product development should vary according to the existing product mix and the determinants cited above. Marketing decision-makers

**FIGURE 10 – 3**

**Forms of Product Development**

|  | Old Product | New Product |
|---|---|---|
| **Old Market** | Product Improvement | Product Development |
| **New Market** | Market Development | Product Diversification |

Source: Charles E. Meisch, "Marketers, Engineers Should Work Together in 'New Product' Development Departments," *Marketing News* (November 13, 1981), p. 10; earlier discussion of these strategies is credited to H. Igor Ansoff, "Strategies for Diversification," *Harvard Business Review* (September–October 1957), pp. 113–124; see also Philip Kotler, *Principles of Marketing* 2nd ed. (Englewood Cliffs, NJ: Prentice-Hall, 1983), pp. 34, 52.

also need to look at the firm's current market position. Figure 10–3 provides a means for looking at overall product development strategy. Four forms of product development are suggested: product improvement, market development, product development, and product diversification.

A **product improvement strategy** refers to *a modification in existing products*. Tide is an example of a product that has undergone constant product improvement over the years. Because of such improvements it continues as a leading product. Another example is the "Quality Is Job One" program established by Ford. And this was apparently more than just a slogan: Ford's products are now more competitive with Japanese cars.

> **product improvement strategy**
> A modification in existing products.

A **market development strategy** concentrates on *finding new markets for existing products*. Market segmentation (discussed in Chapters 3 and 4) is a useful tool in such an effort. Penetrating the home market with the fax machine — a product already established in the office — illustrates such a strategy.

> **market development strategy**
> Finding new markets for existing products.

A **product development strategy** refers to *introducing new products into identifiable or established markets*. Chrysler's Magic Wagon, for example, was a tremendous success because it provided consumers with a spacious vehicle that was as easy to drive, and as comfortable, as a car.

> **product development strategy**
> Introducing new products into identifiable or established markets.

Sometimes the new product is the firm's first entry in a particular market. In other cases, firms choose to introduce new products into markets in which they have already established positions, in an attempt to increase overall market share. These new offerings are called *flanker brands*.

**Product diversification strategy** refers to *the development of new products for new markets*; the introduction of the VCR is an example. In some cases, the new target markets complement existing markets; in others, they do not.

> **product diversification strategy**
> The development of new products for new markets.

New products should be consistent with the firm's overall strategic orientation. Assume that a beverage firm has set four strategic requirements for a new product:

1. It must appeal to the under-21 age segment.

2. It must use off season or excess capacity.

---

## A·P·P·L·Y·I·N·G  T·H·E  C·O·N·C·E·P·T·S

### *Does the World Really Want a . . . ?*

Here are some new products and services that may or may not make it in today's competitive marketplace. What do you think about their chances of success?

- *Career Guard*. John Lorriman was a $40 000-a-year executive who fought with his boss constantly. Eventually he was fired, and a new-product idea was generated. Lorriman began developing an insurance policy that pays a person's salary for two years if he or she is laid off or fired because of personality conflicts, takeover, or bankruptcy. Career Guard, which is designed for executives earning $25 000 or more, also provides legal help and employment assistance. The cost is 1.3 percent of the person's salary.
- *Pick Point Enterprises*. A small firm, Pick Point

Enterprises, is now offering lighted tennis balls. This new product is made of translucent plastic and contains a chemical that radiates light, much as a firefly does.

- *Juicie Treat*. Rosebud Products has introduced just the thing for Fido. Juicie Treat is a drink for dogs that is made of vitamin-enriched sugar water but has the smell of beef bouillon. It can also be mixed with dog food and sells for double the price of milk.

Source: Peggy Berkowitz, "These Days, You Don't Have to Be the Boss's Kid to Get Job Insurance," *Wall Street Journal* (April 7, 1982); "Business Bulletin," *Wall Street Journal* (January 28, 1982), p. 1; and "Arf! Gimme a Virgin Bullshot," *Newsweek* (April 12, 1982), p. 64.

3. It must successfully penetrate a new product category for the firm.

4. It could simply be a "cash cow" that funds other new products.[12]

Each of these criteria would fit in well with the orientation, skills, and resources of the firm.

# The Organizational Structure for New-Product Development

As the above section indicates, new-product planning is a complex area. The critical nature of product-planning decisions requires an effective organizational structure to make them. A prerequisite for efficient product innovation is an organizational structure designed to stimulate and co-ordinate new-product development. New-product development is a specialized task that requires the expertise of many departments. A company that delegates new-product development responsibility to the engineering department often discovers that engineers sometimes design products that are good from a structural standpoint but poor in terms of consumer needs. Many successful medium and large companies assign new-product development to one or more of the following: (1) new-product committees, (2) new-product departments, (3) product managers, or (4) venture teams.

## New-Product Committees

The most common organizational arrangement for new-product development is the *new-product committee.* Such a committee typically comprises representatives of top management in such areas as marketing, finance, manufacturing, engineering, research, and accounting. Committee members are less concerned with conceiving and developing new-product ideas than with reviewing and approving new-product plans.

Since key executives in the functional areas are committee members, their support for a new-product plan is likely to result in its approval for further development. However, new-product committees tend to be slow, are generally conservative, and sometimes compromise in order to expedite decisions so that members may get back to their regular company responsibilities.

## New-Product Departments

To overcome the limitations of the new-product committee, a number of firms have established a separate, formally organized department responsible for all phases of a product's development within the firm, including making screening decisions, developing product specifications, and co-ordinating product testing. The head of the department is given substantial authority and usually reports to the president or to the top marketing officer.

## Product Managers

**product managers**    Individuals assigned one product or product line and given responsibility for determining its objectives and marketing strategies.

**Product managers** (also called **brand managers**) are *individuals assigned one product or product line and given responsibility for determining its objectives and marketing strategies.* Procter & Gamble assigned the first product manager back in 1927 when it made one

## A·P·P·L·Y·I·N·G  T·H·E  C·O·N·C·E·P·T·S

### A Typical Product Manager Under 30

Joe Antonelli graduated from Dalhousie University eight years ago with a major in political science. He then transferred to York University's MBA program. After graduating with good marks two years later, he accepted a position with a large consumer-goods manufacturer.

Joe's first assignment was as brand manager for a liquid sugar substitute. Although he reported directly to the marketing vice-president, Joe was completely in charge of the product and made decisions about an optimal promotional mix for the product, its price, its distribution channels, and even its chemical content.

Joe found it difficult at first, but his marketing efforts resulted in a market share increase of more than two percentage points in a 15-month period. He also averaged 50 hours a week on the job.

Joe's salary increased steadily. In less than a year he had been promoted to product manager for a more important part of the firm's business. His new job involved the responsibility for all of the firm's cake mixes and for the frosting line. Another raise accompanied this promotion.

This job is both stimulating and challenging. In effect, Joe runs a miniature company within the larger firm, with all the problems and decisions of a one-product firm. His next promotion will place him in charge of a group of four to six product managers.

## I·S·S·U·E·S  I·N  I·N·T·E·R·N·A·T·I·O·N·A·L  M·A·R·K·E·T·I·N·G

### Getting Closer to Men

Gillette's new Sensor razor incorporates some revolutionary shaving technology. Men who use the razor rave about it. Store managers report that it's "flying off the shelves" — 5 million units were sold in one recent month alone.

Sensor's success shows that long-term research and development programs can pay off. Gillette spent more than $200 million and 13 years developing the new shaving system. Along the way, it applied for 22 patents and developed a new manufacturing process using lasers to weld the blades to the support bar. For television and print advertising during the year in which Sensor was introduced, it budgeted up to $110 million. Never before had the company spent so much to launch a single product.

Developing the Sensor was a gamble for Gillette; the idea was to induce users of disposable razors to convert to shaving systems, which are much more profitable. But disposable razors are very popular — they account for 40 percent of men's spending on shaving products — and Gillette ran the risk of cutting into sales of its own disposable brand, Good News. In addition, management was reluctant to make a huge investment in manufacturing and marketing while its existing razors were still making enormous profits.

The level of risk was reduced by careful attention to the needs and opinions of consumers.

Sensor is turning out to be a global as well as a national success. It is advertised with the same visuals around the world — only the voice-over changes. The same dialogue (in 26 different languages) is used in Japan, Europe, and the United States. Gillette is building a worldwide mass-market brand while saving millions in packaging, advertising, and other production and marketing costs.

Sources: James Cox, "Sensor: Five Million Chins and Counting," *USA Today* (February 6, 1990); Alison Fahey, "Sensor Sales Sharp," *Advertising Age* (May 7, 1990), p. 60; Jack Falvey, "How the King Maintains His Edge," *Wall Street Journal* (April 23, 1990); Keith H. Hammonds, "How a $4 Razor Ends Up Costing $300 Million," *Business Week* (January 29, 1990), pp. 62–63; Joshua Levine, "Global Lather," *Forbes* (February 5, 1990), pp. 146–148; Ellen Neuborne, "Buyers in a Lather over Sensor," *USA Today* (February 5, 1990) and "Products of the Year," *Fortune* (December 4, 1989), p. 168.

person responsible for Camay soap.[13] The role of product manager is now widely accepted by marketers. Johnson & Johnson, Canada Packers, and General Mills are examples of firms that employ product managers.

Product managers are deeply involved in setting prices, developing advertising and sales promotion programs, and working to provide assistance to sales representatives in the field. Although product managers have no line authority over the field sales force, they share the objective of increasing sales for the brand, and managers try to help salespeople accomplish their task. In multiproduct companies, product managers are key people in the marketing department. They provide individual attention to each product, while the firm as a whole has a single sales force, a marketing research department, and an advertising department that all product managers can use.

In addition to performing product analysis and planning, the product manager must use interpersonal skills and sales skills to gain the co-operation of people over whom he or she has no authority. This occurs with levels above the manager, as well as with those in sales and advertising.

Besides having primary responsibility for marketing a particular product or product line, the product manager is often also responsible for new-product development, creating new-product ideas, and making recommendations for improving existing products. These suggestions become the basis for proposals submitted to top management.

The product manager system is open to one of the same criticisms as the new-product committee: new-product development may get secondary treatment because of the manager's time commitments for existing products. Although a number of extremely successful new products have resulted from ideas submitted by product managers, it cannot be assumed that the skills required for marketing an existing product line are the same as those required for successfully developing new products.[14]

## Venture Teams

An increasingly common technique for organizing new-product development is the use of venture teams.[15]

**venture-team concept** An organizational strategy for developing new products through combining the management resources of technology, capital, management, and marketing enterprise.

The **venture-team concept** is *an organizational strategy for developing new products through combining the management resources of technology, capital, management, and marketing expertise.*[16] Like new-product committees, venture teams are composed of specialists from different functions in the organization: engineering representatives for expertise in product design and the development of prototypes; marketing staff members for development of product-concept tests, test marketing, sales forecasts, pricing, and promotion; and financial accounting representatives for detailed cost analyses and decisions concerning the concept's probable return on investment.

Unlike new-product committees, venture teams do not disband after every meeting. Members are assigned to the project as a major responsibility, and the team possesses the necessary authority to both plan and carry out a course of action.

As a means of stimulating product innovation, the team is typically separated from the permanent organization and is also linked directly with top management. One company moved its three-member venture team from its divisional headquarters to the corporate head office. Since the venture-team manager reports to the division head or to the chief administrative officer, communications problems are minimized and high-level support is assured.

The venture team usually begins as a loosely organized group of members with common interest in a new-product idea. Team members are frequently given released time during the workday to devote to the venture. If viable product proposals are developed, the venture team is formally organized as a task force within a venture department or as a task force reporting to a vice-president or to the chief executive officer. When the commercial potential of new products has been demonstrated, the products may be assigned to an existing division, may become a division within the company, or may serve as the nucleus of a new company. The flexibility and authority of the venture team allows the large firm to operate with the manoeuvrability of smaller companies.

## Stages in the New-Product Development Process

New-product development strategy should be built upon the existing business strategy of the company. Companies that have successfully launched new products are more likely to have had a formal new-product process in place for some time. They are also more likely to have a strategic plan, and be committed to growth through internally developed new products.[17]

Once the firm is organized for new-product development, it can establish procedures for evaluating new-product ideas. The product development process may be thought of as involving seven stages: (1) development of overall new-product strategy, (2) new-product idea generation, (3) screening, (4) business analysis, (5) final product development, (6) test marketing, and (7) commercialization. At each stage, management faces the decision to abandon the project, continue to the next stage, or seek additional information before proceeding further.[18] The process is illustrated in Figure 10–4.

**FIGURE 10 – 4**

**Seven Stages of the New-Product Development Process**

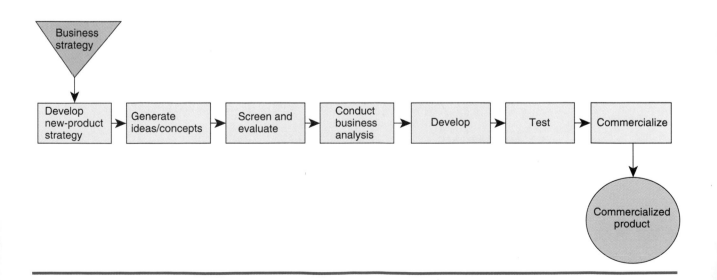

## New-Product Strategy

New-product strategy links corporate objectives to the new-product effort, provides direction for the new-product process, and identifies the strategic roles in the product line that the new products should play. It also helps set the formal financial criteria to be used in measuring new-product performance and in screening and evaluating new-product ideas.[19]

## Idea Generation

New-product development begins with an idea. Ideas emanate from many sources: the sales force, marketing employees, research and development (R & D) specialists, competitive products, retailers, inventors outside the company, and customers who write letters asking "Why don't you...?" It is extremely important for the firm to develop a system of stimulating new ideas and for rewarding persons who develop them.[20]

## Screening

This crucial stage involves separating ideas with potential from those incapable of meeting company objectives. Some organizations use checklists to determine whether product ideas should be eliminated or subjected to further consideration. These checklists typically include such factors as product uniqueness; availability of raw materials; and compatibility of the proposed product with current product offerings, existing facilities, and capabilities. In other instances, the screening stage consists of open discussions of new-product ideas among representatives of different functional areas in the organization. This is an important point in the product development process, since any product ideas that go beyond this point will cost the firm considerable time and money.[21] Figure 10–5 presents some basic criteria used in the screening process.

FIGURE 10 – 5

**Basic Criteria for Preliminary Screening**

1. The item should be in a field of activity in which the corporation is engaged.
2. If the idea involves a companion product to others already being manufactured, it should be made from materials to which the corporation is accustomed.
3. The item should be capable of being produced on the type and kind of equipment that the corporation normally operates.
4. The item should be easily handled by the corporation's existing sales force through the established distribution pattern.
5. The potential market for the product should be at least $ _____.
6. The market over the next five years should be expected to grow at a faster rate than the GNP.
7. Return on investment, after taxes, must reach a minimun level of _____ percent.

Source: Reprinted from William S.Sachs and George Benson, *Product Planning and Management* (Tulsa, OK: Penn Well Books, 1981), p. 231.

## Business Analysis

Product ideas that survive the initial screening are then subjected to a thorough business analysis. This involves assessing the potential market, its growth rate, and the likely competitive strength of the new product. Decisions must be made in determining the compatibility of the proposed product with such company resources as financial support for necessary promotion, production capabilities, and distribution facilities.

Concept testing, or the consideration of the product idea prior to its actual development, is an important aspect of the business analysis stage. **Concept testing** is *a marketing research project that attempts to measure consumer attitudes and perceptions relevant to the new-product idea.* Focus groups (see Chapter 5) and in-store polling can be effective methods for assessing a new-product concept.

**concept testing**    A marketing research project that attempts to measure consumer attitudes and perceptions relevant to a new-product idea.

## Product Development

Those product ideas with profit potential are then converted into a physical product. The conversion process becomes the joint responsibility of development engineering, which is responsible for developing the original concept into a product, and the marketing department, which provides feedback on consumer reactions to alternative product designs, packages, features, colours, and other physical appeals. Numerous changes may be necessary before the original mock-up is converted into the final product.

The series of revisions, tests, and refinements should result in the ultimate introduction of a product with a greater likelihood of success. Some firms use their own employees as a sounding board and obtain their reactions to proposed new-product offerings. Employees at Levi Strauss test new styles by wearing them and providing feedback. A shoe manufacturer asks its workers to report regularly over an eight-week testing period on shoe wear and fit.[22]

But occasionally attempts to be first with a new product result in the premature introduction of new products. Kellogg and several other cereal makers experienced this problem some years ago, when they all failed in attempts to introduce freeze-dried fruit cereal. In their rush to be first on the market with the new offering, they all failed to perfect the product. The small, hard pellets of real fruit took too long to reconstitute in the bowl. Millions of bowls of cereal went into garbage cans.[23]

## Test Marketing

To determine consumer reactions to their products *and* to the proposed marketing plan under normal shopping conditions, a number of firms test-market their new offerings. Up to this point, consumer information has been obtained by submitting free products to consumers, who then gave their reactions. Other information may have been gathered by asking shoppers to evaluate competitive products, but test marketing is the first point at which the product must perform in a "real-life" environment.

**Test marketing** involves *selecting usually one to three cities or television-coverage areas considered reasonably typical of the total market, and introducing a new product in this area with a total marketing campaign.* A carefully designed and controlled test allows management to develop estimates of the effectiveness of marketing-mix decisions and projections of sales following full-scale introduction.

Some firms omit the test-marketing stage and move directly from product development to full-scale production. They cite three problems with test marketing:

**test marketing**    The selection of areas considered reasonably typical of the total market, and introducing a new product to such areas to determine consumer response before marketing the product nationally.

1. Test marketing is expensive. As one marketing executive pointed out,

   > it's very difficult to run a little [test market] for six months or a year in three or four markets across the [country] and then project what your sales volume is going to be two or three years in the future, mainly because you're testing in such small localities, generally to keep your costs down.
   >
   > You simply can't afford to test your product in markets like [Toronto or Montreal]. So you run your test in [smaller cities]. And your test costs are over $1 million even in places like that.[24]

2. Competitors who learn about the test market many disrupt the findings by reducing the price of their products in the test area, distributing cents-off coupons, installing attractive in-store displays, or giving additional discounts to retailers to induce them to display more of their products

   Test marketing a new product also communicates company plans to competitors before the product's introduction. The Kellogg Company discovered a new product with suspected sales potential by learning of a test marketing of a new fruit-filled tart designed to be heated in the toaster and served hot for breakfast. Kellogg rushed a similar product into full-scale production and became the first national marketer of the product they named Pop Tarts.

3. Long-lived durable goods (such as dishwashers, hair dryers, and VCRs) are seldom test-marketed, due to the major financial investment required for the development, the need to develop a network of dealers to distribute the products, and the parts and servicing required. A company such as Whirlpool invests from $1 million to $33 million in the development of a new refrigerator. To develop each silicon chip in an Apple microcomputer costs approximately $1 million and takes from one to fifteen months. Producing a prototype for a test market is simply too expensive, so the "go/no-go" decision for the new durable product is typically made without the benefit of test-market results.[25]

A decision to skip the test-marketing stage should be based on there being a very high likelihood of the product's success. The costs of developing a new detergent from idea generation to national marketing have been estimated at *$10 million*. Even though a firm will experience losses on any product that passes the initial screening process but is not introduced, it will still be much better off if it stops as soon as it discovers that the product cannot succeed. Otherwise, it may be faced with a failure like Corfam, an artificial leather that Du Pont introduced; the company suffered losses of more than *$100 million* over the lengthy period it tried to make Corfam a success.

## Commercialization

The few product ideas that have survived all the steps in the development process are now ready for full-scale marketing. Marketing programs must be established, outlays for production facilities may be necessary, and the sales force, middlemen, and potential customers must become acquainted with the new product.

New-product development should follow the step-by-step approach outlined in Figure 10–4. Systematic planning and control of all phases of development and introduction can be accomplished through the use of such scheduling methods as the Program Evaluation and Review Technique (PERT) and the Critical Path Method (CPM). These techniques map out the sequence in which each step must be

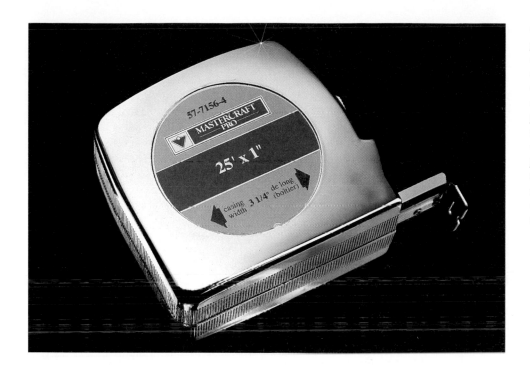

*Canadian Tire's Mastercraft products are identifiable by brand name and distinctive symbols. Customers can be assured of a consistent level of quality for all Mastercraft products, from paints to power tools. Deciding which products should become part of such a product line, or developing new product identifications in the mind of the consumer, is one of the tasks of the marketing manager.*

taken and show the time allotments for each activity. Detailed PERT and CPM flow charts not only will assist in co-ordinating all activities in the development and introduction of new products, but can also highlight the sequence of events that will be the most critical in scheduling.

## Product Deletion Decisions

While many firms devote a great deal of time and resources to the development of new products, the thought of eliminating old products from the firm's line is painful for many executives. Often sentimental attachments to marginal products prevent objective decisions to drop products with declining sales. Management finds it difficult to bury an old friend.

If waste is to be avoided, product lines must be pruned, and old products must eventually be eliminated from the firm's line. This decision is typically faced in the late-maturity and early-decline stages of the product life cycle. Periodic reviews of all products should be conducted in order to prune weak products or to justify their retention.

In some instances a firm will continue to carry an unprofitable product so as to provide a complete line of goods for its customers. Even though most supermarkets lose money on such bulky, low-unit-value items as salt, they continue to carry it to meet shopper demands.

Shortages of raw materials have prompted some companies to discontinue producing and marketing previously profitable items. Du Pont dropped an antifreeze from its product line due to raw material shortages.

Other cases arise in which profitable products are dropped because of failure to fit into the firm's existing product line. The development of automatic washing machines necessitated the development of a low-sudsing detergent. The Monsanto

Company produced the world's first low-sudsing detergent in the 1950s, naming it All. All was an instant success, and Monsanto was swamped with orders from supermarkets throughout the nation. But the Monsanto sales force was primarily involved with the marketing of industrial chemicals to large-scale buyers. A completely new sales force was required to handle a single product. Nine months after the introduction of All, Procter & Gamble introduced the world's second low-sudsing detergent and named it Dash. The Procter & Gamble sales force already handled hundreds of products and could spread the cost of contacting dealers over each of those products. Monsanto had only All. Rather than attempting to compete, Monsanto sold All in 1958 to Lever Brothers, a Procter & Gamble competitor with a marketing organization capable of handling the product.[26]

# Product Identification

Manufacturers identify their products through the use of brand names, symbols, and distinctive packaging. So also do large retailers such as Canadian Tire, with its line of Mastercraft products, and Simpsons and The Bay with their Beaumark brand. Almost every product that is distinguishable from another contains a means of identification for the buyer. Even a 5-year-old can distinguish a Chiquita banana from other ones. And the California Fruit Growers Exchange literally brands its oranges with the name Sunkist. The purchasing manager for a construction firm can turn over an ordinary sheet of roofing and find the name and symbol for Domtar. Choosing means of identification for the firm's output often represents a major decision area for the marketing manager.

## Brands, Brand Names, and Trademarks

**brand**   A name, term, sign, symbols, or design (or some combination thereof) used to identify the products of one firm and to differentiate them from competitive offerings.

**brand name**   Words, letters, or symbols that make up a name used to identify and distinguish the firm's offerings from those of competitors.

**trademark**   A brand that has been given legal protection and has been granted solely to its owner.

A **brand** is *a name, term, sign, symbol, or design (or some combination thereof) used to identify the products of one firm and to differentiate them from competitive offerings*. A **brand name** is that part of the brand consisting of *words, letters, or symbols making up a name used to identify and distinguish its firm's offerings from those of its competitors*.[27] The brand name is, therefore, that part of the brand that may be vocalized. A **trademark** is *a brand that has been given legal protection and has been granted solely to its owner*. Thus, the term trademark includes not only pictorial design but also the brand name.[28] Many thousands of trademarks are currently registered in Canada.

For the consumer, brands allow repeat purchases of products that have been found satisfactory. The brand assures a uniform quality and identifies the firm producing the product. The purchaser associates the satisfaction derived from a carbonated soft drink with the brand name Pepsi-Cola.

For the marketing manager, the brand serves as the cornerstone around which the product's image is developed. Once consumers have been made aware of a particular brand, its appearance becomes further advertising for the firm. The Shell Oil Company symbol is instant advertising to motorists who view it while driving. Well-known brands also allow the firm to escape some of the rigours of price competition. Although any chemist will confirm that all ASA tablets contain the same amount of the chemical acetylsalicylic acid, Bayer has developed so strong a reputation that it can successfully market its Aspirin at a higher price than competitive products. Similarly, McDonald's "golden arches" attract customers to its outlets.

## What Constitutes a Good Brand Name?

Good brand names are easy to pronounce, recognize, and remember.[29] Short names like Coke, Gleem, Dash, and Kodak meet these requirements. Multinational marketing firms face a particularly acute problem in selecting brand names: a brand name that works terrifically well in one country may prove disastrous in another due to language problems.

For 21 years, Nissan Motor Corporation marketers struggled with an easily mispronounced brand name — "Datsun" — for its cars and trucks. Nissan found that in English-speaking nations some people pronounced the *a* like the *a* in *hat*, while others pronounced it like the *o* in *got*, and the difference hindered brand recognition. Finally, Nissan marketers decided to change the name of all its automobile products to Nissan beginning with its Stanza model in 1982. Total costs of the change — effected in more than 135 countries — are estimated to have been as high as $150 million.[30]

Every language has "O" and "K" sounds, and "okay" has become an international word. Every language also has a short "a," so that Coca-Cola and Texaco are good in any tongue. An American advertising campaign for E-Z washing machines failed in the United Kingdom because the British pronounced "Z" as "zed," as we do in Canada.

The brand name should give the buyer the right connotation. Mercury Marine presents favourable images of boating pleasures. The Craftsman name used on the Sears line of quality tools also produces the correct image. Accutron suggests the quality of the high-priced and accurate timepiece made by the Bulova Watch Company. But what can the marketing manager do if the brand name is based on a strange-sounding company name? Sometimes the decision may be to poke fun at this improbable name, as in a promotional campaign built around the theme "With a name like Koogle, it has to be good!"

## The Brand Name Should Be Legally Protectable

S.C. Johnson and Son, makers of OFF, lost a court case against Bug Off since it was held that OFF was an improper trademark because it was not unusual enough to distinguish it from other similar products.[31]

*When all offerings in a class of products become generally known by the brand name of the first or leading brand in that product class*, the brand name may be ruled a descriptive **generic name**, after which the original owner loses exclusive claim to it. Generic names like cola, nylon, zipper, kerosene, linoleum, escalator, and shredded wheat were once brand names.

**generic name** A brand name over which the original owner has lost exclusive claim because all offerings in the associated class of products have become generally known by the brand name (usually that of the first or leading brand in the product class).

Bayer's Aspirin is the only ASA tablet permitted to carry that protected trademark in Canada. All other acetylsalicylic acid tablets are called ASA. In the United States, because Bayer did not protect its trade name, the generic name "aspirin" is given to all acetylsalicylic acid tablets. Most drug purchasers there would not know what an ASA tablet is.

There is a difference between brand names that are legally generic and those that are generic in the eyes of many consumers. Jell-O is a brand name owned exclusively by General Foods. But to most grocery purchasers the name Jell-O is the descriptive generic name for gelatin dessert. Legal brand names — such as Formica, Xerox, Frigidaire, Kodak, Frisbee, Styrofoam, Coke, Kleenex, Scotch Tape, Fiberglas, Band-Aid, and Jeep — are often used by consumers as descriptive names. Xerox is such a well-known brand name that it is frequently used as a verb. British and Australian consumers often use the brand name Hoover as a verb for vacuuming.

To prevent their brand names from being ruled descriptive and available for general use, companies must take deliberate steps to inform the public of their exclusive ownership of brand names. They may resort to legal action in cases of infringement. The Eastman Kodak Company developed a series of advertisements around the theme "If it isn't an Eastman, it isn't a Kodak." The Coca-Cola Company uses the ® symbol for registration immediately after the names Coca-Cola and Coke and sends letters to newspapers, novelists, and other writers who use the name Coke with a lowercase first letter, informing them that the name is owned by Coca-Cola.[32] These companies face the ironic dilemma of attempting to retain the exclusive rights to a brand name that, chiefly due to the success of their own marketing efforts, has become generic to a large market segment.

Since any dictionary word may eventually be ruled to be a generic name, some companies create new words to use for brand names. Such brand names as Keds, Rinso, and Kodak have obviously been created by their owners.

## Measuring Brand Loyalty

Brands vary widely in consumer familiarity and acceptance.[33] While a boating enthusiast may insist on a Mercury outboard motor, one study revealed that 40 percent of homemakers could not identify the brands of furniture in their own homes.[34]

Brand loyalty may be measured in three stages: brand recognition, brand preference, and brand insistence.

**brand recognition**   The first stage of brand loyalty; situation whereby a firm has developed enough publicity for a brand that its name is familiar to consumers.

**Brand recognition** is a company's first objective for newly introduced products — *to make them familiar to the consuming public*. Often the company achieves this goal through advertising. Sometimes it uses free samples or coupons offering discounts for purchases. Several new brands of toothpaste have been introduced on college campuses through free samples contained in Campus Pacs. Once the consumer has used the product, it moves from the "unknown" to the "known" category, and (provided the consumer was satisfied with the trial sample) he or she is more likely to repurchase it.

**brand preference**   The second stage of brand loyalty; situation in which, based on previous experience, consumers will choose a product rather than one of its competitors — if it is available.

**Brand preference** is the second stage of brand loyalty. Because of previous experience with the product, *consumers will choose it rather than competitors — if it is available*. Even if students in a classroom prefer Coca-Cola as a means of quenching their thirst, almost all of them will quickly switch to Pepsi-Cola or 7-Up when they discover that the vending machine has no Coke and the nearest supply is two buildings away. Companies with products at the brand-preference stage are in a favourable position with respect to competing in their industries.

**brand insistence**   The ultimate stage of brand loyalty; occurs when consumers will accept no alternatives and will search extensively for the product.

The ultimate stage in brand loyalty is **brand insistence**, which occurs when *consumers will accept no alternatives and will search extensively for the product*. Such a product has achieved a monopoly position with this group of consumers. Even though brand insistence may be the goal of many firms, it is seldom achieved. Only the most exclusive specialty goods attain this position with a large segment of the total market.

*The importance of brand loyalty*   A study of 12 patented drugs (including well-known drugs like Librium and Darvon) illustrates the importance of brand loyalty. The research indicated that patent expiration had minimal effect on the drugs' market

## A·P·P·L·Y·I·N·G  T·H·E  C·O·N·C·E·P·T·S

### *What's in a Name Change?*

For five years, executives at Alberta Gas Trunk Line Co. Ltd. toyed with the idea of changing the company's name. Alberta Gas Trunk, with its connotations of bewhiskered Victorians in frock coats tending rusted pipe, was hardly suitable for a company with more than $1 billion in annual revenues, diversified energy interests, and a mandate to build the Canadian portion of the Alaska Highway gas pipeline. But at a meeting in March 1980, executives hit on an obvious choice — a name that connotes newness or life in a host of languages.

The formal changeover to "Nova, An Alberta Corporation" cost $2 million in media and regulatory expenses, equivalent to about half a day's revenues. "Nobody could ever get the old name right; it was old-fashioned and far too long," says Nova senior vice-president Dianne Hall. "We also felt it was time to tell all Canadians just how multifaceted we are."

If the change helps protect Nova's share price from day-to-day stock market shocks, the three-month campaign will have been worthwhile. Not only that, the company is sure that the $1 million spent on advertising alone — including five television commercials and print ads in everything from rural weeklies to *Time* magazine — will erase forever any popular impression that the company is either a Crown corporation or a foreign-controlled resource monger.

Vancouver-based Intercorp Marketing Ltd. retained the Alberta Gas Trunk logo but came up with the six-part interlocking puzzle block — representing Nova's manufacturing, gas transmission, research, oil, petrochemical, and pipeline development interests — as a visual symbol of strength and diversity. Hall says that in general the feedback from shareholders and investment dealers has lived up to expectations. The francophone version of the campaign even elicited congratulations from Hydro-Québec.

Source: Adapted from Martin Keeley, "What's in a Name Change? For Nova, a Cool $2 Million," *Canadian Business* (February 1981), pp. 22–23.

shares or price levels, a resiliency credited to the brand loyalty for the pioneer product in the field.[35] Another measure of the importance of brand loyalty is found in the Brand Utility Yardstick used by the J. Walter Thompson advertising agency. These ratings measure the percentage of buyers who remain brand-loyal even if a 50 percent cost savings is available from generic products. Beer consumers were very loyal, with 48 percent refusing to switch. Sinus-remedy buyers were also brand-loyal, with a 44 percent rating. By contrast, only 13 percent of the aluminum-foil buyers would not switch to the generic product.[36]

Some brands are so popular that they are carried over to unrelated products because of their marketing advantages. *The decision to use a popular brand name for a new product entry in an unrelated product category* is known as **brand extension**. This should not be confused with line extension (discussed earlier in this chapter), which refers to adding new sizes, styles, or related products. Brand extension, by contrast, refers only to carrying over the brand name.

> **brand extension**   The decision to use a popular brand name for a new product entry in an unrelated product category.

Examples of brand extension are abundant in contemporary marketing. Deere & Co.'s insurance line prominently features the John Deere brand made famous in the farm machinery business. In fact, John Deere Insurance proudly notes: "Our name is the best insurance you can buy." Similarly, General Foods is extending its Jell-O brand. In some markets the company now has Jell-O Pudding Pops, Jell-O Slice Creme, and Jell-O Gelatin Pops.

## Choosing a Brand Strategy

Brands may be classified as family brands or individual brands. A **family brand** is *one brand name used for several related products*. E.D. Smith markets dozens of food

> **family brand**   Brand name used for several related products.

products under the E.D.Smith brand. Black and Decker has a complete line of power tools under the Black and Decker name. Johnson & Johnson offers parents a line of baby powder, lotions, plastic pants, and baby shampoo under one name.

On the other hand, such manufacturers as Procter & Gamble market hundreds of products with **individual brands** (for example, Tide, Cheer, Crest, Gleem, Oxydol, and Dash). Each such item is *known by its own brand name rather than by the name of the company producing it or an umbrella name covering similar items*. Individual brands are more expensive to market, since a new promotional program must be developed to introduce each new product to its target market.

**individual brand**   Brand that is known by its own brand name rather than by the name of the company producing it or an umbrella name covering similar items.

Using family brands allows promotional outlays to benefit all products in the line. The effect of the promotion is spread over each of the products. A new addition to the products marketed by the H.J. Heinz Company gains immediate recognition due to the well-known family brand. Family brands also facilitate the task of introducing the product — for both the customer and the retailer. Since supermarkets carry an average of nearly 10 000 items in stock, they are reluctant to add new products unless they are convinced of potential demand. A marketer of a new brand of turtle soup would have to promise the supermarket-chain buyer huge advertising outlays for promotion and evidence of consumer buying intent before getting the product into the stores. The Campbell Soup Company, with approximately 85 percent of the market, would merely add the new flavour to its existing line and could secure store placements much more easily than could a company using individual brand names.

Family brands should be used only when the associated products are of similar quality — or the firm risks the danger of harming its product image. Using the Mercedes brand name on a new, less expensive auto model might severely tarnish the image of the other models in the Mercedes product line.

Individual brand names should be used for dissimilar products. Campbell Soup once marketed a line of dry soups under the brand name Red Kettle. Large marketers of grocery products (such as Procter & Gamble, General Foods, and Lever Brothers) employ individual brands to appeal to unique market segments. Unique brands also allow the firm to stimulate competition within the organization and to increase total company sales. Product managers are also freer to try different merchandising techniques with individual brands. Consumers who do not prefer Tide may choose Dash or Oxydol rather than purchase a competitor's brand.

## National Brands or Private Brands?

**national brand (manufacturer's brand)**   A brand promoted and distributed by a manufacturer.

Most of the brands mentioned in this chapter have been **manufacturers' brands**, also commonly termed **national brands**. But, to an increasing extent, large wholesalers and retailers operating over a regional or national market are placing their own brands on the products that they market. These *brands offered by wholesalers and retailers* are usually called **private brands**. Eaton's carries its own brands, such as Viking, Birkdale, Haddon Hall, Eatonia, and Teco. Safeway store shelves are filled with such company brands as Edwards, Town House, Empress, and Taste Tells. Safeway brands represent a large percentage of all products in an average Safeway supermarket.

**private brands**   A brand promoted and distributed by a retailer or wholesaler.

For a large retailer such as Eaton's, The Bay, or Canadian Tire, private brands allow the firm to establish an image and to attain greater control over the products that it handles. Quality levels, prices, and availability of the products become the responsibility of the retailer or wholesaler who develops a line of private brands.

Even though the manufacturers' brands are largely presold through national promotional efforts, the wholesaler and retailer may easily lose customers, since the same products may be available in competing stores. But only Eaton's handles the Viking line of appliances. By eliminating the promotional costs of the manufacturers' brands, the dealer may be able to offer a private brand at a lower price than the competing national brands — or make higher margins. Both consumers and the company benefit. As private brands achieve increasing brand loyalty they may even enable a retailer to avoid some price competition, since the brand can be sold only by the brand owner.

## Battle of the brands

Competition among manufacturers' brands and the private brands offered by wholesalers and large retailers has been called the "battle of the brands." Although the battle appears to be intensifying, the marketing impact varies widely among industries. One survey showed that private brands represented 36 percent of the market in replacement tires but only 7 percent in portable appliances. A full 52 percent of shoe sales involve private brands. For example, Agnew Surpass and Bata stores distribute their own private brands. Department stores capture about 53 percent of heavy appliance sales, most of which are private brands.[37]

Retailers with their own brands become customers of the manufacturer, who place the chains' private brands on the products that the firm produces. Such leading corporations as Westinghouse, Armstrong Rubber, and Heinz obtain an increasingly larger percentage of total sales through private labels.

Manufacturers often debate whether they should serve the private brand market. On the one hand, potential orders are large, so marketing efforts can be reduced. On the other hand, the manufacturer can become dependent on one or two retailers, rather than remaining independent by serving a broad range of customers.

## A·P·P·L·Y·I·N·G T·H·E C·O·N·C·E·P·T·S

### *The Story Behind Generic Food Products*

What really lurks behind those mystery products wrapped in plain, no-name packages? Each generic product has its own story, says David Nichol, president of the Ontario division of Toronto-based Loblaws Ltd. Some items are produced by the same people who make the leading name brands. In fact, sometimes the products are the same as the national brands because the manufacturers often sell their extra stock to supermarkets.

But in most cases, generic products are made for the supermarket chains to their specifications — the supermarkets decide everything from the quality of the product to the packaging. Usually generic products are a lower quality than the national brands, and that is why they cost less. Supermarket executives make no secret about this fact. They simply say they are providing customers with a choice that is not offered by the major manufacturers.

Generics provide the minimum standards to get the job done. A bleach, for example, will have a lower acid content; a chocolate-chip cookie will have fewer chips. Almost all the major grocery manufacturers make no-frill, generic products — even those that have a chunk of the market grabbed by the generics. It is one way to make use of otherwise surplus capacity. No-frill products are also produced by custom manufacturers that will make almost anything if the price is right.

Nichol said the no-frill pancake mix carried by Loblaws comes from Robin Hood Multifoods Ltd. of Montreal. Robin Hood developed the product some time ago, but found it could not compete with the more popular Aunt Jemima brand, produced by Quaker Oats Co. of Canada Ltd. of Peterborough, Ont. So Robin Hood has been content to make the mix for Loblaws as a generic. This is one generic product that has a quality comparable to the national brand, Mr. Nichol said.

Source: Paul Taylor, "Chains Decide Grade of Generic Produced to Their Specifications," *Globe and Mail* (April 14, 1980).

## Generic Products

*Food and household staples characterized by plain labels, little or no advertising, and no brand names* are called **generic products**. Generic products were first sold in Europe, where their prices were as much as 30 percent below brand-name products. By 1979, they had captured 40 percent of total volume in European supermarkets.

This new version of private brands has received significant acceptance in Canada. Surveys indicate that both professional, college-educated consumers and lower-income, blue-collar consumers are heavy purchasers of generics. Canned vegetables are the most commonly purchased generic product, followed by canned fruits and paper goods. Shoppers are indicating considerable willingness to forgo the known quality levels of regular brands in exchange for the lower prices of the generics.[38] Thus in the retail food industry, private brands seem to be caught between the success of generic products and the continuing influence of national brands. According to one major retailer, private brands seem to have slipped from the minds of consumers. Since they are unique to each retail chain, some firms are beginning to develop special advertising campaigns to re-emphasize them.[39] Loblaw's "President's Choice" campaign is one example of such an approach.

# Packaging

In a very real sense the package is a vital part of the total product. Indeed, in an overcrowded supermarket, packaging very often *is* the significant difference between one product and another. Take Nabob, for example. Nabob coffee was packaged in a new type of tough, vacuum-seal package that gave the coffee greater freshness. "Five years ago our market share [of the ground coffee market] was 5 percent" says John Bell, vice-president of marketing. "Today we have 26 percent.[40]

Packaging represents a vital component of the total product concept. Its importance can be inferred from the size of the packaging industry. Approximately $9.1 billion is spent annually on packaging in Canada.[41,42] A study of packaging costs in the food industry[41,42] found that total packaging costs as a percentage of net processed food sales range from 4 to 59 percent, averaging about 22 percent. In cases where packaging costs appeared disproportionately high, cost of ingredients (e.g., salt) were found to be very low.

The package has several objectives, which can be grouped into three general categories: (1) protection against damage, spoilage, and pilferage; (2) assistance in marketing the product; and (3) cost-effectiveness.

### Protection against Damage, Spoilage, and Pilferage

The original purpose of packaging was to offer physical protection. The typical product is handled several times between manufacture and consumer purchase, and its package must protect the contents against damage. Perishable products must also be protected against spoilage in transit, in storage, or while awaiting selection by the consumer.

Another important role provided by many packages for the retailer is in preventing pilferage, which at the retail level is very costly. Many products are packaged with oversized cardboard backings too large to fit into a shoplifter's pocket or purse. Large plastic packages are used in a similar manner on such products as cassette tapes.

## Assisting to Market the Product

Package designers frequently use marketing research in testing alternative designs. Increasingly scientific approaches are used in designing a package that is attractive, safe, and esthetically appealing. Kellogg, for instance, has been known to test the package for a new product as well as the product itself.[13]

In a grocery store containing as many as 15 000 different items, a product must capture the shopper's attention. Walter Margulies, chairman of Lippincott & Margulies advertising agency summarizes the importance of first impressions in the retail store: "Consumers are more intelligent [these days], but they don't read as much. They relate to pictures." Margulies also cites another factor: one of every six shoppers who needs eyeglasses does not wear them while shopping. Consequently, many marketers offering product lines are adopting similar package designs throughout the line in order to create more visual impact in the store. The adoption of common package designs by such product lines as Weight Watchers foods and Planter's nuts represents attempts to dominate larger sections of retail stores the way Campbell does.[44]

Packages can also offer the consumer convenience. Pump-type dispensers facilitate the use of products ranging from mustard to insect repellent. Pop-top cans provide added convenience for soft drinks and for other food products. The six-pack carton, first introduced by Coca-Cola in the 1930s, can be carried with minimal effort by the food shopper.

A growing number of firms provide increased consumer utility with packages designed for reuse. Peanut butter jars and jelly jars have long been used as drinking glasses. Bubble bath can be purchased in plastic bottles shaped like animals and suitable for bathtub play. Packaging is a major component in Avon's overall marketing strategy. The firm's decorative reusable bottles have even become collectibles.

## Cost-Effective Packaging

Although packaging must perform a number of functions for the producer, marketer, and consumer, it must accomplish them at a reasonable cost. Packaging currently represents the single largest item in the cost of producing numerous

*Everything about Loblaw's "no-name" products is geared toward presenting a low cost alternative to the consumer. The packaging is stark and minimal, implying that savings made by avoiding fancy labels were passed on to the consumer. In Loblaw's "No Frills" stores, products are usually presented in their original packing cartons, to save additional costs. The "less is more" strategy has added up to a good share of the generic food market for Loblaw's.*

products. For example, it accounts for 70 percent of the total cost of the single-serving packets of sugar found in restaurants. However, restaurants continue to use the packets because of the saving in wastage and in washing and refilling sugar containers.

An excellent illustration of how packaging can be cost-effective is provided by the large Swedish firm Tetra-Pak, which pioneered aseptic packaging for products like milk and juice. Aseptic packaging wraps a laminated paper around a sterilized product and seals it off. The big advantage of this packaging technology is that products so treated can be kept unrefrigerated for months. Aseptically packed sterilized milk, for instance, will keep its nutritional qualities and flavour for six months. With 60 percent of a supermarket's energy bill going for refrigeration, aseptic packaging is certainly cost-effective. The paper packaging is also cheaper and lighter than the cans and bottles used for unrefrigerated fruit juices. Handling costs can also be reduced in many cases.[45] These containers have recently been criticized because of ecological concerns over recycling. Tetra-Pak has responded aggressively, showing that their containers can be recycled into such items as picnic furniture.

## A·P·P·L·Y·I·N·G  T·H·E  C·O·N·C·E·P·T·S

### Environmentally Safer Packaging

Procter & Gamble has introduced a new, less expensive, more environmentally compatible package for eight of its liquid products. The company estimates that 15 to 25 percent of consumers who use those products will choose to buy them in the new format. That would mean five million fewer plastic bottles — about 700 fewer dump trucks — going to Canadian dumps annually.

Environmental groups say the company's expectation of consumer acceptance of the new packaging seems very conservative. Canadians are far more concerned about the environment than P&G realizes, said officials with Pollution Probe and Friends of the Earth.

P&G is selling Tide liquid laundry detergent, Ivory and Ultra Joy dishwashing liquids, Downy fabric softener, Mr. Clean liquid cleaner, Mr. Clean Magik spray, liquid Spic and Span, and Scope Mouthwash in refill pouches, called Enviro-Paks.

A majority of Canadians now rate environmental issues, including the garbage crisis, as the country's primary problem. The new packages use 70 to 85 percent less plastic than the regular rigid plastic bottles now in use and should cost consumers about 15 percent less, said Douglas Grindstaff, president of P&G in Canada.

P&G did limited consumer tests of the packaging in Canada and has been selling its fabric softener in West Germany in refill pouches for two years. From that experience it concluded that "clearly, not everybody is prepared to put up with the inconvenience" of cutting open a refill pouch and pouring the contents into a bottle, Grindstaff said.

The pouches are similar to milk bags but about twice as thick and designed with gussets so they can stand unsupported on grocery-store and home shelves. They are made from a plastic laminate — which combines low-density polyethylene and polyester — at P&G's Hamilton plant.

Production of the new packaging represents a response to increasing public concerns about the environment, officials said. P&G prints a toll-free telephone number on its packages and says the number of consumer calls it receives about environmental concerns is growing rapidly.

Also on the environmental front, P&G has developed an environmental policy; established a team of senior managers to initiate, co-ordinate, and track environmental projects; reduced and eliminated some packaging materials; begun coding its plastics so they can be identified for recycling; developed two-in-one products (for example, a combination detergent and bleach); and converted some products to larger-size packages.

"We are also well on our way to converting all of our cardboard packages to recycled fibres. All of our laundry detergent cartons are already 100 percent recycled fibres," Grindstaff said.

Source: Adapted from Patricia Lush, "Tide's in, Plastic's Out in Environmentally Safer Pouches," *Globe and Mail* (September 6, 1989).

## Labelling

Sometimes the label is a separate item applied to the package, but most of today's plastic packages contain the label as an integral part of the package. Labels perform both a promotional and an informational function. A **label** in most instances *contains (1) the brand name or symbol, (2) the name and address of the manufacturer or distributor, (3) information about product composition and size, and (4) information about recommended uses of the product.*

Government-set and voluntary packaging and label standards have been developed in most industries. The law requires a listing of food ingredients, in descending order of the amounts used, and the labels of such companies as the Del Monte Corporation now show specific food values and include a calorie count and a list of vitamins and minerals. In other industries (such as drugs, fur, and clothing), federal legislation requires the provision of various information and prevents false branding. The marketing manager in such industries must be fully acquainted with these laws and must design the package and label in compliance with these requirements.

The informational aspect of a label is particularly noteworthy. People who condemn all types of elaborate or fancy packaging fail to realize that the information on the label and the nature of the container enhance the product itself. In some cases, the dispenser is almost as important as the contents and is really an integral part of the total "product." Furthermore, with the advent of self-service nearly everywhere, the information on the label takes the place of a salesperson. Self-service improves marketing efficiency and lowers costs.

**label**  The part of a package that contains (1) the brand name or symbol, (2) the name and address of the manufacturer or distributor, (3) information about product composition and size, and (4) information about recommended uses of the product.

## Universal Product Code (UPC)

The Universal Product Code (UPC) designation is another very important point of a label or package. Most grocery items now display the zebra-stripe UPC on the label or package. The **Universal Product Code**, which was introduced as an attempt to cut expenses in the supermarket industry, is *a code readable by optical scanners that can print the name of the item and the price on the cash-register receipt.*

While the initial cost of UPC scanners is high — about $125 000 for a four-lane supermarket — they do permit considerable cost savings. The advantages include:

**Universal Product Code**  A code readable by optical scanners that can print the name of the item and the price on the cash-register receipt.

1. Labour saving (because products are no longer individually priced).
2. Faster customer check-out.
3. Better inventory control, since the scanners can be tied to inventory records.
4. Easier marketing research for the industries involved with it.
5. Fewer errors in entering purchases at the check-out counter.

It is obvious that the Universal Product Code is going to play an even greater role in product management over the next few years.

## Product Safety

If the product is to fulfill its mission of satisfying consumer needs, it must above all be safe. Manufacturers must design their products in such a way as to protect not only children but all consumers who use them. Packaging can play an important role in product safety. The law requires that bottle tops on dangerous products such as pharmaceuticals be child-proof (some are virtually parent-proof). This safety feature has reduced by two-thirds the number of children under five years of age who swallow dangerous doses of ASA. Prominent safety warnings on the labels of such potentially hazardous products as cleaning fluids and drain cleaners inform users about the dangers of these products and urge purchasers to store them out of the reach of children. Changes in product design have reduced the dangers involved in the use of such products as lawn mowers, hedge trimmers, and toys.

The need for fire-retardant fabrics for children's sleepwear was recognized long before federal regulations were established. While fire-retardant fabrics were available, the problems lay in how to produce them to meet consumer requirements for softness, colour, texture, durability, and reasonable cost. Monsanto spent seven years and millions of dollars in research before introducing a satisfactory fabric in 1972. Today government flame-retardancy standards are strictly enforced.

Federal and provincial legislation has long played a major role in promoting product safety. The **Hazardous Products Act**, passed in 1969, was a major piece of legislation that consolidated previous legislation and set significant new standards for product safety. The Act defines a hazardous product as any product that is included in a list (called a schedule) compiled by Consumer and Corporate Affairs Canada or Health and Welfare Canada. Any consumer product considered to be a hazard to public health or safety may be listed in the schedule. Figure 10–6 lists some of the main items and outlines the regulations that affect them.

The Act itself comprises just 15 clauses. Those relating to criminal penalties and seizure put sharp teeth in the law. Inspectors designated under the Act have powers of search and seizure. Hazardous products inspectors may enter, at any reasonable time, any place where they reasonably believe a hazardous product is manufactured, prepared, packaged, sold, or stored for sale. They may examine the product, take samples, and examine any records believed to contain information relevant to enforcement of the Act. Products that an inspector has reasonable grounds to believe are in contravention of the Act may be seized.

These regulatory activities have prompted companies to voluntarily improve safety standards for their products. For many companies, safety has become a very important ingredient in the broader definition of product.

**Hazardous Products Act**    A major piece of legislation that consolidated previous legislation and set significant new standards for product safety; defines a hazardous product as any product that is included in a list (called a schedule) compiled by Consumer and Corporate Affairs Canada or Health and Welfare Canada.

---

**FIGURE 10 – 6**

### Some Hazardous Products Act Regulations

Bedding may not be highly flammable.

Children's sleepwear, dressing gowns, and robes must meet flammability standards.

Children's toys or equipment may not contain toxic substances (such as lead pigments) beyond a prescribed limit.

Two plastic balloon-blowing kits containing organic solvents are banned.

Certain household chemical products must be labelled with appropriate symbols to alert consumers to their hazards.

Hockey helmets must meet saftey standards to protect young hockey players.

Pencils and artists' brushes are regulated to limit lead in their decorative coating.

Matches must meet saftey standards for strength and packaging.

Safety glass is mandatory in domestic doors and shower enclosures.

Liquid drain cleaners and furniture polishes containing petroleum-based solvents must be sold in child-proof packaging.

Toys and children's playthings must comply with safety standards.

Crib regulations provide for increased child saftey.

# Summary

A product mix is the assortment of product lines and individual offerings available from a marketer. A product line is a series of related products, and an individual offering is a single product offered within that line. Product mixes are assessed in terms of width and depth of assortment. Width of assortment refers to the variety of product lines offered, while depth refers to the extent of the line. Firms usually produce several related products rather than a single product in order to achieve the objectives of growth, optimal use of company resources, and increased company importance in the market.

The organizational responsibility for new products in most large firms is assigned to new-product committees, new-product departments, product managers, or venture teams. New-product ideas evolve through seven stages before their market introduction: (1) development of new-product strategy, (2) idea generation, (3) screening, (4) business analysis, (5) product development, (6) test marketing, and (7) commercialization.

New products experience a decay curve from idea generation to commercialization. Only one of 58 new-product ideas typically makes it all the way to commercialization. The success of a new product depends on a host of factors and can result from any of four alternative product development strategies: product improvement, market development, product development, and product diversification.

While new products are added to the line, old ones may face deletion from it. The typical causes for product eliminations are unprofitable sales and failure to fit into the existing product line.

Product identification may take the form of brand names, symbols, distinctive packaging, and labelling. Effective brand names should be easy to pronounce, recognize, and remember; they should give the right connotation to the buyer; and they should be legally protectable. Brand loyalty can be measured in three stages: brand recognition, brand preference, and finally, brand insistence. Marketing managers must decide whether to use a single family brand for their product line or to use an individual brand for each product. Retailers have to decide the relative mix of national and private brands as well as generic products that they will carry.

Modern packaging is designed to (1) protect against damage, spoilage, and pilferage; (2) assist in marketing the product; and (3) be cost-effective. Labels identify the product, producer, content, size, and uses of a packaged product. Most products also contain a Universal Product Code designation so that optical checkout scanners can be used.

Product safety has become an increasingly important component of the total product concept. This change has occurred through voluntary attempts by product designers to reduce hazards and through strict requirements established by Consumer and Corporate Affairs Canada.

## ▊KEY TERMS

| | | |
|---|---|---|
| product mix | market development strategy | concept testing |
| product line | product development strategy | brand |
| individual offering | product diversification strategy | brand name |
| cannibalizing | product managers | trademark |
| line extension | venture-team concept | generic name |
| product improvement strategy | test marketing | brand recognition |

brand preference
brand insistence
brand extension
family brand

individual brand
national brand
private brand
generic product

label
Universal Product Code
Hazardous Products Act

# REVIEW QUESTIONS

1. What is meant by a product mix? How is the concept used in making effective marketing decisions?
2. Why do most business firms market a line of related products rather than a single product?
3. Explain the new-product decay curve.
4. Outline the alternative organizational structures for new-product development.
5. Identify the steps in the new-product development process.
6. What is the chief purpose of test marketing? What potential problems are involved in it?
7. List the characteristics of an effective brand name. Illustrate each characteristic with an appropriate brand name.
8. Identify and briefly explain each of the three stages of brand loyalty.
9. What are the objectives of modern packaging?
10. Explain the chief elements of the Hazardous Products Act.

# DISCUSSION QUESTIONS AND EXERCISES

1. General Foods gave up on Lean Strips, a textured vegetable protein strip designed as a bacon substitute, after eight years of test marketing. Lean Strips sold well when bacon prices were high but poorly when they were low. General Foods hoped to offer a protein analogue product line that also included Crispy Strips, a snack and salad dressing item. Consumers liked the taste of Crispy Strips but felt it was too expensive for repeat purchases, and the product was abandoned before Lean Strips' demise. General Foods decided to concentrate on new product categories instead of on individual items like Lean Strips. What can be learned from General Foods' experience with Lean Strips?
2. A firm's new-product idea suggestion program has produced a design for a portable car washer that can be attached to a domestic garden hose.

Outline a program for deciding whether the product should be marketed by the firm.
3. Campbell Soup Company's Belgian candy company, Godiva Chocolates, introduced a designer line called "Bill Blass Chocolates." The premium chocolates sold for $14 a pound. Relate this action to the material discussed in Chapter 10.
4. Exxene, a $1 million manufacturer of antifog coatings for goggles, was sued for trademark infringement by Exxon Corp. The oil company giant claimed that it had nearly exclusive rights to the letters "Exx," regardless of what followed them. Four and a half years later, a jury awarded Exxene $250 000 in damages instead. Exxon filed an appeal. Relate this case to the discussion of trademarks.

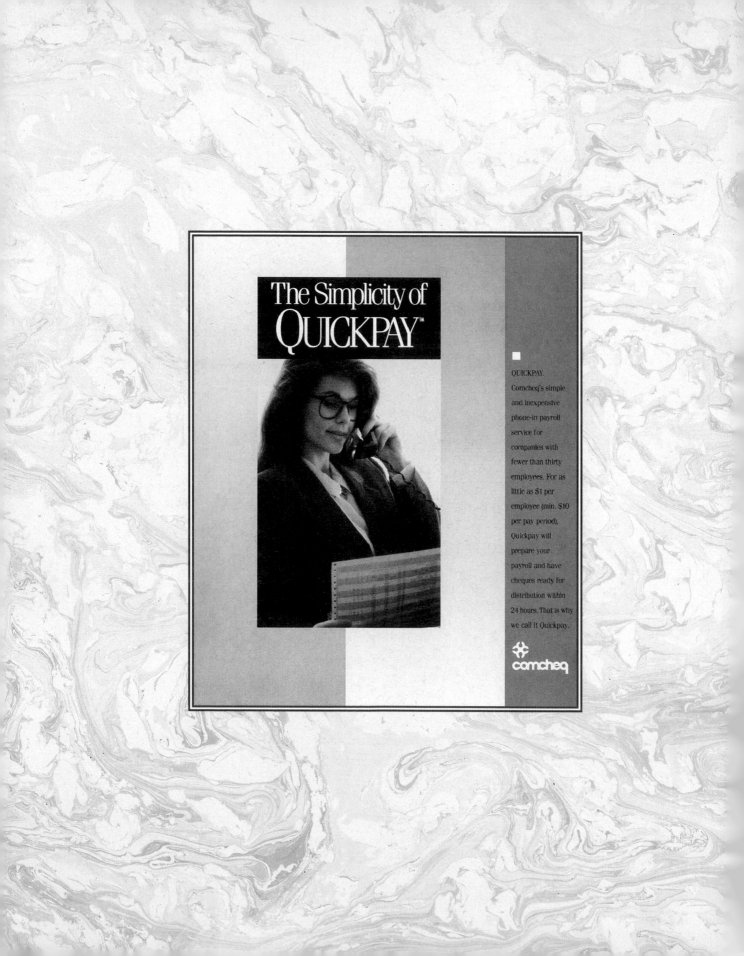

C H A P T E R     11

# Services

## CHAPTER OBJECTIVES

1. To elaborate on the discussion of products by exploring the "service product."
2. To discuss the similarities and differences between goods and services.
3. To explain the four main characteristics of services.
4. To outline the major issues that must be addressed by marketers for each of the characteristics of services.
5. To show the main methods marketers use to address these issues.

IN 1967 Bill Loewen, a young chartered accountant, noticed that one aspect of the organization he worked for was inefficient. The data processing people refused to recognize that automated payrolls could be handled more efficiently and effectively by independent service bureaus. They said that computer programs were long and unwieldy, and the number of forms and cheque requirements made payroll jobs too complex. Besides, most of the big payrolls in town were already well in hand.

However, Loewen's eye was not on the corporate giant; rather, he saw great potential in smaller-to medium-sized payrolls. He searched in vain for such a service. Finally, after finding nothing to his liking, he devised his own computerized payroll system, launching it with Fidelity Trust.

The key to the whole concept was the cheque — the ability to draw on one bank account maintained by the service company. Loewen's fresh approach increased the efficiency of computer operations, since fewer forms and fewer transactions were necessary. Customers were also saved such tedious aspects of payroll management as signing cheques and reconciling bank accounts.

That was more than two decades ago. His entrepreneurial drive, astuteness, and shrewd business decisions have combined to make Comcheq Services Canada's largest independent payroll-services company. Its customer base has grown from a modest four payrolls in 1968 to more than 6500 (from 4500 clients) today. Comcheq has expanded into other services and several countries from this base.

301

Besides having an entrepreneurial vision, and the motivation to build the business, Bill Loewen himself represents a very important reason that the business has grown. In a business that requires total integrity and trust, the man personifies such characteristics. "Bill epitomizes what a quiet leader should be," says Harri Jansson, senior vice-president, commercial and corporate banking at the Bank of Montreal. "He stays in the background and usually avoids the spotlight, yet he is not hesitant to take a controversial stand and speak his mind on matters of importance. He is Mr. Integrity as far as I am concerned — you can always take him at his word."

Loewen's firm is a good example of what an effective service organization can do. Customers' needs can be better served with services tailored to meet them. They are willing to buy such a service, provided that it is economically beneficial, and that they can have confidence in the service firm. People have to trust the service well enough to buy it *before* they will try it.[1]

# Introduction

As Chapter 1 states, a service too is a product. For the most part, discussions about the marketing of goods apply to services as well. Some, in fact, would argue that since they *are* products, services should not be treated in a separate chapter. But services have a number of important special characteristics that differentiate them from goods.

Figure 11–1 clarifies the relationships among these concepts. General marketing notions, approaches, and theories apply to both goods and services. However, some techniques and ideas are relatively exclusive to services marketing; others, to goods marketing. And within either type of marketing, distinctions may also be made among various industries or various marketing situations.[2]

The service sector today is so large that a good understanding of it is necessary. In Canada, services account for more than 47 percent of consumer expenditures (compared with 15.6 percent for durable goods, 10.2 percent for semi-durables, and 27.1 percent for nondurable goods). A recent report published by the General Agreement on Tariffs and Trade (GATT) estimates that total trade in services among that organization's 96 nations has reached $560 billion (U.S.)[3]

# Services versus Goods

**service** A product without physical characteristics; a bundle of performance and symbolic attributes designed to produce consumer want satisfaction.

A **service** is *a product without physical characteristics — a bundle of performance and symbolic attributes designed to produce consumer want satisfaction.* Berry states that "the pivotal difference between goods businesses and services businesses is that goods businesses sell *things* and service businesses sell *performances.*"[4] In other words, goods are produced, whereas services are performed.

Despite the relatively clear-cut definition of a service, many products have *both* intangible and tangible attributes. For example, a pail of fertilizer sold by a farm-supply dealer to a farmer seems like a pure good. However, if that dealer also provides expertise — for example, counselling about its application — a service is

FIGURE 11-1

**Services Marketing in Context**

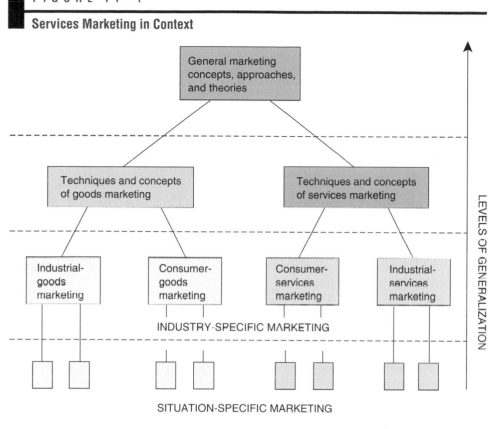

Source: A. Rushton and D. Carson, The Marketing of Services: Managing the Intangibles, *European Journal of Marketing* (1989), p.25. M.C.B. University Press Ltd.

added. Consequently, it is more accurate to consider products as falling on a spectrum between "tangible elements dominant" and "intangible elements dominant" (see Figure 11-2).

## Buying Promises

As mentioned earlier, potential customers often have difficulties conceptualizing the service product, because it has no physical properties. Basically, they are buying promises. No product trial or return is possible. Three types of product properties are attached to every good or service: search qualities, experience qualities, and credence qualities.[5] Products that can be physically examined and compared are high in *search* qualities. Others are primarily assessed on the basis of the *experience* of using them. They include a large proportion of both tangible and intangible attributes. Products with *credence* qualities are those for which, even after purchasing, the buyer must simply trust that the supplier has performed the correct service. Figure 11-3 shows this range of product properties. In intangibles, credence (buying a promise) and experience qualities dominate, while search qualities are central for tangible products.

# A·P·P·L·Y·I·N·G  T·H·E  C·O·N·C·E·P·T·S

## The Business of Going Away

A question for businessman's Trivial Pursuit: what is the world's biggest civilian industry? The answer, it seems, is travel and tourism. It has worldwide sales of some $2 trillion. Quite staggering — that is 5% of all global sales of goods and services.

In a recent study of some 200 developed and developing countries by Wharton Econometric Forecasting Associates on behalf of American Express, a charge card to travel agency business whose commercial interest is self-evident, travel and tourism was found to be the biggest industry by almost any measure. Its definition of the industry is broad (including such things as railways, sightseeing buses, taxicabs, hotels, restaurants, theatres and museums), but the figures remain impressive — however they are added up.

If travel and tourism were a country, its GNP would rank fifth in the world after the United States, the Soviet Union, Japan and West Germany. Value added, the industry's direct contribution to GNP, is worth nearly $950 billion: $516 billion in employee wages; $268 billion in cash available for investment and dividends; and a whopping $166 billion in tax payments — more than the GNP of Austria or Belgium.

In most of the 200 countries studied by the Wharton group this is also more than the added value of agriculture, steel, electronics, and other more-familiar industries whose grandees are frequently consulted by governments when trying to decide economic and social policy.

The industry is also the largest employer in almost every country, accounting for one out of every 16 jobs worldwide. It purchases some $1 trillion worth of goods and services each year. And its new capital expenditure of $280 billion, 7% of the world total, is larger than many key manufacturing industries, such as cars and textiles.

Where do the industry's raw materials, travellers and tourists, come from? Businesses and governments spend some $600 billion a year on travel and associated "tourist" costs such as accommodation and food. That is about 2% of their total costs. The rest, nearly $1.3 trillion, is spent by people travelling at their own expense. Time for another holiday to do your bit for the world economy?

Source: "The Business of Going Away," *The Economist* (April 15, 1989), p. 73. © 1989 *The Economist Newspaper*. Reprinted by permission.

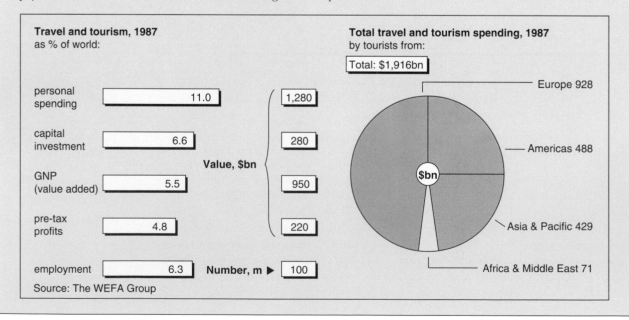

**Travel and tourism, 1987**
as % of world:

| | |
|---|---|
| personal spending | 11.0 |
| capital investment | 6.6 |
| GNP (value added) | 5.5 |
| pre-tax profits | 4.8 |
| employment | 6.3 |

Value, $bn

| |
|---|
| 1,280 |
| 280 |
| 950 |
| 220 |

Number, m ▶ 100

Source: The WEFA Group

**Total travel and tourism spending, 1987**
by tourists from:

Total: $1,916bn

$bn

Europe 928
Americas 488
Asia & Pacific 429
Africa & Middle East 71

FIGURE  11 – 2

## Goods and Services: Scale of Elemental Dominance

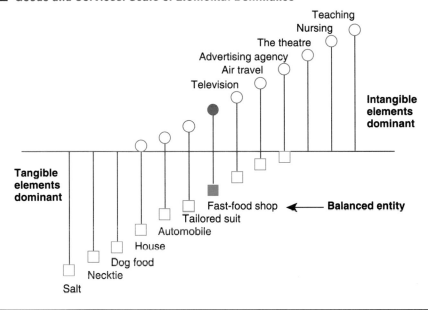

Source: A. Rushton and D. Carson, The Marketing of Services, p.29. M.C.B. University Press Ltd.

FIGURE  11 – 3

## Intangibility and Customer Evaluation

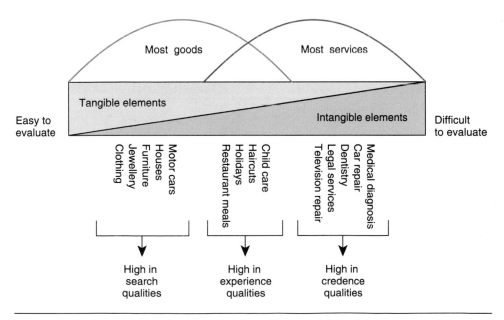

Source: A. Rushton and D. Carson, The Marketing of Services, p.31. M.C.B. University Press Ltd.

# Characteristics of Services

Four unique characteristics of services distinguish them from goods; *intangibility*; *inseparability of production and consumption*; *heterogeneity*; and *perishability*.

## Intangibility

A service is intangible. Unlike goods, which can be displayed before the sale, services cannot be seen, smelled or touched. The student who goes to a counsellor for assistance in deciding what kind of a career to choose cannot foretell the result of that counselling service. Bateson believes that besides being physically intangible, services can also be mentally intangible, because it is sometimes hard for the human mind to grasp them.[6]

The intangibility of services creates a number of marketing problems: (1) Services cannot be stored. (2) They cannot be protected through patents. (3) It is difficult to readily display or communicate services. (4) Prices are harder to set.

***Services cannot be stored.***    A Canadian Airlines plane provides a transportation service for 90 people to fly from Montreal to Vancouver. Revenue from empty seats is lost forever.

***Services cannot be protected through patents.***    Patents apply to physical objects. Thus, because they are intangible, services are ineligible for a patent. This can create a real problem for a services marketer, since the service can easily be copied.

***It is hard to readily display or communicate services.***    It is easy to show a good, allowing potential customers to hold, handle, or try it out before purchase. That way, they can get a good idea of whether or not the good will satisfy their needs. In the case of a service, a purchaser must purchase in order to experience it.

---

### A·P·P·L·Y·I·N·G  T·H·E  C·O·N·C·E·P·T·S

## *Look-alike Competition in the Lending Field*

Unlike their buttoned-down predecessors, lending institutions are no longer content to sit back and wait for prospective borrowers to come to them. Every bank or trust-company branch now holds a clutch of slick posters and brochures encouraging credit-worthy customers to use more and more of their borrowing power. Want a vacation loan? A Toronto-Dominion Bank flyer displays a picture of a happy couple lounging poolside and inviting you to come on in and talk to the loans officer. A yacht's more your style? Try Bank of Montreal, which declares its willingness to talk about loans for everything from canoes to cruisers.

There is now tremendous competition in the banking industry. The upshot of two decades of turmoil has been a lending field crowded with look-alike competitors. Banks, trust companies, and credit unions once occupied distinct roles. Now many offer similar services. If something is working for a competitor, it is easy to offer something similar. For the consumer, this is good news, as competition brings about new innovations. For the banking industry, there must be much more attention to consumers if one is to get a share of the market.

Source: Adapted from Ian McGugan, "Debt Service with a Smile," *Financial Post Magazine* (March 1989), pp. 52–53.

*The service in this Japanese restaurant is affected by a myriad of factors. The server must adopt several roles in this situation — acting as waiter, cook, and maybe even performance artist    to satisfy diners' expectations. He depends on the consistency of various factors, such as the quiet co-operation of the diners and the freshness of the food, to present a satisfactory service.*

***Prices are difficult to set.***    At the best of times, pricing is complex. In the case of a good, the components of each product can be costed out, which helps in determining what it is worth. Costing out, say, an accountant's services proves much more complex.

### Marketing strategies to solve the problems of intangibility

Some of the above-mentioned problems cannot be avoided. But certain marketing strategies can help resolve others, particularly the problem of marketing communication. Because services are so intangible, many marketers *stress tangible cues* in advertising and selling. For example, advertisements for long-distance phone calling dramatize the pleasure on the face of a loved one receiving a call. Marketing messages should also *use personal sources more than nonpersonal sources.* Thus a recommendation for life insurance would likely be more persuasive if it came from John Hanchuck, rather than the more impersonal Life Insurance Council. The personal source adds tangibility to the service.

Services marketers also have found that it is helpful to *stimulate word-of-mouth communications*. If a purchaser can be induced — through the superior service received or by other incentives — to speak to friends and acquaintances positively about a service, that service will tend to be purchased by those people. *Engaging in postpurchase communications* is a related useful strategy. For example, a provider of financial counselling services might write a letter to a new client assuring the client of the wise choices she or he made.

Service marketers also try to *create a strong image* of their organization. This is a very important approach affecting choice of a service. Since potential purchases cannot physically evaluate the product offered, they may be reassured that they are purchasing a service from a well-known organization.

Finally, with respect to the difficulty of setting prices, it has been found useful to *develop a strong cost accounting system*. Such a system enables an accurate and realistic analysis of various costs involved in the operation. This information provides a strong foundation for setting the ultimate price of the service.

## Inseparability of Production and Consumption

Whereas goods are first produced, then sold, and then consumed, services are first sold, then produced and consumed simultaneously.[7] The **customer** therefore **has an active role during production** of the service. For instance, professional legal counselling is consumed at the same time as the service of providing legal advice is performed. The client raises questions, seeks opinions, and responds with the details required by the lawyer.

The inseparability of production and consumption also results in marketing problems: (1) Consumers are involved in production, so performance depends on the quality of input from the customer, as well as on the relationship between the customer and the provider; this problem was discussed in the previous paragraph. (2) Other consumers are involved in production. (3) Centralized mass production of services is difficult.

*Other consumers are involved in production.*   Many services are offered in a setting with other people present. For example, the service provided by a restaurant server is performed not just for one customer, but for many simultaneously. This fact can have a number of positive and negative influences on the service actually experienced by the individual buyer. For instance, the presence of others can distract a server, or create so much pressure that service is negatively affected.

*Centralized mass production of services is difficult.*   Services are normally provided where the people are. Whereas Honda might have one or two factories to serve the entire country, Royal Bank must have many "little factories" (branches) in each city. Cost efficiencies and standardization are therefore difficult to achieve because there are so many producers (people) involved.

### Marketing strategies to solve the problems of inseparability

With services, since production and consumption occur simultaneously and in the same place, production personnel have a tremendous impact on consumers' perceptions of product acceptability. It is therefore essential to *emphasize the selection and training of public-contact personnel*. Personnel not only have to perform the service well, but must be able to interact in a positive manner with the customer. The famous Avis "We Try Harder" program was based on this principle.

*Multi-site locations* may help offset the fact that services cannot be "sent" from a warehouse to a retail outlet. Banking, travel counselling, and other such services must be produced and consumed where consumers shop. Developing, managing, and maintaining so many locations is a major task for the marketer. This is one of the reasons why employment in the service sector is so high. There is a high probability that readers will find careers in one or another of the service industries.

*Managing customers* also helps to make the "inseparability" condition positive for both buyer and seller. Customers can be "managed" by guiding, directing, and facilitating their movements and interactions in the service situation. For example, banks channel the flow of customers to tellers through specially laid-out channels. Restaurants provide chairs for, or seat waiting customers in lounges while they wait for their table to become available.

## Heterogeneity

Services are highly variable. Because they are performed by a provider, who is a fallible human being, they are difficult to standardize. Service providers can vary in skill and training, and individual performance can vary from day to day. Furthermore, performance varies from individual to individual. A customer may pay the same price for a hair styling at the same shop on subsequent dates from two different people, with far from similar outcomes.

The main marketing problem arising from heterogeneity is that **standardization and quality control are difficult to achieve**. Services marketers try to overcome this problem by *industrializing the service or customizing it*. To industrialize a service, Levitt

**FIGURE 11-4**

**Unique Service Features and Resulting Marketing Problems and Solutions**

| Unique Service Features | Resulting Marketing Problems | Marketing Strategies to Solve Problems |
|---|---|---|
| Intangibility | 1. Services cannot be stored.<br>2. Cannot protect services through patents.<br>3. Cannot readily display or communicate services.<br>4. Prices are difficult to set. | 1. Stress tangible cues.<br>2. Use personal sources more than nonpersonal sources.<br>3. Simulate or stimulate word-of-mouth communications.<br>4. Create strong organizational image.<br>5. Use cost-accounting to help set prices.<br>6. Engage in post-purchase communications. |
| Inseparability | 1. Consumer involved in production.<br>2. Other consumers involved in production.<br>3. Centralized mass production of services difficult. | 1. Emphasize selection and training of public-contact personnel.<br>2. Manage consumers.<br>3. Use multisite locations. |
| Heterogeneity | 1. Standardization and quality control difficult to achieve. | 1. Industrialize service.<br>2. Customize service. |
| Perishability | 1. Services cannot be inventoried. | 1. Use strategies to cope with fluctuating demand.<br>2. Make simultaneous adjustments in demand and capacity to achieve a closer match between the two. |

Source: Adapted from Valarie A. Zeithaml, A. Parasuraman, and Leonard L. Berry, "Problems and Strategies in Services Marketing," *Journal of Marketing* (Spring, 1985), p. 35

has suggested substituting organized, preplanned systems for individual service operations. For example, a travel agency could offer prepackaged vacation tours to remove the need for the selling, tailoring, and haggling involved in customization.[8] Customization — the opposite of industrialization — is another possible solution. If each service is produced for an individual customer, the problem of standardization disappears.

## Perishability

A service cannot be stored. No service can be produced before required, and then stocked up to meet future demand. Whatever is not used when available is wasted. Motel rooms not occupied, airline seats not purchased, and telephone line capacity not used cannot be reclaimed. Because of this, service businesses frequently find it difficult to balance supply and demand. The fact that **services cannot be inventoried** is a major problem with services.

The problem of perishability can be solved to some degree by *using strategies to cope with fluctuating demand*. Restaurants, airlines, and other service businesses often give special discounts to those who use the service in periods of low demand. This shifts some demand from high to low periods. A second approach to the perishability problem is to *make simultaneous adjustments in demand and capacity to achieve a closer match between the two*. Capacity can often be increased by adding staff or equipment at peak times. This approach may be used simultaneously with the previous solution.

Figure 11–4 summarizes the foregoing discussion of features that are unique to services, the resulting marketing problems, and suggested marketing solutions. Ziethaml et al. (from whose important study Figure 11–4 is adapted) found that service firms did not view most of the problems as especially serious. The authors speculated that this viewpoint may be founded on the providers' being used to facing these problems. Or, the problems may not in fact be as significant as they first seem.

### A·P·P·L·Y·I·N·G  T·H·E  C·O·N·C·E·P·T·S

## Service Positioning

As with firms that market goods, a service firm should have a clear strategy focusing on a specific target market. Shouldice hospital near Toronto is a good example. Shouldice's doctors perform more operations (on the average) annually than do doctors elsewhere, while its nurses attend several times more patients than they would in the nation's other hospitals. To the surprise of its competitors, Shouldice produces quality service. Shouldice's ex-patients even hold an annual reunion to commemorate their treatment experience.

Shouldice segmented the patient market according to people's complaints and concentrated on hernia surgery, which is inexpensive to perform. Shouldice's doctors have become highly competent and efficient at providing its core services. Earning favourable word-of-mouth from former patients, the hospital successfully positions its product as the "Shouldice experience" — welcome received at check-in, the behaviour of fellow patients, and the attentiveness and perceived competence of doctors and nurses.

Source: Adapted from W.H. Davidow and B. Uttal, "Service Companies: Focus or Falter," *Harvard Business Review* (September–October 1988), p. 28.

# Other Strategies in Services Marketing

## Internal Marketing

Traditionally, the marketing mix is thought to be oriented toward the external market. While services do face a competitive external environment, they must also contend with an internal market — those who provide the service. Since service producers interact so directly with consumers, the way they feel about their task within the marketing strategy is extremely important. In fact, their feelings directly influence the quality of the service they perform. Berry has suggested that "internal marketing means applying the philosophy and practices of marketing to the people that serve the external customer so that (1) the best possible people can be employed and retained, and (2) they will do the best possible work."[9]

The objective of the internal marketing function is to develop motivated, customer-conscious, market-oriented, and sales-minded employees. The successful service company must first sell the job to its employees before it can sell its services to customers.[10]

## Managing Evidence

As discussed earlier, prospective customers like to associate tangibles with a service for cues as to its quality. Marketers, therefore, must try to manage tangibles to convince customers about the service.

Goods marketing tends to give prime emphasis to creating abstract associations with the product. Services marketers, on the other hand, should focus on enhancing and differentiating the "realities" through manipulation of tangible cues. The management of evidence comes first for service marketers.[11] There are several ways that the evidence can be managed.

*The environment*    Services are totally integrated with their environment. The physical setting — where the service is performed — has a great influence on the customer's mentality. The physical milieu should be intentionally created so as to provide the appropriate situation-specific atmosphere to impress the customer. For example, even though two lawyers might provide identical services, customers still differentiate between the two by the environmental differences. If one decorates her office with leather and subdued carpeting, and the other has plain painted offices with steel-and-formica furniture, customers will judge them accordingly.

*Appearance of service providers*    The appearance of service providers also affects customers' perception of the product. Salespeople in an optical shop wearing white "doctor-style" smocks will look more "professional" than those with ordinary attire.

*Service pricing*    Research confirms that there is a high tendency for customers to perceive a direct relationship between price and quality for service.[12] Price is seen as an index of quality. Professional practitioners may charge an unusually high price for their services in order to assure clients. Setting the right price can be critical in differentiating one service from the crowd.

*The physical setting in which a service is performed has a major impact on the customer's perception of the service. If the same clothes displayed in this fashionable boutique were being sold at a neighbourhood garage sale, the expectations of service and price would be totally different. The atmosphere and service provided in the expensive boutique lend credence to the higher prices charged.*

*The Century 21 jacket acts as an effective marketing aid both inside and outside the company. It serves as a visual aid to current clients and future prospects, and strengthens a sense of corporate identity within the organization. In this way, Century 21 hopes to establish a strong image in the public eye — when consumers are looking for real estate services, they'll remember the distinctive jackets and Century 21.*

## Organizational Responsibility for Marketing

In many service firms, the organizational responsibility for marketing may be considerably different than in manufacturing companies. In any company there may be confusion about what marketing is. It is frequently considered to be what the marketing department does. Marketing is, however, often carried out by others in the company to some degree. This confusion may be much more acute for service firms than for manufacturing firms and may in fact constitute an organizational dilemma. In many professional service organizations, the marketing department's role may be limited to handling advertising, sales promotion, and some public relations. The "sales force" comprises those people who are in direct contact with customers (for example, the branch managers and tellers in a bank). Except for the people in the marketing department, however, staff members are not hired for their marketing know-how but for their ability to produce services. *Yet the person who produces a service must also be able to market that service.* In most cases, what is needed is not professional salespeople but service workers who sell — in effect, producer–sellers.

### A·P·P·L·Y·I·N·G   T·H·E   C·O·N·C·E·P·T·S

## *Corporate Uniforms Now "Image" Tools*

The corporate uniform is emerging as a new arrow in the image-maker's quiver.

Far from being synonymous with a lack of imagination and excessive corporate discipline, uniforms (these days labelled "career apparel") are often a symbol of a strong and successful corporate culture.

They are becoming especially popular on the front lines of service businesses (such as travel agencies, airlines, real estate agencies, hotels, and now banks and trust companies).

Probably one of the best-known uniforms in North America is Century 21 Real Estate's gold jacket. Don

Lawby, chief operating officer and regional director, says the company's famous jacket is "synonymous with success" — a "walking business card" consistent with the number-one image Century 21 tries to create.

"People like to talk about real estate. They spot our jacket, and eventually this does business for us," Lawby says, adding that this can happen in the oddest places — including company lavatories and hotel lobbies.

Source: Excerpted from Lisa Grogan, "Corporate Uniforms Now 'Image' Tools," *Financial Post* (September 9–11, 1989).

*What kind of future will we leave to our children?*
*For here, in this same picnic clearing, I, too,*
*played as a child.*

*Now, surrounded by the trees of my youth,*
*I wondered if our children, too, so full of spirit and*
*promise, would some day return with their children.*
*To this same shelter, this peace of mind.*

For over 140 years, we've helped Canadians achieve financial peace of
mind through insurance and investment opportunities.

LIFE INSURANCE ∼ RETIREMENT PLANNING ∼ INVESTMENT SERVICES ∼ GROUP INSURANCE

**CANADA LIFE**

*"Peace of mind" is a difficult product to market, due to the intangible and highly personal nature of this experience. Yet, this is exactly what Canada Life is seeking to promote in this ad in order to remain competitive in the Canadian insurance industry. By associating itself with a peaceful family scene done in soft pastel tones, Canada Life hopes to persuade consumers to consider its services.*

## A·P·P·L·Y·I·N·G  T·H·E  C·O·N·C·E·P·T·S

### Start Hustling or Lose Market, Insurers Warned

Canada's insurance companies have been told they are not reaching many potential clients and that they therefore risk losing market share to banks and trust companies. A recent study suggests that most consumers remain unaware of the insurers' message, despite their heavy marketing campaigns.

The result, the study's authors say, is a strategic hole that will be plugged by outsiders if the insurance industry is unable to respond. In a national survey of 2000 Canadians by Thompson Lightstone & Co., 55 percent of respondents had not been contacted by an insurance agent in the past 18 months. "Simply put, the industry appears not to be doing an adequate job of reaching out to get its message across to Canadians," the study says.

Source: Excerpted from Andy Willis, "Start Hustling or Lose Market, Insurers Warned," *Financial Post* (October 30, 1989).

The dilemma arises when service firms are insufficiently aware of the need to have personnel who are able to adequately perform both marketing and service-production functions. Furthermore, when the workload is high, too little time may be spent on marketing — an imbalance that will likely have very serious long-term consequences for the organization.

## Summary

In Canada, services account for over 47 percent of consumer expenditures. A service is a product without physical characteristics; it is a bundle of performance and symbolic attributes designed to produce consumer want satisfaction.

Four unique characteristics of services distinguish them from goods. These are intangibility, the inseparability of production and consumption, heterogeneity, and perishability. Services' intangibility results in four types of marketing problems: services cannot be stored, protected through patents, or readily displayed, and service prices are more difficult to set. Marketers try to associate services with tangible things to overcome their intangibility. They also rely more on personal recommendations, word-of-mouth promotion, and postpurchase communications in their marketing efforts.

The inseparability of production and consumption results in three challenges: consumers themselves are involved in production, other consumers are often also involved in production, and centralized mass production of services is difficult. It is therefore important to select and train public-contact personnel carefully. Managing customers in the buying/production setting helps to make it a positive experience. And the service firm may need many locations.

Services' heterogeneity makes standardization and quality control difficult to achieve. Services marketers try to overcome this problem by either industrializing the service or customizing it.

Finally, because services are perishable, they cannot be inventoried. In trying to even out demand, service firms may, for example, offer lower prices at off-peak times. Additional human and other resources may be used at peak times.

Internal marketing — that is, marketing to employees involved in the production–selling process — helps ensure that front-line personnel understand and support the service firm's marketing strategy. The strategy totally breaks down if it is not supported at the level at which it is produced and consumed.

Service marketers are very conscious of their need to manage the evidence to support the firm's strategy and claims. This is done through making sure that the physical environment, the appearance of service personnel, and the service's pricing give a consistent message.

## ▌K E Y  T E R M S

| | | |
|---|---|---|
| service | experience qualities | perishability |
| tangible attributes | credence qualities | internal marketing |
| intangible attributes | inseparability | managing the evidence |
| search qualities | heterogeneity | producer–seller |

# REVIEW QUESTIONS

1. If a service is a product, and a good is a product, why is a service not a good?
2. What proportion of consumer expenditures goes to goods and what proportion to services?
3. Outline and explain the three types of properties that are attached to every product.
4. What are the four main characteristics unique to services?
5. Describe the main marketing problems that arise because services are intangible.
6. List the methods by which services marketers counteract the intangibility problems.
7. Outline the marketing problems that arise because services are heterogeneous, and describe how marketers may respond to such problems.
8. Delineate the rationale for a service firm's involvement with internal marketing.
9. Describe ways in which services marketers can "manage the evidence" to enhance customer response.
10. Explain why the organization of the marketing function may be different in a service firm.

# DISCUSSION QUESTIONS AND EXERCISES

1. Prepare a brief report on the marketing activities conducted by a local lawyer. Describe how these activities have changed from five years ago, and what they will probably be like five years from now.
2. Describe the last transportation service you purchased. What was your impression of the way in which the service was marketed? How could the firm's marketing effort have been improved?
3. Commonwealth Holiday Inns of Canada had an advertising program with the slogan "The best surprise is no surprise." What did this slogan mean, and why did the firm feel it necessary to have such a campaign?
4. Outline a marketing mix for the following service firms:
   a. local radio station
   b. independent insurance agency
   c. local housekeeping/cleaning service
   d. funeral home
5. Identify three or four service firms and propose methods by which they could overcome problems with the perishability of their respective services.

# VIDEO CASE 11    Azure Seas

Cruising is big business. Cruise ships carried 3.5 million passengers in 1988, up 500 000 from the previous year. Since 1980, the growth in numbers of passengers has averaged 14 percent annually. Furthermore, research has shown that 30 to 50 million Americans are interested in taking a cruise, including 90 percent of the 10 million people who had previously done so.

What explains the popularity of cruising? Kirk Lanterman, chairman of the Cruise Lines International Association, puts it this way: "Cruising is hot. It's a vacation experience that offers surprising value and affordability and, at the same time, provides the type of luxurious pampering and attention that you might find only in the most expensive and exclusive resorts around the world."

While the growth of cruising over the past decade is impressive, cruise line executives note that 95 percent of all Americans have not sailed. This statistic suggests a tremendous market potential for the industry. As a result, cruise lines have been adding ships and berths since 1980. Some 40 new cruise ships were introduced between 1980 and 1990. Ten new vessels with 8000 berths were added in 1988 alone. A total of 31 000 new berths were added to the industry's capacity during the 1980s, and 43 older ships were refurbished.

One of these refurbished ships was the *Azure Seas*, which operates out of Los Angeles. The *Azure Seas* was purchased by Western Cruise Lines (now known as Admiral Cruises, Inc.) for $30 million and refurbished at a cost of an additional $7 million. The 604-foot-long, 78-foot-wide vessel has 9 decks and can reach a top speed of 20 knots. The *Azure Seas* carries more than 300 passengers, who are served by a crew of 300 to 350.

The company planned to introduce a new concept to West Coast cruising — the short (three-to four-day) cruise. The *Azure Seas* would sail from Los Angeles to Ensenada, Mexico, with varying intermediate stops. The ship's 1988 sailing schedule is shown below.

### Three-Night Friday Cruise

| | | | |
|---|---|---|---|
| Depart: | Los Angeles | Friday | 7:45 p.m. |
| Arrive: | Catalina Island | Saturday | 9:00 a.m. |
| Depart: | Catalina Island | Saturday | 3:30 p.m. |
| Arrive: | Ensenada | Sunday | 9:00 a.m. |
| Depart: | Ensenada | Sunday | 6:30 p.m. |
| Arrive: | Los Angeles | Monday | 8:00 a.m. |

### Four-Night Monday Cruise

| | | | |
|---|---|---|---|
| Depart: | Los Angeles | Monday | 4:45 p.m. |
| Arrive: | San Diego | Tuesday | 9:00 a.m. |
| Depart: | San Diego | Tuesday | 3:30 p.m. |
| Arrive: | Catalina Island | Wednesday | 9:00 a.m. |
| Depart: | Catalina Island | Wednesday | 3:30 p.m. |
| Arrive: | Ensenada | Thursday | 9:00 a.m. |
| Depart: | Ensenada | Thursday | 6:30 p.m. |
| Arrive: | Los Angeles | Friday | 8:00 a.m. |

Western's management was quite familiar with the short-cruise concept. Western's sister company, Eastern Cruise Lines (now also called Admiral Cruises), had long operated short cruises on the East Coast. As Alex Currie, Western's general manager, remarked: "We thought we were the short-cruise experts." However, things were different on the West Coast and the firm had to adapt its service strategy to succeed. Short cruises were sold in the East as a recreational and resort experience, but that idea did not work with West Coast (predominantly California) consumers, who were accustomed to such resort areas as Malibu and Tahoe. Management's strategy had to be different for the West Coast market.

Western decided to test market its short-cruise concept with the area travel agents who would market the cruises. The emphasis was on an affordable, total cruise experience. The travel agents were receptive to the concept and the *Azure Seas* venture was launched with extensive advertising in the travel sections of newspapers.

The target market was called the "Golden Core" by Western executives and was defined as the Los Angeles metropolitan area. Western soon discovered that 70 percent of its passengers came from the so-called Golden Core, and 70 percent of these were first-time cruisers. So the biggest market segment for the *Azure Seas* was first-time cruisers from Los Angeles, who constituted about half of all passengers. Western Cruise Lines also used newspaper advertising throughout an 11-state western region. As part of its effort, Western offered a sea-jet program that included airfare to Los Angeles.

While Western's marketing strategy was well planned, the firm encountered some problems a few years later. The *Azure Seas*' bottom line had not met expectations in the previous quarter, and fall bookings were also running behind schedule. Furthermore, marketing research revealed that only 4 percent of Los Angeles–area travellers recognized the name *Azure Seas*. By contrast, Princess Line had an 80 to 90 percent recognition factor. Western's management attributed this difference to the popular "Love Boat" television series, which featured a Princess vessel. The question facing Western's executives was how to better use their $1 million advertising budget to overcome these problems.

In a meeting with its advertising agency, Western's management decided to conduct a two-week test of television advertising as an alternative to traditional newspaper advertising. The television commercials, which were used only in the Los Angeles area, stressed affordability, food, and service. The results of the experiment were impressive. Revenues jumped 40 percent. Still, management decided to play it cautious. The company cut the commercials after the initial trial run to see what would happen. The result was that sales declined. When television advertising was reintroduced, sales went up. In fact, during one period, sales actually rose an astounding 80 percent. In addition, a new marketing research study showed that public awareness of the *Azure Seas* shot up from 4 percent to 13 percent. As a result of this test, television advertising was continued.

In the late 1980s, Admiral Cruises underwent several changes, merging with other lines and splitting off some lines. During the same period, competition in the West Coast/Mexico cruise market intensified. As of March 1991 the *Azure Seas* had moved into the Caribbean and had abandoned the short-cruise format.

## Questions

1. How would you place a cruise on the goods–services continuum?
2. What type of segmentation strategy was demonstrated in this video case?
3. How did market segmentation help Western Cruise Line's marketers?
4. How did Western Cruise Lines attempt to influence the consumer behaviour of potential buyers?

SOURCES    "1988 Shapes Up As Biggest Ever for New Cruise Ships," *Seattle Times* (January 23–24, 1988), p. 8 (special Travel Show section: data source was Cruise Lines International Association); *Supercruise,* 1988 Admiral Seas brochure; "Cruises: TV Is Becoming the Industry Medium of Choice," *Adweek* (September 14, 1987), p. FP38; Gail DeGeorge, "Carnival Cruise Lines Is Making Waves," *Business Week* (July 6, 1987), p. 34; Update interview with Paul Bockhorst of Admiral Cruises, Inc., April 1991; and William G. Flanagan with Evan McGinn, "Man the Pumps," *Forbes* (December 10, 1990), pp. 116–128.

## CAREER PROFILE

### Kevin T. Scanlon

Robert Bosch Inc.
Product Manager
Power Tool Division

**Education:**

Ryerson Polytechnical Institute
Bachelor of Business Management (Marketing Major)
Graduation — 1986

Ryerson's Marketing Program offered an excellent, logical framework for the development of the most important marketing skills: listening, interpretation, co-operation, organization, and risk management. I learned these skills through the courses completed to get my degree; the group work, which helped develop my "people" skills: the practical client work offered by Ryerson's Marketing Management course; and the experience of working for Ryerson's Business Consulting Service.

The path to my present position involved starting with large responsibilities in a small firm, Safety House of Canada. As Marketing Manager, I had to use every skill my education had fostered to establish, organize, and run Safety House's first formal Marketing Department. This challenge exposed me to many new tasks: I developed my abilities in supervising, copywriting, print promotion production, premium production, trade show planning and management, packaging design, direct-mail, public relations, media planning and purchase, pricing, and product management.

Through proven performance in this position, I earned a promotion to Executive Vice President, responsible for 45 staff members. During my tenure there, the firm experienced a 230 percent increase in sales, along with a reduction in expenses; together, these changes added up to an overall improvement in profitability. Why did I leave Safety House and join Robert Bosch Inc.? I wanted to return to my first love — marketing.

By choosing to work first at a small company before "graduating" to a global firm, I was able to obtain very practical education in a broad range of marketing techniques, and then move from that testing ground to a position where I could further apply my skills. My formal education helped, as well. I have been able to effectively put into practice the knowledge and systems I picked up in classes as varied as Industrial Planning, Retail Pricing, and Export Marketing. And supplemental courses such as English and Statistics also helped, by honing my writing style and mathematical abilities. My current responsibilities call on these latter skills a lot, whether in

pricing, promotion, writing copy for catalogues and brochures, or implementing the marketing plan for the sale of Robert Bosch Inc. power tools across Canada.

My education and experience also taught me that good marketing doesn't require a huge budget. What it does require is a personal commitment to listen to the customer, to communicate effectively the advantages of the firm's product package (price, quality, sufficient inventory, terms of sale, buyer/seller partnership, and so on), and to take a long-range view of the customer's needs.

Over the next 10 years I hope to reach the position of Sales and Marketing Manager, Director of Marketing, or General Manager with a firm of the same calibre as the one that now employs me.

# Pricing

CHAPTER 12
### Price Determination
●
CHAPTER 13
### Managing the Pricing Function

Pricing is a variable of the marketing mix that assumes widely different roles. It requires a considerable amount of science, as well as art, to manage. Part Five consists of two chapters on this critical element in the marketing mix. Chapter 12 examines the role of pricing in the marketing mix as well as price determination in both theory and practice. Chapter 13 examines various pricing decisions that have to be made, as well as the overall management of this function.

C H A P T E R   12

# Price Determination

## CHAPTER OBJECTIVES

1. To identify the major categories of pricing objectives.
2. To explain the concept of elasticity and the determinants of the degree of price elasticity for a product or service.
3. To identify the practical problems involved in applying price theory concepts to actual pricing decisions.
4. To explain the major approaches to price setting.
5. To list the major advantages and shortcomings of using break-even analysis in pricing decisions.
6. To explain the superiority of the marketing approach to pricing.
7. To illustrate a pricing model.

**A** PRICING decision has opened a major opportunity in the hotel market. The idea that business firms as well as families would be interested in budget accommodation has been proven by several relatively new chains. Prior to the 1980s, only individual "mom and pop" motels offered low-priced accommodation. Today there are about half a dozen chains that specialize in the field.

Economy hotels generally do without swimming pools, bars, room service and many other traditional amenities. All they try to offer are clean, comfortable rooms at rates well below those charged by full-service hotels — as little as $37.88 a night. As a result, they are now the fastest-growing segment of Canada's $3-billion annual motel and hotel business. They are led by the country's three largest budget chain operators — Journey's End Corp.; Calgary-based Relax Hotels and Resorts Ltd.; and Venture Inns Inc. of Toronto.

The budget hotels were an immediate hit with low- to middle-management business travellers and with vacationing families. Now, corporate travellers are increasingly turning to such hotels. For example, Venture Inns, which operates hotels in Ontario, lists among its corporate clients The Molson Cos. Ltd., IBM

Canada Ltd., and Honda Canada Inc. Said Pierre Belanger, Voyageur Quebec director of transportation systems: "When a business uses hotels and motels as much as we do, one of the primary considerations has to be price."

Journey's End executives share that view. One executive said, "Affordability is the cornerstone of our business. That's what brought people to us in the first place. And that is what is going to keep customers coming back."[1]

Pricing decisions can create opportunities or problems for a company. A good decision, such as the one implemented by the budget hotel chains, has resulted in a great deal of new business. It was a pricing decision based on a careful and accurate assessment of market needs.

---

# Introduction

Part Four examined the first critical element of a firm's marketing mix: the determination of the products and services to offer the target market. Part Five focuses on price — the second element of the marketing mix. Determination of profitable and justified prices is the result of pricing objectives and various approaches to setting prices. These topics are discussed in this chapter. The following chapter focuses upon management of the pricing function and discusses pricing strategies, price–quality relationships, and both industrial pricing and the pricing of public services. The starting place for examining pricing strategy is to understand the meaning of the term *price*.

**price**   The exchange value of a good or service. The value of an item is what it can be exchanged for in the marketplace.

**Price** is *the exchange value of a good or service, the value of an item being what it can be exchanged for in the marketplace.* This implies that the value is ultimately determined by customers. In earlier times, the price of an acre might have been twenty bushels of wheat, three cattle, or a boat. Price is a measure of what one must exchange in order to obtain a desired good or service. When the barter process was abandoned in favour of a monetary system, price became the amount of money required to purchase an item. As David Schwartz has pointed out, contemporary society uses a number of terms to refer to price:

> Price is all around us. You pay *rent* for your apartment, *tuition* for your education, and a *fee* to your physician or dentist.
>
> The airline, railway, taxi, and bus companies charge you a *fare*; the local utilities call their price a *rate*; and the local bank charges you *interest* for the money you borrow.
>
> The price for taking your car on the ferry to Prince Edward Island or Vancouver Island is a *toll*, and the company that insures your car charges you a *premium*.
>
> Clubs or societies to which you belong may make a special *assessment* to pay unusual expenses. Your regular lawyer may ask for a *retainer* to cover her services.
>
> The "price" of an executive is a *salary*; the price of a salesperson may be a *commission*; and the price of a worker is a *wage*.
>
> Finally, although economists would disagree, many of us feel that *income taxes* are the price we pay for the privilege of making money![2]

All products have some degree of *utility*, or want-satisfying power. While one individual might be willing to exchange the utility derived from a colour television for a vacation, another may not be willing to make that exchange. Prices are a mechanism that allows the consumer to make a decision. In contemporary society, of course, prices are translated into monetary terms. The consumer evaluates the utility derived from a range of possible purchases and then allocates his or her exchange power (in monetary terms) so as to maximize satisfaction. Pricing may be the most complicated aspect of the marketing manager's job. It is difficult to determine the price needed to realize a profit. But an even greater problem is that of determining the meaning of price and its role in society.

Price is fundamental to many aspects of the economic system. Price often serves as a means of regulating economic activity. The employment of any or all of the four factors of production (land, labour, capital, and entrepreneurship) is dependent upon the price received by each.

For an individual firm, prices (along with the corresponding quantity that will be sold) represent the revenue to be received. Prices, therefore, influence a company's profit as well as its use of the factors of production. Early written accounts refer to attempts to develop a fair, or just, price. The "fair price" differs dramatically depending on one's perspective. If you are buying gasoline in Thunder Bay you will have one set of criteria to judge whether the price is fair. If you are driving late at night on a deserted highway north of Lake Superior and the tank is nearly empty, another price perception emerges.

# Price and the Marketing Mix

Just as price is highly important in affecting economic activity, it is a central consideration in the development of a marketing mix. A key question when setting a price is, "What is the role of price in this marketing mix?" One marketing strategy will assign a major role to price as a means of attracting customers and sales. The discount food chain, Save-On Foods, is an example. Towards the other end of the spectrum, the marketing strategy of Accura uses high price as a signal of the value of that fine car. In another marketing mix, price will play a much less important role. It can thus be seen that there are different possible *objectives* for price.

## Pricing Objectives

Pricing objectives are a crucial part of a means-end chain from overall company objectives to specific pricing policies and procedures (see Figure 12–1). The goals of the firm and the marketing organization provide the basis for the development of pricing objectives, which must be clearly established before pricing policies and procedures are implemented.

A firm may have as its primary objective the goal of becoming the dominant supplier in the domestic market. Its marketing objective might then be to achieve maximum sales penetration in all sales regions. The related pricing goal would be sales maximization. This means-end chain might lead to the adoption of a low-price policy implemented through provision of the highest cash and trade discounts in the industry.

Pricing objectives vary from firm to firm. In a recent U.S. study, marketers identified the primary and secondary pricing objectives of their companies. Meeting competitive prices was most often mentioned, but many marketers ranked two

*"Honest Ed's" discount department store in Toronto has taken the low-price policy to its logical extreme. By offering some of the lowest prices in town, and cutting back on customer service, owner Ed Mirvish hopes to maximize sales. As his sign says: "Please don't bother our help. They have their own problems. Serve yourself and save a lot of money."*

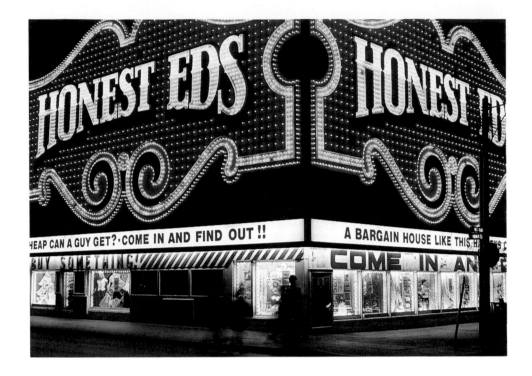

FIGURE 12–1

**The Role of Pricing Objectives in Contemporary Marketing**

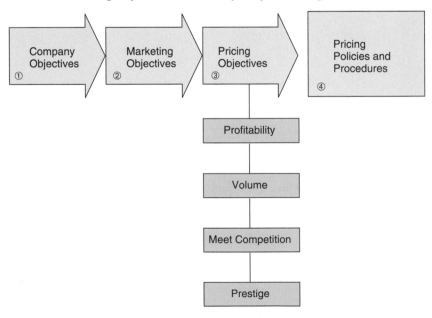

## FIGURE 12-2

### Primary and Secondary Pricing Objectives of Firms

| Pricing Objective | Percentage of Respondents Ranking the Item | | |
| --- | --- | --- | --- |
| | As Primary Objectives | As Secondary Objectives | As Either Primary or Secondary Objective |
| Meeting competitive price level | 38.3 | 43.0 | 81.3 |
| Specified rate of return on investment | 60.9 | 17.2 | 78.1 |
| Specified total profit level | 60.2 | 17.2 | 77.4 |
| Increased market share | 31.3 | 42.2 | 73.5 |
| Increased total profits above previous levels | 34.4 | 37.5 | 71.9 |
| Specified rate of return on sales | 47.7 | 23.4 | 71.1 |
| Retaining existing market share | 31.3 | 35.9 | 67.2 |
| Serving selected market segments | 26.6 | 39.1 | 65.7 |
| Creation of a readily identifiable image for the firm and/or its products | 21.9 | 41.4 | 63.3 |
| Specified market share | 15.6 | 40.6 | 56.2 |
| Other | 5.5 | — | 5.5 |

Source: *Pricing Objectives and Practices in American Industry: A Research Paper.* ©1979 by Louis E. Boone and David L. Kurtz; all right reserved.

profitability-oriented objectives higher: a specified rate of return on investment and specified total profit levels. These two objectives ranked first and second as *primary* pricing objectives. The findings are shown in Figure 12–2.

Pricing objectives can be classified into four major groups: (1) profitability objectives; (2) volume objectives; (3) competition-meeting objectives; and (4) prestige objectives. Profitability objectives include profit maximization and target return goals.

## Profitability Objectives

Businesses need to make profits in order to survive. How much profits? In classical economic theory, the traditional pricing objective has been to *maximize profits*.[3] In terms of actual business practice, this means that profit maximization is the basic objective of individual firms.

Profits, in turn, are a function of revenue and expenses:

$$\text{Profits} = \text{Total Revenues} - \text{Total Costs}$$

And revenue is determined by the selling price and the quantity sold:

$$\text{Total Revenue} = \text{Price} \times \text{Quantity Sold}$$

Price, therefore, should be increased up to the point where it causes a disproportionate decrease in the number of units sold. A 10 percent price increase that results in only an 8 percent cut in volume adds to the firm's revenue. However, a 10 percent hike that causes an 11 percent sales decline reduces total revenue.

**profit maximization** The point where the addition to total revenue is just balanced by an increase in total cost.

This approach is referred to as *marginal analysis*. The point of **profit maximization** is where *the addition to total revenue is just balanced by an increase in total cost*. This is a valuable concept, which the reader should understand. Making it work, however, is not so easy. The basic problem centres on the difficulty in achieving this delicate balance between marginal revenue and marginal cost. As a result, relatively few firms actually achieve the objective of profit maximization. A significantly larger number prefer to direct their efforts toward goals that are more easily implemented and measured.

Consequently, target return objectives have become quite common in industry, particularly among the larger firms where public pressure may limit consideration of the profit maximization objective.[4] Telephone and other utility companies are an example of this phenomenon. **Target return objectives** may be *either short-run or long-run goals and usually are stated as a percentage of sales or investment*. A company, for instance, may seek a 15 percent annual rate of return on investment or an 8 percent rate of return on sales. A specified return on investment was the most commonly reported pricing objective in Figure 12–2.

**target return objectives** Either short-run or long-run goals, usually stated as a percentage of sales or investment.

Goals of this nature also serve as useful guidelines in evaluating corporate activity. One writer has aptly expressed it: "For management consciously accepting less than maximum profits, the target rate can provide a measure of the amount of restraint. For firms making very low profits, the target rate can serve as a standard for judging improvement."[5] Furthermore, they are more likely to result in a more stable and planned profit pattern for the company. This contrasts with a profit maximization approach, which can be very unstable.

Target return objectives offer several benefits to the marketer. As noted above, they serve as a means for evaluating performance. They also are designed to generate a "fair" profit, as judged by management, stockholders, and the general public as well. When using such target objectives, managements should avoid a short-term perspective. For example, if a product has contributed according to target for a time and now faces price competition, it still could be making a good contribution to overhead and should not be arbitrarily dropped.

## Volume Objectives

**sales maximization** The pricing philosophy analyzed by economist William J. Baumol. Baumol believes that many firms attempt to maximize sales within a profit constraint.

Some writers argue that a better explanation of actual pricing behaviour is William J. Baumol's belief that firms attempt to **maximize sales** within a given profit constraint.[6] In other words, they set *a minimum floor at what they consider the lowest acceptable profit level and then seek to maximize sales* (subject to this profit constraint) in the belief that increased sales are more important to the long-run competitive picture. The company will continue to expand sales as long as their total profits do not drop below the minimum return acceptable to management.

Another volume-related pricing objective is the **market share objective** — that is, the goal is set to *control a specific portion of the market for the firm's product*. The company's specific goal can be to maintain or increase its share of a particular market. For example, a firm may desire to increase its 10 percent share of a particular market to 20 percent.[7] As Figure 12–2 indicates, about two-thirds of all responding firms list retaining existing market share as either a primary or secondary pricing objective.

Market share objectives can be critical to the achievement of other objectives. High sales, for example, may mean more profit. The extensive *Profit Impact of Market Strategies* (*PIMS*) project conducted by the Marketing Science Institute analyzed more than 2000 firms and revealed that two of the most important factors influencing profitability were product quality and a large market share.

**market share objective** To control a specific portion of the market for the firm's product.

## Meeting Competition as a Pricing Objective

**Status quo objectives** — *objectives based on the maintenance of stable prices* — are the basis of the pricing philosophy for many enterprises. This philosophy usually stems from a desire to minimize competitive pricing action. The maintenance of stable prices allows the firm to concentrate its efforts on non-price elements of the marketing mix such as product improvement or promotion. Canada Packers de-emphasized price competition and developed an advertising campaign emphasizing product features that differentiated its product, Tenderflake lard, from the competition. As a result, market share and profits increased significantly. They were even able to raise prices gradually. Status quo objectives remain a significant factor in pricing.

**status quo objectives** Objectives based on the maintenance of stable prices.

## Prestige Objectives

Another category of pricing objectives unrelated to either profitability or sales volume is that of prestige objectives. **Prestige objectives** involve *the establishment of relatively high prices in order to develop and maintain an image of quality and exclusiveness*. Such objectives reflect marketers' recognition of the role of price in the creation of an overall image for the firm and its products and services. It appears that Birks and Holt Renfrew follow this strategy. Many luxury perfume manufacturers also use prestige pricing to connote quality. And Rolls-Royce has opted for a higher-price image with its Cabriolet convertible model, priced at approximately $150 000. While some marketers set relatively high prices in order to maintain a prestige image with their consumers, others prefer the opposite approach of developing a low-price image among customers.

**prestige objectives** The establishment of relatively high prices in order to develop and maintain an image of quality and exclusiveness.

## Price Determination

There are three general approaches to determining price. One is price derivation, based on theoretical economic analysis. A second is the cost-plus approach, where the costs of producing the product are determined, and a margin of profit is added on. The third method is the marketing approach. The marketing approach is built upon aspects of the economic-analysis and cost-plus methods, and adds an important marketing dimension to come up with a realistic price.

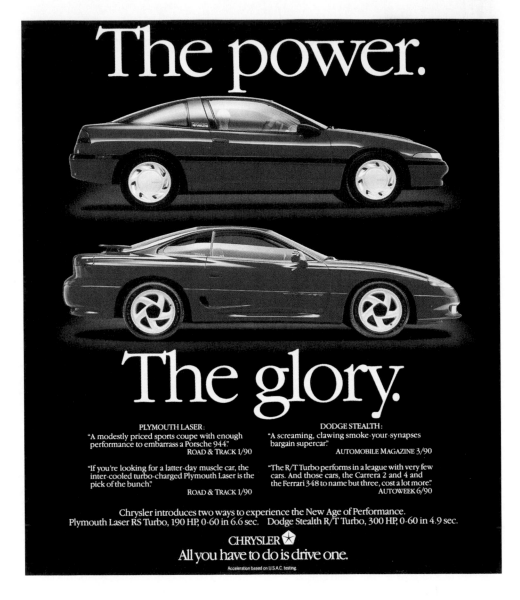

## Price Determination in Economic Theory

Few businesses follow economic theory strictly in setting prices. Because of this, some students ask why we should bother with reviewing the economic approach to pricing. The reason is that *the concepts of economic price theory are essential to understand, and apply to almost any pricing situation*. These concepts are important building blocks that help us understand what is going on in a particular pricing situation.

The microeconomic approach, or price theory, assumes a profit maximization objective and leads to the derivation of correct equilibrium prices in the marketplace. Price theory considers both supply and demand factors and thus is a more complete analysis than what is typically found in practice.

*Demand* refers to a schedule of the amounts of a firm's product or service that consumers will purchase at different prices during a specific period. *Supply* refers to a schedule of the amounts of a product or service that will be offered for sale at different prices during a specified time period. These schedules may vary for different types of market structures.

## Market Structures

There are four types of market structures: pure competition, monopolistic competition, oligopoly, and monopoly. Very briefly, **pure competition** is *a market structure where there is such a large number of buyers and sellers that no one of them has a significant influence on price*. Other characteristics of pure competition include a homogeneous product and ease of entry for sellers, and complete and instantaneous information.

This marketing structure is largely theoretical in contemporary society; however, some uncontrolled sectors of the agricultural commodity sector exhibit many of the characteristics of such a market, and provide the closest example of it.

**Monopolistic competition** is also *a market structure with a large number of buyers and sellers*. However, in this market there is *some degree of heterogeneity in good and/or service and usually geographical differentiation*. The existence of differentiation allows the marketer some degree of control over price. Most retail stores fall into this category, which partially explains why small retailers can exist with prices 5 to 10 percent higher than their larger competitors.

An **oligopoly** is *a market structure in which there are relatively few sellers*. Each seller may affect the market, but no one seller controls it. Examples are the automobile, steel, tobacco, and petroleum-refining industries. Because of high start-up costs, new competitors encounter significant entry barriers. **Oligopsony** is the other side of the coin: *a market where there are only a few buyers*.

A **monopoly** is *a market structure with only one seller of a product with no close substitutes*. Anti-combines legislation has tended to eliminate all but *temporary* monopolies, such as those provided by patent protection, and *regulated* monopolies, such as the public utilities (telephone, electricity, gas). Regulated monopolies are granted by government in markets where competition would lead to an uneconomic duplication of services. In return for this monopoly, government regulates the monopoly rate of return through regulatory bodies such as the Canadian Transport Commission, the Canadian Radio-television and Telecommunications Commission, the National Farm Products Marketing Council, and provincial public utility regulatory commissions.

**pure competition** A market structure where there is such a large number of buyers and sellers that no one of them has a significant influence on price.

**monopolistic competition** A market structure with a large number of buyers and sellers where heterogeneity in product and/or service and (usually) geographical differentiation allow the marketer some control over price.

**oligopoly** A market structure in which there are relatively few sellers.

**oligopsony** A market where there are only a few buyers.

**monopoly** A market structure with only one seller of a product with no close substitutes.

## Revenue, Cost, and Supply Curves

Within each of these market structures the elements of demand, costs, and supply must be considered. The demand side of price theory is concerned with *revenue curves*. *Average revenue* (AR) is obtained by dividing *total revenue* (TR) by the *quantity* (Q) associated with these revenues:

$$AR = \frac{TR}{Q}$$

The average revenue line is actually the demand curve facing the firm. *Marginal revenue* (MR) is the change in total revenue ($\Delta$TR) that results from selling an additional unit of output ($\Delta$Q). This can be shown as:

$$MR = \frac{\Delta TR}{\Delta Q}$$

In order to complete the analysis, the supply curves must be determined for each of these market situations. A firm's cost structure determines its supply curves. Let us examine each of the cost curves applicable to price determination.

**average cost**    Obtained by dividing total cost by the quantity associated with this cost.

**Average cost** (AC) is obtained by dividing total cost by the quantity (Q) associated with the total cost. *Total cost* (TC) is composed of both fixed and variable components. *Fixed costs* are those costs that do not vary with differences in output, while *variable costs* are those that change when the level of production is altered. Examples of fixed costs include executive compensation, depreciation, and insurance. Variable costs include raw materials and the wages paid production workers.

**average variable cost**    The total variable cost divided by the related quantity.

**marginal cost**    The change in total cost that results from producing an additional unit of output.

**Average variable cost** (AVC) is simply the total variable cost (TVC) divided by the related quantity. Similarly, *average fixed cost* (AFC) is determined by dividing total fixed costs (TFC) by the related quantity. **Marginal cost** (MC) is the change in total cost ($\Delta$TC) that results from producing an additional unit of output ($\Delta$Q). Thus, it is similar to *marginal revenue*, which is the change in total revenue resulting from the production of an incremental unit. The point of profit maximization is where marginal costs are equal to marginal revenues.

These cost derivations are shown in the following formulas:

$$AC = \frac{TC}{Q} \quad AFC = \frac{TFC}{Q}$$
$$AVC = \frac{TVC}{Q} \quad MC = \frac{\Delta TC}{\Delta Q}$$

The resulting *cost curves* are shown in Figure 12–3. The marginal cost curve (MC) intersects the average variable cost curve (AVC) and average cost curve (AC) at the minimum points.

### A·P·P·L·Y·I·N·G  T·H·E  C·O·N·C·E·P·T·S

## Pricing Policies Create Twilight Zone in Soviet Stores

What Canadian shopper wouldn't love to walk into a grocery store and find that the prices of beef, chicken, vegetables, fruit, and other basic food items were the same as 30 years ago?

A journey into the Twilight Zone? Maybe in Canada, but this is the situation in Soviet state-run stores, called gastronomes.

In a bid to defy the laws of supply and demand, the Soviet government has kept most prices frozen for three decades or more. Soviet consumers have become so used to these prices that any attempt to allow market forces to prevail is fraught with political risk. In 1990, a kilo of beef in a state store cost 1.90 rubles ($3.80 at the official exchange rate), the same as it did yesterday, last month, last year, and in 1960.(Sometimes the beef looks as if it has been sitting there since 1960.)

The state pricing system covers almost everything. The official prices are moulded, embossed, or forged on to the bottoms of plastic and metal manufactured goods at the factory. Hidden inflation is the result of the fact that most people cannot find anything to buy

at the official state prices, and thus they must look elsewhere, including the black market, to put food on the table.

Go back for a moment to the state gastronome, a cruel misnomer. The yellowing cardboard price signs are unchanged. But the signs often are the only things sitting on the shelf or in the meat and dairy cases. Hundreds of thousands of Muscovites roam from store to store each day in the hope of being in the right spot when a food delivery truck rolls in.

This week, the Central Market in Moscow received fresh produce from private co-operatives in Georgia, Armenia, and other agricultural areas to the south. But the produce is extremely expensive; a single lemon, for instance, can cost as much as two rubles ($4.00). Often, however, there is no other choice. The state fruit and vegetable stands at the Central Market are empty of all but some pathetic three-litre bottles of pickled beets.

Source: Adapted from Jeff Sallot, "Twilight Zone in Soviet Stores," *Globe and Mail* (June 22, 1990).

FIGURE 12–3

## Cost Curves

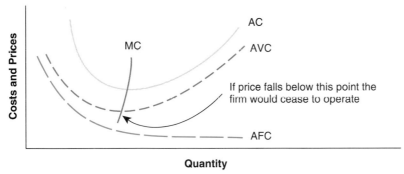

In the short run a firm will continue to operate even if the price falls below AC, provided it remains above AVC. Why is this rational market behaviour? If the firm were to cease operations after the price fell below AC, it would still have some fixed costs, but *no* revenue. Any amount received above AVC can be used to cover fixed costs. The manager is acting rationally by continuing to produce as long as price exceeds AVC since this is minimizing losses. If price falls below AVC the manager would cease operation because continued operation would result in real losses from out-of-pocket costs per unit, with no control of fixed costs. The **supply curve**, therefore, is *the marginal cost curve above its intersection with AVC* since this is the area of rational pricing behaviour for the firm.

**supply curve** The marginal cost curve above its intersection with the average variable cost.

How, then, are prices set in each of the product market situations? Figure 12–4 shows how prices are determined in each of the four product markets. The point of profit maximization (MC = MR) sets the equilibrium output (Point A), which is extended to the AR line to set the equilibrium price (Point B). In the case of pure competition, AR = MR, so price is a predetermined variable in this product market.

## The Concept of Elasticity in Pricing Strategy

Although the intersection of demand and supply curves determines the equilibrium price for each of the market structures, the specific curves vary. To understand why, it is necessary to understand the concept of elasticity.[8]

**Elasticity** is *a measure of responsiveness of purchasers and suppliers to changes in price.* The *price elasticity of demand* is the percentage change in the quantity of a product or service demanded, divided by the percentage change in its price. A 10 percent increase in the price of eggs that results in a 5 percent decrease in the quantity of eggs demanded yields a price elasticity of demand for eggs of 0.5.

**elasticity** A measure of responsiveness of purchasers and suppliers to changes in price.

## Elasticity Terminology

Consider a case in which a one percent change in price causes more than a one percent change in the quantity supplied or demanded. Numerically, that means an elasticity greater than one. When the elasticity of demand or supply is greater than one, it is termed *elastic*.

If a one percent change in price results in less than a one percent change in quantity, a good's elasticity of supply or demand will be numerically less than one

FIGURE 12 – 4

**Price Determination in the Four Product Markets**

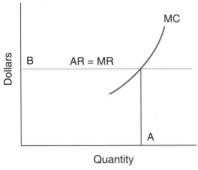

**Pure Competition**

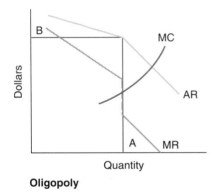

**Monopolistic Competition**

**Oligopoly**

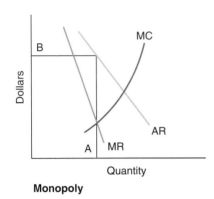

**Monopoly**

and is called *inelastic.* The demand for eggs in the example above is inelastic. The demand for gasoline is relatively inelastic. There was a recent period when retail gasoline prices rose 50 percent, but gasoline sales fell by only about 8 percent.

An extreme case occurs when the quantity supplied or demanded does not change at all when the price changes. Then the supply or demand is called perfectly inelastic.

The case in which a one percent change in price results in exactly a one percent change in quantity is called *unit* (or *unitary*) *elastic.*

## Determinants of Elasticity

Why is the elasticity of supply or demand high for some products and services and low for others? What constitute the specific determinants of demand elasticity?[9]

One factor determining the elasticity of demand is the availability of substitutes. If a product or service has close substitutes, the demand tends to be elastic. The demand for olive oil, for instance, is more elastic than it would be if other salad oils were not available as substitutes. The demand for cars is less elastic than it would be if good public transportation were available everywhere. A related factor is the

*Gasoline prices are relatively inelastic. Since gasoline is essential to the operation of cars and other vehicles, people are likely to keep on buying it despite an increase in price. How does this situation affect the marketing of gasoline as a commodity?*

availability of more important complements. The demand for motor oil, for example, tends to be inelastic, because it is a complement to the more important good, gasoline.

Elasticity of demand is also influenced by whether a product or service is a necessity or a luxury. For example, dining out is a luxury for most people. If restaurant prices increase, most people can respond by eating at home instead. By contrast, eggs and milk are considered necessities, so price changes have less effect on consumption, at least in the short run.

Elasticity is further influenced by the portion of a person's budget that is spent on a product or service. Matches, for example, are no longer really a necessity, and good substitutes exist. Nonetheless, the demand for matches is thought to be very inelastic because people spend so little on them that they hardly notice a price change. However, the demand for housing and transportation is not perfectly inelastic even though they are necessities. Both occupy a large part of people's budgets, so a change in price cannot be ignored.

Elasticity of demand is also affected by the time perspective under consideration. Demand is often less elastic in the short run than in the long run. Consider the demand for home heating fuel. In the short run, when the price goes up, people find it difficult to cut back on the quantity they use. They are accustomed to living at a certain temperature, dressing a certain way, and so forth. Given time, though, they may find ways to economize. They can better insulate their homes, form new habits of dressing more warmly, or even move to a warmer climate.

All the factors mentioned here are only tendencies; yet often the tendencies reinforce one another. The classic case of inelastic demand is salt, which has no good substitute, is a nutritional necessity, and uses a very small part of one's budget. Sometimes, though, the rules just do not seem to fit. Alcohol and tobacco, which are not necessities and do occupy a large share of some personal budgets, also are subject to notoriously inelastic demand.

## Elasticity and Revenue

There is an important relationship between the elasticity of demand and the way that total revenue changes as the price of a product or service changes. Suppose Montreal wants to find a way to raise more money for the public transportation system. One possible fund-raising method is to change the transit fare, but should it be raised or lowered? The correct answer depends on the elasticity of demand for subway rides. A 10 percent decrease in fares is sure to attract more riders, but unless there is more than a 10 percent increase in riders, total revenue will fall. A 10 percent increase in fares will bring in more money per rider, but if more than 10 percent of the riders are lost, revenue will fall. A price cut will increase revenue only if demand is *elastic*, and a price increase will raise revenue only if demand is *inelastic*.

## Practical Problems in Applying Price Theory

From the viewpoint of the marketer, price theory concepts are sometimes difficult to apply in practice. What are their practical limitations?

1. Many firms do not attempt to profit-maximize. Economic analysis is subject to the same limitations as the assumptions upon which it is based – for example, the proposition that all firms attempt to maximize profits.

2. It is difficult to estimate demand curves. Modern accounting procedures provide the manager with a clear understanding of his or her cost structure. The manager, therefore, can readily comprehend the supply side of the price equation. But it is difficult to estimate demand at various price levels. Demand curves must be based upon market research estimates that are often not as exact as cost figures. Although the demand element can be identified, it is often difficult to measure in the real-world setting.[10]

3. Inadequate training and communications hinder price theory in the real world. Many businesspersons lack the formal training in economics to be able to apply its concepts to their own pricing decisions. On the other hand, many economists remain essentially theorists devoting little interest or effort to real-world pricing situations. This dual problem significantly hinders the use of economic theory in actual pricing practice.[11]

In spite of these problems it is very useful for pricing decision-makers to consider whether demand for their product is elastic or inelastic, what kind of market structure they are operating in, and other related theoretical matters.

# Cost-Plus Price Setting

For many firms, price determination tends to be based upon some form of the cost-plus approach.

**cost-plus pricing** Pricing technique using base cost figure per unit to which is added a markup to cover unassigned costs and to provide a profit.

**Cost-plus pricing** uses some *base cost figure per unit to which is added a markup to cover unassigned costs and to provide a profit.* The only real difference in the multitude of cost-plus techniques is the relative sophistication of the costing procedures employed. For example, the local clothing store may set prices by adding a 40 percent markup to the invoice price charged by the supplier. This markup is expected to cover all other expenses, as well as permit the owner to earn a reasonable return on the sale of the garments.

In contrast to this rather simple pricing mechanism, a large manufacturer may employ a pricing formula that requires a computer to handle the necessary calculations for a sophisticated costing procedure. But in the end the formula still requires someone to make a decision about the markup. The clothing store and the large manufacturer may be vastly different with respect to the *cost* aspect, but they are remarkably similar when it comes to the *markup* side of the equation.

The above discussion demonstrates a major problem associated with cost-oriented pricing. "*Costs should not determine prices, since the proper function of cost in pricing is to determine the profit consequences of pricing alternatives.*"[12] That is, costs in the long run only determine the floor for the price. Unfortunately, this is not always understood by some companies.

## Full-Cost Pricing

The two most common cost-oriented pricing procedures are the full-cost method and the incremental-cost method. *Full-cost pricing* uses all relevant variable costs in setting a product's price. In addition, it considers an allocation of the fixed costs that cannot be directly attributed to the production of the specific item being priced. Under the full-cost method, if job order 515 in a printing plant amounts to 0.000127 percent of the plant's total output, then 0.000127 percent of the firm's overhead expenses are allocated to this job. This approach, therefore, allows the pricer to recover all costs plus the amount added as a profit margin.

The full-cost approach has two basic deficiencies. First, there is no consideration of the demand for the item or its competition. Perhaps no one wants to pay the price that the firm has calculated. Second, any method of allocating overhead, or fixed expenses, is arbitrary and may be unrealistic. In manufacturing, overhead allocations are often tied to direct labour hours. In retailing, the mechanism is sometimes floor area in each profit centre. Regardless of the technique, it is difficult to show a cause-and-effect relationship between the allocated cost and most products.

## Incremental-Cost Pricing

One way to overcome the arbitrary allocation of fixed expenses is by *incremental-cost pricing*, which attempts to use only those costs directly attributable to a specific output in setting prices. For example, consider a small manufacturer with the following income statement:

| Sales (10 000 units at $10) | | $100 000 |
|---|---|---|
| Expenses | | |
| Variable | $50 000 | |
| Fixed | 40 000 | 90 000 |
| Net Profit | | $ 10 000 |

Suppose that the firm is offered a contract for an additional 5000 units. Since the peak season is over, these items can be produced at the same average variable cost. Assume that the labour force would be idle otherwise. In order to get the contract, how low could the firm price its product?

Under the full-cost approach the lowest price would be $9 each. This is obtained by dividing the $90 000 in expenses by an output of 10 000 units. The full-cost pricer would consider this a profitless situation. One study indicated that this method of calculation and the subsequent decision were typical of many small businesses: "A common practice is to use full costs, not as a flexible point at which the price is to be set, but as a floor below which the price will not be allowed to fall — a reference point to which flexible markups are added."[13]

The incremental approach, on the other hand, would permit a price of anywhere from $5.01 upwards depending on the competition.[14] If competition were strong, a price of $5.10 would be competitive. This price would be composed of the $5 variable cost related to each unit of production, plus a 10 cents per unit contribution to fixed expenses and overhead. With these conditions of sale, note the revised income statement:

|  |  |  |
|---|---|---|
| Sales (10 000 at $10 plus 5 000 at $5.10) |  | $125 500 |
| Expenses |  |  |
| Variable (15 000 × $5) | $75 000 |  |
| Fixed | 40 000 | 115 000 |
| Net Profit |  | $ 10 500 |

Profits were increased under the incremental approach. Admittedly, the illustration is based on two assumptions: (1) the ability to isolate markets so that selling at the lower price would not affect the price received in other markets; and (2) the absence of certain legal restrictions on the firm. The example, however, does show that profits can sometimes be enhanced by using the incremental approach.

### Limitations of Cost-Oriented Pricing

While the incremental method eliminates one of the problems associated with full-cost pricing, it fails to deal effectively with the basic malady: *cost-oriented pricing does not adequately account for product demand.*

The problem of estimating demand is as critical to these approaches as it is to classical price theory. To the marketer, the challenge is to find some way of introducing demand analysis into cost-plus pricing. It has also been pointed out that a well-reasoned approach to pricing is, in effect, a comparison of the impact of a decision on total sales receipts, or revenue, and on total costs. It involves the increase or decrease in revenue and costs, not just of the product under consideration, but of the business enterprise as a whole.[15]

## Marketing Approaches to Pricing

Marketing is an eclectic discipline. It draws good ideas from many sources. A *marketing approach to pricing* is no exception. A marketing approach recognizes the numerous valuable concepts developed by economic theory. Especially valuable are the concepts of demand estimation and price elasticity. Cost accounting is also considered essential in pricing. Without a thorough understanding of costs, a firm's pricing policies can soon go awry.

A marketing approach to pricing adds the dimension of *consumer analysis* to the foregoing approaches. For example, this approach might accept that a profit margin of, say, 35 percent would be desirable for the firm. It also considers potential demand

*To market its Chlorothene SM Solvent, Dow Chemical Canada set its price for a planned target market. The product was targeted to plant managers who purchase solutions for metal-cleaning applications. Given this target market and a relatively stable demand curve, how do you think the price strategist arrived at a price that would maximize sales and profits?*

for the product, as well as price elasticity. It goes beyond these consideration, however. The marketing approach asks the question of *how potential consumers would respond* to such a price. Would this price cross some possible psychological threshold, and be viewed as much higher than it really is? Or would the proposed price seem so low that it would negatively affect its image and sales? The astute marketer asks a host of other questions based on the unique perspective of consumer orientation.

From a marketing perspective, a product that is new to the world, as opposed to being merely new to the company, passes through distinctive stages in its life cycle. The appropriate pricing policy is likely to be different at each stage.[16] Perhaps the most difficult task is establishing an initial price for the product. In later stages of the product life cycle, pricing is complicated enough, but at that point, strategic decisions hinge largely on decisions to meet or beat the competition in various ways.

## A pricing decision flow chart

A good example of one marketing approach to pricing is G. David Hughes's pricing procedure for new products (see Figure 12–5). This procedure can be used for market entries that are new to the company as well. It adds a number of marketing considerations as well as taking into account many of the points considered in this chapter.[17]

**Establish the range of acceptable prices.** The first step is to establish a price range that is consistent with corporate values, objectives, and policies. The pricing policies of top executives who are risk-takers may be different from those of risk-averters. The range of prices will be predicated on the company's desire to establish a discount image or a quality image. Similarly, a decision to use a prestige channel of distribution will determine channel discount structures, which in turn will be reflected in a final price.

**Set price for a planned target market.** As with virtually all marketing mix decisions, the pricing process has to be developed with a specific target market in mind. Given some estimate of the demand curve for the target segment, the price strategist attempts to identify the price that will maximize sales or profits.

**Estimate demand for the brand.** This price is then positioned against competitive prices to determine expected market share. If this share is too small, the strategist will go back to the generic demand (i.e., primary demand, or those needs that can be met by a product category) and select a new price.

**Estimate competitor's reactions.** Once a price is selected that provides what seems to be an acceptable sales volume, the next task is to estimate how competitors will react. A very low price may cause a price war in an oligopoly. An exceptionally high price may attract lower-priced competition. If either of these responses would destroy the basic marketing strategy, the strategist must go back and select a new price.

**Consider public policy implications.** Unfavourable reactions from the public may take many forms. Provincial or federal authorities may look on a given price strategy in a monopoly-type situation as unconscionable and therefore subject to legislation or regulation. Consumerists may regard a price as excessive and boycott all of the company's products. Labour unions may regard a price increase as an indication that the company can now afford to raise wages.

**Test the price against financial goals.** The next test is to see if the pricing strategy will meet financial goals such as return on investment (ROI), target rate of return on sales, or a payback period. Failure to meet financial goals sends the pricing strategist back to the generic-demand curve to select a new price for analysis. In actual practice, the strategist will probably have tested the price against the financial goals before proceeding to the positioning of the price among other brands, because rough calculations can be based on previous experience. In fact, it is desirable to make profit plans as early as the concept stage during new-product development. These plans can be continually updated as the product passes through the development stages.

**Evaluate its congruence in the mix.** The selected price must be evaluated in terms of the product, channel, advertising, and personal-selling strategies that will be used in the market segment in question. The role of price in the marketing mix should be specifically identified, and all elements of the mix must blend together. Any inconsistencies must be reconciled by altering the price or one of the other elements of the mix.

A low price is appropriate when the product category is at the mature stage in its cycle. A low price may also be appropriate when there is little promotion, the

F I G U R E   1 2 – 5

## Pricing Decision Flow Chart

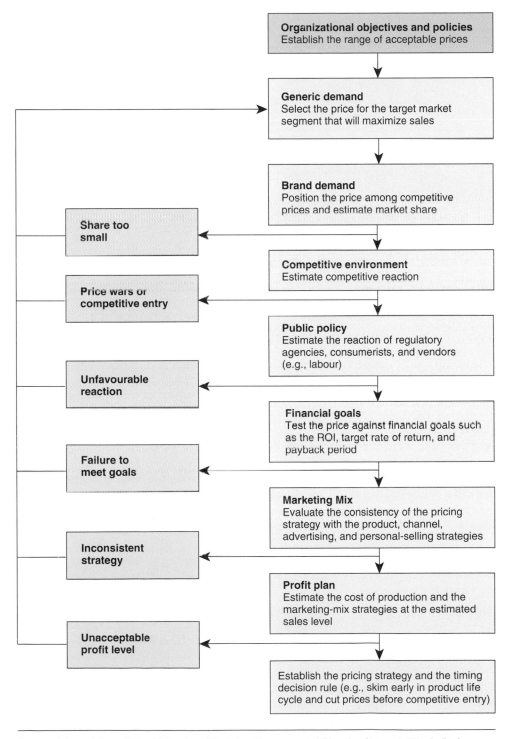

Source: Adapted from G. David Hughes, *Marketing Management: A Planning Approach* (Menlo Park, CA: Addison-Wesley, 1978), p.325.

*By marketing his meat at prices like $2.98 and $1.98, this retailer hopes to achieve a psychological advantage over his competition. Since this strategy is widely used by retailers, however, some consumers have become acclimated or even suspicious of this practice.*

product is mass-produced, market coverage is intense, production is capital intensive, technological change is slow, the product is needed to complete the product line, few services are offered, the product is disposable, or the life cycle is short.[18]

**Develop a profit plan.** The cost of production and the cost of the marketing-mix strategy at the estimated sales level provide inputs for the profit plan. An inadequate profit may send the strategist back to the setting of a new price or to the reduction of the cost of other elements in the marketing mix.

**Finalize actual price and timing.** The last stage in the process is to establish the final price. This is done in light of the preceding steps, but it also takes into specific consideration the actual prices of competing products. For example, the profit plan calculation might indicate a price of $71.87, but the final price offered to the market might be $69.95. This might be chosen for psychological reasons (it sounds less expensive), or to meet the prices of competitors. If a high-priced skimming strategy (described in Chapter 13) has been chosen, a timing decision should also be reached in order to be ready to cut prices when predetermined conditions occur.

Many procedures that are used to determine price are not this elaborate. The foregoing is one of a number of similar possible processes that may be employed.

## Break-even Analysis: A Useful Tool in Pricing

**break-even analysis** A means of determining the number of products or services that must be sold at a given price in order to generate sufficient revenue to cover total costs.

**Break-even analysis** is *a means of determining the number of products or services that must be sold at a given price in order to generate sufficient revenue to cover total costs.* Figure 12–6 shows calculation of the break-even point graphically. The total cost curve includes both fixed and variable segments, and total fixed cost is represented by a horizontal shaded bar. Average variable cost is assumed to be constant per unit as it was in the example used for incremental pricing.

The break-even point is the point at which total revenue ($TR$) just equals total cost ($TC$). It can be found by using the following formulas:

$$\frac{\text{Break-even Point}}{\text{(in Units)}} = \frac{\text{Total Fixed Cost}}{\text{Per-unit Selling Price} - \text{Average Variable Cost}}$$

$$= \frac{\text{Total Fixed Cost}}{\text{Per-unit Contribution to Fixed Cost}}$$

$$\frac{\text{Break-even Point}}{\text{(in Dollars)}} = \frac{\text{Total Fixed Cost}}{1 - \dfrac{\text{Variable Cost per Unit}}{\text{Selling Price}}}$$

In our earlier example, a selling price of $10 and an average variable cost of $5 resulted in a per-unit contribution to fixed costs of $5. This figure can be divided into total fixed costs of $40 000 to obtain a break-even point of 8000 units, or $80 000 in total sales revenue:

$$\frac{\text{Break-even Point}}{\text{(in Units)}} = \frac{\$40\ 000}{\$10 - \$5} = \frac{\$40\ 000}{\$5} = 8000 \text{ units}$$

$$\frac{\text{Break-even Point}}{\text{(in Dollars)}} = \frac{\$40\ 000}{1 - \dfrac{\$5}{\$10}} = \frac{\$40\ 000}{0.5} = \$80\ 000$$

$$\frac{\text{Break-even Profit Point (in Dollars)}}{} = \frac{\$40\ 000 + 10\% \text{ on Sales } (\$8000)}{1 - \dfrac{\$5}{\$10}} = \frac{\$48\ 000}{0.5} = \$96\ 000$$

Break-even analysis is an effective tool for marketers in assessing the required sales in order to cover costs and achieve specified profit levels. It is easily understood by both marketing and nonmarketing executives and may assist in deciding whether

**FIGURE 12 – 6**

**Break-even Chart**

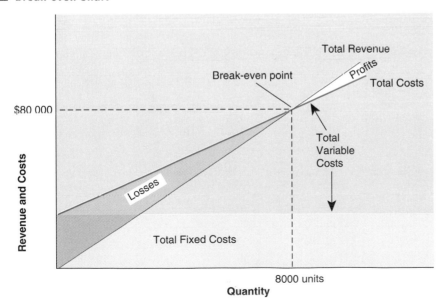

required sales levels for a certain price are in fact realistic goals. Extending this analysis a bit further, a simple profit breakdown is also shown in the example. If a 10 percent profit on sales were desired, sales of $96 000 would be required. More data would be needed if a return on investment or some other measure was used as a profitability target. However, it is not without shortcomings.

First, the model assumes that costs can be divided into fixed and variable categories. Some costs, such as salaries and advertising outlays, may be either fixed or variable depending upon the particular situation. In addition, the model assumes that per-unit variable costs do not change at different levels of operation. However, these may vary as a result of quantity discounts, more efficient utilization of the work force, or other economies resulting from increased levels of production and sales. Finally, the basic break-even model does not consider demand. It is a cost-based model and does not directly address the crucial question of whether consumers will actually purchase the product at the specified price and in the required quantities to break even or to generate profits. The challenge of the marketer is to modify break-even analysis and the other cost-oriented approaches to pricing in order to introduce demand analysis. Pricing must be examined from the buyer's perspective. Such decisions cannot be made in a management vacuum in which only cost factors are considered.

## The Dynamic Break-even Concept

**dynamic break-even analysis** Combines the traditional break-even analysis model with an evaluation of consumer demand.

In Figure 12–6, the break-even analysis was based upon the assumption of a constant $10 retail price regardless of quantity. What happens when different retail prices are considered? **Dynamic break-even analysis** *combines the traditional break-even analysis model with an evaluation of consumer demand.*

Figure 12–7 summarizes both the cost and revenue aspects of a number of alternative retail prices. The cost data are based upon the costs utilized earlier in the basic break-even model. The expected unit sales for each specified retail price are obtained from consumer research. The data in the first two columns of Figure 12–7 represent a demand schedule by indicating the number of units consumers are expected to purchase at each of a series of retail prices. This data can be superimposed onto a break-even chart in order to identify the range of feasible prices for consideration by the marketing decision-maker. This is shown in Figure 12–8.

**FIGURE 12–7**

**Revenue and Cost Data for Dynamic Break-even Analysis**

| | Revenues | | Costs | | | |
|---|---|---|---|---|---|---|
| Price | Quantity Demanded | Total Revenue | Total Fixed Cost | Total Variable Cost | Total Cost | Total Profit (or loss) |
| $14 | 3 000 | $ 42 000 | $40 000 | $ 15 000 | $ 55 000 | ($13 000) |
| 12 | 6 000 | 72 000 | 40 000 | 30 000 | 70 000 | 2 000 |
| 10 | 10 000 | 100 000 | 40 000 | 50 000 | 90 000 | 10 000 |
| 8 | 14 000 | 112 000 | 40 000 | 70 000 | 110 000 | 2 000 |
| 6 | 26 000 | 156 000 | 40 000 | 130 000 | 170 000 | (14 000) |

FIGURE 12 – 8

## Dynamic Break-even Chart Reflecting Costs and Consumer Demand

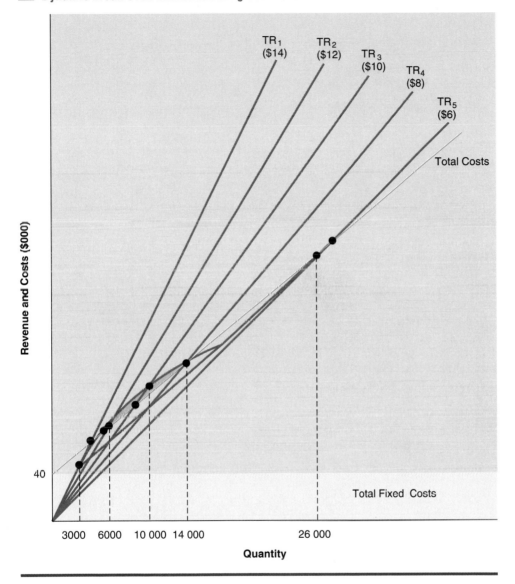

As Figure 12–8 indicates, the range of profitable prices exists from a low of approximately $8 (TR$_4$) to a high of $12 (TR$_2$), with a price of $10 (TR$_3$) generating the greatest projected profits. Changing the retail price produces a new break-even point. At a relatively high $14 retail price, the break-even point is 4445 units; at a $10 retail price the break-even point is 8000 units; and at a $6 price, 40 000 units must be sold in order to break even.

The contribution of dynamic break-even analysis is that it forces the pricing decision-maker to consider whether the consumer is likely to purchase the required number of units of a product or service that will achieve break-even at a given price. It demonstrates that a larger number of units sold does not necessarily produce added profits, since — other things being equal — lower prices are necessary to stimulate added sales. Consequently, it necessitates careful consideration of both costs and consumer demand in determining the most appropriate price.

## Working with Prices: Markups, Markdowns, and Turnover

In working with prices, marketers often must consider three basic concepts: markups, markdowns, and turnover. An ability to handle these is essential for many day-to-day marketing decisions.

### Markups

**markup**    The amount a producer or channel member adds to cost in order to determine the selling price.

A **markup** is *the amount a producer or channel member adds to cost in order to determine the selling price*. It is typically stated as either a percentage of the selling price or of cost. The formulas used in calculating markup percentages are as follows:

$$\text{Markup Percentage on Selling Price} = \frac{\text{Amount Added to Cost (the Markup)}}{\text{Price}}$$

$$\text{Markup Percentage on Cost} = \frac{\text{Amount Added to Cost (the Markup)}}{\text{Cost}}$$

Consider an example from retailing. Suppose an item selling for $1.00 has an invoice cost of $0.60. The total markup is $0.40. The markup percentages would be calculated as follows:

$$\text{Markup Percentage on Selling Price} = \frac{\$0.40}{\$1.00} = 40\%$$

$$\text{Markup Percentage on Cost} = \frac{\$0.40}{\$0.60} = 67\%$$

To determine selling price when only cost and markup percentage on selling price are known, the following formula is utilized:

$$\text{Price} = \frac{\text{Cost in Dollars}}{100\% - \text{Markup Percentage on Selling Price}}$$

In the example cited above, price could be determined as $1.00:

$$\text{Price} = \frac{\$0.60}{100\% - 40\%} = \frac{0.60}{60\%} = \$1.00.$$

Similarly, the markup percentage can be converted from one basis (selling price or cost) to the other by using the following formula:

$$\text{Markup Percentage on Selling Price} = \frac{\text{Markup Percentage on Cost}}{100\% + \text{Markup Percentage on Cost}}$$

$$\text{Markup Percentage on Cost} = \frac{\text{Markup Percentage on Selling Price}}{100\% - \text{Markup Percentage on Selling Price}}$$

Again, using the data from the example above, the following conversions can be made:

$$\text{Markup Percentage on Selling Price} = \frac{67\%}{100\% + 67\%} = \frac{67\%}{167\%} = 40\%$$

$$\text{Markup Percentage on Cost} = \frac{40\%}{100\% - 40\%} = \frac{40\%}{60\%} = 67\%$$

## Markdowns

A related pricing issue that is particularly important to retailers is markdowns. Markups are based partially on executive judgments about the prices consumers are likely to pay for a given product or service. If buyers refuse to pay the price, however, the marketer must take a **markdown**, a reduction in the price of the item. For purposes of internal control and analysis, the markdown percentage is computed as follows:

**markdown**   A reduction in the price of an item.

$$\text{Markup Percentage} = \frac{\text{Markdown}}{\text{``Sale'' (New) Price}}$$

Suppose no one was willing to pay $1.00 for an item and the marketer decided to reduce the price to $0.75. The markdown percentage would be:

$$\text{Markdown Percentage} = \frac{\$0.25}{\$0.75} = 33\frac{1}{3}\%$$

From a customer's viewpoint, this is only a 25% reduction, which is known as the "off-retail percentage." This is the percentage that should be quoted in advertisements. Markdowns are also used for evaluative purposes. For instance, department managers or buyers in a large department store could be evaluated partially on the basis of the average markdown percentage on the product lines for which they are responsible.

## Turnover

All too often, traditional markup and markdown percentages lead to competitive inertia within an industry. Standard percentages are too frequently applied to all items in a given category regardless of factors such as demand.

**stock turnover** The number of times the average inventory is sold annually.

A method for avoiding competitive inertia is to use flexible markups that vary with **stock turnover** — *the number of times the average inventory is sold annually*. The figure can be calculated by one of the following formulas. When inventory is recorded at retail:

$$\text{Stock Turnover} = \frac{\text{Sales}}{\text{Average Inventory}}$$

When inventory is recorded at cost:

$$\text{Stock Turnover} = \frac{\text{Cost of Goods Sold}}{\text{Average Inventory}}$$

Store A, with \$100 000 in sales and an average inventory of \$20 000 (at retail), would have a stock turnover of 5. Store B, with \$200 000 in sales, a 40 percent markup rate, and an average inventory of \$30 000 (at cost), would have a stock turnover of 4.

**Store A**

$$\text{Stock Turnover} = \frac{\$100\ 000}{\$20\ 000} = 5$$

**Store B**

| | |
|---|---|
| \$200 000 | Sales |
| −80 000 | Markup (40 percent) |
| \$120 000 | Cost of Goods Sold |

$$\text{Stock Turnover} = \frac{\$120\ 000}{\$30\ 000} = 4$$

While most marketers recognize the importance of turnover, they often use it more as a measure of sales effectiveness than as a pricing tool. However, it can be particularly useful in setting markup percentages if some consideration is given to consumer demand.

Figure 12–9 indicates the relationship between stock turnover and markup. Above-average turnover, such as for grocery products, is generally associated with relatively low markup percentages. On the other hand, higher markup percentages typically exist in such product lines as jewellery and furniture where relatively lower annual stock turnover is common and inventory and overhead costs must be covered through higher margins.

This chapter has described the basic considerations for determining a price. The next chapter continues the discussion and delves into issues concerning the managing of pricing.

FIGURE 12–9

**Relationship between Markup Percentage and Stock Turnover**

| *Stock Turnover Rate in Relation to the Industry Average* | *Markup Percentage in Relation to the Industry Average* | *Product Example* |
|---|---|---|
| High | Low | Soft Drinks |
| Average | Average | Motor Oil |
| Low | High | Sports Cars |

# Summary

Price — the exchange value of a good or service — is important because it regulates economic activity as well as determining the revenue to be received by an individual firm. As a marketing mix element, pricing is one of those grey areas where marketers struggle to develop a theory, technique, or rule of thumb on which they can depend. It is a complex variable because it contains both objective and subjective aspects. It is an area where precise decision-making tools and executive judgment meet.

Pricing objectives should be the natural consequence of overall organizational goals and more specific marketing goals. They can be classified into four major groupings: (1) profitability objectives, including profit maximization and target return; (2) volume objectives, including sales maximization and market share; (3) competition-meeting objectives; and (4) prestige objectives.

There are three approaches to pricing: economic price theory, the cost-oriented approach, and the marketing approach. Economic price theory is difficult to implement in actually setting prices; however, it provides a number of important basic concepts. Some of these are demand, price elasticity, and marginal revenue and cost.

The cost-oriented method of pricing recognizes that costs must be known before a price can be set. However, sometimes getting at the real cost may be difficult. A cost-oriented approach to pricing also takes little notice of demand or a host of other issues consumers consider important.

The marketing approach to pricing builds on the economic and cost-oriented methods, but it adds a number of important dimensions pertaining to the way consumers perceive and respond to prices. Two useful tools for setting prices are break-even analysis and the pricing decision flow chart.

## KEY TERMS

| | | |
|---|---|---|
| price | monopolistic competition | elasticity |
| profit maximization | oligopoly | cost-plus pricing |
| target return objectives | oligopsony | break-even analysis |
| sales maximization | monopoly | dynamic break-even analysis |
| market share | revenue curves | marketing-oriented pricing |
| status quo objectives | average cost | markup |
| prestige objectives | average variable cost | markdown |
| customary prices | marginal cost | stock turnover |
| pure competition | supply curve | |

## REVIEW QUESTIONS

1. Identify the four major categories of pricing objectives.
2. Categorize each of the following into a specific type of pricing objective:
   a. 8 percent increase in market share
   b. 5 percent increase in profits over previous year
   c. prices no more than 5 percent higher than prices quoted by independent dealers
   d. 20 percent return on investment (before taxes)
   e. highest prices in product category to maintain favourable brand image

**f.** following price of most important competitor in each market segment
3. Outline the basis of the marketing approach to pricing.
4. What market situations exist for the pricing of the following products:
    **a.** telephone service
    **b.** Candu nuclear reactors
    **c.** golf clubs
    **d.** steel
    **e.** potatoes
    **f.** dishwashers
    **g.** tape recorders
    **h.** skis
5. Explain the concept of elasticity. What are the determinants of the degree of price elasticity for a good or service?

6. What are the practical problems involved in attempting to apply price theory concepts to actual pricing decisions?
7. Explain the advantages of using incremental-cost pricing rather than full-cost pricing. What potential drawbacks exist?
8. Explain the relationship between markups and stock turnover rates.
9. Explain the primary benefits of using break-even analysis in price determination. What are the shortcomings of the basic break-even model?
10. In what ways is dynamic break-even analysis superior to the basic model?

## DISCUSSION QUESTIONS

1. "To use a cost-oriented approach to pricing is always a mistake." Please discuss.
2. The role of price in the marketing mix varies. Please explain.
3. Give an example of how considering price elasticity of demand can improve a pricing decision.
4. Select a relatively new product (or hypothetical new one) and develop a price for it, using the pricing-decision flow chart.
5. Select a product such as cameras. Visit five different types of stores to determine the prices charged for the same product. Write a brief report on your findings, and explain the price differences, if any.

## PRICING EXERCISES

1. A retailer has just received a new kitchen appliance invoiced at $28. The retailer decides to follow industry practice for such items and adds a 40 percent markup percentage on selling price. What retail price should the retailer assign to the appliance?
2. If a product has a markup percentage on selling price of 28 percent, what is its markup percentage on cost?
3. An economic downturn in the local area has seriously affected sales of a retailer's line of $150 dresses. The store manager decides to mark these dresses down to $125. What markdown percentage should be featured in advertising this sale item?
4. A store with an average inventory of $50 000 (at cost) operates on a 40 percent markup percentage on selling price. Annual sales total $750 000. What is the stock turnover rate?
5. What is the break-even point in dollars and units for a product with a selling price of $25, related fixed costs of $126 000, and per-unit variable costs of $16?

# ■ MICROCOMPUTER EXERCISE
## ■ Markups and Markdowns

**Directions:** Use the Menu Item titled "Markups" on the *Foundations of Marketing* disk to solve Problems 1 through 3. Use the Menu Item titled "Markdowns" to solve Problems 4 through 6.

1. A Chatham, Ontario, music store sells compact discs for $19 each. The retailer purchases the disks for $13 each. What are the music store's markup percentage on selling price and markup percentage on cost?

2. A Thunder Bay children's clothing store always adds a 40-percent markup (based on selling price) for its children's jeans. A shipment of jeans just arrived, carrying an invoice cost of $11 per pair. What should be the retail selling price for the new jeans?

3. A Banff art dealer uses a markup percentage on selling price of 50 percent for its art prints. What would be the markup percentage on cost for the prints?

4. A period of growing unemployment has adversely affected the sales of $350 suits in a local men's clothing store. The manager decides to mark down these suits to $280. What markdown percentage should be featured in advertising for the sale items?

5. An Oshawa retailer paid $120 per dozen for a particular brand of men's ties. The store attempted to sell these ties at $21 each, but sales have been disappointing. In an attempt to stimulate additional sales, the store manager decides to mark down the ties to $15. Determine the store's markdown percentage on the ties.

6. A Squamish, B.C., furniture dealer has reduced the price on a dining-room suite from $1600 to $1200. What markdown percentage should be featured in advertising for the item?

# ■ MICROCOMPUTER EXERCISE
## ■ Break-even Analysis

Break-even analysis is a useful tool in pricing strategy. It can be used to determine the sales volume (either in dollars or units) that must be achieved at a specified price to generate sufficient revenues to cover total production and marketing costs. Target-profit returns, either in absolute dollar amounts or in percentages of sales, can also be included in the break-even model. Modified break-even analysis is a technique for including assessments of consumer demand into the basic break-even model. By considering estimated sales at several different possible prices, modified break-even analysis aids the marketing decision-maker in determining the required volume needed to break even at various prices. It also shows whether such sales can be achieved.

**Directions:** Use the Menu Item titled "Break-even Analysis" on the *Foundations of Marketing* disk to solve the following problems.

1. Federated Manufacturing of Burnaby, B.C., is considering the possible introduction of a new product. The marketing-research staff estimates that the product

could be marketed at a price of $20. Total fixed costs are $120 000 and the average variable costs are calculated to be $14.

  a.  What is the break-even point in units for the proposed product?

  b.  Federated's controller has suggested a target-profit return of $90 000 for the proposed product. How many units must be sold to break even and achieve this target return?

  c.  The national sales manager at Federated made a counter-proposal of a 10 percent return on sales as a realistic expectation for the proposed new product. How many units must be sold to break even and achieve the return specified by the national sales manager?

  d.  How would your answers to Questions A, B, and C change if the proposed price were increased to $23?

2.  Sunshine Industries of Edmonton, Alta., has developed the following sales estimates for a proposed new gag gift designed to be marketed through direct-mail sales.

| Proposed Selling Price | Sales Estimates, in Units |
| --- | --- |
| $4.00 | 27 500 |
| $5.00 | 11 000 |
| $7.50 | 7 500 |
| $10.00 | 2 500 |
| $12.00 | 1 400 |

The new product has total fixed costs of $30 000, and a $3.50 variable cost per unit.

  a.  Which of the prices listed above would be profitable to Sunshine Industries?

  b.  The marketing-research director also estimates that an additional $0.25-per-unit promotion allocation would produce the following increases in sales estimates: 34 500 units at a $4.00 selling price; 14 000 units at $5.00; 8 500 units at $7.50; 3 000 units at $10.00; and 1 750 units at $12.00. Indicate the feasible range of prices if this proposal is implemented and it results in the predicted sales increases.

  c.  Indicate the feasible price or prices if the $0.25-per-unit additional proposal is not implemented, but management insists upon a $12 500 target return.

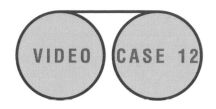

## VIDEO CASE 12  Yamaha Motorcycles

When marketers at Japan's second largest motorcycle maker decided to create the world's fastest, most exciting motorcycle, they were all too aware of the impact their decision would have on the firm's future sales and profits. Their company, Yamaha, had suffered greatly during the 1982 to 1984 downturn in the motorcycle market, losing billions of yen during this period. High tariffs, aimed at protecting Harley-Davidson, the sole U.S. motorcycle maker, from bankruptcy, had worsened Yamaha's competitive position. If the new bike proved to be a mistake, it could cripple the company. Consequently, months of intensive planning went into the new product's development.

A total of 14 different focus groups were used to review preliminary plans for the motorcycle that would be called the V-MAX. Feedback from these groups revealed that consumers who rode the big 1200cc motorcycles wanted a "muscle car" machine, a motorcycle that would rekindle the imagery of the hot rods of the 1950s era. Focus group participants were excited about the V-MAX design; they stated that it looked powerful, a machine that would impress others *if* it could deliver on its promise of power.

The power issue was in the hands of Yamaha engineers, who responded by developing an engine that would produce 135 to 140 horsepower, one of the most powerful on the market. The new bike had the right name, the right look, and it delivered the necessary power. Now it was time to move on to another major — but difficult — decision: the price tag to attach to the V-MAX.

In early planning meetings, John Porter, Yamaha's assistant product manager for the V-MAX, emphasized his belief that consumers in this market segment "want the fastest and are prepared to pay for it — they volunteered prices of $4000, $5000, $5500. If it can deliver the performance, and it is executed in quality, $5500 is not going to be unreasonable."

"Usually the customer has a pretty specific idea of what he wants in terms of price to pay, and usually that price is about 25 percent lower than the actual cost," said Dennis Stefani, Yamaha USA's manager of product planning. "Usually [we have] to look for ways to get the cost down and give him the kind of features he's looking for, or ways to make that motorcycle as exciting as possible, so that he's more willing to pay the extra money for that motorcycle."

Yamaha marketers had to consider a number of elements in deciding how to price the new product. In addition to consumer expectations concerning the price for this type of motorcycle, they had to consider the prices of competing brands offered by such companies as Honda, Kawasaki, Suzuki, BMW, and Harley-Davidson, as well as the retail prices of other products in their own motorcycle line. Production costs, as well as the costs of transporting the V-MAX from Japan to North America, set a floor for price considerations. Another factor involved margins for dealers who handled the line. Marketing expenses, including distribution and promotion, represented additional costs to consider. Another factor involved pricing objectives and whether relatively high prices should be used as a component of the product's overall image and to achieve prestige objectives. Finally, all of these factors had to be calculated in terms of the yen–dollar exchange rate and the impact of the tariff.

After considering all the factors, Yamaha marketers decided to price the V-MAX at $5299, which placed it near, but not at, the top of the market. By 1987, the retail price increased to $5899, and in 1988 it reached $6400.

Promotional activities were designed to emphasize the unique appearance of the V-MAX, whose "muscle-car" look made it as different from other motorcycles as Ferraris are from other cars. At the same time, the advertising had to portray the bike's ability to deliver on its performance promise.

The advertising campaign featured ads set in a 1950s-era carhop, complete with the muscle cars after which it is styled. In the advertisements, though, all eyes are on the V-MAX. The ads and the bike itself succeeded in bringing an increased number of shoppers to Yamaha retail dealerships. Marketing research revealed that they liked the V-MAX's combination of unique styling and high performance, and the image the ad conveyed of V-MAX owners. Interviews with actual purchasers showed that all the agonizing over price had paid off: Most purchasers thought the bike was reasonably priced.

Although first-year sales of the V-MAX exceeded expectations, Harley-Davidson has proven to be a formidable competitor in the 700cc or larger engine market. Yamaha assistant product manager John Porter summarizes the recent sales results: "While sales initially were quite good, somewhere on the order of 5000 bikes, we overproduced in the second year." In 1988, the decision was made to offer the V-MAX in a limited edition of only 1500 bikes at higher prices. The combination of restricted supply and higher prices was intended to further enhance the V-MAX image.

At its September 1990 sales meeting, Yamaha announced an innovative option for the V-MAX: full insurance coverage for the first year of ownership, included in the price of $7999. Without the insurance, the bike is available for $7414. Thus, the option is highly desirable both because of the tremendous saving over outside insurance coverage (which can range up to $2500) and because it is amortized over the life of the vehicle loan. Although it is not available in all states, the option has proven popular where it is available and underscores Yamaha's innovative spirit.

SOURCE    John A. Conway, "Harley Back in Gear," *Forbes* (April 20, 1987), p. 8; Norman Mayersohn, "Brute Bikes," *Popular Mechanics* (December 1985), pp. 106–112; "Yamaha Plays a Different Tune," *The Economist* (November 9, 1985), pp. 96–97; and Beth Bogart, "Harley-Davidson Trades Restrictions for Profits," *Advertising Age* (August 10, 1987), p. S-27; Dave Ahlers of Yamaha Motor Company, [update interview] May 1991.

## Questions

1. Relate the discussion of Yamaha's pricing decision for the V-MAX to the chapter discussion of price determination.

2. What pricing objectives are involved in the Yamaha pricing decision?

3. What is the relationship between costs and the final price set for the V-MAX? Do you feel that demand for the motorcycle is price elastic? Defend your answer.

4. Yamaha marketers are attempting to increase the motorcycling marketplace by attracting families to motorcycling. Is the V-MAX likely to assist them in these efforts? Why or why not?

5. Some people argue that Yamaha marketers could have expanded the sales potential of the V-MAX significantly had they selected a lower retail price. Do you agree? Explain your answer.

# Managing the Pricing Function

1. To identify the various pricing policy decisions that must be made by the marketer.
2. To explore the implications of skimming and penetration strategies.
3. To describe how prices are quoted.
4. To contrast negotiated prices and competitive bidding.
5. To explain the importance of transfer pricing.
6. To describe pricing in the public sector.

THERE is a sense of anticipation in opening mail. Often one is disappointed with the contents. However, correspondence providing an unexpected financial windfall is always destined to pique attention. Thousands of Canadians who believed themselves to be recipients of personalized cheques for $1500 from Ford Canada would doubtless agree. Closer reading of the letter, however, revealed that there were strings attached: the cheque, in fact, was a discount certificate to be used toward the purchase of one of Ford's $35 000-plus luxury models.

Ford is not alone in its imaginative use of price to pitch the consumer. Cash-back rebates, interest-rate breaks, free options such as air conditioning and even Florida vacations have become a fact of life in marketing cars. An important trend in the incentive wars is cut-cost financing. The higher the interest rate goes, the more appealing such offers are. For example, when interest rates were hovering around 13.5 percent, General Motors developed a campaign offering "One Sweet Deal" in the form of 9.9 percent financing of all new GM cars and compact pickups.

Ironically, incentives have allowed auto makers to prosper from prices that were destined to fall anyway. Efficiency gains introduced to the industry during the last several years have lowered production costs. But instead of slashing prices directly, auto makers chose to deluge buyers with promises of special deals.

With increased rebate competition the interest provoked by rebates diminishes over time. Thus, the effectiveness of this pricing tool has declined. Even so, auto makers must continue to use rebates to preserve their all-important market shares. Says the president of the Motor Vehicle Manufacturers Association: "If you lose market share you may never get it back."[1]

Promotional pricing moves thus often have short-term benefits as well as sometimes less desirable long-term outcomes. The management of the pricing variable is challenging, because there are so many possible aspects to consider.

---

# Introduction

The previous chapter introduced the concept of price and outlined the three main approaches to determining a price. Beyond this, however, there are many other pricing issues that the manager must understand. These include the setting of pricing policies, strategic decisions as to the level at which price should be set, and numerous day-to-day issues in pricing management. These will be the subject of this chapter.

# Pricing Policies

**pricing policy**    A general guideline based on pricing objectives that is intended for use in specific pricing decisions.

**price structure**    An outline of the selling price and the various discounts offered to middlemen.

Pricing policies are important for the proper management of pricing. They provide the overall framework and consistency needed in pricing decisions. A **pricing policy** is *a general guideline based on pricing objectives that is intended for use in specific pricing decisions*. Price policies affect the **price structure**, which is *an outline of the selling price and the various discounts offered to middlemen*. Price structure decisions take the selected price policy as a given, and specify the discount structure details. Price policies have great strategic importance, particularly in relation to competitive considerations. They are the bases on which pricing decisions are made. Future Shop, for example, has a policy that says that it will never be undersold, and that if a customer buys from it and then finds a lower price, a portion of the price difference will be refunded.

Many businesses would be well advised to spend more managerial effort in the establishment and periodic review of their pricing policies. Some years ago, a top executive aptly referred to the study and determination of prices as "creative pricing":

> Few businessmen, I am sure, would deny that every well-run business should have a price policy. We give a great deal of thought and planning to our engineering, manufacturing, advertising, and sales promotion policies. Certainly the same kind of careful study and planning should be directed toward the formulation of those price policies that will best serve the various long-run objectives of our businesses. I call pricing based on such a well-formulated policy "creative pricing." There are probably better ways of saying it, but this term comes pretty close to describing what I believe to be the true function of pricing.[2]

Pricing policies provide a focus in dealing with varied competitive situations. The type of policy is dependent upon the environment within which the pricing decision must be made. The types of policies to be considered are skimming versus penetration pricing, price flexibility, relative price levels, price lining, and promotional prices. They should all be arrived at through the use of a pricing procedure similar to those described in Chapter 12.

## Skimming versus Penetration Pricing Policies

In the pricing of new products the initial price that is quoted for an item may determine whether or not the product will eventually be accepted in the marketplace. The initial price also may affect the amount of competition that will emerge. Consider the options available to a company pricing a new product. They may price at the level of comparable products, very high, or very low. Figure 13–1 illustrates that the market is made up of different layers of potential customers with varying degrees of willingness and ability to pay depending on whether prices are higher or lower.

A **skimming pricing** policy chooses *a high entry price.* The name is derived from the expression "skimming the cream." The plan is to sell first to consumers who are willing to pay the highest price, then reduce the price (perhaps introduce a less fancy model) and then market to the next level, and so on. One purpose of this strategy is to allow the firm to recover its development costs quickly. The assumption is that competition will eventually drive the price to a lower level, as was the case, for example, with compact discs.

A skimming policy, therefore, attempts to maximize the revenue received from the sale of a new product before the entry of competition. Ballpoint pens were introduced shortly after World War II at a price of about $20. Today the best-selling ballpoint pens are priced at less than $1. Other examples of products that have been

**skimming pricing**   To sell first to consumers who are willing to pay the highest price, then reduce the price.

## FIGURE 13 – 1

### The Market for Product X

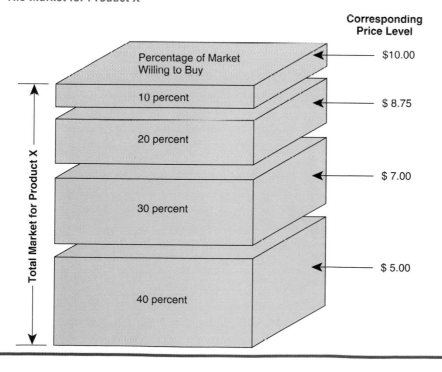

Corresponding Price Level

Percentage of Market Willing to Buy — $10.00

10 percent — $ 8.75

20 percent

30 percent — $ 7.00

— $ 5.00

40 percent

Total Market for Product X

*The mass production of home computers and other high-technology equipment has affected the pricing of these items. When home computers were first introduced, a skimming policy was possible due to the lack of competition in the field. However, with the increased penetration of this market by a number of firms, the market was flooded with home computer options; price reductions resulted.*

introduced using a skimming policy include television sets, Polaroid cameras, videocassette recorders, home computers, and pocket calculators. Subsequent price reductions allowed the marketers of these products to appeal to additional market segments that are more price sensitive.

A skimming strategy permits the marketer to control demand in the introductory stages of the product's life cycle and to adjust its productive capacity to match demand. A danger of low initial price for a new product is that demand may outstrip the firm's production capacity, resulting in consumer and intermediary complaints and possibly permanent damage to the product's image. Excess demand occasionally results in poor-quality products as the firm strives to satisfy consumer desires with inadequate production facilities.

During the late growth and early maturity stages of the product life cycle the price is reduced for two reasons: (1) the pressure of competition and (2) the desire to expand the product's market. Figure 13–1 shows that 10 percent of the market for Product X would buy the item at $10, while another 20 percent would buy at $8.75. Successive price declines will expand the firm's market as well as meet new competition.

A skimming policy has one chief disadvantage: it attracts competition. Potential competitors, who see the innovating firms make large returns, also enter the market. This forces the price even lower than it might be under a sequential skimming procedure. However if a firm has patent protection — as Polaroid had — or a proprietary ability to exclude competition, it may use a skimming policy for a relatively long period. Figure 13–2 indicates that 14.4 percent of the respondents in one pricing study used a skimming policy. Skimming also appears to be more common in industrial markets than in consumer markets.

**Penetration pricing** is the opposite policy in new-product pricing. It results in *an entry price for a product lower than what is believed to be the long-term price.* The pricing study shown in Figure 13–2 suggests that penetration pricing is used more often in consumer markets. Soaps and toothpastes are often good examples of this kind of

**penetration pricing**    An entry price for a product lower than what is believed to be the long-term price.

FIGURE 13 – 2

**Use of New-Product Pricing Strategies**

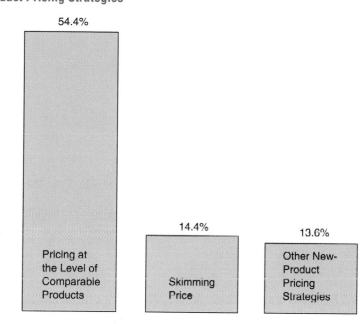

Source: *Pricing Objectives and Practices in American Industry: A Research Report* © 1979 by Louis E. Boone and David L. Kurtz; all rights reserved.

A·P·P·L·Y·I·N·G  T·H·E  C·O·N·C·E·P·T·S

## Cut-rate Dealer Claims Firms out to 'Zap' Him

A cut-rate automobile parts retailer that sells to consumers for half of what they pay elsewhere is asking Ottawa to investigate its complaints that the large parts distributors are trying to put it out of business.

Roger Duchesne, chairperson of Club Zap, said that major parts distributors are bringing pressure on manufacturers not to sell to Club Zap. Since distribution of parts is dominated by a few companies, in some cases they have succeeded in getting the manufacturer to boycott Club Zap, Duchesne complained at a news conference.

Within ten months after it was established, Club Zap had attracted 6500 consumers who buy memberships for $20 a year, and they had purchased $1.3 million worth of parts. Club Zap has a suburban Montreal warehouse with about $750 000 worth of parts and a service centre to install items such as brakes and mufflers.

Traditionally, prices are affected by the channel markup structure. Manufacturers sell to warehouse distributors, who sell to "jobbers" (wholesalers), who sell to garages or stores to sell to consumers. A manufacturer's price of $12 for an item, for example, reaches an average of $100 for the customer, Duchesne said. "It's a racket," Duchesne added. "A starter costing an average $168 at a dealer or parts store can be picked up at Club Zap for $83."

Dennis DesRosiers, an automobile-industry analyst from Toronto, says, "Manufacturers are reticent to deal with these clubs, and rightfully so, because the manufacturer undermines his traditional network."

Source: Adapted from Allan Swift, "Cut-Rate Dealer Claims Firms out to 'Zap' Him," *Calgary Herald* (September 6, 1989).

*Flexible pricing is still alive and well in Canada's open-air and farmers' markets. Individual bargaining is prevalent here due to the relatively simple nature of the market transactions. But even in the more complex wholesale and industrial sectors, price flexibility is an option that can open interesting sales and marketing opportunities.*

pricing. For instance, a new-formula shampoo and conditioner could be introduced with a cents-off label, to induce consumers to try it out.

The premise is that an initially lower price will help secure market acceptance. Since the firm later intends to increase the price, brand popularity is crucial to the success of a penetration policy. One advantage of such a policy is that it discourages competition from entering, since the prevailing low price does not suggest the attractive returns associated with a skimming policy.

Penetration pricing is likely to be used in instances where demand for the new product or service is highly elastic and large numbers of consumers are highly price sensitive. It is also likely to be used in instances where large-scale operations and long production runs result in substantial reductions in production and marketing costs. Finally, penetration pricing may be appropriate in instances where the new product is likely to attract strong competitors when it is introduced. Such a strategy may allow it to reach the mass market quickly and capture a large share of the market before the entry by competitors. With penetration pricing, the marketers will likely forgo some profits, at least in the short run.

The key decision, of course, is when to move the price to its intended level. Consumers tend to resist price increases; therefore, correct timing is essential. The solution depends upon the degree of brand loyalty that has been achieved. Brand loyalty must be at the point where a price increase would not cause a disproportionate decrease in customers. A series of modest price changes, rather than a single large hike, also can retain customers. Often, firms will use cents-off deals to enter at a lower price. These can then be phased out more easily.

A firm may, of course, decide to use neither a skimming nor a penetration price. It may try to price a new product at the point where it is intended to sell in the long run. All three new-product pricing strategies are common, but it can be seen from Figure 13–2 that this last strategy was chosen in 54 percent of new-product pricing situations.

**Most Canadian Retailers Follow a One-Price Policy**

Source: Reprinted by permission of Newspaper Enterprise Association.

## Price Flexibility

Marketing executives must also determine company policy with respect to **flexible pricing**. Is the firm going to have just one price or pursue *a variable price policy* in the market? As a generalization, *one-price policies* characterize situations where mass selling is employed, and *variable pricing* is more common where individual bargaining typifies market transactions, for example, the purchase of a car.

A one-price policy is common in Canadian retailing since it facilitates mass merchandising. For the most part, once the price is set, the manager can direct his or her attention to other aspects of the marketing mix. Flexible prices, by contrast, are found more in wholesaling and industrial markets. This does not mean that price flexibility exists only in manufacturing industries. A study of the retail home appliance market concluded that persons who had purchased identical products from the same dealer had often paid different prices for them. The primary reasons for the differences were customer knowledge and bargaining strength.[3]

While variable pricing has the advantage of flexibility in selling situations, it may result in conflict with the Combines Act provisions. It may also lead to retaliatory pricing on the part of competitors, and it is not well received by those who have paid the higher prices.

## Relative Price Levels

Another important pricing policy decision concerns the relative price level. Are the firm's prices to be set above, below, or at the prevailing market price? In economic theory this question would be answered by supply and demand analysis. However, from a practical viewpoint, marketing managers *administer* prices. In other words, they subjectively set the markup percentages to achieve the price level desired.[4] The decision-maker must still develop a basic policy in regard to relative price levels. A fine clothing store, such as Harry Rosen, would probably have a policy of pricing at a level higher than most other clothing retailers.

**flexible pricing**   A variable price policy

**Some Marketers Set Their Prices above the Prevailing Market Price**

"All I need is one good customer."

*Following the competition* is one method of negating the price variable in marketing strategy, since it forces competition to concentrate on other factors. Some firms choose to price below or above competition. These decisions are usually based on a firm's cost structure, overall marketing strategy, and pricing objectives.

# Pricing Practices

## Price Lining

Most companies sell a varied line of products. An effective pricing strategy should consider the relationship among the firm's products rather than view each in isolation. Specifically, **price lining** is *the practice of marketing merchandise at a limited number of prices*. For example, a clothier might have a $195 line of men's suits and a $325 line. Price lining is used extensively in retail selling. It can be an advantage to

**price lining**    The practice of marketing merchandise at a limited number of prices.

*The Chevrolet Cavalier Wagon and Corvette ZR-1 serve the medium- and high-priced markets, respectively. The Cavalier Wagon appeals to families looking for a medium-priced, reliable vehicle, while the Corvette is marketed for those with a greater disposable income who are looking for a prestige car. Chevrolet appeals to both these markets by offering a line of products in both these price ranges.*

both retailer and customer. Customers can choose the price range they wish to pay, then concentrate on all the other variables, such as colour, style, and material. The retailer can purchase and offer specific lines rather than a more generalized assortment.

Price lining requires that one identify the market segment or segments to which the firm is appealing. For example, a suitcase manufacturer may see its market not as all luggage, but as the "medium-priced, hard-side" portion of the luggage trade. The firm must decide how to *line* its product prices. A dress manufacturer might have lines priced at $89.95, $159.95, and $199.95. Price lining not only simplifies the administration of the pricing structure, but also alleviates the confusion of a situation where all products are priced separately. Price lining is really a combined product/price strategy.

One problem with a price-line decision is that once it is made, retailers and manufacturers have difficulty in adjusting it. Rising costs, therefore, put the seller in the position of either changing the price lines, with the resulting confusion, or reducing costs by production adjustments, which opens the firm to the complaint that "XYZ Company's merchandise certainly isn't what it used to be!"

## Promotional Prices

A **promotional price** is *a lower-than-normal price used as an ingredient in a firm's selling strategy.* In some cases promotional prices are recurrent, such as the annual shoe store sale: "Buy one pair of shoes, get the second for one cent." Or a new pizza restaurant may have an opening special to attract customers. In other situations a firm may introduce a promotional model or brand to allow it to compete in another market.

Most promotional pricing is done at the retail level.[5] One type is **loss leaders**, *goods priced below cost to attract customers* who, the retailer hopes, will then buy other regularly priced merchandise. The use of loss leaders can be effective.

> Probably one of the best innovators of this pricing method was Cal Mayne. He was one of the first men to systematically price specials and to evaluate their effect on gross margins and sales. Mayne increased sales substantially by featuring coffee, butter, and margarine at 10 percent below cost. Ten other demand items were priced competitively and at a loss when necessary to undersell competition. Still another group of so-called secondary demand items were priced in line with competition. Mayne based his pricing policy on the theory that a customer can only remember about 30 prices. Keep prices down on these items and the customer will stay with you.[6]

**promotional price**    A lower-than-normal price used as an ingredient in a firm's selling strategy.

**loss leader**    Goods priced below cost to attract customers.

## A·P·P·L·Y·I·N·G  T·H·E  C·O·N·C·E·P·T·S

### *Have Retail Price Promotions Gone Too Far?*

There was a time when a discounted price was rare. It probably meant that there was something wrong with the product. Today discounting is the rule.

What have we been teaching our customers? They now refuse to buy unless we give them a deal. They do not trust us to give them value; it always has to be negotiated. This is especially true with the purchase of automobiles.

Lord Sieff, a former president of Marks and Spencer, writes in his memoirs of the company's experience when it first came to Canada: "If in the U.K. we found it possible to reduce the price of an article we would state on the promotion ticket that the price was being reduced but that this reduction in price did not mean there was any change in the quality.

"We found that in Canada this kind of statement had no effect on the customer and sales remained as before, but if we put a large ticket with 'regular price $25' slashed through with a bold stroke and underneath 'new reduced price $19.95,' sales would soar."

Twenty years of giving into the quick fix of reduced price has lured customers into promotion dependency. Even worse, we have convinced ourselves that we cannot sell a product at the regular price. This has done North American business incredible harm because it changes our marketing focus. Instead of looking for extra quality and charging a fair price, we are content with average quality and a negotiable price. Nearly all retailers — from the local grocery store to nationwide department chains — run continuous weekly promotions. Half a century of this unrelenting barrage has taught us not to buy at the regular price but to hang on for the deal. It's time to change.

Do you agree with this?

Source: Adapted from John Oldland, "Let's Make a Deal and Other Hoopla," *Marketing* (February 6, 1989), p. 33.

---

The ethical or moral implications of this practice are not being considered here. Some studies have indeed reported considerable price confusion on the part of consumers. One study of consumer price recall reported that average shoppers misquoted the price they last paid for coffee by over 12 percent, toothpaste by over 20 percent, and green beans by 24 percent. While some people hit the prices exactly, others missed by several hundred percent.[7] The use of loss leaders is common in several branches of retailing today.

Three potential pitfalls should be considered when one faces a promotional pricing decision:

1. The Competition Act may prohibit some types of promotional pricing practices. (See Chapter 2.)

2. Some consumers are little influenced by price appeals, so promotional pricing will have little effect on them.[8]

3. Continuous use of an artificially low rate may result in its being accepted as customary for the product. Bic pens were introduced as a low-price product (with corresponding manufacturing costs). It would be extremely difficult to raise their prices significantly now.

### Psychological Pricing

**psychological pricing** Pricing based on the belief that certain prices or price ranges are more appealing to buyers than others.

**Psychological pricing** is based on *the belief that certain prices or price ranges are more appealing to buyers than others*. There is, however, no consistent research foundation for such thinking. Studies often report mixed findings.[9] Prestige pricing, mentioned in Chapter 12, is one of many forms of psychological pricing.

### The High-Class Nickel Discount

When the proprietor of a restaurant runs a newspaper ad for a meal costing less than $7, the price usually ends in 9 — $5.99, for example — to imply a discount. A price in the $7 to $10 range usually ends in 5.

We owe the discovery of these facts of restaurant life to Lee Kreul, a professor at Purdue's School of Consumer and Family Sciences, who analyzed 467 prices from 242 restaurants advertised in 24 newspapers around the country. Restaurateurs switch from 9 to 5 as prices go up, he thinks, because at higher price levels "it takes more than 1 cent to create the discount illusion" and because patrons interested in paying more than $7 for a meal might think a price ending in 9 suggests "discounts, low quality, or hurried service."

Source: Jack C. Horn, "The High-Class Nickel Discount," *Psychology Today* (September 1982); reprinted by permission.

**Odd pricing** is a good example of the application of psychological pricing. *Prices are set ending in numbers not commonly used for price quotations.* A price of $16.99 is assumed to be more appealing than $17 (supposedly because it is a lower figure).

Originally odd pricing was used to force clerks to make change, thus serving as a cash control device within the firm.[10] Now it has become a customary feature of contemporary price quotations. For instance, one discounter uses prices ending in 3 and 7 rather than 5, 8, or 9, because of a belief that customers regard price tags of $5.95, $6.98, $7.99 as *regular* retail prices, while $5.97 and $6.93 are considered *discount* prices.

**odd pricing** Prices are set ending in numbers not commonly used for price quotations.

## Unit Pricing

Consumer advocates have often pointed out the difficulty of comparing consumer products that are available in different-size packages or containers. Is an 800 g can selling for 75 cents a better buy than two 450 g cans priced at 81 cents or another brand that sells three 450 g cans for 89 cents? The critics argue that there should be a common way to price consumer products.

**Unit pricing** is a response to this problem. Under unit pricing all prices are stated *in terms of some recognized unit of measurement* (such as grams and litres) or a standard numerical count. There has been considerable discussion about legislating mandatory unit pricing. The Consumers' Association of Canada has endorsed unit pricing, and many of the major food chains have adopted it.

**unit pricing** All prices are stated in terms of some recognized unit of measurement (such as grams and litres) or a standard numerical count.

The real question, of course, is whether unit pricing improves consumer decisions.[11] One study found that the availability of unit prices resulted in consumer savings and that retailers also benefited when unit pricing led to greater purchases of store brands. The study concluded that unit pricing was valuable to both buyer and seller and that it merited full-scale use.[12] Unit pricing is a major pricing policy issue that must be faced by many firms.

## The Price-Quality Concept

One of the most researched aspects of pricing is the relationship between price and the consumer's perception of the product's quality.[13] In the absence of other cues,

*Some retailers, such as IKEA Canada, conduct consumer tests of their own products to convince customers of their quality and durability. Furniture purchasers at any major IKEA store can watch stress and endurance tests being conducted with their own eyes, rather than merely reading the final published results. Since IKEA markets its furniture on a low-price, self-serve basis, these tests help to alleviate any consumer concerns about product quality.*

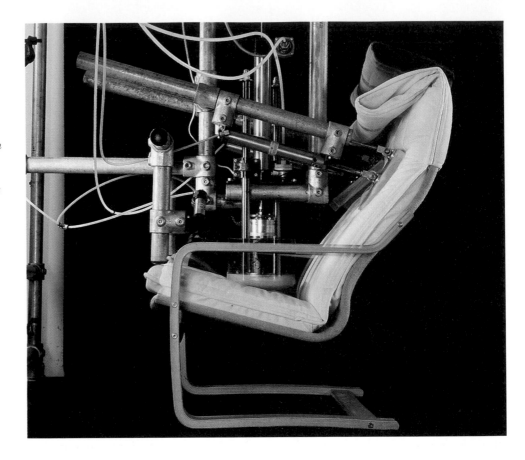

price is an important indication for the consumer in the perception of the product's quality.[14] The higher the price, the better the buyer believes the quality of the product to be. One study asked 400 people what terms they associated with the word *expensive*. Two-thirds of the replies were related to high quality, such as *best* and *superior*.[15] The relationship between price and perceived quality is a well-documented fact in contemporary marketing.

Probably the most useful concept in explaining price-quality relationships is the idea of **price limits**.[16] It is argued that consumers have *limits within which product quality perception varies directly with price*. A price below the lower limit is regarded as too cheap, while one above the higher limit means it is too expensive. Most consumers do tend to set an acceptable price range when purchasing goods and services. The range, of course, varies, depending upon consumers' socio-economic characteristics and buying dispositions. Consumers, nonetheless, should be aware that price is not necessarily an indicator of quality. Alberta Consumer and Corporate Affairs summarized seven price–quality research studies, six covering *Consumer Reports* analyses of 932 products between 1940 and 1977, and one for 43 products tested by *Canadian Consumer* between 1973 and 1977. It found that while there was a positive relationship between price and quality, the correlation was low (Spearman rank correlation = .25). In addition, about 25 percent of products tested had a negative price–quality relation. That is, products ranked lower in performance had higher prices than products deemed superior by the Canadian and U.S. consumer testing organizations.[17]

**price limits**    Limits within which product quality perception varies directly with price.

# Price Quotations

How prices are quoted depends on many factors, such as cost structures, traditional practice in the particular industry, and the policies of individual firms. In this section we shall examine the reasoning and methodology behind price quotations.

The basis upon which most price structures are built is the **list price**, *the rate normally quoted to potential buyers*. List price is usually determined by one or a combination of the methods discussed in Chapter 12. The sticker prices on new automobiles are good examples. They show the list price for the basic model, then add the list price for the options that have been included.

**list price**   The rate normally quoted to potential buyers.

## Discounts, Allowances, and Rebates

*The amount that a consumer pays* — the **market price** — may or may not be the same as the list price. In some cases discounts or allowances reduce the list price. List price is often used as the starting point from which discounts that set the market price are derived. Discounts can be classified as cash, quantity, or trade.

**market price**   The amount that a consumer pays.

**Cash discounts** are those *reductions in price that are given for prompt payment of a bill.* They are probably the most commonly used variety. Cash discounts usually specify an exact time period, such as "2/10, net 30." This would mean that the bill is due within 30 days, but if it is paid in 10 days, the customer may subtract 2 percent from the amount due. Cash discounts have become a traditional pricing practice in many industries. They are legal provided that they are granted all customers on the same terms. Such discounts were originally instituted to improve the liquidity position of sellers by reducing accounts receivable, lower bad-debt losses, and reduce the expenses associated with the collection of bills. Whether these advantages outweigh the relatively high cost of capital involved in cash discounts depends upon the seller's need for liquidity as well as alternative sources (and costs) of funds.

**cash discounts**   Reductions in price that are given for prompt payment of a bill

**Trade discounts**, which are also called *functional discounts,* are *payments to channel members or buyers for performing some marketing function normally required of the manufacturer.* These are legitimate as long as all buyers in the same category, such as wholesalers and retailers, receive the same discount privilege. Trade discounts were initially based on the operating expenses of each trade category, but have now become more of a matter of custom in some industries. An example of a trade discount would be "40 percent, 10 percent off list price" for wholesalers. In other words, the wholesaler passes the 40 percent on to his or her customers (retailers) and keeps the 10 percent discount as payment for activities such as storing and transporting. The price to the wholesaler on a $100 000 order would be $54 000 ($100 000 less 40% = $60 000 less 10%). Note the sequence in which the discount calculations are made.

**trade discounts**   Payments to channel members or buyers for performing some marketing function normally required of the manufacturer.

**Quantity discounts** are *price reductions granted because of large purchases.* These discounts are justified on the grounds that large-volume purchases reduce selling expenses and may shift a part of the storing, transporting, and financing functions to the buyer. Quantity discounts are lawful provided they are offered on the same basis to all customers.

**quantity discounts**   Price reductions granted because of large purchases.

Quantity discounts may be either noncumulative or cumulative. Noncumulative quantity discounts are one-time reductions in list price. For instance, a firm might offer the discount schedule in Figure 13–3. Cumulative quantity discounts are reductions determined by purchases over a stated time period. Annual purchases of

The Toronto Symphony

*The Toronto Symphony Orchestra, like many musical or theatrical groups, offers quantity discounts on its ticket prices. If six concerts are chosen, a 30 percent discount is offered, and if three or four concerts are selected, there is a 20 percent discount. In this way, the TSO hopes to attract a larger audience and provide greater exposure for its performances.*

**FIGURE 13 – 3**

**A Noncumulative Quantity Discount Schedule**

| Units Purchased | Price |
| --- | --- |
| 1 | List price |
| 2–5 | List price less 10 percent |
| 6–10 | List price less 20 percent |
| over 10 | List price less 25 percent |

$25 000 might entitle the buyer to an 8 percent rebate, while purchases exceeding $50 000 would mean a 15 percent refund. These reductions are really patronage discounts since they tend to bind the customer to one source of supply.

Allowances are similar to discounts in that they are deductions from the price the purchaser must pay. The major categories of allowances are trade-ins and promotional allowances. **Trade-ins** are often used in the sale of durable goods such as automobiles. They permit a reduction without altering the basic list price by *deducting from the item's price an amount for the customer's old item that is being replaced.*

**Promotional allowances** are *extra discounts offered to retailers so that they will advertise the manufacturer along with the retailer.* They are attempts to integrate promotional strategy in the channel. For example, manufacturers often provide advertising and

**trade-ins** Deductions from an item's price of an amount for the customer's old item that is being replaced.

**promotional allowances** Extra discounts offered to retailers so that they will advertise the manufacturer along with the retailer.

sales-support allowances for other channel members. Many manufacturers offer such allowances to retail dealers.

**Rebates** are *refunds by the seller of a portion of the purchase price.* They have been used most prominently by automobile manufacturers eager to move models during periods of slow sales. Manufacturers' rebates are sometimes used to stimulate sales of small appliances such as coffee brewers or hair dryers.

## Geographic Considerations

Geographic considerations are important in pricing when the shipment of heavy, bulky, low unit-cost materials is involved. Prices may be quoted with either the buyer or seller paying all transportation charges or with some type of expense sharing.

> The way in which this problem is handled can greatly influence the success of a firm's marketing program by helping to determine the scope of the geographic market area the firm is able to serve, the vulnerability of the firm to price competition in areas located near its production facilities, the net margins earned on individual sales of the product, the ability of the firm to control or influence resale prices of distributors, and how difficult it is for salesmen in the field to quote accurate prices and delivery terms to their potential customers.[18]

The seller has several alternatives in handling transportation costs.

**F.O.B. plant** or *F.O.B. origin* pricing provides a price that does not include any shipping charges. *The buyer must pay all the freight charges.* The seller pays only the cost of loading the merchandise aboard the carrier selected by the buyer. The abbreviation F.O.B. means *Free on Board*. Legal title and responsibility pass to the buyer once the purchase is loaded and a receipt is obtained from the representative of the common carrier.

Prices may also be shown as F.O.B. origin — freight allowed. *The seller permits the buyer to subtract transportation expenses from the bill.* The amount the seller receives varies with the freight charges charged against the invoice. This alternative, called **freight absorption**, is commonly used by firms with high fixed costs (who need to maintain high volume) because it permits a considerable expansion of their market, since a competitive price is quoted regardless of shipping expenses.

*The same price (including transportation expenses) is quoted to all buyers* when a **uniform delivered price** is the firm's policy. Such pricing is the exact opposite of F.O.B. prices. This system is often compared to the pricing of a first-class letter, which is the same across the country. Hence, it is sometimes called *postage-stamp pricing*. The price that is quoted includes an *average* transportation charge per customer, which means that distant customers are actually paying a lesser share of selling costs while customers near the supply source pay what is known as *phantom freight* (the average transportation charge exceeds the actual cost of shipping).

In **zone pricing**, which is simply a modification of a uniform delivered pricing system, *the market is divided into different zones and a price is established within each.* Canadian parcel post rates depend upon zone pricing. The primary advantage of this pricing policy is that it is easy to administer and enables the seller to be more competitive in distant markets. Figure 13–4 shows how a marketer in Winnipeg might divide its market into geographic segments. All customers in zone 1 would be charged $10 per unit freight, while more distant customers would pay freight costs based on the zone in which they are located.

**rebates** Refunds by the seller of a portion of the purchase price.

**F.O.B. plant pricing** The buyer must pay all the freight charges.

**freight absorption** The seller permits the buyer to subtract transportation expenses from the bill.

**uniform delivered price** The same price (including transporting expenses) is quoted to all buyers.

**zone pricing** The market is divided into different zones and a price is established within each.

FIGURE 13–4

**Zone Pricing for a Winnipeg Firm**

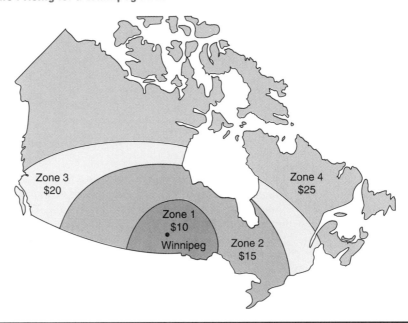

## Negotiated Prices and Competitive Bidding

Many situations involving government and industrial procurement are not characterized by set prices, particularly for nonrecurring purchases such as a defence system for the armed forces. Markets such as these are growing at a fast pace. Governmental units now spend nearly half of Canada's GDP!

**competitive bidding**  Buyers request potential suppliers to make price quotations on a proposed purchase or contract.

**specifications**  A description of the item or job that the buyer wishes to acquire.

**Competitive bidding** is a *process by which buyers request potential suppliers to make price quotations* on a proposed purchase or contract.[19] **Specifications** give a *description of the item (or job)* that the government or industrial firm wishes to acquire. One of the most important tasks in modern purchasing management is to describe adequately what the organization seeks to buy. This generally requires the assistance of the firm's technical personnel, such as engineers, designers, and chemists.

Competitive bidding strategy should employ the concept of *expected net profit*, which can be stated as:

$$\text{Expected Net Profit} = P \ (\text{Bid} - \text{Costs})$$

where P = the probability of the buyer accepting the bid.

Consider the following example. A firm is contemplating the submission of a bid for a job that is estimated to cost $23 000. One executive has proposed a bid of $60 000; another, $50 000. It is estimated that there is a 40 percent chance of the buyer accepting bid 1 ($60 000) and a 60 percent chance that bid 2 ($50 000) will be accepted. The expected net profit formula indicates that bid 2 would be best since its expected net profit is the higher of the two.

Bid 1

$$ENP = 0.40 \ (\$60\ 000 - \$23\ 000)$$
$$= 0.40 \ (\$37\ 000)$$
$$= \$14\ 800$$

Bid 2

$$ENP = 0.60 \ (\$50\ 000 - \$23\ 000)$$
$$= 0.60 \ (\$27\ 000)$$
$$= \$16\ 200$$

The most difficult task in applying this concept is the estimation of the likelihood a certain bid will be accepted. But this is not a valid reason for failing to quantify one's estimate. Prior experience often provides the foundation for such estimates.

In some cases industrial and governmental purchasers use **negotiated contracts** instead of inviting competitive bidding for a project. In these situations, the *terms of the contract are set through talks between the buyer and a seller.* Where there is only one available supplier or where contracts require extensive research and development work, negotiated contracts are likely to be employed.

> **negotiated contract**     The terms of the contract are set through talks between the buyer and a seller.

Some provincial and local governments permit their agencies to negotiate purchases under a certain limit, say, $500 or $1000. This policy is an attempt to reduce cost since obtaining bids for relatively minor purchases is expensive and there is little prospect of large savings to the agency involved.

The fear that inflation may have unknown effects on the economic viability of prices has become a major deterrent to companies bidding for or negotiating contracts. One response has been to include an **escalator clause**[20] that allows the seller *to adjust the final price based on changes in the costs of the product's ingredients between the placement of the order and the completion of construction or delivery of the product.* Such clauses typically base the adjustment calculation on the cost-of-living index or a similar indicator. While an estimated one-third of all industrial marketers use escalator clauses in some of their bids, they are most commonly used with major projects involving long time periods and complex operations.

> **escalator clause**     Allows the seller to adjust the final price based on changes in the costs of the product's ingredients between the placement of the order and the order's completion.

## The Transfer Pricing Problem

One pricing problem peculiar to large-scale enterprises is that of determining an internal **transfer price** — that is, *the price for sending goods from one company profit centre to another.*[21] As a company expands, it usually needs to decentralize management. Profit centres are then set up as a control device in the new decentralized operation. **Profit centres** are *any part of the organization to which revenue and controllable costs can be assigned, such as a department.*

> **transfer price**     The price for sending goods from one company profit centre to another.

> **profit centre**     Any part of the organization to which revenue and controllable costs can be assigned, such as a department.

In large companies the centres can secure many of their resource requirements from within the corporate structure. The pricing problem becomes what rate should Profit Centre A (maintenance department) charge Profit Centre B (sales department) for the cleaning compound used on B's floors? Should the price be the same as it would be if A did the work for an outside party? Should B receive a discount? The answer to these questions depends upon the philosophy of the firm involved.

The transfer pricing dilemma is an example of the variations that a firm's pricing policy must deal with. Consider the case of UDC-Europe, a Universal Data Corporation subsidiary that itself has 10 subsidiaries. Each of the 10 is organized on a

*Should public transit be free? This notion has been proposed by city planners as a possible way to reduce traffic congestion and pollution. If municipal or provincial governments assumed the full cost of public transit, the argument goes, they'd see returns in terms of social and environmental benefits. What advantages and disadvantages do you see with this pricing policy?*

geographic basis, and each is treated as a separate profit centre. Intercompany transfer prices are set at the annual budget meeting. Special situations, like unexpected volume, are handled through negotiations by the subsidiary managers. If complex tax problems arise, UDC-Europe's top management may set the transfer price.[22]

## Pricing in the Public Sector

The pricing of public services has also become an interesting, and sometimes controversial, aspect of contemporary marketing.[23]

Traditionally, government services either were very low-cost or were priced using the full-cost approach: users paid all costs associated with the service. In more recent years there has been a tendency to move toward incremental or marginal pricing, which considers only those expenses specifically associated with a particular activity. However, it is often difficult to determine the costs that should be assigned to a particular activity or service. Governmental accounting problems are often more complex than those of private enterprise.

Another problem in pricing public services is that taxes act as an *indirect* price of a public service. Someone must decide the relative relationship between the direct and indirect prices of such a service. A shift toward indirect tax charges (where an income or earnings tax exists) is generally a movement toward charging on the *ability-to-pay* rather than the *use* principle.

The pricing of any public service involves a basic policy decision as to whether the price is an instrument to recover costs or a technique for accomplishing some other social or civic objective. For example, public health services may be priced near zero so as to encourage their use. On the other hand, parking fines in some cities are high so as to discourage use of private automobiles in the central business district. Pricing decisions in the public sector are difficult because political and social considerations often outweigh the economic aspects.

# Summary

Pricing policies are important for the proper management of pricing. A pricing policy is a general guideline based on pricing objectives that is intended for use in specific pricing decisions. Pricing policies discussed in this chapter are: skimming versus penetration policies, price flexibility, and relative price level policies.

Various pricing practices are commonly involved in the management of pricing: price lining, setting promotional prices, psychological pricing, and unit pricing. There is a strong relationship between price and the perceived quality of a product. In the absence of other cues, price is used by consumers as an important indicator of product quality.

Price quotations take many forms. Discounts and allowances are taken off the list price as an incentive to pay cash. Trade discounts are given for volume and quick payment, and discounts are given for quantity purchases. Geographic considerations affect prices in other situations.

Sometimes prices are arrived at through competitive bidding, a situation in which several buyers quote prices on the same service or good. At other times prices are set in negotiated contracts. Within large companies, transfer pricing can be an issue. Here a company sets prices for transferring goods or services from one company profit centre to another.

As governments become more cost conscious, pricing of public services is becoming more common. Because of the public nature of these service and the complexity of government operations, such pricing is often difficult and controversial.

## KEY TERMS

pricing policy
skimming pricing
penetration pricing
flexible pricing
price lining
promotional pricing
loss leader
psychological pricing
odd pricing
unit pricing
price limits

list price
market price
cash discount
trade discount
cumulative and noncumulative
 quantity discounts
trade-in
promotional allowance
rebate
F.O.B. plant

freight absorption
uniform delivered price
zone pricing
competitive bidding
specifications
negotiated contract
escalator clause
transfer price
profit centre

## REVIEW QUESTIONS

1. List and discuss the reasons for establishing price policies.

2. What are the benefits and pitfalls derived from using a skimming approach to pricing?

3. Under what circumstances is penetration pricing most likely to be used? What are its advantages and disadvantages?
4. When would a one-price policy and when would a variable price policy be more appropriate?
5. When does a price become a promotional price? What are the pitfalls in promotional pricing?
6. What is the relationship between prices and consumer perceptions of quality?

7. How are prices likely to be quoted?
8. Contrast the freight absorption and uniform delivered pricing systems.
9. Contrast negotiated prices and competitive bidding.
10. What types of decisions must be made in the pricing of public services? What role could escalator clauses play in this area?

# DISCUSSION QUESTIONS AND EXERCISES

1. What type of new-product pricing would be appropriate for the following items:
   a. a new deodorant
   b. a fuel additive that increases fuel efficiency by 50 percent
   c. a new pattern of fine china
   d. a new ultrasensitive burglar, smoke, and fire alarm
   e. a new video game
2. How are prices quoted for each of the following:
   a. a Canadian Airlines ticket to Montreal
   b. a fireplace installation by a local contractor
   c. a new jogging suit from a sportswear retailer
   d. a new Nissan pick-up truck
3. Comment on the following statement: Unit pricing is ridiculous because everyone ignores it.
4. Prepare a list of arguments that might be used in justifying a negotiated contract instead of requiring competitive bids.
5. What criteria should be considered for transfer pricing in a large corporation like Westinghouse Electric?

# MICROCOMPUTER EXERCISE
## Competitive Bidding

Expected net profit is a very useful concept in a competitive-bidding situation. Expected net profit is equal to the probability of the buyer accepting the bid times the residual of the bid minus the costs.

**Directions:** Use the Menu Item titled "Competitive Bidding" on the *Foundations of Marketing* disk to solve the following problems.

1. Nancy Terry, the sales manager for Winnipeg Editorial Advisors, wishes to submit a bid on a freelance writing project. She estimates that her firm would actually spend $15 000 completing the project. Terry has prepared two alternative proposals, one for $20 000 and the other for $25 000. Assume she estimates that there is a 70 percent chance of the publisher accepting the $20 000 bid, but only a 40 percent chance of acceptance of the higher bid. Use expected-net-profit analysis to determine which bid Terry should submit to the publisher

2. The president of Red Deer Industries would like to earn an expected net profit of $15 000 on a project for the province of Alberta. The estimated cost of completing the project is $10 000.
   a. What probability of acceptance is being assigned if the president submits a bid of $35 000?
   b. What probability of acceptance is being assigned if the president submits a bid of $40 000?

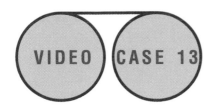

# Looking Good Calendar Co.

Pricing a product looks like a relatively simple task: Add up the production and marketing costs, then pick a price that will guarantee a profit. But costs do not determine prices, and control over the price frequently does not rest with the producer — the caprices of the market set the price. "Pricing is simply how much money you get for your product," says Dr. Richard H. Buskirk, director of the entrepreneurship program of the University of Southern California. "It's not a matter of what you ask for. All sorts of people ask high prices. Those are just wishes. Price is what you get for it." Nobody would pay $10 000 for a mousetrap, no matter how well made or effective it may be, unless trapping a mouse became a $10 000 problem. Henry Ford succeeded not just because he found a cheaper way of making cars if he made a lot of them, but also because an equal number of people actually bought cars at the price he asked.

Says Buskirk, "Costs determine the floor, but what costs really determine are whether you stay in business and whether or not you make a profit. The market determines your price. Hey, the market doesn't care whether you paid a million dollars for a product...or it cost you one dollar. Let's say I look something over and it's worth ten dollars to me. I'll pay you ten. I don't care what it cost you. If it cost you a hundred, that's your tough luck. If it costs you a dime, what difference does it make? It's worth ten [dollars] to me."

Jim and Nick Colachis, founders of Looking Good Calendar Co., were aware of the facts of pricing when they developed their first male calendar at the University of Southern California. Although many people scoffed at their plan, they persevered because they knew that college women wanted their product. Their posters were torn down and rehung in dormitory rooms; when they ran a full-page ad in the campus newspaper, the *Daily Trojan*, women took stacks of papers so that they could wallpaper their rooms with the ad. Even so, the Colachis brothers kept asking themselves, "Will it work?" They showed female students a sample of the calendar and asked what they would be willing to pay for it. The answers showed that they would willingly pay a price in line with that of other calendars. However, the Colachis brothers decided to price their calendar at $5.95 because, as Nick said, "most of the other calendars in the store were selling for $6.95, so why not $1 cheaper?"

The strategy worked: The USC bookstore bought 3500 as its initial order, instead of the five or six dozen the Colachis brothers had expected it to order. "We made $12 000 in about a minute," Nick said. "It was a good feeling." The low price and high quality of the calendar enabled Looking Good to sell its production run quickly and use the proceeds to expand and develop its product line. They continued this policy, and by 1988 they offered fourteen different calendars, still priced about $1 below the competition's. Sales had soared to over $2 million per year.

A completely different approach is necessary for a product with an inverse demand curve. "Inverse demand curves, they're a favourite topic of mine because it goes contrary to the traditional theory of demand," says Buskirk. "On an inverse demand curve, if you lowered price, it would hurt your sales." Perfume exhibits an inverse demand curve. Most perfume is given as a gift; the higher the price, the more highly valued the gift. If a man buys a $1 bottle of perfume as a gift for his wife, what is he saying? Unless that dollar represents a significant sacrifice for him, it is not likely that the gift will be appreciated.

Opus One recognizes that a high-priced product must live up to its price. Although the customer wants to pay a lot for the product, it still must be better than a similar product at a lower price. Opus One is a joint venture between the Robert Mondavi Winery and Mouton Rothschild, the French winery, using California grapes and Bordeaux technology. Says Michael Mondavi, "We know our wines are higher-priced. We also believe they're higher quality and quality is remembered long after the price is forgotten. And by God, you'd better have the quality in the bottle every single time." Priced at over $40 per bottle, the wines sell out within a few weeks of release. Says Buskirk, "Obviously the market's willing to pay it."

AT&T had a completely different problem when it introduced direct dialling. The lowered pricing and convenience of the new service increased usage, and profits, considerably. The government forced the company to pass some of the profits on to its customers by lowering its prices. This further increased usage and profits, placing AT&T in the embarrassing position of continually lowering prices while increasing profits. There are many businesses that wish they had that kind of problem.

The pricing of meat is another interesting example. It is not difficult to see that the prices of various cuts of beef are not related to the cost of producing them. On a given steer, all the cuts cost the same per pound to produce. The problem here is that they cannot all be sold at the same price because they are not all of equal quality. If your price on filet is too low, you'll be up to your ears in chuck and round in no time at all. If your price for filet is too high, it doesn't sell and the meat rots. Says Buskirk, "That whole steer has to sell. . . . If it doesn't sell. . .as fresh,. . . you can clear the whole beef through ground beef very easily and that's the most sensitive price. . . .By lowering that price just a little bit, sales volume can skyrocket."

"Markets set prices," says Buskirk, "not costs. If you have a good product — the right product for the market — it's designed well, you promoted it right, you got good distribution, you'll get your price. But if you are weak in any of those other areas, you have to shade the price. So price is really a thermometer by which we measure how good you are at the rest of your marketing efforts."

## Questions

1. What pricing strategy is being used by Looking Good for its calendars? Justify the choice of this strategy.

2. Suggest methods by which the Colachis brothers can continue to grow and protect their product concept from competitors.

3. Relate an example from this case to each of the following price concepts: (a) trade discounts, (b) promotional allowances, (c) psychological pricing, (d) product line pricing.

4. Discuss the price–quality relationship as it relates to the pricing of beef. What other factors might serve to offset this relationship?

5. Discuss the impact of increased production costs on the ability of Looking Good, Opus One, and beef retailers to continue their current pricing strategies.

SOURCES    *Great Expectations: A Case Study in Marketing and Forecasting* and *What the Market Will Bear: Great Moments in Pricing* [television program], produced by Coast Telecourses, Coast Community College District.

## CAREER PROFILE

### Lori De Cou

Province of British Columbia
Music '91
Marketing Co-ordinator

**Education:**
British Columbia Institute of Technology
Marketing/Tourism Program
Graduation — 1990

I graduated just over a year ago from BCIT's two-year Marketing/Tourism program and currently work as a marketing co-ordinator for Music '91, British Columbia's biggest tourism promotion since Expo '86.

At BCIT I learned a number of things from which I draw daily to do my job effectively. Although many of the specific courses I took provided me with good background information, the biggest lessons I learned stemmed from the BCIT environment. BCIT prides itself on providing job-ready graduates, and I think it achieves this by creating a "work" environment at school. Besides coping with an intense workload, students are required to work in groups and are frequently called on to make oral presentations. This experience goes a long way toward developing one's self-confidence.

As a marketing co-ordinator for Music '91, I work with local media, community organizers, and tourism centres to promote different Music '91 events throughout British Columbia. My first experience with marketing for the tourism industry came in the form of class exercises. After breaking British Columbia into tourism regions, we examined what each individual area had to offer — and, more important, analyzed the region's effectiveness at selling its resources. We then conducted case studies of small communities or of tourism-related industries, after which we drew up marketing plans to entice visitors from other provinces and other countries. Of course, the approach we used would be the same for marketing any product: evaluate, critique the present marketing plan, establish a budget, identify a market, and so on.

The best single piece of advice that I could give students is this: "You will get out of your education only what you put into it." The textbook facts are important, but you can always return to the text as a point of reference. Many of the most valuable skills school can help you learn cannot be found in a book: seize every opportunity to practise working with others, decision-making, time management, and communicating confidently. You probably won't regret it.

As for my future, I hope to move on to another mega-project, or to settle into the marketing department of some corporation.

P A R T   S I X

# Distribution

CHAPTER 14
## Channel and Distribution Strategy

•

CHAPTER 15
## Wholesaling

•

CHAPTER 16
## Retailing

This section deals with the third element of the marketing mix, focusing on the activities and institutions involved in moving products and services to the firm's chosen target market. Chapter 14 introduces the basic concepts related to channels, as well as the related physical distribution. Chapters 15 and 16 analyze wholesalers and retailers, the marketing institutions that go to make up marketing channels.

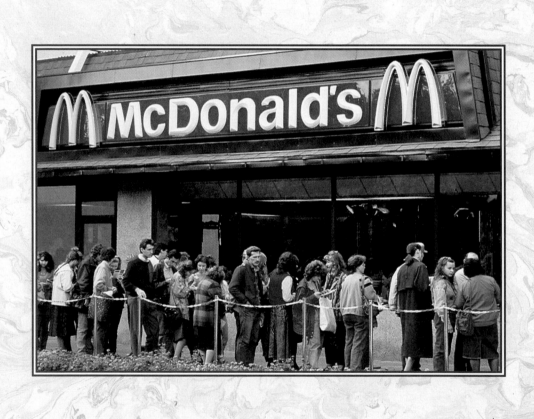

C H A P T E R 14

# Channel and Distribution Strategy

## C H A P T E R   O B J E C T I V E S

1. To relate channel strategy to the other variables of the marketing mix.
2. To relate channel strategy to the concept of total quality management.
3. To explain the role of distribution channels in marketing strategy.
4. To describe the various types of distribution channels.
5. To outline the major channel strategy decisions.
6. To discuss conflict and co-operation in the distribution channel.
7. To integrate operations within a physical distribution system to the functioning of marketing channels.

WHEN there are none of the usual channels of distribution, what do you do? This was the problem faced by McDonald's when it wanted to obtain equipment for its new store in Moscow. As one example of the many problems that had to be overcome, it faced the question of finding the best way to move the 25 tons of equipment that go into a typical McDonald's outlet from the West to downtown Moscow.

"No problem," said executives of freight forwarder Danzas AG of Switzerland. Danzas, one of Europe's largest forwarders, took on the Soviet job for Franke GmbH, a company based in Sackingen, West Germany, which has produced more than 1000 kitchens for McDonald's. The forwarder arranged for VEB Deutrans, a German trucking company, to load six trailers with a full McDonald's kitchen and make the 1600-mile trip through winter snows toward Nuremberg, Leipzig, and Warsaw. At the Soviet border, Danzas was the first company ever to declare that it was importing a McDonald's restaurant into Russia.

Even though the Gorky Street McDonald's is one of the largest ever opened, overwhelming demand immediately produced long lines at the restaurant's 28 cash registers. "It has been a smashing success," said one executive of the forwarder. "Customers there told our people that they like it because they only have to wait in line for an hour." More than 15 000 people a day are now eating in the one store.

As channels and physical distribution become more efficient in the Soviet Union, people will ultimately experience the same speed of service found in other parts of the world.

---

# Introduction

Marketing channels create time, place, and ownership utility in a direct way. Let's take the example of swimwear. Products for the coming spring and summer have already been produced in the months of December and January, and are en route to retail stores throughout the continent. Information from the marketing department has allowed swimwear manufacturers to identify preferences for new colours, styles, and fabrics and to produce products of the highest quality for each market. However, swimwear of even the highest quality will fail to generate adequate sales unless it is delivered to the right place (place utility), at the right time (time utility), and with appropriate legal requirements (ownership utility). Swimwear meeting consumers' quality expectations, available in the appropriate outlet the first warm day in April, accompanied by a sales receipt indicating ownership, will be able to provide buyers with form, time, place, and ownership utility — and a little later they'll slip it on, tiptoe across a sunny beach, and dip a pale toe into the chilly water.

A manufacturer of swimwear must therefore work out a clear channel strategy in order for the entire distribution process to work. Let us now consider basic channel strategy as the starting point for a discussion of the distribution function and its role in the marketing mix. Emphasis will be placed on the role of total quality management (*TQM*) in channel strategy. More North American organizations are learning that what they do prior to supplying the customer has a tremendous influence on performance, measured by cost or customer responsiveness. TQM takes the customer's needs and wants (as stated in the customer's own words) and seeks to preserve them as information is passed to process and manufacturing units. Products are produced that possess superior technical features and meet the needs and wants of customers.

This chapter covers such basic issues as the role and types of distribution channels; channel strategy and composition as a means of assuring total quality management; logistics functions performed within the marketing channel; and conflict and co-operation in the distribution channel.[1] Chapters 15 and 16 deal with wholesaling and retailing, the marketing institutions in the distribution channel. This section begins with a look at what marketers call distribution channels.

Carson luggage is made in Ottawa, Staedtler pens and erasers come from Germany, plywood is produced in British Columbia, and Timex watches are assembled in Toronto. All are sold throughout Canada. In each case, some method must be devised to bridge the gap between producer and consumer. Distribution channels provide the purchaser with a convenient means of obtaining the products that he or she wishes to buy. **Distribution channels** (also called marketing channels) are *the paths that goods — and title to these goods — follow from producer to consumer*.[2] Specifically,

**distribution channel**    The paths that goods — and title to these goods — follow from producer to consumer.

the term *channels* refers to the various marketing institutions and the interrelationships responsible for the flow of goods and services from producer to consumer or industrial user. Intermediaries are the marketing institutions in the distribution channel. A **marketing intermediary**, or middleman, is *a business firm operating between the producer and the consumer or industrial purchaser*. The term therefore *includes both wholesalers and retailers*.

**Wholesaling** is *the activities of persons or firms who sell to retailers, other wholesalers, and industrial users but not significant amounts to ultimate consumers*. The terms *jobber* and *distributor* are considered synonymous with wholesaler in this book.

Confusion can result from the practices of some firms that operate both wholesaling and retailing operations. Sporting goods stores, for example, often maintain a wholesaling operation in marketing a line of goods to high schools and colleges as well as operating retail stores. For the purpose of this book, we will treat such operations as two separate institutions.

A second source of confusion is the misleading practice of some retailers who claim to be wholesalers. Such stores may actually sell at wholesale prices and can validly claim to do so. However, *stores that sell products purchased by individuals for their own use and not for resale* are by definition **retailers**, not wholesalers.

**marketing intermediary**    A business firm operating between the producer and the consumer or industrial purchaser.

**wholesaling**    The activities of persons or firms who sell to retailers, other wholesalers, and industrial users but not in significant amounts to ultimate consumers.

**retailer**    A store that sells products purchased by individuals for their own use and not for resale.

# The Role of Distribution Channels in Marketing Strategy

Distribution channels play a key role in marketing strategy since they provide the means by which goods and services are conveyed from their producers to consumers and users. The importance of distribution channels can be explained in terms of the utility that is created and the functions that are performed.

## The Functions Performed by Distribution Channels

The distribution channel performs several functions in the overall marketing system.[3] These include facilitating the exchange process; sorting to alleviate discrepancies in assortment; standardizing transactions; holding inventories; assisting in the search process; and transporting materials and finished products.[4]

### Facilitating the exchange process

The evolution of distribution channels began with the exchange process described in Chapter 1. As market economies grew, the exchange process itself became complicated. With more producers and more potential buyers, intermediaries came into existence to facilitate transactions by cutting the number of marketplace contacts. For example, if ten orchards in the Okanagan valley each sell to six supermarket chains, there are a total of 60 transactions. If the producers set up and market their apples through a co-operative, the number of contacts declines to 16. This process is described in detail in Chapter 15.

### Sorting to alleviate discrepancies in assortment

Another essential function of the distribution channel is to adjust discrepancies in assortment. For economic reasons, a producer tends to maximize the quantity of a limited line of products, while the buyer needs a minimum quantity of a wide selection of alternatives. Thus, there is a discrepancy between what the producer has to offer and what the customers want. **Sorting** is *the process that alleviates discrepancies in*

**sorting**    The process that alleviates discrepancies in assortment by re-allocating the outputs of various producers into assortments desired by individual purchasers.

FIGURE 14–1

## The Sorting Process

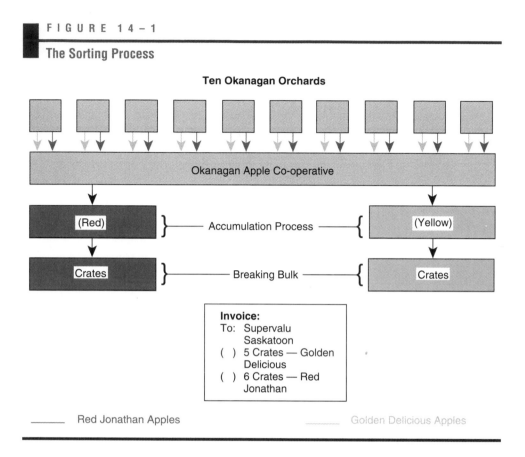

**Ten Okanagan Orchards**

Okanagan Apple Co-operative

(Red) } Accumulation Process { (Yellow)

Crates } Breaking Bulk { Crates

**Invoice:**
To: Supervalu
    Saskatoon
( ) 5 Crates — Golden
    Delicious
( ) 6 Crates — Red
    Jonathan

———— Red Jonathan Apples                    ———— Golden Delicious Apples

*assortment by re-allocating the outputs of various producers into assortments desired by individual purchasers.*

Figure 14–1 shows an example of the sorting process. First, an individual producer's output is divided into separate homogeneous categories such as the various types and grades of apples. These apples are then combined with the similar crops of other orchards, a process known as *accumulation*. These accumulations are broken down into smaller units or divisions, such as crates of apples. This is often called *breaking bulk* in marketing literature. Finally, an assortment is built for the next level in the distribution channel. For example, the Okanagan co-operative might prepare an assortment of five crates of Golden Delicious and six crates of Red Jonathan apples for Supervalu supermarket in Saskatoon.

### Standardizing the transaction

If each transaction in a complex market economy were subject to negotiation, the exchange process would be chaotic. Distribution channels standardize exchange transactions in terms of the product, such as the grading of apples into types and grades, and the transfer process itself. Order points, prices, payment terms, delivery schedules, and purchase lots tend to be standardized by distribution channel members. For example, supermarket buyers might have on-line communications links with the co-operative cited in Figure 14–1. Once a certain stock position is reached, more apples would automatically be ordered from either the co-operative's current output or its cold storage.

## Holding inventories

Distribution channel members hold a minimum of inventories to take advantage of economies of scale in transporting and to provide a buffer for small changes in demand.

## The search process

Distribution channels also accommodate the search behaviour of both buyers and sellers. (Search behaviour was discussed earlier in Chapter 7). Buyers are searching for specific products and services to fill their needs, while sellers are attempting to find what consumers want. A college student looking for some Golden Delicious apples might go to the fruit section of Supervalu in Saskatoon. Similarly, the manager of that department would be able to provide the Okanagan co-operative with information about sales trends in his or her marketplace.

## Physically distributing products

Storing products in convenient locations for shipment to wholesale and retail establishments allows firms to embody time utility in the product. Place utility is created primarily by transporting the product. Customer satisfaction is heavily dependent on reliable movement of products to ensure their availability. Eastman Kodak Company committed a major marketing blunder in the late 1970s when it launched a multi-million dollar advertising campaign for its new instant camera before adequate quantities had been delivered to retail outlets. Many would-be purchasers visited the stores and, when they discovered that the new camera was not available, bought a Polaroid instead. By providing consumers with time and place utility, physical distribution contributes to implementing the marketing concept.

# Types of Distribution

Literally hundreds of marketing channels exist today; however, there is no one marketing channel that is superior to all others. "Best" for Electrolux vacuum cleaners may be direct from manufacturer to consumer through a sales force of 1000 men and women. The "best" channel for frozen french fries may be from food processor to agent intermediary to *merchant wholesaler* (a wholesaler who takes title) to supermarket to consumer. Instead of searching for a "best" channel for all products, the marketing manager must analyze alternative channels in the light of consumer needs and competitive restraints to determine the optimum channel or channels for the firm's products.[5]

Even when the proper channels have been chosen and established, the marketing manager's channel decisions are not ended. Channels, like so many of the other marketing variables, change, and today's ideal channel may prove obsolete in a few years.

For example, the typical channel for motor oil until the 1960s was from oil company to company-owned service stations, because most oil was installed there. But a significant number of oil purchases are now made by motorists in automotive supply stores, discount department stores, and even supermarkets, as today many motorists install motor oil themselves. Others use rapid oil-change specialty shops. And the channel for Shell, Esso, Texaco, Quaker State, and Castrol must change to reflect these changes in consumer buying patterns.

*Dow Chemical Canada markets its Dowper solvent directly to the dry cleaners who are its final users. Many industrial producers follow this model, especially where technical support is required. A direct line between producer and end user is preferable when technical specifications or rigorous performance requirements apply.*

Figure 14–2 depicts the major channels available for marketers of consumer and industrial products. In general, industrial products channels tend to be shorter than consumer goods channels on account of geographic concentrations of industrial buyers, a relatively limited number of purchasers, and the absence of retailers from the chain. The term *retailer* refers to consumer goods purchases. Service channels also tend to be short because of the intangibility of services and the need to maintain personal relationships in the channel.

## Direct Channel

The simplest, most direct marketing channel is not necessarily the best, as is indicated by the relatively small percentage of the dollar volume of sales that moves *directly from the producer to the consumer*. Less than 5 percent of all consumer goods are candidates for the producer-to-consumer channel. Dairies, Tupperware, Avon cosmetics, and numerous mail-order houses are examples of firms whose marketing moves directly from manufacturer to the ultimate consumer.

Direct channels are much more important in the industrial goods market, where most major installations and accessory equipment — and many of the fabricated parts and raw materials — are marketed through *direct contacts between producer and user*.

## All-Aboard Channel

Probably the longest channel is *from producer to agent to wholesaler to retailer to consumer*. Where products are produced by a large number of small companies, a unique intermediary appears to perform the basic function of bringing buyer and seller together — the agent, or broker. **Agents** are, in fact, *wholesaling intermediaries, but they differ from the typical wholesaler in that they do not take title to the goods.*

**agent** A wholesaling intermediary who differs from the typical wholesaler in that the agent does not take title to the goods.

F I G U R E   1 4 – 2

## Alternative Distribution Channels

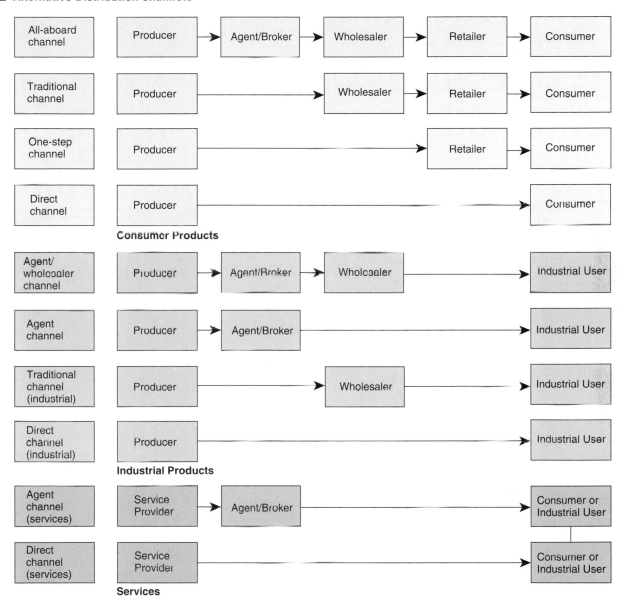

**Consumer Products**

- All-aboard channel: Producer → Agent/Broker → Wholesaler → Retailer → Consumer
- Traditional channel: Producer → Wholesaler → Retailer → Consumer
- One-step channel: Producer → Retailer → Consumer
- Direct channel: Producer → Consumer

**Industrial Products**

- Agent/wholesaler channel: Producer → Agent/Broker → Wholesaler → Industrial User
- Agent channel: Producer → Agent/Broker → Industrial User
- Traditional channel (industrial): Producer → Wholesaler → Industrial User
- Direct channel (industrial): Producer → Industrial User

**Services**

- Agent channel (services): Service Provider → Agent/Broker → Consumer or Industrial User
- Direct channel (services): Service Provider → Consumer or Industrial User

They merely represent the producer or the regular wholesaler (who does take title to the goods) in seeking a market for the producer's output or in locating a source of supply for the buyer. A canner of vegetables in Ontario has 6000 cases of string beans to sell. The firm informs the food brokers (agents) regularly used in various provinces of this fact. A broker in the Maritimes ascertains that the Maritime supermarket chain Sobey's will buy 800 cases. The broker takes the order, informs the canner, and if the price is acceptable, the canner ships the order to Sobey's. The canner bills Sobey's and sends a commission cheque (approximately 3 percent of the sale price) to the food broker for the service of bringing buyer and seller together.

## One-step Channel

This channel is being used more and more, and in many instances it has taken the place of the traditional channel. When large retailers are involved, they are willing to take on many functions performed by the wholesaler — consequently, goods move *from producer to retailer to consumer*.

## Traditional Channel (Consumer)

The traditional marketing channel for consumer goods is *from producer to wholesaler to retailer to user*. It is the method used by literally thousands of small manufacturers or companies producing limited lines of products and by as many or more small retailers. Small companies with limited financial resources use wholesalers as immediate sources of funds and as a marketing arm to reach the hundreds of retailers who will stock their products. Smaller retailers rely on wholesalers as *buying specialists* to ensure a balanced inventory of goods produced in various regions of the world.

   The wholesaler's sales force is responsible for reaching the market with the producer's output. Many manufacturers also use sales representatives to call on the retailers to assist in merchandising the line. These representatives serve the manufacturer as sources of market information and influence, but will generally not make the sales transaction. If they do initiate a sale, they give it to a wholesaler to complete.

## Agent/Wholesaler Channel

*Producer to agent to wholesaler to industrial user*. Similar conditions often exist in the industrial market, where small producers often use a channel to market their offerings. The agent wholesaling intermediary, often called a manufacturer's representative or manufacturer's agent, serves as an independent sales force in contacting large, scattered wholesalers and some key industrial buyers. For example, a manufacturer of specialty industrial tapes might use agents to sell to industrial wholesalers and to encourage the wholesaler's sales force to push the product to industrial users.

## Agent Channel

Where the unit sale is small, merchant wholesalers must be used to cover the market economically. By maintaining regional inventories, they can achieve transportation economies by stockpiling goods and making the final small shipment over a small distance. But where the unit sale is large and transportation costs account for a small percentage of the total product costs, the *producer to agent to industrial user* channel may be employed. The agent wholesaling intermediaries become, in effect, the company's sales force. For example, a producer of special castings might engage agents who are already calling on potential customers with other lines to represent it as well.

## Traditional Channel (Industrial)

Similar characteristics in the industrial market often lead to the use of *wholesalers between the manufacturer and industrial purchaser*. The term industrial distributor is commonly used in the industrial market to refer to those wholesalers who take title to the goods they handle. These wholesalers are involved in the marketing of small

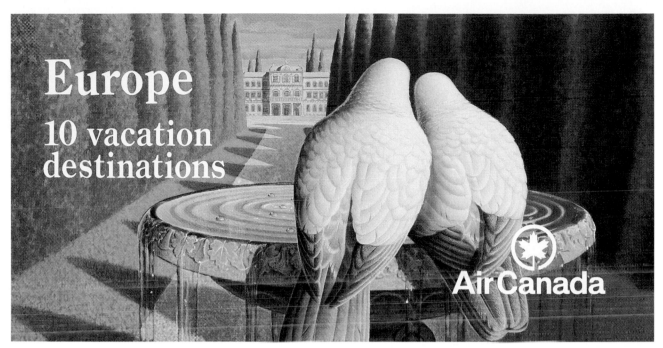

accessory equipment and operating supplies, such as building supplies, office supplies, small hand tools, and office equipment.[6] For example, in an effort to orient its own sales force toward high-priority computer products, IBM has turned to industrial distributors. The IBM industrial distributors sell only two products: a moderately priced display terminal and a desk-top printer. IBM continues to sell its entire product line, but it concentrates on items with higher priority.[7]

## Direct Channel (Services)

Distribution of services to both consumers and industrial users is usually simpler and more direct than for industrial and consumer goods. In part, this is due to the intangibility of services; the marketer of services does not often have to worry about storage, transportation, and inventory control. Shorter channels, often direct from service provider to consumer or industrial user, are typically used.

Many services can only be performed on a direct basis, and personal relationships between performers and users are very important. Consumers will remain clients of the same bank, automobile repair shop, or hair stylist as long as they are reasonably satisfied. Likewise, public accounting firms and attorneys are retained on a relatively permanent basis by industrial buyers.

## Agent Channel (Services)

When *service providers use marketing intermediaries to reach consumers or industrial users,* these are usually *agents or brokers.* Common examples include insurance agents, securities brokers, travel agents, and entertainment agents.

For instance, travel and hotel packages are sometimes created by intermediaries and then marketed at the retail level by travel agents to both vacationers and firms wanting to offer employee incentive awards.

*Travel agents act as agents for air carriers such as Air Canada and often post their advertisements. Today, few people deal directly with Air Canada or other carriers, but prefer to buy their tickets from a travel agent who provides a wide range of services. This arrangement is also better from the producer's point of view, since a wider range of customers can be reached in this manner.*

## A Special Note on Channel Strategy for Consumer Services

A dominant reason for patronage of many consumer services, such as banks, motels, and auto rental agencies, is convenient location. It is absolutely essential that careful consideration be given to selecting the retail site. For example, banks are being sensitive to consumers' needs when they locate branches in suburban shopping centres and malls. The installation of automated electronic tellers that enable customers to withdraw funds and to make deposits when a bank's offices are closed is a further example of attempts to provide convenience.

## Multiple Channels

An increasingly common phenomenon is the use of more than one marketing channel for similar products. These *multiple channels* (or dual distribution) are utilized when the same product is marketed both to the ultimate consumer and industrial users. Dial soap is distributed through the traditional grocery wholesaler to food stores to the consumer, but a second channel also exists, from the manufacturer to large retail chains and motels that buy direct from the manufacturer. Competition among retailers and other intermediaries striving to expand lines, profitability, and customer service has created these multiple channels.

In other cases, the same product is marketed through a variety of types of retail outlets. A basic product such as a paintbrush is carried in inventory by the traditional hardware store; it is also handled by such nontraditional retail outlets as auto accessory stores, building supply outlets, department stores, discount houses, mail-order houses, supermarkets, and variety stores. Each retail store may utilize a different marketing channel.

Firestone automobile tires are marketed:

1. directly to General Motors, where they serve as a fabricated part for new Chevrolets;
2. through Firestone stores, company-owned retail outlets;
3. through franchised Firestone outlets;
4. from the factory to tire jobbers to retail gas stations.

Each channel enables the manufacturer to serve a different market.

## Reverse Channels

**reverse channels**    The paths goods follow from consumer to manufacturer or to marketing intermediaries.

While the traditional concept of marketing channels involves movement of products and services from producer to consumer or industrial user, there is increasing interest in reverse channels. **Reverse channels** are *the paths goods follow from consumer to manufacturer or to marketing intermediaries*. William G. Zikmund and William J. Stanton point out several problems in developing reverse channels in the *recycling* process.

> The recycling of solid wastes is a major ecological goal. Although recycling is technologically feasible, reversing the flow of materials in the channel of distribution — marketing trash through a "backward" channel — presents a challenge. Existing backward channels are primitive, and financial incentives are inadequate. The consumer must be motivated to undergo a role change and become a producer — the initiating force in the reverse distribution process.[8]

*Boy Scouts collect aluminum cans from a beach as part of a recycling campaign organized by Reynolds Aluminum. These aluminum cans are following a reverse channel from consumer to manufacturer. By participating in or initiating projects like these, the consumer can become a producer in the reverse distribution process.*

Reverse channels will increase in importance as raw materials become more expensive, and as additional laws are passed to control litter and the disposal of packaging materials such as soft-drink bottles. In order for recycling to succeed, four basic conditions must be satisfied:

1. a technology must be available that can efficiently process the material being recycled;
2. a market must be available for the end product — the reclaimed material;
3. a substantial and continuing quantity of secondary product (recycled aluminum, reclaimed steel from automobiles, recycled paper) must be available;

## A·P·P·L·Y·I·N·G  T·H·E  C·O·N·C·E·P·T·S

### A Multiple Channel Problem in the Miniblind Business

Rainbow Window Fashions, Inc., a successful small manufacturer of venetian blinds, was organized by Louis Sterner when he realized that the growing market for one-inch miniblinds was not being satisfied. About 90 percent of miniblind sales were custom-made orders, which typically took up to five weeks to fill.

Sterner decided to produce and stock quality miniblinds that would be available for immediate installation. However, his new enterprise had a distribution problem. Small, independent stores sold the most miniblinds, but brand recognition came from acceptance by department stores. Sterner felt he needed this recognition to establish Rainbow's position in the marketplace. His dilemma was complicated by

the fact that department store buyers were reluctant to accept brands sold by the smaller stores.

Sterner decided to offer two brands: the Rainbow label went to department stores, while smaller retailers got stripped-down versions of the miniblind under the Streamline brand. The firm's small sales force was able to penetrate both of these distribution channels successfully. Today, Rainbow Window Fashions is growing by about $2 to $3 million annually.

Source: Sanford L. Jacobs, "How Enterpreneur Exploited Chance the Big Firms Ignored," *Wall Street Journal* (March 1, 1982).

4. a marketing system must be developed that can bridge the gap between suppliers of secondary products and end users on a profitable basis.[9]

In some instances, the reverse channel consists of traditional marketing intermediaries. In the soft-drink industry, retailers and local bottlers perform these functions. In other cases, manufacturers take the initiative by establishing redemption centres. A concentrated attempt by the Reynolds Metals Company in one area permitted the company to recycle an amount of aluminum equivalent to 60 percent of the total containers marketed in the area. Other reverse-channel participants may include community groups, which organize "clean-up" days and develop systems for rechannelling paper products for recycling, and specialized organizations developed for waste disposal and recycling.

***Reverse channels for product recalls and repairs***    Reverse channels are also used for product recalls and repairs. Ownership of some products (for example, tires) is registered so that proper notification can be sent if there is a product recall. In the case of automobile recalls, owners are advised to have the problem corrected at their dealership. Similarly, reverse channels have been used for repairs to some products. The warranty for a small appliance may specify that if repairs are needed in the first 90 days, the item should be returned to the dealer. After that period, the product should be returned to the factory. Such reverse channels are a vital element of product recalls and repair procedures.

## Facilitating Agencies in the Distribution Channel

**facilitating agency**    An agency that provides specialized assistance for regular channel members (such as producers, wholesalers, and retailers) in moving products from producer to consumer.

A **facilitating agency** *provides specialized assistance for regular channel members (such as producers, wholesalers, and retailers) in moving products from producer to consumer.* Included in the definition of facilitating agencies are transportation companies, warehousing firms, financial institutions, insurance companies, and marketing research companies.

# Physical Distribution in the Marketing Channel

**physical distribution**    A broad range of activities concerned with efficient movement of products from the source of raw materials to the production line and, ultimately, to the consumer.

**Physical distribution** or logistics involves a broad range of *activities concerned with efficient movement of finished products from the source of raw materials to the production line and, ultimately, to the consumer.* Physical distribution activities include such crucial decision areas as customer service, inventory control, materials handling, protective packaging, order processing, transportation, warehouse site selection, and warehousing. Physical distribution is important to marketers because its activities represent roughly half of all marketing costs. A second — and equally important — aspect is the role physical distribution activities play in providing *customer service.* Robert Woodruff, former president of Coca-Cola, emphasized the role of physical distribution in his firm's success when he stated that his organization's policy is to "put Coke within arm's length of desire."

## Components of the Physical Distribution System

A system may be defined as an organized group of parts or components linked together according to a plan to achieve specific objectives. The physical distribution system contains the following elements:

## Customer service

What level of customer service should be provided? Customer service standards are the quality-of-service levels the firm's customers will receive. For example, a customer service standard of one firm might be that 60 percent of all orders will be shipped within 48 hours after they are received, 90 percent in 72 hours, and all orders within 96 hours. Setting the standards for customer service to be provided is an important marketing channel decision. Customers are often other channel members as well as final consumers. Inadequate customer service levels may mean dissatisfied customers and loss of future sales.

## Transportation

How will the products be shipped and by what carrier? The transportation system in Canada is a regulated industry, much like the phone and power industries. The federal and provincial governments perform both promotional and regulatory functions to maintain a viable Canadian transportation system. Transport Canada, a government agency within the federal bureaucracy, supports technological developments associated with the airways, waterways, and highways in Canada. Analogous agencies operate at the provincial level of government, although the scope and magnitude of their promotional support is significantly lower than that provided by the federal government. The Canadian Transport Commission (CTC), an agency of the federal government, is responsible for the air, rail, pipeline, and inland water components of the transportation industry. Each province has a transportation regulatory agency whose functions are equivalent to those of the CTC. In general, the purpose of government intervention in the transportation sector is to assure the development of a sound, efficient transportation infrastructure while protecting the public against abusive tactics.

Three legal forms of transportation carriers exist to provide linkages between the various channel members: *common, contract,* and *private. Common carriers* must "hold themselves out" to serve the general public for a fee. They must receive appropriate regulatory authority to perform transport service, and must adhere to guidelines and rules as to rate setting, mergers, application of accounting procedures, and financial dealings. Although common carriers perform transportation services between each of the marketing channel intermediaries, nonetheless they most frequently operate between manufacturers, wholesalers, and retailers moving goods of high value.

*Contract carriers* do not offer their services to the public at large. Rather, they enter into contractual arrangements with select customers. All rates and charges are included in the contractual instrument along with additional terms and conditions associated with the provision of service. Although regulatory requirements for contract carriers are significantly less than for common carriers, rules and standards are in effect at both the federal and provincial levels of government to delineate the scope of their authority to perform transportation services. Contract carriers tend to operate between raw material suppliers and manufacturers, and between manufacturers, rather than between wholesalers, retailers, and final customers, since they tend to be commodity and final goods consolidators rather than break-bulk operators.

*Private carriers* are not providers of transportation for a market fee. Instead they perform transportation services for a particular firm and may not solicit other transportation business. The test to determine whether a carrier is a private or a for-hire carrier is to ask whether the "primary business" is transportation or not. Legal

*Pipeline transportation is an efficient means of moving natural gas or oil. It has little utility for the marketing of manufactured goods, however, and points out the importance of choosing a transportation system suited to a particular product. The creative use of available transportation resources can have a major impact on the overall marketing plan.*

status is dependent on the percentage of revenues accruing from transportation activities or the ratio of transportation to non-transportation-related assets. Owing to the exclusive nature of their operations, and the fact that transportation is incidental to the main operations of the firm, private carriers are not subject to economic regulation by either the federal or provincial governments. They are, however, subject to federal and provincial safety regulations as are others who use transportation facilities.

There are five major transportation alternatives, referred to as modes, that link the various channel intermediaries. These are *railways, trucking, water carriers, pipelines*, and *air freight*. Railways are the largest transporters (as measured by tonne-kilometres of freight) and are considered the most efficient mode in moving bulk commodities over long distances. They are readily available in most locations in North America, although line abandonment has reduced considerably the operating systems of the major rail carriers over the past three decades. Likewise, railways are quite flexible in that many different commodities, raw materials, liquids, grains, as well as finished goods can be safely and efficiently moved.

Trucking companies compete with railways in several product categories; however, where speed, flexibility, and frequency of service are important, motor carriers often outperform rail carriers. The truck shows its inherent advantage in moving high-valued goods short to intermediate distances. While the rate per tonne-kilometre is often greater for truck than for rail carrier, the service advantages provided by truck often more than compensate for the added expenditures. Furthermore, the variety of available trucking technologies provides the shipper with a broad array of options in transporting goods to market. No other mode rivals trucking in the range of transportation options.

Water carriers are much like rail carriers in that they tend to perform best in moving bulky low-valued commodities long distances. Whether along the inland waterway system, the Great Lakes, or in international commerce, water carriers tend to carry bulk cargoes at rather low speeds. They do possess the advantage in international commerce of moving freight of all kinds as no other mode can, given present technologies. Rates per tonne-kilometre tend to be lowest for this mode, reflecting in part the relatively low value per unit of weight of cargoes typically carried by water. The exception to this general case is the provision of container service for medium- to high-valued goods. Container ships provide manufacturers the opportunity of extending market channels to locations that are quite distant from sourcing and producing sites. The presence of scale economies in production and distribution permit effective competition with local production.

Air freight is often referred to as "premium transportation" because of the high-cost–high-service nature of the mode. Speed is the single most important factor in the selection of air over other freight carriers, and the rate per tonne-kilometre tends to be among the highest of all modes. Cut flowers from southern U.S. growing fields, fresh seafood from Vancouver, and component parts urgently needed for a downed assembly line in Ontario are examples of the types of goods often moved by air freight carriers. In recent years, growth in demand for expedited small parcel and parcel post service has exploded, and companies like Emery Worldwide and Federal Express have developed as a response to this demand.

Pipeline transportation is the mode least likely to be used within a marketing channel except in specific industries such as oil extraction and refining, coal extraction, and in industries where raw commodities can be pulverized into small pellets or a powder, mixed with water, and transported in suspension.

## Inventory control

How much inventory should be maintained at each location? Inventory control analysts have developed a number of techniques that aid the physical distribution manager in effectively controlling inventory costs. The most basic is the **EOQ (economic order quantity)** model. This technique emphasizes a *cost trade-off between two fundamental costs involved with inventory: inventory holding costs and order costs.* As Figure 14–3 indicates, these two cost items are then "traded off" to determine the optimum order quantity of each product.

**EOQ (economic order quantity)** A model that emphasizes a cost trade-off between inventory holding costs and order costs.

FIGURE 14-3

## The EOQ Model

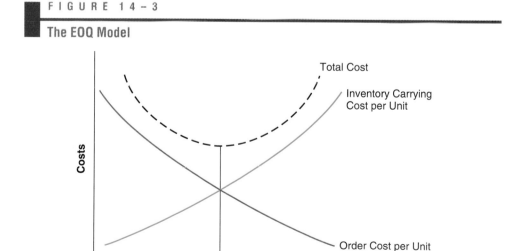

No aspect of physical distribution strategy has experienced the changes brought by acceptance of the TQM philosophy as much as inventory practice and policy. Once it is recognized that significant resources are often tied up in inventory, it should come as no surprise that some of the new frontiers in distribution cost savings have accrued from minimizing inventory holding costs. The Japanese capitalized on this simple idea several decades ago with the implementation of *Just-In-Time (JIT)* inventory systems. The basic idea is to identify stocking levels that meet peak efficiency minimums and to trade off higher transportation expenditures for reduced inventory holding expenditures.

The concept can be visualized in the following illustration. Imagine a young couple entering an automobile dealership in Calgary. They have a vague idea of the features they would like to have in their dream car and have sought out the services of an informed representative to assist them in their purchase decision. The representative activates her computer and asks the young couple for the specific features they would like in their automobile: exterior and interior colours, fabric content, stereo system, wheel type, suspension, and so forth. As the couple discuss the various options, the representative enters the information into the computer. Once the features have all been selected, the representative pushes a button and a simulated version of the automobile with the designated features is superimposed on the colour monitor. Assuming the couple agree on the features and a transaction occurs, the representative activates orders to the various component suppliers and assembly plants to begin assembly of the automobile. An order is sent to the battery manufacturer, the stereo manufacturer, the engine manufacturer, and to all other component suppliers who contribute to the production of the ordered automobile. From these sub-assembly plants the various components are produced and then shipped to the next unit in the manufacturing chain. The important point is that inventories are not held in large amounts anywhere in the manufacturing or marketing channel. Instead, upon receiving the order, the sub-assembler produces the component and transports it in minimum efficient lot sizes to the next assembler in the channel. The JIT method results in significant reductions in inventory costs even though transport costs may increase. Just as important as reducing inventory costs, however, are the gains accruing from reductions in setup and changeover times in procedures and equipment modifications, in more rapid response to changes in market conditions, and the increased awareness of total quality management by using the most recent technologies in producing component parts.

### Materials handling

How do we develop efficient methods of handling products in the factory, warehouse, and transport terminals? All the activities associated with moving products among the manufacturer's plants, warehouses, wholesalers, retailers, and transportation company terminals are called materials handling. Two important innovations have developed — *combining as many packages as possible into one load* (**unitization** and *combining several unitized loads* (**containerization**) — which have revolutionized the materials handling field. The materials handling system must be thoroughly coordinated in order that plants and warehouses that service the various channel intermediaries perform effectively.

**unitization** Combining as many packages as possible into one load.

**containerization** Combining several unitized loads.

### Warehousing

Where will the products be located? How many warehouses should be utilized? Warehouses lend themselves exceptionally well to automation, with the computer as the heart of the operation. *Distribution warehouses* are designed to assemble then redistribute products, whereas **break-bulk warehouses** *receive consolidated shipments from a central distribution centre, and distribute smaller shipments to individual customers in more limited areas.* Another type of warehouse, the *storage warehouse*, stores products for moderate to long periods of time in an attempt to balance supply and demand for producers and purchasers.

These components are interrelated, and decisions made in one area affect the relative efficiency of other areas. For this reason alone, an efficient physical distribution system must be implemented in order for a TQM strategy to function effectively.

**break-bulk warehouse**    One that receives consolidated shipments from a central distribution centre, and then distributes them in smaller shipments to individual customers in more limited areas.

## The Objective of Physical Distribution

The objective of a firm's physical distribution system is to produce a specified level of customer service while minimizing the costs involved in physically moving and storing the products and raw materials from production or extraction locations to the point where the end product is ultimately purchased. To achieve this, the physical distribution manager makes use of three basic concepts: (1) the total cost approach, (2) the use of cost trade-offs, and (3) the avoidance of suboptimization.

The premise that all relevant factors in physically moving and storing products should be considered as a whole and not individually forms the basis of the *total-cost approach*. Thus, a firm may incur higher transportation costs and in so doing lower its inventory costs. The basic question to ask is whether the *cost trade-off* between the two physical distribution activities has resulted in an actual lowering of total physical distribution costs. To the extent that total distribution costs are higher after the substitution of more transportation for inventory resources, the distribution system is likely to be suboptimizing. *Avoidance of suboptimization* requires that the elements of the physical distribution system be employed in the proportions that generate the least total costs for a given level of customer service.

The integration of these three basic concepts forms what is commonly referred to as the *physical distribution concept*. The uniqueness of the physical distribution concept is not in the individual functions that are performed to assure customer satisfaction; rather, it stems from the integration of all of these functions into a unified whole. In a way, the physical distribution concept is a movement/storage-oriented version of the *total quality management concept*. Whereas the physical distribution concept applies to activities and institutions within the channel that physically move material and information from point to point, the total quality management concept applies to *all* management activities involved in creating, moving, and marketing a product.

# Channel Strategy Decisions

Marketers face several channel strategy decisions. The selection of a specific distribution channel is the most basic of these, but the level of distribution intensity and the issue of vertical marketing systems must also be addressed.

## Selection of a Distribution Channel

What makes a direct channel (manufacturer to consumer) best for the Fuller Brush Company? Why do operating supplies often go through both agents and merchant wholesalers before being purchased by the industrial firm? Why do some firms employ multiple channels for the same product? The firm must answer many such questions when it determines its choice of marketing channels. The choice is based on an analysis of the market, the product and the producer, and various competitive factors. Each is often of critical importance, and all are often interrelated.

### Market factors

A major determinant of channel structure is whether the product is intended for the consumer or the industrial market. Industrial purchasers usually prefer to deal directly with the manufacturer (except for supplies or small accessory items), but most consumers make their purchases from retail stores. Products sold to both industrial users and the consumer market usually require more than one channel.

The geographic location and the needs of the firm's potential market will also affect channel choice. Direct sales are possible where the firm's potential market is concentrated in a few regions. Industrial production tends to be concentrated in a relatively small geographic region, making direct contact possible. The small number of potential buyers also increases the feasibility of direct channels. Consumer goods are purchased by every household everywhere. Since consumers are numerous and geographically dispersed, and purchase a small volume at a given time, intermediaries must be employed to market products to them efficiently.

In Canada, population distribution is an extremely influential factor in channel decisions. For example, the markets for fishing nets are on the two coasts, with smaller markets on the Great Lakes, Lake Winnipeg, and a few other large lakes. The Rockies and the Canadian Shield effectively divide markets and strongly offset channels of distribution. Our relatively smaller and widely dispersed centres of population tend to result in less specialized wholesaling and retailing institutions than in the United States and other developed, heavily populated countries. This, of course, may limit the range of channel opportunities available to the marketing manager.

Order size will also affect the marketing channel decision. Manufacturers are likely to employ shorter, more direct channels in cases where retail customers or industrial buyers place relatively small numbers of large orders. Retail chains often employ buying offices to negotiate directly with manufacturers for large-scale purchases. Wholesalers may be used to contact smaller retailers.

Shifts in consumer buying patterns also influence channel decisions. The desire for credit, the growth of self-service, the increased use of mail-order houses, and the greater willingness to purchase from door-to-door salespeople all affect a firm's marketing channel.[10]

### Product factors

Product characteristics also play a role in determining optimum marketing channels. *Perishable products*, such as fresh produce and fruit, and fashion products with short life cycles, *typically move through relatively short channels* direct to the retailer or to the ultimate consumer. Old Dutch Potato Chips are distributed by company salespeople–truck drivers direct to the retail shelves. Each year Hines & Smart Corporation ships over 2 million kg of live lobsters by air, in specially designed insulating containers, directly to restaurants and hotels throughout North America.

Complex products, such as custom-made installations or computer equipment, are typically sold direct from the manufacturer to the buyer. As a general rule, *the more standardized a product, the longer the channel will be*. Such items will usually be marketed by wholesalers. Also, products requiring regular service or specialized repair services usually avoid channels employing independent wholesalers. Automobiles are marketed through a franchised network of regular dealers whose employees receive regular training on how to service their cars properly.

Another generalization concerning marketing channels is that *the lower the unit value of the product, the longer the channel.* Convenience goods and industrial supplies with typically low unit prices are frequently marketed through relatively long channels. Installations and more expensive industrial and consumer goods go through shorter, more direct channels.

### Producer factors

Companies with adequate resources — financial, marketing, and managerial — will be less compelled to utilize intermediaries in marketing their products.[11] A financially strong manufacturer can hire its own sales force, warehouse its products, and grant credit to the retailer or consumer. A weaker firm relies on intermediaries for these services (although some large retail chains may purchase all of the manufacturer's output, making it possible to bypass the independent wholesaler). Production-oriented firms may be forced to utilize the marketing expertise of intermediaries to replace the lack of finances and management in their organization.

A firm with a broad product line is better able to market its products directly to retailers or industrial users since its sales force can offer a variety of products to the customers. Larger total sales allow the selling costs to be spread over a number of products and make direct sales more feasible. The single-product firm often discovers that direct selling is an unaffordable luxury.

The manufacturer's need for control over the product will also influence channel selection. If aggressive promotion for the firm's products at the retail level is desired, the manufacturer will choose the shortest available channel. For new products the manufacturer may be forced to implement an introductory advertising campaign before independent wholesalers will handle the item.

### Competitive factors

Some firms are forced to develop unique marketing channels because of inadequate promotion of their products by independent intermediaries. Avon concentrated on house-to-house selling rather than being directly involved in the intense competition among similar lines of cosmetics in traditional channels. This radical departure from the traditional channel resulted in tremendous sales by the firm's thousands of neighbourhood salespeople. Similarly, Honeywell discovered about 15 years ago that its $700 home security system, Concept 70, was being inadequately marketed by the traditional wholesaler-to-retailer channel and switched to a direct-to-home sales force.

Figure 14–4 summarizes the factors affecting the choice of optimal marketing channels and shows the effect of each characteristic upon the overall length of the channel.

## Determining Distribution Intensity

Adequate market coverage for some products could mean one dealer for each 50 000 people. On the other hand, Procter & Gamble defines adequate coverage for Crest toothpaste as almost every supermarket, discount store, drugstore, and variety store plus many vending machines.

FIGURE 14–4

## Factors Affecting Choice of Distribution Channels

| Factor | Channels Tend to Be Shorter When: |
|---|---|
| **Market Factors** | |
| Consumer market or industrial market | Users are in industrial market |
| Geographic location of market target | Customers are geographically concentrated |
| Customer service needs | Specialized knowledge, technical know-how, and regular service needs are present |
| Order size | Customers place relatively small number of large orders |
| **Product Factors** | |
| Perishability | Products are perishable, either because of fashion changes or physical perishability |
| Technical complexity of product | Products are highly technical |
| Unit value | Products have high unit value |
| **Producer Factors** | |
| Producer resources — financial, managerial, and marketing | Manufacturer possesses adequate resources to perform channel functions |
| Product line | Manufacturer has broad product line to spread distribution costs |
| Need for control over the channel | Manufacturer desires to control the channel |
| **Competitive Factors** | |
| Need for promotion to channel members | Manufacturer feels that independent intermediaries are inadequately promoting products |

## Intensive distribution

**intensive distribution** A form of distribution that attempts to provide saturation coverage of the potential market.

Producers of convenience goods who *attempt to provide saturation coverage of their potential markets* are the prime users of **intensive distribution**. Soft drinks, cigarettes, candy, and chewing gum are available in convenient locations to enable the purchaser to buy with a minimum of effort.

Bic pens can be purchased in thousands of retail outlets in Canada. TMX Watches of Canada Ltd. uses an intensive distribution strategy for its Timex watches. Consumers may buy a Timex in many jewellery stores, the traditional retail outlet for watches. In addition, they may find Timex in discount houses, variety stores, department stores, hardware stores, and drugstores.

Mass coverage and low unit prices make the use of wholesalers almost mandatory for such distribution. An important exception to this generalization is Avon Products, which operates direct to the consumer through a nationwide network of neighbourhood salespeople who purchase directly from the manufacturer, at 60 percent of the retail price, and service a limited area with cosmetics, toiletries, jewellery, and toys.

It must be remembered that while a firm may wish for intensive distribution, the retailer or industrial distributor will carry only products that make a profit. If demand is low the producer may have to settle for less than complete market coverage.

## Selective distribution

As the name implies, **selective distribution** involves *the selection of a small number of retailers to handle the firm's product line.* By limiting its retailers, the firm may reduce its total marketing costs, such as those for sales force and shipping, while establishing better working relationships within the channel. This practice may also be necessary to give the retailers an incentive (through having a product available to a limited number of sellers) to carry the product and promote it properly against many competing brands. Co-operative advertising (where the manufacturer pays a percentage of the retailer's advertising expenditures and the retailer prominently displays the firm's products) can be utilized to mutual benefit. Marginal retailers can be avoided. Where product service is important, dealer training and assistance is usually forthcoming from the manufacturer. Finally, price-cutting is less likely since fewer dealers are handling the firm's line.

**selective distribution** The selection of a small number of retailers to handle the firm's product line.

## Exclusive distribution

When *manufacturers grant exclusive rights to a wholesaler or retailer to sell in a geographic region,* they are practising **exclusive distribution**, which is an extreme form of selective distribution. The best example of exclusive dealership is the automobile industry. For example, a city of 100 000 might have a single Toyota dealer or one Cadillac agency. Exclusive dealership arrangements are also found in the marketing of some major appliances and in fashion apparel. Powerful retailers may also negotiate to acquire exclusive distribution.

**exclusive distribution** The granting of exclusive rights by manufacturers to a wholesaler or retailer to sell in a geographic region.

Some market coverage may be sacrificed through a policy of exclusive distribution, but this is often offset through the development and maintenance of an image of quality and prestige for the products, with more active attention by the retailer to promote them, and the reduced marketing costs associated with a small number of accounts. Producers and retailers co-operate closely in decisions concerning advertising and promotion, inventory to be carried by the retailers, and prices.

## The legal problems of exclusive distribution

The use of exclusive distribution presents a number of potential legal problems. Three problem areas exist — exclusive dealing, tied selling, and market restriction. Each will be examined briefly.

**Exclusive dealing** *prohibits a marketing intermediary* (either a wholesaler or, more typically, a retailer) *from handling competing products.* Through such a contract the manufacturer is assured of total concentration on the firm's product line by the intermediaries. For example, an oil company may consider requiring all dealers to sign a contract agreeing to purchase all of their accessories from that company.

**exclusive dealing** An arrangement whereby a supplier prohibits a marketing intermediary (either a wholesaler or, more typically, a retailer) from handling competing products.

The legal question is covered in Part IV of the Competition Act, which prohibits exclusive dealing by a major supplier if it is likely to:

1. impede entry into or expansion of a firm in the market;
2. impede introduction of a product into or expansion of sales of a product in the market; or

3. have any other exclusionary effect in the market, with the result that competition is or is likely to be lessened substantially.[12]

**tied selling**   An arrangement whereby a supplier forces a dealer who wishes to handle a product to also carry other products from the supplier or to refrain from using or distributing someone else's product.

**market restriction**   An arrangement whereby suppliers restrict the geographic territories for each of their distributors.

A second problem area is **tied selling**. In this case *a supplier might force a dealer who wishes to handle a product to also carry other products from the supplier or to refrain from using or distributing someone else's product*. Tied selling is controlled by the same provision as exclusive dealing.

The third legal issue of exclusive distribution is the use of **market restriction**. In this case *suppliers restrict the geographic territories for each of their distributors*. The key issue is whether such restrictions substantially lessen competition. If so, the Restrictive Trade Practices Commission has power to order the prohibition of such practices. For example, a *horizontal territorial restriction*, where retailers or wholesalers agree to avoid competition in products from the same manufacturer, would likely be declared unlawful.

## Vertical Marketing Systems

The traditional marketing channel has been described as a "highly fragmented network in which vertically aligned firms bargain with each other at arm's length, terminate relationships with impunity, and otherwise behave autonomously."[13] This

**FIGURE 14-5**

**Three Types of Vertical Marketing Systems**

| *Type of System* | *Description* | *Examples* |
|---|---|---|
| Corporate | Channel owned and operated by a single organization | Bata Shoes<br>Firestone<br>Sherwin-Williams<br>Singer<br>McDonald's (partial) |
| Administered | Channel dominated by one powerful member who acts as channel captain | Kodak<br>General Electric<br>Corning Glass |
| Contractual | Channel co-ordinated through contractual agreements among channel members | *Wholesaler-Sponsored Voluntary Chain:*<br>IGA<br>Canadian Tire<br>Independent Druggists Alliance (IDA)<br>Allied Hardware<br>*Retail Co-operative:*<br>Associated Grocers<br>*Franchise Systems:*<br>McDonald's (partial)<br>Century 21 Real Estate<br>AAMCO Transmissions<br>Coca-Cola bottlers<br>Ford dealers |

potentially inefficient system of distributing goods in some industries is gradually being replaced by **vertical marketing systems** — "*professionally managed and centrally programmed networks pre-engineered to achieve operating economies and maximum impact.*"[14] In other words, a vertical marketing system (VMS) is the use of various types of economic power to attain maximum operating efficiencies, deep market penetration, and sustained profits. Vertical marketing systems produce economies of scale through their size and elimination of duplicated services. Three types prevail: corporate, administered, and contractual. They are depicted in Figure 14–5.

**vertical marketing systems**
Professionally managed and centrally programmed networks pre-engineered to achieve operating economies and maximum impact.

## Corporate System

When there is single ownership of each stage of the marketing channel, a *corporate vertical marketing system* exists. Holiday Inn owns a furniture manufacturer and a carpet mill. Bata Shoes owns a retail chain of shoe stores. Many McDonald's food outlets are corporate-owned.

## Administered System

Channel co-ordination is achieved through the exercise of economic and "political" power by a dominant channel member in an *administered vertical marketing system.*[15] Canadian General Electric has a network of major appliance dealers who aggressively display and promote the line because of its strong reputation and brand. Although independently owned and operated, these dealers co-operate with the manufacturer because of the effective working relationships enjoyed over the years and the profits to be realized from selling the widely known, well-designed, broad range of merchandise.

## Contractual System

The most significant form of vertical marketing is the *contractual vertical marketing system.* It accounts for nearly 40 percent of all retail sales. Instead of the common ownership of channel components that characterizes the corporate VMS or the relative power relationships of an administered system, the contractual VMS is characterized by formal agreements between channel members. In practice there are three types of agreements: the wholesaler-sponsored voluntary chain, the retail co-operative, and the franchise.[16]

### Wholesaler-sponsored voluntary chain

The wholesaler-sponsored voluntary chain represents an attempt by the independent wholesaler to preserve a market for the firm's products through the strengthening of the firm's retailer customers. In order to enable the independent retailers to compete with the chains, the wholesaler enters into a formal agreement with a group of retailers whereby the retailers agree to use a common name, have standardized facilities, and purchase the wholesaler's products. The wholesaler often develops a line of private brands to be stocked by the members of the voluntary chain. A common store name and similar inventories allow the retailers to achieve cost savings on advertising, since a single newspaper advertisement promotes all retailers in the trading area. IGA, with a membership of approximately 800 food stores, is a good example of a voluntary chain.

*Harvey's is a well-known franchise in the fast-food sector. A customer entering any Harvey's franchise can expect the same level of product quality and service even though the stores are run by different owners. These franchise owners benefit from the unique marketing strategies that promote Harvey's hamburgers and other products.*

### Retail co-operatives

A second type of contractual VMS is the retail co-operative, which is established by a group of retailers who set up a wholesaling operation to compete better with the chains. A group of retailers purchase shares of stock in a wholesaling operation and agree to purchase a minimum percentage of their inventory from the firm. The members may also choose to use a common store name, such as Home Hardware, and develop their own private brands in order to carry out co-operative advertising.

Buying groups like wholesaler-sponsored chains and retail co-operatives are not a new phenomenon in the Canadian distribution industry. They date back at least 50 years, some having evolved from the co-operative movement of the early years of the century. Under the Combines Investigation Act, suppliers may charge different prices for different volumes of purchases, so long as these prices are available to all competing purchasers of articles of like quantity and quality. And suppliers have done so; it is common practice to offer volume rebates. Thus buying groups improved the small retailers' bargaining position with their suppliers, thus increasing competition for their large rivals.

In some cases, buying groups have failed because of difficulties with organization and management. In others, the buying group concept has worked very well, with some groups now as large as the chains. The chains themselves have now formed their own buying groups. Recently, five of these large buying groups in the food industry represented some 14 000 stores, and accounted for about 85 percent of all retail food sales in Canada. This development leads to the concern that while buying groups may improve the balance of market power in some areas, there is a possibility of abuse of power in others.[17]

## Franchising

A third type of contractual VMS is the **franchise**. A franchise is *an agreement whereby dealers (franchisees) agree to meet the operating requirements of a manufacturer or other franchiser*. The dealer typically receives a variety of marketing, management, technical, and financial services in exchange for a specified fee.

**franchise** An agreement whereby dealers (franchisees) agree to meet the operating requirements of a manufacturer or other franchiser.

Although franchising attracted considerable interest beginning in the late 1960s, the concept actually began 100 years earlier when the Singer Company established franchised sewing machine outlets. Early impetus for the franchising concept came after 1900 in the automobile industry.[18] The soft-drink industry is another example of franchising, but in this case the contractual arrangement is between the syrup manufacturer and the wholesaler bottler.

The franchising form that created most of the excitement both in retailing and on Wall Street in the late 1960s was the retailer franchise system sponsored by the service firm.[19] McDonald's Corporation is an excellent example of such a franchise operation. McDonald's brought together suppliers and a chain of hamburger outlets. It provided a proven system of retail operation (the operations manual for each outlet weighs over a kilogram) with a standardized product and ingenious promotional campaigns. This enabled prices to be offered through the franchiser's purchasing power on meat, buns, potatoes, napkins, and other supplies. In return the franchisee pays a fee for the use of the name (over $150 000 for McDonald's) and a percentage of gross sales. Other familiar examples include Hertz, Avis, Kentucky Fried Chicken, Pizza Hut, and Weight Watchers.

McDonald's has several stores in operation in every major centre and has expanded its menu to include such items as Egg McMuffin, hotcakes, scrambled eggs, and McChicken. These efforts are aimed at obtaining even more of the millions of dollars Canadians spend annually in restaurants.

Fast-food franchising has already proven itself in the international market. In Tokyo, London, Rome, Paris, and Moscow, McDonald's hamburgers are consumed daily. Kentucky Fried Chicken has opened nearly 500 restaurants in Canada and in such locations as Manila and Munich, Nice and Nairobi. In some countries adjustments to the North American marketing plans have been made to match local needs. Although their menu is rigidly standardized in Canada, McDonald's executives approved changes to the menu in outlets in France. Kentucky Fried chicken replaced french fries with mashed potatoes to satisfy their Japanese customers.[20]

Although many franchises are profitable, the infatuation with the franchising concept and the market performance of franchise stocks have lured dozens of newcomers into the market who have failed. Lacking experience and often with a well-known celebrity's name as their sole asset, many of these firms have disappeared almost as quickly as they entered the market.[21]

The median investment for a franchise varies tremendously from one business area to another. A pet-sitting franchise might sell for as low as $9500, whereas a restaurant franchise will likely average over $250 000. The great bulk of the nation's franchises are in the "traditional" franchise areas such as auto dealers, service stations, and soft-drink bottlers. Figure 14–6 shows the proportion of sales accounted for by the various franchise categories.

Despite the many franchise opportunities available, there are few specific regulations with respect to the proper disclosure of information to prospective franchisees. It is worthwhile to evaluate the opportunity carefully before investing.

VMS — whether in the form of corporate, administered, or contractual systems — are already becoming a dominant factor in the consumer goods sector of the

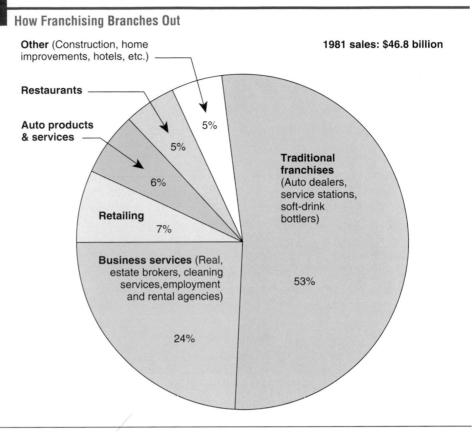

FIGURE 14 – 6

**How Franchising Branches Out**

**Other** (Construction, home improvements, hotels, etc.)

**Restaurants**

**Auto products & services**

**Retailing**

**1981 sales: $46.8 billion**

5%

5%

6%

7%

**Traditional franchises** (Auto dealers, service stations, soft-drink bottlers)

53%

**Business services** (Real, estate brokers, cleaning services,employment and rental agencies)

24%

Source: *The Financial Post Report on Franchising* (October 8, 1983), p. S1, from information provided by Statistics Canada, Merchandising & Services Division.

Canadian economy. Over 60 percent of the available market is currently in the hands of retail components of VMS.

Leadership and co-operation in the marketing channel are necessary for the successful implementation of marketing strategy. Channel leadership is a function of one's power within the distribution channel, and the most powerful often becomes the dominant and controlling member of the channel — the *channel captain*. Historically, the role of channel captain belonged to the manufacturer or wholesaler, since retailers tended to be both small and locally oriented. However, retailers are increasingly taking on the role of channel captain as large retail chains assume traditional wholesaling functions and even dictate product design specifications to the manufacturer.

Distribution channels must be organized and regarded as a systematic co-operative effort if operating efficiencies are to be achieved. In a sense, the forward-thinking organizations are those that form strategic alliances between channel members in order to take advantage of the competitive attributes each possesses. These alliances include direct channel participants as well as facilitating agencies such as transportation companies, legal organizations, and the like. No longer is it likely that completely independent channel players will dominate the competition in globally oriented industries. Organization and co-operation between independent entities within the channel is a must today.

Co-operation and mutual understanding based on enlightened self-interest are far from the reality of channel relations, according to numerous authors. Instead, many channel relationships are marked by intense rivalry and conflict. *Channel conflict* can evolve from a number of sources:

> A manufacturer may wish to promote a product in one manner...while his retailers oppose this. Another manufacturer may wish to get information from his retailers on a certain aspect relating to his product, but his retailers may refuse to provide this information. A producer may want to distribute his product extensively, but his retailers may demand exclusives. A supplier may force a product onto its retailers, who dare not oppose, but who retaliate in other ways, such as using it as a loss leader. Large manufacturers may try to dictate the resale price of their merchandise; this may be less or more than the price at which the retailers wish to sell it. Occasionally a local market may be more competitive for a retailer than is true nationally. The manufacturer may not recognize the difference in competition and refuse to help this channel member. There is also conflict because of the desire of both manufacturers and retailers to eliminate the wholesaler.[22]

## Summary

Distribution channels refer to the various marketing institutions and the interrelationships responsible for the physical and title flow of goods and services from producer to consumer or industrial user. Wholesaling and retailing intermediaries (or middlemen) are the marketing institutions in the distribution channel.

Distribution channels bridge the gap between producer and consumer. By making products and services available when and where the consumer wants to buy, and by arranging for transfer of title, marketing channels create time, place, and ownership utility. Marketing channels indirectly add to the creation of form utility through the provision of information regarding consumer preferences.

Physical distribution functions are performed throughout the channel by each of the participants. They include numerous activities, such as establishing customer service standards, transporting products, order processing, inventory control, materials handling, and warehousing.

Total Quality Management is a philosophy that has taken root in North American industry. The customers' preferences serve as the core of this philosophy. They inform management within each unit of the organization of the decisions that need to be made in order to produce and distribute products that are compatible with these preferences. The marketing channel is an important component of the TQM concept, since form, time, place, and ownership utility are affected by channel member performance.

Distribution channels also perform such specific functions as (1) facilitating the exchange process; (2) sorting to alleviate discrepancies in assortment; (3) standardizing the transaction; (4) holding inventories; and (5) accommodating the search process.

A host of alternative distribution channels are available for makers of consumer products, industrial products, and services. They range from contacting the consumer or industrial user directly to using a variety of intermediaries. Multiple channels are also increasingly commonplace today. A unique distribution system — the reverse channel — is used in recycling, product recalls, and in some service situations.

Channel leadership is primarily a matter of relative power within the channel. The channel leader that emerges is called the channel captain.

Basic channel strategy decisions involve channel selection, the level of distribution intensity, and the use of vertical marketing systems. The selection of a distribution channel is based on market, product, producer, and competitive factors. The decision on distribution intensity involves choosing from among intensive distribution, selective distribution, or exclusive distribution. The issue of vertical marketing systems also has to be explored by the marketing manager. There are three major types of vertical marketing systems: corporate, administered, and contractual, this third including wholesaler-sponsored chains, retail co-operatives, and franchises.

## KEY TERMS

| | | |
|---|---|---|
| TQM | physical distribution | exclusive distribution |
| distribution channel | common carrier | exclusive dealing |
| marketing intermediaries | contract carrier | tied selling |
| wholesaling | EOQ | market restriction |
| retailer | JIT | vertical marketing systems |
| sorting | unitization | (VMS) |
| agent | containerization | franchise |
| industrial distributor | break-bulk warehouse | channel captain |
| reverse channels | intensive distribution | channel conflict |
| facilitating agencies | selective distribution | |

## REVIEW QUESTIONS

1. What types of products are most likely to be distributed through direct channels?
2. Which marketing channel is the traditional channel? Give some reasons for its frequent use.
3. Why would manufacturers choose more than one channel for their products?
4. What role does the marketing channel play in the application of the Total Quality Management (TQM) concept?
5. Distinguish between common, contract, and private legal forms of transportation.
6. What is the basic idea behind a Just-In-Time inventory system?
7. Why would any manufacturer deliberately choose to limit market coverage through a policy of exclusive coverage?
8. Explain and illustrate each type of vertical marketing system.
9. What advantages does franchising offer the small retailer?
10. In what ways could the use of multiple channels produce channel conflict?

## DISCUSSION QUESTIONS AND EXERCISES

1. Chipwich, an ice cream and chocolate-chip cookie snack, is marketed via vendor carts as well as supermarkets. Relate Chipwich's distribution strategy to the material presented in this chapter.
2. Which degree of distribution intensity is appropriate for each of the following:
   a. *Maclean's*
   b. Catalina swimwear
   c. Irish Spring soap
   d. Johnson outboard motors

e. Cuisinart food processors

f. Kawasaki motorcycles

g. Waterford crystal

3. Outline the distribution channels used by a local firm. Why were these particular channels selected by the company?

4. Prepare a brief report on the dealer requirements for a franchise that has units in your area.

5. One generalization of channel selection mentioned in the chapter was that low unit value products require long channels. How can you explain the success of a firm (such as Avon) that has a direct channel for its relatively low unit value products?

6. Discuss the inherent advantages of each of the five modes of transportation discussed in the text. What products would likely be transported by each mode?

# MICROCOMPUTER EXERCISE
## Decision Tree Analysis

A useful method for making decisions in an uncertain marketing environment is *decision tree analysis*. This is a quantitative technique used in identifying alternative courses of action, assigning probability estimates for the profits or sales associated with each alternative, and indicating the course of action with the highest profit or sales. In order to use this the marketer must be able to estimate the likelihood of occurrence of each alternative. In addition, he or she must assign financial payoffs (sales, profits, or losses) for the various alternative courses of action.

The following example illustrates how decision tree analysis works. A Montreal-based firm is in the process of choosing one of two possible wholesalers to distribute its Christmas novelty items. A marketing research consultant retained by the firm has prepared both a best-case and worst-case forecast for each wholesaler. The researcher estimates a probability of 50/50 for occurrence of the "best" and "worst" cases. The potential sales volumes for the two wholesalers are shown in Table A.

The problem can be illustrated as a type of decision tree lying on its side, as shown in Table B. Each branch represents a different possible course of action. In this example, the expected revenue from a decision to use the first wholesaler in the firm's distribution channel is $2.5 million. This determination is made by first multiplying expected revenue from the occurrence of the "best case" forecast by the .5 probability of such a forecast being realized. Next the expected revenue is multiplied by the .5 probability that the "worst case" forecast will occur. Finally, the expected values of the two outcomes are combined for a total of $2.5 million ($1.5 million plus $1 million). A similar series of calculations is made for the possible use of the second wholesaler, producing a total expected revenue of $3 million.

# TABLE A

| Forecast | First Wholesaler | Second Wholesaler |
|---|---|---|
| Best Case | $3 million | $5 million |
| Worst Case | $2 million | $1 million |

■ T A B L E   B

| Decision to Analyze | Courses of Action | Possible Outcomes | Expected Revenue or Profit |
|---|---|---|---|
| | Yes | "Best Case" Occurs | .5(3 000 000) = 1 500 000 |
| | | No "Best Case" Occurs | .5(2 000 000) = 1 000 000 |
| | | | $2 500 000 |
| Use the First Wholesaler? | No | "Best Case" Occurs | .5(5 000 000) = 2 500 000 |
| | | No "Best Case" Occurs | .5(1 000 000) = 500 000 |
| | | | $3 000 000 |

In this example, the decision to utilize the second wholesaler as a component of the firm's distribution channel produces a slightly larger net expected value of revenues. Unless the firm's marketers feel that the data being used in the forecast are incorrect, they should begin serious negotiations with the second wholesaler.

**Directions:** Use the Menu Item titled "Decision Tree Analysis" on the *Foundations of Marketing* disk to solve each of the following problems.

1. A consumer-goods company headquartered in Mississauga, Ont., believes that it can increase its current $60 million annual sales volume to as much as $73 million if it replaces its current selective distribution with a strategy of intensive distribution. While the firm's vice-president of marketing believes that the probability of such a sales increase is only 30 percent, she is also convinced that no possibility exists for sales to fall below $60 million if the firm converts to an intensive distribution. If the firm elects to continue its selective distribution, there is a 90/90 chance that sales will rise to $65 million. Recommend a course of action for the firm, based upon the decision tree analysis model.

2. A Regina firm with $20 million in annual sales is considering bypassing its independent wholesaling intermediaries and setting up its own retail outlets. If the new distribution arrangement is successful, the firm's management estimates that next year's sales will increase to $23 million. The likelihood of sucess is calculated to be 60 percent. Management estimates that sales will decline to $17 million if the new distribution system is unsuccessful. If the firm chooses to continue its current distribution channel, sales volume is given a 60/90 chance to remain at $20 million and a 40/90 chance to drop to $19 million. Should the Regina firm set up its own retail outlets?

3. A Kingston-based industrial-supplies firm is seriously considering the replacement of its current network of industrial distribution with its own sales force. The firm's marketing vice-president believes that the establishment of a quality sales force could increase next year's sales to $50 million — $10 million more than the "best case" scenario of $40 million in sales expected under the current distribu-

tion system. In addition, he feels that this sales increase can be achieved with no increase in selling costs. But the vice-president also believes that the conversion to a new distribution channel could cause next year's sales to decline to $20 million unless the firm is successful in attracting, training, and motivating high-quality sales representatives. This compares to $35 million that he feels is the minimum the current system will provide. Since management is confident of its ability to create an effective selling organization, it assigns a 70-percent probability of success for the new sales force. If the current system is retained, management projects a 50 percent probability of earning $40 million in sales and an equal probability of dropping to $35 million. Use the decision tree analysis to suggest a course of action for the firm.

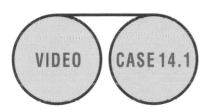

# VIDEO  CASE 14.1     Famous Amos

Today many people recognize Wally "Famous" Amos, the man who gave his name to the original gourmet cookie. The company founded by Amos has achieved virtual nationwide distribution of several flavours of its cookies in stores, and has scattered retail stores worldwide, with franchises in Japan, Australia, and Canada, as well as the United States.

In 1975, Wally Amos was just another talent agent trying to succeed in Hollywood. However, he soon developed another calling. Friends told him that the cookies he made were so good that he should sell them, and eventually Amos took their advice. Some of these friends backed up their advice by investing $25 000 in his venture, the Famous Amos Chocolate Chip Cookie Company, and the world's first gourmet cookie shop opened in 1975. It was an instant success. By 1981, sales had reached $7 million, and grew to $10 million in 1985.

News of Famous Amos spread by word of mouth, and in a classic example of pull-through demand, consumers would walk into stores and ask the owners why they did not stock Famous Amos cookies. The company relied solely on this informal sort of marketing for its first five years.

When Amos started his company, he had made no plans for such growth. His first retail "hot bake" shop appeared to be earning a profit and, after all, in his words, "All I wanted to do was make a living." Consumer demand grew and requests began to pour in from other areas, but Amos did not have the funds to expand his cookie shop concept into a chain. He also wanted to avoid the risk of expanding through borrowing funds. Then the idea struck him — just as it had McDonald's Ray Kroc 20 years earlier: franchising. The firm distributed its frozen dough directly to the franchised "hot bake" shops located in suburban shopping centres and downtown walk-in locations.

Amos also used other distribution alternatives to get the cookies into supermarkets, convenience outlets, "mom-and-pop" stores, and gift shops that make up the Famous Amos market, by contracting with an independent wholesale distributor. This distribution channel saved the company the cost of starting its own network, while giving it access to an already established distribution system, without which the young company might have failed. Even though many store owners were unhappy about doing business with products offering such a low markup, consumer demand was so strong that retailer complaints soon fell to a trickle and distribution became more widespread.

Famous Amos has tailored its cookies to its markets. Frozen dough is shipped directly to the firm's franchised "hot bake" shops. For supermarkets, it offers several different sizes of cookies, and sets up racks for the packages in the fresh baked goods section, rather than on the cookie shelf. For convenience stores, one- and two-ounce bags were created to save space and to encourage impulse sales. It now makes several flavours of cookies (oatmeal-based cookies are the nation's best sellers), and in its retail stores, it has soft cookies available.

Demand was created in part by the cookie's taste. The gourmet cookie shop concept was entirely novel, and to outlast the novelty, Famous Amos cookies had to be good. But while consumers like the taste of the cookies (a recent *Consumer Report* test rated Famous Amos's chocolate chip cookies one of the best-tasting brands available), much of the success of Famous Amos is based on effective personal marketing. Wally Amos's winning grin gleams from each package of Famous Amos cookies, and his presence seems to give the cookies an identity that its competitors lack. John Rosica, a public relations executive with the company, called Wally "a perpetual promotion." In recognition of his role in the company's success, the Smithsonian's Collection of Advertising History includes his Panama hat and brightly-patterned Indian gauze shirt.

By the late 1980s interest in the gourmet cookie had waned, so that only a few locations could support bake shops devoted exclusively to cookies. Famous Amos decided to change its placement from gourmet cookie to high-quality family cookie. Package sizes were changed from 2 ½-, 7-, and 16-ounce packages to a 12-ounce size for wholesale distribution to grocery store outlets and a 30-ounce size for food-club stores. A 2-ounce package was also developed to be sold through vending machines. As of 1991 there were only a few bake shop franchises operating fifteen stores, and Famous Amos was restricting itself to making finished cookies.

Even though Amos sold his ownership interest in the firm in 1985, Famous Amos continues to rely solely on promotions that feature Wally. Among the most successful promotions have been its efforts at cause marketing. The company worked in conjunction with literacy councils in several cities, having stores contribute a percentage of profits to literacy programs. Such promotions resulted in greatly increased sales, including a 38 percent sales jump in Philadelphia.

## Questions

1. What distribution channels are used in the marketing of Famous Amos cookies? Draw each channel and label all components.

2. What changes would be made in the chart in Question 1 to reflect the distribution channels existing in the mid-1980s, before the decline of the gourmet cookie concept?

3. Explain the impact of Famous Amos's channel strategy on the firm's growth. How should his strategy be adapted to achieve continued growth?

4. Although Famous Amos has largely ignored mass-market promotions, the firm recently began advertising on television. Explain how such promotion aids the firm's distribution strategy.

SOURCES    Michael King, "To Sell or Not to Sell..." *Black Enterprise* (June 1987), pp. 287–290; Gail Buchetter, "Happy Cookie," *Forbes* (March 10, 1986), pp. 176–178; *Consumer Reports* (February 1985), pp. 69–72; Keith Lively of Famous Amos, [update interview] May 1991.

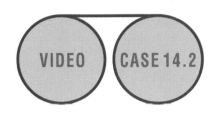

# Arrowhead Drinking Water Co.

Bottled water got a big boost in the late 1970s when the importers of Perrier launched a $4-million advertising campaign promoting their sparkling spring water as an alternative to soft drinks and alcoholic beverages. The campaign spoke to a receptive audience — a growing number of health-conscious and fitness-minded North Americans concerned about water pollution and purity, and showing a preference for low-calorie, alcohol-free beverages.

The advertising blitz not only helped Perrier become the market leader in bottled water sales; it also fuelled an explosive growth in the industry, as other bottled water marketers began aggressively promoting their mineral water, club soda, seltzer, and sparkling water. The market responded by buying bottled water in record numbers.

Today the bottled water market is the fastest growing segment of the beverage business. According to the Beverage Marketing Corporation, bottled water sales grew 15 percent each year from 1983 to 1986, and then continued to grow at an annual rate of 10 percent. The bottled water market's growth during the past decade has attracted competitors such as PepsiCo and other national soft-drink, beer, and spirits marketers. Perrier, eager to maintain its market leadership and increase its market share, acquired Arrowhead Drinking Water Co. from Beatrice Foods in 1987. The acquisition not only doubled Perrier's market share to 21 percent, it also broadened the firm's presence in the nonsparkling water market.

Arrowhead, based in Monterey Park, California, is a major regional distributor of jug water. Jug water is marketed primarily as a substitute for tap water through two channels: through supermarkets in 1 and 2.5-gallon containers, and delivered directly to consumers in 5-gallon bottles for their water coolers. Though jug water lacks the sparkle of its specialty counterparts, it accounts for the lion's share — 77 percent — of all U.S. bottled water sales. In 1985, Arrowhead entered the sparkling water market by introducing Arrowhead Springs Sparkling Water in 1.5-liter bottles and six-packs of 10-ounce bottles. A year later, the company extended the line by adding Ozarka Sparkling Water.

Perrier's marketing success can be attributed to its promotional efforts, but Arrowhead's accomplishments as a bottled water marketer are tied mainly to a superior product and an efficient distribution system that brings mountain spring water to customers' homes and offices and to supermarkets in Arizona, California, Hawaii, and Nevada.

Arrowhead's beginnings date to the early 1800s when David Smith built a health spa at Arrowhead Springs. Visitors flocked there to bathe in — and drink — the supposedly restorative mineral water. As customer demand for the drinking water increased, Smith began piping water down the mountainside and, in 1905, started bottling it in the basement of the spa's hotel and shipping it to customers.

Today, Arrowhead gathers water from seven springs in the San Bernardino Mountains. From these sources, water flows through 7-mile pipelines to storage reservoirs, where it is loaded by gravity within 25 minutes into 64 000-gallon-capacity tanker trucks that transport it to Arrowhead's bottling plant. The tankers operate 24 hours a day, seven days a week. While alternative methods such as railroad and pipeline have been tried, trucks have proven to be the most efficient way to transport the water supply needed to satisfy Arrowhead's customer demand.

At the bottling plant, water is pumped through several filtration stages to produce three different products: spring, distilled, and fluoridated water. In a computer-controlled bottling room, sanitized bottles are rapidly filled and capped. Five-gallon bottles are individually crated, while smaller containers are packed in boxes. Boxes and crates are unitized to ensure that forklift operators can move them safely and efficiently from the production line to the warehouse or delivery yard.

Arrowhead generates most of its sales from the delivery of 5-gallon water bottles directly to consumers. Satisfying these customers is the firm's top priority, and Arrowhead's route salespeople do more than deliver water. They are responsible for soliciting new business and completely servicing existing accounts. They control their own truck inventory and make daily adjustments to accommodate last-minute customer requests, collect money, update orders, and balance their books. Route salespeople receive support from telephone operators in the order processing department who answer customer inquiries, transmit called-in orders, and set up delivery schedules. Because deliveries are scheduled at 14-day intervals, route salespeople must ensure that each delivery will satisfy a two-week demand. "The route salesperson is really the backbone of the company," says Larry Fried, director of marketing. "If it weren't for the route salespeople, Arrowhead wouldn't even exist. They're the most important part of the company."

Since home delivery involves high transportation and labour costs, it takes up a large part of Arrowhead's expense budget. To contain delivery costs, Arrowhead marketers chose a different approach for grocery-store customers. Rather than investing in a fleet of delivery trucks, Arrowhead offers the grocery trade a freight allowance as an incentive for retailers to pick up products at Arrowhead's warehouse.

To compete profitably with other bottled water companies and municipal water systems and yet maintain its high level of customer service, Arrowhead marketers strive for operating efficiency in inventory control, materials handling, packaging and warehousing. Marketers plan for inventory needs by preparing detailed 1-, 5-, and 10-year forecasts of consumer demand, which enable them to estimate the type of water and number of bottles that will be needed. These estimates assist planners in the purchase of bottles, containers, boxes, crates, and other operating equipment and supplies, and in determining future warehousing needs.

Arrowhead marketers balance their large capital investment expenses by maintaining a minimum inventory of 5-gallon bottles. Bill Lindop, manager of production operations, states that the inventory plan operates on the principle of one day for empty bottles to be filled, one day for full bottles on the route trucks to be delivered, and a quarter to a half day for bottles on hand as backup. To the extent possible, bottles are taken directly from the production line and loaded on delivery trucks to avoid double handling.

Because the production process for the bottled water sold to supermarkets is slower than that for the 5-gallon bottles, these products are warehoused to ensure that enough is available when the retailers need them. To balance production output with retail demand, Arrowhead marketers try to maintain a three- to four-day supply of 1- and 2.5-gallon bottles and several weeks' supply of sparkling water. They move inventory on a first-in, first-out basis to keep the product as fresh as possible on supermarket shelves. They also encourage retailers to keep their own backroom inventories of high-volume drinking water to meet customer demand.

As Arrowhead's distribution requirements have increased through the years, so have their costs for loading and unloading delivery trucks — a process that originally required route salespeople to stay with their trucks during the one to one and a half hours of loading. To reduce loading expenses, Arrowhead marketers asked their engineers to develop a more cost-efficient system. They designed a straddle trailer that moves hundreds of bottles at one time. "With the straddle trailer, it's a 15-minute turnaround time," says Lindop, "so you're saving between an hour and an hour and 15 minutes, not only of the drivers' time, but the capital investment on the equipment that you can keep on the road, which is about $150 000 worth of equipment."

In making packaging decisions, Arrowhead marketers consider production-line efficiency as well as the rate of product turnover. All aspects of marketing home-delivered bottled water are geared to the 5-gallon size — the industry standard since the turn of the century. Changes in bottle size would involve millions of dollars of new production equipment. Without changing the size, Arrowhead has significantly improved 5-gallon productivity by changing from a 14-pound glass bottle to a 3-pound polycarbonate bottle. With the lighter bottle, route salespeople carry one ton less a day in weight and have fewer lifting-related injuries, while delivery trucks get much better gas mileage.

When Arrowhead introduced its sparkling water, marketers decided to package the 1.5-litre plastic bottles in 8 bottle cases, even though the industry standard for sparkling water in glass bottles was 12 per case. Their decision, which took into account the advice of industry suppliers and other experts, was based on providing the best distribution economies throughout the system.

## Questions

1. Arrowhead marketers use multiple distribution channels in reaching the firm's customers. Draw a diagram of each channel used and label each part.

2. Relate each of the components of the physical distribution system to the way that Arrowhead provides mountain spring water to customers.

3. What are Arrowhead's physical distribution objectives? Identify several possible sources for suboptimization to occur and explain how the total cost approach is used by Arrowhead marketers to avoid the occurrence of suboptimization.

4. Which transportation factors discussed in the chapter might have affected Arrowhead's decision to switch from the use of railroad cars to trucks in transporting water from its source to the bottling plant?

5. Which of Arrowhead's marketing decisions have improved the effectiveness and efficiency of the firm's physical distribution system?

SOURCES    Beverage Marketing Corp., *1987 Annual Industry Survey*; Marcy Magiera, "Bottled Waters Spring Up," *Advertising Age* (September 21, 1987), pp. 24, 83; "Water, Water Everywhere," *Consumer Reports* (January 1987), pp. 42–47; Larry Wilarski of Arrowhead Drinking Water Co., [update interview] May 1991.

C H A P T E R   15

# Wholesaling

## CHAPTER OBJECTIVES

1. To relate wholesaling to the other variables of the marketing mix.
2. To identify the functions performed by wholesaling intermediaries.
3. To explain the channel options available to a manufacturer who wants to bypass independent wholesaling intermediaries.
4. To identify the conditions under which a manufacturer is likely to assume wholesaling functions rather than use independents.
5. To distinguish between merchant wholesalers and agents and brokers.
6. To identify the major types of merchant wholesalers and instances where each type might be used.
7. To describe the major types of agents and brokers.

**A** NEW Winnipeg wholesale operation has arisen from the ashes of Merchant's Consolidated Ltd. Merchant's had been placed into receivership 10 months previously.

Joe Profeta, Ron Block, and Gordon Muth — former Merchant's managers — decided to resurrect the Carry 'N Save division. Like its predecessor, Independent Wholesale Inc.'s Carry 'N Save Division supplies groceries, sporting goods, and building and hardware products to independent retailers.

Profeta and his partners believe Independent Wholesale can fill the void that was created when Merchant's was forced to close its doors. "There is a big need for this," he added. "That's why we're here."

He explained that hundreds of smaller, independent retailers across Canada — operations like small-town grocery, hardware, general, and sporting goods stores — depended on Merchant's to supply them with products. When Merchant's went under, many of its regular customers were forced to order their supplies from Eastern Canadian–based distributors. "That meant long delays in getting their shipments, as well as added freight costs," he said.

"Others were unable to find new suppliers," he added. "Most of those companies in Eastern Canada want large-volume accounts. If you are a small account they don't want to bother with you. But that won't happen with Independent Wholesale," he added. "We'll sell to any organization or retailer that has a sales tax number. We're going to look after the little guy. Also the in-between guy and the big guy."

Profeta said what Independent Wholesale will strive to offer is "service, selection, and value." Retailers will have the option of buying their supplies by the single unit or by the case, he said. And they can either pick up their order or, if it's a larger order, Independent will deliver it.[1]

The demise of Merchant's and the rise of Independent Wholesale illustrate some key ideas about wholesaling. First, wholesaling is a large and important business sector that most people are relatively unaware of. Second, wholesaling performs an essential function. Without a wholesaler, it is actually impossible for some smaller retailers to obtain merchandise to sell. Third, the delivery function applies only to larger orders, even at the wholesale level. There is a large cash-and-carry trade with smaller retailers.

## Introduction

Wholesaling is the initial marketing institution in most channels of distribution from manufacturers to consumer or industrial user. Chapter 14 introduced the basic concepts of channel strategy, primarily from the manufacturer's viewpoint. Attention now shifts to the institutions within the distribution channel.

Wholesaling intermediaries are a critical element of the marketing mixes of many products, but many intermediaries are also separate business entities with their own marketing mixes. A good starting point for the discussion is to look at the terminology used in wholesaling.

## Wholesaling Activities

**wholesalers**    Wholesaling intermediaries who take title to the products they handle.

**wholesaling intermediaries**    Intermediaries who assume title, as well as agents and brokers who perform important wholesaling activities without taking title to the products.

Wholesaling involves the activities of persons or firms who sell to retailers and other wholesalers or to industrial users, but not in significant amounts to ultimate consumers. The term **wholesaler** (or merchant intermediary) is applied only to *those wholesaling intermediaries who take title to the products they handle*. **Wholesaling intermediaries** (or wholesaling middlemen) is a broader term that describes not only *intermediaries who assume title*, but also *agents and brokers who perform important wholesaling activities without taking title to the products*. Under this definition, then, a wholesaler is a *merchant intermediary*.

## Wholesaling Functions

The route that goods follow on the way to the consumer or industrial user is actually a chain of marketing institutions — wholesalers and retailers. Only 3 percent of the dollar value of all goods sold to the ultimate consumer is purchased directly from the manufacturer. The bulk of all products sold passes through these marketing institutions.

An increasing number of consumer complaints about high prices is heard each year. The finger of guilt is often pointed at wholesalers and retailers, the intermediaries who allegedly drive prices up by taking "high profits." Discount stores often advertise that their prices are lower since they buy direct and eliminate the intermediaries and their profits. Chain stores often assume wholesaling functions and bypass the independent wholesalers.

Are these complaints and claims valid? Are wholesaling intermediaries anachronisms doomed to a swift demise? Answers to these questions can be formulated by considering the functions and costs of these marketing intermediaries.

## Wholesaling Intermediaries Provide a Variety of Services

A marketing institution will continue to exist only so long as it fulfills a need by performing a required service. Its death may be slow, but it is inevitable if other channel members discover that they can survive without it. Figure 15–1 examines a number of possible services provided by wholesaling intermediaries. It is important to note that numerous types of wholesaling intermediaries exist and that not all of them provide every service listed in Figure 15–1. Producers–suppliers and their customers, who rely on wholesaling intermediaries for distribution, select those intermediaries providing the desired combination of services.

The list of possible services provided by wholesaling intermediaries clearly indicates the provision of marketing utility — time, place, and ownership — by these intermediaries. The services also reflect the provision of the basic marketing functions of buying, selling, storing, transportation, risk-taking, financing, and market information.

The critical marketing functions — transportation and convenient product storage; reduced costs of buying and selling through reduced contacts; market information; and financing — form the basis of evaluating the efficiency of any marketing intermediary. The risk-taking function is present in each of the services provided by the wholesaling intermediary.

*Transportation and product storage*   Wholesalers transport and store products at locations convenient to customers. Manufacturers ship products from their warehouses to numerous wholesalers, who then ship smaller quantities to retail outlets convenient to the purchaser. A large number of wholesalers and most retailers assume the inventory function (and cost) for the manufacturer. The retailer benefits through the convenience afforded by local inventories, and the manufacturer's cash needs are reduced since the firm's products are sold directly to the wholesaler or retailer.

At the wholesale level, costs are reduced through making large purchases from the manufacturer. The wholesaler receives quantity discounts from the manufacturer — along with reduced transportation rates, since economical carload or truckload shipments are made to the wholesaler's warehouses. At the warehouse the wholesaler breaks bulk into smaller quantities and ships to the retailer over a shorter distance than would be the case if the manufacturer filled the retailer's order directly from a central warehouse.

*The advantages of product storage for both the manufacturer and the retailer are evident in this wholesale mattress warehouse. A retail furniture outlet can purchase a few mattresses from a local warehouse like this on a regular basis, without having to pay for extra storage space. The wholesaler may assume the inventory function for the manufacturer, making it well worth the latter's while to sell to wholesalers.*

*Cost reductions*   Costs are often lowered when intermediaries are used, since the sales force of the retailer or wholesaler can represent many manufacturers to a single customer. As Figure 15–2 indicates, the number of transactions between manufacturers and their customers are markedly reduced through the introduction of an intermediary (a wholesaler or retailer). Reduced market contacts can lead to lowered marketing costs. When a wholesaling intermediary is added, the number of transactions in this illustration is reduced from 16 to 8, thereby creating economies of scale by providing an assortment of goods with greater utility and at lower cost than without such an intermediary.

*Information*   Because of their central position between the manufacturer and retailers or industrial buyers, wholesalers serve as important information links. Wholesalers provide their retail customers with useful information about new products. They also supply manufacturers with information concerning market reception of their product offerings.

*Financing*   Wholesalers provide a financing function as well. Wholesalers often provide retailers with goods on credit. By purchasing products on credit, retailers can minimize their cash investments in inventory and pay for most of their purchases as the goods are being sold. This allows them to benefit from the principle of *leverage*; a minimum investment inflates their return on investment. A retailer with an investment of $1 million and profits of $100 000 will realize a return on investment (ROI) of 10 percent. But if the necessary invested capital can be reduced to $800 000 through credit from the wholesaler, and if the $100 000 profits can be maintained, the retailer's ROI increases to 12.5 percent.

FIGURE 15-1

**Possible Wholesaling Services for Customers and Producers–Suppliers**

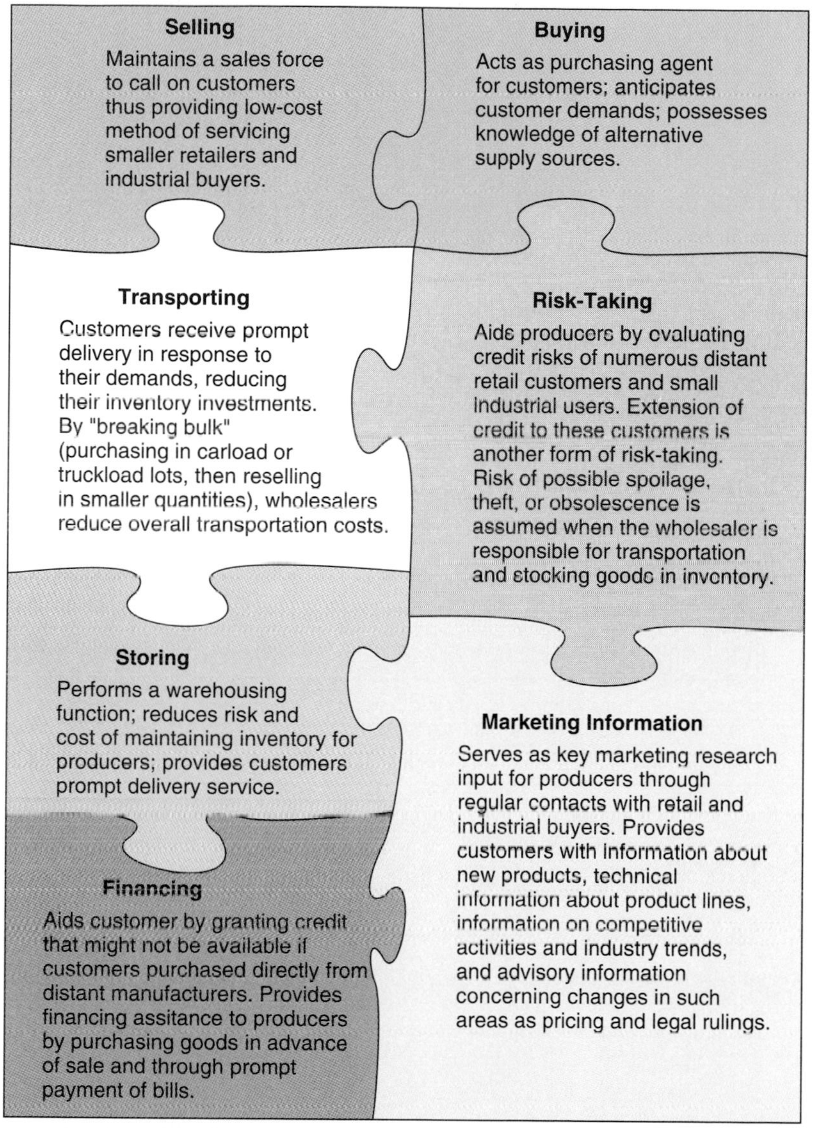

**Selling**

Maintains a sales force to call on customers thus providing low-cost method of servicing smaller retailers and industrial buyers.

**Buying**

Acts as purchasing agent for customers; anticipates customer demands; possesses knowledge of alternative supply sources.

**Transporting**

Customers receive prompt delivery in response to their demands, reducing their inventory investments. By "breaking bulk" (purchasing in carload or truckload lots, then reselling in smaller quantities), wholesalers reduce overall transportation costs.

**Risk-Taking**

Aids producers by evaluating credit risks of numerous distant retail customers and small industrial users. Extension of credit to these customers is another form of risk-taking. Risk of possible spoilage, theft, or obsolescence is assumed when the wholesaler is responsible for transportation and stocking goods in inventory.

**Storing**

Performs a warehousing function; reduces risk and cost of maintaining inventory for producers; provides customers prompt delivery service.

**Marketing Information**

Serves as key marketing research input for producers through regular contacts with retail and industrial buyers. Provides customers with information about new products, technical information about product lines, information on competitive activities and industry trends, and advisory information concerning changes in such areas as pricing and legal rulings.

**Financing**

Aids customer by granting credit that might not be available if customers purchased directly from distant manufacturers. Provides financing assitance to producers by purchasing goods in advance of sale and through prompt payment of bills.

Wholesalers of industrial goods provide similar services for the purchasers of their goods. In the steel industry, intermediaries called metal service centres currently market approximately one-fifth of the steel shipped by Canadian mills. Such a centre may stock as many as 6500 items for sale to many of the thousands of major metal users who buy their heavy-usage items in large quantities directly from the steel mills, but who turn to service centres for quick delivery of special orders and other items used in small quantities. While an order from the mills may take 90 days for delivery, a service centre can usually deliver locally within 24 to 48 hours. Such service reduces the investment needed in stock.

FIGURE 15 – 2

## Achieving Transaction Economy with Wholesaling Intermediaries

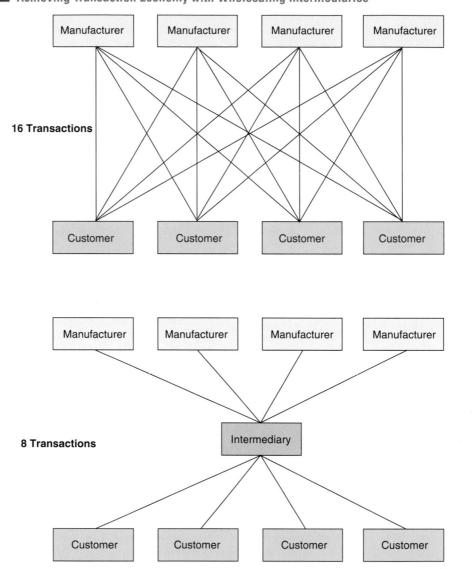

## Who Should Perform Distribution Channel Functions?

While wholesaling intermediaries often perform a variety of valuable functions for their producer, retailer, and other wholesale clients, these functions could be performed by other channel members. Manufacturers may choose to bypass independent wholesaling intermediaries by establishing networks of regional warehouses, maintaining large sales forces to provide market coverage, serving as sources of information for their retail customers, and assuming the financing function. In some instances, they may decide to push the responsibility for some of these functions through the channel on to the retailer or the ultimate purchaser. Large retailers who choose to perform their own wholesaling operations face the same choices.

A fundamental marketing principle is that marketing functions must be performed by some member of the channel; they may be shifted, but they cannot be eliminated. Either the larger retailers who bypass the wholesaler and deal directly with the manufacturer will assume the functions previously performed by wholesaling intermediaries, or these functions will be performed by the manufacturer. Similarly, a manufacturer who deals directly with the ultimate consumer or with industrial buyers will assume the functions of storage, delivery, and market information previously performed by marketing intermediaries. Intermediaries themselves can be eliminated from the channel, but the channel functions must be performed by someone.

The potential gain for the manufacturer or retailer who might be considering bypassing wholesaling intermediaries can be estimated from the profit structure of the wholesaling industry. After-tax profitability runs about 1.7 percent on income, and 11.4 percent on equity.[2] These amounts could theoretically be saved *if* channel members performed the wholesale functions as efficiently as independent wholesaling intermediaries. Such savings could be used to reduce retail prices, to increase the profits of the manufacturer or retailers, or both. In general, profit levels are low. High turnover is therefore a necessity to provide adequate returns on investment.

# Types of Wholesaling Intermediaries

As mentioned previously, various types of wholesaling intermediaries are present in different marketing channels. Some provide a wide range of services or handle a broad line of products, while others specialize in a single service, product, or industry. Figure 15–3 classifies wholesaling intermediaries based on two characteristics: *ownership* (whether the wholesaling intermediary is independent, manufacturer-owned, or retailer-owned) and *title flows* (whether title passes from the manufacturer to the wholesaling intermediary or not). There are, in turn, three basic types of ownership: (1) independent wholesaling, which can involve either merchant wholesalers (who do take title to goods) or agents and brokers (who do not);[3] (2) manufacturer-owned sales branches and offices; and (3) retailer-owned co-operatives and buying offices.

## Manufacturer-Owned Facilities

Increasing volumes of products are being marketed directly by manufacturers through company-owned facilities. There are several reasons for this trend. Some products are perishable; some require complex installation or servicing; others need more-aggressive promotion; still others are high-unit-value goods that the manufac-

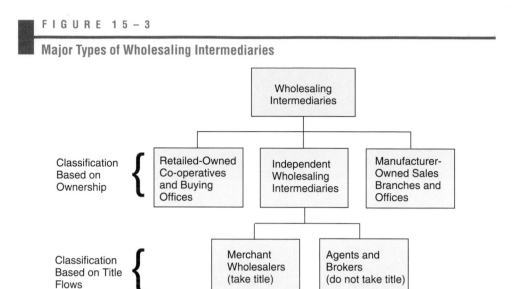

FIGURE 15–3

**Major Types of Wholesaling Intermediaries**

turer wishes to control through the channel directly to the purchaser. Among the industries that have largely shifted from using independent wholesaling intermediaries to using company-owned channels are paper, paint, lumber, construction materials, piece goods, and apparel manufacturers.[4] More than 50 percent of all industrial goods are sold directly to users by the manufacturer, and slightly more than one-third of *all* products are marketed through manufacturer-owned channels.[5]

This does not mean that independent wholesalers are being squeezed out. Their numbers remain in the thousands, and their volume of trade in the billions of dollars.

***Sales branches and offices*** The basic distinction between sales branches and sales offices is that the **sales branch** of a company *carries inventory, and processes orders to customers from available stock.* The branch duplicates the storage function of the independent wholesaler and serves as an office for sales representatives in the territory. Sales branches are prevalent in the marketing of commercial machinery and equipment, petroleum products, motor vehicles, and chemicals.

A **sales office,** by contrast, *does not carry stock but serves as a regional office for the firm's sales personnel.* Maintaining sales offices in close proximity to the firm's customers helps reduce selling costs and improve customer service. The firm's listing in the local telephone directory and yellow pages may result in sales for the local representative. Many buyers will choose to telephone the office of a supplier of a needed product rather than take the time to write letters to distant suppliers.

Since warehouses represent a substantial investment in real estate, smaller manufacturers and even larger firms developing new sales territories may choose to use **public warehouses.** These are *independently owned storage facilities.* For a rental fee the manufacturer may arrange to store its inventory in one of the nation's many public warehouses for shipment by the warehouse to customers in the area. The warehouse owner will break bulk (divide up a carload or truckload), package inventory into smaller quantities to fill orders, and even bill the purchaser for the

**sales branch**
Manufacturer-owned facility that carries inventory and that processes orders to customers from available stock.

**sales office**
Manufacturer-owned facility that does not carry stock but serves as a regional office for the firm's sales personnel.

**public warehouse**
Independently owned storage facility.

manufacturer. The public warehouse can provide a financial service for the manufacturer too, by issuing a warehouse receipt for the inventory. The receipt can then be used as collateral for a bank loan.

***Other outlets for the manufacturer's products***    In addition to using a sales force and regionally distributed sales branches, manufacturers often market their products through trade fairs and exhibitions and merchandise marts. **Trade fairs** or trade exhibitions are *periodic shows at which manufacturers in a particular industry may display their wares for visiting retail and wholesale buyers.* The Montreal toy show and the Toronto, Montreal, and Calgary furniture shows are annual events for both manufacturers and purchasers of toys and furniture.

A **merchandise mart** provides space for *permanent exhibitions at which manufacturers may rent showcases for their product offerings.* One of the largest is Place Bonaventure in Montreal, which is approximately a block square and is several storeys high. Thousands of items are on display there. A retail buyer can compare the offerings of dozens of competing manufacturers and make many purchase decisions in a single visit to a trade fair or merchandise mart.

## Independent Wholesaling Intermediaries

As has been mentioned earlier, there are many independent wholesaling intermediaries. Figure 15–4 shows that they are flourishing. They perform vital functions in the marketing of goods and services, and their role and categorization should be understood clearly. These intermediaries may be divided into two categories: **merchant wholesalers**, who *take title to the products*, and **agents and brokers**, who *may take possession of the products, but who do not take title to them.* Merchant wholesalers account for 84.9 percent of all sales handled by independent wholesalers. As Figure 15–5 indicates, they can be further classified as full- or limited-function wholesalers.

*Full-function merchant wholesalers* provide a complete assortment of services for retailers or industrial purchasers. They are found in convenient locations, thus allowing their customers to make purchases on short notice. To minimize their customers' inventory requirements, they usually maintain a sales force who regularly call on retailers, make deliveries, and extend credit to qualified buyers. In the

**trade fairs**    Periodic shows at which manufacturers in a particular industry display their wares for visiting retail and wholesale buyers.

**merchandise mart**    Permanent exhibition at which manufacturers rent showcases for their product offerings.

**merchant wholesalers**    Wholesaling intermediaries who take title to the products.

**agents and brokers**    Wholesaling intermediaries who may take possession of the products, but who do not take title to them.

**FIGURE 15 – 4**

### Wholesale Trade by Type of Operation, 1983 and 1986

| Type of Operation | Number of Establishments | | Volume of Trade (billions of $) | | Percentage of Volume of Trade | |
|---|---|---|---|---|---|---|
| | 1983 | 1986 | 1983 | 1986 | 1983 | 1986 |
| Merchant wholesalers | 47 482 | 62 189 | 148.34 | 199.7 | 83.2 | 84.9 |
| Agents and brokers | 4 806 | 4 534 | 29.98 | 35.5 | 16.8 | 15.1 |
| Total | 52 288 | 66 723 | 179.32 | 235.2 | 100.0 | 100.0 |

Source: Statistics Canada, *Market Research Handbook* 1990 (Cat. No.63-224). By permission of the Minister of Supply and Services Canada.

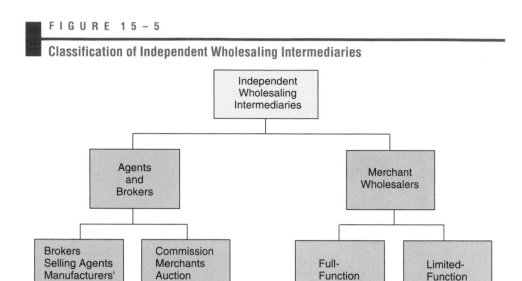

FIGURE 15 – 5

**Classification of Independent Wholesaling Intermediaries**

industrial-goods market, the full-function merchant wholesaler (often called an *industrial distributor*) usually markets machinery, less-expensive accessory equipment, and supplies.

Full-function merchant wholesalers prevail in industries where retailers are small and carry large numbers of relatively inexpensive items, none of which is stocked in depth. The hardware, drug, and grocery industries have traditionally been serviced by them.

A unique type of service wholesaler emerged after World War II as supermarkets began to stock high-margin nonfood items. Since the supermarket manager possessed little knowledge of such products as toys, housewares, paperback books, records, and health and beauty items, the **rack jobber** provided the necessary

**rack jobber**    Wholesaler who provides the racks, stocks the merchandise, prices the goods, and makes regular visits to refill the shelves.

---

A·P·P·L·Y·I·N·G  T·H·E  C·O·N·C·E·P·T·S

### A Wholesaler Must Be Versatile

National Drugs, a typical merchant wholesaler, offers its drugstore customers a range of services. These include accounting, merchandising, site location, store design, and financing. For a fee that seldom exceeds a few hundred dollars, National will assist a retail customer in analyzing everything from market share, cash flow, and current profit position to evaluations of proposed store locations. Retail stores can even obtain a daily printout of individual department performance as compared with expectations. National has developed standards of performance through experience and can use them to point out trouble spots. For instance, paper goods such as paper towels and toilet paper take up a substantial amount of selling space, yet average a gross profit of only 13 percent. By comparison, toothpaste chalks up gross profits of 25 percent and pocket novels deliver 30 percent. Magazines produce only 20 percent, but the great volume sold makes it worthwhile to stock them.

National Drugs not only serves many independent drugstores, but has diversified through the direct ownership of large drugstores. These compete directly with franchise chain stores such as Shoppers Drug Mart, which have bypassed the independent wholesaler by establishing their own wholesaling operations across Canada.

expertise. This wholesaler *provides the racks, stocks the merchandise, prices the goods, and makes regular visits to refill the shelves*. In essence, the rack jobber rents space from the retailer on a commission basis. Rack jobbers have expanded into drug, hardware, variety, and discount stores.

Since full-function merchant wholesalers perform a large number of services, their costs are sometimes as high as 20 percent of sales. Attempts to reduce the costs associated with dealing with the full-function wholesaler have led to the development of a number of *limited-function* intermediaries.

Four types of limited-function merchant wholesalers are cash-and-carry wholesalers, truck wholesalers, drop shippers, and direct-response wholesalers.

**Cash-and-carry wholesalers** perform most wholesaling functions except financing and delivery. They first appeared on the marketing stage in the grocery industry during the Depression era of the 1930s. In an attempt to reduce costs, retailers drove to the wholesaler's warehouse, paid cash for their purchases, and made their own deliveries. By eliminating the delivery and financing functions, cash-and-carry wholesalers were able to reduce operating costs to approximately 9 percent of sales.

**cash-and-carry wholesaler**
Limited-function merchant wholesaler who performs most wholesaling functions except financing and delivery.

---

### A·P·P·L·Y·I·N·G  T·H·E  C·O·N·C·E·P·T·S

## *Is This a True Wholesaler?*

Costco Wholesale Corporation, based in Seattle, opened its eighth Canadian store recently in Winnipeg. The outlet is a mammoth, 120 000-square-foot metal box on St. James Street.

About 3600 items are carried. These include everything from toilet paper (by the case) to diamond rings, groceries (including perishables), office supplies, furniture, major appliances, and electronic equipment.

Only major national brands are handled, and Costco has serious quality and customer satisfaction guarantees.

It also has extraordinary pricing policies. The company actually guarantees that its prices average between 30 percent and 50 percent cheaper than anywhere else for nonfood items, and between 10 percent and 15 percent cheaper for food items.

Besides volume buying, the secret behind Costco's ability to charge such low prices is simple but comprehensive. Ed Maron, the company's senior vice-president and general manager of Canadian operations, says, "We have eliminated every cost we consider nonessential."

And when he says every cost, he means every cost. Most products are presented on wooden skids in the same cartons the manufacturers shipped them in. The floors are bare concrete; no glitzy promotional signage distracts the eye and no mannequins display clothing.

No credit cards are accepted, everything is cash and carry, and there is no delivery. The boxes in which the product is originally shipped are used by customers to carry out the goods. There is virtually no sales staff (what you see is what you get).

The operation has already spent all it plans to spend on advertising (announcing the opening), and there is next to no capital expense involved in distributing or storing goods. Manufacturers ship directly to each of Costco's 64 warehouses throughout the U.S. and Canada, and the product goes directly onto the floor.

Costco operates as a membership club, with annual fees of $30 for business members and $35 for private individuals who are employed by government or who have a connection with some credit unions and a few other organizations. The company says that the primary market for Costco is the business and retail customer who would normally buy from traditional wholesalers. The total operation grossed more than $4 billion in 1989.

Maron says Costco traditionally takes a bit of the market share from several different markets, but the ones that will probably most feel the effect are the wholesaler/distributors and cash-and-carry discount houses.

One small-business owner at Costco was heard to say that his expense for coffee for his office staff will be about 10 percent of what he spends with his current coffee supplier.

Source: Adapted from Martin Cash, "New Kid on 'Wholesale City' Block," *Winnipeg Free Press* (November 1, 1990).

Although feasible in servicing small stores, such wholesalers have generally proven unworkable for the large-scale operation. The chain store manager is unwilling to perform the delivery function, and the cash-and-carry operation typically operates today as one department of a regular full-service wholesaler.

**Truck wholesalers**, or truck jobbers, *market perishable food items*, such as bread, tobacco, potato chips, candy, and dairy products. They make regular deliveries to retail stores and simultaneously perform the sales, delivery, and collection functions. The relatively high cost of operating a delivery truck and the low dollar volume per sale account for their relatively high operating costs of 15 percent. The truck wholesaler does provide aggressive promotion for these product lines.

The **drop shipper** *takes orders from customers and places them with producers, who then ship directly to the customer*. Although drop shippers take title to the products, they never physically handle — or even see — the goods. Since they perform no storage or handling function, their operating costs are a relatively low 4 to 5 percent of sales.

Drop shippers operate in fields where the product is bulky and customers make purchases in carload lots. Since transportation and handling costs represent a substantial percentage of the total cost of such products as coal and lumber, drop shippers do not maintain an inventory and thereby eliminate the expenses of loading and unloading carload shipments. Their major service is in developing a complete assortment for customers. For example, drop shippers constitute a highly skilled group of sellers of lumber products from British Columbia. While the major forest-product firms, such as MacMillan-Bloedel and British Columbia Forest Products, have their in-house lumber traders, independent drop shippers compete head to head with them in selling the output of independent sawmills to Eastern Canada and the United States.

The **direct-response wholesaler** is a limited-function merchant wholesaler who *relies on catalogues rather than a sales force to contact retail, industrial, and institutional customers*. Purchases are made by mail or telephone by relatively small customers in outlying areas. Mail-order operations are found in the hardware, cosmetics, jewellery, sporting goods, and specialty food lines, as well as in general merchandise.

**truck wholesaler**   Limited-function merchant wholesaler who markets perishable food items.

**drop shipper**   Limited-function merchant wholesaler who takes orders from customers and places them with producers, who then ship directly to the customer.

**direct-response wholesaler**   Limited-function merchant wholesaler who relies on catalogues rather than a sales force to contact retail, industrial, and institutional customers.

**FIGURE 15–6**

**Services Provided by Merchant Wholesalers**

| Services | Full-Function Wholesalers | Cash-and-Carry Wholesalers | Truck Wholesalers | Drop Shippers | Direct-response Wholesalers |
|---|---|---|---|---|---|
| Anticipates customer needs | Yes | Yes | Yes | No | Yes |
| Carries inventory | Yes | Yes | Yes | No | Yes |
| Delivers | Yes | No | Yes | No | Yes (by mail) |
| Provides market information | Yes | Rarely | Yes | Yes | No |
| Provides credit | Yes | No | No | Yes | Sometimes |
| Assumes ownership risk by taking title | Yes | Yes | Yes | Yes | Yes |

Figure 15–6 compares the various types of merchant wholesalers in terms of the services they provide. Full-function merchant wholesalers and truck wholesalers are relatively high-cost intermediaries because of the number of services they perform, while cash-and-carry wholesalers, drop shippers, and direct-response wholesalers provide fewer services and thus have relatively low operating costs.

***Agents and brokers*** A second group of independent wholesaling intermediaries — the agents and brokers — may or may not take possession of the products they handle, but they never take title to them. They normally perform fewer services than the merchant wholesalers and are typically involved in bringing together buyers and sellers. Agent wholesaling intermediaries may be classified into five categories — commission merchants, auction houses, brokers, selling agents, and manufacturers' agents.

Commission merchants predominate in the marketing of agricultural products. The **commission merchant** *takes possession when the producer ships goods to a central market for sale.* The commission merchant acts as the producer's agent and receives an agreed-upon fee when a sale is made. Since customers will inspect the products and prices may fluctuate, the commission merchant is given considerable latitude in making decisions. The owner of the goods may specify a minimum price, but the commission merchant will sell them on a "best price" basis. The commission merchant deducts the appropriate fee from the price and the balance is remitted to the original seller.

A valuable service in such markets as used cars, livestock, antiques, works of art, fur, flowers, and fruit is performed by agent wholesaling intermediaries known as **auction houses**. They *bring buyers and sellers together in one location and allow potential buyers to inspect the merchandise before purchasing.* A commission, often based on the sale price, is charged by the auction company for its services. Auction houses tend to specialize in merchandise categories such as agricultural products and art. Sotheby's is a world-famous auction house specializing in art and related products.

The task of **brokers** is to *bring buyers and sellers together.* They operate in industries characterized by a large number of small suppliers and purchasers — real estate, frozen foods, and used machinery, for example. They may represent either buyer or seller in a given transaction, but not both. The broker receives a fee from the client when the transaction is completed. The service performed is finding buyers or sellers and negotiating for exchange of title. The operating expense ratio for the broker, which may be as low as 2 percent, rises depending on the services performed.

Because brokers operate on a one-time basis for sellers or buyers, they cannot serve as an effective marketing channel for manufacturers seeking regular, continuing services. A manufacturer who seeks to develop a more permanent channel using agent wholesaling intermediaries must evaluate the services of either the selling agent or the manufacturers' agent.

For small, poorly financed, production-oriented manufacturers, the **selling agent** may prove an ideal marketing channel. These wholesaling intermediaries have even been referred to as independent marketing departments, since they are *responsible for the total marketing program for a firm's product line.* They typically have full authority over pricing decisions and promotional outlays, and they often provide financial assistance for the manufacturer. The manufacturer can concentrate on production and rely on the expertise of the selling agent for all marketing activities.

Selling agents are common in the textile, coal, sulphur, and lumber industries. Their operating expenses average about 3 percent of sales.

**commission merchant** An agent wholesaling intermediary who takes possession when the producer ships goods to a central market for sale.

**auction house** An agent wholesaling intermediary who brings buyers and sellers together in one location and allows potential buyers to inspect the merchandise before purchasing.

**broker** A wholesaling intermediary who brings buyers and sellers together; operates in industries with a large number of small suppliers and purchasers.

**selling agent** A wholesaling intermediary who is responsible for the total marketing program for a firm's product line.

**manufacturers' agent**   An independent salesperson who works for a number of manufacturers of related but noncompeting products.

Instead of a single selling agent, a manufacturer may use a number of manufacturers' agents. A **manufacturers' agent** is essentially *an independent salesperson who works for a number of manufacturers of related but noncompeting products* and receives a commission based on a specified percentage of sales. Manufacturers' agents can be thought of as an independent sales force. Although some commissions may be as high as 20 percent of sales, they usually average between 6 and 7 percent. Unlike the selling agent, who may be given exclusive world rights to *market* a manufacturer's product, the manufacturers' agent *sells* in a specified territory.[6]

Manufacturers' agents reduce their selling costs by spreading the cost per sales call over a number of different products. An agent in the plumbing supplies industry may represent a dozen different manufacturers.

Producers may use manufacturers' agents for several reasons. First, when they are developing new sales territories, the costs of adding new salespeople to "pioneer" new territories may be prohibitive. The agents, who are paid on a commission basis, can perform the sales function in the new territories at a much lower cost to the manufacturer.

Second, firms with unrelated lines may need to employ more than one channel. One line of products may be marketed through the company's sales force. A second, unrelated line might be marketed through independent manufacturers' agents. This is particularly common where the unrelated product line is a recent addition and the regular sales force has no experience with the products.

Finally, small firms with no existing sales force may turn to manufacturers' agents in order to have access to the market. A newly organized firm producing pencil sharpeners may use office equipment and supplies manufacturers' agents to reach retail outlets and industrial purchasers.

Although the importance of selling agents is now very limited because many manufacturers desire better control of their marketing programs, the volume of sales handled by manufacturers' agents has increased substantially.

The various types of agents and brokers are compared in Figure 15–7.

**FIGURE 15–7**

**Services Provided by Agents and Brokers**

| Services | Commission Merchants | Auction Houses | Brokers | Manufacturers' Agents | Selling Agents |
|---|---|---|---|---|---|
| Anticipates customer needs | Yes | Some | Some | Yes | Yes |
| Carries inventory | Yes | Yes | No | No | No |
| Delivers | Yes | No | No | Infrequently | No |
| Provides market information | Yes | Yes | Yes | Yes | Yes |
| Provides credit | Some | No | No | No | Some |
| Assumes ownership risk by taking title | No | No | No | No | No |

## Retailer-Owned Facilities

Retailers have also assumed numerous wholesaling functions in attempts to reduce costs or to provide special service. Independent retailers have occasionally banded together to form buying groups in order to achieve cost savings through quantity purchases. Other groups of retailers have established retailer-owned wholesale facilities by forming a co-operative chain. Larger chain retailers often establish centralized buying offices to negotiate large-scale purchases directly with manufacturers for the members of the chain.

## Independent Wholesaling Intermediaries — A Durable Marketing Institution

Many marketing observers of the 1920s felt that the end had come for the independent wholesaling intermediaries as chain stores grew in importance and attempted

---

### A·P·P·L·Y·I·N·G  T·H·E  C·O·N·C·E·P·T·S

## *Why Airwick Closed Its Sales Offices*

Airwick Industries is a well-known manufacturer and marketer of household cleaners and deodorizers. Its product line, led by Carpet Fresh and Stick-Ups products, generated approximately $220 million in sales internationally in 1980.

Success in the consumer market led Airwick to establish a professional-product division to market a variety of disinfectants, cleaning agents, odour counteractants, insecticides, and environmental sanitation products for airports, government installations, hospitals, hotels and motels, industrial plants, nursing homes, office complexes, restaurants, and retail stores. Airwick's original distribution network consisted entirely of independent wholesaling intermediaries. In the 1970s, the firm began purchasing many of the independents with the idea of eventually converting entirely to company-owned distribution facilities. By 1980, a network consisting of independent wholesaling operations and company-owned offices had been developed.

But Airwick managers were unable to detect improved performance in those areas where company-owned facilities operated. In addition, independent wholesalers were expressing growing dissatisfaction with what they considered at least the potential of unfair competition from Airwick's sales offices. At that point, Airwick decided to close the sales offices and establish new independent distributors. John Updegraph, division president, summed up the decision this way: "We felt it was better to ride one horse successfully rather than risk falling on our faces riding two horses at the same time."

Updegraph recognized that the new distribution structure meant that Airwick was relinquishing some control, but he felt that the advantages outweighed the limitations. "In some ways, it is actually better to have the sales of your products handled by private entrepreneurs. These independent distributors run their own businesses and if anyone wants to turn a profit, they do. The more they push our products, the more money they make.

"Also, when you market your products through distributors you eliminate numerous management headaches. In fact, we found that Airwick is even stronger now because the distributors know we are behind them 100 percent."

Supporting the change are programs that help distributors hire and train salespeople, manage time and territories, control inventory and receivables, increase sales effectiveness, install better accounting systems, and make computer records conversions.

"Before the phase-out we were not able to do very much in the way of advertising and promotion support for the distributors. But now we can direct more attention to those areas," Updegraph said.

"What's important is that you maintain good marketing and sales efforts and continue to cultivate good management. It doesn't really matter what type of distribution channel you use."

Source: Adapted with permission from Bernard F. Whalen, "Airwick Drops Sales Offices to Increase Sales," *Marketing News* (February 8, 1980), p. 6, published by the American Marketing Association.

to bypass them. From 1929 to 1939 the independents' sales volume dropped, but it has increased again since then.

Figure 15–4 shows how the relative numbers and shares of total independent wholesale trade volumes changed over two recent years. The growth shows that independent wholesaling intermediaries are far from obsolete. Their continued importance is evidence of the ability of independent wholesaling intermediaries to adjust to changing conditions and changing needs. Their market size proves their ability to continue to fill a need in many marketing channels.

## Summary

Wholesaling is one of the two major institutions that make up many firms' marketing channels. (The second is retailing.) Wholesaling includes the activities of persons or firms who sell to retailers and other wholesalers or to industrial users but who do not sell in significant amounts to ultimate consumers.

Three types of wholesaling intermediaries are manufacturer-owned facilities, independent wholesaling intermediaries, and retailer-owned facilities. In the middle category are merchant wholesalers and agents and brokers. Merchant wholesalers take title to products they handle. Agents and brokers may take possession, but do not take title to the products. Merchant wholesalers include full-function wholesalers (for example, rack jobbers) and limited-function wholesalers (such as cash-and-carry wholesalers, truck wholesalers, drop shippers, and direct-response wholesalers). Since they do not take title, commission merchants, auction houses, brokers, selling agents, and manufacturers' agents are classified as agent wholesaling intermediaries.

The operating expenses of wholesaling intermediaries vary considerably, depending on the number of services provided and the costs involved. These services may include storage facilities in conveniently located warehouses, market coverage by a sales force, financing for retailers and sometimes for manufacturers, market information for retailers and manufacturers, transportation, and management services, sales training, and merchandising assistance and advice for retailers.

While the percentage of wholesale trade by manufacturer-owned facilities has increased since 1958, independent wholesaling intermediaries continue to account for a significant proportion of total wholesale trade. They accomplish this by continuing to provide desired services to manufacturers and retailers.

## ◼ K E Y   T E R M S

| | | |
|---|---|---|
| wholesaler | merchant wholesaler | direct-response wholesaler |
| wholesaling intermediary | agents and brokers | commission merchant |
| sales branch | rack jobber | auction house |
| sales office | cash-and-carry wholesaler | broker |
| public warehouse | truck wholesaler | selling agent |
| trade fair | drop shipper | manufacturers' agent |
| merchandise mart | | |

## ■ R E V I E W   Q U E S T I O N S

1. Distinguish between a wholesaler and a retailer.
2. In what ways do wholesaling intermediaries assist manufacturers? How do they assist retailers?
3. Explain how wholesaling intermediaries can help retailers increase their returns on investment.
4. Distinguish between sales offices and sales branches. Under what conditions might each type of facility be used?
5. What role does the public warehouse play in distribution channels?

6. Distinguish merchant wholesalers from agents and brokers.
7. Why is the operating-expense ratio of the merchant wholesaler higher than that of the typical agent or broker?
8. In what ways are commission merchants and brokers different?
9. Distinguish between a manufacturers' agent and a selling agent.
10. Under what conditions would a manufacturer use manufacturers' agents for a distribution channel?

## ■ D I S C U S S I O N   Q U E S T I O N S   A N D   E X E R C I S E S

1. Match each of the following industries with the most appropriate wholesaling intermediary:
   _____ Groceries
   _____ Potato chips
   _____ Coal
   _____ Grain
   _____ Antiques
   a. Drop shipper
   b. Truck wholesaler
   c. Auction house
   d. Manufacturers' agent
   e. Full-function merchant wholesaler
   f. Commission merchant

2. Comment on the following statements: Drop shippers are good candidates for elimination. All they do is process orders. They don't even handle the goods.
3. Prepare a brief (five-page) report on a wholesaler in your local area.
4. The term *broker* also appears in the real estate and securities fields. Are such brokers identical to the agent wholesaling intermediaries described in this chapter?
5. Interview a truck wholesaler or a rack jobber. Report to the class on this person's job within the wholesaling sector.

## ■ M I C R O C O M P U T E R   E X E R C I S E

### ■ Inventory Turnover

**Directions:** Use the Menu Item titled "Inventory Turnover" on the *Foundations of Marketing* disk to solve each of the following problems.

1. A Brandon, Manitoba, wholesaling intermediary carries an average inventory recorded at cost of $5 million. Its total cost of goods sold is $27.5 million. What is the firm's inventory-turnover rate?

2. A Lethbridge, Alberta, wholesaler started 1992 with an inventory of $4 million at retail. During the year, the wholesaler decided to reduce its overall inventory position. The firm ended 1992 with a $3 million inventory (at retail). Sales in 1992 were $36 million. What was the wholesaler's inventory-turnover rate for the year?

3. A wholesaler in Quebec City had a $22 million cost-based inventory on January 1, 1992, but was able to reduce it to $20 million by the end of the year. The firm has a 20 percent markup percentage on selling price. In 1992, sales volume totalled $90 million. Calculate the wholesaler's 1992 inventory-turnover rate.

# VIDEO CASE 15 Northern Produce Co./Mushrooms, Inc.

It is 4 o'clock on a Monday morning when Joey Weiss arrives at the Central Produce Market in Los Angeles. With the eye of an experienced buyer, Joey moves quickly from stall to stall, assessing the quality and quantity of fresh fruits and vegetables displayed by many suppliers. The produce he buys in large volume must fill the orders of hundreds of restaurant, hotel, and grocery-store customers that expect delivery of their daily supply of fresh produce within a few hours.

Joey Weiss is president of Northern Produce Co./Mushrooms, Inc. of Los Angeles. As a full-function merchant wholesaler, Northern takes title to the produce it distributes and provides a broad range of services for customers and suppliers. Joey and his brother Barry are third-generation owners of a family business that was set up by their father and grandfather in 1938, as a wholesaler of fresh produce. In the 1950s, the Weiss family expanded their business by distributing cultivated mushrooms. During the late 1970s, they moved into specialty produce, buying and selling fresh herbs and such exotic fare as miniature vegetables, edible flowers, and unusual varieties of wild cultivated mushrooms. Today the company has 85 employees and rings up annual sales of $20 million.

Northern buys produce to service more than 400 customers, including Vons, Safeway, and other major retail food stores; Irvine Ranch specialty markets; Hilton and Sheraton hotels; Royal Viking cruise ships; and some of Southern California's most fashionable restaurants.

To satisfy diverse customer needs, Joey buys from alternative supply sources. Buying decisions take into account fluctuating market conditions and the seasonal availability of many produce items. Joey buys about half the firm's inventory during his early-morning trips to three produce markets in Los Angeles. He frequently revisits the markets at the end of the day to plan his buying strategy for the following day. When he finds fruits and vegetables in plentiful supply at the end of a day, he knows that he will have more bargaining power the next morning.

Joey buys many specialty and off-season items directly from food brokers, shippers, and growers in other countries. To reduce the air freight costs on some imported produce, Joey has imported seeds from Europe and lined up farmers in the United States to grow such crops as edible flowers, white carrots, haricots verts (French green beans), and radiccio (a red Italian lettuce).

Each produce shipment arriving at Northern's two warehouses is inspected carefully to ensure that the merchandise is not damaged or spoiled. The quality check reduces the company's risk of taking title to produce it may not be able to sell to customers. Fruits and vegetables that pass inspection are moved to refrigerated areas and placed on pallets. Warehouse workers continually rotate inventory, a system that helps alleviate confusion about which produce is brought in to be cooled and which is going out to be delivered to customers. Other warehouse workers sort through bulk packages of produce and repack them so that customers receive produce that is uniform in size, colour, and degree of ripeness.

The high quality of Northern's produce is especially important to its cruise-ship customers, who have proliferated in recent years. Not only must the ships have top-quality produce to satisfy their discriminating clientele, but there is no way for Northern to make good on defective produce when the ship is at sea. Joey is justly proud of the large amount of repeat business he gets from the ships.

Northern maintains a fleet of 25 refrigerated delivery trucks, each one handpainted with a giant mural of different fruits and vegetables. For many customers, prompt delivery is as important as produce quality and price. A cruise-ship customer says, "We need to be able to ensure that the product is delivered to us when the wholesaler says he will deliver to us. A truck stopped on the freeway is of no use to us because the ship must sail on time."

Northern Produce takes pride in its reputation of being a service-oriented wholesaler. Says Joey, "We tell our customers that if they need two or three deliveries a day, they will have them." The company also sends out several delivery trucks to the same geographic area to ensure that produce is delivered to customers when they want it. Produce is shipped by air to customers in faraway places — for example, the Grand Hyatt Hotel in New York and cruise ships in Europe, Peru, Tahiti, Hawaii, and Japan.

Another service Northern provides for customers is financing. Customers are given up to 30 days to pay for merchandise. If they bought directly from brokers or the market, they would have to pay within a week.

Keeping customers informed is a top priority of Northern's eight full-time salespeople. Because Northern specializes in exotic produce, much of which may be unfamiliar to many customers, salespeople regularly contact customers, explaining new items in detail so that customers understand their features and uses. In addition to servicing existing accounts, salespeople continually monitor the opening of new hotels, restaurants, and specialty food stores in an effort to bring in new business.

## Questions

1. Explain why Northern Produce is classified as a full-function merchant wholesaler.
2. How does Northern Produce attempt to reduce the risks it assumes in taking title to goods?
3. What functions does Northern Produce perform in linking producers with customers?
4. Competition among chic restaurants is fierce. To remain competitive, chefs constantly look for new ideas to attract their upscale clientele. Do you think Northern Produce could make a difference in the success or failure of a restaurant? Why or why not?
5. Which marketing mix elements do you think contributed most to the growth of Northern Produce? Which elements will be most important to the wholesaler's future growth and expansion?

SOURCES    Telephone interviews with Joey and Barry Weiss, February 18 and 19, 1988; update interview with Joey Weiss, May 1991.

CHAPTER 16

# Retailing

## CHAPTER OBJECTIVES

1. To relate retailing to the other variables of the marketing mix.
2. To outline the decision framework for retailing.
3. To distinguish between limited-line retailers and general merchandise retailers.
4. To identify and explain each of the five bases for categorizing retailers.
5. To identify the major types of mass merchandisers.
6. To explain the types of nonstore retailing.
7. To distinguish between chain and independent retailers and to identify several industries dominated by chains.
8. To contrast the three types of planned shopping centres.

NOISE and chaos are being deliberately cultivated by Oshawa Group Ltd. in its stores. The company has spent millions of dollars making more of its Food City outlets look less like supermarkets.

Gone is the too-tidy, almost clinical atmosphere of traditional grocery stores. What shoppers really want, Oshawa reckons, is a bit of the noise and chaos that enliven traditional farmers' markets. And so, using a mix of intuition and consumer research, the company has come up with a way to fabricate at least some of that market atmosphere. The new format includes aisles named after local streets, fish and meat departments made to look like open storefronts, and a gazebo-covered produce department.

So far, at least, the studious clutter of the revamped stores is bringing in a tidy return. At the store most recently renovated, sales are up 40 percent from the year-ago level, to $15 a square foot each week. And the average customer order is running at $37, compared with an industry average of $20 to $25.

Most of the renovation costs are in new equipment for delicatessens and the like, with about $600 000 spent on the more decorative items, such as imitation outdoor billboards on the walls around the store.

"They've put a lot of thought into it and they've done it well," says John Winter, a retailing analyst who heads John Winter Associates Ltd. "This is the innovation of the 1990s."

"Your street name is probably hanging up there [above an aisle]," Winter notes. "You're not looking for the munchies, you're looking for Maclean Ave."

Even the elevator music traditionally broadcast in so many stores has come in for some change. To add "the sound of the street," speakers hidden behind the shelves play recent pop music with vocals, while those around the perimeter — by the fish market and deli — play instrumental tunes only. The sound-tracks mix at intersections.[1]

The Food City renovations reflect the constant change that occurs in the retail world. Retailing represents one of marketing's most dynamic aspects. Retailers who do not keep in touch with the trends in the marketplace will find themselves losing out to competitors such as Food City.

## Introduction

In a very real sense, retailers *are* the marketing channel for most consumers, since consumers have little contact with manufacturers and almost none with the wholesaling intermediaries. The services provided — location, store hours, quality of salespeople, store layout, selection, and returns, among others — often figure even more importantly than the physical product in buying decisions.

Retailers are both customers and marketers in the channel. They market goods and services to ultimate consumers and also are the consumers for wholesalers and manufacturers. Because of their critical location in the channel, retailers may perform an important feedback role in obtaining information from customers and transmitting it to manufacturers and other channel members.

Retailing is the "last step of the marketing channel" for the consumer goods manufacturer. Whether the manufacturer has established a company-owned chain of retail stores or uses several of the thousands of retail stores in Canada, the success of the entire marketing strategy rides on the decisions of consumers in the retail store.

**retailing**   All the activities involved in the sale of goods and services to the ultimate consumer.

**Retailing** may be defined as *all the activities involved in the sale of goods and services to the ultimate consumer*. Retailing involves not only sales in retail stores, but also several forms of nonstore retailing. These include telephone and direct-response sales, automatic merchandising, and direct house-to-house solicitations by salespersons.

## Evolution of Retailing

Early retailing in Canada can be traced to the voyageurs, to the establishment of trading posts by the Hudson's Bay Company and others, and to pack peddlers who literally carried their wares to outlying settlements. After the trading post days, the Hudson's Bay and other retailers evolved into the institution known as the *general store*. The general store was stocked with general merchandise to meet the needs of a small community or rural area. Here customers could buy clothing, groceries, feed, seed, farm equipment, drugs, spectacles, and candy. The following account provides a good description of this early retail institution:

> The country store was in many respects a departmental store on a small scale, for a well-equipped store contained a little of everything. On one side were to be seen shelves well filled with groceries, crockery-ware, and a few patent medicines, such as blood purifiers, painkillers, and liniments; on the other side, a well assorted stock of dry goods, including prints, woollens, muslins, calico, cottons, etc. At the back, a lot of hardware, comprising nails, paints, oils, putty, glass, and garden tools, as well as an assortment of boots and shoes — from the tiny copper-toe to the farmer's big cowhide. In the back room, at the rear end of the store, were to be found barrels of sugar and New Orleans molasses, crates of eggs, and tubs of butter and lard. With this miscellaneous mixture — tea, coffee, dry goods, codfish, and boots and shoes — the odour of the country store was truly a composite one, and trying to the olfactory organs of the visitor. The country merchant was usually a man in good circumstances, for he was obliged in most cases to give a year's credit, the farmers paying their bills in the fall of the year, after the "threshing" or the "killing"; their only source of revenue at any other time being from butter and eggs, which their wives took to the country store, usually once a week, and exchanged for store goods. Perhaps there was no more popular place of meeting than the country store. After the day's work was over, it was customary for many of the men in the neighbourhood, especially the farmers' hired men, who had no other place of amusement to go to, to gather here. Even if they did not have occasion to buy anything, they would drop in for a few minutes to while away the time; have a chat, see someone they wished, hear politics discussed, and generally learn all the latest news. The society of the country store had a peculiar fascination for many of them, for there generally happened to be some one there who was gifted with the faculty of cracking jokes, telling funny yarns, or interesting stories; besides it was a comfortable place, especially on the long winter evenings, when they would gather around on the big box stove, lounge on the counters, sit on the boxes and barrels, puff away at their pipes, chew tobacco, and chaff one another to their heart's content.[2]

The basic needs that caused the general store to develop also doomed this institution to a limited existence. Since the general store keepers attempted to satisfy the needs of customers for all types of "store-bought" goods, they carried a small assortment of each good. As the villages grew, the size of the market was large enough to support stores specializing in specific product lines, such as groceries, hardware, dry goods, and drugs. Most general stores either converted into more specialized limited-line stores or closed. But the general store did, and in some rural areas still does, fill a need for its customers. General stores are still operated profitably in less developed countries where income levels cannot support more specialized retailers and in some isolated parts of Canada as well.

## Innovation in Retailing

Retailing operations are remarkable illustrations of the marketing concept in operation. Retail innovations often develop as attempts to better satisfy particular consumer needs.

As consumers demand different bundles of satisfactions from retailers, new institutions emerge to meet this demand. The supermarket appeared in the early 1930s to meet consumer desires for lower prices. Convenience food stores today meet the consumer's desire for convenience in purchasing and after-hours availability. Discount houses and catalogue stores reflect consumer demands for lower prices and a willingness to give up services. Department stores provide a wide variety of products and services to meet the demands of their clientele. Vending machines, door-to-door retailers, and mail-order retailing offer buyers convenience. Planned shopping centres provide a balanced array of consumer goods and services and include parking facilities for their customers. Canada's 165 000 retailing establishments are involved in developing specific marketing mixes designed to satisfy chosen market targets.[3]

# Marketing Strategy in Retailing

The retailer's decision-making process, like the producer's and wholesaler's, centres on the two fundamental steps of (1) analyzing, evaluating, and ultimately selecting a *target market*, and (2) developing a *marketing mix* designed to satisfy the chosen market target profitably. In other words, the retailer must develop a product offering to appeal to the chosen consumer group, set prices, and choose a location and method of distribution. Finally, the retailer has to develop a marketing communications strategy.[4]

## The Target Market

Like other marketers, retailers must start by selecting the target market to which they wish to appeal. Marketing research is often used in this aspect of retail decision-making. For example, retailers entering new countries, or even new markets in the same country, have been surprised that the target market of their home location apparently does not exist in the new location. Canadian Tire expanded to the larger U.S. market with the purchase of White Stores, Inc.,[5] but found U.S. market acceptance of virtual carbon copies of the successful Canadian stores so limited that the firm abandoned that market after significant losses. Marketing research can help a company adjust to a new environment faster.

Sometimes a retailer finds it necessary to shift target markets. For example, stores established to serve specialty markets such as skiers or snowmobilers have found that lack of snow or changes in consumer recreation habits have forced them to expand or change their offerings to serve more viable target markets. Market selection is as vital an aspect of retailers' marketing strategy as it is for any other marketer.[6]

## Goods Service Strategy

Retailers must also determine and evaluate their offerings with respect to the following:

1. general goods/service categories
2. specific lines
3. specific products
4. inventory depth
5. range of assortment

These decisions are determined by the size of the retailer, as well as whether the store tends to concentrate on convenience, shopping, or specialty goods. Other

marketing factors can influence goods and/or service offerings. For instance, Toys "Я" Us distinguishes itself by specializing and providing great breadth and depth of assortment.

Product strategy evolves to meet competition and changing consumer needs. The success of Loblaw's Superstores forced Safeway to develop their large Food For Less establishments. On a more limited scale, a decision by K mart to provide a special area devoted to patio equipment would likely have to be matched by Woolco.

## Retail Pricing Strategy

Pricing is another critical element of the retailing mix. The essential decisions concern relative price levels. Does the store want to offer higher-priced merchandise (as Holt Renfrew does) or lower-priced items (like Zellers)? Some of the larger department stores such as Woodwards have clearly opted for a higher-price strategy, but try simultaneously to serve some of the lower-priced market targets with basement and warehouse outlets.

Other pricing decisions concern markups, markdowns, loss leaders, odd pricing, and promotional pricing. The retailer is the channel member with direct responsibility for the prices paid by consumers. As Chapters 12 and 13 pointed out, the prices that are set play a major role in buyer perceptions of the retail market.

## Location and Distribution Decisions

Real estate professionals often say that there are three critical factors for establishing a retail establishment: "location, location, and location." A store must be in an appropriate location for the type and price of merchandise carried. Small service outlets such as dry cleaners have discovered that there is a difference between being on the "going to work" side of a busy street and the "going home" side. Other retailers have found success in small "strip"-type neighbourhood shopping centres that are close to where people live. These centres continue to flourish despite the advent of larger suburban community shopping centres.[7]

**retail trade area analysis**
Studies that assess the relative drawing power of alternative retail locations.

**Retail trade area analysis** refers to *studies that assess the relative drawing power of alternative retail locations*. For example, shoppers might be polled as to where they live, how they get to the stores they shop at, how long it takes, how often they shop, and the like. Similarly, the credit charges of an existing store might be plotted to show what its service area is.

Another technique to use is the law of retail gravitation, sometimes called Reilly's law after its originator, William J. Reilly.[8] The **law of retail gravitation**, originally formulated in the 1920s, *delineates the retail trade area of a potential site on the basis of distance between alternative locations and relative populations*. The formula is:

**law of retail gravitation**
Principle that delineates the retail trade area of a potential site on the basis of distance between alternative locations and relative populations.

$$\frac{\text{Breaking Point}}{\text{in km from A}} = \frac{\text{km between A and B}}{1 + \sqrt{\dfrac{\text{Population of B}}{\text{Population of A}}}}$$

Assume a retailer is considering locating a new outlet in Town A or Town B, which are located 60 km from each other. The population of A is 80 000 and the population of B is 20 000. One question that concerns the retailer is where people living in a small rural community located on the highway between the two towns 25 km from B are likely to shop.

According to the law of retail gravitation, these rural shoppers would most likely shop in A even though it is 10 km farther away than B. The retail trade area of A extends 40 km toward B, and the rural community is located only 35 km away.

$$\frac{\text{Breaking Point}}{\text{in km from A}} = \frac{60}{1 + \sqrt{\dfrac{20\ 000}{80\ 000}}} = \frac{60}{1 + \sqrt{.25}} = \frac{60}{1.5} = 40$$

The formula can be applied inversely to find B's trade area, yielding a figure of 20 km, which falls 5 km short of the rural community.

$$\frac{\text{Breaking Point}}{\text{in km from B}} = \frac{60}{1 + \sqrt{\dfrac{80\ 000}{20\ 000}}} = \frac{60}{1 + \sqrt{4}} = \frac{60}{3} = 20 \text{ km}$$

The complete trade area for A or B could be found by similar calculations with other communities.

The application of this technique is limited in an area of urban sprawl, regional shopping centres, and consumers who measure distances in terms of travel time. As a result, a contemporary version of retail trade analysis has been offered by David Huff.

Huff's work is an interurban model that assesses the likelihood that a consumer will patronize a specific shopping centre. Trading areas are expressed in terms of a series of probability contours. The probability that a consumer will patronize a specific shopping centre is viewed as a function of centre size, travel time, and the type of merchandise sought.[9] Such models are more often used for structuring decision-making than as a precise, predictive tool.

*Other distribution decisions*    Retailers are faced with a variety of other distribution decisions, largely in order to ensure that adequate quantities of stock are available when consumers want to buy. The definition of "adequate" will vary with the service strategy of the retailer. Since the cost of carrying inventory is high, a high-margin full-service retailer will likely have a greater depth and range of merchandise than a low-margin, limited-line, high-volume outlet.

## Retail Image and Promotional Strategy

**Retail image** refers to *the consumer's perception of a store and of the shopping experience it provides*.[10] Promotional strategy is a key element in determining the store's image with the consumer. Another important element is the amenities provided by the retailer — the so-called "atmospherics."

**retail image** The consumer's perception of a store and of the shopping experience it provides.

Promoting a store with screaming headlines about fantastic once-in-a-lifetime sale prices creates a substantially different image than using a subdued, tasteful illustration of obviously stylish, elegant clothing. Similarly, walking into a discount store redolent of caramel popcorn produces an image dramatically different from that of entering a beautifully carpeted boutique.

Regardless of how it is accomplished, the objective of retailer promotional strategy should be to align the consumer's perception of the store with other elements of the retailing mix: retail image should match the target market that is selected.

## Categorizing Retailers

The nation's retailers come in a variety of forms. Since new types of retail operations continue to evolve in response to the changing demands of their markets, no

### A·P·P·L·Y·I·N·G  T·H·E  C·O·N·C·E·P·T·S

#### Sharper Focus Needed for Retailing in the 1990s

"Retailers in the 1990s must develop a sharp 'brand' focus and design their stores, train and motivate their people, shape their co-op advertising, and choose their products to reinforce that focus." So said Tony Miller to the International Council of Shopping Centres conference. In his presentation, Miller made the following comments and predictions about retailing:

- The malling of North America is virtually complete. As a result more developers these days don't just build, rent, then sell. They are more likely to create an image, then perhaps rebuild and work harder still to build an even stronger image.
- What developers are doing is turning their malls into brands with their own particular equities.
- "Branded" malls must work to become "destinations" in their own right, like Toronto's Eaton Centre and the West Edmonton Mall.
- The two biggest segments of the market, baby boomers and WOOFs (well-off older folks) are going to become even more discerning in their buying

habits. Baby boomers are picky, and they have more complicated purchasing criteria, such as a growing concern about the environmental impact of the things they buy.

- The boomers and the WOOFs want quality, value, and honesty; they want the substantial rather than the transitory. The 1980s were a disappointing period of glitz, and these people now want more substance. These target markets now get what they want, and very importantly, they won't dither around in getting it.
- The decline in the importance of mass marketing will continue, so marketers must have a more precise understanding of who they want to sell to, and why.
- We must understand consumers not as a generic mass, but as clearly defined groups, and ideally, we must extend our understanding down to the level of the individual.

Source: Adapted from Stan Sutter, "End Fight Between Brand and Retail," *Marketing* (March 26, 1990), p. 34.

FIGURE 16–1

**Bases for Classifying Retailers**

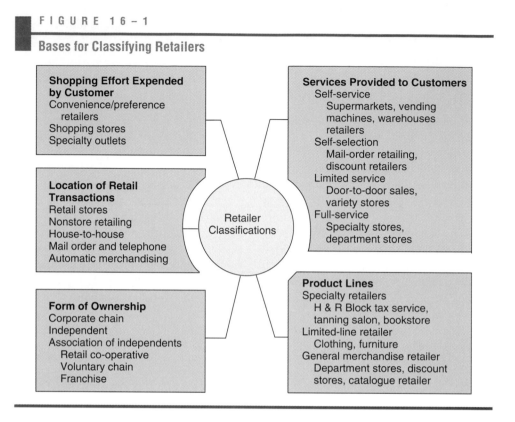

**Shopping Effort Expended by Customer**
Convenience/preference
    retailers
Shopping stores
Specialty outlets

**Services Provided to Customers**
Self-service
    Supermarkets, vending
    machines, warehouses
    retailers
Self-selection
    Mail-order retailing,
    discount retailers
Limited service
    Door-to-door sales,
    variety stores
Full-service
    Specialty stores,
    department stores

**Location of Retail Transactions**
Retail stores
Nonstore retailing
House-to-house
Mail order and telephone
Automatic merchandising

Retailer Classifications

**Form of Ownership**
Corporate chain
Independent
Association of independents
    Retail co-operative
    Voluntary chain
    Franchise

**Product Lines**
Specialty retailers
    H & R Block tax service,
    tanning salon, bookstore
Limited-line retailer
    Clothing, furniture
General merchandise retailer
    Department stores, discount
    stores, catalogue retailer

universal classification has been devised. The following characteristics or bases can be used in categorizing them:

1. shopping effort expended by customers
2. services provided to customers
3. product lines
4. location of retail transactions
5. form of ownership

Any retailing operation can be classified using each of these five bases. A 7-Eleven store may be classified as a convenience store (category 1); self-service (category 2); relatively narrow product lines (category 3); in-store retailing (category 4); and a member of a corporate chain (category 5). Figure 16–1 illustrates the bases for classifying retail operations.

## Retailers Classified by Shopping Effort

A classification of consumer goods based on consumer purchase patterns in securing a particular product or service was presented in Chapter 9. This system can be extended to retailers by considering the reasons consumers shop at a particular retail outlet. The result is a classification scheme in which retail outlets, like consumer goods, are categorized as convenience–preference, shopping, or specialty.[11] The type of retail outlet has a significant influence on the marketing strategies the retailer should select. *Convenience–preference retailers* focus on conve-

**FIGURE 16-2**

**Classification of Retailers on the Basis of Customer Service Levels**

| Self-Service | Self-Selection | Limited-Service | Full-Service |

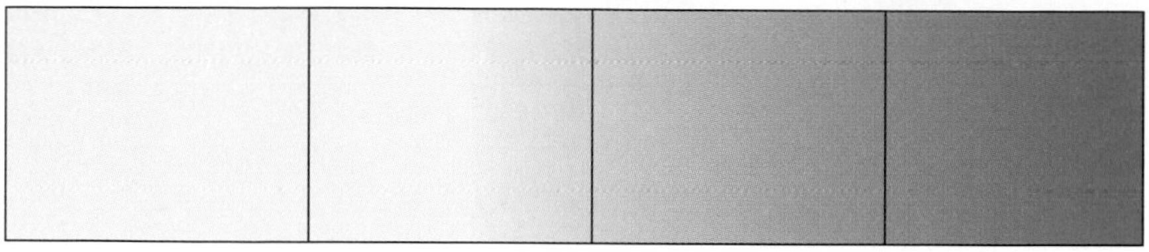

**Characteristics**

| Very few services | Restricted services | Limited variety | Wide variety of services |
|---|---|---|---|
| Price appeal | Price appeal | of service | Fashion merchandise |
| Staple goods | Staple goods | Less price appeal | Specialty merchandise |
| Convenience goods | Convenience goods | Shopping goods | |

**Examples**

| Warehouse retailing | Discount retailing | Door-to-door | Specialty stores |
|---|---|---|---|
| Supermarkets | Variety stores | Telephone sales | Department stores |
| Mail-order | Mail-order retailing | Variety stores | |
| Automatic vending | | | |

Source: Adapted from Larry D. Redinbaugh, *Retailing Management: A Planning Approach*, p. 12, Copyright © 1976 McGraw-Hill Book Company. Used with the permission of McGraw-Hill Book Company.

nient locations, long store hours, rapid checkout service, and adequate parking facilities. Small food stores, gasoline retailers, and some barber shops may be included in this category.

*Shopping stores* typically include furniture stores, appliance retailers, clothing outlets, and sporting goods stores. Consumers will compare prices, assortments, and quality levels of competing outlets before making a purchase decision. Managers of shopping stores attempt to differentiate their outlets through advertising, window displays and in-store layouts, knowledgeable salespeople, and appropriate merchandise assortments.

*Specialty retailers* provide some combination of product lines, service, and reputation that results in consumers' willingness to expend considerable effort to shop there. Holt Renfrew and Birks have developed a sufficient degree of loyalty among many shoppers to be categorized as specialty retailers.

The foregoing categories are not absolute. The most exclusive specialty store carries handkerchiefs, and many supermarkets have gourmet food departments.

## Retailers Classified by Services Provided

Some retailers seek a differential advantage by developing a unique combination of service offerings for the customers who compose their target market. Retailing operations may be classified according to the extent of the services they offer. Figure 16-2 indicates the spectrum of retailer services from virtually no services (self-service) to a full range of customer services (full-service retailers).

Since the self-service and self-selection retailers provide few services to their customers, retailer location and price are important factors. These retailers tend to specialize in staple and convenience goods that are purchased frequently by customers and require little product service or advice from retail personnel.

*This sporting goods store provides a far wider range of soccer balls than a department store would. By offering a limited line of goods, this store can attract people like this father and son, who may be looking for the "perfect" soccer ball, as well as professional athletes who want to select quality merchandise from a complete line of products.*

The full-service retail establishments focus more on fashion-oriented shopping goods and specialty items and offer a wide variety of services for their clientele. As a result, their prices tend to be higher than those of self-service retailers due to the higher operating costs associated with the services.

## Retailers Classified by Product Lines

Perhaps the most commonly used method of categorizing retailers is to consider the product lines they handle. Grouping retailers by product lines produces three major categories: limited-line stores, specialty stores, and general merchandise retailers. Figure 16–3 shows retail trade for various types of outlets. From this it can be seen that Canadians spend most on food and automobiles.

### Limited-Line Retailers

**limited-line store** Retailer that offers a large assortment of a single line of products or a few related lines of products.

*A large assortment of a single line of products or a few related lines of products* are offered in **limited-line stores**. Their development paralleled the growth of towns when the population grew sufficiently to support them. These operations include such retailers as furniture stores, hardware stores, grocery stores and supermarkets, appliance stores, and sporting goods stores. Examples of limited-line stores include Sherwin-Williams (paints), Leon's and House of Teak (furniture), Radio Shack (home electronics), Agnew Surpass and Bata (shoes). Calculator World (electronic calculators), D'Allaird's (ready-to-wear), and Coles (books).

These retailers choose to cater to the needs of a specific target market — people who want to select from a complete line in purchasing a particular product. The marketing vice-president of one limited-line firm summarized the limited-line retailer's strategy this way: "Sears can show customers three types of football, but we can show them 40.[12] Most retailers are in the limited-line category.

FIGURE 16 – 3

## Total Retail Sales, by Kind of Business, 1987 and 1988

| Kind of business | 1987 | 1988 | Percentage change 1988/1987 |
|---|---|---|---|
| | \$000 000 | | |
| **All Stores — Total** | 153 732.8 | 165 190.4 | + 7.5 |
| Combination stores (groceries and meat) | 26 775.1 | 27 903.4 | + 4.2 |
| Grocery, confectionery, and sundries stores | 7 690.9 | 8 287.8 | + 7.8 |
| All other food stores | 2 805.7 | 2 996.3 | + 6.8 |
| Department stores | 12 906.0 | 13 271.1 | + 2.8 |
| General merchandise stores | 3 063.8 | 3 109.3 | + 1.5 |
| General stores | 2 263.5 | 2 414.8 | + 6.7 |
| Variety stores | 1 073.6 | 1 056.9 | − 1.6 |
| Motor vehicle dealers | 32 248.1 | 35 917.5 | +11.4 |
| Used car dealers | 1 032.6 | 1 190.2 | +15.3 |
| Service stations | 12 276.8 | 12 732.9 | + 3.7 |
| Garages | 1 699.1 | 1 879.1 | +10.6 |
| Automotive parts and accessories stores | 3 440.3 | 3 766.8 | + 9.5 |
| Men's clothing stores | 1 583.1 | 1 718.7 | + 8.6 |
| Women's clothing stores | 3 256.4 | 3 374.2 | + 3.6 |
| Family clothing stores | 2 244.0 | 2 392.9 | + 6.6 |
| Specialty shoe stores | 300.0 | 315.1 | + 5.0 |
| Family shoe stores | 1 196.4 | 1 284.0 | + 7.3 |
| Hardware stores | 1 609.9 | 1 824.0 | +13.3 |
| Household furniture stores | 1 879.3 | 2 031.0 | + 8.2 |
| Household appliance stores | 634.8 | 697.0 | + 9.8 |
| Furniture, TV, radio, and appliance stores | 1 683.7 | 1 715.8 | + 1.9 |
| Pharmacies, patent medicine and cosmetics stores | 6 691.5 | 7 459.1 | +11.5 |
| Book and stationery stores | 896.2 | 1 018.8 | +13.7 |
| Florists | 581.9 | 615.3 | + 5.7 |
| Jewellery stores | 1 136.9 | 1 215.0 | + 6.9 |
| Sporting goods and accessories stores | 2 342.3 | 2 668.5 | +13.9 |
| Personal accessories stores | 2 396.9 | 2 573.2 | + 7.4 |
| All other stores | 18 024.1 | 19 758.4 | + 9.6 |

Source: Statistics Canada, Bulletin 63-006, December 1990, p. 103.

*The supermarket*    Until the 1920s, food purchases were made at full-service grocery stores. Store personnel filled orders (often from a shopping list presented to them), provided delivery services, and often granted credit to their customers. The supermarket eliminated these services in exchange for lower prices, and it quickly revolutionized food shopping in Canada and much of the world.[13]

## Survival Techniques for the Nineties No. 1: Differentiate, Then Deliver

In mass retailing it doesn't matter if you're in the grocery business, the oil business, the car business, or the discount department store business, the critical issues are the same. Competition is ruthless, as are low-margin pricing policies, similar product lines, saturation of retail outlets, and a market that's not growing. It's a tough, tough place to make money today.

Not only is it tough, but retailers have abused the perception of regular price. This creates mistrust on the part of the consumer. Retailers have created many of their own problems with the prevalence of short-term selling tactics, shoddy employment practices, a win/lose adversarial negotiation style with their goods and service suppliers, and the destruction of the concept of customer service.

There are really two ways to derive long-term competitive advantage. Either a business is the legitimate low-cost provider in the marketplace, or it must develop strategies to differentiate itself from the competition.

There are some good examples of retailers developing differentiation. Canadian Tire offers a legitimate proposition to its customers: it is the place for people to shop for automotive and hardware supplies. Toys "Я" Us offers every toy available: it sells assortments of toys, not price.

If a business advertises an image differentiating itself from others, that image must be delivered.

Source: This and the other "survival techniques" are adapted from Arthur Smith, "Survival Techniques for the Nineties," *Marketing* (January 22, 1990), pp. 20, 22.

**supermarket**  Large-scale, departmentalized retail store offering a large variety of food products.

A **supermarket** can be defined as *a large-scale, departmentalized retail store offering a large variety of food products* such as meats, produce, dairy products, canned goods, and frozen foods in addition to various nonfood items. It operates on a *self-service* basis and emphasizes price and adequate parking facilities. Supermarket customers typically shop once or twice a week and make fill-in purchases between each major shopping trip. Supermarkets account for 71.8 percent of food store sales in Canada.

In recent years supermarkets have become increasingly competitive. One Ontario supermarket attempted to increase its share of the market through a well-publicized price-cutting program. The ramifications were quickly felt in other areas of the country where branches of competing chains operate. Retaliation by other supermarkets was swift, and temporary price cuts ensued — as well as reductions in profits. Supermarket profits average only about 1 percent of sales after taxes. However, a high turnover of 20–26 times per year provides attractive returns on investment.

With a razor-thin profit margin, supermarkets compete through careful planning of retail displays in order to sell more merchandise per week and reduce the amount of investment in inventory. Product location is studied carefully in order to expose the consumer to as much merchandise as possible (and increase impulse purchases). In an attempt to fight the tendency of consumers to eat many of their meals outside the home, supermarkets have begun to feature their own delicatessens and bakeries and to devote ever increasing portions of their stores to nonfood items. Nonfood products such as toys, toiletries, magazines, records, over-the-counter drugs, and small kitchen utensils are carried for two reasons: (1) consumers have displayed a willingness to buy such items in supermarkets, and (2) supermarket managers like them because they have a higher profit margin than the food products. Nonfood sales have grown substantially as a percentage of supermarket sales.

Another change is an increased emphasis on warehouse stores, box stores (carrying a very limited line of high-volume items, which customers carry out in discarded boxes), and food barns. All of these provide fewer items within a narrower range of size and brand options than conventional supermarkets.

*By specializing in a narrow line of products, the owner of this bakery can develop a level of expertise that would be hard to achieve in a large grocery store. This is usually accompanied by more personalized service than that received in larger stores, especially if the owner is independent. Such a combination of advantages can add up to a good share of the local market, even in today's competitive environment.*

## Specialty Stores

A **specialty store** typically *handles only part of a single line of products.* However, this narrow line is stocked in considerable depth. Such stores include meat markets, shoe stores, bakeries, furriers, and luggage shops. Although some of these stores are operated by chains, most are run as independent small-scale operations. The specialty store is perhaps the greatest stronghold of the independent retailer, who can develop expertise in providing a very narrow line of products for his or her local market.

Specialty stores should not be confused with specialty goods, for the specialty store typically carries convenience and shopping goods. The label "specialty" comes from the practice of handling a specific, narrow line of merchandise.

**specialty store**    Retailer that handles only part of a single line of products.

## General Merchandise Retailers

*Department stores*    The department store is actually a series of limited-line and specialty stores under one roof. A **department store**, by definition, is *a large retail firm that handles a variety of merchandise* that includes men's and boys' wear, women's wear and accessories, household linens and dry goods, home furnishings, appliances, and furniture. It serves the consumer by acting as a one-stop shopping centre for almost all personal and household items.

A distinguishing feature of the department store is indicated by its name. The entire store is *organized around departments* for the purposes of service, promotion, and control. A general merchandising manager is responsible for the entire store's product planning. Reporting to the merchandising manager are the buyers who manage each department. The buyers typically run the departments almost as independent businesses and are given considerable discretion in merchandising and layout decisions. Acceptance of the retailing axiom that "well-purchased goods are half sold" is indicated in the department manager's title of *buyer*. The buyers,

**department store**    Large retailer that handles a variety of merchandise.

452     Part Six/Distribution

particularly those in charge of high-fashion departments, spend a considerable portion of their time making decisions concerning the inventory to be carried in their departments.

The department store has been the symbol of retailing since the turn of the century. It started in Canada with Timothy Eaton in 1869, when he purchased the 4-metre wide dry-goods store and stock of William Jennings for $6500. Eaton established a one-price cash policy (instead of bargaining and paying in produce) and formulated the famous "goods satisfactory or money refunded" guarantee. By 1929, half the retail sales in Canada were made at Eaton's.[14]

Today, almost every urban area in Canada has one or more department stores associated with its downtown area and its major shopping areas. Department stores have had a major impact in many cities. For example, as recently as 1969, Eaton's received 40 percent of every retail dollar (except groceries) in Winnipeg.[15]

The impact of department stores on urban life is not confined to Canada. Such stores are, of course, widespread in the United States. European shoppers associate London with Harrod's and Paris with Au Printemps. Australians associate Melbourne and Sydney with Myer.

Department stores are known for offering their customers a wide variety of services such as charge accounts, delivery, gift wrapping, and liberal return privileges. In addition, approximately 50 percent of their employees and some 40 percent of their floor space are devoted to nonselling activities. As a result, department stores have relatively high operating costs, averaging between 45 and 60 percent of sales.

Department stores have faced intense competition in the past 30 years. Their relatively high operating costs make them vulnerable to such new retailing innovations as discount stores, catalogue merchandisers, and hypermarkets (discussed later in this section). In addition, department stores are typically located in downtown business districts and experience the problems associated with limited parking, traffic congestion, and urban migration to the suburbs.

Department stores have displayed a willingness to adapt to changing consumer desires. Addition of bargain basements and expansion of parking facilities were attempts to compete with discount operations and suburban retailers. Also, department stores have followed the movement of the population to the suburbs by opening major branches in outlying shopping centres. Canadian department stores have led other retailers in maintaining a vital and dynamic downtown through modernization of their stores, extended store hours, emphasis on attracting the trade of tourists and people attending conventions, and focusing on the residents of the central cities.

**Variety stores**    Retail *firms that offer an extensive range and assortment of low-priced merchandise* are called **variety stores**. Some examples are Woolworth and Stedmans. The nation's variety stores account for only about 0.64 percent of all retail sales. Variety stores have steadily declined in popularity. Many have evolved into or have been replaced by other retailing categories such as discounting.

**variety store**    Retailer that handles an extensive range and assortment of low-priced merchandise.

**Mass merchandisers**    Mass merchandising has made major inroads on department store sales during the past two decades by emphasizing lower prices for well-known brand-name products, high turnover of goods, and reduced services. **Mass merchandisers** often stock a *wider line of products than department stores, but they usually do not offer the depth of assortment in each line.* Major types of mass merchandisers are discount houses, hypermarkets, and catalogue retailers.

**mass merchandiser**    Retailer that often stocks a wider line of products than department stores, but usually does not offer the depth of assortment in each line.

*Discount houses*   The birth of the modern **discount house** came at the end of World War II when a New York operation named Masters discovered that a very large number of customers were willing to shop at a store that *did not offer such traditional retail services as credit, sales assistance by clerks, and delivery, in exchange for reduced prices*. Within a very brief period retailers throughout the country followed the Masters formula and either changed over from their traditional operations or opened new stores dedicated to discounting. At first the discount stores were primarily involved with the sale of appliances, but they have spread into furniture, soft goods, drugs, and even food.

Discount operations had existed in previous years, but the early discounters usually operated from manufacturers' catalogues, with no stock on display and often a limited number of potential customers. The new discounters operated large stores, advertised heavily, emphasized low prices on well-known brands, and were open to the public. Elimination of many of the "free" services provided by traditional retailers allowed the discount operations to reduce their markups to 10 to 25 percent below their competitors. And consumers, who had become accustomed to self-service by shopping at supermarkets, responded in great numbers to this retailing innovation. Conventional retailers such as Kresge and Woolworth joined the discounting practice by opening their own K mart and Woolco stores.

As the discount houses move into new product areas, a noticeable increase in the number of services offered as well as a corresponding decrease in the discount margin is evident. Carpeted floors are beginning to appear in discounters' stores, credit is increasingly available, and many discounters are even quietly dropping the term *discount* from their name. Even though they still offer fewer services, their operating costs are increasing as they become similar to the traditional department stores. Some have even moved into the "best" shopping areas, and now offer such name brands as Seiko watches, Puma running shoes, and Pentax cameras.

*Hypermarkets*   **Hypermarkets** are giant *mass merchandisers that operate on a low-price, self-service basis and carry lines of soft goods, hard goods, and groceries*. Hypermarkets are sometimes called superstores, although this latter term has also been used to describe a variety of large retail operations.[16] The *hypermarché*, or hypermarket, began in France and has since spread to Canada and the United States to a limited degree. The Hypermarché Laval outside Montreal was the first to open and had 19 500 m$^2$ of selling space (11 to 15 times the size of the average supermarket) and 40 checkouts. A typical hypermarket is like a shopping centre in a single store. It sells food, hardware, soft goods, building materials, auto supplies, appliances, and prescription drugs, and has a restaurant, a beauty salon, a barber shop, a bank branch, and a bakery. Many of these superstores are currently in operation throughout the world. It appears that they are more popular in Europe than in North America. This is likely because North America already had many large, well-developed shopping centres before the hypermarket concept arrived.

*Catalogue retailers*   One of the major growth areas in retailing in the past decade has been that of catalogue retailing. **Catalogue retailers** *mail catalogues to their customers and operate from a showroom* displaying samples of their products. Orders are filled from a backroom warehouse. Price is an important factor for catalogue store customers, and low prices are made possible by few services, storage of most of the inventory in the warehouse, reduced shoplifting losses, and handling products that are unlikely to become obsolete — such as luggage, small appliances, gift items, sporting equipment, toys, and jewellery. The largest catalogue retailer in Canada is

**discount house**   Retailer that, in exchange for reduced prices, does not offer such traditional retail services as credit, sales assistance by clerks, and delivery.

**hypermarket**   Mass merchandiser that operates on a low-price, self-service basis and carries lines of soft goods, hard goods, and groceries.

**catalogue retailer**   Retailer that mails catalogues to its customers and operates from a showroom displaying samples of its products.

*Teleshopping is the latest concept in the area of general-merchandise marketing. Shoppers can select products from an assortment displayed on a TV or computer screen, and then order them from a central distribution centre. This may be the catalogue retailing of the future, using video screens instead of the printed page.*

Consumers Distributing. (Mail-order catalogue retailing is discussed later in this chapter.)

## Retailers Classified by Location of Retail Transaction

A fourth method of categorizing retailers is by determining whether the transaction takes place in a store. While the overwhelming majority of retail sales occur in retail stores, nonstore retailing is important for many products. Nonstore retailing includes direct house-to-house sales, mail-order retailing, and automatic merchandising machines. These kinds of sales account for about 1.7 percent of all retail sales.

### House-to-House Retailing

**house-to-house retailer**
Retailer that sells products by direct contact between the retailer–seller and the customer at the home of the customer.

One of the oldest marketing channels was built around *direct contact between the retailer–seller and the customer at the home of the customer* — **house-to-house retailing**. It provides maximum convenience for the consumer and allows the manufacturer to control the firm's marketing channel. House-to-house retailing is a minor part of the retailing picture, with less than 1 percent of all retail sales.

House-to-house retailing is conducted by a number of different merchandisers. Manufacturers of such products as bakery and dairy products and newspapers utilize this channel. Firms whose products require emphasis on personal selling and product demonstrations may also use it. Such products and services would include, for example, cosmetics (Avon), vacuum cleaners (Electrolux), household brushes (Fuller Brush Company), encyclopedias (World Book), and insurance.

---

## A·P·P·L·Y·I·N·G  T·H·E  C·O·N·C·E·P·T·S

### Mom (and Former Lawyer) Turns Concept into Winner

Cindy Eeson had never been to a Tupperware or Mary Kay home sales party before she launched her children's clothing business. But something told the former lawyer that direct marketing was the approach to take. As a result, the youthful 38-year-old has turned her home-based clothing venture into a business that should record more than $1 million in sales next year.

"Maybe we'll be the McDonald's of kids' clothing," Eeson says of her firm, Kids Only Clothing Club Inc., which she started in 1988.

Eeson has always had a passion for sewing. She worked in costume design for a time after earning a university arts degree. But it wasn't until after the birth of her third child that she considered starting her own business: designing, manufacturing, and selling children's clothes.

Retailers responded enthusiastically to her handpainted clothing creations, but she decided she wanted to carry the project through to completion herself.

After carefully researching the direct-selling market and looking at companies like Tupperware and Mary Kay Cosmetics, Eeson launched Kids Only. "I thought, this is the start of something, and if I'm lucky I'll be the first one out there," she said. "I know I won't be the last."

Working initially out of her attic, Eeson sold $120 000 worth of clothing through home parties in her first full year of operation. Her second year of business was conducted from a basement-level factory space in a small shopping centre; she expected sales to top $500 000.

Sixty-five consultants, every one a parent, sell Eeson's creations at home parties in cities across Canada. The orders are made up in Calgary and shipped to the representatives within three weeks.

The clothes are bright, loose and flowing, and designed to grow with the child. Eeson's creations feature adjustable waistbands, reinforced knees, and extendable cuffs that allow for six inches of vertical growth. Eeson says Kids Only takes the frustration out of shopping for busy parents. They can browse through her colourful brochures and look at samples of outfits without dragging their sometimes unwilling children from store to store.

Source: Adapted from Anna Geddes, "Mom Turns Concept into Winner," *Winnipeg Free Press* (June 14, 1990).

---

Some firms — such as Tupperware, and Stanley Home Products — use a variation called *party-plan selling* where a customer gives a party and invites several neighbours and friends. During the party a company representative makes a presentation of the product, and the host or hostess receives a commission based on the amount of products sold. Another version depends heavily on the *personal influence network* and "positive thinking" techniques — for example, Amway and Shaklee. Friends and acquaintances are recruited to recruit others and sell merchandise. A commission scheme on sales made by recruits makes it generally more profitable for sponsors to aggressively solicit recruits than to sell products themselves.

The house-to-house method of retailing would appear to be a low-cost method of distribution. No plush retail facilities are required; no investment in inventory is necessary; and most house-to-house salespersons operate on a commission basis. In fact, this method is an extremely high-cost approach to distribution. Often the distribution cost of a product marketed through retail stores is half that of the same product retailed house-to-house. High travel costs, the problems involved in recruiting and training a huge sales force that generally has a high turnover, nonproductive calls, several layers of commissions, and the limited number of contracts per day result in high operating expenses.

## Mail-Order Retailing

The customers of **mail-order merchandisers** can *place merchandise orders by mail, by telephone, or by visiting the mail-order desk of a retail store.* Goods are then shipped to the customer's home or to the local retail store.

**mail-order merchandiser**
Retailer that offers its customers the option of placing merchandise orders by mail, by telephone, or by visiting the mail-order desk of a retail store.

Many department stores and specialty stores issue catalogues to seek telephone and mail-order sales and to promote in-store purchases of items featured in the catalogues. Among typical department stores, telephone and mail-generated orders account for 15 percent of total volume during the Christmas season.

Mail-order selling began in Canada in 1894 when Eaton's distributed a slim 32-page booklet to rural visitors at the Canadian National Exhibition in Toronto. That first catalogue contained only a few items, mostly clothing and farm supplies. Simpsons soon followed, and mail-order retailing became an important source of products in isolated Canadian settlements.

Even though mail-order sales represent only a small percentage of all retail sales, it is an important channel for many consumers who desire convenience and a large selection of colours and sizes.

With the demise of the Eaton's catalogue sales operations in 1976, apparently due to a failure to introduce effective cost and inventory control measures, Sears became the one major mail-order catalogue marketer left in Canada. Sales have been strong. Catalogue sales contributed at least a third to Simpsons-Sears' $3.1 billion in sales in 1982. Sears now has nearly 1300 catalogue sales offices across Canada and produces 11 catalogues a year, with a combined distribution of 45 million.[17]

Mail-order houses offer a wide range of products — from novelty items (Regal Gifts) to sporting equipment (S.I.R.). The growing number of women who work outside the home, increasing time pressures, and a decline in customer service in some department stores augur well for catalogue sales.

## Automatic Merchandising

*Automatic vending machines* — the true robot stores — are a good way to purchase a wide range of convenience goods. These machines accounted for over 424.5 million in sales in Canada.[18] Approximately 213 000 vending machines are currently in operation throughout the country.

While automatic merchandising is important in the retailing of some products, it represents less than 1 percent of all retail sales. Its future growth is limited by such factors as the cost of machines and the necessity for regular maintenance and repair. In addition, automatically vended products are confined to convenience goods that are standardized in size and weight with a high rate of turnover. Prices for some products purchased in vending machines are higher than store prices for the same products.

# Retailers Classified by Form of Ownership

The fifth method of classifying retailers is by ownership. The two major types are corporate chain stores and independent retailers. In addition, independent retailers may join a wholesaler-sponsored voluntary chain, band together to form a retail co-operative, or enter into a franchise arrangement through contractual agreements with a manufacturer, wholesaler, or service organization. Each type has its special characteristics.

## Chain Stores

**chain stores**   Groups of retail stores that are centrally owned and managed and that handle the same lines of products.

**Chain stores** are *groups of retail stores that are centrally owned and managed and that handle the same lines of products.* The concept of chain stores is certainly not new; the Mitsui chain was operating in Japan in the 1600s. Woodwards, Zellers, The Bay, and Reitman's have operated in Canada for many years.

The major advantage possessed by chain operations over independent retailers is economies of scale. Volume purchases through a central buying office allow such chains as Provigo and Save-On-Foods to obtain lower prices than independents. Since a chain such as Provigo has hundreds of retail stores, specialists in layout, sales training, and accounting systems may be used to increase efficiency. Advertising can also be effectively used. An advertisement in a national magazine for Eaton's promotes every Eaton's store in Canada.

Chains (excluding food stores) account for approximately one-third of all retail stores and their dollar volume of sales amounts to 42 percent of all retail sales. At present, chains dominate four fields: department stores, variety stores, shoe stores, and food stores.[19] Figure 16–4 lists the 10 largest retailers in Canada.

Many of the larger chains have expanded their operations to the rest of the world. Sears now has branch stores in Spain, Mexico, and several countries in South America. Safeway operates supermarkets in Germany, the United Kingdom, and Australia. Bowring's has expanded internationally, as has Marks & Spencer. Direct retailers such as Avon and Tupperware have sales representatives in Europe, South America, and Southeast Asia.

## Independent Retailers

Independents have attempted to compete with chains in a number of ways. Some independents were unable to do so efficiently and went out of business. Others have joined retail co-operatives, wholesaler-sponsored voluntary chains, or franchise

FIGURE 16 – 4

### Canada's Largest Retailers

| Consumer Product Retailers | Revenues 1989 ($000s) | Rank within Industry Sector | Net Income 1989 ($000s) | Rank within Industry Sector | Total Assets 1989 ($000s) | Rank within Industry Sector | Percentage Return on Shareholders' Equity | Number of Employees |
|---|---|---|---|---|---|---|---|---|
| Loblaw Companies Ltd. | 7 934 000 | 1 | 70 000 | 6 | 2 040 000 | 3 | 10.0 | 39 500 |
| Provigo Inc. | 6 139 000 | 2 | 10 700 | 19 | 1 110 700 | 6 | 2.8 | 15 000 |
| Hudson's Bay Co. | 4 771 328 | 3 | 121 908 | 4 | 3 897 653 | 1 | 10 3 | 65 000 |
| Sears Canada Inc. | 4 562 300 | 4 | 106 100 | 5 | 3 168 500 | 2 | 11.4 | — |
| Canada Safeway Ltd. | 4 198 581 | 5 | 144 946 | 3 | 1 256 910 | 5 | — | 24 000 |
| Canadian Tire Corp., Ltd. | 2 956 842 | 6 | 149 616 | 2 | 1 730 342 | 4 | 17.1 | 25 000 |
| Great Atlantic & Pacific Co. of Canada | 2 258 803 | 7 | 29 329 | 10 | 464 891 | 12 | 17.6 | 18 000 |
| F.W. Woolworth Co. Ltd | 2 257 546 | 8 | 64 311 | 7 | 800 055 | 7 | 14.9 | 27 000 |
| Zellers Inc. | 2 150 000 | 9 | 179 500 | 1 | 757 000 | 8 | — | 15 000 |
| Dylex Ltd. | 1 718 265 | 10 | (60 701) | 36 | 741 409 | 9 | — | 23 248 |

Source: *The Financial Post 500* (Summer, 1990), p. 153.

*All shopping malls have stores and restaurants, but not many include an indoor amusement park. Fantasyland, at the West Edmonton Mall, includes a two-hectare, $90 million addition that features an indoor lake complete with submarines and artificial rubber trees. Quite a departure from the first department store in Canada, which was opened by Timothy Eaton in 1869.*

operations. Still others have remained in business by exploiting their advantages of flexibility in operation and knowledge of local market conditions. The independents continue to represent a major part of Canadian retailing.

# Shopping Centres

## Planned Shopping Centres

**planned shopping centre**
Group of retail stores planned, co-ordinated, and marketed as a unit to shoppers in a particular geographic trade area.

A pronounced shift of retail trade away from the traditional downtown retailing districts and toward suburban shopping centres developed after 1950. A **planned shopping centre** is a *group of retail stores planned, co-ordinated, and marketed as a unit to shoppers in a particular geographic trade area*. These centres followed population shifts to the suburbs and focused on correcting many of the problems involved in shopping in the downtown business districts. Ample parking and locations away from the downtown traffic congestion appeal to the suburban shopper. Additional hours for shopping during the evenings and on weekends facilitate family shopping.

### Types of shopping centres

There are three types of planned shopping centres. The smallest and most common is the *neighbourhood shopping centre*, which most often comprises a supermarket and a group of smaller stores such as a drugstore, a laundry and dry cleaner, a small appliance store, and perhaps a beauty shop and barbershop. Such centres provide convenient shopping for perhaps 5000 to 15 000 shoppers who live within a few minutes' commuting time of the centre. Such centres typically contain 5 to 15 stores whose product mix is usually confined to convenience goods and some shopping goods.

## A·P·P·L·Y·I·N·G  T·H·E  C·O·N·C·E·P·T·S

### *Survival Techniques for the Nineties, No. 2: Loyalty Marketing*

Loyalty marketing is the process of providing incentives to customers so that they will want to return again and again. Such activities are sometimes called "continuity programs." The development of a loyalty-marketing program is more important for those companies or industries in a commodity-like business, where there is less ability to differentiate by product. Customer loyalty today equals the best sale price.

Airlines started the continuity programs. Their objective was to attract and maintain their principal customer, the business traveller, using frequent-flyer programs. These programs have become so important to the airlines, due to the loyalty factors, repeat business, and the marketing value of the frequent-flyer list, that they can't afford to drop them.

One of the most outstanding loyalty programs is the Zellers Club Z program. Zellers developed the first on-line frequent-buyer system (points are given with purchases) in North America. The initial objectives of Club Z included specific financial targets for market penetration, customer shopping frequency, incremental purchase, and new customers. Not only were these targets exceeded, but the program continues to outperform expectations.

Another goal was to increase the frequency of purchase of everyday consumables. Zellers wanted to find a way to drive up sales of such things as shampoo or toothpaste rather than having to "give them away" in order to get customers back into the store.

On an individual customer basis, Zellers wanted to build frequency per customer and spending per customer. The Club Z program enabled the company to delineate a specific day in the week, hour in the day, or department in the store where it could give double points. For example, the fashion department gave double points on Valentine's Day.

Club Z also provides a database so that Zellers knows exactly where Club Z members live and how much they spend. Zellers can thus identify profiles of individuals who are good consumers, and target them. Loyalty programs like this one enable a firm to add an important degree of differentiation to its offerings that truly builds loyalty.

Source: Excerpted from a presentation by Arthur Smith, former executive vice-president of Zellers in *Marketing* (January 22, 1990), p. 20.

---

*Community shopping centres* typically serve 20 000 to 100 000 persons in a trade area extending a few kilometres in each direction. These centres are likely to contain 15 to 50 retail stores, with a branch of a local department store or a large variety store as the primary tenant. In addition to the stores found in a neighbourhood centre, the community centre is likely to have additional stores featuring shopping goods, some professional offices, and a branch of a bank.

The largest planned centre is the *regional shopping centre*, a giant shopping district of at least 30 000 m$^2$ of shopping space, usually built around one or more major department stores and containing as many as 300 smaller stores. In order to be successful, regional centres must be located in areas where at least 150 000 people reside within 30 minutes' driving time of the centre. Characteristically, they are temperature-controlled, enclosed facilities. The regional centres provide the widest product mixes and the greatest depth of each line.

Such a centre is the West Edmonton Mall, located in Jasper Place, a suburb of Edmonton. Said to be the largest shopping centre in the world, the West Edmonton Mall is located in a densely populated area and is easily accessible to both cars and pedestrians. Catering to a range of suburban clientele, the stores at this mall offer a variety of quality merchandise to their customers.

Planned shopping centres account for approximately 40 percent of all retail sales in Canada. Their growth has slowed in recent years, however, as the most lucrative locations are occupied and the market for such centres appears to have been saturated in many regions. Recent trends have developed toward the building of smaller centres in smaller cities and towns.

**Scrambled Merchandising Is Common in Modern Retailing**

*"No used cars? What kind of a drugstore is this anyway?"*

Source: Masters Agency.

## Scrambled Merchandising

A fundamental change in retailing has been the steady deterioration of clear-cut delineations of retailer types. Anyone who has attempted to fill a prescription recently has been exposed to the concept of **scrambled merchandising** — *the retail practice of carrying dissimilar lines to generate added sales volume*. The large mass-merchandising drugstore carries not only prescription and proprietary drugs, but also gifts, hardware, housewares, records, magazines, grocery products, garden supplies, even small appliances. Gasoline retailers now sell bread and milk; super-markets carry antifreeze, televisions, cameras, and stereo equipment.

Scrambled merchandising was born out of retailers' willingness to add dissimilar merchandise lines in order to offer additional higher-profit lines, as well as to satisfy consumer demands for one-stop shopping. It complicates manufacturers' channel decisions because attempts to maintain or increase a firm's market share mean, in

**scrambled merchandising**
The retail practice of carrying dissimilar lines to generate added sales volume.

most instances, that the firm will have to develop multiple channels to reach the diverse retailers handling its products.

# The Wheel-of-Retailing Hypothesis

M.P. McNair attempted to explain the patterns of change in retailing through what has been termed the **wheel of retailing**. According to this hypothesis, *new types of retailers gain a competitive foothold by offering lower prices to their customers through the reduction or elimination of services*. Once they are established, however, they evolve by adding more services, and their prices gradually rise. Then they become vulnerable to a new low-price retailer who enters with minimum services — and the wheel turns.

Most of the major developments in retailing appear to fit the wheel pattern. Early department stores, chain stores, supermarkets, and discount stores all emphasized limited service and low prices. In most instances, price levels have gradually increased as services have been added.

There have been some exceptions, however. Suburban shopping centres, convenience food stores, and vending machines were not developed on a foundation of low-price appeals. However, the wheel pattern has been present often enough in the past that it should serve as a general indicator of future developments in retailing.[20]

**wheel of retailing** Hypothesized process of change in retailing, which suggests that new types of retailers gain a competitive foothold by offering lower prices through the reduction or elimination of services; but once established, they add more services and their prices gradually rise, so that they then become vulnerable to a new low-price retailer with minimum services — and the wheel turns.

## Trends in Retailing

A number of trends are currently emerging that may greatly affect tomorrow's retailer. One is the possibility of **teleshopping** — *ordering merchandise that has been displayed on home television sets or computers*. Cable television currently reaches 69 percent of Canadian homes, and it has the potential of revolutionizing many retail practices if interactive teleshopping through cable television becomes possible. A similar concept is shopping through an interactive personal computer. In Manitoba, the Grassroots system, which uses Telidon technology, enables farmers to obtain precise weather reports for their farm locality. This same system is linked with several retailers, including The Bay, Sears, Sports Mart, and Compu Store. Selected items are listed, along with prices, and orders can be placed through the computer network. Sears and S.I.R., a sporting goods catalogue retailer, both offer customers the chance to place a catalogue order through the Grassroots system after browsing through the printed catalogue. Similarly, patrons may use the system to order tickets for the Jets' hockey games.

**teleshopping** Ordering merchandise that has been displayed on home television sets or computers.

Teleshopping obviously offers an exciting new dimension for retailing, but it is not without its drawbacks. A survey conducted for *Marketing News* found that only 10 percent of 2163 respondents expressed positive attitudes about teleshopping. Reasons for the low acceptance varied, but included a desire to inspect the product personally, a preference for going out to shop, and the fear of being tempted to purchase unneeded items.[21]

Teleshopping via an interactive cable system is likely to be most effective for products where sight, feel, smell, and personal service are not important in the purchase decision.[22]

In the future, retail executives believe that catalogue stores, direct mail, discount houses, and telephone selling are likely to offer growth opportunities. Medium-sized discount stores may be giving way to extremely large hypermarket discounters on one hand and specialty stores on the other. The furniture warehouse retailer (such

## I·S·S·U·E·S  I·N  I·N·T·E·R·N·A·T·I·O·N·A·L  M·A·R·K·E·T·I·N·G

### IKEA Makes Furniture Shopping Easy and Fun

IKEA's home furnishings stores have been described as "Disneyland for adults." The company uses every possible inducement to get customers to come in and stay. As a result, almost no one leaves empty-handed.

The idea behind IKEA (the words rhyme) is simple: to sell quality Scandinavian furniture at prices that almost anyone can afford. This idea is so universally appealing that in 1990 IKEA attracted 100 million customers to its 88 stores in 20 countries. More than 70 percent of the company's sales come from countries outside Scandinavia.

The stores are huge warehouse-style buildings covering 100 000 or more square feet, decorated in bold blue and yellow (the colors of the Swedish flag) and filled with china, plants, wallpaper, flooring, carpets, lighting, and furniture that customers assemble themselves. About 12 000 items are available.

IKEA attracts customers in a variety of ways. It sells well-designed merchandise in self-service stores at extremely low prices. All purchases are available on the spot — usually. (Out-of-stock items are the company's main problem.) Once the customer is in the store, all obstacles to purchase are removed: catalogues, tape measures, pencils and paper, and shopping carts are provided; strollers are available, or children may be left in a nursery (which offers free diapers); a restaurant/café serves Swedish food at moderate prices; there are automatic teller machines in the stores; and customers can borrow automobile roof racks. By encouraging customers to take their purchases home with them, IKEA saves money on shipping, storage, and assembly.

IKEA's cut-rate pricing is combined with mass mailings and multimedia advertising. Whenever it opens a new store, IKEA blitzes the area with billboards and sends catalogues to all homes within a 40-mile radius. It spends nearly half its annual marketing budget on direct mail, publishing 27 different catalogues in 12 languages.

Sources: Cara Appelbaum, "How IKEA Blitzes a Market," *Marketing Week* (June 11, 1990), pp. 18–19; Janet Bamford with A. Dunlap Smith, "Why Competitors Shop for Ideas at IKEA," *Business Week* (October 9, 1989), p. 88; Seth Chandler, "Swedish Marketers Going Global," *Advertising Age* (April 16, 1990), p. 38; and Diane Harris, "Money's Store of the Year," *Money* (December 1990), pp. 144–150.

---

as Leon's) is regarded as a major threat to established furniture outlets. Other limited-line retailers are likely to generate new competition for the consumers' general merchandise business.

A renewed emphasis on the pleasurable aspects of shopping is another trend that should accelerate in the next few years. Department stores are increasingly emphasizing boutiques and specialty shops within the department store itself. This will allow them to provide more individualized service and to appeal to specific kinds of customers.

The future of specialty stores appears bright. Their share is expected to increase into the 1990s.[23] However, the *number* of small, independent specialty stores is expected to continue to decline. Those that survive will become stronger and will generate the increase in sales volume.

## Summary

Retailers are vital members of the distribution channel for consumer products. They play a major role in the creation of time, place, and ownership utility. Retailers can be categorized on five bases: (1) shopping effort expended by customers; (2) services provided to customers; (3) product lines; (4) location of retail transactions; and (5) form of ownership.

Retailers — like consumer goods — may be divided into convenience, shopping, and specialty categories based upon the efforts shoppers are willing to expend in purchasing products. A second method of classification categorizes retailers on a spectrum ranging from self-service to full-service. The third method divides retailers into three categories: limited-line stores, which compete by carrying a large assortment of one or two lines of products; specialty stores, which carry a very large assortment of only part of a single line of products; and general merchandise retailers, such as department stores, variety stores, and such mass merchandisers as discount houses, hypermarkets, and catalogue retailers — all handling a wide variety of products.

A fourth classification method distinguishes between retail stores and nonstore retailing. While more than 97 percent of total retail sales in Canada take place in retail stores, such nonstore retailing as house-to-house retailing, mail-order establishments, and automatic merchandising machines are important in marketing many types of products.

A fifth method of classification categorizes retailers by form of ownership. The major types include corporate chain stores, independent retailers, and independents who have banded together to form retail co-operatives or to join wholesaler-sponsored voluntary chains or franchises.

Chains are groups of retail stores that are centrally owned and managed and that handle the same lines of products. Chain stores dominate retailing in four fields: department stores, variety stores, food stores, and shoe stores. They account for more than a third of all retail sales.

Retailing has been affected by the development of planned shopping centres and the practice of scrambled merchandising. Planned shopping centres are a group of retail stores planned, co-ordinated, and marketed as a unit to shoppers in their geographic trade area. Shopping centres can be classified as neighbourhood, community, and regional centres. Another significant development is scrambled merchandising, the practice of carrying dissimilar lines in an attempt to generate additional sales volume.

The evolution of retail institutions has generally supported the wheel-of-retailing hypothesis, which holds that new types of retailers gain a competitive foothold by offering lower prices to their customers through the reduction or elimination of services. Once they are established, however, they add more services and their prices generally rise. They then become vulnerable to the next low-price retailer. Among the emerging trends in retailing is teleshopping conducted through interactive cable television.

## ▮ K E Y   T E R M S

| | | |
|---|---|---|
| retailing | department store | mail-order merchandiser |
| retail trade area analysis | variety store | chain stores |
| law of retail gravitation | mass merchandiser | planned shopping centre |
| retail image | discount house | scrambled merchandising |
| limited-line store | hypermarket | wheel of retailing |
| supermarket | catalogue retailer | teleshopping |
| specialty store | house-to-house retailer | |

## REVIEW QUESTIONS

1. Discuss the evolution of retailing.
2. Outline the framework for decisions in retailing.
3. Outline the five bases for categorizing retailers.
4. How are limited-line and specialty stores able to compete with such general merchandise retailers as department stores and discount houses?
5. Identify the major types of general merchandise retailers.
6. Give reasons for the success of discount retailing.
7. Identify and briefly explain each of the types of nonstore retailing operations.
8. Why has the practice of scrambled merchandising become so common in retailing?
9. Outline the wheel-of-retailing hypothesis.
10. Discuss the current development of and potential for teleshopping.

## DISCUSSION QUESTIONS AND EXERCISES

1. Computers are one of the fastest-growing aspects of retailing. Computer outlets include Radio Shack, Computerland, Computer Connection, MicroAge, and Computer Innovations. Relate this growth to the concepts discussed in this chapter.
2. Xerox has opened stores to serve small businesses and professionals like attorneys, physicians, dentists, and chartered accountants. How would you classify these stores?
3. Assume that a retailer is considering opening an outlet in Town A, population 144 000. The retailer wants to know how far his trade area would extend toward Town B (population 16 000), 72 km away. Apply the law of retail gravitation to the retailer's problem.
4. List several examples of the wheel of retailing in operation. List examples that do not conform to the wheel hypothesis. What generalizations can be drawn from this exercise?
5. What is your assessment of the future of teleshopping through interactive cable television?

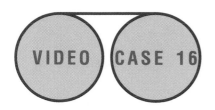

VIDEO CASE 16 South Coast Plaza

In the past 50 years the rapid increase in automobile ownership has combined with the tremendous pace of urbanization to favour the proliferation of shopping malls. Two characteristics of shopping malls have given them distinct advantages over the traditional downtown retail districts they replace. Being newly developed on vacant land, they can provide the parking facilities desired by car-dependent consumers, and because they are under a single owner, the facilities can be developed and occupied very rapidly. Typically, shopping mall development requires the establishment of a flagship or anchor store — often a large department store — which is given land, or sold land at a nominal price, to draw shoppers and as an inducement to other businesses to locate at the mall. The remaining land is kept by the mall's developers and leased to other retailers. By retaining ownership, the developers can control the mix of businesses, their location, and the amenities provided by the mall.

South Coast Plaza, in Costa Mesa, California, was developed in this way in the early 1960s by Henry Segerstrom, whose family had owned land in Orange County since the late nineteenth century. At the time that South Coast was developed, there were no other central retailers in Orange County. South Coast's strategy was cautious. A conventional mix of businesses was developed, based on anchor operations by Sears and the May Company. This approach proved to be a sound one, and the Plaza's operations provided higher-than-expected profits.

By the late 1970s the population and affluence of Orange County had risen to the point where South Coast officials felt it was time to expand. Since South Coast Plaza was no longer the only mall in the area, Segerstrom saw the expansion as an opportunity to reposition South Coast to attract the most affluent segments of the population and thus distinguish the Plaza from other malls. High-end retailers were courted; I Magnin opened in 1977, Nordstrom in 1978, and Saks in 1979. At the same time, elite stores like Cartier, Mark Cross, and Rizzoli were attracted to the mall. South Coast Plaza had established itself as a unique, high-quality shopping mall.

South Coast Plaza chooses its retailers carefully, and the price tags on their goods are not the main criterion in this choice. South Coast looks for retailers with a strong commitment to customer service, retailers who see South Coast Plaza as a very desirable location. It handles its own leasing, shunning brokers in order to retain control. "It is my opinion you shouldn't lease sitting behind the desk answering a telephone," says Segerstrom. "You should be out in the market seeing what's going on, finding the retailers that are exciting and new, and we try to do that."

That is precisely how Segerstrom found Nordstrom. During a visit to Seattle he had discovered the Nordstrom store and had been very favourably impressed by it. The Nordstrom family was considering expansion outside the Northwest but did not think Southern California was the right area; moreover, Nordstrom was usually the anchor store when located in a mall. After four years of discussions, Segerstrom finally convinced the family to bring a store to South Coast Plaza. Today the South Coast Nordstrom has the highest volume of sales per square foot of any store over 100 000 square feet in California.

Nordstrom is a perfect match for South Coast Plaza. Founded in 1901, it has always stressed service, value, and quality. When salespeople are trained, instead of merely being given a book of instructions they are taught how to make the customer happy. They are taught to go from department to department with the customer and to record purchases so that they can better advise the same customer in the future. Nordstrom even offers a personal shopper service in which sellers are available by appointment and stay with their customers as long as they are needed. This service is particularly helpful at rush times, such as the Christmas season.

It is apparent that the anchor store concept is no longer applicable to South Coast Plaza. Each of the stores has to draw customers in its own right. South Coast is careful to maintain a mix of stores, and this mix is dynamic because leases usually run for relatively short (five-year) periods. The range of stores in the mall is considerable, from tool retailers (Brookstone) through a foreign-exchange and precious-metals dealer (Deak-Pereira) to art museum stores (New York's Metropolitan Museum of Art), as well as the more expected clothiers (Barney's) and athletic-clothing retailers (Foot Locker).

While the mix is controlled, the location of stores within the mall often has more to do with space availability than with planning. Three toy stores — FAO Schwartz, Sesame Street, and Disney — are close to each other and to the mall's carousel and other children's stores. Although it was not planned as such, the result is a mini-mall for children and is immensely successful. Parents with children, especially children in strollers, do not like walking the length of the mall to get to the next store. The proximity of these related stores makes it possible to buy the kids some clothing and mollify them with a trip to the toy store without taking all day to do it.

South Coast Plaza functions like a huge department store. Each shopper experiences the mall differently: a family hurries past; a group of teenagers search for friends; a man buys a book and stands under a light reading intently; a middle-aged couple buys a wedding gift for a nephew and then has dinner at a gourmet restaurant. Each shopper feels that South Coast was made for him or her, that it is the right place to go to satisfy his or her needs, because so many of the retailers are target stores. Because of its size, however, South Coast can offer amenities beyond those available to a single department store — including a branch of the Laguna Art Museum.

Once a pioneer in the fledgling shopping mall industry, South Coast Plaza today maintains its leadership by going beyond the real estate management philosophy of its competitors. It is not unreasonable to call South Coast Plaza a retail operations manager because of its canny control of its tenant mix and its careful shaping of its image. As long as its owners continue to sensitively monitor the pulse of retailing, South Coast should continue to prosper.

## Questions

1. A mall could be considered a special form of retailer practising scrambled merchandising. Why would this be a desirable approach to mall operation?
2. Discuss the following methods of categorizing retailers as each applies to South Coast Plaza:
   a. shopping effort expended by customers
   b. services provided to customers
   c. product lines
   d. location of retail transactions
   e. form of ownership
3. What does South Coast Plaza offer its tenants that they would not get from a competing mall?
4. Discuss the importance of location within South Coast Plaza to its retailers. Would the importance of location be the same for retailers that are target stores as it would for those that draw customers from the mall traffic?

SOURCES   Mary Ann Galante, "Barneys N.Y. to Open South Coast Plaza Store," *Los Angeles Times* (May 23, 1989); Anne Michaud, "Met Museum to Open Store in Costa Mesa Mall," *Los Angeles Times* (July 4, 1990); and John Needham, "Mall Accidentally Corners the Toy Scene," *Los Angeles Times* (November 23, 1990).

## CAREER PROFILE

### Lolita Norton

CIBC
Marketing Division

**Education:**
Centennial College
Marketing Management
President, Centennial College Marketing
Graduation — 1985

I was a "mature student." Although I had work experience, I wanted a career in a more creative and people-oriented field. Marketing, I decided, met both these criteria. And the marketing program at Centennial College provided me with the hands-on experience and the accreditation that would prepare me for a position in this field.

After graduation I accepted a position with a sales promotion agency. Several months later I learned that the CIBC had an opening in a new department for a sales consultant. I applied for and was offered this job; it ultimately evolved into that of National Account Manager, with responsibility for more than $900 million in VISA sales.

Why did the bank hire me? A combination of factors led to its decision: my schooling in marketing, my banking experience, and some previous sales experience were all instrumental.

I have found various facets of Centennial's Marketing program applicable to different parts of my job. The Personal Selling course taught me the skills needed to effectively sell the CIBC's traditional image — and, more important, the services the bank offers. The course on Retail Marketing proved useful, too, since I now deal primarily with retailers. Understanding how they operate and how I can best help them gives me a decided advantage.

The CIBC marketing department has grown considerably over the past 10 years, with many areas becoming more specialized. My degree definitely boosted my confidence: I feel it prepared me well to understand the complex dynamics of marketing and the interrelationships among its many components.

To people considering this type of career, I usually suggest that any sales experience — or a customer service–related job in a retail or service environment — would make a good start.

Recently I was promoted to a newly created position with Merchant Sales as Manager, Technical Support. Changing requirements and rapidly developing technology should render this a challenging and exciting opportunity. I hope the experience will position me to become a consultant to retailers, working independently or at a higher level within CIBC or another financial institution or service provider.

# PART SEVEN
# Marketing Communications

CHAPTER 17
## Marketing Communications Strategy
•
CHAPTER 18
## Applying Marketing Communications

Probably, the most visible component of marketing is advertising. This is just one component of the mix of variables used by the marketer to communicate with current and potential customers. Marketers are often quick to express opinions about marketing communications, but in reality, marketing communications strategy is quite complex. Part Seven concludes with a chapter dealing with some of the basic concepts of applying marketing communications.

C H A P T E R　17

# Marketing Communications Strategy

## CHAPTER OBJECTIVES

1. To explain the concept of the marketing communications mix.
2. To relate the marketing communications mix and the marketing mix.
3. To identify the primary determinants of a marketing communications mix.
4. To contrast pulling communications strategies with pushing communications strategies.
5. To list the objectives of marketing communications.
6. To explain the primary methods of developing a marketing communications budget.
7. To consider marketing communications in the light of some of the public criticisms that are sometimes raised about them.

MARKETING communications are used to accomplish important components of the marketing plan. One such task is the positioning of Pepsi-Cola as a suitable drink for the breakfast table. The soft-drink giant has developed Pepsi A.M., a cola drink with about 28 percent more caffeine per ounce than regular Pepsi but 77 percent less than coffee or tea. At time of writing, the product was being test marketed. The reader will know, by whether or not it is on the shelves, if the campaign was successful or not.

Soft-drink makers say they capture only a fraction of the market for beverages consumed in the morning, and industry analysts say recent declines in coffee consumption provide an opening for soft-drink marketers. Coffee was included in 38 percent of the breakfasts eaten at home, according to a recent survey. That was down from 44 percent just four years previously. Carbonated soft-drinks, however, were included in only 2 percent of the breakfasts.

A beverage-industry analyst said it is hard to break consumer habits. "These things are not done overnight. It takes years to train people that a soft drink in the morning is just as good as or better than coffee," he said.[1]

Such a change will happen only if the market is really ready for the new idea; and that is more likely to occur if every aspect of the marketing mix is tuned to the market. Marketing communications will likely fulfill an especially significant role in that process.

## Introduction

**marketing communications**
All messages that inform, persuade, and influence the consumer in making a purchase decision.

**Marketing communications**, the fourth variable in the marketing mix, is defined as *all messages that inform, persuade, and influence the consumer in making a purchase decision.* Figure 17–1 depicts the relationship between a firm's marketing communications strategy and the other elements of the overall marketing plan.

The marketing manager sets the goals and objectives of the firm's communications approach in accordance with overall organizational objectives and the goals of the marketing organization. Then, based on these goals, the various elements of marketing communications — advertising, personal selling, sales promotion, publicity, and public relations — are formulated in a co-ordinated plan. This plan, in turn, becomes an integral part of the total marketing strategy for reaching selected consumer segments. Finally, the feedback mechanism, in such forms as marketing research and field reports, closes the system by identifying any deviations from the plan and by suggesting modifications or improvements.

### FIGURE 17–1

**Integrating the Marketing Communications Plan into the Total Marketing Mix**

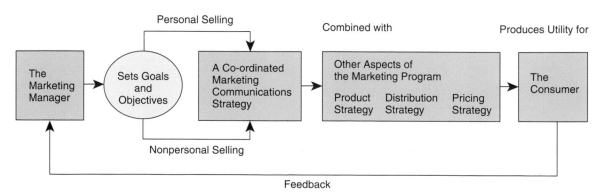

# The Communications Process

Figure 17–2 shows a generalized communications process using terminology borrowed from radio and telecommunications.[2] The sender is the *source* of the communications system, since he or she seeks to convey a *message* (a communication of information or advice or a request) to a *receiver* (the recipient of the communication). The message must accomplish three tasks in order to be effective:

1. It must *gain the attention* of the receiver.
2. It must *be understood* by both the receiver and the sender.
3. It must *stimulate* the needs of the receiver and *suggest* an appropriate method of satisfying these needs.[3]

The message must be *encoded,* or translated into understandable terms, and transmitted through a communications medium. *Decoding* is the receiver's interpretation of the message. The receiver's response, known as *feedback,* completes the system. Throughout the process, *noise* can interfere with the transmission of the message and reduce its effectiveness.

In Figure 17–3 the marketing communications process is applied to promotional strategy. The marketing manager is the sender in the system. The message is encoded in the form of sales presentations, advertisements, displays, or publicity releases. The *transfer mechanism* for delivering the message may be a salesperson, the advertising media, or a public relations channel.

The decoding step involves the consumer's interpretation of the sender's message. This is the most troublesome aspect of marketing communications, since consumers often do not interpret a promotional message in the same way as does its sender. Because receivers are likely to decode messages based on their own frames of

**FIGURE 17–2**

**A Generalized Communications Process**

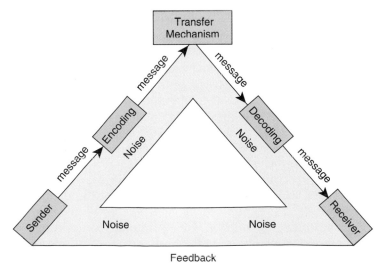

FIGURE 17 – 3

## The Process of Marketing Communications

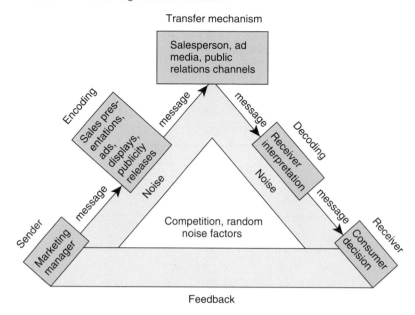

reference or individual experiences, the sender must be careful to ensure that the message is properly encoded to match the target audience.

*Feedback* is the receiver's response to the message. It may take the form of attitude change, purchase, or nonpurchase. In some instances a firm may use marketing communications to create a favourable attitude toward its new products or services. Such attitude changes may result in future purchases. In other instances, the objective of the communication is to stimulate consumer purchases. Such purchases indicate positive responses to the firm, its product/service offerings, its distribution channels, its prices, and its promotion. Even nonpurchases can serve as feedback to the sender. They may result from ineffective communication in that the message was not believed, not remembered, or failed to persuade the receiver that the firm's products or services are superior to its competitors. Feedback can be obtained from field sales reports and such techniques as marketing research studies.

*Noise* represents interference at some stage in the communications process. It may result from such factors as competitive promotional messages being transmitted over the same communications channel, misinterpretation of a sales presentation or an advertising message, receipt of the promotional message by the wrong person, or random noise factors, such as people conversing — or leaving the room — during a television commercial.

Figure 17–4 illustrates the steps in the communications process with several examples of promotional messages. Although the types of promotion vary from a highly personalized sales presentation to such nonpersonal promotion as television advertising and two-for-one coupons, each form of promotion goes through each stage in the communications model.

FIGURE 17 – 4

**Examples of Marketing Communications**

| Type of Promotion | Sender | Encoding | Transfer Mechanism | Decoding by Receiver | Feedback |
|---|---|---|---|---|---|
| Personal selling | Sharp Business Products | Sales presentation on new model office copier | Sharp sales representative | Office manager and employees in local firm discuss Sharp sales presentation and those of competing suppliers | Order placed for the Sharp copier |
| Two-for-one coupon (sales promotion) | Wendy's Hamburgers | Wendy's marketing department and advertising agency | Coupon insert to weekend newspaper | Newspaper reader sees coupon for hamburger and saves it | Hamburgers purchased by consumers using the coupon |
| Television advertising | Walt Disney Enterprises | Advertisement for a new family-entertainment animated movie is developed by Disney's advertising agency | Network television during programs with high percentage of viewers under 12 years old | Children see ad and ask their parents to take them to movie; parents see ad and decide to take children | Movie ticket purchased |

# Components of the Marketing Communications Mix

The marketing communications mix, like the marketing mix, involves properly blending numerous variables in order to satisfy the needs of the firm's target market and achieve organizational objectives. While the marketing mix comprises product, price, marketing communications, and distribution elements, the marketing communications mix is a subset of the overall marketing mix. In the case of the marketing communications mix, the marketing manager tries to achieve the optimal blending of various communications elements in order to accomplish information and persuasion objectives. The components of the **marketing communications mix** are *personal selling and nonpersonal selling (including advertising, sales promotion, and public relations)*.[4]

Personal selling and advertising are the most significant elements, since they usually account for the bulk of a firm's marketing communications expenditures. A discussion of each of these elements is presented in the chapters that follow. Here only a brief definition will be given in order to set the framework for the overall discussion of promotion.

**marketing communications mix**
The blending of personal selling and nonpersonal selling (including advertising, sales promotion, and public relations) by marketers in an attempt to accomplish information and persuasion objectives.

A firm's annual report can be used as an effective public relations tool, while also imparting information to shareholders. The theme for Du Pont Canada's 1990 annual report was "Delivering Results through People." In it, the company featured people like Don Corbett (pictured here), whose skills had contributed to the firm in a special way. In this manner, Du Pont hoped to foster a stronger corporate culture within the firm, and to create a favourable attitude toward Du Pont Canada in the wider community.

## Personal Selling

**personal selling**   A seller's promotional presentation conducted on a person-to-person basis with the buyer.

**Personal selling** may be defined as *a seller's promotional presentation conducted on a person-to-person basis with the buyer*. It is a direct face-to-face form of promotion. Personal selling was also the original form of promotion. Today it is estimated that 600 000 people in Canada are engaged in this activity.

## Nonpersonal Selling

Nonpersonal selling is divided into advertising, sales promotion, and public relations. Advertising is usually regarded as the most important of these forms.

**advertising**   Paid nonpersonal communication through various media by business firms, nonprofit organizations, and individuals who are in some way identified with the advertising message and who hope to inform or persuade members of a particular audience.

**Advertising** may be defined as *paid nonpersonal communication through various media by business firms, nonprofit organizations, and individuals who are in some way identified with the advertising message and who hope to inform or persuade members of a particular audience*.[5] It involves the mass media, such as newspapers, television, radio, magazines, and billboards. Business realizes the tremendous potential of this form of communication, and advertising has become increasingly important in marketing. Mass consumption makes advertising particularly appropriate for products that rely on sending the same message to large audiences.

**sales promotion**   Those marketing activities, other than personal selling, mass media advertising, and publicity, that stimulate consumer purchasing and dealer effectiveness.

**Sales promotion** includes "*those marketing activities, other than personal selling, mass media advertising, and publicity, that stimulate consumer purchasing and dealer effectiveness*, such as displays, shows and expositions, demonstrations, and various nonrecurrent selling efforts not in the ordinary routine."[6] Sales promotion is usually practised together with other forms of advertising to emphasize, assist, supplement, or otherwise support the objectives of the promotional program. It is growing in importance.

**Public relations** is *a firm's effort to create favourable attention and word-of-mouth* among various publics — including the organization's customers, suppliers, shareholders, and employees; the government; the general public; and the society in which the organization operates. Public relations programs can be either formal or informal. Every organization, whether or not it has a formalized, organized program, must be concerned about its public relations.

**public relations**     A firm's effort to create favourable attention and word-of-mouth.

# Factors Affecting the Marketing Communications Mix

Since quantitative measures to determine the effectiveness of each component of the communications mix in a given market segment are not available, choosing a proper mix of communications elements is one of the most difficult tasks facing the marketing manager. Factors affecting the mix are (1) the nature of the market; (2) the nature of the product; (3) the product's stage in the product life cycle; (4) price; and (5) funds available.

## Nature of the Market

The marketer's target audience has a major impact on what type of promotion will work best. In cases where there is a limited number of buyers (as, for example, with a manufacturer of printing presses), personal selling may prove highly effective. However, markets characterized by a large number of potential customers scattered over a large geographic area may make the cost of contact by personal salespeople prohibitive; in such instances, marketers may make extensive use of advertising (as, for example, is done for Kodak film). The type of customer also affects the marketing communications mix. A target market made up of industrial purchasers or retail and wholesale buyers is more likely to require personal selling than one consisting of ultimate consumers.

## Nature of the Product

A second important factor in determining an effective marketing communications mix is the product itself. Highly standardized products with minimal servicing requirements are less likely to depend on personal selling than are higher-priced custom products that are technically complex and require servicing. Consumer goods are more likely to rely heavily on advertising than are industrial goods. Within each product category, marketing communications mixes vary.

For instance, installations typically involve heavy reliance on personal selling when compared to the marketing of operating supplies. Convenience goods rely heavily on manufacturer advertising, and personal selling plays only a small role. On the other hand, personal selling is often more important in the marketing of shopping goods, and both personal selling and nonpersonal selling are important in the marketing of specialty goods. Finally, personal selling is likely to be more important in the marketing of products characterized by trade-ins.

## Stage in the Product Life Cycle

The marketing communications mix must also be tailored to the stage in the product life cycle. In the introductory stage, heavy emphasis is placed on personal selling to inform the marketplace of the merits of the new product or service. Salespeople contact marketing intermediaries to secure interest and commitment to handle the new product. Trade shows and exhibitions are frequently used to inform and educate prospective dealers and ultimate consumers. Any advertising at this stage is largely informative, and sales promotional techniques, such as samples and cents-off coupons, are designed to influence consumer attitudes and stimulate initial purchases.

As the product or service moves into the growth and maturity stages, advertising becomes more important in attempting to persuade consumers to make purchases. Personal-selling efforts continue to be directed at intermediaries in an attempt to expand distribution. As more competitors enter the marketplace, advertising stresses product differences in an attempt to persuade consumers to purchase the firm's brand. Reminder advertisements begin to appear in the maturity and early decline stages.

## Price

The price of the product is a fourth factor in the choice of marketing communications mixes. Advertising is a dominant mix component for low-unit-value products due to the high costs per contact involved in personal selling. The cost of an industrial sales call, for example, is now estimated at nearly $230.[7] As a result, it has become unprofitable to promote lower-value products through personal selling. Advertising, by contrast, permits a low promotional expenditure per sales unit, since it reaches mass audiences. For low-value consumer products, such as chewing gum, colas, and snack foods, advertising is the only feasible means of promotion.

## Funds Available

A very real barrier to implementing any marketing communications strategy is the size of the budget. A 30-second television commercial costs an average packaged-goods company $86 000[8] to shoot, and one showing nationally during a Grey Cup game can cost $6000 or more. Even though the message is received by millions of viewers and the cost per contact is relatively low, such an expenditure would exceed the entire promotional budget of thousands of firms. For many new or smaller firms, the cost of national mass advertising is prohibitive, so they are forced to seek less-expensive, less-efficient methods. One common approach involves initially using smaller, local media. Neighbourhood retailers may not be able to advertise in metropolitan newspapers or on local radio and television stations; apart from personal selling, therefore, their limited promotional budgets may be allocated to an eye-catching sign, one of the most valuable promotional devices available to small retailers.

Figure 17–5 summarizes the factors that influence the determination of an appropriate marketing communications mix.

## Marketing Communications Strategy — Pull or Push?

**pulling strategy**   A promotional effort by the seller to stimulate final-user demand, which then exerts pressure on the distribution channel.

Essentially, there are two marketing communications policies that may be employed: a pulling strategy and a pushing strategy. A **pulling strategy** is a *promotional effort by the seller to stimulate final-user demand, which then exerts pressure on the distribution channel.* The plan is to build consumer demand for the product by means of advertising so

FIGURE 17-5

## Factors Influencing the Marketing Communications Mix

| | Emphasis on | |
|---|---|---|
| *Factor* | *Personal Selling* | *Advertising* |
| *Nature of the Market* | | |
| Number of buyers | Limited number | Large number |
| Geographic concentration | Concentrated | Dispersed |
| Type of customer | Industrial purchaser | Ultimate consumer |
| *Nature of the Product* | | |
| Complexity | Custom-made, complex | Standardized |
| Service requirements | Considerable | Minimal |
| Type of good | Industrial | Consumer |
| Use of trade-ins | Trade-ins common | Trade-ins uncommon |
| *Stage in the Product Life Cycle* | | |
| | Introductory and early growth stages | Latter part of growth stage and maturity and early decline stages |
| *Price* | High unit value | Low unit value |

that channel members will have to stock the product to meet that demand. If a manufacturer's advertising efforts result in shoppers' requesting the retailer to stock an item, they will usually succeed in getting that item on the retailer's shelves, since most retailers want to stimulate repeat purchases by satisfied customers. A pulling strategy may be required to motivate marketing intermediaries to handle a product when they already stock a large number of competing products. When a manufacturer decides to use a pulling strategy, personal selling is often largely limited to contacting intermediaries, providing requested information about the product, and taking orders. Advertising and sales promotion are the most commonly used elements of promotion in a pulling strategy.

By contrast, a **pushing strategy** relies more heavily on personal selling. Here, the objective is the *promotion of the product first to the members of the marketing channel, who then participate in its promotion to the final user.* This can be done through co-operative advertising allowances, trade discounts, personal-selling efforts by the firm's sales force, and other dealer supports. Such a strategy is designed to produce marketing success for the firm's products by motivating representatives of wholesalers and/or retailers to spend a disproportionate amount of time and effort in promoting these products to customers.

While these are presented as alternative policies, it is unlikely that very many companies will depend entirely on either strategy. In most cases marketers employ a mixture of the two.

Timing is another factor to consider in the development of a promotional strategy. Figure 17–6 shows the relative importance of advertising and selling in different periods of the purchase process. During the pretransactional period (before the actual sale) advertising is usually more important than personal selling. It is often argued that one of the primary advantages of a successful advertising program is that

**pushing strategy** The promotion of the product first to the members of the marketing channel, who then participate in its promotion to the final user.

FIGURE 17 – 6

Relative Importance of Advertising and Selling

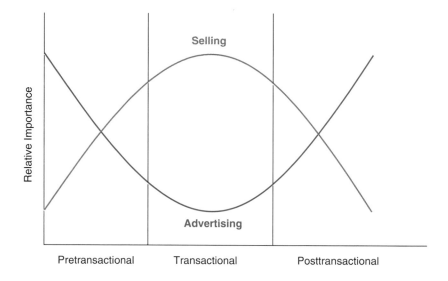

Source: Harold C. Cash and W.J.E. Crissy, "The Salesman's Role in Marketing," *The Psychology of Selling*, Vol. 12 (Personnel Development Associates, Box 3005, Roosevelt Field Station, Garden City, NY 11530). Reprinted by permission.

it assists the salesperson in approaching the prospect. Personal selling becomes more important than advertising during the transactional phase of the process. In most situations personal selling is the actual mechanism of closing the sale. In the post-transactional stage advertising regains primacy in the communication effort. It serves as an affirmation of the customer's decision to buy a particular good or service as well as a reminder of the product's favourable qualities, characteristics, and performance.

## Marketing Communications Objectives

Management has always found that determining exactly what it expects marketing communications to achieve is a perplexing problem. Generally, strategy for this mix element should be oriented toward achieving clearly stated, measurable communications objectives.

The specific objective varies with the situation. However, the following can be considered objectives of marketing communications: (1) to provide information; (2) to increase demand; (3) to differentiate the product; (4) to accentuate the value of the product; and (5) to stabilize sales. Note that it is generally too simplistic to state the objective of advertising and promotion merely in terms of "increasing sales."

*When Jay Udow graduated from Commerce in 1986, he decided the first product he had to sell was himself. To inform the market about the availability of his services, he rented a billboard to advertise his skills. No one can say he's not creative with his job-hunting techniques.*

## Providing Information

The traditional function of marketing communications was to inform the market about the availability of a particular product. Indeed, a large part of modern marketing communications effort is still directed at providing product information

FIGURE 17 – 7

**Promotion Can Help Marketers Achieve Demand Objectives**

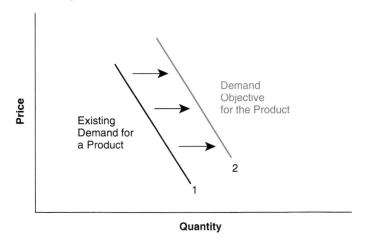

Source: Richard H. Buskirk, *Principles of Marketing: The Management View*, 3rd ed. Copyright © 1961, 1966, 1970, by Holt, Rinehart and Winston, Inc. Adapted and reprinted by permission of Holt, Rinehart and Winston, Inc.

## FIGURE 17–8

### Advertising to Stimulate Demand

*Cadbury's "thick" bar ads were very successful in the three years they were run. With slogans like "Prehistorthick" and "Birds of a Feather Thick Together," this campaign raised the demand for the product. Their success in influencing the market spawned a number of "thick" competitors, which prompted Cadbury to change their lead slogan to "the Thick of the Crop."*

to potential customers. An example of this is the typical university or college extension course program advertisement appearing in the newspaper. Its content emphasizes informative features, such as the availability of different courses. Southam Business Information has employed an interesting idea in advertising to potential business advertisers. It shows the back of a station wagon covered with bumper stickers, then makes the point: "To communicate effectively, deal with one idea at a time." By doing this, it educates potential advertisers, as well as showing how Southam can help.

The informative function often requires repeated customer exposures. For instance, "in a...study concerning customer acceptance of a new durable good, it was found that...at least several months were required after introduction (and accompanying promotion) before consumers became generally aware of the item and somewhat familiar with its characteristics."[9]

## Stimulating Demand

The primary objective of most marketing communications efforts is to increase the demand for a specific brand of product or service. This can be shown by using the familiar demand curves of basic economics (see Figure 17–7). Successful promotion can shift demand from schedule 1 to schedule 2, which means that greater quantities can be sold at each possible price level. Cadbury Schweppes Powell accomplished this with its "Thick" bars, in a campaign that brought the chocolate bars to a position among the top five brands in the Canadian market.[10] Figure 17–8 illustrates advertising with the chief goal of stimulating demand.

FIGURE 17 – 9

**Product Differentiation**

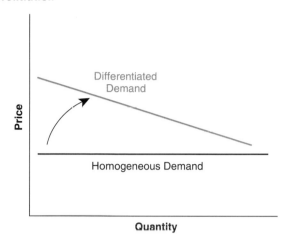

Source: Lee E. Preston, *Markets and Marketing: An Orientation* (Glenview, IL: Scott, Foresman, 1970), p. 196. Copyright © 1970 by Scott, Foresman and Company. Adapted by permission.

## Differentiating the Product

Product differentiation is often an objective of the firm's marketing communications efforts. Homogeneous demand, represented by the horizontal line in Figure 17 9, means that consumers regard the firm's output as no different from that of its competitors. In such cases the individual firm has no control over such marketing variables as price. A differentiated demand schedule, by contrast, permits more flexibility in marketing strategy, such as price changes.

For example, McCain's, a producer of frozen vegetables, advertises the dependable high quality and good taste of its products. This differentiates these products from others. Consequently, some consumers wanting these attributes are willing to pay a higher price for McCain's than they would for other brands. Similarly, the high quality and distinctiveness of Cross pens are advertised, resulting in Cross's ability to ask for and obtain a price 100 times that of some disposable pens. With the exception of commodities, most products have some degree of differentiation, resulting in a downward-sloping demand curve. The angle of the slope varies somewhat according to the degree of product differentiation.

## Accentuating the Value of the Product

Marketing communications can point out ownership utility to buyers, thereby accentuating the value of a product. The good or service might then be able to command a higher price in the marketplace. For example, status-oriented advertising may allow some retail clothing stores to command higher prices than others. The demand curve facing a prestige store may be less responsive to price differences than

FIGURE 17–10

**Promotion Can Accentuate the Value of the Product**

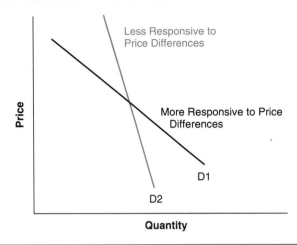

that of a competitor without a quality reputation. The responsiveness to price differences is shown in Figure 17–10.

## Stabilizing Sales

A company's sales are not uniform throughout the year. Fluctuations can occur for cyclical, seasonal, or other reasons. Reducing these variations is often an objective of the firm's marketing communications strategy. Lee E. Preston elaborates:

> Advertising that is focused on such attitudinal goals as "brand loyalty" and such specific sales goals as "increasing repeat purchases" is essentially aimed at stabilizing demand. The prominence of such goals in the current literature and in advertising planning discussions suggests that stabilizing demand and insulating the market position of an individual firm and product against unfavourable developments is, in fact, one of the most important purposes of promotional activity at the present time.[11]

## Budgeting for Marketing Communications Efforts

Marketing communications budgets can differ not only in amount but also in composition.[12] Industrial firms generally invest a larger proportion of their budgets in personal selling than in advertising, while the reverse is usually true of most producers of consumer goods.

A simple model showing the productivity of marketing communications expenditures is shown in Figure 17–11. In terms of sales revenue, initial expenditures on marketing communications usually result in increasing returns. There appear to be some economies associated with larger expenditures. These economies result from such factors as the cumulative effects of repeated communications and repeat sales.

Evidence suggests that sales initially lag behind advertising for structural reasons (filling up the retail shelves, low initial production, lack of buyer knowledge). This produces a threshold effect, where there are no sales but lots of initial investment in advertising. A second phase might produce returns (sales) proportional to a given marketing communications expenditure; this would be the most predictable range.

Finally, the area of diminishing returns is reached when an increase in marketing communications expenditure does not produce a proportional increase in sales.[13]

## Establishing a Budget

Theoretically, the optimal method of allocating a marketing communications budget is to expand it until the cost of each additional increment equals the additional incremental revenue received. In other words, the most effective allocation procedure is to increase expenditures until each dollar of expense is matched by an additional dollar of profit (see Figure 17–11). This procedure — called *marginal analysis* — results in the maximization of the input's productivity. The difficulty arises in identifying this optimal point. In practice, doing so is virtually impossible.

The more traditional methods of allocating a marketing communications budget are by percentage of sales, fixed sum per unit, meeting competition, and task-objective methods.[14]

*Percentage of sales* is a very common (but dangerous) way of allocating budgets. The percentage can be based on either past (for example, the previous year) or forecasted (current year) sales. While the simplicity of this plan is appealing, it is not an effective way of achieving the basic communications objectives. Arbitrary percentage allocations (whether applied to historical or future sales figures) fail to allow the required flexibility. Furthermore, such reasoning is circular, for the advertising allocation is made to depend on sales, rather than vice versa, as it should be. Consider, for example, the implications of a decline in sales.

FIGURE 17-11

**Marketing Communications Sales Curve**

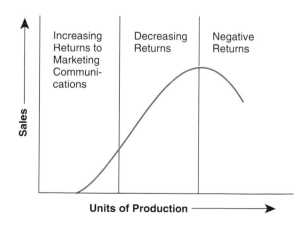

Source: Adapted from John C. Narver and Ronald Savitt, *The Marketing Economy: An Analytical Approach*, p. 294. Copyright © 1971 by Holt, Rinehart and Winston, Inc. Reprinted by permission of Holt, Rinehart and Winston, Inc.

The *fixed sum per unit* approach differs from percentage of sales in only one respect: it applies a predetermined allocation to each sales or production unit. This also can be set on either a historical or a forecasted basis. Producers of high-value consumer durable goods, such as automobiles, often use this budgeting method.

Another traditional approach is simply to match competitors' outlays — in other words, *meet competition* — on either an absolute or a relative basis. However, this kind of approach usually leads to a status quo situation at best, with each company retaining its market share. Meeting the competition's budget does not necessarily relate to the objectives of promotion and, therefore, seems inappropriate for most contemporary marketing programs.

**task-objective method**   A sequential approach to allocating marketing communications budgets that involves two steps: (1) define the particular goals that the firm wants the marketing communications mix to accomplish and (2) determine the amount and type of marketing communications activity required to accomplish each of these objectives.

The **task-objective method** of developing a marketing communications budget is *based on a sound evaluation of the firm's communications objectives*, and is thus better attuned to modern marketing practices. It involves two sequential steps.

1. The organization must *define the realistic communication goals* the firm wants the marketing communications mix to accomplish — for example, a 25 percent increase in brand awareness, or a 10 percent rise in consumers who realize that the product has certain specific differentiating features. The key is to specify quantitatively the objectives to be accomplished. They then become an integral part of the marketing communications plan.

2. The organization must *determine the amount and type of marketing communications activity required to accomplish each of these objectives*. The units thus identified, when combined, become the firm's budget.

A crucial assumption underlies the task-objective approach: that the productivity of marketing communications expenditures is measurable. That is why the objectives must be carefully chosen, quantified, and co-ordinated with the rest of the marketing mix. Generally, an objective like "We wish to achieve a 5 percent increase in sales" is an ill-conceived marketing objective, because a sale is the culmination of the effects of *all* elements of the marketing mix. A more appropriate advertising objective might be "To make 30 percent of the target market aware of the facilities available at the health spa."

## Measuring the Effectiveness of Marketing Communications

It is widely recognized that part of a firm's marketing communications effort is ineffective. John Wanamaker, a successful nineteenth-century retailer, once observed, "I know half the money I spend on advertising is wasted; but I can never find out which half."

Measuring the effectiveness of marketing communications has become an extremely important research question, particularly among advertisers. Studies aimed at this measurement objective face several major obstacles, among them the difficulty of isolating the effect of the marketing communications variable.

Most marketers would prefer to use a **direct-sales results test** to measure the effectiveness of marketing communications. Such a test attempts to *ascertain for each dollar of promotional outlay the corresponding increase in revenue*. The primary difficulty involves controlling the other variables that operate in the marketplace. A $1.5-million advertising campaign may be followed by an increase in sales of $20 million. However, this shift may have more to do with a sudden price hike by the firm's leading competitor than with the advertising expenditure. Therefore, advertisers are turning to establishing and assessing achievable, measurable objectives.

With the increasing sophistication of marketing analysts, analytical techniques, and computer-based marketing information systems, banks of historical data on marketing communications expenditures and their effects are being subjected to ever more scrutiny. More and more is being learned about measuring and evaluating the effects of marketing communications activity. While the technical literature in marketing reveals much of what is happening in this critical area, firms are reluctant to release much of this information. Not only do they wish to keep their proprietary (privately held) information about how the market works to themselves for competitive reasons, but they do not want competitors knowing the methods and decision routines used in planning marketing communications activity.

Other methods of assessing marketing communications effectiveness include inquiring about the product, about changes in attitudes toward the product, and about improvements in public knowledge and awareness. One indicator of probable advertising effectiveness would be the elasticity or sensitivity of sales to marketing communications based on historical data concerning price, sales volume, and advertising expenditures.

It is difficult for the marketer to conduct research in a controlled environment like that which can be set up in other disciplines. The difficulty of isolating the effects of marketing communications causes many to abandon all attempts at measurement. Others, however, turn to indirect evaluation. These researchers concentrate on quantifiable factors, such as recall (how much is remembered about specific products or advertisements) and readership (the size and composition of the audience). But it remains difficult to relate these variables to sales. Does extensive ad readership actually lead to increased sales? Another problem is the high cost of research in promotion. To assess the effectiveness of marketing communications expenditures correctly may require a significant investment.

## The Value of Marketing Communications

Various aspects of marketing communications have often been the target of criticism. A selection of these would include the following:

"Advertising contributes nothing to society."
"Most advertisements and sales presentations insult my intelligence."
"Promotion 'forces' consumers to buy products they cannot afford and do not need."
"Advertising and selling are economic wastes."
"Salespeople and advertisers are usually unethical."

Consumers, public officials, and marketers agree that all too often many of these complaints are true.[15] Some salespeople do use unethical sales tactics. Some product advertising is directed at consumer groups that can least afford to purchase the particular item. Many television commercials are banal and annoying.

While such components of the marketing communications mix as advertising can certainly be criticized on many counts, it is important to remember that marketing communications plays a crucial role in modern society. This point is best explained by looking at the importance of marketing communications on the business, economic, and social levels.

**Marketing Communications Is an Essential Part of the Mix**

Source: *Marketing* (April 10, 1989), p. 4.

## Business Importance

Marketing communications has become increasingly important to business enterprises — both large and small. The long-term rise in outlays for advertising and other communications elements is well documented and certainly attests to management's faith in the ability of marketing communications to affect sales. It is difficult to conceive of an enterprise that does not attempt to promote its product or service in some manner or another. Most modern institutions simply cannot survive in the long run without promotion. Business must communicate with the public.

Nonbusiness enterprises have also recognized the importance of this variable. The Canadian government is now the largest advertiser in Canada, promoting many programs and concepts. Religious organizations too have acknowledged the importance of promoting what they do. Even labour organizations have used marketing communications channels to make their viewpoints known to the public at large. In fact, advertising now plays a larger role in the functioning of nonprofit organizations than ever before.

## Economic Importance

Advertising has assumed a degree of economic importance, if for no other reason than that it is an activity that employs thousands of people.[16] More importantly, however, effective advertising has allowed society to derive benefits not otherwise available. For example, the criticism that "advertising costs too much" views an individual expense item in isolation. It fails to consider that item's possible effect on other categories of expenditures.

Marketing communications strategies that increase the number of units sold permit economies in the production process, thereby lowering the production costs assigned to each unit of output. Lower consumer prices then allow these products to become available to more people. Similarly, researchers have found that advertising subsidizes the informational content of newspapers and the broadcast media.[17] In short, advertising pays for many of the enjoyable entertainment and educational aspects of contemporary life, as well as lowering product costs.

## Social Importance

Criticisms such as "most advertising messages are tasteless" and "advertising contributes nothing to society" sometimes ignore the fact that there is no commonly accepted set of standards or priorities existing within our social framework. We live in a varied economy characterized by consumer segments with differing needs, wants, and aspirations. What is tasteless to one group may be quite informative to another. Advertising is faced with an "averaging" problem that escapes many of its critics. The one generally accepted standard in a market society is freedom of choice for the consumer. Customer buying decisions will eventually determine what is acceptable practice in the marketplace.

Advertising has become an important factor in the campaigns to achieve such socially oriented objectives as stopping smoking and promoting family planning, physical fitness, and the elimination of drug abuse. Advertising performs an informative and educational task that makes it extremely important in the functioning of modern society. As with everything else in life, it is how one uses advertising, not advertising itself, that is critical.

# Summary

This chapter has provided an introduction to marketing communications, the fourth variable in the marketing mix. The marketing communications system includes the sender, the message, encoding, the transfer mechanism, decoding, the receiver, feedback, and noise. The major components of the marketing communications strategy are personal selling and nonpersonal selling (advertising, sales promotion, and public relations). These elements are discussed in the next chapter.

Developing an effective communications strategy is a complex matter. The elements of marketing communications are related to the type and value of the product being promoted, the nature of the market, the stage of the product life cycle, and the funds available, as well as to the timing of the communications effort. Personal selling is used primarily for industrial goods, for higher-value items, and during the transactional phase of the purchase decision process. Advertising, by contrast, is used primarily for consumer goods, for lower-value items, and during the pretransactional and posttransactional phases.

A pushing strategy, which relies on personal selling, attempts to promote the product first to the members of the marketing channel, who then participate in its promotion to the final user. A pulling strategy concentrates on stimulating final-user demand, primarily through mass media advertising and through sales promotion. The increased demand then induces channel members to stock the product.

The five basic objectives of marketing communications are to (1) provide information, (2) stimulate demand, (3) differentiate the product, (4) accentuate the value of the product, and (5) stabilize sales.

There are several methods used in establishing marketing communications budgets. However, the task-objective method makes the most sense and promises the best management of resources.

Although the target of much criticism, advertising plays an important role in business, economic, and social activities.

## KEY TERMS

| | | |
|---|---|---|
| marketing communications | sales promotion | pushing strategy |
| marketing communications mix | public relations | task-objective method |
| personal selling | pulling strategy | direct-sales results test |
| advertising | | |

## REVIEW QUESTIONS

1. Relate the steps in the theoretical communications process to marketing communications strategy.
2. Explain the concept of the marketing communications mix and its relationship to the marketing mix.
3. Identify the major determinants of a marketing communications mix and describe how they affect the selection of an appropriate blend of promotional techniques.
4. Compare the five basic objectives of marketing communications. Cite specific examples.
5. Explain the concept of noise in marketing communications and discuss its causes.
6. Under what circumstances should a pushing strategy be used in promotion? When would a pulling strategy be effective?
7. What are the primary objectives of marketing communications?
8. Identify and briefly explain the alternative methods for developing a marketing communications budget.
9. How should a firm attempt to measure the effectiveness of its marketing communications efforts?
10. Identify the major public criticisms sometimes directed toward advertising. Prepare a defence for each criticism.

## DISCUSSION QUESTIONS AND EXERCISES

1. "Perhaps the most critical communications question facing the marketing manager concerns when to use each of the components of marketing communications." Comment on this statement, and relate your response to the goods classification, product value, stage in the product life cycle, price, and the timing of the promotional effort.

2. What mix of marketing communications variables would you use for each of the following?
   a. Champion spark plugs
   b. Weedeater lawn edgers
   c. a management consulting service
   d. industrial drilling equipment
   e. women's sports outfits
   f. customized business forms
3. Develop a hypothetical marketing communications budget for the following firms. Ignore dollar amounts by using percentage allocations to the various elements (for example, 30 percent to personal selling, 60 percent to advertising, and 10 percent to public relations).
   a. Tilden Rent-A-Car
   b. Holiday Inns
   c. a manufacturer of industrial chemicals

d. Great-West Life Assurance Company
4. Should doctors, dentists, and lawyers be prohibited from promoting their services through media like direct mail and newspaper advertisements? How do these professionals currently promote their services?
5. When paperback book sales suffered a downturn, several major publishers adopted new marketing communications strategies. One firm began using 30-cents-off coupons to promote its romance series. Another company, on the other hand, established a returns policy that rewarded dealers who showed high sales. The new policy also contained penalties to discourage low-volume buying by retail book outlets. Relate these marketing communications strategies to the material discussed in this chapter.

## MICROCOMPUTER EXERCISE
### Promotional Budget Allocations

While marketing communications budgeting is always difficult, the development of computer-based models has made it less of a problem than it has been in the past. The problems that follow focus on the budgeting methods discussed in this chapter.

**Directions:** Use the Menu Item titled "Promotional Budget Allocations" on the *Foundations of Marketing* disk to solve each of the following problems.

1. Medicine Hat Enterprises (MHE) was founded in 1987 in Medicine Hat, Alberta. As indicated in Table A, both the firm's sales and its marketing communications expenditures grew considerably during a five-year period. The 1992 sales forecast is $7 000 000. Table B shows the annual sales and marketing communications expenditures of the firm's four major competitors.

**TABLE A**

**Growth of Sales and Marketing Communications Expenditures for Medicine Hat Enterprises**

| Year | Annual Sales | Marketing Communications Expenditures |
|---|---|---|
| 1987 | $ 500 000 | $ 24 000 |
| 1988 | 900 000 | 40 000 |
| 1989 | 2 200 000 | 80 000 |
| 1990 | 3 500 000 | 150 000 |
| 1991 | 4 900 000 | 196 000 |

TABLE B

## Annual Sales and Marketing Communications Expenditures of MHE's Major Competitors

| Competitor | Annual Sales | Expenditures |
|---|---|---|
| Lethbridge Manufacturing | $1 200 000 | $725 000 |
| The Camrose Corp. | 4 500 000 | 250 000 |
| Edmonton Consolidated | 8 000 000 | 500 000 |
| Golden Enterprises | 6 500 000 | 425 000 |

**a.** What percentage of 1992 sales should MHE include in its 1992 marketing communications budget if the budget is based on the percentage allocated for 1991 sales? How many dollars would be allocated to marketing communications?

**b.** Suppose the firm's marketers decide to use the average percentage allocated for marketing communications over the past five years. They determine this average by calculating total sales and total marketing communications outlays since 1987 and then dividing total marketing communications outlays by total sales. What percentage would be included in the 1992 marketing communications budget? How many dollars would be allocated to marketing communications?

**c.** MHE's marketers are also considering basing their marketing communications budget on the average marketing communications outlays of their major competitors. What percentage would be used for marketing communications if this approach were implemented?

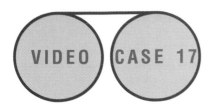

# VIDEO CASE 17  Apple Computer, Inc.

"I've always believed that marketing must begin with a great product. So now, wouldn't you like to see one? Ladies and gentlemen, inside this small, handsome case rests one of the great visions of our company — the Apple IIc."

With those words, John Sculley, president and chief executive officer of Apple Computer, Inc., introduced the company's newest personal computer to 4000 dealers, industry analysts, and members of the press during a product rollout extravaganza in San Francisco back in 1984. The big, splashy event, complete with rock music and laser lights, was Apple's way of generating excitement for its new product. "We think we can put on great events," says Del Yocam, executive vice-president, "and so we like the idea of capturing individuals' entire attention — their focus — whether it's for a day or a period of time. It helps them concentrate on Apple; whether it's the Macintosh group or the Apple II group, it is Apple. They feel a part of the family."

Event marketing — expensive, unconventional approaches to advertising, sales promotion, and personal selling — and innovative product design have helped Apple stay afloat in the high-risk personal computer market. Apple co-founders Steven Jobs and Stephen Wozniak, who designed the first Apple personal computer in 1976, are credited with developing this multibillion-dollar market. Apple sales grew rapidly during the late 1970s and early 1980s. But by 1983, the company was in trouble, losing market share to IBM, which had entered the personal computer market in 1981. Two years later, IBM dominated the market, driving out many large and small competitors and causing others to reposition their products as IBM-compatibles.

Apple intended to survive the shakedown. In 1983, John Sculley was recruited from PepsiCo to bring professional management to Apple, consistency to its product line, and order to its marketing efforts. Under Sculley's direction, Apple changed its entire product line in 100 days, increased its advertising budget of $15 million in 1983 to $100 million in 1984, and embarked on an attention-getting promotional campaign. Sculley says, "We couldn't have taken that big risk of changing our products and gone with technology that was radically different from where IBM and the rest of the industry were headed unless we had the boldness and voice of big events."

Sculley's promotional plan of staging big events was based on an assessment of Apple's products and the industry. In the early 1980s, the personal computer industry was in its infancy. The products were expensive, in the introductory stage of the product life cycle, and embodied high technology that most people did not understand. Sculley believed that advertising for personal computers was ineffective because it was filled with high-tech jargon that baffled almost everyone other than computer experts. He planned to increase Apple sales by using big events that would differentiate Apple from other computer companies and communicate a single message to consumers and retailers: Apple was a winning company with vision and bold products.

In promoting the Apple IIc to consumers, Apple marketers faced the considerable problem of how to communicate the compact computer's tremendous power, which was impossible to explain simply in a 30-second commercial. To show the computer's power, Apple's advertising agency created a commercial illustrating how the IIc could control all the operating systems — air conditioning, security, fire alarms, elevators, and turbines — in a 50-storey office building, a feat that requires far more power than a typical personal computer purchaser would need for home or classroom use.

"Apple will use advertising in outrageous ways to communicate very fundamental messages," said Sculley. In 1984, the company had an important message to communicate. Apple had developed the Macintosh, an innovative computer with its own proprietary operating system, and decided to position it as an alternative to the IBM PC, whose MS/DOS operating system was then the standard in the personal computer industry. To launch the Macintosh, Apple marketers used a single advertising event. They bought $2 million worth of Super Bowl advertising on January 22 to air "1984," a television commercial that likened IBM to the Big Brother in George Orwell's futuristic novel *1984*. Apple's message was: "On January 24th, Apple Computer will introduce Macintosh. And you'll see why 1984 won't be like *1984*."

Like all of Apple's big events, the "1984" commercial was designed to make people curious about the product before it actually hit the marketplace. For the first Macintosh promotion, Mike Murray, director of marketing, said, "We needed to have a message that was so strong and so radical that people would say, 'What was that?'...We needed to use IBM almost as a punching bag during 1984 so we could draw attention to why we were saying Macintosh could be positioned as an alternative to the IBM PC." The commercial did indeed draw attention. It was given much of the credit for generating $100 million in Macintosh sales within the 10 days following the commercial's one-time airing.

To back its advertising claim that Macintosh was "the first personal computer anyone can learn to use overnight," Apple marketers ran the promotion "Test Drive a Macintosh," which invited consumers to visit one of Apple's more than 2000 authorized dealers and take a Macintosh home overnight to try it out. Apple's innovative advertising resulted in 1984 sales of $1.5 billion, a 54 percent increase over 1983 sales.

Since the firm's beginning, Apple marketers have targeted their products at the home and educational markets. They have given hundreds of computers to elementary and high schools as part of their long-term strategy of converting student users into future buyers. But with the Macintosh, Apple marketers aimed at appealing to a new target group — business users. The business market, according to Sculley, comprises "the biggest market with the highest profit and the fastest growth in the personal computer industry."

In order to sell to the business market, Apple marketers refocused their promotional efforts on personal selling and publicity, changing the flavour of their advertising. Apple formed a new national sales force by recruiting 350 salespeople to sell Macintosh products to corporations. To generate favourable publicity, Apple managers held meetings for industry analysts and business consultants, during which new products were explained well in advance of their launch. Advertisements directed at business users emphasized detailed product information and solutions to problems. To communicate this information effectively, Apple marketers decided to use more print advertising than television commercials. As Apple added new Macintosh software and equipment aimed at business users, the timing of promotions became an important factor, so that promises made in advertising and public events were translated into meeting product-delivery deadlines.

In 1990 Apple introduced three new low-priced models, providing a new generation of entry-level machines promoted by a $25-million television and print advertising campaign. In the first quarter of 1991 orders were outstripping an already expanded production facility. Apple also recognized that most of its sales to consumers were for business or educational uses, and it concentrated its promotional efforts on those segments.

Today, largely owing to its ability to promote its products effectively, Apple is a successful corporation. It is maintaining its leadership position in the educational market while gaining widespread acceptance in the business market.

SOURCES    Apple Computer, Inc., 1987 *Annual Report*, p. 24; Brian O'Reilly, "Growing Apple Anew for the Business Market," *Fortune* (January 4, 1988), pp. 36–37; Katherine M. Hafner, "Apple Goes for a Bigger Bite of Corporate America," *Business Week* (August 24, 1987), pp. 74–75; Apple Computer Inc., *1990 Annual Report*; Apple Computer, Inc., *1991 First-Quarter Report*; Christy Fisher, "Battle Moves to the Home Front," *Advertising Age* (November 12, 1990), pp. S-1–S-2; Bradley Johnson, "Mac Leaves Home," *Advertising Age* (October 15, 1990), p. 6; and Brenton R. Schlender, "Yet Another Strategy for Apple," *Fortune* (October 22, 1990), pp. 81–87.

## Questions

1. Give examples of how Apple marketers have used both pushing and pulling strategies in their marketing communications efforts.

2. Explain how the nature of Apple's product and the industry influenced the firm's marketing communications strategy.

3. Relate the marketing communications elements discussed in the chapter to Apple's different target markets.

4. What are Apple's marketing communications objectives in targeting the consumer market? The business market?

5. The chapter discussed several methods marketers use in setting marketing communications budgets. Which method did John Sculley use when he raised Apple's advertising budget to $100 million? Discuss Sculley's decision in terms of Apple's competition and personal computers' position in the product life cycle.

# Applying Marketing Communications

## CHAPTER OBJECTIVES

1. To identify the categories of advertisements.
2. To list and discuss the various advertising media.
3. To describe the process of creating an advertisement.
4. To identify the methods of sales promotion.
5. To classify the three basic types of selling.
6. To discuss the characteristics of successful salespersons.
7. To outline the seven steps in the sales process.
8. To specify the functions of sales management.

**A** SMALL Alberta firm wants to add Snap, Crackle, and Pop to advertising campaigns around the world. The three elves, which have been part of Rice Krispies promotions for decades, are among dozens of figures created in larger-than-life costume form at the International Mascot Corp. (IMC) manufacturing plant in Edmonton.

IMC's lineup of characters includes such staples of Saturday-morning television as Tony the Tiger, Freddie and Eddie Shreddie, the Crayola Crayon, and the cartoon character Archie.

"Kids go nuts — they love the characters," says Carol Reader, product manager for children's cereals at Toronto-based Kellogg Canada Inc., which owns 20 different mascots from IMC. A two-metre-tall (seven-foot) mascot of Tony the Tiger, whose striped orange face has appeared on packages of Kellogg's Frosted Flakes for 37 years, drew a crowd of children at a promotional appearance at Toronto's Ontario Place during the summer.

"It's a way to channel information to the public in a very inoffensive way," IMC President Brian Baker says. "If your product is geared to children, they will relate to the character. Through that, they are being reminded of a product, and the parents are as well.''

The mascots weigh 20 to 25 pounds, depending on the character, and cost from $1500 (for a simple head shape and matching body) to $6000 (for a complete suit with all the options, including a battery-powered, motorized cooling vest and fan units controlled by the performer).

Reader says mascots are ''quite cost-effective'' when compared with the high costs of television advertising.[1] The way that this company's promotional characters fit in with corporate advertising clearly illustrates the concept of the marketing communications mix. Other components of the mix can be blended with advertising to strengthen the message being transmitted in the mass media. In this case, we find not only ingenious promotion, but also gentle ''personal'' (animal?) selling.

# Introduction

As we saw in Chapter 17, marketing communications consists of both personal and nonpersonal elements. This chapter will discuss the main components of these two elements. The most predominant components are advertising and personal selling.

# Advertising

If you sought to be the next prime minister of Canada, you would need to communicate with every possible voting Canadian. If you had invented a new calculator and went into business to sell it, your chances of success would be slim without informing and persuading students and business of your calculator's usefulness. In both these situations you would discover, as have countless others, that you would need to use advertising to communicate to buyers or voters. In the previous chapter, advertising was defined as paid nonpersonal communication through various media by business firms, nonprofit organizations, and individuals who are in some way identified in the advertising message and who hope to inform or persuade members of a particular audience.

Today's widespread markets make advertising an important part of business. Since the end of World War II, advertising and related expenditures have risen faster than have gross domestic product and most other economic indicators. Furthermore, about 8500 people are employed in advertising, according to Statistics Canada.[2]

Three advertisers — the Government of Canada, Procter & Gamble, and General Motors of Canada — spent more than $50 million each for advertising in 1988. Figure 18–1 ranks the top advertisers in Canada. It is particularly noteworthy that governments, both federal and provincial, are such a major force in Canadian advertising. The government is still the nation's largest advertising spender. It spent $32.5 million more than the number-two spender, Procter & Gamble. Total 1990 advertising media expenditures were about $10.2 billion. This means that about $392 is spent on advertising each year for every person in Canada.[3]

FIGURE 18-1

## The Top 10 Advertisers in Canada

| Rank | Name | Revenue (in millions of dollars) |
|------|------|----------------------------------|
| 1 | Government of Canada | 91.3 |
| 2 | Procter & Gamble | 58.6 |
| 3 | General Motors of Canada | 52.5 |
| 4 | Gulf & Western | 44.6 |
| 5 | RJR | 42.3 |
| 6 | John Labatt Limited | 42.1 |
| 7 | The Molson Companies | 41.1 |
| 8 | The Thomson Group | 40.1 |
| 9 | Cineplex Odeon Corporation | 38.8 |
| 10 | Government of Ontario | 37.9 |

Source: Adapted from *Marketing* (April 10, 1989); original data source was Media Management Services (Toronto).

Advertising expenditures vary among industries and companies. Cosmetics companies are often cited as an example of firms that spend a high percentage of their funds on advertising and promotion. Management consultants Schonfeld & Associates studied more than 4000 firms and calculated their average advertising expenditures as a percentage of both sales and gross profit margin. Estimates for selected industries are given in Figure 18-2. Wide differences exist among industries. Advertising spending can range from one-fifth of 1 percent (as is the case with iron and steel foundries) to more than 7 percent of sales (as in the detergent industry).

## A·P·P·L·Y·I·N·G  T·H·E  C·O·N·C·E·P·T·S

### A Vote for Advertising

In June 1990, the Supreme Court of Canada recognized the public's right to free commercial speech. It struck down prohibitions on advertising by the Royal College of Dental Surgeons of Ontario as a violation of freedom of expression. The ruling applies equally to other professionals such as lawyers, accountants, and architects.

In the spirit of the Charter of Rights and Freedoms, the court ruled that advertising restrictions set by professional governing bodies are unconstitutional, unless they are protecting consumers.

The Canadian Advertising Foundation supported the decision, and commented, "To make informed decisions consumers must know what services are available to them. Keeping consumers in ignorance of available services does not benefit any profession. Advertising by professionals should result in better services at lower prices."

Source: Adapted from Canadian Advertising Foundation, "A Vote for Advertising," *Pulse* (Summer 1990), p. 5.

FIGURE 18-2

## Estimates of Average Advertising to Sales in 10 Industries

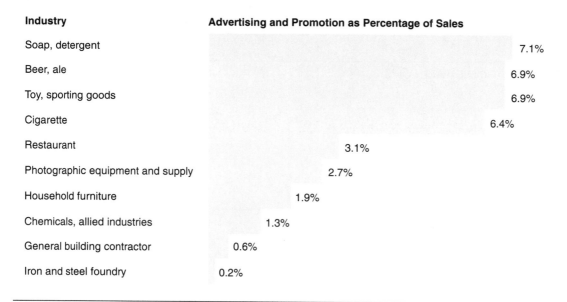

| Industry | Advertising and Promotion as Percentage of Sales |
|---|---|
| Soap, detergent | 7.1% |
| Beer, ale | 6.9% |
| Toy, sporting goods | 6.9% |
| Cigarette | 6.4% |
| Restaurant | 3.1% |
| Photographic equipment and supply | 2.7% |
| Household furniture | 1.9% |
| Chemicals, allied industries | 1.3% |
| General building contractor | 0.6% |
| Iron and steel foundry | 0.2% |

Source: Schonfeld & Associates, Inc., 120 S. La Salle St., Chicago 60603, (312) 236-5846; survey conducted in 1982.

## Historical Development

Some form of advertising aimed at boosting product sales has probably existed since the development of the exchange process.[4] Most early advertising was vocal. Criers and hawkers sold various products, made public announcements, and chanted advertising slogans like this one (now familiar to many as a nursery rhyme):

> One-a-penny, two-a-penny, hot-cross buns
>   One-a-penny, two for tuppence, hot-cross buns

Signs were also used in early advertising. Most were symbolic and used to identify products or services. In Rome a goat signified a dairy; a mule driving a mill, a bakery; a boy being whipped, a school.

Later the development of the printing press greatly expanded advertising's capability. A 1710 advertisement in the *Spectator* billed one dentifrice as "the Incomparable Powder for cleaning of Teeth, which has given great satisfaction to most of the Nobility and Gentry in England."

Many early newspapers carried advertising on their first page. Most of the advertisements would be called classified ads today — they featured spouses looking for wandering partners, householders looking for servants, and the like. However, some future national advertisers also began to use newspaper advertising at this time.

One identifying feature of advertising in the last half of the twentieth century is its concern for researching the markets that it attempts to reach. Originally, advertising research dealt primarily with media selection and the product. Then, advertisers

**Advertising Is a Necessary Investment, Not an Expense**

Copyright © 1983, Newspaper Enterprise Association.

became increasingly concerned with aiming their messages more specifically through determining the appropriate *demographics* (such characteristics as the age, sex, and income level of potential buyers). Now, understanding consumer behaviour has become an important aspect of advertising strategy. Psychological influences on purchase decisions — often called *psychographics* — can be useful in describing potential markets for advertising appeals. As described in Chapter 3, these influences include such factors as lifestyle and personal attitudes. Increased knowledge in these areas has led to improved advertising decisions.

The emergence of the marketing concept, with its emphasis on a company-wide consumer orientation, saw advertising take on an expanded role as marketing communications assumed greater importance in business. Advertising provides an efficient, inexpensive, and fast method of reaching the much-sought-after consumer. Its extensive use now rivals that of personal selling. Advertising has become a key ingredient in the effective implementation of the marketing concept.

## Advertising Objectives

Traditionally the objectives of advertising were stated in terms of direct sales goals. A more realistic approach, however, is to view advertising's communications objectives as being *to inform, persuade, and remind* potential customers of the product. Advertising seeks to condition the consumer so that he or she has a favourable viewpoint toward the promotional message. The goal is to improve the likelihood that the customer will buy a particular product. In this sense, advertising illustrates the close relationship between marketing communications and promotional strategy.

In instances where personal selling is the primary component of a firm's marketing mix, advertising may be used in a support role to assist the salespeople. Much of Avon's advertising is aimed at assisting the neighbourhood salesperson by strengthening the image of Avon, its products, and its salespeople. Figure 18–3 illustrates the important role advertising can play in opening doors for the sales force by preparing customers for the sales call.

FIGURE 18 – 3

**Use of Advertising to Assist Personal Selling**

*Personal selling is important in the sale of industrial products, such as Du Pont Canada's Lorox DF herbicide. To assist sales representatives like Chantal Kilsdonk (right), Du Pont promoted its new "Toss-n-go" soluble bag, which dissolves in water when dropped into a herbicide sprayer (eliminating contact by the user). Promotion of this new product advantage gives Chantal an added edge when she makes her sales calls.*

## Advertising Planning

Advertising planning begins with effective research. Research results allow management to make strategic decisions, which are then translated into tactical execution — budgeting, copywriting, scheduling, and the like. Finally, there must be some feedback mechanism for measuring the effectiveness of the advertising. The elements of advertising planning are shown in Figure 18–4.

There is a real need for following a sequential process in advertising decisions. Novice advertisers are often guilty of being overly concerned with the technical aspects of advertisement construction, while ignoring the more basic steps such as market analysis. The type of advertisement that is employed in any particular situation is related largely to the planning phase of this process.

FIGURE 18 – 4

**Elements of Advertising Planning**

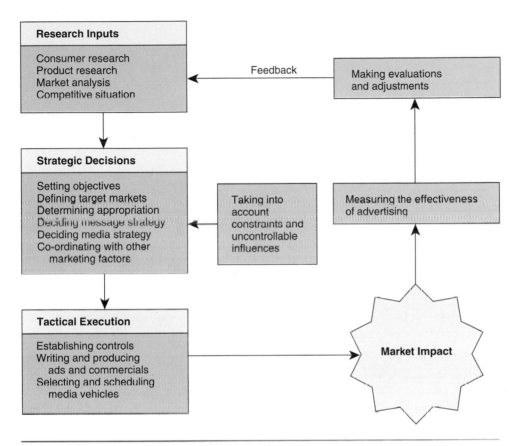

Source: Adapted from S. Watson Dunn and Arnold M. Barban, *Advertising: Its Role in Modern Marketing*, 5th ed. (Hinsdale, IL: Dryden Press, 1982), p. 202. Copyright © 1982 by CBS College Publishing. Reprinted by permission.

# Positioning

The concept of positioning was discussed in Chapter 4. It involves developing a marketing strategy aimed at a particular segment of the market in order to achieve a desired position in the mind of the prospective buyer. A variety of positioning strategies is available to the advertiser. An object can be positioned, in the following ways:

1. By attributes. (Crest is a cavity fighter.)

2. By price/quality. (Sears is a value store.)

3. By competitor. ("Avis is only number two in rent-a-cars, so why go with us? We try harder.")

4. By application. (Gatorade is for quick, healthful energy after exercise and other forms of physical exertion.)

---

## I·S·S·U·E·S  I·N  I·N·T·E·R·N·A·T·I·O·N·A·L  M·A·R·K·E·T·I·N·G

### H.J. Heinz Moves into China

Heinz has converted its dominant products — ketchup and Weight Watchers diet meals — into global brands and has entered new markets around the world. By 1991, 40 percent of its revenues came from overseas. But perhaps its most innovative move has been to make and sell an instant rice cereal for babies in China.

Heinz has a lot going for it in the Chinese market. For one thing, 22 million babies are born in China each year — six times the number born in the United States. For another, under China's one-child-per-family policy a child born in that nation stands a good chance of being an only child and the apple of its parents' eye — or, as the Chinese say, their "little emperor."

For the parents of these infants, a Western baby food high in vitamins and minerals is well worth the relatively high price of 75 cents a box (an expensive purchase for a worker earning $40 a month). To attract their attention, Heinz has produced high-quality television commercials in a market where most advertising is done via newspapers and billboards. The commercials show happy babies being cuddled by their mothers, with a message assuring viewers of the product's nutritional value. The fact that Heinz's cereal is precooked and instant — in contrast to less expensive products that need to be cooked — makes it more appealing to families in which both parents work outside the home.

Heinz began making instant cereal in a small plant in Guangzhou (formerly Canton) in 1986. The venture is already profitable — a surprise in a country where it usually takes a decade to turn a profit. In fact, its margins are comparable to those of the parent company, prompting Heinz to begin a search for a second factory site.

Sources: Patrice Duggan, "Feeding China's 'Little Emperors,'" *Forbes* (August 6, 1990), pp. 84–85; Gregory L. Miles, "Heinz Ain't Broke, But It's Doing a Lot of Fixing," *Business Week* (December 11, 1989), pp. 84, 85, 88; and Alicia Swasy, "Heinz's O'Reilly Drives Hard for Growth," *Wall Street Journal* (February 7, 1991).

---

## A·P·P·L·Y·I·N·G  T·H·E  C·O·N·C·E·P·T·S

### The Fight against Sexist Ads

Some key players who are in a position to influence advertising are beginning to recognize the dangers of portraying women as sex objects. Two small but significant and encouraging incidents indicate that a change may be in the wind. It may even lead to some more thoughtful advertising.

Both incidents were the result of a string of controversial ads that were blasted by women's groups for demeaning women. Some of the ads were pulled or modified in a bid to turn down the heat.

Incident No. 1 involved the Brewers of Ontario, a trade group. It commissioned a consultant to probe the possibility of reviewing advertising guidelines dealing with sexual stereotyping, lifestyle scenarios, and other issues. It is expected that the review would eventually involve all advertisers.

The probe is at a preliminary stage, and there are still plenty of marketers who swear by their predictable girlwatching/boywatching ads. But a light has gone on.

Incident No. 2 involved a major ad agency, Young & Rubicam. The agency recently invited Media-Watch, a feminist ad watchdog, to help it avoid sexist ads.

The agency wanted to make sure that it didn't fall into the trap of sexism, thus risking financial losses — not to mention a black eye — for clients. After a review of a number of proposed ads, suggestions for change were made in some. "It was definitely helpful to us," Ken Solomon, an official at Young & Rubicam, says about the consultation. "To know these things in advance can certainly save clients a lot of money."

Realistically, it's probably not so much the rules that need to be revised as the marketers' attitudes. Some marketers rationalize their heavy use of bodies in overly suggestive poses and predicaments with a "me-too" argument — everyone else is doing it.

Surely there has to be some moral responsibility on the part of advertisers. They are not just selling a product — they are selling an image of popular culture. Promoting attitudes that involve worshipping the body beautiful as a prize to be won with the right product is simply unacceptable. Such a culture creates illusionary expectations.

Source: Adapted from Marina Strauss, "Small Victories in Fight Against Sexist Ads," *Globe and Mail* (October 12, 1990).

5. By product user. (Mercedes-Benz automobiles are for discriminating executives.)
6. By product class. (Carnation Instant Breakfast is a breakfast food.)[5]

# Categories of Advertisements

Essentially, there are two basic types of advertisements: product and institutional. The former type can be subdivided into informative, persuasive, and reminder-oriented categories.

**Product advertising** deals with *the nonpersonal selling of a particular good or service*. It is the type we normally think of when the subject of advertising comes up in a conversation. **Institutional advertising**, by contrast, is concerned with *promoting a concept, idea, or philosophy, or the goodwill of an industry, company, or organization*. It is often closely related to the public relations function of the enterprise.[6] An example of institutional advertising appears in Figure 18–5.

**product advertising**
Nonpersonal selling of a particular good or service.

**institutional advertising**
Promoting a concept, idea, or philosophy, or the goodwill of an industry, company, or organization.

## Informative Product Advertising

All advertising seeks to influence the audience, as does any type of communication. **Informative product advertising** *seeks to develop demand through presenting factual information on the attributes of the product and/or service*. For example, an advertisement for a new type of photocopy machine would attempt to persuade through citing the various unique product and/or service features of that copier. Informative product advertising tends to be used in promoting new products, since a major requirement in such cases is to announce availability and characteristics that will satisfy needs. Thus it is often seen in the introductory stages of the product life cycle. Figure 18–6 shows an advertisement for Dow Chemical that uses a factual approach to persuade people to use that service.

**Informative product advertising**
Advertising that seeks to develop demand through presenting factual information on the attributes of a product and/or service.

## Persuasive Product Advertising

In **persuasive product advertising** *the emphasis is on using words and/or images to try to create an image for a product and to influence attitudes about it*. In contrast to informative product advertising, this type of advertising contains little objective information. Figure 18–7 shows an advertisement for a Ford vehicle. While it gives a little objective information, the main thrust is persuasion. Coke and Pepsi use persuasive techniques in their lifestyle advertisements featuring a group of happy people enjoying the product. Persuasive advertising is generally used more after the introductory stage of the product life cycle.

**persuasive product advertising**
Advertising that emphasizes using words and/or images to try to create an image for a product and to influence attitudes about it.

## Reminder-Oriented Product Advertising

The goal of **reminder-oriented product advertising** is *to reinforce previous promotional activity by keeping the product's or service's name in front of the public*. It is used in the maturity period as well as throughout the decline phase of the product life cycle. An example of a reminder-oriented slogan is Coke's well known "You can't beat the real thing." Figure 18–8 illustrates the general relationship between the type of advertising and the stage of the life cycle.

**reminder-oriented product advertising**     Advertising whose goal is to reinforce previous promotional activity by keeping the product or service name in front of the public.

### FIGURE 18-5

### An Example of Institutional Advertising

*By promoting its people, rather than a specific product, Shell Canada has chosen an institutional form of advertising. All the people cited in this ad are involved in community groups that support Shell's statement that it is "Caring Enough to Make a Difference." By promoting community goodwill in this fashion, Shell Canada hopes to give its corporate image a more personal touch.*

# Shell people.
# They're making a difference.

Meet some special Shell people. On their own time, they're putting their talents and efforts to work for their communities as volunteers.

*"You can continue to make a contribution to your world, to your community and to your neighbourhood."* Bill Hughes, retired Toronto Shell employee, volunteers his time and skills to ten different community services. At Senior Link, for example, Bill is helping to pioneer a dynamic new alternative in the housing and care of senior citizens.

*"You get more out of it than you ever put in."* Myra Drumm, Calgary Shell employee, is a volunteer at the Tom Baker Cancer Centre. Trained to work one-on-one with newly-diagnosed cancer patients, Myra is a listener, a source of support, and a friend in a time of crisis.

*"I had time that I could give to someone else."* Jean-Paul Blais, Montréal Shell employee, is a volunteer with The Compassionate Friends of Québec where he gives 'self-help' support and understanding to parents who have lost children. Jean-Paul is also a 'Big Brother'.

The Shell Community Service Fund provides financial support to community groups in which these and other Shell people volunteer their time and efforts.

For more information on our activities, please call (403) 691-3198.

Shell Canada
**Caring Enough to Make a Difference.**

FIGURE 18 – 6

## An Example of Informative Product Advertising

We'd like to strip away any misconceptions about Chlorinated Solvents.

*Informative ads are often used by industrial manufacturers to present factual information about a product. This ad for chlorinated solvents from Dow Chemical Canada is targeted at purchasing agents for metal-cleaning applications. Information regarding the benefits of the solvent are outlined in a straightforward fashion, so the purchasing agent can make an informed decision about the product.*

Much has been written about the differences between industrial solvents. About how aqueous solvents are more economical than chlorinated solvents. About how fluorocarbon solvents are safer than their chlorinated counterparts. Much *has* been written. But now it's time to set the record straight.

**SAFETY**

Any industrial solvent, when mishandled is unsafe. However, the degree of hazard is dependent upon handling procedures and the level of exposure. With proper engineering controls in place to minimize exposure the hazard becomes negligible. In this respect, chlorinated solvents systems are more efficiently controlled and, therefore, maintain better levels of exposure.

**STABILITY**

Fact is, all industrial solvents can break down. Proper degreaser practices with normal solvent makeup and equipment cleanouts best determine a solvent's lifespan. Chlorinated solvents are, in reality, exceptionally stable. They are specially inhibited for vapour degreasing. Plus, the inhibitor system stays intact throughout degreasing and distilling cycles. When properly handled, chlorinated solvents can be used almost indefinitely.

**RECYCLING**

Chlorinated solvents can be recycled in standard distillation equipment with no loss in inhibitor effectiveness allowing you to reuse them again and again.

**ECONOMY**

When overall systems are compared, chlorinated solvents save you money because, 1) they're recyclable, 2) they don't require expensive water treatment, rinsing or drying equipment, 3) they use up much less floor space and 4) they don't require energy intensive refrigeration. In fact, actual degreaser studies show that for most applications *total* costs are lower for chlorinated solvent systems.

**EFFICIENCY**

No argument here. Chlorinated solvents are overall the most effective industrial solvents in use today. They are unparalleled when it comes to solvency of organic residue, petroleum based oils, greases and waxes, fats, resins, gums and rosin fluxes. They clean without pitting, corroding, oxidizing, staining, etching or dulling metals. In fact, people using other solvent systems often combine them with chlorinated solvents to improve performance.

When you look at the facts, for most applications chlorinated solvents simply outperform their rivals – in safety, stability, economy and effectiveness. At Dow, we're proud to offer a wide range of chlorinated solvents to answer most specialized needs. Because we believe they're still the best bet in industrial cleaning solvents today. And the facts prove it.

Dow encourages its customers to review their applications of Dow products from the standpoint of human health and environmental concern. To help ensure that Dow products are not used in ways other than as intended or tested, Dow personnel are willing to assist customers in dealing with ecological and product safety considerations. Your Dow representative can arrange the proper contacts.

**DOW CHEMICAL CANADA INC.**

## FIGURE 18-7

### An Example of Persuasive Product Advertising

Looking to get away from it all? Escape the pressures of urban living? In a new 4-door Explorer, there's no such thing as city limits.

Powered by a spirited 4.0 L V6, Explorer's body-on-frame construction delivers a more stable, solid ride. Handling is surprisingly responsive. And with the longest wheel base in its class, four-door Explorer's all round performance is smooth, despite the geography.

Aerodynamic styling helps reduce interior noise to a whisper. Standard rear anti-lock brakes make quick work of any unexpected 4×4 stops along the way. And with Explorer's exclusive push button 4-wheel drive, the real adventure begins where the pavement ends.

One look inside its new ergonomically designed interior and you'll discover that Explorer is the first of its kind to successfully combine car-like comfort with truck-style

ruggedness. It's packed full of car-like luxury.

With the largest interior in its class, you'll never feel cramped discovering wide open spaces. There's comfortable seating for five. Six with the optional split bench front seat. Lower the rear seats and watch the largest cargo space in its class unfold before your eyes. A versatile function liftgate makes loading and unloading a breeze. We even built Explorer lower to the ground, so that getting in is just one small step away. It's features like these that made Explorer, 4 Wheeler Magazine's first choice. So don't miss your calling. Discover how easy escaping can be in any of the four or uniquely styled two door models.

There's a Ford or Mercury dealer in your neck of the woods.

**Quality is Job 1.**

# Escape the concrete jungle.

1991 Explorer

*"Escape the Concrete Jungle": The idea of "getting away from it all," coupled with a striking image of the Ford vehicle that will accomplish this dream, appeals to almost everyone. While it does furnish some objective information, the main thrust of this ad is persuasive.*

## Institutional Advertising

As mentioned earlier, institutional advertising seeks to increase public knowledge of a concept, idea, philosophy, industry, or company. In the early 1980s the oil industry was experiencing a degree of unfavourable publicity. One firm's communications director said, "We decided we had a story to tell."[7] Consequently, the company tripled its corporate advertising budget to $3 million and undertook an extensive program to educate the public about the company's contributions to society. Other firms, such as Volkswagen, have continuously advertised their innovativeness and reliability.

## Media Selection

One of the most important decisions in developing an advertising strategy is media selection. A mistake at this point can cost a company literally millions of dollars in ineffectual advertising. Media strategy must achieve the communications goals mentioned earlier.

FIGURE 18 - 8

**Relationship between Advertising and the Product Life Cycle**

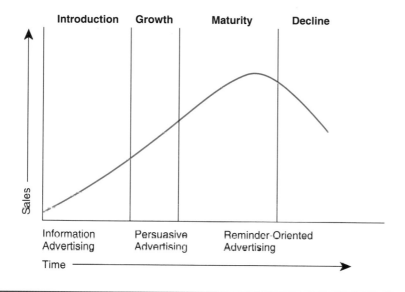

Research should identify the target market, determine its size and characteristics, and then match the target with the audience and effectiveness of the available media. The objective is to achieve adequate media coverage without advertising beyond the identifiable limits of the potential market. Finally, alternative costs are compared to determine the best possible media purchase.

There are numerous types of advertising media, and the characteristics of some of the more important ones will be considered here.[8] The advantages and disadvantages of each are shown in Figure 18–9.

## Newspapers

About 26 percent of Canada's total advertising revenues, the largest share received by any of the media, is spent on advertising in newspapers (including weekend supplements).[9] The primary advantages of newspapers are flexibility (advertising can be varied from one locality to the next), community prestige (newspapers have a deep impact on the community), intense coverage (in most places about nine out of ten homes can be reached by a single newspaper), and reader control of exposure to the advertising message (unlike audiences of electronic media, readers can refer back to newspapers). The disadvantages are a short lifespan, hasty reading (the typical reader spends only 20 to 30 minutes on the newspaper), and poor reproduction.

## Magazines

Magazines are divided into such diverse categories as consumer magazines, farm and business publications, and directories. They account for about 12 percent of all advertising. The primary advantages of periodical advertising are target markets;

FIGURE 18–9

## Advantages and Disadvantages of the Various Advertising Media

| Media | Advantages | Disadvantages |
|---|---|---|
| Newspapers | Flexibility<br>Community prestige<br>Intense coverage<br>Reader control of exposure<br>Co-ordination with<br>national advertising<br>Merchandising service | Short lifespan<br>Hasty reading<br>Poor reproduction |
| Magazines | Selectivity<br>Quality reproduction<br>Long life<br>Prestige associated with<br>some magazines<br>Extra services | Lack of flexibility |
| Television | Great impact<br>Mass coverage<br>Repetition<br>Flexibility<br>Prestige | Temporary nature of<br>message<br>High cost<br>High mortality rate for<br>commercials<br>Evidence of public distrust<br>Lack of selectivity |
| Radio | Immediacy<br>Low cost<br>Practical audience<br>selection<br>Mobility | Fragmentation<br>Temporary nature of<br>message<br>Little research information |
| Outdoor Advertising | Quick communication of<br>simple ideas<br>Repetition<br>Ability to promote products<br>available for sale nearby | Brevity of the message<br>Public concern over esthetics |
| Direct Mail | Selectivity<br>Intense coverage<br>Speed<br>Flexibility of format<br>Complete information<br>Personalization | High cost per person<br>Dependency on quality of<br>mailing list<br>Consumer resistance |

Source: Based on Dunn and Barban, *Advertising*, pp. 513–577.

selectivity of targets markets; quality reproduction; long life; the prestige associated with some magazines; and the extra services offered by many publications. Canadian consumer magazines have pioneered many controlled distribution techniques. Our Postal Code system, with its six-digit Forward Sortation Area (FSA) and Local Delivery Unit (LDU), can be linked with census data at the Enumeration Area (EA) to produce well-defined circulation clusters based on demographics, life cycles,

---

### A·P·P·L·Y·I·N·G  T·H·E  C·O·N·C·E·P·T·S

## *How a Multifaceted Campaign Works*

The opening of Brettons' new flagship store in downtown Toronto provides a good example of the development and use of a marketing communications mix.

To announce the opening of its new store, Brettons used many media, including magazines, subway posters, billboards, radio, newspapers, direct mail, and public relations.

Toronto issues of *Flare* and *Maclean's* included special sections with a mix of ads and "advertorial" (an advertisement set up to look like an editorial). Local radio stations were used first for "teaser" ads (designed to stimulate interest, but not reveal the sponsor), and then for "launch" (opening) advertisements. In addition, a direct mailing went to 200 000 households.

Furthermore, Brettons launched a national charge-card campaign, with 700 000 applications distributed through a combination of mailing lists, postal drops, and the Toronto editions of *Flare* and *Maclean's*. The first 15 000 new cardholders in Toronto were offered a year's free subscription to *Flare*.

Brettons — which specializes in fashions, accessories, gifts, and cosmetics — handled the campaign in-house, rather than turning it over to an advertising agency. Instead, the firm got assistance as needed from G&G Advertising, Toronto. Strategic Objectives, Toronto, handled the PR program.

Source: Adapted from "Brettons Launch," *Marketing* (September 25, 1989), p. 4.

---

or other interest activity profiles.[10] The primary disadvantage is that periodicals lack the flexibility of newspapers, radio, and television.

## Television

Television is the second largest advertising medium. It now accounts for about 14 percent of total advertising volume. Television advertising can be divided into three categories: network, national spot, and local spot. The Canadian Broadcasting Corporation, the Canadian Television Network, and Global Television are the three national networks. Network advertising usually accounts for over two-thirds of the total television advertising expenditures. A national "spot" refers to non-network broadcasting used by a general advertiser (for example, Black & Decker might choose to place an advertisement in several cities across the country, without buying time from a total television network). Local spots, primarily used by retailers, consist of locally developed and sponsored commercials. Television advertising offers the following advantages: impact, mass coverage, repetition, flexibility, and prestige. Its disadvantages include the temporary nature of the message, high costs, high mortality rates for commercials, some evidence of public distrust, and lack of selectivity.

## Radio

Advertisers using the medium of radio can also be classified as network or local advertisers. Radio accounts for about 7 percent of total advertising volume. The advantages of radio advertising are immediacy (studies show that most people regard radio as the best source for up-to-date news); low cost; flexibility; practical, low-cost audience selection; and mobility (radio is an extremely mobile broadcast medium). Radio's disadvantages include fragmentation (for instance, Montreal has about 19 AM and FM stations), the unavailability of the advertising message for future reference, and less research information than for television.

## Direct Mail

Sales letters, postcards, leaflets, folders, broadsides (which are larger than folders), booklets, catalogues, and house organs (periodical publications issued by an organization) are all forms of direct-mail advertising. The advantages of direct mail include selectivity, intensive coverage, speed, format flexibility, complete information, and the personalization of each mailing piece. Direct mail purchasers also tend to be consistent buyers by mail.[11] A disadvantage of direct mail is its high cost per reader. Direct mail advertising also depends on the quality of the mailing list.[12] Often those unfamiliar with the efficacy of direct mail condemn it all as "junk mail." They are very surprised to find that many people respond positively to direct mail. In fact, marketing research surveys consistently show a majority who say they prefer to receive it. Effectively used, direct mail is a successful and lucrative marketing tool.

## Outdoor Advertising

Posters (commonly called billboards), painted bulletins or displays (such as those that appear on building walls), and electric spectaculars (large illuminated — sometimes animated — signs and displays) make up outdoor advertising. Accounting for 6 percent of advertising volume, this form of advertising has the advantages of quickly communicating simple ideas, repetition, and the ability to promote products that are available for sale nearby. Outdoor advertising is particularly effective in metropolitan and other high-traffic areas. Disadvantages of the medium are the brevity of its message and public concern over esthetics; however, as Figure 18–10 shows, a simple message can be extremely powerful.

# Organizing the Advertising Function

While the ultimate responsibility for advertising decisions often rests with top marketing management, the organization of the advertising function varies among companies. A producer of a technical industrial product may be served by a one-person operation primarily concerned with writing copy for trade publications. A consumer-goods company, on the other hand, may have a large department staffed with advertising specialists.[13]

The advertising function is usually organized as a staff department reporting to the vice-president (or director) of marketing. The *director of advertising* is an executive position heading the functional activity of advertising. The individual filling this slot should not only be a skilled and experienced advertiser; he or she must also be able to communicate effectively within the organization. The success of a firm's promotional strategy depends on the advertising director's willingness and ability to communicate both vertically and horizontally. The major tasks typically organized under advertising include advertising research, art, copywriting, media analysis, and, in some cases, sales promotion.

## Advertising Agencies

**advertising agency** A marketing specialist firm that assists the advertiser in planning and preparing its advertisements.

Many advertisers also make use of an independent advertising agency. The **advertising agency** is *a marketing specialist firm that assists the advertiser in planning and preparing its advertisements.* There are several reasons why advertisers use an agency for at least a portion of their advertising. Agencies are typically staffed with highly qualified

## FIGURE 18-10

### An Award-Winning Billboard

# STUCK JUNE 30 AND STILL HOLDING

# TRY BAND·AID FABRIC
BRAND

*Johnson & Johnson*

*Johnson & Johnson's successful "stuck and still holding" ad campaign was designed by the Young & Rubicam advertising agency in Montreal. The simple message, with the product highlighted by two massive black arrows, takes full advantage of the outdoor billboard medium it was intended for. It also issues an attention-grabbing challenge, giving Johnson & Johnson the chance to prove the quality of their product.*

specialists who provide a degree of creativity and objectivity that is difficult to maintain in a corporate advertising department. In some cases using an agency reduces the cost of advertising, since the agency does not require many of the fixed expenses associated with internal advertising departments. Effective use of an advertising agency requires a close relationship between advertiser and agency.

## Creating an Advertisement

The final step in the advertising process is the development and preparation of an advertisement, which should flow logically from the promotional theme selected. It should thus be a complementary part of the marketing mix, with its role in total marketing strategy carefully determined. In addition, major factors to consider when preparing an advertisement are its creativity, its continuity with past advertisements, and possibly its association with other company products.[14]

What should an advertisement accomplish? Regardless of the exact appeal that is chosen, an advertisement should (1) gain attention and interest, (2) inform and/or persuade, and (3) eventually lead to buying action.

Gaining attention should be productive. That is, the reason for gaining consumers' attention should be to instill some recall of the product. Consider the case of the Gillette Company, which had a chimpanzee shave a man's face in a commercial. After tests in two cities, one Gillette man observed, "Lots of people remembered the chimp, but hardly anyone remembered our product. There was fantastic interest in the monkey, but no payoff for Gillette."[15] The advertisement gained the audience's attention but it failed to lead to buying action. An advertisement that fails to gain and hold the receiver's attention is ineffectual.

Information and persuasion is the second factor to consider when creating an advertisement. For example, insurance advertisements typically specify the features of the policy and may use testimonials in attempting to persuade prospects.

Stimulating buying action, however, is often difficult since an advertisement cannot actually close a sale. Nevertheless, if the first two steps have been accomplished, the advertising has likely been well worthwhile. Too many advertisers fail to suggest how the receiver of the message can buy the product if he or she so desires.

## Comparative Advertising

**comparative advertising**
Advertising that makes direct promotional comparisons with leading competitive brands.

**Comparative advertising** *makes direct promotional comparisons with leading competitive brands.* The strategy is best employed by firms that do not lead the market. Most market leaders prefer not to acknowledge that there are competitive products. Procter & Gamble and General Foods, for instance, traditionally have devoted little of their huge promotional budgets for comparative advertising. But many firms do use it extensively. An estimated 23 percent of all radio and television commercials make comparisons to competitive products. Here are some examples:

- Scope mouthwash prevents "medicine breath," but Listerine is never mentioned.
- Minute Maid lemonade is better than the "no-lemon lemonade," a reference to General Foods' Country Time brand.
- Suave antiperspirant will keep you just as dry as Ban Ultra Dry does and for a lot less.
- Nationwide, more Coca-Cola drinkers prefer the taste of Pepsi.

Marketers who contemplate using comparative advertising in their promotional strategies should take precautions to ensure that they can substantiate their claims, because comparison advertising has the potential of producing lawsuits. Advertising experts disagree about this practice's long-term effects. The conclusion is likely to be that comparative advertising is a useful strategy in a limited number of circumstances.[16]

## Retail Advertising

Retail advertising is all advertising by stores that sell goods or services directly to the consuming public. While accounting for a sizeable portion of total advertising expenditures, retail advertising varies widely in its effectiveness.

The basic problem is that advertising is often treated as a secondary activity, particularly in smaller retail stores. Store managers in these stores are usually given the responsibility of advertising as an added task, to be performed along with their normal functions. Advertising agencies have traditionally been used rarely by retailers.

More recently, however, larger retailers have been spending more than ever on advertising, and they are going to agencies to buy the needed expertise.[17] One reason for this is that Canadians spend 42 percent of their consumer dollars in chain stores. Consequently, there is great incentive to promote a chain store nationally, as well as to stress its private brands.

**co-operative advertising**    The sharing of advertising costs between the retailer and manufacturer or wholesaler.

**Co-operative advertising** involves *the sharing of advertising costs between the retailer and the manufacturer or wholesaler.* For example, General Mills may pay 50 percent of the cost of the 50 cm$^2$ of a chain's weekly newspaper ad that features a Betty Crocker cake mix special.

Co-operative advertising initially evolved because many newspapers offered lower rates to local advertisers than to national advertisers. Later, co-operative advertising was seen as a method of inducing retailers to share in the costs of advertising. From the retailer's viewpoint, co-op advertising permits a store to secure additional advertising that it would not otherwise have.

## Assessing the Effectiveness of an Advertisement

For many firms, advertising represents a major expenditure, so it is imperative to determine whether a campaign is accomplishing its promotional objectives. Determining advertising's effectiveness, however, is one of the most difficult undertakings in marketing. It consists of two primary elements — pre-testing and post-testing.[18]

### Pre-testing

**Pre-testing** is *the assessment of an advertisement's effectiveness before it is actually used*. It includes a variety of evaluative methods. For example, to test magazine advertisements, the ad agency Batten, Barton, Durstine & Osborn cuts ads out of advance copies of magazines and then "strips in" the ads it wants to test. Interviewers later check the impact of the advertisements on the readers who receive free copies of the revised magazine. There are many other techniques used for testing advertising.

**pre-testing** The assessment of an advertisement's effectiveness before it is actually used.

### Post-testing

**Post-testing** is *the assessment of advertising copy after it has been used*. Pre-testing is generally a more desirable testing method than post-testing because of its potential cost savings. But post-testing can be helpful in planning future advertisements and in making adjustments to current advertising programs.

**post-testing** The assessment of advertising copy after it has been used.

In one of the most popular post-tests, the *Starch Readership Report*, interviewers ask people who have read selected magazines whether they have read various ads in them. A copy of the magazine is used as an interviewing aid, and each interviewer starts at a different point in the magazine. For larger ads, respondents are also asked about specifics such as headlines and copy. All readership or recognition tests assume that future sales are related to advertising readership.

Regardless of the exact method used, marketers must realize that pre-testing and post-testing are expensive and must, therefore, plan to use them as effectively as possible.

## Sales Promotion Methods

The second type of nonpersonal selling is sales promotion. As we learned in Chapter 17, sales promotion may be defined as those marketing activities, other than personal selling, advertising, and publicity, that stimulate consumer purchasing and dealer effectiveness. It includes such activities as displays, shows and exhibitions, demonstrations, and various nonrecurrent promotional efforts not in the ordinary routine.[19]

Sales promotion techniques may be used by all members of a marketing channel — manufacturers, wholesalers, and retailers — and are typically targeted at specific markets. For example, a manufacturer such as Texize Corporation might combine trial sample mailings of a new spot remover to consumers with a sales contest for wholesalers and retailers who handle the new product. In both instances, the sales promotion techniques are designed to supplement and extend the other elements of the firm's promotional mix.

Firms that wish to use sales promotion can choose from various methods — point-of-purchase advertising; specialty advertising; trade shows; samples, coupons, and premiums; and contests. More than one of these options may be used in a single promotional strategy, but probably no promotional strategy has ever used all the options in a single program. While they are not mutually exclusive, sales promotion methods are generally employed on a selective basis.

## Point-of-Purchase Advertising

*Displays and demonstrations that seek to promote the product at a time and place closely associated with the actual decision to buy* are called **point-of-purchasing advertising**. The in-store promotion of consumer goods is a common example. Such advertising can be extremely useful in carrying forward a theme developed in another element of promotional strategy. A life-sized display of a celebrity used in television advertising, for instance, can become a realistic in-store display. Another example is the L'eggs store displays, which completely altered the pantyhose industry.

**point-of-purchase advertising** Displays and demonstrations that seek to promote the product at a time and place closely associated with the actual decision to buy.

## Specialty Advertising

**Specialty advertising** is a sales promotion medium that *utilizes useful articles to carry the advertiser's name, address, and advertising message* to reach the target customers.[20] The origin of specialty advertising has been traced to the Middle Ages, when wooden pegs bearing the names of artisans "were given to prospects to be driven into their walls and to serve as a convenient place upon which to hang armor."[21]

**specialty advertising** Sales promotion medium that utilizes useful articles to carry the advertiser's name, address, and advertising message.

Examples of contemporary advertising specialties carrying a firm's name include calendars, pencils, pens, paperweights, matchbooks, personalized business gifts of modest value, pocket diaries, shopping bags, memo pads, ash trays, balloons, measuring sticks, key rings, glasses, and hundreds of other items.

## Trade Shows

To influence channel members and resellers in the distribution channel, it has become a common practice for a seller to participate in a *trade show*, exposition, or convention. These shows are often organized by an industry's trade association and may be part of the association's annual meeting or convention. Vendors serving the particular industry are invited to the show to display and demonstrate their products for the association's membership. An example would be the professional meetings attended by college professors in a given discipline, at which the major textbook publishers exhibit their offerings to the channel members in their marketing system.

## Samples, Coupons, and Premiums

The distribution of samples, coupons, and premiums is probably the best-known sales promotion technique. *Sampling* involves free distribution of an item in an attempt to obtain consumer acceptance. This may be done on a door-to-door basis, by mail, through demonstrations, or as an insertion into packages containing other products. Sampling is especially useful in promoting new products.

*Coupons* offer a discount, usually some specified price reduction, from the next purchase of a product. Coupons are readily redeemable with retailers, who also receive an additional handling fee. Mail, magazine, newspaper, or package insertion are standard methods of distributing coupons.[22]

*Premiums*, bonus items given free with the purchase of another product, have proven effective in getting consumers to try a new product or a different brand.[23] Service stations, for example, use glassware, ice scrapers, and beach balls to convince noncustomers to try their brand. Premiums are also used to obtain direct-mail purchases. The value of premium giveaways runs into millions of dollars each year.

## Contests

Firms may sponsor contests to attract additional customers, offering substantial cash or merchandise prizes to call attention to their products. A company might consider employing a specialist in developing this type of sales promotion because of the variety and complexity of schemes available.

## Personal Selling

Personal selling was defined in Chapter 17 as a seller's promotional presentation conducted on a person-to-person basis with the buyer. Selling is an inherent function of any business enterprise. Accounting, engineering, personnel management, and other organizational activities are useless unless the firm's product can be sold to someone. Thousands of sales employees bear witness to selling's importance in the Canadian economy. While advertising expenses in the average firm may represent from 1 to 3 percent of total sales, selling expenses are likely to equal 10 to 15 percent of sales. In many firms, personal selling is the single largest marketing expense.

**FIGURE 18–11**

**Factors Affecting the Importance of Personal Selling in the Promotional Mix**

| | *Personal Selling* is likely to be more important when: | *Advertising* is likely to be more important when: |
|---|---|---|
| Consumer is: | geographically concentrated, relatively small numbers | geographically dispersed, relatively large numbers |
| Product is: | expensive, technically complex, custom-made, special handling required, trade-ins frequently involved | inexpensive, simple to understand, standardized, no special handling, no trade-ins |
| Price is: | relatively high | relatively low |
| Channels are: | relatively short | relatively long |

As Chapter 17 pointed out, personal selling is likely to be the primary component of a firm's marketing communications mix when customers are concentrated geographically; when orders are large; when the products or services are expensive, technically complex, and require special handling; when trade-ins are involved; when channels are short; and when the number of potential customers is relatively small. Figure 18–11 summarizes the factors affecting personal selling's importance in the overall marketing communications mix.

## Categories of Selling

The sales job has evolved into a professional occupation. Today's salesperson is more concerned with helping customers select the correct product to meet their needs than with simply selling whatever is available. Modern professional salespeople advise and assist customers in their purchase decisions. Where repeat purchases are common, the salesperson must be certain that the buyer's purchases are in his or her best interest, or else no future sales will be made. The interests of the seller are tied to those of the buyer.

Not all selling activities are alike. While all sales activities assist the customer in some manner, the exact tasks that are performed vary from one position to another. Three basic types of selling can be identified: (1) order processing, (2) creative selling, and (3) missionary sales.

Most sales jobs do not fall into any single category. Instead, we often find salespersons performing all three types of selling to a certain extent. A sales engineer for a computer firm may be doing 50 percent missionary sales, 45 percent creative selling, and 5 percent order processing. In other words, most sales jobs require their incumbents to engage in a variety of sales activities. However, most selling jobs are classified on the basis of the primary selling task that is performed. We shall examine each of these categories.

### Order Processing

**order processing**    Selling at the wholesale and retail levels; involves identifying customer needs, pointing out the need to the customer, and completing the order.

**Order processing** is most often typified by selling at the wholesale and retail levels. Salespeople who handle this task must do the following:

1. *Identify customer needs*: for instance, a soft-drink route salesperson determines that a store that normally carries inventory of 40 cases has only 7 cases left in stock.
2. *Point out the need* to the customer: the route salesperson informs the store manager of the inventory situation.
3. *Complete (or write up) the order*: the store manager acknowledges the situation; the driver unloads 33 cases; the manager signs the delivery slip.

Order processing is part of most selling jobs and becomes the primary task where needs can be readily identified and are acknowledged by the customer. Selling life insurance usually requires more than simple order processing. However, one insurance company reported that during a period of civil unrest in Belfast, Northern Ireland, one of their representatives, Danny McNaughton, sold 208 new personal-accident income-protection policies in a week. McNaughton averaged one sale every 12 minutes of his working day.[24] Apparently, the need for insurance was readily recognized in Belfast.

## Creative Selling

When a considerable degree of analytical decision-making on the part of the consumer is involved in purchasing a product, the salesperson must skillfully solicit an order from a prospect. To do so, creative selling techniques must be used. New products often require a high degree of **creative selling**. The seller *must make the buyer see the worth of the item.* Creative selling may be the most demanding of the three tasks.

**creative selling** Selling that involves making the buyer see the worth of the item.

## Missionary Selling

**Missionary selling** is an indirect type of selling; people *sell the goodwill of a firm and provide the customers with technical or operational assistance.* For example, a toiletries-company salesperson may call on retailers to look after special promotions and overall stock movement, although a wholesaler is used to take orders and deliver merchandise. In more recent times, technical and operational assistance, such as that provided by a systems specialist, have also become a critical part of missionary selling.

**missionary selling** Selling that emphasizes selling the firm's goodwill and providing customers with technical or operational assistance; manufacturer's sales representative may help familiarize wholesalers and retailers with the firm's products and aids in-store displays and promotional planning.

# Characteristics of Successful Salespeople

The saying "Salespeople are born, not made" is untrue. Most people have some degree of sales ability. Each of us is called upon to sell others his or her ideas, philosophy, or personality at some time. However, some individuals adapt to selling more easily than others. Selling is not an easy job; it involves a great deal of hard work. Many college and university graduates find it to be an extremely rewarding and challenging career.

Effective salespersons are self-motivated individuals who are well prepared to meet the demands of the competitive marketplace. The continuing pressure to solve buyers' problems requires that salespeople develop good work habits and exhibit considerable initiative.

Successful sales representatives are not only self-starters, they are knowledgeable businesspersons. Sales personnel are also in the peculiar position of having their knowledge tested almost continually. Sales success is often a function of how well a salesperson can handle questions. Salespeople must know their company, their products, their competition, their customers, and themselves. They must also be able to analyze customer needs and fit them with products and services that satisfy those requirements.

# The Sales Process

The sales process involves seven steps. While the terminology may vary, most authorities agree on the following sequence:

1. prospecting and qualifying
2. approach
3. presentation
4. demonstration
5. handling objections

6. closing

7. follow-up

## Prospecting and qualifying

**prospecting**    Identifying potential customers.

**Prospecting** — *identifying potential customers* — is difficult work that often involves many hours of diligent effort. Prospects may come from many sources: previous customers, friends and neighbours, other vendors, nonsales employees in the firm, suppliers, and social and professional contacts. New sales personnel often find prospecting frustrating, since there is usually no immediate payoff. But without prospecting there are no future sales. Prospecting is a continuous process because there will always be a loss of some customers over time, a loss that must be compensated for by the emergence of new customers or the discovery of potential customers who have never been contacted. Many sales management experts consider prospecting to be the very essence of the sales process.

**qualifying**    Determining that the prospect is really a potential customer.

**Qualifying** — *determining that the prospect is really a potential customer* — is another important sales task. Not all prospects are qualified to become customers. Qualified customers are people with both the money and the authority to make purchase decisions.[25] A person with an annual income of $25 000 may wish to own a $100 000 house, but this person's ability to actually become a customer must be questioned.

## Approach

**approach**    The initial contact between the salesperson and the prospective customer.

Once the salesperson has identified a qualified prospect, he or she collects all available information relative to the potential buyer and plans an **approach** — *the initial contact between the salesperson and the prospective customer*. All approaches should

---

### A·P·P·L·Y·I·N·G  T·H·E  C·O·N·C·E·P·T·S

## *The Changing Face of Selling*

The term *salesperson* all too often conjures up unpleasant visions. But the tasks of the modern salesperson are so different and so complex. Take, for example, the case of Louis J. Manara, a superb salesperson employed by American Cyanamid. The changes that have occurred in Manara's job were depicted in a *Fortune* article as follows:

When Manara began selling chemicals for Cyanamid, the job was relatively straightforward. The salesman was assigned a territory and dispatched to tap every possible customer. He was told little about his division's goals, nothing about the profitability of his bag of products. His marching orders were uncomplicated: sell all you can, as fast as you can.

But in the past decade the salesperson's job has become vastly more complex — so much so that a number of executives believe a new job title is required. "Salesman is just too narrow a word," says one marketing manager. Gordon Sterling, Manara's division president, pinpoints the basic change. "Ten years ago, it was sales, sales, sales," he says. "Now we tell our salespeople: don't just sell — we need information. What do our customers need? What is the competition doing? What sort of financial package do we need to win the order?"

Probing for market intelligence is not the only new duty. Manara is also expected to mediate disputes between Cyanamid's credit department, newly vigilant in these times of costly money, and slow-paying customers. He has to sort out customer complaints concerning Cyanamid products. He must keep abreast of fast changes in both government regulations and world chemical markets.

In brief, the sales representative's job requires applying informed management skills to solving customers' problems.

Source: Hugh D. Menzies, "The New Life of a Salesman," *Fortune* (August 11, 1980), p. 173. Reprinted by permission.

be based on comprehensive research. The salesperson should find out as much as possible about the prospect and the environment in which the prospect operates.

## Presentation

When the salesperson *gives the sales message to a prospective customer*, he or she makes a **presentation**. The seller describes the product's major features, points out its strengths, and concludes by citing illustrative successes.[26] The seller's objective is to talk about the product or service in terms meaningful to the buyer — that is, to discuss benefits rather than technical specifications. Thus the presentation is the stage where the salesperson relates product features to customer needs.

**presentation** The act of giving the sales message to a prospective customer.

The presentation should be clear and concise, and should emphasize the positive. For example, consider how, many years ago, a young college president presented an idea to industrialist Andrew Carnegie:

> One of the buildings of Wooster University burned down one night. On the following day the youthful, boyish-looking president, Louis E. Holden, started to New York City to see Andrew Carnegie. Without wasting a minute in preliminaries he began: "Mr. Carnegie, you are a busy man and so am I. I won't take up more than five minutes of your time. The main building of Wooster University burned down night before last, and I want you to give us $100 000 for a new one." "Young man," replied the philanthropist, "I don't believe in giving money to colleges." "But you believe in helping young men, don't you?" urged Holden. "I'm a young man, Mr. Carnegie, and I'm in an awful hole. I've gone into the business of manufacturing college men from the raw material and now the best part of my plant is gone. You know how you would feel if one of your big steel mills were destroyed right in the busy season." "Young man," responded Mr. Carnegie, "raise $100 000 in 30 days and I'll give you another." "Make it 60 days and I'll go you," replied Holden. "Done," assented Carnegie. Holden picked up his hat and started for the door. As he reached it, Carnegie called after him, "Now remember, it's 60 days only." "All right, sir, I understand." Holden's call had consumed just four minutes. The required $100 000 was raised within the specified time, and when handing over his check, Carnegie said, laughing, "Young man, if you ever come to see me again, don't stay so long. Your call cost me just $25 000 a minute."[27]

## Demonstration

Demonstrations can play a critical role in a sales presentation. A demonstration ride in a new automobile allows the prospect to become involved in the presentation. It awakens customer interest in a way no amount of verbal presentation can. Demonstrations supplement, support, and reinforce what the sales representative has already told the prospect. The key to a good demonstration is planning. A unique demonstration is more likely to gain a customer's attention than a "usual" sales presentation. But such a demonstration must be well planned and executed if a favourable impression is to be made. One cannot overemphasize the need for the salesperson to check and recheck all aspects of the demonstration before delivering it.

## Handling objections

A vital part of selling involves handling objections. It is reasonable to expect a customer to say, "Well, I really should check with my family," or "Perhaps I'll stop back next week," or "I like everything except the colour." A good salesperson, however, should use each objection as a cue to provide additional information to the prospect. In most cases an objection such as "I don't like the bucket seats" is really the prospect's way of asking what other choices or product features are available. A customer's question reveals an interest in the product. It allows the seller an opportunity to expand a presentation by providing additional information.

### Closing

**closing**  The act of asking the prospect for an order.

The moment of truth in selling is the **closing**, for this is when the salesperson *asks the prospect for an order*. A sales representative should not hesitate during the closing. If he or she has made an effective presentation, based on applying the product to the customer's needs, the closing should be the natural conclusion.

A surprising number of sales personnel have a hard time actually asking for an order. But to be effective they must overcome this difficulty.

### Follow-up

**follow-up**  The postsales activities that often determine whether a person will become a repeat customer.

The *postsales activities that often determine whether a person will become a repeat customer* constitute the sales **follow-up**. To the maximum extent possible, sales representatives should contact their customers to find out if they are satisfied with their purchases. This step allows the salesperson to psychologically reinforce the person's original decision to buy. It gives the seller an opportunity, in addition to correcting any sources of discontent with the purchase, to secure important market information, and to make additional sales. Automobile dealers often keep elaborate records on their previous customers. This allows them to remind individuals when they might be due for a new car. One successful travel agency never fails to telephone customers on their return from a trip. Proper follow-up is a logical part of the selling sequence.

## Managing the Sales Effort

**sales management**  Securing, maintaining, motivating, supervising, evaluating, and controlling the field sales force.

The selling function is made effective through **sales management**, which is defined as *securing, maintaining, motivating, supervising, evaluating, and controlling the field sales force*. The sales manager is the link between the firm and the marketplace through the sales force. The sales manager has a challenging task that involves interpreting and implementing company strategy through a diverse group of sales representatives. Similarly, since the sales force also represents the customer, the sales manager is required to represent customers' and sales representatives' needs and concerns to senior management.

The sales manager performs seven basic managerial functions: (1) recruitment and selection, (2) training, (3) organization, (4) supervision, (5) motivation, (6) compensation, and (7) evaluation and control. Each of these is an elaborate and demanding task; unfortunately describing them in detail is beyond the scope of this book. There are many books on sales management that an interested reader can refer to.

## Summary

Advertising should generally seek to achieve communications goals rather than direct sales objectives. It strives to inform, persuade, and remind the potential consumer of the good or service being promoted.

Advertising planning starts with effective research, which permits the development of a strategy. Tactical decisions about copy and appropriate format to express the message are then made. Finally, advertisements should be evaluated, and appropriate feedback provided to management. There are four basic types of advertisements: informative product advertising, persuasive product advertising, reminder-oriented product advertising, and institutional advertising.

A major decision in developing an advertising strategy is the selection of the mix of media — newspapers, periodicals, television, radio, outdoor advertising, and direct mail — that will be employed to attract the attention of the target market.

An advertisement's effectiveness may be assessed using either pre-testing or post-testing methods.

The principal methods of sales promotion are point-of-purchase advertising; specialty advertising; trade shows; samples, coupons, and premiums; and contests.

Personal selling is inherent in most business enterprises. Selling activities can be categorized as order processing, creative selling, or missionary selling. Most sales-people do all three, but the emphasis changes with different selling jobs.

The seven steps in the sales process are prospecting and qualifying, the approach, presentation, demonstration, handling objections, closing, and follow-up. Sales managers play a challenging linking role between management and the marketplace via the sales force.

## KEY TERMS

product advertising
institutional advertising
informative product advertising
persuasive product advertising
reminder-oriented product
  advertising
advertising agency
comparative advertising

co-operative advertising
pre-testing
post-testing
sales promotion
point-of-purchase advertising
specialty advertising
order processing
creative selling

missionary selling
prospecting
qualifying
approach
presentation
closing
follow-up
sales management

## REVIEW QUESTIONS

1. Explain the wide variation in advertising expenditures as a percentage of sales in the industries shown in Figure 18–2.
2. Describe the primary objectives of advertising.
3. List and discuss the four basic types of advertising. Cite an example of each type.
4. What are the advantages and disadvantages of each of the advertising media?
5. List and discuss the principal methods of sales promotion.

6. Identify the factors affecting the importance of personal selling in the marketing communications mix.
7. Identify the three categories of selling, and give examples of each.
8. Identify the characteristics of successful salespersons.
9. What are the steps in the sales process? Which step would take the most time?

## DISCUSSION QUESTIONS AND EXERCISES

1. Develop an argument favouring *or* opposing the use of comparative advertising by a marketer who is currently preparing an advertising plan. Make any assumptions necessary.

2. What specialty advertising would be appropriate for the following?
   a. an independent insurance agent
   b. a retail furniture store

c. Xerox

d. a local radio station

3. Categorize the types of selling involved in the following.

   a. office equipment selling

   b. support for Christmas Seals promotion sponsored by a local Rotary Club

   c. a fast-food franchise

   d. used cars

   e. cleaning products to be used in plant maintenance

4. Who was the best salesperson you ever encountered? What made this person stand out in your thinking?

5. Select three outstanding magazine advertisements, and three that you consider poor. Analyze each and explain why it falls into its respective category.

# MICROCOMPUTER EXERCISE

## Cost per Thousand (CPM)

CPM, or the cost per thousand, is an important media-selection tool. It allows advertisers to evaluate options within a specific advertising media.

**Directions:** Use the Menu Item titled "CPM" on the *Foundations of Marketing* disk to solve the following problems.

1. Aubrey Edwards has decided to use radio advertising to promote his Winnipeg sporting goods store. He is targeting his advertising at people between 18 and 49 years of age. Edwards has decided to run his commercials during the morning and afternoon hours — the so-called drive time, during which people are commuting to and from work. He has assembled the data shown in Table A about the stations that offer the blend of programming designed to attract listeners in his target market.

   a. Which of the four radio stations has the lowest overall CPM? Which is the most expensive in terms of overall CPM?

   b. Which of the four stations has the lowest CPM for listeners between the ages of 18 and 34? Which is the most expensive for this age category?

   c. Which of the four stations will reach the total audience at the lowest CPM?

### TABLE A

**Members of Edwards's Target Market in Radio Audience**

| Radio Station | Total Audience | Listeners Aged 18–34 | Listeners Aged 35–49 | Cost of 30-Second Commercial |
|---|---|---|---|---|
| CFND | 22 500 | 7 000 | 5 000 | $ 90 |
| CFAM | 36 000 | 6 000 | 8 000 | $120 |
| CFOX | 50 000 | 35 500 | 11 500 | $200 |
| CJUB | 75 000 | 17 000 | 20 000 | $225 |

2. Linda Morrison is the product manager for Model 101, a sophisticated new microcomputer specifically designed for business applications. Model 101's programs assume that the user is knowledgeable about business and finance and has

some hands-on computer experience. Morrison is evaluating six magazines to use in advertising Model 101. She has collected the data shown in Table B.

a. Which magazine has the lowest overall CPM? Which is most expensive in terms of overall CPM?

b. If Morrison defines her target market as consisting only of college graduates, which of the six magazines would offer her the lowest CPM?

c. If Morrison decides to focus solely on people who hold managerial or administrative positions, which magazine would allow her to reach this target at the lowest CPM? Which would be most expensive in terms of CPM?

■ TABLE B

**Members of Model 101's Target Market in Magazine Readership**

| Magazine | Total Readers | Managerial/ Administrative | College Graduates | Black and White Page Rates |
|---|---|---|---|---|
| Computer Pro | 2 000 000 | 1 000 000 | 750 000 | $20 000 |
| Top Byte | 1 150 000 | 525 000 | 390 000 | $15 000 |
| Office Today | 2 575 000 | 1 500 000 | 425 000 | $17 500 |
| The Micro Manager | 600 000 | 400 000 | 250 000 | $10 000 |
| Today's Computer | 4 250 000 | 1 100 000 | 850 000 | $35 000 |
| Future Computer | 2 500 000 | 750 000 | 500 000 | $13 000 |

# Santa Anita Park

Thoroughbred horse racing is the most heavily attended sport in the United States. Robert Strub, President of Santa Anita Park, explains why: "One of the interesting things about thoroughbred racing — it's a participative sport. The public actually participates because they make their wager. They affect the odds, and therefore affect the amount of money that's going to be bet on this horse or that horse. I think the greatest thing we have to offer the public is a great sport. For people who like horses, people who like to see a real contest and have the excitement of watching the horses pound down the stretch, and root for the horse they put their wager on, it's one of the most exciting things a person can do. Once in a while, I turn around and look back at the crowd and take my eyes off the racetrack just to see what the people are doing. And they're jumping up and down, they're screaming, they're yelling, they're pounding their friends on the back, doing everything they can to root their horse home. I think this is exciting for people."

Strub knows, however, that Santa Anita needs to do more than just race horses in order to survive. "We live in a community with a tremendous population base," he says, "but it's also one of the great sports capitals of the world, so it's very competitive. People have lots of things to do and we have to offer something that they want to come out and see and participate in." Because of that competition, which comes from virtually every other known leisure activity, Santa Anita must sell itself to the public in order to encourage its current patrons to return more often and to attract new patrons.

To achieve these goals, Santa Anita uses promotions, heavy advertising, and direct selling through a group sales department. Effective use of promotion requires knowledge of the population segments to which a service or product appeals. Horse racing appeals to a mix that represents the entire population, though with a lower proportion of the younger segments and a high proportion of the older ones. To increase patronage both now and in the future, therefore, a promotion should be aimed at the younger segments of the population.

The specific promotion programs used by Santa Anita include premium giveaways, discount admission coupons, entertainment events, and contests. Promotions are carefully integrated into Santa Anita's advertising program and are fully analyzed for their effectiveness. Moreover, the costs of each promotion are compared to any increases in profit or attendance that may be attributable to the promotion. Records are kept on a daily basis. Thus, a promotion that brings new customers to the park but costs more than those customers spend can be analyzed for its long-term effects on patronage and profit. Careful planning of promotion and advertising resources is especially important because of the short (four-month) season.

Sports facilities often use premium-giveaway programs to attract repeat patronage. Hollywood Park, one of Santa Anita's major competitors, offers giveaways once or twice a week. Patrons there have come to expect a giveaway every time they enter the park, and the premiums are unremarkable. Santa Anita uses higher-quality merchandise, such as an all-leather key case with a pocket for parimutuel tickets or money. Like most of the giveaways, the case has Santa Anita's name on it and is of high enough quality to actually be used after the patron's visit.

Although giveaway promotions occur roughly every two weeks, they are carefully timed. Holidays are prime candidates for giveaways, because they attract families that might choose some other pastime without the added inducement of the gift. The giveaways are distributed by members of local PTAs or charities, and Santa Anita sends a cheque to the organization involved. The volunteers are friendly and cheerful, and Santa Anita's contribution to a worthy cause enhances its public image.

Discount admission coupons — printed in newspapers and distributed to about 200 000 previous patrons by direct mail — also serve to attract repeat customers. The redemption rate for the direct-mail coupons is higher than the rate for those included in newspaper ads. Santa Anita considers the loss of 50 or 75 cents off the $2.25 admission price insignificant, since the park obtains 80 percent of its income from betting.

Unlike giveaways and discount admission coupons, entertainment events attract new patrons. Such events have been particularly effective in attracting families, young people, and Hispanic patrons. The Hispanic community in Southern California is growing rapidly, and drawing these customers not only increases patronage but adds to its diversity. Entertainment events are typically held before and between races in the infield section of the park, which the target groups usually prefer. Comedy shows and a "Latin Fiesta" have both been effective. Advertising for the latter event was carried on Spanish-speaking radio and television broadcasts.

Entertainment events at Santa Anita are not expected to make money. It is even expected that the costs of running them will exceed the earnings from the new patrons, especially in view of the fact that customers in the target segments seldom place bets. However, it is hoped that the new patrons will return in the future and that as they age and become more affluent they will begin betting.

Contests appeal to both new and repeat patrons. As originally presented, a contest called "The Key to the Mint" awarded between $10 000 and $25 000 to the winners. After a number of contests had been held, Santa Anita changed the event so that the winnings are no longer fixed in advance. Instead, five winners are selected and invited to the track's winner's circle. There they choose their own prize from 100 identical money bags. All the bags contain at least $1000, but a few contain larger amounts ranging up to $100 000. It is felt that this approach generates more excitement.

The future is almost certain to bring further increases in competition for discretionary spending, as well as further competition for the land on which Santa Anita Park is located, resulting in proportionately higher taxes. The park will probably have to further expand its patronage in order to survive. By maintaining a flexible sales promotion mix, Santa Anita can hold and expand its existing market segments and penetrate new ones.

SOURCES    "Off and Running: A Case Study in Promotional Strategy [television program], produced by Coast Telecourses, Coast Community College District.

## Questions

1. Horse racing generates its own publicity in the form of sportscasts and newspaper sports pages. What does Santa Anita do, or what could it do, to generate additional publicity?
2. Betting, which generates most of Santa Anita's income, is an adult activity. Why would the track want to attract families?
3. What advantages does Santa Anita's giveaway program have over Hollywood Park's?
4. Since most of Santa Anita's income is generated by betting, why not lower the admission fee permanently instead of using one-time discount admission coupons?

**VIDEO** **CASE 18.2**   Lipton & Lawry's

Top management at Lipton & Lawry's raves about the firm's sales force. After all, the L&L sales organization is largely responsible for generating annual sales of more than $1.3 billion for the Unilever subsidiary and maintaining market shares of more than 80 percent for several L&L products. Admittedly, the strong consumer franchise enjoyed by such buyer favourites as Lipton's teas and dried soups, Lawry's blended seasonings, and Wishbone salad dressings is a decided advantage, but the marketing leadership at Lipton & Lawry's works hard to ensure that its salespeople are well prepared to meet customer needs.

Newly hired field sales personnel must complete a rigorous 27-week training program. The first week of training is spent orienting the new sales representatives, giving them a broad understanding of L&L and the markets it serves. The second week takes them into the field to observe experienced salespeople in action. This is followed by another week of specialized training sessions on selling skills, including three days during which they engage in simulated selling situations. Their performances are recorded on videotape and critiqued by experienced sales representatives who conduct the training activities. The next 24 weeks constitute a period of gradually increased responsibility for the trainees. During this period they accompany various L&L sales representatives in calling on established accounts and prospects. At the end of six months, the new sales representatives attend a week-long L&L national training seminar. Here they work on fine-tuning their sales and customer-service skills.

The training program is heavily weighted toward time spent in the field with experienced sales representatives. The approach is a logical one, since the L&L salespeople spend most of their workdays there, representing the company to the retail merchants they call on.

Periodic sales meetings are a fact of life for today's professional salesperson, but poorly planned or unnecessary meetings are blamed as timewasters by the sales forces of many firms. This is not the case at Lipton & Lawry's. "We never have a sales meeting unless there is a reason to have a meeting," says Frank Cleveland, a district sales manager. "The two primary reasons you have sales meetings are, one, to discuss the work plan and the strategies that surround it, and the other reason would be due to motivation: challenging people and showing them how they can accomplish the things that need to be accomplished if the programs we have are properly implemented."

Such programs may involve heavy increases in seasonal advertising, special in-store promotions, use of recipe giveaways, and coupons. To make certain that the sales force believes in the products it represents, members of the L&L sales organization frequently travel to company headquarters, where they participate in blind taste tests of new products. Such participation is useful in involving them in the product development process, providing conviction about product strengths, and supplying them with information about the strengths and weaknesses of competing brands.

Each sales representative is responsible for selling the entire Lipton & Lawry's product line — approximately 250 items, ranging from seasoning salts to taco shells. The L&L sales organization is divided into four regions. Within each region are four or five districts, which are in turn divided into business units.

At the national level, the national sales manager is responsible for direct sales to grocery chains, such as Safeway and A&P. (Separate divisions are used to market the L&L lines to company buyers for mass merchandisers and drugstore chains.)

Each sales unit is staffed by a business manager (who calls on the major accounts located in its geographic area) and a retail unit manager (who oversees between 6 and 10 of the approximately 35 salespersons in each district). Some units also have senior sales representatives, who are responsible for calling on smaller chain-store accounts located in the unit's territory. Each district also has a district sales administrator to handle computer-related activities and a district sales trainer, who is responsible for co-ordinating training activities for newly hired salespeople and continuing training activities for experienced sales reps.

L&L sales representatives are compensated on a straight salary basis. However, they can earn bonuses of up to an additional 25 percent of their base salaries, depending on total sales in the district. Merchandisers, approximately 10 in each district, receive hourly wages, but they can also earn bonuses of up to 10 percent of their annual wages depending on district sales.

Selling at Lipton & Lawry's is a two-phase operation. First, the national sales manager and the various unit business managers must sell the product to headquarters buyers of various food chain retailers. Then the retail sales force takes over to meet the needs of the individual stores.

L&L salespeople frequently work in two-person teams consisting of the sales representative and a merchandiser. The latter's responsibilities consist of replacing the physical stock on store shelves, setting up special cardboard displays (known as shippers) of L&L products, and checking inventory, thereby saving the store manager both time and labour costs. Both the merchandiser and the salesperson are trained to spot display opportunities for L&L brands within the store.

The unit retail sales manager performs a number of functions, including sales assistance, motivation, and performance evaluation. Several days will be spent in the field with each sales representative over a three-month period, during which the unit sales manager will assist the salesperson in making difficult sales, handling problems, and conducting on-the-spot performance reviews through what L&L calls curbstone review. Such reviews take place immediately following a sales call and consist of a summarization by the manager of positive components of the sales call and suggestions for improvement. The intent, of course, is to aid the sales professional in becoming even more effective. As district sales manager Frank Cleveland points out, "If you're with us a year or 15 years, you're still always learning and growing."

Techniques such as the taste tests and curbstone reviews are intended to enhance motivation. Financial rewards such as the potential bonus are also used. Sales awards are also part of the salesperson motivation formula, and L&L marketers give them on national, regional, district, and business unit levels. All phases of the sales representative's job — selling, merchandising, and customer service — are evaluated in choosing the award winners. Suzanne Valker, a senior sales representative who has won the salesperson of the year award, summed up her goal as a Lipton & Lawry's salesperson this way: "You want to help the customer."

SOURCES    "'Tis the Seasoning: A Case Study in Selling," [television program], produced by Coast Telecourses, Coast Community College District; update interview with John Heil, Lawry/Lipton Foods, May 1991.

## Questions

1. Draw the Lipton & Lawry's, Inc. sales organization chart. Discuss how such an organization facilitates the management of the sales force.
2. This sales force is only one part of the firm's marketing communications mix. Discuss how the rest of the mix might be designed to blend with the existing sales management system.

## CAREER PROFILE

### Vince Polloway

3M Canada Inc.
Sales Representative

**Education:**

Red River Community College
C&I Sales
Graduation — 1977

I knew early that I wanted a career in sales: my first taste of this work involved serving as advertising manager for my high-school yearbook. I sold advertising space to businesses, thereby bringing down the book's price so that students could afford it. That invaluable experience allowed me to test the waters, so to speak, without committing myself. And I found I loved it!

Certain that this was "my" field, I applied to the Marketing Program at Red River Community College. There I acquired a foundation of knowledge that encouraged me to pursue my goal with confidence. And sure enough, soon after graduating I joined the team at 3M Canada as a sales representative. I now represent 3M in three sizeable territories: Thunder Bay/N.W. Ontario, Manitoba, and Southern Saskatchewan. In the latter area I have a network of direct and indirect distributors.

One exciting aspect of my job involves direct marketing: I conduct in-store promotions in major stores and I often work at trade show booths. These activities demand that I be comfortable doing a lot of public speaking. So I'm grateful that the program at Red River taught me many of the finer points of getting and holding an audience's attention, then persuading them to consider and eventually to purchase the product. One exercise, I remember, involved obtaining a product from a manufacturer, learning all its key selling points, and demonstrating it in class. Our confidence as public speakers grew with each presentation before our peers.

The class on Advertising and Demonstration taught me how to use the limited amount of floor space available at trade shows to effectively get passers-by to notice our booth.

Because Red River Community College played such a major role in my success, I frequently return there to present seminars [on Scotch Communication and Data Recording] to the Business Administration students. I'm always happy to answer any questions students may have about entering the sales field.

I plan to continue with 3M. I enjoy having a job that allows me to choose the direction I want to take. I hope to expand my territory and to take on new and exciting challenges.

My advice for anyone considering a career like mine? Approach people who are already in the industry; they make great sources of feedback and information about the different types of sales — field, telemarketing, industrial, services, retail — and may help you discover which would best suit you. And don't be discouraged by poor results in the beginning. Learn from them, and try again.

Thus far, this book has dealt with the fundamental components of marketing. The reader may see the coverage as having been extensive, but there are many other important aspects of marketing. The chapters in this final section introduce three of them. Chapter 19 discusses the application of marketing in the international environment. Chapter 20 illustrates that marketing can be applied to not-for-profit organizations such as charities, religious groups, associations, and government organizations.

The final chapter reiterates a theme introduced in Chapter 1: the focus of marketing planning and implementation should be the consumer. Today's competitive environment requires that the management and implementation of every facet of the marketing program must go far beyond "adequate." A fervent commitment to total quality management in marketing is a requirement for long-term success; and the ultimate judge of quality management in marketing is the consumer.

# Global Marketing

## CHAPTER OBJECTIVES

1. To introduce some of the fundamental concepts that underlie global business.
2. To identify aspects of marketing strategy of major importance in the global marketplace.
3. To outline the environment for international business.
4. To consider the marketing mix in light of competition in a global environment.
5. To illustrate the importance of trading blocs.
6. To outline various approaches to global marketing taken by companies.

NOT long after the Canada–U.S. Free Trade Agreement (FTA) was signed, Du Pont Canada kick-started its free-trade strategy by committing $159 million to Canadian capital expansion projects. Du Pont saw free trade as a crucial step in the right direction for being more competitive in world markets.

About the same time as Du Pont decided to boost its capital budget, Northern Telecom Ltd. (NorTel), of Mississauga, Ontario, already a world player, was grappling with a different problem — too many plants. Four days after the Du Pont decision, NorTel announced it would cut costs by transferring or laying off up to 2500 employees. In their different ways, Du Pont and NorTel symbolize the coming shakeout in North American markets, as firms scramble to take advantage of wider trading opportunities in a global economy.

For many companies, the Free Trade Agreement is part of the trend toward globalization — a move that will alter the map of world manufacturing, imperil some Canadian plants and thousands of jobs, and create opportunities for others. In boardrooms across the country, executives are wondering where to build the factories of the future. Will it be Buffalo, New York; Markham, Ontario; Seoul, South Korea; or Richmond, British Columbia? It is difficult to predict the future. However, it seems almost certain that many low-skilled manufacturing jobs in Canada will be lost to offshore competition.

NorTel has been competing successfully in the global marketplace for years and says that its strategy is simple — get close to the most demanding leading-edge customers in the world. They will force the company to develop the best quality and most advanced products. NorTel believes in the axiom, "leading-edge customers make leading suppliers."

What has happened with NorTel is that jobs have moved from the factory to the design and service ends of the firm's business. The company has found that it spends increasingly more of its revenue on installing the product, servicing it for the customer, and making and designing its successor than on product manufacturing.[1]

One thing is certain: the competitive environment is changing. That change may be ascribed to many factors. But the root of it is the trend toward the global marketplace. Companies can no longer choose to compete only in their own local market. Even if they ignore the opportunities in the international market, they will find themselves confronted with international competitors in their own back yards. Canadian businesses ignore the global market at their peril.

# Introduction

International trade is vital to a nation and its marketers for several reasons. International business expands the market for a country's or firm's products and thus makes possible further production and distribution economies. An added benefit to an exporting firm with global trade experience is that it can compete more effectively with foreign competitors who enter this market at a later date. Furthermore,

---

### I·S·S·U·E·S  I·N  I·N·T·E·R·N·A·T·I·O·N·A·L  M·A·R·K·E·T·I·N·G

## *Using Joint Ventures Successfully*

Decentralization and joint ventures have paid off for London-based pharmaceuticals giant Glaxo Holdings. Glaxo supplies its international operations with funding, legal services, insurance, and technical support. Managers of its 70 companies in 150 countries are free to set their own research and development and marketing goals. Glaxo has no reason to complain about the results: since 1981 its annual sales have risen from about $1 billion to nearly $5.6 billion.

A key factor in Glaxo's success is its strategy of entering into joint ventures. Beginning in Japan in the 1970s, Glaxo has entered into marketing partnerships with companies in several countries, including Canada, South Korea, and the Soviet Union. In some cases it has formed alliances with competitors in which the companies market each other's products.

Glaxo's joint ventures are important in light of current trends in the pharmaceuticals industry. Until recently the key to profitability was discovering or

developing new drugs like Glaxo's Zantac, which is used in the treatment of ulcers and is the world's best-selling drug. Today, however, the pace of technological change in the industry is so rapid that the profitable lifetime of any single drug is much shorter than in the past. It is therefore advantageous for a company to be large enough so that it can sell new drugs in large volumes as rapidly as possible.

These conditions mean that selling drugs globally is now at least as important as investing in research and development. Glaxo's numerous joint ventures and marketing alliances enable it to launch a new drug in markets throughout the world, thereby profiting more quickly from the research and development efforts of its component companies.

Sources: "The Doctors' Dilemma," *The Economist* (January 27, 1990), pp. 69–70; Christopher Elias, "Glaxo Is Swallowing Market for Prescription Drugs in U.S.," *Insight* (November 12, 1990), pp. 35–37.

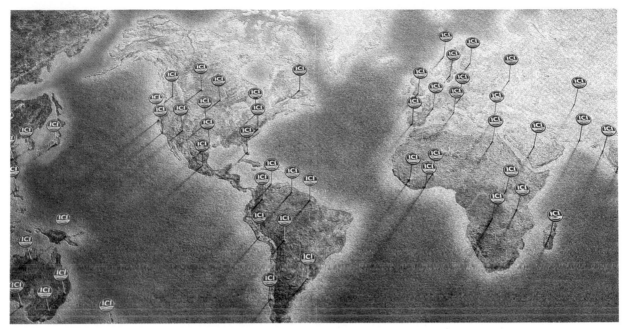

## Who says the earth is covered mostly by water?

Three-quarters of the earth is covered by water. But five-sixths of the earth's countries are covered by ICI. We're everywhere. From Australia and New Zealand to Canada and Italy. In 150 countries, to be precise. With over 130,000 employees.

Which makes ICI Canada part of the most international science-based company on earth.

But not only do we cover the world. We cover the world of technology.

Everything from agricultural products that ensure the healthy growth of food—to forest products that go into just about every page of newsprint in Canada.

From explosives that help the mining industry dig up metals from under the earth—to paints that cover almost everything on top of it.

From lubricants that grease the wheels of transport and commerce—to fabric treatments that dress up the world of haute couture.

Altogether, 33,000 inventions and 150,000 patents carry our name. No wonder we're one of the few companies with the technology, reach and drive to be a powerful competitor in a marketplace which is increasingly global.

Since we're everywhere, we can market our technology wherever it's needed. And that makes ICI Canada a formidable competitor in international circles.

After all, as citizens of the world, we believe our responsibility goes farther than one country. Across the seven seas, in fact. **What we make is a world of difference.**

**ICI Canada Inc.**

international involvement will be the only way many firms can survive in the competitive world marketplace. Global marketing can also mean more jobs at home. It is estimated that some 30 000 to 40 000 new jobs are supported by every billion export dollars.

Some Canadian companies are heavily dependent on their ability to sell their products abroad. For manufacturers like General Motors, MacMillan Bloedel, Alberta and Southern Gas, and others, the majority of sales dollars come from customers in other countries.

Some two million Canadians — one in five of the labour market — work in areas directly or indirectly related to export trade. Thus, there is a good chance that every single Canadian has a close connection with export trade through family or friend. Thirty cents of every dollar of our gross national product (GNP) comes from our exports.

Our exports pay for the things we import to meet our high standard of living expectations — our morning orange juice, fresh vegetables in winter, wool and cotton clothes, TV sets, cars, and computers. On another level, exports also pay for the interest and dividends on foreign investment, for the deficit on tourism, for access to foreign technologies, and for the borrowing that different levels of government use to finance our economic development.[2]

In other words, foreign trade is important to Canada from both the *exporting* and *importing* viewpoints. International trade is more important to the economy of some countries than others. Countries such as the United Kingdom, Belgium, the Scandinavian countries, and New Zealand are heavily dependent upon international trade.

*ICI Canada Inc. is part of an international company that produces everything from agricultural products to explosives. Canada's participation in this network means that Canadian science and technology can be marketed (through ICI) on a global scale. It also ensures a competitive edge, and provides a base for production and distribution facilities.*

FIGURE 19-1

## Canada's Major Trading Partners

### Growth in Exports and Imports, 1979–89

| | Export Value | | Import Value | |
|---|---|---|---|---|
| | *% Change 1979–89* | *$Million 1989* | *% Change 1979–89* | *$Million 1989* |
| U.S. | +130 | 103 732 | +110 | 93 322 |
| **EUROPE** | | | | |
| Switzerland | +290 | 719 | +86 | 600 |
| Norway | +127 | 635 | +780 | 785 |
| France | +103 | 1 260 | +159 | 2 017 |
| Belgium/Luxembourg | +84 | 1 231 | +135 | 567 |
| Sweden | +84 | 319 | +145 | 939 |
| Spain | +83 | 398 | +220 | 567 |
| Italy | +50 | 1 096 | +216 | 2 012 |
| Netherlands | +42 | 1 533 | +227 | 823 |
| Britain | +41 | 3 538 | +145 | 4 604 |
| West Germany | +30 | 1 777 | +138 | 3 708 |
| **AUSTRALIA** | +85 | 1 032 | +34 | 618 |
| **JAPAN** | +117 | 8 472 | +291 | 8 262 |
| **NEWLY INDUSTRIALIZED ECONOMIES (NICs)** | | | | |
| Taiwan | +750 | 882 | +350 | 2 352 |
| Hong Kong | +637 | 1 014 | +172 | 1 161 |
| South Korea | +336 | 1 592 | +427 | 2 441 |
| Singapore | +112 | 243 | +207 | 503 |
| **EMERGING NICs** | | | | |
| Indonesia | +371 | 295 | +356 | 192 |
| Thailand | +289 | 340 | 1 224 | 420 |
| Malaysia | +235 | 219 | +232 | 320 |
| Philippines | +159 | 219 | +162 | 205 |
| **OTHER** | | | | |
| Mexico | +154 | 600 | +706 | 1 680 |
| China | +85 | 1 116 | +606 | 1 182 |
| Saudi Arabia | +34 | 337 | −80 | 253 |
| India | +32 | 297 | +140 | 224 |
| Brazil | +24 | 521 | +261 | 1 130 |
| U.S.S.R. | −11 | 685 | +83 | 118 |
| Algeria | −26 | 292 | −66 | 30 |
| **TOTAL** | +112 | 138 934 | +120 | 134 255 |

Source: *The Financial Post 500* (Summer 1990), p.21.

On the other hand, although the United States is both the largest exporter and the largest importer in the world, exports only account for about 7.7 percent of its gross national product. Compare this to the percentages for Belgium (46 percent) and West Germany (23 percent). Canadian exports account for about 30 percent of our GNP. The leading trade partners of Canada are shown in Figure 19–1. The United States is clearly our chief trading partner, supplying about 69.5 percent of our imports and buying about 74.7 percent of our exports. Note also the very large percentage increases in exports to Pacific Rim countries.

There are both similarities and differences between international and domestic marketing. This chapter examines characteristics of the global marketplace, environmental influences on marketing, and the development of an international marketing mix.

## Measuring a Country's International Trade Activity

Since imports and exports are important contributors to a country's economic welfare, governments and other organizations are concerned about the status of various components of international marketing. The concepts of balance of trade and balance of payments are a good starting point for understanding international business.

### Balance of Trade

A nation's **balance of trade** is determined by *the relationship between a country's exports and its imports*. A favourable balance of trade (trade surplus) occurs when the value of a nation's exports exceeds its imports. This means that, other things being equal, new money would come into the country's economic system via the sales abroad of the country's products. An unfavourable balance of trade (trade deficit), by contrast,

**balance of trade** The relationship between a country's exports and its imports.

---

### A·P·P·L·Y·I·N·G  T·H·E  C·O·N·C·E·P·T·S

## Coke's International Distribution System Helps It Thrive in Marketing Nightmare

Coca-Cola Co. could not have choreographed a more convincing demonstration of its omnipresence.

Two out-of-place Americans and their Brazilian guide are stuck in the flooded Amazon rain forest, their canoe wedged in the gnarled jungle growth and the outboard motor dead. It is steamy, tempers are short and, except for the cursing in English and Portuguese, the only sound is the screeching of monkeys.

Suddenly, from out of the shadows, glides a battered canoe carrying a dark-skinned youngster. Without a word, the girl slides the lid off a beat-up Styrofoam cooler. Inside are yellow cacao pods — and icy-cold Coca-Cola.

Robert Winship Woodruff, the company patriarch who pledged to put a Coke within arm's reach of the

world, could only have dreamed of a moment like this. The appearance of 13-year-old Shirley Batista da Silva in the middle of nowhere, peddling Cokes to help support her family — and to buy a spandex swimsuit for herself — is vivid evidence of Coca-Cola's unmatched ability to sell soft drinks the world over.

Even though Brazil is a marketing nightmare, with government corruption, crippling price controls, astronomical inflation, and grinding poverty, Coca-Cola survives. It now accounts for 57 percent of all soda-pop sold in the country, which is already the company's third-largest market, behind the United States and Mexico.

Source: Adapted from Melissa Turner, "Coke Thrives in Marketing Nightmare of Brazil," *Globe and Mail* (August 18, 1989). Reprinted with permission from Cox News Service.

FIGURE 19 – 2

## Canada's Balances in Goods Trade and Export Volumes

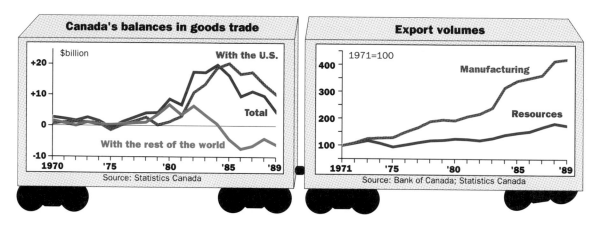

Source: *The Financial Post 500* (Summer 1990), p.18.

results when imports are in excess of exports. The net money flow then would be outward, other things being equal. On the whole, Canada has maintained a favourable balance of trade. (See Figure 19–2.)

## Balance of Payments

**balance of payments**  The flow of money into or out of a country.

A country's balance of trade plays a vital role in determining its **balance of payments**, *the flow of money into or out of a country*. However, other factors are also important. A favourable balance of payments indicates that there is a net money inflow; an unfavourable balance of payments means a net money flow out of the country.

The balance of payments is also affected by such factors as tourism, military expenditures abroad, investment abroad, and foreign aid. A money outflow caused by these factors may exceed the money inflow from a favourable balance of trade and leave a nation with an unfavourable balance of payments.

In recent years Canada has had an unfavourable balance of payments, even when the nation had a favourable balance of trade. Foreign travel and interest on foreign borrowings have contributed to this situation.

## Exchange Rate Adjustments

**exchange rate**  The rate at which a nation's currency can be exchanged for other currencies or gold.

When the real value of a currency is out of line with international currencies in terms of relative buying power, the **exchange rate**, *the rate at which a nation's currency can be exchanged for other currencies or gold*, may change. (See the discussion of the hamburger standard in the accompanying box for an unusual but practical example.) Some countries try to fix the exchange rate. In Canada we have a floating rate. Fluctuations in the exchange rate have a significant impact on both the balance of trade and balance of payments. Because of this, government policy may lead to efforts to stem significant fluctuations by buying or selling foreign — i.e., U.S. — currency.

Foreign claims on Canadian currency led to the devaluation of the Canadian dollar in the late 1970s and early 1980s. **Devaluation** occurs *when a nation reduces the value of its currency in relation to gold or some other currency*. Devaluation of the dollar has the effect of making Canadian products less expensive abroad and trips to Canada cheaper for foreign visitors. On the other hand, imports are more expensive. **Revaluation**, a less typical case, occurs *when a country adjusts the value of its currency upward*. Either of these actions may force firms to modify their world marketing strategies. In the early 1990s, the Canadian dollar ranged upward to more than $U.S. 84.6. This increase made Canadian products more expensive to U.S. buyers, and exports to the United States dropped significantly.

**devaluation**    Situation in which a nation reduces the value of its currency in relation to gold or some other currency.

**revaluation**    Situation in which a country adjusts the value of its currency upward.

## Global Marketing: Some Basic Concepts

The Pacific island republic of Nauru has only a few thousand people but has one of the richest deposits of phosphate in the world. Australia has vast grazing lands, while Hong Kong's 4.1 million people are crowded into a small area that has become one of the most urbanized territories in the world. Hong Kong is a world trader in its own right as well as a source of foreign exchange for the People's Republic of China through handling many of China's goods. Kuwait has rich oil fields but few other industries or resources. Should these countries try to diversify their product base in order to increase self-sufficiency?

These situations lead to arguments that nations are usually better off if they specialize in certain products or marketing activities. By doing what they do best, nations are able to exchange the products not needed domestically for foreign-made

---

**A·P·P·L·Y·I·N·G  T·H·E  C·O·N·C·E·P·T·S**

### *A Practical Measure of the Rate of Exchange:* The Economist's "Hamburger Standard"

It is time to update our McDonald's hamburger standard. We launched it three years ago as a ready reckoner of whether currencies are at their correct exchange rates. Big-Mac watchers rely on the theory of purchasing-power parity (PPP), which argues that in the long run the exchange rate between two currencies is "in equilibrium" (i.e., at PPP) when it equalizes the prices of a basket of similar goods and services in both countries.

Our basket is just a Big Mac. The burger's virtue is that it is produced locally with little change in recipe in 50 countries. So international-distribution costs are not the distorting factor which they would be if we used, say, the price of this newspaper in different countries, as a few readers have suggested.

However, we have made one change. A year ago our estimates of the dollar's Mac-PPPs were based on the New York price of a hamburger. We have now found that the price of a Big-Mac varies much more in

## Big MacCurrencies

| Currency | Hamburger prices* in local currency | Implied PPP** of the dollar | Actual exchange rate 11/04/89 | % over (+) or under (−) valuation of the dollar |
|---|---|---|---|---|
| Australia | A$2.10 | 1.04 | 1.24 | +19 |
| Belgium | BFr 90 | 45 | 39.5 | −12 |
| Britain | £1.26 | 0.62 | 0.59 | −5 |
| Canada | C$2.15 | 1.06 | 1.19 | +13 |
| Denmark | DKr 24.75 | 12.3 | 7.33 | −40 |
| France | FFr 17.70 | 8.76 | 6.37 | −27 |
| Holland | FL5.10 | 2.52 | 2.13 | −15 |
| Hong Kong | Hk$7.60 | 3.76 | 7.78 | +107 |
| Ireland | IR£1.30 | 0.64 | 0.71 | +11 |
| Italy | Lire 3300 | 1634 | 1382 | −15 |
| Japan | ¥370 | 183 | 133 | −27 |
| Singapore | S$2.80 | 1.39 | 1.96 | +41 |
| South Korea | Won 2400 | 1188 | 666 | −44 |
| Spain | Ptas 280 | 139 | 117 | −16 |
| Sweden | SKr 21 | 10.4 | 6.41 | −38 |
| United States*** | $2.02 | — | — | — |
| West Germany | DM 4.30 | 2.13 | 1.89 | −11 |
| Yugoslavia | Dinar 7000 | 3465 | 9001 | +160 |

*Prices may vary between branches
**Purchasing-power parity: foreign price divided by dollar price
***Average of New York, Chicago, San Francisco, and Atlanta

Source: McDonald's

America than within other countries. The recommended American price before tax is $1.55; in central Manhattan our correspondent had to fork out a top-of-the-range $2.48 ($2.29 before tax). So this time we have used the average post-tax price in four American cities — $2.02.

In Tokyo a Big Mac costs ¥370. Dividing this by the dollar price yields a Mac-PPP of $1=¥183, compared with a current exchange rate of ¥133. In other words, the dollar is undervalued by 27 percent. The dollar is also 11 percent undervalued against the D-mark, which has a Mac-PPP of DM2.13, but it is almost spot on against sterling. This in turn implies that the pound's PPP against the D-mark is DM3.44 — i.e., its actual rate is 7 percent too low. British manufactures thus have little need to squeal. Mr Nigel Lawson, the chancellor of the exchequer, can safely aim for a stronger pound. In contrast to sterling, most of the EMS currencies, like

the French franc and the lira, look overvalued against the D-mark.

The currencies of Hongkong and Singapore still look too cheap against the dollar — one reason that America's trade deficit remains huge. But Mac-PPPs do not support Washington's call for South Korea to continue to upvalue its currency. The dollar appears to be 44 percent undervalued against the won. Indeed, Seoul has the dearest Big Macs in our sample. American Big-Mac watchers should focus their attention closer to home: Big Macs are 12 percent dearer in the United States than in its leading trade partner, Canada — i.e., the American dollar needs to fall against the Canadian one.

Source: "The Hamburger Standard," *The Economist* (April 15, 1989), p. 86. © 1989 The Economist Newspaper Ltd. Reprinted by permission.

goods that are needed. Nauru could attempt to develop a tourist trade, but it has opted for specializing in phosphate mining. This allows a higher standard of living than would be possible through diversified business enterprises.

On the other hand, if "specialization" means sale of nonrenewable resources, a country could find itself without a specialty and have a devastating balance of trade when these resources diminish. For example, Canada has quite a high volume of trade with Japan, and maintains a positive balance of trade. The problem for Canada is that it sells Japan mostly raw materials (coal, wood, pulp, softwood lumber, precious metals, fish, and wheat) while importing manufactured goods (cars, computers, telecommunications equipment, and photographic products). The challenge is to expand exports of finished goods that create more jobs at home.[3]

Specialization by countries sometimes produces odd situations. A classic example was when Britain's Conservative Party issued T-shirts with the party slogan "Put Britain First." Later, it was discovered that the T-shirts were made in Portugal.[4] Similarly, a number of "Buy Canadian" stickers can be found on the rear bumpers of Subarus and Toyotas.

FIGURE 19-3

## Leading Commodities in Canadian Foreign Trade

| Exports | $ millions |
|---|---|
| Total exports | 138 934.3 |
| Motor vehicles | 24 043.9 |
| Pulp and paper products | 7 627.4 |
| Energy products | 2 982.5 |
| Primary metals | 3 454.2 |
| Motor vehicle parts | 10 755.8 |
| Food, feed, beverages, and tobacco | 9 420.0 |
| Wheat | 2 589.4 |
| Lumber | 5 564.4 |
| Machinery, industrial and agricultural | 5 409.2 |
| Metal ores | 5 178 |
| **Imports** | **$ millions** |
| Total imports | 127 485.7 |
| Machinery, industrial and agricultural | 134 96.9 |
| Motor vehicles | 15 221.4 |
| Motor vehicle parts | 16 810.6 |
| Energy products | 4 413 |
| Food, feed beverages, and tobacco | 7 412 |
| Communications and related equipment | 7 608.2 |
| Office machines and equipment | 11 400.2 |
| Personal apparel and accessories | 3 474.8 |
| Chemical and related products | 8 142.3 |

Source: Statistics Canada, *Summary of Canadian International Trade*, Cat. No. 65-001, February 1990, pp. 16–23.

**absolute advantage**
Advantage said to be held by a nation that is the sole producer of a product or that can produce a product for less than anyone else.

**comparative advantage**
Advantage said to be held by a nation that can produce a given item more efficiently than it can produce other products.

An understanding of the concepts of absolute and comparative advantage is vital to the study of world marketing. These explain why countries specialize in the marketing of certain products. A nation has an **absolute advantage** in the marketing of a product if the country *is the sole producer of or can produce the product for less than anyone else*. Since few nations are sole producers and economic conditions rapidly alter production costs, examples of absolute advantage are rare.

The concept of **comparative advantage** is a more practical approach to international trade specialization. A nation has a comparative advantage in an item *if it can produce it more efficiently than other products*. For example, Telecom can produce telephone switching equipment better and cheaper than most other companies in other countries (comparative advantage). Thus, even if other countries can produce such equipment, it would be more efficient for them to concentrate on other products at which they are more efficient. Nations will usually produce and export those goods in which they have the greatest comparative advantage (or least comparative disadvantage) and import those items in which they have the least comparative advantage (or the greatest comparative disadvantage).

Figure 19–3 suggests how the comparative advantage concept works out for Canada. The export commodities tend to be those in which there is a comparative advantage over the trading partners. Being an industrialized nation, with ample natural resources, Canada tends to export manufactured items, such as cars and machinery, and natural resources, such as grain, wood, and ores. By contrast, countries with lower-cost labour tend to specialize in products that require a significant labour content, such as textiles, shoes, and clothing.

Of course, there are also noneconomic reasons for not specializing in certain items. Some countries refuse to specialize their productive efforts because they want to be self-sufficient. The Communist nations have typically followed this pattern, to their disadvantage. Israel is another example. South Africa was forced into this position because of world reaction to its domestic policies. It gradually became clear that it was nearly impossible to be fully self-sufficient. Trade is necessary. Still other nations adopt the self-sufficiency viewpoint only for certain commodities that they regard as important to their long-run development. Canada, for instance, has taken steps to reduce its dependency on foreign oil.

## Competing in the International Market

While some Canadian firms have never ventured outside their own domestic market, others have discovered the challenges as well as the payoffs of marketing abroad. In some ways, marketing in Malaysia is very similar to marketing in Canada. That is, the marketing *principles* discussed in this book apply everywhere. However, the economic environment and culture often result in significant differences in the *implementation* of a marketing plan.

Market size, for example, means different things in different countries. Mexico has a population three and a half times as large as Canada's. However, its potential for many products is quite low since the per capita income is only about $2100, compared with Canada's $13 000. Consequently, a marketer of a prestige product might not be too interested in Mexico. Yet even in such a market, there could well be a very profitable market niche of well-to-do customers.

## Buyer Behaviour

There are many influences on buyer behaviour. Some of these, as was discussed in an earlier chapter, represent various components of the external environment. In international marketing, the culture of the country is often an extremely important factor. Such cultural factors influence not only buyers, but also all business relationships.

The cultural nuances cannot be underestimated. In Japan, for instance, it is considered the height of bad manners to say "no" when asked a question. When a Japanese client asks if it is possible to modify a particular product, one should say, "I'll think about it" or "Let me get back to you in a few days."[5] Marketers must be careful that their marketing strategies comply with local customs, tastes, and buying practices.

Long-term relationships are very important. When, for example, Northern Telecom became the first non-Japanese telephone-equipment supplier to make a major sale to Nippon Telegraph and Telephone with a $250-million seven-year deal, it was the culmination of a four-year marketing effort. Much of this effort was "trust-building" work. The company president alone made eleven trips to Japan within a space of six months.

## Cultural, Economic, and Societal Factors

International marketing is normally affected and influenced by cultural, economic, and societal factors. The economic status of some countries makes them less (or more) likely candidates for international business expansion. Nations with lower per capita income cannot afford the technical equipment necessary in an industrialized society so they may be poor markets for expensive industrial machinery but good markets for agricultural hand tools. Wealthier countries can prove to be prime markets for the products of many Canadian industries, particularly those involved with consumer goods and advanced industrial products.

Many products have failed abroad simply because the producing firm tried to use the same marketing strategy that was successful at home. Consider an advertising strategy based primarily on the use of print media that features testimonials. Such a campaign would offer dim prospects in a less developed nation with a high degree of illiteracy.

North American products do not always meet the needs of foreign consumers. Some products of North American automobile manufacturers have traditionally been rejected by European drivers, who complain of poor handling, high fuel consumption, and poor styling. Since an understanding of local, cultural, economic, and societal variables is not obvious to one used to the Canadian situation, international marketers must carefully monitor these factors in all of the markets in which they operate.

## Trade Restrictions

Assorted trade restrictions also affect world trade. These restrictions are most commonly expressed through tariffs. A **tariff** is a *tax levied against products imported from abroad*. Some tariffs are based on a set tax per unit. Others are figured on the value of the imported product. Tariffs may be classified as either revenue or protective tariffs. *Revenue tariffs* are designed to raise funds for the government. Most

**tariff**    A tax levied against products imported from abroad.

of the revenue of the Canadian government in the early years of Confederation came from this source. *Protective tariffs* are designed to raise the retail price of imported goods to that of similar domestic products or higher. In the past it was believed that a country should protect its infant industries by using tariffs to keep out foreign-made products. Some foreign goods would still enter, but the addition of a high tariff payment would make the domestic products competitive. Protective tariffs are usually higher than revenue tariffs. Different interest groups argue whether or not tariffs should be raised to protect employment and profits in domestic Canadian industry. It is debatable whether, in the long run, such a goal is obtainable through tariff protection.

The **General Agreement on Tariffs and Trade (GATT)** is *an international trade agreement to gradually lower tariffs*. GATT has sponsored eight major tariff negotiations that have reduced the overall level of tariffs by over 33 percent throughout the world. It also established systems for resolving trade disputes between countries. The latest series, the Uruguay Round, has been the most difficult one in which to gain an agreement. The biggest stumbling block was created by strongly held trading bloc positions on the amount of tariff protection and subsidies that could be given to the agricultural sector.

There are other forms of trade restrictions. An **import quota** *sets limits on the amount of products that may be imported in certain categories*. One country may use unofficial quotas to limit imports. When Canadian hog farmers began to take over the U.S. Midwest market, U.S. officials "discovered" that Canadian meat might have certain additives that might be "harmful" and, therefore, restricted imports. The objective of import quotas is to protect local industry and employment and preserve foreign exchange. The ultimate form of a quota is an **embargo**, *a complete ban on importing a particular product*.

Foreign trade can also be regulated by exchange control through a central bank or government agency. **Exchange control** means that *firms gaining foreign exchange by exporting must sell their foreign exchange to the central bank or agency, and importers must buy foreign exchange from the same organization*. The exchange control authority can then allocate, expand, or restrict foreign exchange according to existing national policy.

## Dumping — A Marketing Problem

The term **dumping** is applied to situations where *products are sold at significantly lower prices in a foreign market than in a nation's own domestic market*. If foreign goods sell in Canada for substantially lower prices than Canadian products, the likely consequence is a loss of jobs here. National Revenue, Canada Customs and Excise Branch, investigates alleged cases of dumping. If there is a preliminary determination of dumping, the Deputy Minister submits the finding to the Anti-Dumping Tribunal. The tribunal must make an inquiry within 90 days and issue a finding as to whether dumping is causing or likely to cause national injury to the production in Canada of like goods. This may lead to the imposition of anti-dumping duties by Customs and Excise. The tariff charge is designed to protect Canadian employment by raising the product's price up to what it sells for in its home market.

Some critics have argued that fear of the dumping procedure and its tariff causes many foreign markets to keep their export prices higher than would normally be the case. The result, it is argued, is higher prices for the Canadian consumer. It is likely that dumping will remain a controversial topic in international trade for some time.

**GATT**   (General Agreement on Tariffs and Trade): An international trade agreement to gradually lower tariffs.

**import quota**   A limit set on the amount of products that may be imported in a given category.

**embargo**   A complete ban on importing a particular product.

**exchange control**   Requirement that firms gaining foreign exchange by exporting must sell their foreign exchange to the central bank or agency, and importers must buy foreign exchange from the same organization.

**dumping**   Practice of selling products at significantly lower prices in a foreign market than in the selling nation's own domestic market.

## A·P·P·L·Y·I·N·G  T·H·E  C·O·N·C·E·P·T·S

### Winners and Losers in Dumping War

Between $22 million and $41 million appears to be at stake in a battle between shoe manufacturers and retailers. Based on industry sales figures, that is the amount of annual dumping charges that Revenue Canada has imposed on imported women's footwear from low-cost producers in six countries including China, Taiwan, Brazil, Poland, Yugoslavia, and Romania.

Retailers and import companies argue that much of the new charges will be passed on to consumers, which would lead to price hikes in the range of 30 percent on the shoes affected. But the Shoe Manufacturers' Association of Canada, whose complaints led to the new duties, maintains that the negative impact suggested by retailers is "very much exaggerated," according to association president Nathan Finkelstein.

Both retailers and importers have already launched a public campaign against the dumping charges. "Retail has an oligopoly in this industry," said Nathan Finkelstein. "The bulk of it is controlled by no more than 14 or 15 organizations. Some of the major retailers have been intimidating manufacturers." Finkelstein said he has heard of veiled and unveiled threats to manufacturers — such as talk of reduced orders — in an effort to quiet industry lobbying for these or any other duties.

Sharon Maloney, president of the Canadian Shoe Retailers' Association, said, "I would be very surprised if any direct threats have been made."

Very interesting, but where is the representation for the consumer in all of this?

Source: Adapted from Kenneth Kidd, "Millions at Stake for Shoe Industry in Dumping War," *Globe and Mail* (February 12, 1990).

## Political and Legal Factors

Political factors can greatly influence international marketing. For instance, Colgate's popular Irish Spring soap was introduced in England with a political name change. The British know the product as Nordic Spring.[6] The government of the People's Republic of China encourages foreign firms who are willing to bring investment and new technology into the country — as do many others. However, China might not be quite as open to the direct import of more "frivolous" products such as electric can-openers.

Many nations try to achieve political and economic objectives through international business activities. Like it or not, firms operating abroad often end up involved in, or influenced by, international relations. A dynamic political environment is a fact of life in world business.

Legal requirements complicate world marketing. Indonesia has banned commercial advertisements from the nation's only television channel. It was feared that the advertisements would cause the 80 percent of the population living in rural areas to envy those who resided in cities. All commercials in the United Kingdom and Australia must be cleared in advance. In the Netherlands, ads for candy must also show a toothbrush. Some nations have **local content laws** that *specify the portion of a product that must come from domestic sources.* This may force a manufacturer to ship a product unassembled and to have the assembly done in the host country. These examples suggest that managers involved in international marketing must be well versed in legislation affecting their specific industry.

**local content laws** Laws specifying the portion of a product that must come from domestic sources.

The legal environment for Canadian firms operating abroad can be divided into three dimensions:

1. Canadian law
2. International law
3. Legal requirements of host nations.

*Canadian law*    International marketing is subject to various trade regulations, tax laws, and import/export requirements. One significant provision in the Combines Investigation Act exempted from anticombines laws groups of Canadian firms acting together to develop foreign markets. An example is the cartel of Canadian uranium producers, which was designed to increase prices received in international markets. The intent of allowing this is to give Canadian industry economic power equal to that possessed by foreign cartels. A **cartel** is *the monopolistic organization of a group of firms*. Companies operating under this provision must not reduce competition within Canada and must not use "unfair methods of competition." It is hard to say whether companies can co-operate internationally and remain competitive without collusion in the domestic market. Canadian law also restricts the export of certain strategic goods, such as military hardware, to certain countries.

**cartel**    The monopolistic organization of a group of firms.

*International law*    International law can be found in the treaties, conventions, and agreements that exist among nations. Canada has many **friendship, commerce, and navigation (FCN) treaties**. These treaties *include many aspects of commercial relations with other countries*, such as the right to conduct business in the treaty partner's domestic market.

Other international agreements concern international standards for various products, patents, trademarks, reciprocal tax treaties, export control, international air travel, and international communications. For example, the leading nations of the world established the International Monetary Fund, which has been set up to lend foreign exchange to nations that require it to conduct international trade. This facilitates the whole process of international marketing.

**friendship, commerce, and navigation (FCN) treaties**
Treaties that address many aspects of commercial relations with other countries; such treaties constitute international law.

*Laws of the host nation*    The legal requirements of host nations affect foreign marketers. For example, some nations limit foreign ownership in their business sectors. Global marketers could not operate without obeying the laws and regulations of the countries within which they operate.

## Canadian Government Assistance to Exporters

Exporting is of great importance to a country. It creates jobs and helps bring about a positive balance of trade, thus making the entire economy more prosperous. Consequently, governments have active programs to help companies become more active in the global marketplace. Provincial governments provide information and guidance to businesses and even set up foreign trade offices in major markets such as Japan, Hong Kong, and Britain.

The Canadian government has trade officers in every embassy and consulate around the world. These people seek out opportunities for Canadian goods and services and send this information back to Canada. They also help Canadian businesspeople make the right contacts when travelling abroad. Furthermore, the officers may arrange trade shows that demonstrate Canadian products. For example, in Australia, a large Canadian agricultural equipment show is held in Dubbo, a big agricultural town.

In Canada, External Affairs and International Trade Canada has trade officers in many major cities; these individuals facilitate export planning by Canadian firms, and connect them with the overseas consulates. Their offices are also good sources of secondary data concerning exporting and various countries.

Moreover, through these same offices the Canadian government administers various travel support programs in the form of loans to firms needing to go to a foreign market to initiate trade. If the venture is successful, the loan must be paid back.

The Export Development Corporation (EDC) is a Canadian Crown corporation that provides financial services to Canadian exporters and foreign buyers in order to facilitate and develop export trade.[7] It does this through a wide range of insurance, guarantee, and loan services not normally provided by the private sector.

EDC services are provided for Canadian exporters who are offering competitive products in terms of price, quality, delivery, and service, to help them compete internationally. Exporters in other countries have access to similar support facilities from their governments.

Canadian firms of any size can insure their export sales against nonpayment by foreign buyers. EDC normally assumes 90 percent of the commercial and political risks involving insolvency or default by the buyer, as well as blockage of funds in a foreign country. EDC will also make long-term loans to foreign buyers of Canadian capital goods and services. Funds are paid directly to Canadian suppliers on behalf of the borrower, in effect providing the exporters with cash sales. EDC policy is to achieve maximum private-sector involvement in export financing; it therefore provides 100 percent guarantees to banks and financial institutions to facilitate the exporters' banking arrangements.

## The Marketing Mix in the Global Setting

A fundamental marketing principle is that the marketing mix must be designed to meet the needs of the target market. This holds whether the marketing is done in Canada or a foreign market. Thus, depending on the international situation, some marketing elements may be relatively unchanged, whereas others require significant modification.

Some products seem to be "global" products, and virtually the same marketing mix can be used everywhere. Examples are Levi jeans, Coca-Cola, Rolex watches, and most industrial products. In these cases, a universal comprehension of the product exists or has been developed through international media, or there are common behaviour patterns between countries. A computer is not "culture-bound," whereas a food item, or the place and method of serving it, could be very much an acquired preference moulded by culture. For example, many Germans accustomed to heavy, dark bread might find Canadian mass-produced bread unappetizing.

Adaptation is required for many products — and for managerial styles. Let us consider a few examples of adaptations to the marketing mix.

### Product Decisions

Customer expectations define quality and value, and those expectations are not always the same as they are in Canada. Northern Telecom learned that lesson after it sold its SL-1, or PBX telephone answering and switching system, to a large Japanese department store. Among the features on the product is one called "music on hold." Both Japanese and North American customers are familiar with this. However, familiarity and expectations are two very different things. The Japanese *expect* to hear music under all circumstances while waiting to be connected. The SL-1 gave them music while they waited to be connected to a particular department, but if that call was transferred to somebody else, no music would play. As a result the Japanese callers assumed they had been disconnected and hung up. Rather than trying to reshape the listening habits of 130 million Japanese, the company redesigned their equipment to meet Japanese expectations.

Government-established product standards often differ between countries. Host-country standards obviously must be met. For example, a Canadian marketer of packaged food products must meet specific nutritional label-information requirements. Similarly, electrical products must meet varying codes from country to country. Germany, for example, has very rigid requirements for products such as FAX machines that are connected to the telephone system. Thus, well-known brands accepted in Canada are not allowed in Germany.

## Pricing Decisions

When exporting, a cost-plus approach to pricing can quickly destroy potential opportunities. This is because more intermediaries are often required. If all these intermediaries take a standard markup based on a percentage of the cost they pay, the resulting price escalation can be so large that the product is priced out of the foreign market. This problem can be avoided by reconsidering the internal costing system, as well as whether the standard markups are necessary in this situation.

Because exchange rates fluctuate, marketers must be careful to consider whether the price that they are asking will be enough at the time of delivery. The currency of the deal might devalue, thus possibly wiping out all profits. Because of this, a stable commonly traded currency such as U.S. dollars may be chosen as the currency of payment.

If a country has limited foreign exchange reserves it might not be able to afford to pay for a product in foreign currency. It is sometimes necessary to think about payment in different terms. For example, Northern Telecom will sometimes agree to accept payment in kind from customers.

"Deals often hinge on how willing companies are to set aside more cherished commercial practices and accept payment in the form of copper, sugar cane, bamboo, rice, or even a boatload of figs," says Alan Lytle, Northern Telecom's vice-president of marketing.

## Marketing Communications

In Canada, sales representatives sometimes try to develop rapport with a client by asking about his or her family. In Saudi Arabia, this could be taken as an insult. Advertising messages also vary from country to country. In France, sexually explicit scenes are more common than in Canadian advertising, and the British tend to use more humour.

Because communication is so entwined with culture, the subtle nuances that make messages acceptable or unacceptable should be, at least, monitored by a local communicator before use. Preferably, local communicators should develop the message so that it accords with pre-established company strategy.

## Distribution Decisions

Distribution is one of the major problems in developing a marketing plan for a foreign market. This is especially true if exporting. The logistics of moving products are often very complicated. Fortunately, service firms called freight forwarders specialize in distribution and can be counted on to help solve the physical distribution problem. Obviously, both the service provided and the transportation add to the cost structure and must be reflected in the price or compensated for by reduction in other costs.

Another problem is deciding which are the proper channels of distribution to use. The system may be quite different from what the Canadian marketer is accustomed to. In one country it may be difficult to find the necessary wholesaling intermediaries. In Japan, the opposite is true: channels of distribution normally consist of many layers of wholesalers who sell the product to others of their kind, who finally sell it to the retailer. As in the domestic market, the marketer has to solve the problem of how to persuade the channels to carry and promote the product.

From the foregoing discussion it is clear that the marketing mix is likely to require some adaptation before success in the foreign market can be achieved. An attitude of openness and flexibility is essential. An example of what it takes is illustrated in the accompanying box.

## Company Approaches to Global Marketing

A variety of approaches to global marketing can be seen. Some firms do not get involved at all. Others export occasionally when an order happens to arrive from overseas or possibly when they have some excess product. All of these reasons could be classified as not-committed approaches.

Among firms committed to international business, Warren Keegan has identified four different approaches to involvement in international marketing: ethnocentric, polycentric, regiocentric, and geocentric.[8]

### What It Takes to Do Business Internationally

The reasons for the success of our example firm, Northern Telecom, in the global market are summed up by its vice-president, Mr. Alan Lytle:

If there's one word that sums up the core features of marketing...especially internationally, that word would be 'accommodation.'

Companies who desire international success must be willing to accommodate their products and marketing strategies to the needs of the customer and the attitudes and business practices of the country they're operating in, no matter how demanding they may be.

If that means having to make major and costly product modifications to meet the technical requirements and customer expectations, so be it.

If it means investing years of time and money in order to build trust and establish a presence to win that first contract, than that too has got to be done.

If it means applying a sensitive understanding of cultural behaviour, such as learning the language, then that must be done as well.

And if it means fashioning an appealing financed co-operative marketing package that maximizes the benefits of the products you sell, that must be done.

Only by embracing these kinds of value-charged initiatives can [a company] hope to surmount the complex barriers and challenges of international marketing.

Companies who do [so] will find themselves well on the way to global competitive success. Companies who don't [do so] will sadly discover their respective customers won't care or give a fig for their work.

Source: "Mastering the International Market," p. B12.

*There are still difficulties to be ironed out in the Canada–U.S. Free Trade Agreement (FTA). When the United States imposed a ban on importing live and cooked lobsters, Nova Scotia was faced with a loss to its profitable lobster sales. Canada contended that the ban contravened the FTA, and a panel from both countries was asked to investigate. Their challenge is to rise above nationalist concerns and prepare a report that is fair to both nations.*

**ethnocentric company**    Firm that assumes that its way of doing business in its home market is the proper way to operate, and tries to replicate this in foreign markets.

**polycentric company**    Firm that assumes that every country is different and that a specific marketing approach should be developed for each separate country.

**regiocentric company**    Firm that recognizes that countries with similar cultures and economic conditions can be served with a similar marketing mix.

**geocentric**    Firm that develops a marketing mix that meets the needs of target consumers in all markets.

A company that is **ethnocentric** *assumes that its way of doing business in its home market is the proper way to operate, and it tries to replicate this in foreign markets.* As the previous discussion has shown, such an inflexible approach is likely to severely inhibit the effectiveness of a firm's efforts in another country.

The opposite of the ethnocentric approach is the **polycentric** approach. Companies that are polycentric *assume that every country is different and that a specific marketing approach should be developed for each separate country.* This attitude certainly overcomes the inflexibility of ethnocentricity. For many firms, being insightful enough to see the pitfalls of the ethnocentric approach and being willing to adapt have become the foundation of success and are cause for some pride. Such an approach can be more costly, however, because the marketing must be custom-tailored to each individual country.

As business has become more global in its orientation, managers have found that it is not always necessary to develop a separate plan for each country. A **regiocentric** approach *recognizes that countries with similar cultures and economic conditions can be served with a similar marketing mix.* As has been mentioned earlier, in the case of some products it is possible to take a **geocentric** approach. This means *developing a marketing mix that meets the needs of target consumers in all markets.* Note that this is different from an ethnocentric approach. Depending on circumstances, polycentric, regiocentric, and geocentric strategies can each be appropriate.

A related issue centres on how to serve foreign markets. Should a firm try to do so by exporting only? Or should it take the risk of setting up a manufacturing operation in another country? A firm might also reduce risk by setting up a joint venture with a local company in the market of interest, but that would reduce the control it has over the venture. The exploration of such questions is beyond the scope of this book.

# Integration of World Markets

One country would find it difficult to produce all the goods and services it needed, so international trade occurs. Nevertheless, every country tends to jealously protect its own producers and markets. This results in a maze of laws, tariffs, and restrictions that need to be overcome by trading firms.

GATT has been a significant influence in lowering tariffs and some restrictions. However, some countries decide to go further and make agreements to open their borders for trading with each other. The Free Trade Agreement between Canada and the United States is an example of this. Even though inter-country trade was very large, each country agreed that it would be to the advantage of both to simplify the process.

There are different types of arrangements used to achieve greater economic integration. The simplest approach is a **free trade area**, *where participants agree to free trade of goods among themselves*. Normally such agreements are phased in over a period of time in order to allow companies in both countries to adjust.

A **customs union** *establishes a free trade area plus a uniform tariff for trade with nonmember nations*. The European Community (EC) is the best example of a customs union. Popularly referred to as the Common Market, it comprises Belgium, Britain, Denmark, France, Germany, Greece, Ireland, Italy, Luxembourg, Portugal, The Netherlands, and Spain.

**free trade area** Area (established by agreement among two or more nations) within which participants agree to free trade of goods among themselves.

**customs union** Agreement among two or more nations that establishes a free trade area plus a uniform tariff for trade with nonmember nations.

---

## I·S·S·U·E·S  I·N  I·N·T·E·R·N·A·T·I·O·N·A·L  M·A·R·K·E·T·I·N·G

### *Multinational Economic Integration and World Markets*

A noticeable trend toward multinational economic integration has developed since the end of World War II. The Common Market, or European Community (EC), is the best-known multinational economic community; it goes into effect in 1992.

The EC has formed an economic union, which involves a customs union, and seeks to reconcile all government regulations affecting trade.

Involving 12 countries, 325 million people, and a combined gross national product approaching $5 trillion, the EC is the world's largest common market. Under its provisions, all barriers to free trade will disappear among EC members, making it as simple and painless to ship products between England and Spain as it is to do so between Vancouver and Toronto. Also involved is the standardization of the regulations and requirements businesses must meet. Instead of having to comply with 12 sets of standards, manufacturers will have to comply with just one. Before 1992, varying regulations drove up the cost of doing business by eliminating the possibility of achieving economies of scale. For example, in France, yellow headlights were required on all automobiles; meanwhile, in Italy, white lights were standard. Belgian sausages were outlawed in Germany because of different fat-content requirements. And auto emission standards were different for each country.

Although on the surface the European Community offers the attraction of a larger market, experts predict that the competition will be tougher for North American companies since European firms are expanding to meet the demands of their own market. In addition, North American firms that do not have European distributors or partners may find doing business more difficult. Although the standardization of European products ultimately will make it easier for North American exporters, companies may find themselves scurrying to meet the requirements of the nearly 300 directives that determine what the European market will and will not accept.

Source: "The European Market Juggernaut Is on Track," *Update Magazine* 3 (1990), pp. 29–31; John Hillkirk, "The EC in 1992: 12 Nations, United," *USA Today* (May 7, 1990); see also John K. Ryans, Jr. and Pradeep A. Rau, *Marketing Strategies for the New Europe* (New York: American Marketing Association, 1990); and Brian Reading, "A Greater European Century," *Across the Board* (December 1989), pp. 17–20.

**economic union** Agreement among two or more nations that establishes a free flow not only of goods, but also of people, capital, and services among its member.

As of 1992, the nations of the European Community will go beyond a customs union and form a more integrated **economic union** (commonly referred to as *Europe '92*). Such an agreement *establishes a free flow not only of goods, but also of people, capital, and services.* Even an individual country's control of the value of its own currency and social programs has been given up to some degree. Europe '92 has resulted in a trading bloc that is unparalleled in history: the bloc now constitutes a single giant market of 325 million consumers. The rest of the world watches it with fascination and with some nervousness. Some nations worry that Europe '92 could turn into "Fortress Europe," slamming the door on trade with its members.

The Canada–U.S. *Free Trade Agreement* (*FTA*) reinforces the long-term trading relationship between the two countries. Each country has traditionally been the other's biggest customer. So what prompted the two countries to negotiate such an agreement? In the world marketplace the United States has long been the target of many trading countries. This has resulted in serious negative trade balances for the United States — which, in response, had gradually begun to put significant restrictions on trade. These restrictions were, of course, threatening Canadian business. In addition, the United States often made apparently arbitrary judgments as to whether Canadian firms were trading "fairly" with them. By the 1980s, the potential for further restrictions and arbitrary decisions prompted Canada to seriously negotiate the Free Trade Agreement, which had previously only been under discussion.

Under the agreement, tariffs on certain goods were eliminated as of January 1, 1989, the commencement date. Over a 10-year period, all tariffs will gradually be eliminated according to a timetable. New rules also make it easier for business travellers to obtain visas allowing movement between the two countries.

New rules defining what constitutes a product of Canada or of the United States were also established. Generally, for manufactured products, 50 percent of the direct production costs of the final product must be incurred in Canada or the United

## A·P·P·L·Y·I·N·G T·H·E C·O·N·C·E·P·T·S

### *Some Economic Effects of Global Marketing*

Ms. Batista da Silva haunts the maze of Amazon tributaries peddling Coke to tourists and fishermen seven days a week, except during the three-month rainy season. Selling four cases a day, she makes enough money to help put food on the family table and buy the occasional piece of clothing at the dockside market in Manaus.

Coca-Cola provides her family with an entry into the twentieth century and the material world. Although Coca-Cola has been in the Amazon only a few years longer than she has been alive, the soft drink is woven into the fabric of life in the region.

In the primitive mining camp of Serra Pelada, 2300 kilometres across the rain forest from the floating river shack in Xi Borena where Ms. Batista da Silva and her eight brothers and sisters live, the first images are of an Old West mining town. Well, not quite. The very first image is a black-and-white billboard at the landing strip

that reads: Coca-Cola welcomes visitors to Serra Pelada. Elsewhere in the town there are the red-and-white "Bebe [Drink] Coca-Cola" signs nailed on dozens of shanties. Such is Coca-Cola's reach.

There is another side to this story as well. When necessary, Coca-Cola can point out that it provides 40 000 jobs in Brazil and buys $200 million worth of the country's oranges and coffee each year. And its bottlers spend more than $330 million a year locally on sugar, bottles, steel cans, and other things they need to run their operations.

"The key to the company's success is to think globally but act locally in harmony with the local conditions and within the local parameters," a Coca-Cola executive says.

Source: Adapted from Melissa Turner, "Coke Thrives in Marketing Nightmare of Brazil," *Globe and Mail* (August 18, 1989). Reprinted with permission from Cox News Service.

States for it to qualify as a good of that country. For agriculture, direct export subsidies on goods being shipped to the other partner ended.

Canadian companies can now bid on some U.S. government procurement projects worth $25 000 (U.S.) or more. U.S. bank subsidiaries now have greater access to the Canadian market. Finally, the Canada–United States Trade Commission, with offices in Ottawa and Washington, was created to supervise the agreement. A dispute-settlement mechanism and panels of individuals to review disputes were also established.

This agreement will bring hardships to some industries as companies render their operations more efficient in one country or another, but it presents great opportunities to others willing to seek them out. In Canada, the agreement's value remains a highly controversial issue. Nevertheless, its existence has led both nations to consider extending the agreement to include Mexico. At the time of writing the ultimate outcome of those negotiations was unknown.

The evolution of Europe '92 and free trade in North America have made other nations such as Japan somewhat concerned about the possible negative effects of trading blocs on those outside them. Japan is said to be working on an East Pacific Trade Zone, which would include dynamic economies like South Korea, Taiwan, Hong Kong, Singapore, and several other countries in the region.[9]

The global marketplace is dynamic and exciting. It is now clear that growth for most firms will depend on some involvement in foreign marketing. The movement toward the globalization of business is accelerating. It will create many opportunities for the student of marketing who wants to become active in the world marketplace.

## Summary

International marketing is growing rapidly. Many Canadian firms are now engaged in some type of international marketing activity. Foreign trade is essential to Canada from both the exporting and importing perspectives.

International business involvement is often considered in terms of a nation's balance of trade (the relationship between its exports and imports) and balance of payments (the flow of money into or out of the country). The exchange rate — the rate at which a currency can be exchanged for other currencies or gold — affects the attractiveness of the price of a country's products abroad, as well as the country's international buying power.

One basic concept in world trade is absolute advantage (a country is the sole producer or can produce a product for less than anyone else). An associated concept is comparative advantage (a country can produce a product more efficiently than other products). These concepts, as well as non-economic considerations such as the political aim of self-sufficiency, determine the products in which a nation specializes.

The principles of marketing that apply at home also apply abroad. However, because of different economic and cultural circumstances, the marketing mix often has to be adapted. Different approaches to the global market can be observed. Some firms show little or no commitment to becoming involved in developing opportunities in other countries' markets. Others follow an ethnocentric approach, assuming that the procedures developed at home will also be the best procedures abroad. A polycentric approach is the opposite: for each market a separate marketing program is developed. Companies with a regiocentric approach develop a marketing plan to fit the commonalities of countries in a region. Sometimes it is possible to use a geocentric approach and develop a common marketing program that will fit all countries.

Large trading blocs such as the European Community and the bloc created by the Free Trade Agreement between Canada and the United States are beginning to have a significant impact on world trade. From the perspective of global marketers, the question arises as to whether or not these blocs will facilitate trade beyond their boundaries.

## KEY TERMS

| | | |
|---|---|---|
| exporting | tariff | ethnocentric |
| importing | GATT | polycentric |
| balance of trade | import quota | regiocentric |
| balance of payments | embargo | geocentric |
| exchange rate | exchange control | free trade area |
| devaluation | dumping | customs union |
| revaluation | local content laws | economic union |
| absolute advantage | cartel | Free Trade Agreement (FTA) |
| comparative advantage | FCN treaties | |

## REVIEW QUESTIONS

1. Why is global marketing important (a) to Canadian firms and (b) to the Canadian economy?
2. What types of products are most often marketed abroad by Canadian firms?
3. Is the marketing mix likely to be different in the global context than in the domestic situation?
4. Describe methods for measuring a nation's international trade activity.
5. Describe the various approaches taken by companies to international marketing.
6. Explain how trade restrictions may be employed to restrict or to stimulate international marketing activities.
7. Distinguish between import quotas and embargoes.
8. Explain the international practice of dumping. Why is it controversial?
9. Identify and briefly explain the three basic formats for economic integration.
10. Explain the threats and opportunities presented to Canada by the Free Trade Agreement.

## DISCUSSION QUESTIONS AND EXERCISES

1. Comment on the following statement: "It is sometimes dangerous for a firm to attempt to export its marketing strategy."
2. Give an example — hypothetical or actual — of a firm with the following approach to international marketing. How would the marketing mix for foreign markets compare with that used in the home market?
   a. exporting in response to external demand
   b. ethnocentric approach
   c. polycentric approach
   d. regiocentric approach
   e. geocentric approach
3. The following business opportunity was listed in *CandExport*:[10]

Singapore — A services and supplies company wishes to import *water treatment products for the pharmaceutical, food, and beverages industries.* Contact Randy Yang, Marketing Manager, Jelen Supplies & Services, Singapore.

Assume that you work for a company that supplies such products. Outline the possible opportunities that such a venture might bring to your firm, and then list the problems. What steps should be taken to fully follow up on this advertisement?

4. Assume that you market a product in Canada on which there is a 20 percent U.S. tariff. There is also a 25 percent Canadian tariff for products coming from the United States. Both will, in two years, be tariff-free under the terms of the Free Trade Agreement. What challenges and opportunities will be involved in such a change? What should your company do in anticipation of the changes?

5. Discuss the following statement: "If elected, we will get Canada out of the Free Trade Agreement with the United States."

## VIDEO CASE 19    Carl's Jr.

In 1988 the Carl's Jr. restaurant chain had more than 600 outlets in California. Management decided that the time was ripe for expansion into a foreign market in the Far East. For some time Friendly Corporation of Osaka had been pursuing Carl's Jr. for a franchise; it had commissioned several marketing studies that showed that Japanese tourists in California liked Carl's Jr. hamburgers. Carl's Jr. decided to give Friendly its franchise, and the first overseas outlet opened in Osaka in 1989. As of 1991 a total of five outlets have been opened, and six more are scheduled for opening.

Because the idea was to give the Japanese a brief encounter with California life, it was necessary to preserve the ambience and menu of the home chain as much as possible. However, both participants in the venture knew that changes would have to be made. Beef is a high-priced commodity in Japan, but the Japanese perceive the hamburger as a snack, so the size of the hamburger patty was reduced by 25 percent, keeping the cost within bounds while better matching the market's needs. Because perfect beef patties were not available locally, they were initially imported from the United States. Subsequently, an agreement was made with a Japanese firm to process Japanese, Australian, and American beef for the franchises. Bacon proved to be a greater problem, however, because Japanese-made bacon doesn't become crisp when it is fried. Since crisp bacon is an essential textural element of the Carl's Jr. menu, the authentic original is imported from the United States. Sauces such as ketchup and mustard were initially produced locally because Japanese laws ban many of the preservatives used in the American products, but the sauces have since been reformulated and are shipped from the United States.

The physical environment is also different in Japan. Land generally costs more, so the physical size of the outlets must be smaller. But local building codes and the smaller average size of Japanese customers allow smaller aisles, especially in the kitchen areas, decreasing waste space. Efficient kitchen layout is important in the Carl's Jr. operation, and the home office retained control of the design, working closely with Japanese architects. While much of the equipment for the first outlets had to be shipped from the United States, the layout was successfully reduced to meet Japanese space constraints. Subsequent outlets are being fabricated in Japan, with only a few pieces of specialized equipment coming from the United States.

Carl's Jr. has since decided to expand into Malaysia (with MBF International, one outlet to open in 1991) and Mexico (with Carl's Jr. de Monterrey, one outlet open and one more to open in 1991), and these locations require different changes. For instance, because of Malaysia's large Muslim population, beef must be slaughtered under the "halal" system. And because Muslims do not eat pork, bacon could not be used. Experiments with soy bacon and beef bacon were tried, but neither proved entirely satisfactory. Rather than compromise the quality of the burger, Carl's Jr. decided to omit the bacon altogether. The smoky taste of the sauce prevents the omission from affecting the burger's flavour significantly, although the texture is changed. When plans are made to expand into other Far Eastern countries, such as Singapore, bacon can be reintroduced without debasing the Malaysian product.

The Mexican market is quite different from the Japanese and Malaysian markets. Because Mexicans crave larger amounts of meat, the size of the patty has not been changed. The bacon double cheeseburger is being heavily promoted and is selling well.

In all the overseas locations, only a portion of Carl's Jr.'s original menu is offered. This makes it easier to start up new outlets and establish supply networks, but it also leaves room for future additions to the menu and for the associated promotional campaigns. Other Far Eastern, European, and South American countries are being investigated as targets for expansion.

## Mikoshi Japanese Noodle House

Satoshi Sakurada, founder of MOS Food Services of Japan, also looked overseas for expansion opportunities. However, the home chain itself is partly a result of global marketing.

In 1962 Sakurada was living in Los Angeles as a salesperson for the Japanese firm Nikko Securities. During this time he often lunched on the Southern California chili-and-beef concoction called the Tommy burger. Ten years later, when McDonald's had just opened its first restaurant in Japan, Sakurada decided that it was time to introduce his concept of the hamburger to Japan.

After working tirelessly to promote the idea of his hamburger and winding up in a hospital suffering from exhaustion, Sakurada developed his successful approach, which is summed up in the company acronym HDC, "hospitality, deliciousness, and cleanliness." There is no question about the intended market for the MOS burger and its siblings, the teriyaki burger, the soy burger, and the rice burger; outlets are located in local neighbourhoods, not in expensive tourist and business districts like Tokyo's Ginza. But the American slant of the food gives the chain enough of an international touch for it to outrank both Kentucky Fried Chicken and McDonald's with the most number of outlets in Japan — more than a thousand.

How, then, could Sakurada expand operations overseas? Bringing the transformed Tommy burger back to its birthplace didn't seem wise, especially in view of the tremendous competition in the American burger market and the health-related issues constantly being raised against the burger. The answer was not to export the product itself, but instead to export the business idea — a chain of small, clean, orderly outlets selling a quality product that had a degree of exoticism but could be tailored to the culture in which the outlet was located without destroying the integrity of the dish. For the United States, the solution was the noodle.

Soup and noodles, or ramen, are traditionally paired in Japanese cuisine. Relying on foodstuffs that can be either prepared in advance or rapidly prepared at the last minute, these dishes lend themselves to a high-quality fast-food operation. The basic dishes are low in animal fats and appeal to health-conscious consumers, an increasingly significant percentage of the population. These basic dishes became the basis for the menu of Sakurada's venture, the Mikoshi Japanese Noodle House.

Southern California was chosen for the initial outlets because a wide variety of exotic foods are available there and the sizeable Asian-American community has created a food processing network that is sensitive to ramen's culinary requirements. Although rice flour was initially imported from Japan, local processors were eventually able to provide an acceptable product. As the traditional recipes have not required changes, the basic dishes have not been compromised. However, the toppings for the noodles, always open to some variation in the traditional cuisine, have been modified for American tastes. While a traditional topping based on roast pork is offered, the Yakisoba greens harvest was developed specifically for this market. It consists of traditional yakisoba noodles topped by a fresh green salad with an oil-free dressing. The most popular dish is teriyaki chicken ramen. Teriyaki chicken would be served before or after, or possibly beside, ramen in traditional Japanese cuisine.

While respect for the ramen tradition was a central ingredient of the Mikoshi Noodle House plan, the chain had to establish itself visually as a high-quality fast-food outlet. Thus, Japanese tea-house decor was shunned in favour of California techno-pop. Orders are placed at a register, and then the food is served at a table on real china. Americans are not accustomed to eating Japanese foods, so a card on the table gives instructions to enhance appreciation of the cuisine — for instance, the soup and noodles should be eaten together like hamburger and fries, not sequentially like hamburgers and pie. (Sakurada solved a similar problem in Japan: because the Japanese are reluctant to touch food, the MOS burger is served wrapped in a napkin.)

By the end of 1990, Sakurada had opened three Mikoshi outlets in the Los Angeles area; another was scheduled to open in Brea in 1991. For the present, the California outlets are owned by the American parent corporation, MOS Foods West, but future plans call for franchised outlets, as many as 100 a year, expanding first to San Francisco and then to the East Coast and the Sun Belt.

SOURCES    Christina Lee, "The International Burger," *Los Angeles Times* (January 28, 1991); update interview with Steve Kishi, Carl Karcher Enterprises, May 1991; Teresa Watanabe, "Exporting Fast Food," *Los Angeles Times* (January 7, 1991); update interview with Gretchen Booma, Dentsu Burson-Marsteller, representing the Mikoshi Japanese Noodle House, May 1991.

## Questions

1. Compare the product promotional strategies of the two companies discussed in this case.

2. Choose one of the two companies and explain why it would want to expand beyond its own national boundaries. Explain why it finds its particular foreign market attractive.

3. Explain how Carl's Jr. is exporting more than materials to its overseas franchises. Why is franchising more desirable for Carl's Jr. than overseas marketing or foreign production and marketing? Why would Mikoshi Japanese Noodle House want to open its first outlets itself instead of franchising them?

4. Why did Mikoshi choose California instead of some other location in the United States?

# Not-for-Profit Marketing

1. To outline the primary characteristics of nonprofit organizations that distinguish them from profit-seeking organizations.
2. To show that marketing applies to nonprofit organizations in the same way as it does to businesses.
3. To identify the main categories of marketing in nonprofit settings.
4. To examine the application of the marketing mix in nonprofit situations.

IN July 1988, the Vancouver Symphony Orchestra (VSO) was set adrift — literally. Having filed for bankruptcy just months before, the VSO was on the long road, or in this case, the waterway, back to financial solvency. During Vancouver's annual Sea Festival, more than 100 000 people had the opportunity to see the orchestra, which was playing Tchaikovsky's *1812 Overture*, as it drifted into town on a brightly lit barge while fireworks burst overhead. This promotion was just one in a series of special events staged by the VSO to develop a higher profile and convey an image of greater accessibility to the citizens of its city — citizens who were desperately needed to fill the seats of the Orpheum theatre, where the orchestra performed.

The Vancouver Symphony, a nonprofit organization, was practising marketing. Marketing strategists have long held the view that marketing is not for businesses only. Today, more nonprofit organizations are making use of marketing techniques as they struggle to develop plans for survival.[1]

# Introduction

Too often people look at the *advertising* done by nonprofit organizations (NPOs)[2] and equate it with marketing. By now, the reader will realize that marketing is much more than advertising or selling. Marketing involves the application of the entire marketing mix in accordance with a well-planned marketing strategy.

For example, consider the Heart and Stroke Foundation. Its products are heart disease education and research. There are two target markets for this organization: potential donors and those who need to be educated. Because of this, the Foundation should have two highly interrelated marketing strategies. Both education and research are in accord with people's needs for health information and medical care, but if support for the Foundation's efforts is to continue, the public must perceive the Foundation's products to be valuable.

Potential donor segments must be identified in order to appeal to the various motivations in the population. For those who have heart disease, fear of the disease might be a motivation. Others may simply recognize that this is a worthy cause. Corporate donors may have less obvious motivations to which the Foundation should appeal. Marketing research may be necessary to develop a complete picture of the factors that would create a favourable response to an appeal for funds.

Marketing research may also be needed in order to learn how best to communicate current findings and advice concerning heart disease and to distribute appeal literature.

Another task for the Foundation is to find, manage, and motivate the thousands of volunteers who collect funds for its work. This process has some similarities to sales management in a profit organization but is broader in scope, especially since the motivation of volunteers is different from that of paid employees.

Above all, proper marketing planning will greatly improve the direction and effectiveness of this nonprofit organization. Not only has the Heart and Stroke Foundation discovered the benefits of this approach, but many other nonprofit organizations have also successfully applied marketing thinking to their efforts.

In Chapter 1, marketing was defined as the development and efficient distribution of goods, services, ideas, issues, and concepts for chosen consumer segments. Although much of the text up to now has concentrated on organizations that operate for profit, the activities of the Heart and Stroke Foundation are as representative of modern marketing activities as are the marketing programs of IBM, Wendy's, and Canada Packers. Our definition of marketing is sufficiently comprehensive to encompass nonprofit as well as profit-seeking organizations.

**nonprofit organization (NPO)**
Organization whose primary objective is something other than returning a profit to its owners; also known as a *not-for-profit* organization.

A substantial portion of our economy is composed of **nonprofit organizations (NPOs)** — *those whose primary objective is something other than returning a profit to their owners*. An estimated one out of every ten service workers and one of six professionals are employed in the nonprofit sector. The nonprofit sector includes thousands of religious organizations, human service organizations, museums, libraries, colleges and universities, symphony orchestras and other music organizations, and organizations such as government agencies, political parties, and labour unions. Figure 20–1 depicts one portion of the marketing efforts of one nonprofit organization — the Heart and Stroke Foundation.

Nonprofit organizations can be found in both public and private sectors of society. In the public sector, federal, provincial, and local governmental units and agencies whose revenues are derived from tax collection have service objectives not keyed to profitability targets. One part of External Affairs and International Trade Canada,

FIGURE 20 – 1

**Example of Advertising by a Nonprofit Organization**

*Non-profit advertising often appeals to basic human feelings or experiences that everyone can relate to. In this ad, the Heart and Stroke Foundation exhorts people to give now, not just when a death strikes one's family or friends. By appealing to basic human sentiments and by positioning heart and stroke research as their central objective, the foundation hopes to appeal to a wide cross-section of people. How does this differ from the benefit segmentation analysis carried out by profit-driven companies?*

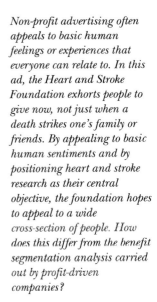

for instance, provides services that facilitate exports of Canadian products. A provincial department of natural resources regulates conservation and environmental programs. The local animal control officer enforces ordinances that protect both people and animals.

Some public-sector agencies may be given revenue or behaviour goals. An urban-transit system might be expected to pay a great deal of its costs out of revenues, for example. But society does not expect these units to routinely produce a surplus that is returned to the taxpayers.

The private sector offers an even more diverse array of nonprofit settings. Art institutes, churches, labour unions, private schools, the United Way, the Rotary Club, and the local country club all serve as examples of private-sector, nonprofit organizations. The diversity of these settings suggests how pervasive organizational objectives other than profitability really are in a modern economy.

The market offering of the nonprofit organization is frequently more nebulous than the tangible goods or service provisions of profit-seeking firms. Figure 20–2 lists social issues and ideas, ranging from family planning to the use of motorcycle helmets, that represent the offerings made by some nonprofit organizations to their publics.

The diversity of these issues suggests the size of the nonprofit sector and the marketing activities involved in accomplishing their objectives. What makes them different from their profit-seeking counterparts?

**FIGURE 20 – 2**

**Social Issues Marketed by Nonprofit Organizations**

| | | |
|---|---|---|
| Abortion rights | Fire prevention | 911 (emergency number) |
| Affirmative action | Fluoridation | Nonsmokers' rights |
| Alcoholism control | Forest fire prevention | Nuclear energy |
| Birth defects | Foster parenthood | Physical fitness |
| Blood | Fraternal organizations | Police, support of |
| Blue laws | Free enterprise | Pollution control |
| Buy Canadian goods | Freedom of the press | Population control |
| Cancer research | French immersion | Prison reform |
| Capital punishment | Gay rights | Religion |
| CARE packages | Housing co-operatives | Right to Life |
| Carpooling | Legalized gambling | Save the whales |
| Child abuse | Literacy | Seatbelt use |
| Child adoption | Littering prevention | Solar energy |
| Consumer co-operatives | Mass transportation | STD hotline |
| Crime prevention | Mental health | Suicide hotline |
| Drunk driving | Metric system | Tax reform |
| Energy conservation | Military recruiting | UNICEF |
| Euthanasia | Motorcycle helmets | United Way |
| Family planning | Museums | |

Source: Most of these issues are listed in Seymour H. Fine, *The Marketing of Ideas and Social Issues* (New York: Praeger, 1981), pp. 13–14.

# Characteristics of Nonprofit Organizations

Nonprofit organizations have a special set of characteristics that affects their marketing activities. Like the profit-oriented service offerings discussed in Chapter 11, *the product offered by a nonprofit organization is often intangible*. A hospital's diagnostic services exhibit marketing problems similar to those inherent in marketing a life insurance policy.

A second feature of nonprofit organizations is that *they must deal with multiple publics*. As Professor Philip Kotler points out,

> nonprofit organizations normally have at least two major publics to work with from a marketing point of view: their clients and their funders. The former pose the problem of *resource allocation* and the latter, the problem of *resource attraction*. Besides these two publics, many other publics surround the nonprofit organization and call for marketing programs. Thus a college can direct marketing programs toward prospective students, current students, parents of students, alumni, faculty, staff, local business firms, and local government agencies. It turns out that business organizations also deal with a multitude of publics but their tendency is to think about marketing only in connection with one of these publics, namely their customers.[3]

A customer or service user *may have less influence than a customer of a profit-seeking (or for-profit) firm*. A government employee may be far more concerned with the opinion of a member of the Cabinet than with that of a service user. Furthermore, nonprofit organizations often possess some degree of monopoly power in a given geographical area. As an individual, a person might object to the local United Way's inclusion of a crisis centre among its beneficiary agencies; but as a contributor who accepts the merits of the United Way appeal, this same person recognizes that a portion of total contributions will go to the agency in question.

---

## A·P·P·L·Y·I·N·G  T·H·E  C·O·N·C·E·P·T·S

### *A Marketing Management Perspective Is Required for Not-for-Profit Groups*

Government funding for the Vancouver Symphony Orchestra (VSO) was cut off in 1987, pending formulation of a valid, feasible business plan. One of the VSO's first steps was to hire the youthful Peter McCoppin as musical advisor and conductor. McCoppin was well aware that his position at the front of the orchestra involved more than just musicianship. He said, "We have to recognize that we are in the field of entertainment. Part of that recognition comes with the public having a rapport with the conductor. If they don't, then it's game over."* With the statement "We are in the field of entertainment," McCoppin avoids marketing myopia. When growth is threatened, it is not because the market is saturated but rather because management suffers from marketing myopia and fails to have the foresight to consider what business it is really in.

The struggle to develop a workable fit between any organization and its changing opportunities is a struggle that ultimately defines strategic marketing planning. Marketing strategy includes a mission statement, goals and objectives, an overview of products or services, plans for growth, the marketing process itself, and control systems. As the VSO became marketing-oriented, the words "marketing strategy" became an important part of its vocabulary — just as they were in the vocabularies of the businesses the VSO courted for support.

*Stephen Godfrey, "On and Off the Podium: A Dynamic Promoter," *Globe and Mail* (November 18, 1990).

Source: Adapted from M. Louise Ripley and George Gilbert, "The Vancouver Symphony Orchestra: Marketing, "*Academy of Marketing Science News* (January 1991), p. 2.

Another problem involves *the resource contributor, such as a legislator or a financial backer, who interferes with the marketing program*. It is easy to imagine a political candidate harassed by financial supporters who want to replace an unpopular campaign manager (the primary marketing position in a political campaign).

Perhaps the most commonly noted feature of the nonprofit organization is its lack of a **bottom line**, which refers to *the overall-profitability measure of performance*. That is, nonprofit organizations have goals other than profit. While a nonprofit organization may attempt to maximize its return from a specific service, less measurable goals such as service level standards are the usual substitute for an overall evaluation. The net result is that it is often difficult to set marketing objectives that are in line with overall organizational goals.

Another characteristic is the *lack of a single clear organizational structure*. Nonprofit organizations often refer to constituencies that they serve, but these are often considerably less exact than, for example, the stockholders of a profit-oriented corporation. Nonprofit organizations often have multiple organizational structures. A hospital might have an administrative structure, a professional organization consisting of medical personnel, and a volunteer organization that dominates the board of trustees. These people may sometimes work at cross-purposes and not be totally in line with the marketing strategy that has been devised.[4]

A final characteristic of the nonprofit sector is that it is sometimes inefficient. Often two or more NPOs work toward the same "cause." For example, there may be several affirmative-action groups. Religious organizations, many with very similar objectives, abound and overlap. This could be seen as a duplication or multiplication of efforts. Clearly, however, there is competition in many cases, and the competition is not only to win a larger portion of the client target market. In fund-raising, for example, the same types of NPOs sometimes compete for donor support. In addition, competition for personnel, such as fund-raisers, also occurs.

While the above factors may also characterize some profit-oriented organizations, they are certainly prevalent in nonprofit settings. These characteristics affect the implementation of marketing efforts in such organizations and must be considered in the development of an overall strategy.

## Types of Nonprofit Marketing

Although nonprofit organizations are at least as varied as profit-seeking organizations, it is possible to categorize them based upon the type of marketing each requires. The three major types of marketing among NPOs are person marketing, idea marketing, and organization marketing.

### Person Marketing

**Person marketing** refers to *efforts designed to cultivate the attention, interest, and preference of a target market toward a person*.[5] This type of marketing is typically employed by political candidates and celebrities.

Leadership campaigns for political parties are good examples of person marketing. Serious contenders conduct research into the various voter segments and develop strategies to reach them. Similarly, in a profit-seeking setting, various

**bottom line** The overall-profitability measure of performance.

**person marketing** Efforts designed to cultivate the attention, interest, and preference of a target market toward a person.

musicians are carefully marketed to subsegments of the total market. The marketing mix for marketing Anne Murray is different from that for k.d. lang.

## Idea Marketing

The second type of nonprofit marketing deals with causes and social issues rather than an individual. **Idea marketing** refers to *the identification and marketing of a cause to chosen consumer segments.*[6] A highly visible marketing mix element frequently associated with idea marketing is the use of *advocacy advertising*, discussed in an earlier chapter. The importance of wearing seatbelts and motorcycle helmets is an idea currently being marketed in several provinces. Antismoking marketing programs have been so successful that many people have quit smoking, and legislation has been passed that forbids smoking in public places.

**idea marketing** The identification and marketing of a cause to chosen consumer segments.

## Organization Marketing

The third type of nonprofit marketing, **organization marketing**, *attempts to influence others to accept the goals of, receive the services of, or contribute in some way to an organization.* Included in this category are *mutual benefit* organizations, such as churches, labour unions, and political parties; *service* organizations, such as colleges and universities, hospitals, and museums; and *government* organizations such as military services, police and fire departments, the post office, and local communities.[7] Figure 20–3 illustrates the efforts of the town of High River to attract businesses to settle in that community. If successful, this advertising effort, along with other marketing mix elements, will create new jobs and stimulate the economic base of the community.

**organization marketing** Attempts to influence others to accept the goals of, receive the services of, or contribute in some way to an organization.

# Understanding of Marketing by Nonprofit Organizations

Nonprofit organizations often have too limited an understanding of marketing. In many cases, marketing is taken to mean simply marketing communications. The development of well-thought-out marketing strategy, as well as consideration of other components of the marketing mix — product development, distribution, and pricing strategies — have too often been largely ignored. Marketing, considered and practised merely as aggressive promotion, is a short-lived, surface-level solution for a variety of organizational problems and objectives. For instance, one university decided to "adopt marketing" and thought it was doing so by planning to release balloons containing scholarship offers. And a "marketing planning" conference for a private school consisted mainly of the development of new slogans for advertisements.

Professor Seymour H. Fine conducted a survey of nonprofit organizations to assess the degree of marketing sophistication present. His findings, illustrated in Figure 20–4, revealed that many respondents were unaware of, or at least reluctant to admit to, the presence of marketing efforts in their organizations.

Nonprofit organizations need to take the time to develop a comprehensive marketing approach. One university, for example, conducted a comprehensive marketing audit that designated strong and weak areas in its product mix (program offerings). It was then possible to develop strategies after the basic parameters of market, resources, and mission had been identified and analyzed.

FIGURE 20-4

## Responses of Selected Nonprofit Organization Representatives

| Nonprofit Organization | Response to the Question "Do you have a marketing department or equivalent?" |
| --- | --- |
| Public health service official | "Marketing fluoridation is not a function of government — promotion and public awareness is." |
| Administrator of regional women's right group | "We have never thought of ourselves as marketing a product. We have people who are assigned equal pay for work of equal value as their 'item.'" |
| Group crusading for the rights of the left-handed | "Don't understand the term [marketing]; we do lobbying, letter writing to appropriate government and commercial concerns. |
| A national centre for the prevention of child abuse | "We disseminate information without the marketing connotation. Besides, demand is too great to justify marketing." |
| Recruiting officer | "Not applicable." |

Source: Adapted from Fine, *Marketing of Ideas*, p. 53.

## The Importance of Marketing to Nonprofit Organizations

Marketing is a late arrival to the management of nonprofit organizations. The practices of improved accounting, financial control, personnel selection, and strategic planning were all implemented before marketing. Nevertheless, nonprofit organizations have begun to accept it enthusiastically. For example, university administrators attend seminars and conferences to learn how better to market their own institutions.

Marketing's rise in the nonprofit sector could not be continued without a successful track record. While it is often more difficult to measure results in nonprofit settings, marketing can already point to examples of success. As an example, the Church of the Nazarene in Canada has used a telemarketing campaign called "Phones For You" to develop a target clientele interested in supporting the start of new churches. And one art gallery's marketing analysis resulted in a definition of two distinct market segments it should serve. Marketing is increasingly an accepted part of the operational environment of successful nonprofit organizations. Figure 20-5 presents a hypothetical job description for a marketing director at a college or university.

FIGURE 20 – 5

**Job Description: Director of Marketing for a University**

---

**Position Title:** Director of Marketing

**Reports to:** A vice-president designated by the president

**Scope:** University-wide

**Position Concept:** The director of marketing is responsible for providing marketing guidance and services to university officers, school deans, department chairpersons, and other agents of the university.

**Functions:** The director of marketing will
1. Contribute a marketing perspective to the deliberations of the top administration in its planning of the university's future
2. Prepare data that might be needed by any officer of the university on a particular market's size, segments, trends, and behavioural dynamics
3. Conduct studies of the needs, perceptions, preferences, and satisfactions of particular markets
4. Assist in the planning, promotion, and launching of new programs
5. Assist in the development of communication and promotion campaigns and materials
6. Analyze and advise on pricing questions
7. Appraise the workability of new academic proposals from a marketing point of view
8. Advise on new student recruitment
9. Advise on current student satisfaction
10. Advise on university fundraising

**Responsibilities:** The director of marketing will
1. Contact individual officers and small groups at the university to explain services and to solicit problems
2. Rank the various requests for services according to their long-run impact, cost-saving potential, time requirements, ease of accomplishment, cost, and urgency
3. Select projects of high priority and set accomplishment goals for the year
4. Prepare a budget request to support the anticipated work
5. Prepare an annual report on the main accomplishments of the office

**Major Liaisons:** The director of marketing will
1. Relate most closely with president's office, admissions office, development office, planning office, and public relations department
2. Relate secondarily with the deans of various schools and chairpersons of various departments

---

Source: Reprinted with permission from Philip Kotler, "Strategies for Introducing Marketing into Nonprofit Organizations," *Journal of Marketing* (January 1979), p. 42, published by the American Marketing Association.

# Developing a Marketing Strategy

The need for a comprehensive marketing strategy rather than a mere increase in marketing communications expenditures has already been noted. Substantial opportunities exist for effective, innovative strategies since there has been little previous marketing effort in most nonprofit settings.

## Marketing Research

Many decisions in nonprofit settings (as well as business) are based on little if any research. Numerous Canadian art galleries arbitrarily establish programs and schedules with little or no reference to audience marketing research.

Adequate marketing research can be extremely important in a variety of nonprofit settings. Resident opinion surveys in some cities have proven valuable to public officials.[8] The analysis of projected population trends has led school boards to build new schools and to phase out others.

## Product Strategy

Nonprofit organizations face the same product decisions as profit-seeking firms. They must choose a product, service, person, idea, or social issue to be offered to their target market. They must decide whether to offer a single product or a mix of related products. They must make product identification decisions. The fact that the United Way symbol and the Red Cross trademark are as familiar as McDonald's golden arches or the Shell logo illustrates the similarity in the use of product identification methods.

A common failure among nonprofit organizations is the assumption that heavy promotional efforts can overcome a poor product strategy or marketing mix. For example, some liberal arts colleges tried to use promotion to overcome their product mix deficiencies when students became increasingly career-oriented. Successful institutions adjust their product offerings to reflect customer demand.

## Pricing Strategy

Pricing is typically a very important element of the marketing mix for nonprofit organizations. Pricing strategy can be used to accomplish a variety of organizational goals in nonprofit settings. These include:

---

### A·P·P·L·Y·I·N·G  T·H·E  C·O·N·C·E·P·T·S

## *Gaining Corporate Support: Essential for Many*

To market its way back from virtual extinction, the Vancouver Symphony Orchestra (VSO) needed to have support from the business community. Canadian Airlines International underwrote the VSO for $200 000 during a three-day gala called "There's Music in the Air." Ed Leclaire, national promotions director for the airline, summed up the sponsorship experience this way: "We saw this as a great opportunity for us; one that made solid business sense. 'There's Music in the Air' was very much a marketing-driven exercise. It gave us an opportunity to step forward and make a stand and show leadership, which fits in with our mission statement. It was a window to reach our target group. It was an opportunity to, in one fell swoop, crystallize what this corporation stands for."[*]

The two marketing strategy components "mission statement" and "target group" are as crucial for the VSO as they are for Canadian Airlines or for Procter & Gamble. The mission statement is the first step of a successful strategic marketing plan; it outlines who the customer is, what is of value to the customer, and what the organization is and should be. The VSO had to consider carefully its mission and its target market. The marketing process then consisted of adjusting the elements of the marketing mix accordingly.

[*]Chris Dafoe, "Corporations Join Music Makers in Search of Perfect Pitch," *Globe and Mail* (November 18, 1990).

Source: Adapted from M. Louise Ripley and George Gilbert, "The Vancouver Symphony Orchestra: Marketing, "*Academy of Marketing Science News* (January 1991) p. 2.

1. *Profit maximization.* While nonprofit organizations by definition do not cite profitability as a primary goal, there are numerous instances in which they do try to maximize their return on a single event or a series of events. The $1000-a-plate political fund-raiser is an example.

2. *Cost recovery.* Some nonprofit organizations attempt only to recover the actual cost of operating the unit. Mass transit, colleges, and bridges are common examples. The amount of recovered costs is often dictated by tradition, competition, and/or public opinion.

3. *Providing market incentives.* Other nonprofit groups follow a penetration pricing policy or offer a free service to encourage increased usage of the product or service. Winnipeg's bus system policy of free fares on special "Dash" buses in the downtown area reduces traffic congestion, encourages retail sales, and minimizes the effort required to use downtown public services.

4. *Market suppression.* Price is sometimes used to discourage consumption. In other words, high prices are used to accomplish social objectives and are not directly related to the costs of providing the product or service. Illustrations of suppression include tobacco and alcohol taxes, parking fines, tolls, and gasoline excise taxes.[9]

## Distribution Strategy

Distribution channels for nonprofit organizations tend to be short, simple, and direct. If intermediaries are present in the channel, they are usually agents, such as an independent ticket agency or a specialist in fund-raising.

Nonprofit organizations often fail to exercise caution in the planning and execution of the distribution strategy. Organizers of recycling centres sometimes complain about lack of public interest when their real problem is an inconvenient location or lack of adequate drop-off points. In a number of cities, this problem has been solved by dropping "blue [recycling] boxes" off to people's homes. By contrast, some public agencies, like health and social welfare departments, have set up branches in neighbourhood shopping centres to be more accessible to their clientele. Nonprofit marketers must carefully evaluate the available distribution options if they are to be successful in delivering their products or in serving their intended consumers.

## Marketing Communications Strategy

It is common to see or hear advertisements from nonprofit organizations such as educational institutions, churches, and public service organizations. A striking example of nonprofit advertising is Figure 20–6, a newspaper advertisement aimed at promoting improved drug awareness.

Marketing communications are affected by a variety of factors including relative involvement in the nonprofit setting, pricing, and perceived benefits.[10] But overall, marketing communications are seen by many nonprofit managers as the primary solution to their marketing problems. As noted earlier, this view is often naive, but it does not diminish the importance of this mix element in a nonprofit setting.

All types of marketing communications elements have been used. The Canadian Forces has used television advertising to attract recruits. Fund-raising for some support groups for the handicapped is done through personal selling over the telephone. Volunteers are an essential part of the marketing program for many

FIGURE 20-6

**A Drug Awareness Advertisement**

*Another campaign from Health and Welfare Canada urges young adults to make their own decisions about drugs. Marketing communications play a large part in the marketing mix employed by this government agency. Can you think of any other areas of the marketing mix that could also be effectively used by Health and Welfare?*

nonprofit organizations. They are used to "sell" (canvass) by phone or in person. Such individuals pose a significant "sales management" problem. With a paid sales force, it is easy to demand certain behaviours on the part of the sales personnel or to provide various financial incentives to affect their behaviour. Similar methods are not as readily available with volunteers. Other stimulation and incentives, such as

public recognition or receptions, are used as substitutes. Even so, it is unlikely that the same effects can be achieved.

Advertising is a desirable marketing communications option. However, because the cost of media is high, fund-raising drives often rely on publicity and public relations efforts, such as appearances on TV talk shows, to promote their product. Charitable groups have used badges, paper flowers, and other specialty advertising items to identify donors or contributions and to promote their particular cause. Marketing communications will remain a key ingredient of most nonprofit organizations' marketing plans.

## The Future of Nonprofit Marketing

While marketing has gained increasing acceptance in the nonprofit sector of society, it is still viewed with suspicion by some of the people involved. The heavy emphasis on marketing communications is one reason. Marketing efforts in nonprofit organizations often lack the sophistication and integration found in the marketing of profit-oriented industries. Marketing is too often seen as the "quick-fix" solution to a more basic problem. To combat this, marketers must market their own discipline in a realistic and socially responsible manner. The client must be made to understand the opportunities, benefits, behaviour modifications, and commitment involved in the adoption of the marketing concept in a nonprofit setting.

## Summary

Nonprofit organizations are those whose primary objective is something other than returning a profit to their owners. Nonprofit organizations are often characterized by the intangible nature of many of their offerings; the multiple publics with whom they must deal; possible inattention to consumer needs; the involvement of resource contributors; the lack of a bottom line; the lack of a clear organizational structure; and often a certain degree of inefficiency.

The three types of nonprofit marketing are person, idea, and organizational marketing. Marketing is now considered to be essential by many nonprofit organizations. These organizations have gone beyond thinking of marketing as merely an equivalent to marketing communications; they now realize that it involves the development of complete marketing plans designed in a way similar to those used in business organizations.

Marketing, while still just a concept to some, is growing in use among nonprofit organizations. In the future many more will discover the value of applying marketing to their problems.

## ▮ K E Y  T E R M S

| | | |
|---|---|---|
| nonprofit organization | person marketing | organization marketing |
| bottom line | idea marketing | |

# REVIEW QUESTIONS

1. What are the primary characteristics of nonprofit organizations that distinguish them from profit-seeking organizations?
2. What is person marketing? Contrast it with marketing of a consumer good such as magazines.
3. Why is idea marketing more difficult than organization marketing?
4. Identify the types of organization marketing and give examples of each.

5. Why is marketing sometimes defined inaccurately in a nonprofit organization?
6. Contrast the product strategy of nonprofit marketing with that of marketing for profit.
7. Identify the pricing goals that are commonly found in nonprofit enterprises.
8. Compare distribution and marketing communications strategies of nonprofit organizations with those used by profit-seeking enterprises.

# DISCUSSION QUESTIONS AND EXERCISES

1. What type of nonprofit organization does each of the following represent:
   a. United Auto Workers
   b. John Doe–for–mayor committee
   c. St. John's Public Library
   d. Stanley Park Zoo (Vancouver)
   e. Save the Whales Foundation
   f. Girl Guides
   g. Easter Seals
2. Figure 20-4 reveals that many nonprofit organization executives have negative attitudes toward marketing. What needs to be done if this is to change?
3. Cite several examples of circumstances when penetrating pricing might be practised by public utilities.

4. How would you assess the marketing performance of the following?
   a. your college or university
   b. War Amps
   c. Canadian Postal Workers Union
   d. Planned Parenthood
   e. the re-election committee of a local MP
5. Outline the marketing program of your college or university. Make any reasonable assumptions necessary. Where are the major strengths and weaknesses of the current program? What recommendations would you make for improving it?

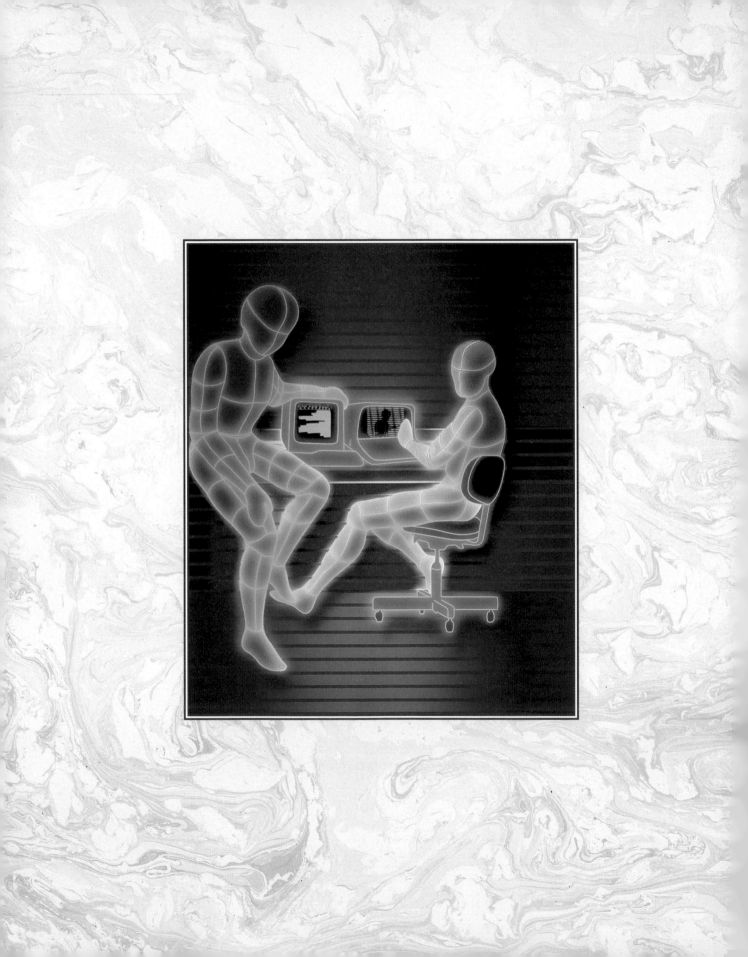

# Total Quality Management in Marketing

"**H**OW is your company performing?" William Brand asked. "Sales and profits are up," the president replied. "In fact, our financial people tell me this year we will have one of our best 'bottom lines' ever!"

Mr. Brand and the president, whose company manufactured computer components, were reviewing the company's recent accomplishments and preparing to plan the company's strategy for next year.

"Today's financial results measure the results of strategic initiatives taken in the past. Are you monitoring the critical factors that will create success in the future?" Brand challenged.

"What do you mean? Aren't strong financial controls the proper measuring tools to monitor business performance?" the president said, somewhat taken aback.

Using financial measures alone is like driving a car while watching the rearview mirror: they tell you where you have been. A manager also needs to look forward, toward building success in the areas that lead to a long-run competitive advantage. These key success factors include product quality and after-sale service, corporate flexibility, and employee innovation.[1]

# Introduction

This whole book is about finding and serving customers profitably. In discussing the issue we have developed an understanding of the many elements involved in the marketing planning process (Figure 21–1). The final aspect of the marketing planning process is control — determining whether the objective of achieving consumer satisfaction has been met. Only by systematically reviewing the outcome of the process can marketers improve the marketing plan. In a recent study of the marketing planning practices of the top 500 Canadian firms, this author found that only 57.8 percent of firms developed a written marketing plan. Furthermore, only 25.4 percent included a postmortem of the past year's results in their current marketing plan.

# The Evaluation and Control Process

Figure 21–2 is a model of the *evaluation and control* process. Since marketing planning and control are closely related components of an effective marketing program, evaluation and control guide performance to conform to the plan.

---

**FIGURE 21 – 1**

**The Marketing Planning Process**

---

**I. SITUATION ANALYSIS**
  **Where are we now?**
A. *Historical Background*
B. *Consumer Analysis*
   — Who are the customers we are trying to serve?
   — What market segments exist?
   — How many consumers are there?
   — How much do they buy and why?
C. *Competitive Analysis*
**II. MARKETING OBJECTIVES**
  **Where do we want to go?**
A. *Sales Objectives*
B. *Profit Objectives*
**III. STRATEGY**
  **How can we get there?**
A. *Product/Service Decisions*
B. *Pricing Decisions*
C. *Distribution Decisions*
D. *Communication Decisions*
E. *Financial Considerations*
F. *Control Aspects*

---

Source: Adapted from Stephen K. Keiser, Robert E. Stevens, and Lynn J. Loudenback, *Contemporary Marketing Study Guide* (Hinsdale, IL: Dryden Press, 1986), p. 482.

A number of elements must be present for evaluation and control to be effective. First, as Figure 21–2 indicates, organizational goals must result in the establishment of standards of performance. Such standards become reference points against which actual performance can be compared. They may take such forms as expected number of sales calls per month, sales, profit, or market-share expectations, or even rankings of consumer awareness. These performance standards have been, and will continue to be, important.

In addition to these standards, marketers need to concentrate on relevant measures that assess whether or not customer satisfaction has been achieved. What is customer satisfaction, really? Here are some answers given by managers:[2]

- "You have to start with the definition of customer satisfaction and quality from the customer perspective. Do the diagnostic work. What are the key factors that drive the customer on the good or service?"

- "The customer doesn't care about your system. The customer cares about satisfaction — having problems handled."

- "Customers don't care how you track their orders. What the customer thinks is 'I need the answer as to what the status of my shipment is, within the hour.' Customers don't care about how you execute, only that you do. They care about the *results*."

Ultimately, there is a common thread in the managers' responses: customer satisfaction comes down to superior performance in serving customers' needs. As the managers' comments imply, organizations have to get beyond lip service to customer satisfaction. One way in which they are doing this is by going into the marketplace and measuring satisfaction regularly. A good example of such an approach is shown in the accompanying box.

---

**FIGURE 21–2**

**Steps in the Process of Evaluation and Control**

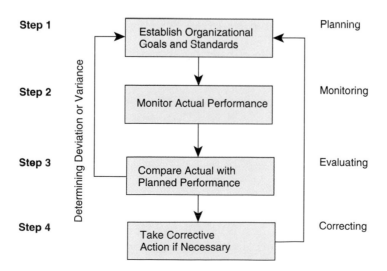

## A·P·P·L·Y·I·N·G  T·H·E  C·O·N·C·E·P·T·S

### Hewlett-Packard's Approach to Customer Satisfaction in Europe

Hewlett-Packard has chosen to use customer satisfaction rather than relying on product features to differentiate itself from its competitors. H-P has established three programs to obtain customer feedback, in order to provide the kind of service that will make a difference. These three programs — customer feedback input, customer satisfaction surveys, and total quality control — compose the H-P customer satisfaction program.

Customer feedback input documents customers' gripes as well as compliments, "because we can learn from positive feedback as well," said Norma Gutierrez, customer satisfaction executive at H-P.

Worldwide "relationship" surveys are administered every 18 months as a way to focus on customers and learn from their comments. The surveys include some product questions but concentrate on asking how satisfied the customer is with the company as a whole, and how H-P rates against its competition.

According to 1990 survey results, worldwide customer satisfaction had improved 3 percentage points over the previous year. "The cheapest way to do business is to do it right the first time," Gutierrez said. "Keeping customers forever makes good business sense."

H-P's quality control program includes "Focus on the Customer," a sort of "baptismal training," Gutierrez explained, "in order to get everyone involved in customer service." She said this is the segment of customer service that takes action based on what customers are saying. "We can say we are listening, but it's not until we take action that things really start happening," she said. Through this quality control program, customer data are used to make improvements and are reflected in the business plan.

Some companies have still not recognized the trend toward making customer service their number one goal. "They haven't quite realized customer service is an effective marketing tool," said another official.

Source: Adapted from Charlotte Klopp and John Sterlicchi, "Customer Satisfaction Just Catching On in Europe," *Marketing News* (May 28, 1990) p. 5.

## Total Quality Management Relates to Marketing Too

**total quality management (TQM)**
Concept that for every customer-impinging activity, nothing less than total quality is acceptable.

The Japanese product invasion throughout the world has created a growing recognition of the importance of quality products. Out of this has emerged the concept of **total quality management** (**TQM**), which emphasizes that *for every customer-impinging activity, nothing less than total quality is acceptable.* Under this philosophy, quality is considered the absolute responsibility of each person in the organization, not something that will be monitored by someone else.

There is empirical evidence to show that when consumers perceive a company's products to be of good quality, greater profits result for that company. This finding came from the Profit Impact of Market Strategies (PIMS) program, which has been carrying out research since 1972 on the relationship between business strategy and business performance, using a database of more than 450 companies and 3000 business units.

However, perceived quality is not the same as the traditional engineering definition of quality, which is "conformance to specifications." Quality must be defined from an external, customer-based viewpoint. Marketing executives must lead their organizations to a better understanding of quality, defined in customer terms.[3] A company's products may be perfectly manufactured, but will fail if they do not meet market requirements.

TQM applies not only to the products that are marketed, but also to the marketing management process. For example, if informed consumers of health-care services see ads proclaiming the high quality of care at a hospital known for its low-quality service, they are likely to think, "Why waste the money on hype when I can't get

The pursuit
of quality is
second nature
to us.

**Bell**
Answering your call

through on the phone to make an appointment?" Furthermore, staff and clinical employees who see the ads might say, "Why put all that money into marketing and nothing into improving the poor quality of care?"[4]

Reassuring the public that you care and provide high-quality service is a sound way to build a customer base and profit, but only if such claims are undeniably true. Among other things, TQM means that quality should be the constant motto of those managing every facet of the marketing program. Total quality means that a good or service totally conforms to the customer's requirements. This, of course, cannot be done without an active program for monitoring *customer satisfaction*.

To take quality from slogan to substance, management should follow these guidelines:

**Ensure that the quality of the good or service is the overriding goal of the organization, in every department**. Every service must be measured against the same standard, and every employee should be working toward zero errors and defects.

**Communicate the goals and standards of quality to all employees, even if they do not deal with the consumer**. The best salespeople cannot make a company liked and profitable if other people in the organization are inefficient or error-prone.

**Train all employees in a voluntary, co-operative atmosphere**. It is woefully inadequate for a vice-president or chief executive officer to announce that "all employees should do their best," without providing training in what that means and how to achieve it.

**Give rewards**. These can be financial or otherwise and should be given to those whose involvement leads to quality improvements and real cost savings.

# Assessing Other Aspects of Marketing Performance: The Marketing Audit

As an aid in determining where an organization stands with respect to providing total quality to its customers, Philip Kotler has devised an auditing system to measure marketing effectiveness. This *marketing audit* is based on five variables: consumer philosophy, integrated marketing organization, adequate marketing information, strategic orientation, and operational efficiency. These activities are defined as follows:[5]

1. *Customer philosophy*: Does management acknowledge the primacy of the market-place and of customer needs and wants in shaping company plans and operations?

2. *Integrated marketing organization*: Is the organization staffed so that it will be able to carry out marketing analysis, planning, and implementation and control?

3. *Adequate marketing information*: Does management receive the kind and quality of information needed to conduct effective marketing?

4. *Strategic orientation*: Does marketing management generate innovative strategies and plans for long-run growth and profitability?

5. *Operational efficiency*: Are marketing plans implemented in a cost-effective manner, and are the results monitored for rapid corrective action?

Figure 21–3 presents a suggested marketing effectiveness audit and a scoring system for assessing overall effectiveness.

---

**FIGURE 21–3**

## The Marketing Effectiveness Audit

---

### Customer philosophy

Score *A. Does management recognize the importance of designing the company to serve the needs and wants of chosen markets?*

0 ☐ Management primarily thinks in terms of selling current and new products to whomever will buy them.

1 ☐ Management thinks in terms of serving a wide range of markets and needs with equal effectiveness.

2 ☐ Management thinks in terms of serving the needs and wants of well-defined markets chosen for their long-run growth and profit potential for the company.

*B. Does management develop different offerings and marketing plans for different segments of the market?*

0 ☐ No.

1 ☐ Somewhat.

2 ☐ To a good extent.

*C. Does management take a whole marketing system view (suppliers, channels, competitors, customers, environment) in planning its business?*

0 ☐ No. Management concentrates on selling and servicing its immediate customers.

1 ☐ Somewhat. Management takes a long view of its channels, although the bulk of its effort goes to selling and servicing the immediate customers.

2 ☐ Yes. Management takes a whole marketing systems view, recognizing the threats and opportunities created for the company by changes in any part of the system.

FIGURE 21-3 (CONTINUED)

## The Marketing Effectiveness Audit

### Integrated marketing organization

*D. Is there high-level marketing integration and control of the major marketing functions?*

0 ☐ No. Sales and other marketing functions are not integrated at the top and there is some unproductive conflict.

1 ☐ Somewhat. There is formal integration and control of the major marketing functions but less than satisfactory co-ordination and co-operation.

2 ☐ Yes. The major marketing functions are effectively integrated.

*E. Does marketing management work well with management in research, manufacturing, purchasing, physical distribution, and finance?*

0 ☐ No. There are complaints that marketing is unreasonable in the demands and costs it places on other departments.

1 ☐ Somewhat. The relations are amicable although each department pretty much acts to serve its own power interest.

2 ☐ Yes. The departments co-operate effectively and resolve issues in the best interest of the company as a whole.

*F. How well organized is the new-product development process?*

0 ☐ The system is ill-defined and poorly handled.

1 ☐ The system formally exists but lacks sophistication.

2 ☐ The system is well structured and professionally staffed.

### Adequate marketing information

*G. When were the latest marketing research studies of customers, buying influences, channels, and competitors conducted?*

0 ☐ Several years ago.

1 ☐ A few years ago.

2 ☐ Recently.

*H. How well does management know the sales potential and profitability of different market segments, customers, territories, products, channels and order sizes?*

0 ☐ Not at all.

1 ☐ Somewhat.

2 ☐ Very well.

*I. What effort is expended to measure the cost-effectiveness of different marketing expenditures?*

0 ☐ Little or no effort.

1 ☐ Some effort.

2 ☐ Substantial effort.

### Strategic orientation

*J. What is the extent of formal marketing planning?*

0 ☐ Management does little or no formal marketing planning.

1 ☐ Management develops an annual marketing plan.

2 ☐ Management develops a detailed annual marketing plan and a careful long-range plan that is updated annually.

*K. What is the quality of the current marketing strategy?*

0 ☐ The current strategy is not clear.

1 ☐ The current strategy is clear and represents a continuation of traditional strategy.

2 ☐ The current strategy is clear, innovative, data-based, and well reasoned.

*L. What is the extent of contingency thinking and planning?*

0 ☐ Management does little or no contingency thinking.

1 ☐ Management does some contingency thinking, although little formal contingency planning.

2 ☐ Management formally identifies the most important contingencies and develops contingency plans.

### Operational efficiency

*M. How well is the marketing thinking at the top communicated and implemented down the line?*

0 ☐ Poorly.

1 ☐ Fairly well.

2 ☐ Successfully.

*N. Is management doing an effective job with the marketing resources?*

FIGURE 21-3 (CONTINUED)

## The Marketing Effectiveness Audit

0 ☐   No. The marketing resources are inadequate for the job to be done.

1 ☐   Somewhat. The marketing resources are adequate, but they are not employed optimally.

2 ☐   Yes. The marketing resources are adequate and are deployed efficiently.

*O. Does management show a good capacity to react quickly and effectively to on-the-spot developments?*

0 ☐   No. Sales and market information is not very current and management reaction time is slow.

1 ☐   Somewhat. Management receives fairly up-to-date sales and market information; management reaction time varies.

2 ☐   Yes. Management has installed systems yielding highly current information and fast reaction time.

**Total score**

*Rating marketing effectiveness*

The auditing outline can be used in this way. The auditor collects information as it bears on the 15 questions. The appropriate answer is checked for each question. The scores are added — the total will be somewhere between 0 and 30. The following scale shows the equivalent in marketing effectiveness:

| | |
|---|---|
| 0–5 | None |
| 6–10 | Poor |
| 11–15 | Fair |
| 16–20 | Good |
| 21–25 | Very good |
| 26–30 | Superior |

To illustrate, 15 senior managers in a large building materials company were recently invited to rate their company using the auditing instrument in this exhibit. The resulting overall marketing effectiveness scores ranged from a low of 6 to a high of 15. The median score was 11, with three-fourths of the scores between 9 and 13. Therefore, most of the managers thought their company was at best "fair" at marketing. Several divisions were also rated. Their median scores ranged from a low of 3 to a high of 19. The higher scoring divisions tended to have higher profitability. However, some of the lower scoring divisions were also profitable. An examination of the latter showed that these divisions were in industries where their competition also operated at a low level of marketing effectiveness. The managers feared that these divisions would be vulnerable as soon as competition began to learn to market more successfully.

An interesting question to speculate on is the distribution of median marketing effectiveness scores for *Fortune* "500" companies. My suspicion is that very few companies in that roster would score above 20 ("very good" or "superior") in marketing effectiveness.

Source: Reprinted with permission from Phillip Kotler, "From Sales Obsession to Marketing Effectiveness," *Harvard Business Review* (November–December 1977), pp. 70–71. Copyright © 1977 by the President and Fellows of Harvard College; all rights reserved.

# Ethics in Marketing: An Important Component of Quality Marketing Management

Marketing planning is based on an understanding of the consumer and the environment. The output of this process is a stream of goods and services designed to serve the needs of the consumer and to return a profit to the company. In this process, marketing plays a significant role in society.

Historically, some marketers have neglected the social issues involved in their activities and have operated on the edge of accepted societal standards of propriety and honesty. Various regulations and licence requirements have been enacted to limit certain marketing practices. Gradually society has decided that it is not willing to tolerate questionable business behaviour. Thus, society now expects that marketers will act in a socially responsible manner.

**Social responsibility** is *the marketer's acceptance of the obligation to consider profit, consumer satisfaction, and the well-being of society as being of equal value in evaluating the performance of the firm*. It is the recognition that marketers must be concerned with the qualitative measures of consumer and social benefits as well as with the quantitative measures of sales, revenue, and profits by which marketing performance has traditionally been measured.

**Marketing ethics** are *the marketer's standards of conduct and moral values*. Ethics involve the decision to do what is morally right. People develop standards of ethical behaviour based on their own systems of values. Their "individual ethics" help them deal with the various ethical questions in their personal lives. However, when they are

**social responsibility** The marketer's acceptance of the obligation to consider profit, consumer satisfaction, and the well-being of society as being of equal value in evaluating the performance of the firm.

**marketing ethics** The marketer's standards of conduct and moral values.

FIGURE 21–4

## A Marketing Code of Ethics

As a member of the American Marketing Association, I recognize the significance of my professional conduct and my responsibilities to society and to the other members of my profession:

1. By acknowledging my accountability to society as a whole as well as to the organization for which I work.

2. By pledging my efforts to assure that all presentation of goods, services, and concepts be made honestly and clearly.

3. By striving to improve marketing knowledge and practice in order to better serve society.

4. By supporting free consumer choice in circumstances that are legal and are consistent with generally accepted community standards.

5. By pledging to use the highest professional standards in my work and in competitive activity.

6. By acknowledging the right of the American Marketing Association, through established procedure, to withdraw my membership if I am found to be in violation of ethical standards of professional conduct.

Source: American Marketing Association, *Constitution and Bylaws*, rev. ed. (Chicago: American Marketing Association, 1977), p. 20. Reprinted by permission.

in a work situation a serious conflict may materialize. Individual ethics may differ from the "organizational ethics" of the employer.

Such conflicts may be resolved to some degree by adherence to professional ethical standards. These standards could be based on a concept of professionalism that transcends both organizational and individual ethics. It depends on the existence of a professional peer group that can exercise collective sanctions on a marketer's professional behaviour. The professional association to which most marketers belong is the American Marketing Association. It has published a Marketing Code of Ethics, as shown in Figure 21–4.

One thing is clear, however: just as total quality expectations are growing for the products marketed, the same standards are expected of the ethical decisions made by marketers. It is recommended that students of marketing think through and develop quality standards of ethical behaviour *before* they are faced with the inevitable ethical dilemmas they will confront in the day-to-day practice of marketing. Such a stance will result in more honourable marketing practices — and a better world.

## The Challenges of Marketing

Marketing is one of the most interesting disciplines. The process of applying marketing thinking in competitive situations could hardly be more challenging. A career in marketing requires great sensitivity to the many variables that must be taken into consideration. Continued success demands the highest levels of creativity on the part of the marketer. And since conditions, people, and the environment are constantly changing, a career in marketing will rarely be boring! The fact that many company presidents began their careers in marketing attests to the breadth of business understanding developed through the profession of marketing.

## Summary

It is not enough to develop a creative and innovative marketing plan. Such a plan should be implemented in a manner consistent with the concept of total quality management. This concept emphasizes that in every stage of production, nothing less than total quality is acceptable. Total quality in marketing results in customer satisfaction. What constitutes customer satisfaction should be determined and relentlessly measured.

Evaluation to determine progress toward objectives, and control to correct deviations, are an essential part of implementing the marketing plan. The marketing audit systematically analyzes every aspect of the marketing program with a view to determining the effectiveness of each program element. It is based on a consideration of five variables: customer philosophy, integrated marketing organization, adequate marketing information, strategic orientation, and operational efficiency.

Total quality management is necessary not only in products and management practices, but also in the ethical approach to doing business. The marketer can follow the guidance of the American Marketing Association code of ethics, but must also develop a personal set of ethical standards by which to make business decisions.

# KEY TERMS

total quality management
evaluation and control
customer satisfaction
marketing audit

customer philosophy
integrated marketing
  organization
social responsibility

marketing ethics
American Marketing Association
  code of ethics

# REVIEW QUESTIONS

1. Explain the significance of emphasizing customer satisfaction.
2. Describe how control fits into the marketing planning process.
3. Illustrate the steps in the marketing evaluation and control process.
4. Outline the total quality management (TQM) concept.
5. Show how the TQM concept applies to product offerings.
6. How does the TQM concept pertain to the management of the marketing effort?
7. Identify the major steps in a marketing audit.
8. Describe several ethical issues a marketer may face.
9. Outline the American Marketing Association code of marketing ethics.
10. How does the TQM concept apply to marketing ethics?

# DISCUSSION QUESTIONS AND EXERCISES

1. Describe what might be included in a meaningful customer satisfaction assessment for the following:
   a. Canadian Airlines
   b. A paint manufacturer
   c. Eaton's
2. Describe the possible problems involved in using the information developed in Question 1 to make a difference in an organization.
3. In detail, describe how the total quality management concept could be applied to the marketing management system of a company with which you have some familiarity.
4. Outline the probable steps in a marketing audit for a local dry cleaning company.
5. Henry Ford II has argued that in a competitive market system, a firm cannot afford to meet the expense of environmental improvements unless competitors are also legally required to follow the same standards. Discuss.

588

## CAREER PROFILE

### Pier Massa

Molson Breweries
National Brand Manager
Coors/Coors Light

**Education:**

M.B.A., University of Toronto, 1987
B.A. (Hons) Economics, University of Toronto, Trinity College, 1983
International Baccalaureate, Lester B. Pearson College of the Pacific (United World College) 1980

Up front, it is my firm belief that in any educational program you get out of it whatever you're willing to put into it. A commitment to learning and applying new solutions to real-world situations are what provide a real leverage point to the graduate of any marketing program; the letters behind your name are incidental.

My business degree provided me with two key benefits. First, I acquired a set of strategic and analytical tools that allow me to do a better job. I frequently use specific techniques I learned in business school whenever I want to assess a situation from a new angle — in other words, every day.

And second, I developed a "total" business perspective. For marketers in particular, an understanding of crossfunctional issues is absolutely critical; numerous marketing initiatives affect other departments and functions, especially production and finance. To be successful in marketing in any organization, one must have a productive rapport with these groups and truly understand their concerns.

To date my career has followed a traditional vertical path. In most marketing jobs, breadth of experience is a real asset, and brand management has provided that. Brand managers assume profit-and-loss responsibilities, which means that the role of brand manager is really that of a "mini" general manager.

My ambitions lie in international/global marketing. The coming together of Europe in '92 and the opportunities stemming from North American trade should make for very exciting times in my field.

# Cases

THE LEFT-HANDED MARKET
CANBANK
GILLETTE
SPORTS EQUIPMENT LIMITED
RETAIL GROCERY PRICES
HOLT RENFREW AND CO. LTD.
DETYZCO, INC.
ACTIVE DETERGENT
TECH FEEDS CORPORATION
SID'S SUNFLOWER SEEDS (1974) LTD.
WORDTECH LIMITED
CREATION TECHNOLOGIES INC.
SYTKO INTERNATIONAL INC.
SPACEMAX
PORTA-BROIL
DURADENT 1-2-3
FEDERATED CHEMICALS LTD.
COMPUTRON, INC.
SOUTHERN CROSS, PTY. LTD.
LIME LIGHT CINEMA
RW PACKAGING (A)
RW PACKAGING (B)
RW PACKAGING (C)
WINTEC ELECTRONICS

# A Note on the Case Method

What is a case? It is a description of a specific situation or incident, which usually requires a decision. It normally includes more than the bare facts of the situation. Varied opinions of individuals involved in the case and background information to which the real decision-maker in the case might have access are also provided.

A case puts you in the role of the decision-maker. Solving a case is like working with the problems that people in actual business situations encounter.

In some ways, the case method of learning is more difficult than the lecture method. Instead of casting the facts into some suitable semi-permanent pedagogical order, the instructor assumes the difficult task of helping students meet new and different problems. The instructor's task becomes one of fostering a facility for approaching and handling new and unstructured situations. The students often find initial difficulties:

> Instead of beginning with...textbook...principles...the student is given a pedestrian description of how the Ward Machine Company put a mechanical shaver on the market.
>
> The initial atmosphere of the classroom does little to restore a feeling of certainty. The behavior of the professor is strangely disconcerting. There is an absence of professorial dicta, a surprising lack of "answers" and "cold dope" which the student can record in his notebook; rather he is asked what *he* thinks, what *he* would do, what problems *he* feels are important.[1]

Despite these difficulties, experience indicates some strong arguments in favour of the case method.

First, it challenges you to use and develop your own insight and knowledge in a realistic situation.[2] Second, as you genuinely apply yourself to the analysis of cases, you will develop abilities to deal successfully with new management problems as they occur in the business world. Thus, your transition from the world of formal education will be easier. Third, the case method gives you an opportunity to experiment with various ways of using your knowledge of the basic principles of the field you are studying.[3]

---

SOURCE    This note is based on M. Dale Beckman, "Evaluating the Case Method," *The Educational Forum* (May 1972), pp. 489–497.

# Preparing a Case

Preparation of a case requires some diligence. It is not enough to skim the case once or twice and then come to class and "shoot from the hip" (or lip), or write down the first solution that comes to mind. Rather, the solution is a progressive process through a methodical and systematic analysis that provides great challenge and interest.

You should read the case several times, starting first with a quick skim to get the overall feel of the situation. Then read it again in more detail as you learn more facts and begin to think about the various aspects of the case. There are several possible approaches to successful case analysis. One alternative is presented below. Use it, but do not try to follow every point slavishly. You are not being asked to "fill in the blanks," but to analyze the case intelligently, using your own judgment and analytical skills fully.

# Suggestions for Development of Case Solutions

**A.** The development of a case solution should be organized into five parts.
   **I.** Summary of Important Facts
   **II.** Problem
   **III.** Analysis
   **IV.** Conclusion
   **V.** Recommendations

*I. Summary of Important Facts*    There are two possible methods of making this summary. You should probably use the first method until you have developed some competence in logically outlining the facts in a case. Then the briefer summary (described in number 2 below) will suffice. The alternative methods are as follows:
1. Outline in logical order the important facts given in the case.
   **a.** Do not merely list miscellaneous facts in the order given in the case.
   **b.** Organize your outline in logical fashion under a few main headings. Possible groupings include: nature of the company and its products; competitive situation; market for the

product; channels of distribution; pricing policies; organization of sales department; policies relating to management of salespeople, etc.

2. Prepare a concise, one-paragraph summary giving a brief picture of the company and the factors that gave rise to the problem to be solved.

## II. Problem
Clearly and concisely state the problem that is to be solved.

1. This may be an exact restatement of the problem given at the end of a case, or
2. The problem may be given to you by your instructor, or
3. You may have to use your own powers of discernment in order to pick out the main problem, because it is not stated in so many words.

## III. Analysis

1. This is the crucial segment in the development of a case. You should make a detailed analysis, leading to your decision and recommendations. You should organize it in accordance with the basic issues or factors in the case.
2. In your analysis, it is necessary and important to consider the weakness of your decision. Consider and present arguments on both sides of the major issue involved.
3. Analytical arguments should be based upon the facts of the case, as well as upon logical and clear-cut reasoning.
4. State clearly any assumptions you make, and give your reasons for making them.
5. Where possible, "push your pencil" and make use of the data. Make creative use of all possible information in the case.
6. Use an objective, unemotional approach in your analysis. This does not mean that you may not be persuasive in your methods of presentation. In fact, you may do an effective "selling" job in your presentation. A logical grouping of related points will help, as will full development of each point. Give your analysis depth, as well as breadth; substantiate major points with minor points. Be sure that you cover each point adequately by explanation or evidence.

## IV. Conclusion
The conclusion should summarize briefly the arguments used in the development of the case analysis. In a written report it is inadequate to simply state that "the arguments above warrant. . . ." It is too much to expect the reader to think back and perhaps reread the report to discover what the arguments were.

## V. Recommendations
State in point form the course of action you believe to be the most sound solution, based on your exhaustive analysis of all alternative possibilities.

B. Common difficulties encountered in case analysis:

I. Students at first have a tendency to repeat the statements in the problem book without reorganizing them and relating them to the problem. Thus the report becomes simply a rehash of the problem. To avoid this the student should keep in mind at all times what the problem is and should constantly think, "What has this to do with the problem?" It is wise also to close the book while writing the report, referring to it only in order to get the accurate facts.

II. Statements of conclusions may be presented without the reasoning that leads to them. So far as the reader is concerned such statements are simply snap judgments and have no more validity than the flipping of a coin. All statements must be *substantiated* by the evidence. A conclusion may be stated at the beginning or at the end of the evidence, but in either case it is necessary to show how the evidence connects with the conclusion. This is done by the use of connectives — "because," "the reason is," and "it follows that."

III. It is tempting to neglect to present evidence that is adverse to the conclusion in the report. However, since the report is to lead to executive action, both sides must be considered and carefully weighed one against the other. Here again, the proper use of connectives is helpful. Such connectives as "notwithstanding," "in spite of," and "be that as it may" indicate that the argument given is subordinate to some other.

IV. Students often fail to carry through the argument to a logical conclusion. This indicates lazy thinking. The careful reader or listener wonders, "So what?" indicating that the analyst has failed to show the pertinence of some statement to the problem solution.

V. Do not use generalizations when specific statements can be made. Most material in the problems is specific, and applies to this particular problem. There is no point in making it general and thus weakening the argument.

VI. Do not use your personal attitude as an argument. Statements such as "I firmly believe" or "It is my considered opinion" are pompous excuses for real arguments.

VII. Students sometimes come up with the conclusion and recommendation that the firm should do the "best thing under the circumstances." Such a recommendation is simply passing the buck and would indicate to the employer a refusal to take responsibility. The reader or listener wants you to decide, not sit on the fence.

---

SOURCE    R. H. Evans and M. D. Beckman, *Cases in Marketing: A Canadian Perspective* (Toronto: Prentice-Hall, 1972), pp. xi–xiii.

# CASE 1

## The Left-Handed Market

Though most people probably do not think of them as a distinct minority group, left-handers have throughout history faced the same discriminations other minority groups have: social stigmatism, ostracism, even burnings at the stake. Many organizations have been formed to champion the cause of left-handers. One of these has tried to provide its members with greater access to products designed specially for them. At the same time the group would like to persuade manufacturers that left-handers are an overlooked segment of the consumer market.

Dean Campbell is chairman and founder of Left-handers International (LHI). He maintains that about 10 percent of the population (2.5 million people in Canada) use only their left hand for most things, while another 5 percent use their left hand for some things. The 15 percent figure will likely increase if the stigma attached to left-handedness decreases.

While other left-handed organizations exist, none has concerned itself specifically with trying to make more left-handed products — from scissors to golf clubs — available. Though many people don't realize it, even an automobile is designed for right-handers.

Part of the problem is that even when products are available for left-handers they tend to be found only at a high price. For example, a power saw, which would normally cost as little as $25.95, when specially designed to be used ambidextrously costs about $225. Pro shops often sell golf clubs for left-handers, but only in the manufacturers' cheapest and most expensive lines. Even then shops seldom keep left-handed models in stock, so that potential buyers cannot try them out before buying, the way right-handers always can.

Companies that do manufacture left-handed products seldom market them seriously. Campbell tried to fill the gap by printing a catalogue of about 80 products for left-handers, including an iron, playing cards, scissors, and even coffee mugs designed so that their messages face the left-handed drinker.

Campbell insists that the group's main goal is to make manufacturers more aware of the left-handed market, hoping they will then produce more merchandise for it and actually market the merchandise so that left-handers can find it.

### Discussion Questions

1. Relate the case to each of the steps of the market-segmentation process shown in Figure 4–2.
2. What types of products could be offered to this market segment? How would you suggest that they be advertised? Distributed?
3. Identify ways in which this market is currently being serviced.
4. Which type(s) of market segmentation should prove most effective in reaching this market? Defend your answer.

SOURCE   Adapted from Kevin T. Higgins, "Southpaws Left Out by Marketers," *Marketing News* (August 10, 1985), p. 6.

# CASE 2

# Canbank

Arnie Johannsen, new product development and merchandising manager at Canbank's Toronto corporate office, was annoyed. He had spent five months and $700 000 developing a new retail product to the point of launch, and now something was terribly wrong.

In October 1990 he had been given the go-ahead to launch his latest product — Canshare, a discount stock brokerage service. With no sign-up charges, it would offer qualifying Canbank customers the opportunity to purchase stocks on the Montreal Stock Exchange, the TSE, VSE, NYSE, and NASDAQ at a discount of between 20 percent to 80 percent of the brokerage fees charged by full-service stock brokers.

The target market was defined as knowledgeable Canbank account holders who would like to buy stocks and who did not require investment counselling. There were 2 500 000 customers in the Canbank system. Arnie expected that 625 000 of these Canbank account holders would take advantage of the new product.

The discount brokerage product concept was not a new one among Canadian banks. The lead bank in this market was the Toronto-Dominion Bank, with its very successful Green Line Investment Services. Among other bank-affiliated competitors were National Bank's Investel, Bank of Montreal's Investor Line, Royal Bank's Action Direct, and Scotia Securities.

To develop a name for the product, Arnie had hired an agency, which provided 200 computer-generated potential brand names. Arnie asked Canbank's lawyers to search these names and found that 150 of them already had been registered for copyright protection. After screening the 50 remaining names, another 45 were rejected as inappropriate for Canbank. The five finalists were presented to Canbank executives, who settled on "Canshare" as the best one to identify their new discount brokerage service.

An agreement was signed with a full-service stock brokerage service to process share transactions gen-erated by Canshare. Neither the broker nor Canbank would offer investment advice.

On October 15, Arnie began planning the introduction of the new product. Promotion was an important part of the plan. A top freelance advertising copywriter was hired to develop promotional copy in English. The French-language copy was created by a Quebec advertising agency, with the content loosely based on the finished English language promotional materials.

On March 18, pamphlets and window posters, together with application forms, were distributed to the Canbank branches nationwide — in plenty of time to be in place for the April 2 advertising campaign launching Canshare. Because of its high cost, television advertising was not used. Instead, media advertising was concentrated on newspaper ads in every major city in Canada. The campaign theme was "Making Your Own Decisions." This was to be followed up with inserts in all account statements mailed during the month of April, and using the same theme. By that time, Canbank had invested $700 000 in the new product.

On April 15, Arnie, feeling like a proud new father, went to Canbank's main branch in Toronto to see first-hand how his "baby" was doing. From the street he felt his first surge of joy. The Canshare poster was displayed in a prominent window position. But his pleasure quickly dissolved when he stepped inside the branch. On checking the literature display he could find no Canshare brochures. Recognizing that the branch's supply of brochures could not possibly be exhausted so soon, even if the product were an instant success, Arnie asked the branch manager where they were.

The branch manager didn't know. Indeed it took him a full five minutes to find them, still sealed in their shipping package. When Arnie asked him why they weren't on display with the bank's other brochures, the manager said, "I was hoping that no one would ask me about Canshare."

After a few short, sharp words with the manager, Arnie stormed out and began checking Toronto's other Canbank branches. To his mounting annoyance he discovered that not one of the branches had Canshare brochures displayed on their information

SOURCE    Dr. Peter M. Banting, McMaster University, Hamilton, Ontario (December 1990).

racks and only a few had display posters in their windows.

That night at the dinner table Arnie related the day's events to his wife. "I honestly believe that the competition from Canbank's own products is worse than the competition Canshare faces from the discount brokerage services of the other banks," Arnie concluded.

## Discussion Questions

1. What corrective measures should Arnie take to "save" Canshare?
2. Outline, step by step, the strategy Arnie should follow for his next new product, to avoid repetition of the problem encountered by Canshare.

# CASE 3

# Gillette

When many people think of marketing they automatically think in terms of the Western world market. But one company — Gillette — has tailored a good deal of its marketing to Third World countries. More than half of all Gillette's sales come from abroad. The company's investment in the Third World has paid off. Since 1969 the proportion of its total sales coming from Africa, Asia, Latin America, and the Middle East has doubled and the dollar volume has increased sevenfold. In that year Gillette first allowed subsidiaries in which the company did not have 100 percent ownership to use their trademarks — the Gillette and Papermate names. The policy was changed largely because Gillette realized it lost precious advertising — for example, on stadium walls when it sponsored televised World Cup soccer matches. And since 1969 the company has built one foreign plant a year in countries such as China, Thailand, Egypt, and India.

In developing countries Gillette first opens a plant that produces razor blades — usually double-edged, which are still popular in the Third World. If these sell well, the company later introduces its shampoos, toothbrushes, pens, and deodorants. Gillette has also introduced products specially designed for Third World consumers, such as Black Silk, a hair relaxer developed for blacks in South Africa and Kenya. But despite Gillette's efforts to diversify its product line, the company's razor blades still provide a third of its revenue and two-thirds of its pretax profit.

Often Gillette sells its regular line of products but packages them differently, mostly because of the financial condition of Third World consumers. For instance, in Latin America Gillette sells Silkience shampoo in half-ounce plastic bubbles because consumers there cannot afford seven-ounce bottles. In Mexico Gillette markets plastic tubs of shaving cream that sell for half the price of the same product sold in North America in aerosol cans. Similarly, in Brazil Gillette sells deodorant in plastic squeeze bottles because they are cheaper than aerosols.

The more complicated problem is to convince Third World men who might not do so otherwise to shave regularly. Gillette sends portable theatres to villages to show movies and commercials that promote daily shaving. In one, made for a Mexican market, a handsome sheriff chases bandits who have kidnapped a woman. The sheriff stops to shave every day on the trail. He gets the woman. At such demonstrations, or in actual shaving demonstrations, free razors are then given to men. The razor blades, of course, must be bought from store owners.

While these tactics may not gain large numbers of converts immediately, the increasing migration of peasants to cities may. In the fields peasants have little reason to shave. Working in an office in the city they do.

## Discussion Questions

1. Why, in your opinion, do Gillette marketers choose to develop a specific marketing strategy for different international markets? What are the disadvantages of a tailored approach such as that used by Gillette?
2. Recommend methods by which Gillette marketers might use the opinion-leader concept in their international marketing efforts.
3. Is reference-group influence important in the purchase of Gillette products? Defend your answer.

SOURCE    David Wessel, "Gillette Keys Sales to Third World Tastes," *The Wall Street Journal* (January 23, 1986), p. 35.

# CASE 4

## Sports Equipment Limited

Sports Equipment Limited has been formed recently as a wholly owned subsidiary of General Chemical Co. General Chemical is a major producer of chemicals, plastics, and textiles. In recent years the chief executive officer of General Chemical has been very keen to enter the consumer leisure market. As a major shareholder he has met with little resistance to his ideas. Rather than developing its own manufacturing facilities, General Chemical has, in the past 10 months, been quietly buying companies engaged in manufacturing sporting goods equipment in Canada. Most, but not all, of these companies produced better quality items but had suffered from poor marketing. After reorganization, General Chemical wants each company to operate autonomously in terms of production. Sports Equipment Limited has been given the responsibility of marketing and distributing the products across Canada. All products are manufactured in Ontario and are sent to Sports Equipment's distribution warehousing facilities in Mississauga, Ontario. Sports Equipment is well financed and organized but is unfamiliar with marketing these products. It has no existing sales force.

### Product Line Description

**Racquets — Classique Racquets**   A fairly complete medium-to-high-price line of tennis, squash, and racquet ball racquets, with no products at the low-priced end of the market.

**Backpacking Equipment — Back Country**   A full line of internal and external frame bags, including a line of day packs, specialty packs (bicycle panniers, soft camera packs, racquet sport bags, etc.), expedition-sized packs, and medium-sized packs. All these products are of superior quality and appeal to the more serious backpacker/hiker. They are priced accordingly.

**Nordic Skiing Equipment — Les Skis du Nord**   A limited line of skis, poles, and boots. The skis are available in wood, fibreglass wrap, and foam core, generally targeted toward the mid-price-range buyer with little appeal to the serious or competitive cross country skier.

**Cycling Accessories — Spoke**   A very high-quality line of cycling skirts, moleskin-lined pants, gloves, pannier packs, helmets, pumps, water bottles, etc., aimed at the more serious cycling enthusiast. The line does not include bicycles.

**Freeze-Dried Foods — Nutri-lite**   A very complete line of freeze-dried foods including meats, vegetables, stews, omelettes, desserts, etc., competitively priced with other manufacturers.

**Fishing Lures — Catch-all**   A full line of fishing accessories including lines, lures, hooks, sinkers, tackle boxes, bait buckets, etc., with a very general appeal. The line does not include rods or reels.

**Hiking Boots — Country Stride**   A limited line of hiking boots directed toward the casual hiker and those who purchase the product because of current fashion trends. Serious backpackers and hikers tend to purchase better quality boots. In the past six months they have developed a new ultralight hiking boot that has been rated as a good-quality boot at an attractive price by a sports magazine. The ultralight boot market is viewed by experts as the future for hiking boots.

When Alice Navarre, Sports Equipment's marketing manager, examined the sales records for these companies, she felt that inadequate channels of distribution were a major problem. She feels that these channels will most likely vary from region to region and will certainly vary according to the line, although certain product lines may be logically grouped. A multichannel approach may be adopted in order to serve all types of retailer.

She decides that a logical process is to first determine the market segment(s) she is trying to reach and the type and intensity of retail distribution she desires, and then work backwards. Obviously, not all products will be distributed to all regions of Canada.

SOURCE   T. Goddard, Conestoga College, Kitchener, Ontario.

Her preliminary research indicates that many retail sporting goods stores are becoming more specialized in specific sports and activities.

## Discussion Questions

1. How would you advise Alice Navarre? Examine the advantages and disadvantages of various channels of distribution.

2. What physical distribution system would you expect Sports Equipment to use? Prepare a map showing the location and area covered for all wholesalers, sales brochures, and/or warehouses. (In preparing your answer, use available secondary data from the library or other sources.)

## CASE 5

# Retail Grocery Prices

In a recent year, the regular sample food basket calculation compiled by Agriculture Canada showed the cross-country prices shown here. Note the range of prices across the country. Note also the sharp drop in prices from November to December in Calgary. As well, observe the differences between months.

SOURCE    Dave Hynes, *Calgary Herald*, (January 18, 1989).

## Discussion Question

1. Discuss the possible reasons for these price differences.

**Food Costs: Average Weekly Cost of a Nutritious Food Basket for a Family of Four**

|  | December | November |
|---|---|---|
| Toronto | $115.90 | $115.43 |
| Montreal | $112.74 | $111.81 |
| Quebec City | $112.29 | $111.29 |
| Thunder Bay | $111.65 | $111.73 |
| Victoria | $111.53 | $110.22 |
| Saint John | $109.28 | $109.45 |
| St. John's | $108.76 | $109.05 |
| Edmonton | $108.67 | $108.04 |
| Vancouver | $108.06 | $107.23 |
| Charlottetown | $107.35 | $106.68 |
| Ottawa | $107.14 | $106.05 |
| Halifax | $104.85 | $106.18 |
| Regina | $103.74 | $103.75 |
| Saskatoon | $101.52 | $101.50 |
| Calgary | $100.53 | $106.42 |
| Winnipeg | $100.20 | $ 98.78 |

Source: Herald Graphic

# CASE 6

# Holt Renfrew and Co. Ltd.

Holt Renfrew and Co. Ltd., the venerable *grande dame* of Canada's retail carriage trade, is expanding its markets beyond its long-established well-heeled clientele.

While Holt is reluctant to relinquish its reputation as a store for the affluent, demographics are creating a rapidly expanding 25-to-45 age bracket that has money to spend and a desire for quality merchandise. The increase in the number of working women has given rise to a large market which Holt wants to tap by providing a wider range of medium-priced merchandise.

Company chairman Lenard Shavick and newly-appointed president Robert Herber hope to double the company's sales within five years. Holt, owned since 1972 by Carter Hawley Hale Stores, Inc., of Los Angeles, keeps its sales and profit figures a closely guarded secret, but Shavick said recently that the five-year sales goal for the company's 18 stores is $100 million. That is about double present volume.

Other merchandisers, from small high-fashion boutiques to major department store chains like The Bay and Eaton's will be watching Holt's moves closely. If Holt increases its market share it will likely be at the expense of other retailers as the selling environment of the 1980s becomes increasingly competitive.

Attempts to broaden its customer base are only one facet of Holt's new growth strategy. The company has also moved its buying, marketing, and merchandising staff from Montreal to Toronto. Moreover, senior personnel ranks have received an influx of fresh blood, with four of the seven occupants of the executive suite hired from outside the company in the past two years.

Shavick contends the result is a powerful new team. "It's very important to have the stars, and we do now," he declares. Shavick, who joined the company in 1946 and rose to the position of president and chief executive officer in 1968, has now become the company chairman. Often accused in the past of running a one-man show, he appears to have con-

verted recently to a more flexible team-oriented management style.

Herber, who joined Holt less than a year ago as executive vice-president after eight years with Hudson's Bay Co. and 16 years with Greatermans' Department Stores of South Africa prior to that, is obviously one of Shavick's "stars." Herber will be based in Toronto, while Shavick and the financial, administrative, and personnel departments will remain in Montreal.

"Toronto is the site of our flagship store and the city with the greatest growth opportunities," says an enthusiastic Herber. "We are looking to expand in the west, and Toronto is the logical base. It's a young city, a cosmopolitan city, and it's full of the kind of people who want to shop at Holt's."

The main Toronto store contributed 22 percent of the company's total sales last year while the downtown Montreal store contributed 19 percent. In addition, Holt's studies show the market of households with annual incomes in excess of $40 000 is 39 percent bigger in Toronto than in Montreal. Within three years the spread is expected to reach 45 percent.

A recent company survey in its Ottawa, Vancouver, and Toronto stores found that 75 percent of Holt's shoppers were working, 76 percent had some college or university education, and 60 percent owned their own house or condominium. The median age was 35 and 85 percent were female. "We are after the market which is well-educated, aware, and prepared to spend money on themselves — the movers and shakers," says Herber.

In broadening its appeal, Holt will concentrate on beefing up merchandise areas such as accessories, women's office wear, and casual clothes for men to augment its suit selection.

But Holt's move to diversify out of an upper-crust market is seen by some observers as a sign that things have not been going as well as they could be in recent years. Specialty boutiques selling exclusive labels are aggressively competing for their share of the high-fashion business, and because of their concentration on a narrower range of merchandise they can often provide greater depth and more personalized service.

---

SOURCE    Adapted from "Holt Woos Shoppers from Both Sides of the Track," *Financial Times* (July 9, 1981).

To counteract this problem, Holt is experimenting with a program of clientele development by initiating contact with customers by telephone or letter, letting them know when merchandise in which they are interested has arrived. Sales personnel will also provide the service of keeping a record of customers' sizes and colour and fashion preferences.

"We want to be different from the department stores," says Herber. "Instead of just standing behind a counter and saying 'may I help you?' we want to provide more personalized service."

## Discussion Question

1. Evaluate the plans to respond to the changing competition and the changing demographic profile of the market.

# CASE 7

# Detyzco, Inc.

"Pet 88 is a nutritionally balanced, frozen dessert for your dog — fortified with vitamins and minerals. Your dog will love it!" are the words used on the package to describe Detyzco's new product aimed at dog lovers. The firm has achieved selected distribution in southwestern Ontario for its products and would like to attain national market coverage.

## Product Development

About three years ago, Peter DeMarco, a poultry science student working at a pet store, casually asked his employer, "Why isn't there a good nutritional ice cream for dogs?" C. Dale Cook, owner of the Pet Palace, responded that he did not know why, but thought that such an idea might be "just crazy enough to sell." With some interest and mostly curiosity they asked William Tyznik, a recognized animal nutritionist at a local university, about the possibility of such a product.

After many trials and experiments over a period of nine months, Tyznik, working with DeMarco, came up with the basic formula at the laboratory level. Cook, who had formerly worked with a major contract research organization, began to get more involved with the process with the objective of taking the product from the laboratory to the marketplace.

The product was tested and retested on dozens of dogs during most of 1986. It was then necessary to develop the production capability to manufacture and package such a product. In 1987, a patent was sought for the product and later that year the product was introduced in the market. The three men involved formed Detyzco, a solely owned corporation, to manufacture and market the product. Their joint resources amounted to a modest $75 000.

## Product Description

Pet 88 Frozen Dog Dessert is packaged in a six-serving carton. Each individual serving is in a four-ounce plastic cup. The product can be served to dogs in its frozen state or thawed in the refrigerator and served as a creamy pudding. Additional information about the product is provided in Figure C7–1, which shows a handout given to potential customers in supermarkets.

## Pricing

The product is currently retail priced at $1.39 per six-pack carton. At this price retailers have a margin of about 25 to 30 percent. Food distributors receive a markup of 15 percent for handling the product from Detyzco to the retailer.

## Promotion

To introduce Pet 88 Frozen Dog Dessert to the market, Detyzco produced a 30-second television advertisement. A brief description of this advertisement is given in Figure C7–2.

A "new business package" consisting of forty 30-second spots and costing a total of $2000 was purchased from a major metropolitan television station. These advertisements were "run of schedule," meaning that the station could fit them into its schedule throughout the broadcasting day as space was available.

The primary purpose of this series of advertisements was to provide credibility to the company and its product in order to help convince retailers to carry the product. It was hoped that customers would ask retailers for the product if it was not on display.

Detyzco also developed a point-of-purchase poster for the product along with a counter card to help promote the product. The same graphic logo was used in all promotional materials, including packaging, to provide continuity to the product presentation.

After initial distribution was achieved, the firm utilized a few radio commercials (following the same general theme of the television advertisements). Copy for these radio commercials was read live by the announcers in an attempt to achieve an individual touch with more spontaneity. Sales for the first quarter amounted to $18 000.

SOURCE    From W. Wayne Talarzyk, ed., *Cases for Analysis in Marketing*, 3rd ed., pp. 19–22. Copyright 1985, CBS College Publishing. Reprinted by permission of CBS College Publishing.

FIGURE C7-1

**Descriptive Product Leaflet**

### Pet 88 Frozen Dog Dessert

Doesn't your dog deserve dessert? Won't you feel better giving "man's best friend" — and yours — a treat that is actually *good* for him?

PET 88 FROZEN DOG DESSERT is a nutritionally complete, well-balanced food made with only the highest quality proteins and with vitamins and minerals added. And it contains *absolutely no sugar*.

PET 88 FROZEN DOG DESSERT can be fed like ice cream or it can be thawed in the refrigerator and spooned over dry dog food. And it can be refrozen for your convenience.

Can't you just imagine how pleased your pet will be to have a change of taste in its diet after eating the same thing meal after meal?

Feed PET 88 FROZEN DOG DESSERT with the confidence that you're feeding the *best*! and have fun watching your pet truly enjoy a *real dessert treat*!

FIGURE C7-2

**Introductory Television Advertisement**

| Video | Audio |
| --- | --- |
| Full head shot of dog | Pet 88 is the newest in dog desserts. It's frozen! |
| Full screen of both packages | Now for the first time you can reward your dog with a tasty dessert that's good for him and absolutely unique. It's frozen! |
| Zoom in on one package with (6) six desserts | Pet 88 is a healthful, nutritious dessert that can be stored easily in your freezer. |
| Model spooning dessert — dog eating dessert | When your dog is ready for this tasty treat, just spoon it into his bowl or serve it over his favourite dry dog food. |
| Full screen of package | So ask your grocer or pet store for Pet 88 — or call 1-800-279-3922. |
| Superimposed phone number | Because doesn't your dog deserve dessert today! |

## Discussion Questions

1. What are the best ways to expand distribution of the product?
2. How should the product be promoted (i.e., types of advertisements and sales promotions)?
3. Where in the store should the product be displayed — in the frozen-food section, with ice cream, or in a separate area?
4. Should the product line be expanded? If so, how?
5. How would it be possible to keep people from opening the packages to see what is inside?
6. Toward what market target should the product be aimed?
7. Should any marketing research be conducted? If so, what type?

## CASE 8

# Active Detergent

Will the public purchase a quality product whose manufacturer doesn't advertise and instead passes the savings on to the consumer? Witco Chemical Corporation looked at the detergent market, which is a mature market, and decided that since a substantial market segment is averse to detergent advertising, it would be willing to choose an unadvertised quality product if it was cheaper.

So far the answer is "no" for Active, a laundry detergent billed by its maker as a consumer's dream product. However, Witco Chemical Corporation's Ultra division has given itself two years to find out if the faith in consumer buying sharpness will pay off through more active Active sales.

Active's makers like to point out that it:

- is the only unadvertised manufacturer's brand on the market, according to company officials;
- was judged equal in quality to leading brand-name detergents in two independently conducted tests;
- sells for at least 20 cents less per package than the leading brands.

The detergent market is dominated by three large manufacturers: Procter & Gamble, Lever Brothers, and Colgate-Palmolive. Each of these companies has several individual brands, each aimed at a different market segment. All brands are supported by very large advertising campaigns.

Up to now, sales of Active aren't promising. Although Rusi Patell, the division's consumer products manager, estimates that sales so far have been 80 percent of what was first anticipated, others aren't so optimistic.

"Sales are really bad," laments product sales manager James Pifer of the food brokerage firm that sells Active to both wholesale and chain supermarkets. "The product itself has real potential, but the idea of not advertising isn't good. Since they don't advertise, they can't get it across to the consumer that Active is real savings," Mr. Pifer argues.

But Witco's net sales for all products were up 50 percent last year. A manufacturer and marketer of a wide range of specialty chemical and petroleum products for industrial and consumer use, Witco doesn't hinge its future on the failure or success of Active. As a result, the company can afford to give the no-advertising approach plenty of time to catch on.

Although Active isn't advertised in the traditional sense, Witco gets its message across with a combination of supermarket appearances and television interviews by the company's consumer economist, Audrey Clifford. Also, the company president and other company officials plan to make speeches to women's and other consumer groups. In addition, newspaper articles are being sought in public relations campaigns.

Despite Active's less-than-encouraging track record at the moment, Witco representatives have no plans to stray from their no-advertising policy, and eventually expect to introduce the product nationally.

The only exception to the no-advertising policy will be some limited advertising to retailers in trade journals in order to acquaint them with the product, Active's strategy, and the additional margins that retailers would make on it.

Witco's approach hinges on the intelligent consumer — the buyer who reads labels, compares prices, and decides accordingly. "Our product originates from a consumer need. The time is right for a consumer approach because the days are gone when people would unconsciously pick things up and buy them without reading the packages and comparing prices," a company representative said.

Others, though, don't give shoppers so much credit. "I just don't think consumers are going to spend enough time to do their own research on any product. They're too used to being sold on something and that is the only way they react," contends Neil Engstrom, a buyer for a supermarket chain. "Active sales have been going poorly; homemakers are strongly loyal to national brands, and the competition in this area is tough. If you want to sell your product, you must fight fire with fire and advertise."

---

SOURCE    Adapted from William A. Babcock, *The Winnipeg Free Press* (August 28, 1975).

## Discussion Questions

1. What are the main features of Witco's marketing mix for Active?

2. What else could Witco do to make its "no-advertising" marketing program more effective?

3. Will Active appeal to a significant segment of consumers?

# CASE 9

# Tech Feeds Corporation

Mike Howard slowly hung up the phone. That was the call he hadn't been waiting for. He knew he had a decision to make, and he also knew that he didn't want to make it.

Earlier in the year, Tech Feeds Corporation (TFC) had signed a contract to act as general contractor to establish a feed mill in Guangdong Province, China. The project had barely gotten under way when it was quickly halted due to the massacre of pro-democracy students in Tiananmen Square, Beijing. Mike had just spoken to a Chinese official from the agriculture ministry (through an interpreter); the ministry requested that TFC return to Guangdong to complete the project. "It is business as usual," claimed the official. Mike felt somewhat differently.

This particular official was new to Mike. When Mike asked about the whereabouts of the two Chinese officials previously responsible for the project, he was told that they had been reassigned. Mike was depressed. He trusted both officials and wished he could have talked to them instead.

## Company Background

The company was established as the Saskatoon Feed Company on June 1, 1936, by the late R.F. "Bob" Cummings. The company was incorporated in 1966 and the name changed to Tech Feeds Corporation. It was felt the new name better reflected how "scientific" the animal feed industry had become. As well, major expansion was planned and a generic business name would be more appropriate.

Mike Howard and his wife had purchased the company from the Cummings family in 1965. Mike owned 51 percent of the outstanding common shares. His wife, Judith, owned an additional 10 percent of the company. The remainder of the shares were sold off over the years to finance expansion. There were now 44 shareholders in total.

SOURCE    This case was prepared by Carter Berezay, MBA, under the supervision of Dr. M. Dale Beckman, as a basis for class discussion rather than to illustrate either effective or ineffective handling of an administrative situation. Where required, names of individuals and certain financial data have been disguised. The funding support of the Centre for International Business Studies, University of Manitoba, is gratefully acknowledged.

In 1965, a new plant was opened at Prince Albert, Saskatchewan, and in 1975 new facilities were opened at Red Deer, Alberta. By 1977, the Saskatoon plant needed upgrading. Construction of new facilities was started and, by 1981, the new plant was in full operation and the old one shut down. Two existing feed plants were purchased in 1978: one in Brandon, Manitoba, and a second in Humboldt, Saskatchewan.

Further expansion took place in 1984, with the construction of a new electronically controlled feed plant at Linden, Alberta. In that same year two new premix plants were built. The larger one, in Saskatoon (with 10 000 tonnes capacity), served the Saskatchewan, Manitoba, and northern U.S. markets. The second premix plant, at Lethbridge, Alberta (with 5 000 tonnes capacity), served the large Alberta market.

In 1986, TFC expanded and adopted a new concept at four prairie locations: Peace River and Drumheller, Alberta, and Kindersley and Melfort, Saskatchewan. Each of these feed plants uses state-of-the-art production equipment. All phases of production are electronically controlled from a centralized computer control room. As well, each plant has a fully integrated management information system that can be accessed at any time from head office in Saskatoon. The entire system was custom designed, developed, and implemented by TFC personnel. An estimated 14 person-years of development went into this effort. In future, as each mill is modernized or a new one built, the custom control/MIS system will be integrated into the plant.

Expansion has not been limited to facilities alone. Specialty feeds, pet foods, liquid supplements, and feed molasses supplement blocks have expanded the company's market. These products are sold all across Canada and some are exported to various northern states.

Sales in 1988 topped $28 000 000. After-tax profits were approximately 1.3 percent of gross sales. This marginal profitability was caused in large part by poor economic conditions in the agriculture industry. Stiff competition had made margins razor-thin in the agrifeed industry. Profitability projections for 1989 did not look much better.

## China (1975–1988)

In the mid-1970s the Chinese government officially recognized that the country was falling behind virtually all economies in the world. Economic development became the government's focus. Self-sufficiency was the stated goal. Agriculture, communications, and energy were designated as priorities.

Chinese entrepreneurs were given the opportunity to start ventures that were profit-driven. Economic incentives were provided in the form of loans aimed at stimulating development. Successful entrepreneurs were given special status. They were officially recognized for their efforts. The result was significant development of efficiently run businesses, as the owners were permitted to keep some of the profits for themselves. Improvements continued, spurred on by more and more entrepreneurs starting and expanding businesses in just about every type of industry. Productivity in privately owned businesses was found to be up to 10 times greater than in similar state-run factories and shops.

The Chinese government also recognized that in order to become self-sufficient China would also need newer technology. To speed the acquisition process, China developed a more open-door policy to foreign companies. Joint-venture projects were initiated: these projects were normally majority-owned by the Chinese. China's growing 1.1 billion population was a magnet for many foreign companies. Due to bureaucratic red tape, the process was agonizingly slow. In spite of this, dozens of joint-venture projects were initiated. For example, IBM, Xerox, Chrysler, Peugot, and Volkswagen AG each invested vast amounts of capital into such projects. They also provided the technology to open modern production plants.

By 1988 China's economic development was rapidly increasing. There was some concern by government officials that their open-door policy would lead to a pro-democracy movement by the Chinese people once they were exposed to foreign capitalist societies. In general, the Chinese government apparently believed it could achieve economic change without political change. The government had clearly been wrong.

## TFC in China

Mike first visited China in 1980, as part of a trade mission led by Canada's major grain companies (who were trying to sell more wheat to China). Because of his related feed business, Mike had been invited along by the Canadian government, which would pay all expenses for the 10-day trip. Although he didn't feel TFC would gain much, Mike had nevertheless decided to go.

At first, he was glad he did. Agriculture development was definitely a "hot button" for the Chinese. Over the next five years Mike returned to China six times to develop contacts. Stan Fong, a PhD graduate from the University of Saskatoon, had been instrumental in helping Mike. Stan said he owed a lot to Saskatchewan, and offered to serve as interpreter on most visits. Mike knew he would have gotten nowhere without him. Stan and his father were extremely well connected in the Chinese government. They controlled several toy and computer factories in Shanghai. Their exports provided much-needed foreign currency for the government.

The Chinese were very interested in TFC's production technology. They had sent four different delegations to visit TFC's modern plants in Canada.

In late 1985, TFC shipped 25 tonnes of hog feed to China for a feed trial. The hogs that were fed the TFC ration gained weight an average of 36 percent faster than those fed regular rations. The Chinese were very impressed. Mike knew it was not only the feed that had produced the dramatic gains. The feeding methods and penning techniques had also been improved. But he didn't bother to tell the Chinese that.

In early 1986 TFC began shipping small volumes of premixes (nutrient concentrates to be mixed with grains to make a ration) to China. It was the fastest way to improve productivity.

In July 1986 TFC was invited to submit a proposal to design, develop, and implement a new feed mill in Guangdong Province. TFC responded with a different idea: rather than send feed all over the province, why not build a premix plant? The premix would be distributed and used with local grains (e.g., corn, soybeans) to provide animal rations. The Chinese accepted TFC's advice: in December a contract to develop a premix plant was signed.

The Chinese government was responsible for plant construction and acquiring all of the equipment. TFC's contract price was $1.3 million. Tech Feeds was to supply technical personnel to oversee all aspects of construction, setup, and ongoing support until the Chinese could operate the plant themselves.

TFC supplied all the software programs to run the plant, including machine control, premix formulation, and management programs. The company had already developed 90 percent of the software for its own premix plants in Canada. With appropriate development and modifications, the entire system was transplanted to the Chinese project.

Tech Feeds sent a total of seven technical personnel to work on the various phases of the plant's development. Two were construction experts: the remaining five were system software specialists.

The plant became fully operational in September 1988, after only a few minor startup problems. On December 7, TFC received the final 10 percent "holdback" payment from the Chinese government.

While the seven specialists were in China, they had taken the opportunity to hold further discussions regarding the construction of feed mills. They learned that the Chinese had a long-term plan to erect five mid-size (50 000 tonne/annum capacity) feed mills in the southern provinces, where livestock production was concentrated. The first plant was scheduled to begin operating in late 1990 or early 1991. The remaining four would be constructed over a five-year period from 1991 through 1995.

TFC personnel had worked closely with the Chinese officials in developing the detailed specifications required for the tendering process. Approximately 34 person-weeks had been spent on this effort at no charge to the Chinese.

The tender for the first feed mill was released on June 6, 1988. Requests for Proposals (RFPs) were sent to eight potential bidders — two Canadian, four American, and two Australian companies or consortiums. The deadline for submission was November 1, 1988. The results: two firms placed no bid, while three of the other submissions did not meet specifications (mainly in the area of software). TFC was short-listed, along with two American consortiums. TFC had submitted the lowest bid — the others were higher by 5 percent and 18 percent, respectively — and was subsequently awarded the contract on January 6, 1989. TFC celebrated its success by having a dinner party for all head-office staff.

The planned schedule was as follows:

Construction Phase: Start: April 3, 1989
End: August 31, 1990

Implementation Phase: Start: July 3, 1989
End: November 30, 1990

Startup Phase: Start: December 3, 1990
End: May 31, 1991

TFC estimated that the project would require 80 person-years of effort. The firm's fee was $1.6 million in total. Included in this amount was the sourcing of all mill equipment: due to sourcing problems encountered with the premix plant, the Chinese required the general contractor to procure all necessary equipment. TFC estimated that landed equipment costs would total $5.9 million. Approximately 75 percent of the machinery would be manufactured in Canada.

TFC's two construction specialists arrived in China on March 24, 1989, to prepare for the startup of the plant construction phase. They had worked only a few short weeks when the violence erupted. Although they were 200 miles from Beijing, they were advised to get out of the country as quickly as possible. They arrived home safely on June 10, 1989.

## Massacre in Beijing

Mike had closely followed the historic events that were happening in China throughout 1989. He pulled out a thick file of information he had gathered since April. Now was a good time to review it. A July 10, 1989, article in *Maclean's* magazine summarized the horror that had occurred in Beijing.

### CHRONOLOGY

15 April 1989, 7:35 AM: Hu Yaobang, Politburo member and former general secretary of the Communist Party of China, dies of a heart attack at age 73.

18 April, 2:00 AM: Four thousand Beijing and People's University students march to Tiananmen Square to place banner calling Hu the "Soul of China" on Monument to the Revolutionary Martyrs.

22 April, 8:30 AM: Fifty thousand students defy government order and stay overnight in Tiananmen Square for Hu's state funeral.

24 April: Tens of thousands of students in Beijing begin class boycott to press home demands for talks with government.

25 April and 26 April: Chinese Television, then the People's Daily, label unrest as conspiracy to negate Communist Party leadership.

27 April: 150 000 students march through streets of Beijing in protest against editorials. Half a million

people line the streets to cheer them on. The government agrees to talks.

4 May: After a week of inconclusive discussions, students hold another big demonstration to mark anniversary of 4 May Movement of 1919. Communist Party boss Zhao Ziyang says government is willing to meet with all sectors of society.

10 May: More than one thousand journalists demand talks to discuss freedom. Students protest against censorship.

13 May, 5:20 PM: Several hundred students begin hunger strike in Tiananmen Square to demand televised talks with government and retraction of People's Daily editorial.

15 May, noon: Soviet leader Mikhail Gorbachev arrives in Beijing for first Sino-Soviet summit in 30 years. Hunger strikers refuse to clear Tiananmen Square. Numbers grow to three thousand.

17 May: A million people march through Beijing in support of hunger strike. Disturbances throughout rest of country.

18 May, noon: Premier Li Peng meets with student leaders to demand they end strike. They tell him they cannot control situation.

19 May, 4:30 AM: Zhao and Li meet hunger strikers in square, but students stay put. Later that day, a riot occurs in remote city of Urumqi.

20 May, midnight: Li calls in army to end chaos. Students end hunger strike but vow to hold Tiananmen. Troops stopped by unarmed civilians. 10:00 AM: Li declares martial law over parts of Beijing.

23 May: A million people march to demand Li resign and martial law be withdrawn. Most soldiers return to bases on outskirts of city.

2 June: Mostly unarmed troops begin to move on Tiananmen Square again. People block them again.

3 June, 2:00 PM: Demonstrators clash with soldiers near Tiananmen Square. Troop convoys begin moving into city. Most blocked. 11:00 PM: Soldiers begin firing on people at Muxidi in west Beijing.

4 June, 2:00 AM: After hours of bloody fighting, soldiers reach Tiananmen Square. 4:00 AM: Students forced to leave, army retakes square. Killing continues for next few days.

Mike pulled out another article, which had been published in the *Globe and Mail* of August 9, 1989. It indicated that the massacre in Beijing was unplanned.

The Tiananmen Square massacre in June was the result of a last-minute decision by a misinformed army and a frightened leadership in the midst of a power struggle, Chinese and Western sources say.

The slaughter of hundreds, perhaps thousands, of reform-seeking demonstrators stunned people in China and the rest of the world. At the time, the massacre seemed inexplicable.

But information pieced together during the past two months from interviews with dozens of witnesses, Chinese military sources, and Western diplomats sheds new light on the events of June 3–4.

Stunning as it seems, the massacre appears to have been unplanned. Chinese sources say that, until minutes before the shooting started on the night of June 3, soldiers were under explicit orders not to fire.

The emerging picture is that the demonstrators were pawns. The massacre was a blunder by the conservative old guard as they moved in immense firepower, including hundreds of tanks and ground-to-air missiles, to depose Communist Party chief Zhao Ziyang's reformist faction. The situation quickly deteriorated because the soldiers were trained for the battlefield, not riot control in a heavily populated city. Both Chinese and Western sources say the troop movements brought China to the brink of civil war.

To be sure, there is no sign that paramount leader Deng Ziaoping regrets the massacre. But the last-minute nature of the decision helps explain why the Chinese themselves were so unprepared.

They permitted foreign journalists to witness the massacre, when they had time to expel them after martial law was first imposed.

Hospitals lacked blood for the wounded and ice for the bodies. Medical staff, even at military hospitals that treated injured soldiers, were called from their beds.

State television, then under military control, was caught without footage. For several days, mainly blank TV screens showed headlines.

Police lacked a coherent plan. They set up roadblocks late, did not issue a wanted list until 10 days after the assault, and did not tighten exit controls until June 20. By then, some dissidents had escaped.

The government was also unprepared for the foreign-policy shock. Diplomats could not reach Foreign Ministry officials for days. During the evacuation of foreigners, even pleas for gasoline went unheeded.

Mr. Deng said the government imposed martial law for its own survival. But as more details emerge, it appears the move was more an excuse to bring in troops to purge Mr. Zhao than a method to deal with the student-led protests.

The two men disagreed over the pace of China's economic reforms. They also disagreed over political reforms, especially those demanded by students.

Mike read one more article, this time from the *Globe and Mail's* September 21, 1989, issue. The World Bank had resumed loaning money to China.

The World Bank will resume making new loans to China in the near future after holding up $780 million (U.S.) in lending after the bloody crackdown on protesters, the bank's president says.

"There are 1.1 billion poor people in China and we don't want to give up contact with them," Barber Conable told reporters.

Mr. Conable held up seven loans after the Chinese crackdown against pro-democracy demonstrators in June but kept disbursing loans already granted. At an average of $2 billion a year, China is the bank's biggest borrower after India.

The annual meeting of representatives of the 152 governments that own the bank and the International Monetary Fund begins today.

China will be represented, and Mr. Conable said resumption of new lending will be among the subjects discussed.

Mr. Conable said the World Bank is not a political body and is analyzing the results of Chinese developments. He noted that its permanent staff in Beijing, withdrawn in June, has now returned.

He believes most of the member governments would like to see the new loans resumed, but prefer not to vote on the issue now.

Mr. Conable said 90 percent of the bank's lending goes to countries where the average earnings of a citizen are less than $400 a year. China receives 15 percent of its loans from the bank in this way.

The rest comes from the group's International Bank for Reconstruction and Development, which makes loans on terms close to those of commercial banks but for much longer periods.

"Who am I to judge?" Mike thought. The Canadian government had not imposed any sanctions against China. He felt he knew why: China was Canada's largest grain buyer next to Russia. Canada could scream and yell at South Africa for apartheid; economically, Canada had very little to lose there. But China was an entirely different story. For example, Northern Telecom had just sold China $100 million worth of communications equipment. The Chinese loan had recently been approved. "If we don't sell them the technology, someone else will" seemed to be the Canadian government's rationale.

"But what kind of government would murder its own people for whatever reason?" wondered Mike. "Who am I to judge?" he repeated to himself.

## Conclusion

Since the middle of June, Mike had kept his technical team busy internally supporting various projects plus generating bids on potential contracts.

While his team had been working in China, TFC had turned down the chance to bid on two feed-mill projects in Hungary. He certainly regretted that now.

In the last few months the company had responded to four RFPs — one each from Russia, Poland, Saudi Arabia, and Jordan. Final decisions for these contracts were to be made in January/February 1990. Mike believed TFC had about a 60 percent chance at winning the Russian contract (TFC was short-listed with one other firm). As for the rest, he felt that TFC's prospects of being awarded a given project were more like 25 percent.

Mike had heard rumours that two of his systems analysts were actively seeking new employment. They clearly suspected that layoffs were likely if new work could not be found soon. With their $50 000-plus salaries, TFC could not be expected to keep them around much longer. Mike did not want to lose any of his key project people; he had spent several years training and developing each of them.

To clarify his thoughts, Mike decided to list what would happen if TFC defaulted on the China contract.

1. Tech Feeds would never again be allowed to do business in China. But with so many people to feed, the country held incredible potential for firms like TFC.

2. Stan Fong would lose face. Mike had a loyalty to Stan, who was the reason TFC had gotten into China in the first place. Were TFC to walk away from the contract, Stan could suffer serious repercussions. At the very least, he stood to lose a lot of credibility with the Chinese bureaucrats.

3. Tech Feeds had not been paid for work done on the project to date. In July it had sent an invoice for a total of $84 400, broken down as follows:

Direct Labour (2 × 41 days × $800/day)
                                    $65 600.00
Direct Expenses (other than per diem)
                                    18 800.00
TOTAL                               $84 400.00

But TFC had never even gotten an acknowledgment that the invoice had been received, let alone a cheque! The Chinese official who had phoned earlier had intimated that payment would be made immediately once the project was under way again. From experience, Mike knew the Chinese were shrewd negotiators: he hadn't even bothered, therefore, to suggest that TFC preferred to be paid "up front" in this instance.

4. The Canadian equipment manufacturers would lose significant sales. Many of these manufacturers were Mike's close business associates.

5. TFC would lose a potential profit of $280 000 on the project — an excellent margin that was due to the firm's having helped write the tender specifications. The specs had been written to include much of the software Tech Feeds had already developed. It was hard to imagine being so fortunate in any future bids.

Mike sat back and thought hard. "TFC actually has relatively little to lose," he realized after reviewing his list. "Unlike the many joint-venture groups, Tech Feeds has no direct investment in China. We can still survive."

Today was Friday. At least he would have the weekend to mull things over. The Chinese official would be calling him on Monday evening.

Mike had Angela Barber, his secretary, arrange a meeting with his technical group for 8:00 AM Monday. At 10:00 he had called a management meeting. At noon a Board of Directors' meeting was scheduled. For each meeting at least the agenda was simple. He wanted to discuss TFC's return to China.

Mike knew that no matter what happened on Monday, the final decision was his. It was 5:50 PM and right now Mike Howard was very, very tired.

## Discussion Questions

1. Should a company's financial health take precedence over ethical issues?
2. What should Mike Howard do?

## CASE 10

# Sid's Sunflower Seeds (1974) Ltd.

## Introduction

Two years ago, Issy Steen, president and owner of Sid's Sunflower Seeds (Sid's) in Regina, Saskatchewan, received a phone call from Bart Lewis, who represented the Licensing Corporation of America (LCA). Steen, the caller asserted, had been granted exclusive rights to use the major-league baseball logo: his product was now the "official sunflower seed of Major League Baseball." Issy recalls that this welcome news elated him, yet he was cautious. The logo would certainly provide his organization with a tremendous opportunity to gain valuable exposure in what, for Sid's, were new markets. However, he had two concerns. First, the potentially rapid growth might put a strain on the firm's internal resources and ability to serve current markets. Second, he questioned his marketing abilities when it came to penetrating these new markets. Issy was nevertheless determined to capitalize, one way or another, on what he felt was a "once-in-a-lifetime opportunity." For two years, Issy wondered if he had made the most of the opportunity.

## Company History

Sid's Sunflower Seeds was founded in 1938 by Sid Bercovich. Bercovich established a small production line in his garage and an office in his house. He ran the business as a hobby and put little effort into growth and expansion. Yet by the end of 1973, gross sales revenues from his single product line had reached $300 000 annually. Market penetration, however, remained confined to Saskatchewan, as Bercovich had no desire to expand geographically.

In 1974, Issy Steen purchased Sid's from Bercovich. Steen did not make any changes to the production process that year; he wanted to learn more about the business before making any major decisions. In 1975, Steen purchased some production and packaging equipment in efforts to increase production efficiency. Production soon outpaced sales. Moreover, he was able to reduce his staff by more than half, thereby significantly increasing his margins. The next logical step for Sid's was to

SOURCE   C. Brooke Dobni, College of Commerce, University of Saskatchewan.

expand its market presence. This would mean going beyond Saskatchewan's borders for the first time in the company's history.

Throughout the late 1970s and the 1980s, Steen continued his process of production rationalization and geographic expansion. He also expanded the firm's product line to include pumpkin seeds and hulled sunflower seeds. Today, Sid's sells more sunflower seeds than any other company in Canada, employs 19 people, and boasts five seed roasters and an automated production process. Through brokers it has developed markets in the northwestern United States, Australia, Europe, the Pacific Rim, and Scandinavian countries. In 1989 alone, Sid's sold more than 3.2 million kilograms of sunflower seeds and exceeded $2.1 million in total sales revenues.

## Strategic Position

By 1989, Sid's had established itself as the number-one producer of sunflower seeds in Canada and the number-two producer overall in North America. The product/market strategy and competitive strategy that contributed to this status can be further outlined as follows:

1. *Product/Market Strategy*: Although Sid's sells a number of products, 85 percent of its revenues are generated from the sale of roasted and salted unhulled sunflower seeds. Steen's philosophy is to market product to "anybody, anywhere" — provided that a sufficient return can be made and that existing accounts are not jeopardized by the marketing efforts. He has categorized his target market as "anyone with teeth who can spit."

2. *Competitive Strategy*: Sid's has taken pride in being the top sunflower-seed producer in Canada. Steen credits this success partly to the firm's competitive strategy. It differentiates its product on the bases of quality, freshness, and superior packaging. Sid's offers a product that is less salty than that of the competition, presenting it as a nut rather than as a seed. At the wholesale and retail level, the emphasis is on distribution and customer service. At the consumer level, Sid's relies on product recognition and brand loyalty for repeat purchases.

But Steen also attributes his company's success to what he calls "sensible and intelligent marketing techniques" — doing the right thing at the right time at the right place. Since the firm must market to wholesalers, retailers, and consumers, a co-ordinated effort is required in order to minimize overlap. Lastly, Sid's prides itself on being able to deliver product on time and in the amounts ordered.

## Operations

Sid's can be classified as a stage-one organization — its operations were characterized by hands-on management. Issy Steen attempted to divide his time between managing the firm and developing new markets. Aaron Steen, Issy's younger brother and the company's sales manager, concentrated on servicing existing accounts and further developing markets in territories where Sid's was already established.

The Sid's management group worked informally, with a minimum of structure and control. The team did what had to be done, often covering for one another. In fact, it was not an unusual sight to see Issy or Aaron Steen load a last-minute order for shipment. All the managers were pressed by the requirements of everyday business. Priority was given to "putting out fires," which often preoccupied a manager's entire day. The installation of an information system in late 1986 had helped smooth out operations, particularly since the plant and the head office in Regina had been separated.

*Marketing* Marketing duties were logically divided between Issy and Aaron Steen. Product-line marketing and maintaining current accounts were Aaron's responsibilities. Aaron also pursued the development of new accounts in existing areas as opportunities presented themselves. Issy concentrated on identifying and developing growth opportunities in new markets.

Up to 1990, Issy had single-handedly developed all export markets and identified other feasible growth opportunities. The development of new markets had always preoccupied Steen. Because theirs was a relatively small company, they had a limited budget to spend on marketing. Sid's thus had to be very selective in its marketing thrusts.

Sid's employed eight sales representatives; all were located in western Canada, and all reported to the sales manager. The reps were paid a wage plus commission, giving them incentive to develop new accounts in their respective territories. Recently, business development in western Canada had been slowing. It appeared that the market was approaching saturation.

*Promotion* Although Sid's had not developed an explicit marketing plan, the company spent approximately 10 percent of its annual revenues on advertising and promotion. At the retail level, campaigns were often aimed at encouraging potential customers to associate eating seeds with their favourite outdoor activities. Other promotion activities included sunflower-seed giveaways, joint promotions with other products such as Coca-Cola, contests, couponing, static displays, and ads in printed and radio media. Sid's also sponsored a number of sporting events and teams, such as Little-League baseball tournaments and baseball teams. Many of these activities were done on a test basis and therefore carried a high price tag. After the completion of a campaign, the management team would sit down and attempt to quantify the costs and the benefits.

*Distribution* Sid's emphasized getting the product to the customer on time, in the quantities ordered, and as cheaply as possible. Since Sid's did not employ truck jobbers, but rather used the common-carrier system, the distribution system was problematic. Aaron spent much of his time "tracking" shipments that became lost in transit.

To reduce shipping costs for shipments smaller than a truckload, Sid's leased a warehouse in Vancouver, British Columbia. Truckload lots were shipped to this warehouse, where they were broken down and distributed to various accounts. All other orders were shipped from the Regina warehouse. Distribution was seen as one area that needed improvement if they were to remain competitive in markets outside western Canada.

*Information Systems* Although limited use was made of the reports that the management information system was capable of generating, a monthly report of sales by product line and area was made available to each manager. Versions of these reports were then filtered to sales reps and production personnel. Quarterly reports, compiled manually by the accounting staff, attempted to determine actual margins by product line.

The system also monitored orders and aided in production scheduling, accounting, and inventory control. However, it was used mostly to input orders, co-ordinate production, generate invoices, and flag overdue accounts.

*Production*   The maximum capacity of the existing Regina plant was 5.5 million kilograms annually. This level could be realized by operating three 8-hour shifts, seven days per week (with one portion of a shift allocated to maintenance). Ideal plant capacity was 4.5 million kilograms annually.

## Marketing Efforts for Sid's: A Renewed Approach

In its constant search for new markets to develop, Sid's has looked to eastern Canada and to the United States. Previous market entry efforts in eastern Canada had been marginally successful, but Sid's had been unable to sustain a presence there due to excessive costs and other nonmitigatable factors. What Sid's needed was a competitive advantage that would allow the organization to sustain a market presence — something that would further differentiate his product from that of the competition. As market growth in western Canada slowed, the issue of new market development became even more important. The opportunity offered by Major League Baseball (MLB) and the Licensing Corporation of America (LCA) certainly sounded attractive.

*The Agreement*   Once negotiated, this licensing agreement would give Sid's the exclusive right (withheld from any of its competitors) to use the MLB logo on packaging and on all other advertising and promotion materials. Further, it would allow the company to represent its product as the official sunflower seed of MLB. In return, Sid's would have to supply sunflower seeds free of charge to players in the dugout and clubhouse areas and pay a royalty of $0.04 to the LCA on each bag of sunflower seeds sold in cities that had major-league baseball teams. Any benefits that accrued outside MLB cities as a result of this agreement would be a bonus to Sid's and of no interest to the LCA. The LCA would in turn pay a royalty to MLB, to be divided among the league's 26 teams. Under the agreement, Sid's would attempt to penetrate all MLB stadiums (with the exception of the Toronto SkyDome) by 1995.

This agreement would not automatically secure concession space for the firm's product in every major-league baseball stadium, nor did it exclude the competition from attempting to gain entry to these stadiums. Negotiations and marketing and promotion efforts to gain entry to each stadium would be up to Sid's. After careful consideration, Steen felt that these issues could be mitigated by the very fact that Sid's would be recognized as the official supplier. The potential long-term benefits, in Steen's estimation, appeared to outweigh the short-term costs.

Sid's and the LCA agreed to terms and signed an agreement in March 1988. The initial agreement was to last five years, with an option to renew for an additional five years if both parties agreed. During the agreement period, the LCA could not enter into similar negotiations with competing firms.

*The Chewing-Tobacco Syndrome*   Four out of ten players in baseball's major leagues use chewing tobacco. This form of tobacco has long been used by baseball players, starting as "a thing to do" that turns into an addiction. No one can really explain how the tradition began. Some suggest that, besides occupying a player's time during long games, chewing tobacco was convenient to spit the juice outdoors.

In 1988, C. Everett Koop, then Surgeon General of the United States, reported that children's use of chewing tobacco had reached epidemic proportions; more than two million Americans under the age of 15 were regular users. Since many MLB players are role models for young Americans, the league had decided to take positive action to eradicate the use of chewing tobacco among its players. While stopping short of banning its use altogether, these efforts included designating baseball stars such as Nolan Ryan of the Texas Rangers to go on television and speak out against its use, and encouraging players to find alternative products that would work as healthier substitutes. MLB hopes that sunflower seeds will serve as one such natural replacement, thus allowing the players to set a new example for America's youngsters. By 1995, it is hoped that the number of players using tobacco will decrease to one or two out of ten.

*Stadium by Stadium*   Stadiums that are homes to MLB teams vary in their policies on concession operating. For example, at the Toronto SkyDome,

## Sid's Sunflower Seeds: Major League Baseball Stadium Penetration, Actual and Proposed

| | | | | Team-Owned |
|---|---|---|---|---|
| **Stadiums in which Sid's Sunflower Seeds Can Be Found as a Concession Item.** | | | | |
| *Stadium* | *Home of (and Division)* | *Location* | *Year Penetrated* | *Concession* |
| ACTUAL | | | | |
| Exhibition Stadium/ | | | | |
| SkyDome(*) | Toronto Blue Jays (ALE) | Toronto, ON | 1988/89 | Yes/No |
| Olympic Stadium | Montreal Expos (NLE) | Montreal, PQ | 1988/89 | Yes |
| Shea Stadium | New York Mets (NLE) | New York, NY | 1990 | Yes |
| Yankee Stadium | New York Yankees (ALE) | New York, NY | 1990 | Yes |
| Fenway Park | Boston Red Sox (ALE) | Boston, MA | 1990 | No |
| Memorial Stadium | Baltimore Orioles (ALE) | Baltimore, MD | 1990 | Yes |
| Astrodome | Houston Astros (NLW) | Houston, TX | 1990 | No |
| | | | | |
| PROPOSED | | | | |
| Tiger Stadium | Detroit Tigers (ALE) | Detroit, MI | 1991 | Yes |
| County Stadium | Milwaukee Brewers (ALE) | Milwaukee, WI | 1991 | Yes |
| Comiskey Park | Chicago White Sox (ALW) | Chicago, IL | 1991 | No |
| Wrigley Field | Chicago Cubs (NLE) | Chicago, IL | 1991 | Yes |
| Oakland–Alameda | | | | |
| Country Coliseum | Oakland Athletics (ALW) | Oakland, CA | 1992 | No |
| Anaheim Stadium | California Angels (ALW) | Anaheim, CA | 1992 | No |
| Candlestick Park | San Francisco Giants (NLW) | San Francisco, CA | 1992 | No |
| Dodger Stadium | Los Angeles Dodgers (NLW) | Los Angeles, CA | 1992 | Yes |
| Kingdome | Seattle Mariners (ALW) | Seattle, WA | 1993 | No |
| Arlington Stadium | Texas Rangers (ALW) | Arlington, TX | 1993 | Yes |
| San Diego Stadium | San Diego Padres (NLW) | San Diego, CA | 1993 | No |
| Hubert Humphrey | | | | |
| Metrodome | Minnesota Twins (ALW) | Minneapolis, MN | 1993 | No |
| Municipal Stadium | Cleveland Indians (ALE) | Cleveland, OH | 1994 | Yes |
| Royals Stadium | Kansas City Royals (ALW) | Kansas City, MO | 1994 | Yes |
| Three Rivers Stadium | Pittsburgh Pirates (NLE) | Pittsburgh, PA | 1994 | No |
| Veteran's Stadium | Philadelphia Phillies (NLE) | Philadelphia, PA | 1995 | No |
| Busch Memorial | | | | |
| Stadium | St. Louis Cardinals (NLE) | St. Louis, MO | 1995 | Yes |
| Riverfront Stadium | Cincinnati Reds (NLW) | Cincinnati, OH | 1995 | No |
| Atlanta–Fulton County | | | | |
| Stadium | Atlanta Braves (NLW) | Atlanta, GA | 1995 | Yes |

(*) The Blue Jays moved to the Toronto SkyDome in mid-season. Sid's Sunflower Seeds are not a listed product of confectioners in the Sky-Dome. As such, their product is not in the SkyDome.
**KEY**: ALE — American League East   ALW — American League West
      NLE — National League East   NLW — National League West

## Sid's Sunflower Seeds (1974) Ltd.

| Income Statements — Years Ended September 30 ($000s) | | | | | | |
|---|---|---|---|---|---|---|
| | *1989* | *1986* | *1982* | *1978* | *1974* | *1973* |
| Sales: | | | | | | |
| Product | 2 136 | 1 656 | 1 102 | 735 | 406 | 300 |
| Other | 3 | 3 | 4 | 2 | – | – |
| Total Sales | 2 139 | 1 659 | 1 106 | 737 | 406 | 300 |
| Cost of Goods Sold: | | | | | | |
| Direct labour | 252 | 194 | 127 | 91 | 55 | 42 |
| Direct material | 397 | 305 | 201 | 145 | 89 | 70 |
| Overhead | 278 | 214 | 140 | 101 | 61 | 47 |
| Freight | 397 | 306 | 201 | 144 | 87 | 64 |
| Depreciation | 75 | 61 | 50 | 38 | 12 | 6 |
| Other | 82 | 66 | 45 | 30 | 6 | 2 |
| Total C.O.G.S. | 1 481 | 1 146 | 764 | 549 | 310 | 231 |
| Gross Profit: | 658 | 513 | 342 | 188 | 96 | 69 |
| Selling and administrative: | | | | | | |
| Wages and fringe | 200 | 180 | 124 | 80 | 45 | 40 |
| Advertising and promotion | 260 | 175 | 115 | 75 | 27 | 10 |
| Expenses | 60 | 44 | 29 | 15 | 6 | 4 |
| | 520 | 399 | 268 | 170 | 78 | 54 |
| Financial: | | | | | | |
| Interest and financial | 42 | 42 | 50 | 35 | 13 | – |
| Other* | – | – | 100 | – | – | – |
| | 42 | 42 | 150 | 35 | 13 | – |
| Earnings (loss) before taxes: | 96 | 72 | (76) | (17) | 5 | 15 |
| Provision for taxes: | 21.8 | 10.8 | – | – | 1.2 | 3.7 |
| Net Income (Loss): | 74.1 | 61.2 | (76) | (17) | 3.8 | 11.3 |

*The expense in 1982 can be attributed an investment by Sid's that failed.

the concessions are owned by the SkyDome Corporation, which has rigid policies concerning product listing. The SkyDome Corporation requires a $5 million exclusive listing and partnership fee just to get a product into the concessions. By contrast, in Montreal's Olympic Stadium, where the Montreal Expos play and own the concession rights, new products can be listed with no up-front fees. Of the 24 U.S. teams, 12 own the concession rights in the stadium they occupy. It is much easier to penetrate stadiums that have team-owned concessions.

The stadiums that Sid's could penetrate would certainly be costly. Steen estimated that he would have to spend between $50 000 and $75 000 per stadium for initial endorsement advertising and promotion expenses. He believed that these would be one-time costs for efforts to establish the product and the name in the ballpark. Listing fees, where such fees are imposed by the concession owners, would boost the cost further. Central to Steen's entry strategy was the ability to get key players and personnel of respective teams to act as official Sid's

## Sid's Sunflower Seeds (1974) Ltd.

| | Balance Sheet (1973–1989) As of September 30 | | | | | |
|---|---|---|---|---|---|---|
| | *1989* | *1986* | *1982* | *1978* | *1974* | *1973* |
| **ASSETS** | | | | | | |
| Cash | 5 025 | 3 000 | 150 | 150 | 1 000 | 500 |
| Accounts Receivable | 281 749 | 258 009 | 175 220 | 105 751 | 58 421 | 40 052 |
| Other Current Assets | 20 351 | 15 272 | 1 100 | 9 872 | 4 500 | 0 |
| Inventory | 250 100 | 190 350 | 142 600 | 89 720 | 42 100 | 19 100 |
| Total Current Assets | 557 225 | 466 631 | 319 070 | 205 493 | 106 021 | 59 652 |
| Fixed Assets | 452 350 | 409 000 | 310 050 | 300 192 | 93 005 | 100 110 |
| Total Assets | 1 009 575 | 875 631 | 629 120 | 505 685 | 199 026 | 159 762 |
| **LIABILITIES** | | | | | | |
| Operating Loan | 153 500 | 150 000 | 105 650 | 71 125 | 42 120 | 25 001 |
| Accounts Payable | 269 269 | 233 296 | 136 552 | 89 747 | 53 354 | 50 900 |
| Other Current Liabilities | 33 052 | 26 756 | 39 200 | 12 651 | 3 052 | 1 250 |
| Total Current Liabilities | 455 821 | 410 052 | 281 402 | 173 523 | 98 526 | 77 151 |
| Term Loans | 175 950 | 220 025 | 244 592 | 260 000 | 70 500 | 0 |
| Total Liabilities | 631 771 | 630 077 | 525 994 | 433 523 | 169 026 | 77 151 |
| Share Capital | 60 000 | 60 000 | 30 000 | 30 000 | 30 000 | 1 500 |
| Retained Earnings | 317 804 | 185 554 | 73 176 | 42 162 | 0 | 81 111 |
| Total Equity | 377 804 | 245 554 | 103 176 | 72 162 | 30 000 | 82 611 |
| **TOTAL LIABILITIES AND OWNER'S EQUITY** | 1 009 575 | 875 631 | 629 170 | 505 685 | 199 026 | 159 762 |

spokesmen and endorse the product. He has done this successfully in Toronto and in Montreal, where Dave Stieb (starting pitcher for Toronto) and Buck Rogers (manager of the Expos), respectively, have endorsed the product and undertaken promotional activities.

## The Next Five Years

Steen and his management were optimistic about the future, particularly where growth potential was concerned. Steen felt that the MLB logo opened the door for tremendous growth opportunities in the United States and the Pacific Rim. Further, it would provide him with the "edge" required to break away from the competition in eastern Canada and the U.S.

Steen's biggest challenge over the next five years will be to develop a marketing plan to gain entry to as many of the stadiums as possible. Clearly Steen had no such plan at the moment. He would obviously have to overcome this problem before he could capitalize on this opportunity.

## Discussion Questions

1. With respect to the MLB opportunity, conceptualize a marketing plan for Sid's Sunflower Seeds. This plan should include specific steps/tasks to be undertaken by Steen, an accompanying budget and time line, and an implementation strategy.
2. Differentiate between short-term and long-term marketing plans. Why do you suppose it is important to do this?
3. What concerns do you have about the future plans for Sid's Sunflower Seeds?

**620**  *Cases*

## Sid's Sunflower Seeds (1974) Ltd.

**Projected Income Statement 1990–1995**
**Years Ended September 30 ($000s)**
***With* MLB Penetration**

| | *1990* | *1991* | *1992* | *1993* | *1994* | *1995* |
|---|---|---|---|---|---|---|
| Sales: | | | | | | |
| Product | 2 446 | 2 760 | 3 290 | 3 888 | 4 752 | 6 364 |
| Other | 3 | 5 | 1 | 1 | 10 | 15 |
| Total Sales | 2 449 | 2 765 | 3 291 | 3 889 | 4 762 | 6 379 |
| Cost of Goods Sold: | | | | | | |
| Direct labour | 279 | 326 | 388 | 458 | 559 | 747 |
| Direct materials | 443 | 517 | 614 | 727 | 884 | 1 181 |
| Overhead | 308 | 360 | 428 | 507 | 617 | 825 |
| Freight | 438 | 512 | 610 | 723 | 880 | 1 177 |
| Depreciation | 75 | 95 | 115 | 200 | 250 | 300 |
| Other | 82 | 100 | 110 | 120 | 130 | 150 |
| Total C.O.G.S. | 1 625 | 1 910 | 2 265 | 2 735 | 3 320 | 4 380 |
| Gross Profit: | 824 | 855 | 1 026 | 1 154 | 1 442 | 1 999 |
| Selling and Administrative: | | | | | | |
| Wages and fringe | 220 | 250 | 300 | 325 | 350 | 375 |
| Advertising and promotion | 350 | 525 | 600 | 650 | 700 | 900 |
| Expenses | 80 | 100 | 100 | 100 | 120 | 140 |
| | 650 | 875 | 1 000 | 1 075 | 1 170 | 1 415 |
| Financial: | | | | | | |
| Interest and financial | 45 | 45 | 180 | 180 | 160 | 110 |
| Other* | 40 | – | – | – | – | 70 |
| | 85 | 45 | 180 | 180 | 160 | 180 |
| Earnings (loss) before taxes: | 89 | (65) | (154) | (101) | 112 | 404 |
| Provision for taxes: | 20.2 | – | – | – | – | 21.8 |
| Net Income (Loss): | 68.8 | (65) | (154) | (101) | 112 | 382 |

*Projected shareholder bonuses and income from operations used for expansionary purposes.

## Sid's Sunflower Seeds (1974) Ltd.

**Projected Income Statement 1990–1995**
**Years Ended September 30 ($000s)**
***Without* MLB Penetration**

| | *1990* | *1991* | *1992* | *1993* | *1994* | *1995* |
|---|---|---|---|---|---|---|
| Sales: | | | | | | |
| Product | 2 250 | 2 550 | 2 870 | 3 160 | 3 456 | 3 848 |
| Other | 3 | 3 | 4 | 5 | 6 | 6 |
| Total Sales | 2 253 | 2 553 | 2 874 | 3 165 | 3 462 | 3 854 |
| Cost of Goods Sold: | | | | | | |
| Direct labour | 265 | 303 | 334 | 366 | 390 | 442 |
| Direct materials | 420 | 482 | 530 | 580 | 619 | 700 |
| Overhead | 293 | 335 | 369 | 404 | 432 | 488 |
| Freight | 415 | 477 | 525 | 576 | 614 | 695 |
| Depreciation | 75 | 95 | 115 | 130 | 145 | 150 |
| Other | 82 | 85 | 85 | 90 | 90 | 95 |
| Total C.O.G.S. | 1 550 | 1 777 | 1 958 | 2 146 | 2 290 | 2 570 |
| Gross Profit: | 703 | 776 | 916 | 1 019 | 1 172 | 1 284 |
| Selling and Aministrative: | | | | | | |
| Wages and fringe | 220 | 230 | 300 | 300 | 320 | 320 |
| Advertising and promotion | 280 | 325 | 350 | 400 | 450 | 550 |
| Expenses | 80 | 80 | 90 | 90 | 100 | 100 |
| | 580 | 635 | 740 | 790 | 870 | 970 |
| Financial: | | | | | | |
| Interest and financial | 40 | 40 | 40 | 38 | 36 | 33 |
| Other* | 40 | 40 | 40 | 60 | 60 | 60 |
| | 80 | 80 | 80 | 98 | 96 | 93 |
| Earnings (loss) before taxes: | 43 | 61 | 96 | 131 | 206 | 221 |
| Provision for taxes | 9.4 | 13.4 | 21.8 | 28.8 | 47.9 | 53.7 |
| Net Income (Loss): | 33.6 | 47.6 | 74.2 | 102.2 | 158.1 | 167.3 |

* Projected shareholder bonuses

# CASE 11

# Wordtech Limited

## Background

In ten years Toronto-based Wordtech Limited has grown from a consultant service bureau that undertook projects in the office automation industry to a product-based company serving the market for document interchange. While Wordtech's product line originated as a hardware-based solution for media transfer, it has since evolved to a software-based line. After several years of sustained growth, sales have plateaued and the Board of Directors now believes that without a clear statement of strategy to take the company into its next decade, growth and profitability will falter.

## Information Exchange: The Challenge

The information industry is huge, and it's growing. It encompasses all sorts of data processing methods: ways to collect, organize, manipulate, store, and communicate information in any form from text to visual images. By the year 2000, an estimated 90 percent of all employed Americans will be contributing somehow to this industry.[1] Over the years since 1964, when the earliest word-processing equipment became available to office workers, considerable technological advances have been made. Word-processing programs now boast many sophisticated formatting features. Many software packages have greatly improved in user-friendliness as well as functionality. And new levels of sophistication are always just around the corner: voice annotation, animation, even video interfaces are currently on the horizon. But all these accomplishments have been accompanied by significant compatibility problems.

Virtually anyone who has ever worked on an office computer is only too painfully aware of the difficulties caused by incompatible platforms, programs, and even program versions. Documents prepared using one type of operating system (say, DOS) cannot be read by machines that run under another operating system (say, UNIX or the system on an Apple Macintosh). Often even users who

work with the *same* operating system on equipment produced by different manufacturers cannot share data: the two platforms may use different storage media (high-density 3.5-inch floppy disks versus low-density 5.25-inch floppies, for example), or two different word-processing programs may have been involved (say, Microsoft *Word for Windows* on one and *WordPerfect* on the other). And to confuse matters still further, even different versions of the same word-processing package may store information differently — making it impossible, say, for a document created in *WordPerfect* version 5.1 to be read by someone who is still using an older version of the program, such as version 4.2.

Some companies try to minimize such problems by standardizing the equipment and programs used by their own employees. But even if they succeed in doing so, the need to communicate with those outside their organization (government agencies, suppliers, clients) generally makes resolving information incompatibilities a continuing challenge. What is needed is some type of "middleware"–technology that performs a "transparent" conversion (that is, one that requires no attention or expertise from the user), allowing a given document to be reviewed on numerous systems, with numerous word-processing programs, no matter what version is being used. And Wordtech, among other firms, has developed just such a solution.

As more and more users want to share documents easily — on a local area network; via electronic data transfer (say, e-mail or electronic bulletin boards such as those offered by CompuServe), and even between home computers and office models — the demand for document-interchange solutions like those developed by Wordtech grows. In 1990, the global market for such products was estimated to comprise more than 17 million users. For a middleware product with a resale value of $200 to $250, the market value would be between $2.4 billion and $3.25 billion. Moreover, the market was expected to triple within five years.

## Wordtech

***Entrepreneurial Beginnings*** In 1980 Dave Brown and Rick King formed Wordtech. Initially the busi-

SOURCE David A. Boag, School of Business, University of Victoria, and Denise Shilling, University of Saskatchewan, with financial support from Industry, Science and Technology Canada.

ness provided consultant services for other organizations and companies. Wordtech advised organizations on selecting equipment and related software, provided training services, and developed systems and software. The business initially experienced steady growth, reaching $2 million in annual sales after five years. But as a project-based company, Wordtech was extremely vulnerable to economic downturns. So Wordtech sought to develop a product that would allow data transfer across different storage media.

With $240 000 from an equity partner, Wordtech began developing a peripheral device to perform conversions among different data formats. In less than four months a prototype was developed. The Wordtech T500 was announced in 1984 and Wordtech became the leading supplier of disk-to-disk conversion hardware during the product's first year of availability. Wordtech serviced more than 2000 customers with this product.

***Company Growth*** From 1983 to 1985, Wordtech grew from 5 to nearly 160 employees. A U.S. marketing subsidiary was established in Boston, MA; at its peak, the subsidiary had more than 45 employees. By 1985, however, Wordtech was losing approximately $1 million a month. In the absence of forecasted sales growth, the U.S. subsidiary's operations were streamlined and the total number of employees was reduced to 60. By October 1990, Wordtech employed approximately 80 people.

***Product-Line Expansion*** In 1985, 80 percent of the company's sales were based on the Wordtech T500 and the Wordtech T600. These products matched the technology of the era, since most businesses

---

**FIGURE C11-1**

**Wordtech Product Line**

| Current Product Line | |
|---|---|
| WORDTECH T600 | Hardware-based system that provides disk-to-disk document interchange and acts as a PC-based gateway system for noncommunicating word-processing systems. |
| WORDSYS 500 | Software solution that is resident on a computer system (mainframes, minicomputers, or network or work stations of microcomputers). Provides on-line users of a shared service with access to document interchange facilities. |
| WORDSERVE | IBM PC- or compatible-based document translation system targeted to service bureaus and large corporate customers who are supplying disk-to-disk document translation services. |
| WORDSHELL | PC menu shell that creates a user-friendly interface. |
| **Future Product Line** | |
| WORDSYS 600 | Spreadsheet-interchange product that provides bi-directional spreadsheet interchange; part of the WODA architecture; permits export/import of cell data, equations, formulas, and formatting commands among various spreadsheet systems. |
| WORDSYS 700 | Graphics-interchange product that provides parameter-driven graphics interchange; part of the WODA architecture; designed to permit full, bi-directional interchange among various parameter-driven graphics systems. |
| WORDSYS 800 | Image-interchange product that will provide bi-directional interchanges for images; part of WODA architecture; designed to permit full, bi-directional interchange among various image-processing systems. |

were using "dedicated" word processors, which required converting input and output among proprietary disk formats. However, as the information industry moved away from dedicated word processors, new obstacles arose for those wanting to exchange documents. Demand increased for products that would allow interfacing among proprietary software packages on various platforms. Wordtech followed these advances in technology and devoted more effort to software products that would perform these tasks.

Working closely with its customers, Wordtech expanded its product line to keep pace with technological developments. Wordtech now supports a

---

**FIGURE C11-2**

**Wordtech Interchange Support Library**

| UNIX-based Formats | | |
|---|---|---|
| Applix/Alis | Cliq Word | Nixdorf Targoon Word |
| NR OFF/TROFF | Philips All Round Script | Primeword |
| Quadratron | Q-One | Samna AMI |
| SGO Lyrix | Uniplex II Plus | Wang WPx |
| Word Era | WordMARC | WordPerfect |

| PC-based Editors | | |
|---|---|---|
| HP AdvanceWrite | Data General CEOwrite | Enable |
| IBM Display Write | IBM DCF/Script | Informix Smart Ware II |
| Line Printer (target) | Lotus/Agenda | Lotus/Manuscript |
| Lotus/Notes | MASS-II | Microsoft Word |
| Microsoft Word for Windows | Microsoft Works | MultiMate Advantage |
| Office Writer | Primeword | PostScript Writer |
| Quadratron Q-One | Sama Word | Uniplex II Plus |
| Wang PC | WordMARC | WordPerfect |
| WordStar | Xerox Writer | |

| Interchange Formats | | |
|---|---|---|
| ASCII (Intelligence) | Bull DSA | Data General CDS |
| DECdx | DEC DDIF | IBM DCA-RCF |
| IBM DCA-FFT | IBM MO:DCA | ISO 6937 |
| Interleaf AML | Keyword:KSIF | Microsoft RTF |
| Navy DIF | NBI Net Archive | ODA/ODIF |
| SGML | Wang WITA | |

| Mac-based Editors | | |
|---|---|---|
| MacWrite | Microsoft Word | PageMaker |
| WordPerfect | | |

| VAX-based Editors | | |
|---|---|---|
| EDT | Mass-11 | TPU |
| WordPerfect | WPS (DECdx) | |

| Communication | | |
|---|---|---|
| Convergent Technologies Xerox 860 (MSDOS) | CPT Comm | Wang OIS/VS Comm |

| Formats | | |
|---|---|---|
| CPT Comm | Xerox 860 (MSDOS) | NBI OASys Archive 1 |

variety of document-processing packages on various dedicated word processors, personal computers, and mainframe- or workstation-based systems (see Figure C11–1). Complete document-interchange products are supported for individual users operating in a PC environment, workgroups using LAN systems, departments operating on VAX or IBM mainframes that use either UNIX or VMS operating systems, or VAX and mainframe operations on UNIX, VAX, and IBM systems (see Figure C11–2). The product line includes both hardware-based and software-based solutions for document interchange, and encompasses more than 45 document-processing formats.

Wordtech's strategy is to provide complete document interchange to meet the customer's specific requirements. If necessary, Wordtech will customize a solution. Management believes that Wordtech uniquely serves as a one-stop solution for the maze of document interchange problems.

Wordtech has kept pace with technological advances. Menu interfaces have been developed to improve user-friendliness. Wordtech maintains support for word-processing packages by staying abreast of upgrades and new releases to the various packages it supports. To extend Wordtech's product line, support for spreadsheets, graphics processing, and image processing is being pursued. By March 1991, WORDSYS 600 will be released; this product will enable bi-directional spreadsheet interchange. Importing and exporting of data, equations, formulas, and formatting commands among various spreadsheet forums will be possible. By July 1991, WORDSYS 700 will be developed; this package will support bi-directional processing of parameter-based graphics.[2] It is important to note, however, that Wordtech currently lags by as much as one year in delivering updates to its products in light of changes in software (e.g., Wordtech lagged by almost 10 months advancements made to one particularly popular word-processing package).

### Structure and Culture of the Organization
The organizational structure of Wordtech comprises three levels (see Figure C11–3). The top level of senior executives includes the president and three vice-presidents. The president, who is the chief executive officer, provides the vision and corporate direction and continues to drive research efforts. He also fulfills the role of vice-president in charge of sales and marketing. A second vice-president is responsible for corporate development and strategic alliances and planning. Another vice-president serves as a general manager responsible for operations, which include accounting, software and hardware development and distribution, quality assurance, customer service, and support. Below these senior executives is a second tier of managers.

Forty-five persons constitute the product development and research team. The team consists of electronics technicians, computer hardware designers, electronics engineers, and computer programmers. About 90 percent are software personnel. The unit is responsible for assembling hardware-based products (e.g., Wordtech T600), programming and developing WORDSYS software-based products, and customer service.

The sales force consists of ten individuals — seven in direct sales and three responsible for dealer, distributor, and corporate sales. Sales offices are located in Toronto, Ottawa, Chicago, Los Angeles, and Dallas. The network is complemented by office automation dealers and computer system dealers, which account for 15 percent of annual sales. Significant growth of European sales is expected; large manufacturers such as Seimens of Germany, Bull of France, Philips of Holland, and Olivetti of Italy have been trained and have agreed to market the product as a value-added product. A customer support group comprising five employees provides customer service and training. A group service bureau that provides one-time conversions employs two people.

### Wordtech's Position in the Information Industry
Wordtech is viewed as a "Switzerland" in the industry. By signing "nondisclosure" agreements with office equipment manufacturers (OEMs) and software developers, Wordtech has developed an excellent rapport with the groups, which has enabled it to remain abreast of technology advances in the document-processing industry. For example, Wordtech has participated as a major contributor in the development of the international standard, ODA (open document architecture). This architecture is a three-tier system with support ranging from text processing (FOD11) to composite document processing (FOD26) to compound document processing (FOD36). Wordtech has demonstrated document interchange capabilities at all levels. These standards are very sophisticated with a focus on future-based text processing.

FIGURE C11-3

## Organizational Structure of Wordtech

A. EXECUTIVE LEVEL

PRESIDENT & CEO
D. Brown

| EXECUTIVE VICE-PRESIDENT S. Jones | VICE-PRESIDENT R. King | DIRECTOR OF TECHNOLOGY A. Grosh | ACTING VICE-PRESIDENT SALES & MARKETING D. Brown |

B. OEM RELATIONS

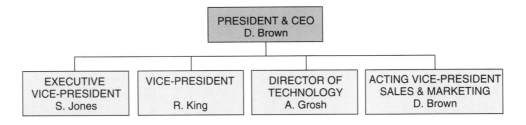

EXECUTIVE VICE-PRESIDENT

| OEM & STRATEGIC MARKETING PROGRAMS | DIRECTOR OF OEM RESALES & TECHNICAL SERVICE |

C. OPERATIONS

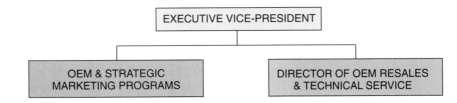

VICE-PRESIDENT & GENERAL MANAGER

| CONTROLLER | SUPERVISOR MANUFACTURING | DIRECTOR SOFTWARE | GENERAL MANAGER, OAS |

D. SALES AND MARKETING

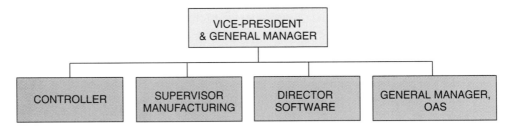
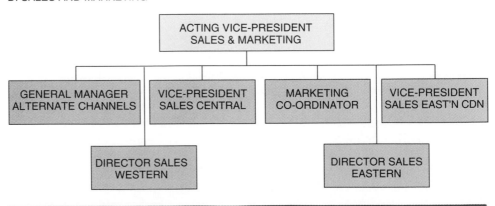

ACTING VICE-PRESIDENT SALES & MARKETING

| GENERAL MANAGER ALTERNATE CHANNELS | VICE-PRESIDENT SALES CENTRAL | MARKETING CO-ORDINATOR | VICE-PRESIDENT SALES EAST'N CDN |

DIRECTOR SALES WESTERN

DIRECTOR SALES EASTERN

Wordtech's products extend beyond these standards to provide a unique link between past and present technologies. Wordtech's perceived competitive strength advantage is its comprehensiveness, and its goal is to incorporate all new features. The scope of Wordtech's architecture is continually being revised and expanded, making document interchange possible among the various commercial word-processing packages. Since not all vendors will be implementing the proposed standards and their products will contain extensions that differentiate them from their competitors, a special interface will be required.

*Customer Review*    Satisfying customer demands has been a key concern for this company. Wordtech takes great pride in producing high-quality packages to meet customer demands. The consensus of a recent customer survey conducted by IBM was positive. Thirty individuals ranging from system programmers to application programmers to business professionals with and without document-processing skills participated in the survey. More than 85 percent were satisfied with the overall quality of the product purchased from Wordtech. Responses to the question, "What did you like best about the product?" included the following comments: "It works"; "easy to use"; "allows conversion from one program to another while retaining format"; "does what it's supposed to do"; "saves me manual work"; "don't have to do a lot of editing"; "user community can use it without assistance"; and "satisfies all our translation needs."[3]

Wordtech attributes its success to its products' simple user interface, the availability of on-line help, the comprehensiveness and accuracy of its document translation, its customer service, and product reliability.

*Competitors and Various Avenues in Document Interchange*    Wordtech's competitors either specialize in a given media conversion or offer a utility that operates on a limited basis. For example, Systems Compatibility Company (SCC) of Chicago has designed a product that provides document interchange among word-processing packages restricted to use on IBM PCs and compatibles. SCC's market focus is on end users; hence it markets a highly discounted product requiring a dealer distribution network. Another business, SoftSwitch, focuses on

electric mail–based gateway software. SoftSwitch markets a high-priced product with a narrow application; it merely serve as a translator to passing documents. Other vendors incorporate a Wordtech product as a utility for their own products; for example, DEC's product ALL-IN-1 uses WORDSYS to enable document interchange among a variety of word-processing packages for the DEC mainframe.

A number of consultant firms provide document-interchange facilities. Wordtech performs some work in this area; however, less than 5 percent of its revenue is generated by this support service. But other organizations purchase Wordtech products to provide such a service; for example, Pivar (Chicago), Whitaker Associates (Ottawa), Access Systems (Australia), and hundreds of others have purchased Wordtech products to offer a one-time conversion service.

### Wordtech's Marketing Strategies

*Wordtech's Customer Base*    Wordtech has installed more than 3000 units worldwide with approximately 100 000 users. Wordtech's customers are primarily Fortune 1000 companies who have defined information system plans. For instance, Bell South provides WORDSYS for more than 30 000 users on its electronic-mail network. As mentioned earlier, more than 17 million users of integrated office systems have been identified as potential clientele for document-interchange utilities.

*Revenue Distribution*    As sales of its hardware solution, WORDTECH T600, are being phased out, Wordtech's focus is shifting toward generating revenues from software-based solutions. In 1984, 95 percent of total sales were related to WORDTECH T600; in 1990, less than 10 percent of total sales came from this package. Only 1 percent of Wordtech's revenue is generated from service contracts (one-time document conversions).

Alliances with OEMs offer an effective way to target the users of integrated office systems without incurring associated selling costs. Accordingly, special OEM revenue-generating relationships have been established. In these relationships, the OEM pays a portion of a negotiated royalty to Wordtech prior to the development process. Once the product is developed, the balance of the royalty is paid. The OEM then integrates the Wordtech product into its product line. The contract with the OEM specifies when sales are to be reported and how royalties will be applied against. Each contract specifies a unique rate and payout period. Contracts of this nature support research and product development and provide additional sales outlets. Wordtech has OEM development contracts with such hardware leaders as DEC, IBM, HP, Wang, Bull, and AT&T.

European sales account for 10 percent of total revenue; and Australian sales, 5 percent. The expected trend will be to double revenue from European and Australian markets. Wordtech has yet to penetrate the Asian market.

### Technology of Wordtech Products

*Architecture* Wordtech's product architecture permits any document to be passed through Wordtech's interchange format when being converted to the required target word processor. The interface is its proprietary architecture entitled Wordtech Open Document Architecture (WODA) and its canonical form Wordtech Standard Interchange Format (WSIF). The concept of this architecture parallels that of IBM DCA, DEC DX, Wang WITA, and DG CDS encoding standards. WODA/WSIF is a superset of all these proprietary standards, which incorporates extensions for other proprietary word processing systems. The process involves deciphering the source word-processor format by performing a source-to-WSIF conversion; from the WSIF, a conversion to the target word-processing package is done to complete document interchange. The result is an accurate document interchange that produces a readable and revisable document.

### Product Development Time Lines

Adding another word-processing package or platform to the interchange library involves 20 to 24 person-weeks. Two interfaces are developed — one to convert a document from the source word-processor format to WSIF, and the other to translate from WSIF back to the word processor's format. Typically, two to four people are involved in a project.

During development, the two interfaces (source-to-WSIF and WSIF-to-target) are programmed concurrently. The process involves a two-to three-week review of the hardware capabilities and software features. An initial review is then completed; this

embodies the customer's design specifications and outlines the details of the interchange. By the tenth or twelfth week of the project, a prototype is developed. The code is then reviewed from the perspective of maintainability and documentation. The final review is completed by the twentieth or twenty-second week; then a "beta" (trial) product is released. Feedback from users of the beta version is incorporated into the final product Wordtech places on the open market. This process is followed whenever a new processor is added or a new version is released.

*Quality Assurance* Quality-assurance tests have more than 30 levels of complexity and involve passing more than 1000 documents from the source word processor to WSIF and then back to the target word processor. The source and target documents are then compared each time. The beta product is then reviewed for performance and maintainability of the code to ensure compliance with the WSIF architecture.

*Research Efforts* Wordtech has analyzed the potential for incorporating spreadsheet and graphics capabilities within the WSIF structure. In reviewing available graphics formats and conversion packages, three person-weeks were used. The company must now decide either to invest the effort to develop the conversion interface or to purchase existing technology that can be annexed to WSIF.

*Programming of Wordtech Products* Product coding has been in the "C" language on a PC network operating in a DOS environment. "C" affords easy portability under several current operating systems on various platforms, and has been an asset in expediting the development of similar interchanges on different environments. Wordtech has also catalogued a set of WSIF templates. Unfortunately, updates containing unique conversion solutions are often not catalogued. The trade-off between documentation and developing maintainable code is related to the time allowed to create the document-interchange software.

Another technical consideration is the transfer or development of code using the state-of-the-art object-oriented "C" ++ programming language. Object-oriented techniques improve software systems by better facilitating the factoring of functionality and related data.[4] The maintainability and extensibility of Wordtech's architecture may be enhanced. Object-oriented programming (OOP) also results in code that is reusable and portable among the variety of available hardware.[5] OOP commitment will involve a learning transition, which may be time-consuming and will require significant organizational support. To minimize the risks in making a transition, a staged approach to migrating to OOP is recommended. A badly managed transition will result in wasted effort and reduced productivity. This is an important consideration since software applications in an OS/2 environment boast of success with OOP techniques.[6]

***Research and Development Strategies***   Document interchange is a technology-intensive industry. Since 1984, Wordtech has invested more than $8 million in product development. This includes development of extensions to the existing proprietary software and hardware, and enhancing product line to

meet the customers' requirements. However, Wordtech has gotten the customer to bear much of its research and development costs. The customer often supplies the required hardware and software involved with document interchange, since most packages are customized to meet the consumer's request. For example, one firm financed the development of a seamless integration between WORDSYS and DEC's ALL-IN-1 stand-alone product. Another required a special version to operate on its own local area network, since the network was a unique development that did not employ an existing integrated operating system.

Research continues on upgrading product lines to support the current technology for document processing. Upgrades are completed within six months of a new product's announcement and are distributed to the customer base. An annual licence fee is assessed the customer for this service. This fee covers the cost of support lines, newsletters, and related services. The licence fee is based on product cost.

## FIGURE C11-4

### Revenue-Expense Profile for 1989-90

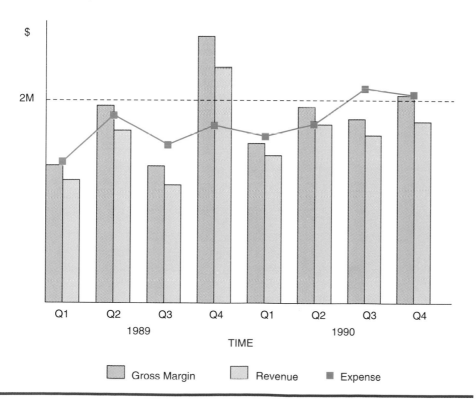

## The Challenge of Increasing Revenue

Wordtech's annual revenues have plateaued in the last three years (see Figure C11–4). Moreover, there is considerable debate within the company as to the future strategies the company should pursue. One faction advocates an infusion of several million dollars from the Board for development and marketing expenses aimed at establishing additional partnerships with OEMs. Another proposed option involves reinforcing existing partnerships — developing a more knowledgeable and dedicated sales force among Wordtech's OEM partners. In contrast to either of these strategies, another group suggests a more cautious growth based on internal cash flows. Indeed, the Board has previously declined to autho-

rize the addition of further debt for expansion. Still others have argued that Wordtech should pursue a technology-based strategy with a view to achieving "first-mover" advantages through innovation in video and voice annotation.

## Discussion Question

1. As the consultant, you have been asked by Wordtech's Board to suggest a tentative prioritization of short-and long-term goals and to identify the mechanisms required to effect such objectives. You will need to consider the technological demands and company capabilities. What should Wordtech do?

# CASE 12

# Creation Technologies Inc.

## Introduction

An important decision faces the management team of Vancouver-based Creation Technologies Inc. in early 1991. Over the past year Creation has acquired Anatek, a manufacturer of hybrid integrated circuits (ICs), also based in Vancouver, that had pursued a new market opportunity with equivocal results. With an almost 50 percent shortfall in actual sales compared to forecast, Creation's managers wonder what to do next. Although at this juncture, Anatek's entry cannot be deemed a failure, it is clear to Creation that at the current level of sales this new business is not viable. Management feels that the company must diversify in order to gain stability. Where and how should this diversification take place? Should it take place at all?

## Company Background

In 1989 Barry Henderson and partner Ian MacLellan formed Creation Studios as a small "B"-level garage recording studio. Their strategy was to intimately understand the music and pro-audio markets through the studio and then apply the resulting market-driven product ideas toward development and manufacturing. In June 1990, the studio moved into 2000 square feet of commercial space and began to target higher-level local and international business. In tandem with the studio expansion, Henderson worked with Anatek, a mid-sized electronics manufacturing company, to develop a line of proprietary music and audio products targeting the performing musician and home-studio markets.

Anatek Electronics Inc. was formed in 1969 by Allan Crawford, as a manufacturer of power supplies for laboratory use. As the electronics industry matured, Anatek too changed to reflect this evolution. With the formation of the Hybrid Division in 1976, Anatek acquired the capability to produce hybrid circuits (see Figure C12–1). Over the next

decade the Hybrid Division grew to become the mainstay of the company. The Power Supply Division was sold in 1983, and the company, renamed Anatek Microcircuits Inc., became fully devoted to the hybrid-circuit market.

In 1987 Anatek was acquired by Linear Technologies Inc. (LTI), of Burlington, Ontario. LTI was the holding company for a group of electronic manufacturers; Anatek and Gennum Corporation were its principal assets. Figure C12–2 shows the relationship that existed between these companies.

Anatek, in the past 20 years, had grown to approximately 80 employees. In 1989, Anatek had gross sales of $5.7 million, with a before-tax income of $100 000. This type of performance was typical of the past years. Marketing of the custom hybrids was done almost solely through manufacturers' representatives. Three internal people at Anatek worked with the reps, with two people travelling out to visit them. Anatek's production facilities were not set up for long-term, high-volume production runs. Due to the nature of the custom business, plant capacity was limited in order to maintain versatility.

Anatek's engineering efforts were dedicated mainly to converting customers' specifications into manufacturing documentation. The engineers on staff were close-knit and would seldom admit they could not do something, but apparently were always overworked. It seemed they constantly faced more problems than they had resources to handle. The formal R&D effort was focused on improving production yields and throughput (process R&D), rather than on developing new products. A considerable amount of the unit's time was spent helping the rest of the engineering department fight fires.

Gennum Corporation, also based in Burlington, Ontario, is a large manufacturer of linear ICs supplying world markets. Its gross annual sales are in the $18 million range. The major product line is a series of audio amplifiers and related devices, which are the principal components in hearing aids. Gennum is a supplier to every major manufacturer of hearing instruments, and is estimated to control 70 percent of the world market for certain hearing-instrument components. Industry experts view Gennum as a technology leader.

SOURCE    David Boag, University of Victoria, and Mitch King, University of Saskatchewan, with financial support from Industry, Science and Technology Canada. This case has been adapted from material supplied by Creation Technologies Inc. and reused with permission of the company.

FIGURE C12–1

## What Is a Hybrid Circuit?

A *hybrid circuit* is a generic name for a circuit board that uses a ceramic plate as its base. Electronic components are mounted on this ceramic plate, and the circuit is formed by applying a conductive film to the plate. The conductive film joins the components electrically to form the required circuit. The hybrid circuit can be a complete circuit in itself, or a component of a larger circuit.

LTI purchased Anatek for several reasons. In the past, Gennum had unsuccessfully tried to diversify into areas other than the hearing-instrument industry. By acquiring another company, LTI could instantly broaden its market base, capabilities, and management pool. Anatek was expected to gain from Gennum's knowledge of hearing instruments. Gennum was to benefit from Anatek's custom-electronics experience. Anatek's entrepreneurial attitude would, it was hoped, inspire Gennum with new products and inject new life into a well-established managerial style.

Although the acquisition did improve Gennum's sales by adding hearing-aid hybrid opportunities, Anatek's operations became less focused and too dependent on Gennum. The existing management was retained and Anatek continued to pursue its own agenda, with annual budget approval being voted on by LTI. While a relationship between Anatek and Gennum existed, synergy between the two

was not as great as had been expected. Although Anatek derived 25 percent of its revenues through the sale of circuits to Gennum, it had not become a preferred customer of Gennum.

By the end of 1990, Anatek was falling into a considerable loss position. With managers being demoted and employee morale at an all-time low, LTI decided to divest itself of the subsidiary and set up its own hearing-aid hybrid facility in Burlington. This decision came at an opportune moment for Henderson and MacLellan, who had been planning to acquire Anatek's music-products division for more than a year. By taking on Anatek's custom-hybrid business as well as its music products, they were able to gain instant cash flow and short-circuit the painful process of setting up manufacturing and distribution from scratch. For Creation this was a considerable growth opportunity. However, going from a garage recording studio with first-year sales of $14 000 to a $4 million high-tech manufacturer in

FIGURE C12–2

## Relationships Between LT1, Gennum, and Anatek

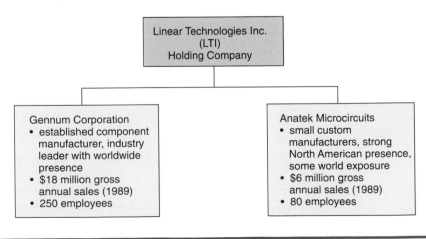

just over 18 months did not occur without presenting some major problems.

Along with Anatek's excellent customer base came uncontrolled manufacturing processes; poor morale; unfocused management with little or no leadership; and purchasing, selling and spending policies that were sure to keep the company in the red. Henderson knew he had to get the right people in the right places and get them motivated to really perform. To address these manufacturing and financial problems Henderson recruited Geoff Reed (formerly with Ernst & Young in Toronto) as vice-president of finance, and Paul Clark (also from Toronto) as vice-president of manufacturing. Clark had been a manufacturing consultant with Northern Telecom, and had worked with George Henry of Hewlett-Packard as its vice-president of manufacturing. Reed and Clark moved out to Vancouver to become partners with Henderson and MacLellan. On March 15, 1991, the group signed a deal with Gennum Corporation to take over Anatek.

One of the reasons Creation feels it must diversify is the instability of the hybrid-circuit market. Hybrids first found widespread use in the early 1970s as a method of interconnecting transistors, resistors, capacitors, and other similar components to form complex circuits. In the mid-1970s, these types of circuits were integrated into single silicon chips, and the end of the hybrid era was predicted. But instead the function of the hybrid circuit changed: it was now used to combine the silicon chips to form even higher-level circuits. When these higher-level circuits were in turn integrated into single chips, the industry's demise was again predicted, but the hybrids survived through adapting to still higher complexities. Similar changes are still going on and Creation must constantly acquire the capability to work with more complex circuits. It is entirely possible, however, that rapid technology change will yet render the hybrid technology altogether obsolete.

As the hybrid market grew and became more technologically mature, its customers also matured. Previously, price had been the most important buying criterion. As customers became wiser, they began to realize the importance of quality and of dependability in a manufacturer. A hybrid house with a reputation for reliability received some customer loyalty.

Figure C12–3 illustrates the shifts that occur in the level of technical difficulty with which Creation works. Line A represents the upper boundary of technical difficulty that is currently addressed by Creation, and Line B represents the lower limit. When a new idea is introduced into the market, Creation's advanced users demand that they be provided with this innovation. This innovation starts out above Line A. Creation must obtain the skills to produce with the innovation. This action shifts Line A upward. As the newly introduced technology gains popularity, Creation's slower-adapting customers also demand it. Soon, no one wants products that use the older technology. This action shifts Line B up. As the working range shifts upward, most depart-

**FIGURE C12–3**

**How Creation Technologies Adapts to Innovation**

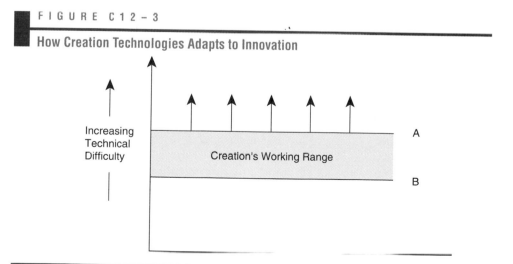

## Hybrid Circuits — Rising Markets, Rising Problems

The opening of new markets and deeper penetration into existing markets have forged advances in hybrid circuit materials, processes, and equipment, posing new challenges and creating a few outsized problems. Among them:

- Thick-film hybrids have gained in telecommunications and are rapidly taking their place with thin films in telephone-system applications. Admission into telephony requires guaranteed reliability for long lifetimes. The reliability in some circuits has been suspect.

- The medical-electronics segment is still growing. Heart pacemakers and other types of implantable systems are natural candidates for further growth, but new FDA safety requirements have slowed new development and costs are affected by mushrooming insurance rates.

- Packaging requirements have escalated as LSI density has pushed hybrids into multilayered structures requiring packages with multiconductive layers. New engineers in the field are said to be unfamiliar with hybrid packages.

Nevertheless, the hybrids field keeps growing and its down cycles are relatively flat. There are multidevice materials sources for specialized applications, providing users with more confidence in turning to the technology.

Source: Excerpted from Nat Snyderman, "Hybrid Circuits — Rising Markets, Rising Problems," *Electronic News* (November 1, 1989).

ments in Creation (such as engineering, production, marketing, and service) must adapt to the changes.

Although the hybrid industry has been able to withstand these changes, some individual firms were not so fortunate. Four of Creation's competitors (Ciro-Craft, RF Hybrids, Lentronics, and Hytec) have ceased operations, while two others (Epitek and HEI) are performing very poorly. Margins are extremely tight as companies undercut each other, trying to maintain production.

At present, there are about 40 hybrid houses in North America. Of these 40, approximately 20 are dedicated to military business, and a good portion of the business of the other 20 also is military. Estimates of the total North American market vary from $100 million to $1 billion.

Previously Anatek had avoided military business altogether. It felt that the "mil-spec" market was quite different from the market it wanted to serve. In its view, a custom commercial hybrid house competing in the military market would be like a fast-food diner trying to switch to gourmet cuisine. Preparation was more difficult, and the presentation totally different.

The company had long sought a proprietary product that would buffer it from its continual need to face internal and external changes. Historically, all

sales had involved large manufacturers such as NCR and Digital. Anatek had been highly dependent on five or six customers for as much as 80 percent of its income, with no guarantee of repeat sales. The idea of a proprietary product that could offset these forces was particularly appealing. After assessing its own strengths, management decided that any new product line should be analog and should be marketed to industrial users. These criteria ensured that the technology required matched design, production, and marketing capabilities. Anatek adopted a strategy of developing a proprietary product or product line and the search began.

### Anatek Enters the Music-Products Industry

Finding a suitable proprietary product was not easy. One area investigated was telecommunications. Components for telephones and for the switching equipment used by telephone companies were considered, developed, and trial marketed with poor results. Other ideas were tried, but it seemed that for every product, something did not fit with the company. Finally, Barry Henderson, Anatek's chief engineer and an avid amateur musician, struck upon a solid prospect. A common problem facing musicians with electronic instruments is the need to process digital music information between musical components. Such processing can be used to remove unwanted noise, blend sounds, or add special effects. After looking at what was available on the market to meet these needs, and with his knowledge of electronics, Henderson developed an initial prototype and approached Anatek with his idea. After listening to Henderson, his co-workers were undecided. The new music product would need to be digitally controlled, and would be sold through retail stores to the public. Thus, neither of the criteria they had established earlier for proprietary product development (that the new product line should be analog and should be marketed to industrial users) was met. However, Henderson's presentation was so strong and enthusiastic that he convinced the Board of Directors to adopt his plan. They felt that his high energy level, his background as both a musician and an engineer, and his strong perception of a need for this product were enough to warrant further investigation. Henderson was therefore named Music-Products Division Manager.

*Introduction of the Music-Products Line*   Several adjustments needed to be made to properly introduce the music-products line. Digital development engineering capability was added, and plans for marketing and distribution were prepared. Research was done to determine price/volume estimates. As Anatek looked for a marketing channel, it found that existing North American distribution networks were not suitable. Using an independent distributor would not allow everyone involved enough margin, while still providing a reasonably priced product. Anatek decided that it would have to set up its own distribution network. It recruited Richard Shier, who was particularly experienced in the retail and music-instrument markets, to meet the challenge. Shier decided to cover the North American market with 13 manufacturers' representatives, who would deal with the retail stores. Two more employees were hired to manage the network. Marketing to other parts of the world (Europe, Japan, Australia) was done through established distributors, whom Shier also had to manage.

In April 1989 Anatek introduced three MIDI (Musical Instrument Digital Interface) products. This family of products was soon expanded to ten and then to seventeen. The products were pocket-sized and so were labelled "Pocket Products." The unique feature of the MIDI products is their low power consumption. This allows the devices to be energized by the MIDI signal, eliminating the need for an external power supply. This was perceived as an important product feature. The products were compact and easy to use; management was confident it had a successful design.

Although the predictions made by marketing for shipping volumes were almost exact while the distribution channels filled, subsequent sales fell well below expected volumes. It was felt that the focus of the advertising campaign was wrong. Product features were highlighted rather than customer benefits. The ads were changed to educate the customer, focusing on benefits. But this approach did not seem to increase sales appreciably. This failure was puzzling, since most customers were extremely happy with Pocket Products. When the MIDI products were demonstrated to musicians, they were impressed and wanted to buy immediately. It seemed that the product was meeting customer needs, once musicians realized their function and value. The obvious question was how to let potential customers know this.

*Corporate Strategy*   From its beginnings, Anatek, and now Creation, has been aggressive with everything it has tried. Entrepreneurial spirit keeps the company looking for constant growth. Sales growth estimates by product area are shown in Figure C12–4 for the years 1991 to 1994. These projections highlight how Creation's management feels the company will grow over the next four years.

Like many entrepreneurial companies, Anatek unfortunately had lacked focus and strategic planning. It had a reactive management style with goals based on the bottom line. This approach developed relatively strong engineering and technology process capabilities, but a limited production throughput. Occasionally, Anatek had appeared unreliable to some customers, when it had bitten off more than it could chew in a project. Creation believes that it brings an entirely new philosophy to the business — flat structure, teamwork, and excellent customer service.

## New Opportunities

Another local electronics company, Newtec, has recently ceased operations. Newtec manufactured electronic gas monitors. The gas-monitoring industry began in order to provide protection from

FIGURE C12−4

**Creation's Sales Growth by Product Area (Planned 1991)**

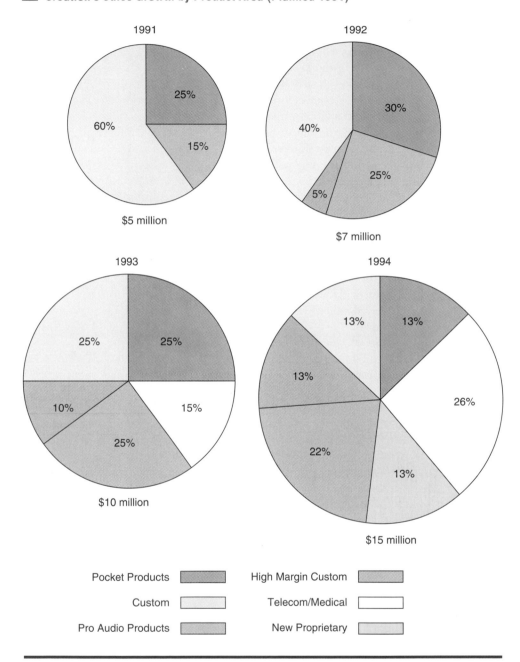

1991

25%
60%
15%

$5 million

1992

30%
40%
5%
25%

$7 million

1993

25%   25%
10%
25%   15%

$10 million

1994

13%   13%
13%   26%
22%
13%

$15 million

| Pocket Products | | High Margin Custom | |
| Custom | | Telecom/Medical | |
| Pro Audio Products | | New Proprietary | |

hazardous gases. Recent concerns about the environment have expanded the use of gas monitors to include the areas of industrial and residential pollution. The current size of the North American market is approximately $540 million, with the world market being around $1 billion. Annual industry growth rates have been averaging 10 percent to 20 percent. Buying cycles in this market are typically long, in the six- to twelve-month range. Creation has the opportunity to purchase Newtec and is investigating this possibility. Newtec's product consists of an expensive gas sensor imported from Japan, coupled with its proprietary but not very original circuits. Newtec was spending as much as 40 percent of its revenue on R&D, trying to develop a gas sensor of its own. It was estimated that another year was needed to come up with a useful sensor of its own. With sales of $2 million, Newtec's product had been well accepted by a few major boat and RV manufacturers. It felt that efforts to penetrate the industrial-safety markets were just beginning to pay off, and this would prove to be a major market. Although the company had disbanded, it still had approximately $100 000 in inventory, offset by some small debts. Newtec could be purchased for the price of its remaining inventory, less debts. It was felt that by cutting out much of Newtec's R&D, and focusing on aggressive sales and better packaging, there was an opportunity to achieve significant profits. Creation's marketing expertise would certainly "fit" this product.

Recently, Creation signed a distributional agreement with Steve Linn, an inventor from California who has developed his own unique MIDI product. This product has a similar function to Creation's present MIDI line, but has an attractive combination of features not previously offered. Currently discussions centre on new product opportunities.

Creation is also looking at new areas in the hybrid-circuit market. A niche exists in hybrid circuits for products that have very tight tolerance and/or use absolutely "leading-edge" technology, including "flip-chip" and "bonding on flex." Meeting this requirement would involve tight design and production tolerances, and a change in the method of marketing.

## Decisions Facing Creation

Henderson and his team need to make a decision. Geoff Reed advises that Creation's financing is not strong enough to attack more than one option. Creation also recognizes that something needs to be done with the music-products line. Sales have been slow. Considerable investment had been made in setting up the distribution channel. Henderson feels that his manufacturers' reps and retail outlets are excellent, a valuable asset. It is still uncertain what marketing improvements need to be made. It appears that anyone who sees a demonstration or uses a Pocket Product likes it. Marketing has developed an instructional videocassette that has been sent to all dealers. The tape demonstrates how the products work.

Should Creation get further involved with the California inventor? His existing products seem good, and Creation's management is discussing first right of refusal for future inventions. It is uncertain how much longer it would take Creation to develop similar products. Using outside development resources would reduce the strains on R&D, but would it be worthwhile to add more products to a line that is in trouble now? Yet maybe a successful new product would increase sales of existing products. Does Newtec have a product with potential? The hazardous-gas monitors seemed more suited for Creation, but there are many unknowns regarding this product.

## Discussion Question

1. A Board of Directors meeting is scheduled shortly. What advice would you give them regarding music products, Newtec, high-tech custom hybrids, and the business strategy in general?

# CASE 13

# Sytko International Inc.

In early November 1990, Les Sytkowski, the founder of Sytko Custom Homes Inc., in anticipation of his December visit to Poland, was reviewing his plans to do business in his native country. Sytko, a Winnipeg-based home building business, was not performing particularly well. Local demand had been declining and, although there was no immediate threat to the survival of the company, its profits had declined substantially and little improvement was expected over the next couple of years. The company needed some change in focus. This was not easy to find in the saturated Canadian housing market.

Les, who had strong feelings toward his native Poland, had first considered a business venture in this formerly communist country in early 1990. In January he had participated in the Conference on New Opportunities for Canadian Business organized in Toronto by the Polish Trade Mission. As a result, he believed he could join the wave of some 1700 new, foreign-owned businesses launched in this eastern European country over the past year. He felt that with his expertise in the home construction industry, he would have a substantial advantage over local competitors. His subsequent visit to Poland in early June confirmed his feelings and allowed him to establish some important business contacts. His upcoming visit was expected to lead to a final decision on the scope and focus of his Polish venture.

## Company Background

Sytko Custom Homes Inc. was founded by Les in 1985. He had originally come to Canada in 1960 with his parents. Although Les was only 6 years old at the time, over the next 30 years he managed to maintain his national ties. He participated in the activities of the Winnipeg Polish community and was fluent in both Polish and English. Les completed

SOURCE    Prepared by Kris Opalinski under the direction of Walter S. Good, as a basis for classroom discussion rather than to illustrate either effective or ineffective handling of an administrative situation. Copyright © 1991 by the Case Development Program, Faculty of Management, University of Manitoba. Support for the development of this case was provided by the Centre for International Business Studies, University of Manitoba, Winnipeg, Canada.

university degrees in political science and economics. He spent a year in Poland during 1978–79 working on a research project that was part of his graduate thesis.

In 1982 Les started his own business. As a student, he had once managed to build a house during the summer and sell it at a profit. Therefore, he had some experience in home building and starting as an independent home builder seemed to be a natural choice to him. His first year in business resulted in the construction and sale of 5 houses. During the Winnipeg housing boom of the mid-1980s Les managed to sell an average of 25 houses annually. His brother Jack joined him in 1985 and the business was incorporated. Les and his wife held a 55 percent share in the business, with Jack having the remaining 45 percent. This capital structure has been maintained.

Sytko custom homes were built exclusively for customers who wanted to have some input at all stages of design and construction of their "single-detached" houses and were also willing and able to finance construction through all its stages. The company's sales averaged $2 million between 1985 and 1989. Sytko was considered small relative to other home builders in Winnipeg, but could be considered as medium-sized in the custom-built segment of the market.

## The Residential Construction Industry in Canada

Residential properties were purchased for the purpose of individual use, renting out, or speculation. The number of apartments built in a given year depended on demographic and economic trends. In 1989 the total value of new residential construction in Canada was estimated at $35 billion. Approximately $21 billion could be attributed to construction of new residential buildings, with the remainder attributable to renovations, alterations, and conversions. In Manitoba these figures were over $1 billion and $400 million, respectively. These dollar sales translated into 216 000 housing units across the country and more than 4000 in Manitoba. However, 1990 brought a drastic decline in both the number of new houses and their dollar value. In Manitoba, it was estimated that the number of units built would be reduced to 2500, with a proportional decline in their dollar value. A further 20 percent decline in national demand was anticipated in 1991 due to the economic downturn, high interest rates, and the introduction of the Goods and Services Tax. Subsequent years were expected to turn around, with projections for 20 percent annual growth (till 1995) due to the economic recovery and an influx of almost 1.5 million new immigrants to Canada. However, Manitoba — being less attractive to the newcomers — was not expected to benefit substantially from this influx. It was anticipated that the local demand for new housing would be maintained at a stable level of 2200 units per year throughout the period of 1992 through 1995.

Residential buildings were classified into four major categories: single detached, semi-detached (including duplexes), apartments (including row housing), and other residential construction (recreational, etc.). Typically, 70 percent of the number of dwelling built in a given year fell into the single-detached category.

## Competition

The residential building industry in Canada was very competitive in nature. There were more than 19 000 companies specializing in residential construction. Of those, almost 800 were in Manitoba. The majority of these companies were subcontractors providing specialized services to "home builders" — companies or individuals who were direct suppliers of residential buildings to the final customer.

To become a home builder specializing in single-detached houses required little initial capital. All construction work could be subcontracted to specialized companies, leaving the home builder with the tasks of co-ordinating and supervising construction work. According to industry sources, all that was initially required was a telephone and a half-ton truck.

The primary basis for competition among firms was price and location. Houses in popular areas provided a higher return, even after accounting for differences in the cost of land and its development. The ability to follow existing trends in design and finishing were unquantifiable factors but, according to some analysts, had some significance in the over-crowded market.

In 1990 there were 196 home builders in Manitoba: 150 could be categorized as small (fewer than 10 employees), 40 as medium-sized (10 to 35), and 6 as large (more than 35). Most of the small companies were local operations; only 5 of the biggest firms had a national focus. The 2500 units built were shared evenly among the three size categories.

The majority of houses were developed by "tract builders" — that is, those who had only a few standard models to choose from. In many cases, companies from this group would start construction without a contract from a purchaser. This group of home builders was particularly vulnerable to changes in the economy. An error in evaluating current economic conditions and any consequent delay in the sale of finished houses could result in bankruptcy.

Sytko Custom Homes Inc. was among some 20 "custom builders" in Manitoba. It was estimated that this segment built some 200 units in 1990 in Manitoba. The competitive factors in this segment were pricing, customer relations, flexibility in adjusting to customer requirements, and quality of work. The fact that a lot of new business resulted from referrals highlights the importance of customer satisfaction.

The risk for these companies came from fluctuations in demand and competition rather than as a result of holding excess inventory, because virtually all financing was arranged by the customer. Overall, it was estimated that 50 percent of new small companies and 25 percent of medium-sized companies did not survive their first five years of operations.

## Buyer Behaviour

Single-family houses were generally available and affordable by the majority of Canadian households in the early 1990s. A well-established market system facilitated exchange and allowed families to change their houses as their needs changed. At the beginning of their working life, young people typically satisfied their need for shelter by renting an apartment. A decision to raise a family was usually followed by the commitment to invest in a house. The increased participation of women in the paid work force helped the average family carry the associated costs. As the family grew, so did its housing needs, a shift that could result in subsequent adjustments to their house size and quality. In addition, variations in employment opportunities across the country resulted in high mobility for Canadians, which further boosted real estate sales. As a result, frequent moves became a landmark of the Canadian lifestyle.

## Sytko Custom Homes Inc.

Over its five-year history Sytko built more than 100 single-detached houses. The company applied simple, wooden-frame technology that did not require a lot of specialized equipment in the construction of its houses. During the good times, company employees were engaged in framing, insulating, and finishing single-family houses under the close supervision of Les or Jack. All specialized work was subcontracted to other companies. The brothers found that only their direct involvement could assure efficiency and the quality of the work. They did not shy away from working on some of the finishing jobs themselves if their schedules permitted. Their business did not follow any kind of strong seasonal pattern, since winter construction became feasible during the 1980s.

A typical contract to construct a custom house would require some preliminary discussions with the customer, ranging from a couple of days up to several months before signing a formal agreement. After two weeks or so during which financing was finalized, construction could begin. Construction work took approximately two months. During good times, the company would have up to 10 houses under construction at the same time.

Over time, the division of responsibilities between the partners gradually changed. Les was primarily involved with customer relations, whereas Jack worked as the direct supervisor of Sytko's employees and dealt with subcontractors. Sytko did not employ any administrative staff. Their office was located at Les's house and run by him and his wife.

The unit price of Sytko's houses ranged from $75 000 to $300 000. A typical unit (a three-bedroom, 1800–2000-square-foot house) was priced between $80 000 and $90 000. Sytko required the customer to provide a 10 percent down payment, allowing the company to subcontract the initial stages of construction. Additional partial payments on completion of subsequent stages allowed the company to reduce its requirement for working capital.

Sytko Custom Homes Inc. established its reputation based on reasonable price, quality of work,

flexibility in adjusting to individual requirements, reliability, and excellent customer service. Les attributed 30 to 40 percent of the firm's new business to referrals from its former customers. The rest came from advertising in newspapers and running show homes.

In Les's opinion it was too risky for the company to pursue other segments of the home building market. "Tract building" was subject to high risks. Construction of apartment buildings required the application of different technology and equipment, neither of which was within the firm's reach. Construction of cottages, farm buildings, and log houses did not seem attractive because of the established competition and the large geographic dispersion of construction sites.

The company managed to make substantial profit throughout the 1980s. Its 10 percent average profit margin on a typical home had resulted in a $200 000 average annual profit over the previous five years. These profits were primarily used for speculation in the local real estate market.

The firm's good performance resulted from carefully scrutinizing all expenses and its owners' experience in determining appropriate prices (acquired after a few initial miscalculations). Their basic pricing method was "cost plus margin" applied against the market.

But the 1990 fiscal year was not as strong as the previous five years. Average prices of houses declined to their 1988 level whereas the cost of materials kept increasing, a circumstance that reduced profit margins to between 2 and 3 percent. With contracts to build only 10 houses during 1990, the company's expected profit shrank to between $20 000 and $30 000. The only factor that could brighten this picture for Les and Jack personally (although not for the company) was that with the decrease in the number of orders they were able to increase their own labour input by laying off several employees.

*The Future*    The only positive element Les saw in the housing environment for the near future was that more baby boomers would probably want to move up to their second and third houses, and this category of buyers was his target group. He expected some improvement in his business — to 15 houses a year — when interest rates decreased and the economy recovered. However, this level of sales was not sufficient to satisfy Les's personal objectives.

Seeing no immediate, attractive business prospects in Canada, Les focused his attention on opportunities in Poland. He had conducted extensive research on that country's market before his June trip. The visit identified some new factors that indicated that Sytko International, his newly established venture, could be successful.

## Poland — General Perspective

The legacy of communism heavily influenced the way business was conducted in Poland in 1990. The year-old noncommunist government, the first in 45 years of Soviet-dominated eastern Europe, inherited an economy that was in a shambles (see Figure C13–1 for comparative statistics on Canada and Poland). A widespread program of reforms attempting to gear the economy to the free-market model had been undertaken.

Austerity measures — including slashing the money supply to reduce a 1000 percent annual inflation rate — were introduced, with surprisingly high support from the population. As a result, unemployment, which had been practically unknown, reached over 1 million in the summer of 1990. In addition, production output dropped by 20 percent and real incomes shrank by 30 percent.

Most businesses in Poland were still state-owned and run by cadres of Communist Party members accustomed to following orders from the top. Most manufacturing sectors were dominated by large, inefficient plants able to control their profits only by raising the prices they charged for their products.

Some changes in ownership had already been initiated but had precipitated a number of problems. These resulted from the lack of investment capacity by individuals and financial institutions. A "socialist mentality," characterized by passive participation in economic and political activities and the expectation that government would play an active role in providing free basic services, remained the prevailing attitude.

However, there were some positive signs of economic recovery. The exchange rate stabilized at a level of zl 9500/US $ throughout most of 1990, despite the continuing high inflation rate. Inflation was curbed from a rate of 40 percent monthly at the beginning of the year to a moderate (by local standards) 1 to 2 percent monthly throughout the third quarter and 3 to 4 percent at the end of the year. Previously, real interest rates had traditionally been negative. The recent central bank rate, however, was 43 percent annually, which was 5 to 6 points above the annual inflation rate. Regional commodity and stock exchanges were being inaugurated almost daily.

New regulations recently introduced by the government were directed toward attracting foreign investment. Although the transfer of profits out of the country was limited to 15 percent of annual volume, this limit was to be waived by the end of 1995. A three-year tax holiday, followed by a 40 percent income tax and a 15 percent withholding tax, a state guarantee for foreign-owned assets, and a provision in the law permitting foreign ownership of real estate, were recent amendments that made Poland's business environment similar to that of the Western economies.

The general advantages of entering the Polish market included low labour costs; a highly educated and skilled labour force; and (potentially) high domestic demand for a wide range of consumer goods and services and for industrial technology, materials and equipment. A willingness to participate in the expected rapid development expressed by private entrepreneurs and a new wave of managers, hastily trained in the market economy, contributed to the new-found feeling of business excitement. Generally, no recurrence of the old, centrally controlled system was anticipated.

However, there were some impediments to foreign-owned businesses operating in Poland. "Red tape" affected almost all areas of business activity. Virtually dozens of permits were required from state and local agencies for almost any business and it took months to obtain them. In many cases the local municipal administration had too much discretion in deciding on vital aspects of business activities, which resulted in corruption. Information on market demand and supply situations was barely available and standards for economic data were different from those applied in North America. Telecommunications was underdeveloped; it was difficult to install a telephone and, once installed, obtaining a connection was also a problem. Quality of products and frequently of subassemblies, as well as that of raw materials, was low and prices were high. Business practices in Poland were ineffective, emphasizing protocol and formal position rather than level of competency. The Poles' lack of knowledge about the market economy (particularly in finance and marketing) made it difficult for Westerners to communicate investment objectives to their local counterparts. In addition, despite Poland's relatively large population, the internal market for many goods and services was very small. Considering average income levels, it was estimated that the total consumer demand for goods and services was no more than US $30 billion annually.

Finally, a significant number of people maintained an unrealistic view of the Polish economy, expecting it to miraculously recover from the deep recession of 1990. This situation could potentially bring on political instability and a demand for populist changes in economic reforms.

**FIGURE C13 – 1**

**Canada and Poland — Comparative Statistics***

|  | Canada | Poland |
|---|---|---|
| **Size (sq. kms.)** | 9 558 160 | 312 677 |
| **Population** | 26.5 million | 38.0 million |
| **Population growth (% per year)** | 1.1% | 0.7% |
| **Structure of population by age:** | | |
| below 20 years of age | 35% | 32% |
| 20–34 | 29% | 25% |
| 35–44 | 16% | 13% |
| 46–64 | 16% | 21% |
| above 64 years of age | 4% | 9% |
| **Life expectancy at birth** | 76.6 | 71.9 |
| **Labour force** | 10.38 million | 17.5 million |
| **Women as % of labour force** | 39.8% | 45.5% |
| **Unemployment rate (1990)** | 8% | 7% |
| **Employment by sector (1988)** | | |
| Agriculture and forestry | 5% | 29% |
| Mining | 2% | 3% |
| Manufacturing | 19% | 25% |
| Construction | 7% | 8% |
| Trade | 19% | 9% |
| Transport, communications, and utilities | 8% | 8% |
| Finance, insurance, and Real estate | 6% | 2% |
| Public administration and other services | 35% | 16% |
| **GDP (1987)** | US $405 billion | US $74 billion |
| **GDP per capita (1987)** | US $15 640 | US $1 950 |
| **Foreign debt (1990)** | — | US $40 billion |
| **Exchange rate per unit US $ (Nov. 1990)** | Can. $1.16 | zloty 9 500 |
| **Number of cars per 1000 population** | 435 | 105 |
| **Percentage of population above 25 years of age with secondary education and above** | 33% | 40% |
| **Exports (1987)** | US $97 billion | US $13 billion |
| **Imports** | US $88 billion | US $15 billion |
| **Average monthly earnings** | US $1 770 | US $115 |

Source: *All statistical data on Canada are based on *Canadian Statistical Review*, 1987–1990 issues. Most data on Poland are based on the 1987–1990 issues of *Rocznik Statystyczny*

## The Construction Market in Poland

The housing problem in Poland had always been acute. Several historical factors contributed to the situation in 1990. World War II destruction required a substantial effort to reconstruct most major cities. The state's emphasis on the development of heavy industry also shifted resources away from housing construction (see Figure C13–2). The centralized decision-making system resulted in the multiplication of mistakes in applying construction technologies and the inefficiency of large, state-owned construction enterprises.

In 1985, there were 12.1 million households in Poland but only 10.4 million dwelling units. By 1987 there were more than 2.4 million households on waiting lists for state and co-operative housing. As a result, the average waiting time for co-operative housing in large cities — where the shortage was the most severe — was reported to be from 14 to 15 years. Traditionally, the number of marriages in a given year exceeded the number of dwelling units built, a difference indicating that the problem was becoming even more acute. Additional pressure was anticipated within the next decade as a result of the migration of some 10 percent of the total work force

FIGURE C13 – 2

### Housing Statistics – Canada and Poland

|  | Canada | Poland |
|---|---|---|
| **Number of households (1986)** | 9 million | 12.1 million |
| **Number of households per dwelling*** | 0.99 | 1.18 |
| **Percentage of households with** | | |
| running water | 99.8% | 80% |
| telephone | 98.4% | 25% |
| **Age structure of housing (1986)** | | |
| Apartments/houses built: | | |
| Before 1946 | 20% | 36% |
| 1946–70 | 39% | 34% |
| 1971–80 | 30% | 19% |
| 1981–86 | 11% | 11% |
| **Number of dwellings completed per year (1983–1988)** | | |
| 1983 | 163 000 | 196 000 |
| 1984 | 153 000 | 196 000 |
| 1985 | 139 000 | 190 000 |
| 1986 | 184 000 | 185 000 |
| 1987 | 218 000 | 191 000 |
| 1988 | 216 500 | 177 000 |
| **Housing standard (1987):** | | |
| Average number of rooms in an apartment | 5.7 | 3.3 |
| Average number of persons per room | 0.5 | 1.1 |
| **Structure of ownership:** | | |
| % of dwellings owned | 62% | 46% |
| % of dwellings rented | 37.5% | 54% |
| % of dwellings on reserve | 0.5% | — |

*Serves as an indicator of nominal demand for housing. Numbers lower than 1.00 indicate that the total number of dwellings available on the market exceeds the number of families.

from small farms to urban centres. This would generate an additional demand for more than 1 million dwelling units within the decade.

The average size of an apartment in Poland was slightly above 50 square metres. At least 30 percent of all apartments had been built before World War II, and a substantial portion of them needed to be replaced by new units.

Until the recent economic and political changes, housing had been subject to allocation rather than free-market forces. Severe limitations had been placed on ownership (only one house or apartment could be legally owned by a family), trade (revenue from the sale of real estate was treated as income for the year without allowing for purchase costs), and private rental (allowed only when the apartment owner was out of the country).

The system of state subsidies, which reduced housing expenditures for the average family, was being changed in 1990. State assistance was to become a

## FIGURE C13–3

### Housing Costs in Poland's Major Urban Centres

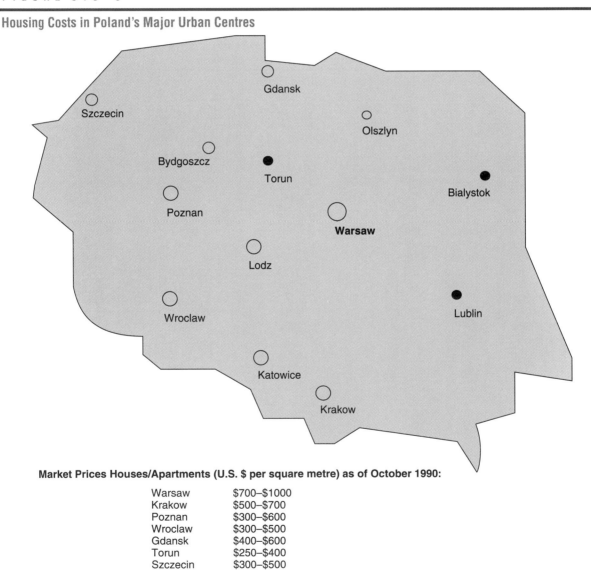

**Market Prices Houses/Apartments (U.S. $ per square metre) as of October 1990:**

| | |
|---|---|
| Warsaw | $700–$1000 |
| Krakow | $500–$700 |
| Poznan | $300–$600 |
| Wroclaw | $300–$500 |
| Gdansk | $400–$600 |
| Torun | $250–$400 |
| Szczecin | $300–$500 |

Source: Current issues of *Rzeczpospolita*.

source of cheaper credit to private investors in place of the direct grants formerly provided to institutional investors, such as housing co-operatives. Despite the housing shortage, the total size of the market in 1990 was estimated at an equivalent of US $1.5 billion to $2.5 billion. The prevailing market price for new apartments was some $300 per square metre.

The dramatic decline in the number of apartments built in 1990 was a direct result of changes in the housing subsidy system, a drastic decrease in individual incomes, and the poor overall financial condition of the construction industry. According to recent reports, extremely high prices (reflecting inefficiencies in the construction industry), accompanied by the low average income level, brought some regional markets to the saturation point (see Figure C13–3).

In 1990 there were still three distinct housing systems in Poland. *State housing* was provided by local governments to low-income individuals and by state enterprises to their employees. A system of direct price subsidies resulted in low housing costs for peo-

ple in this category. *Co-operative housing* was the predominant type of new housing in Poland, accounting for some 70 percent of new apartments. Heavily subsidized in the past, this sector was dominated by large co-operatives that were administrative/distribution entities rather than actual independent organizations of would-be homeowners. *Private housing* was always considered as a supplementary source of apartments and constituted some 20 percent of the total number of housing units built in Poland. Its dollar share of the market, however, was 30 percent, since most units in this category were single-detached houses of larger size. Government subsidies to this category were traditionally limited to low-interest credits.

## Market Segmentation

Compared with the situation in Canada, the following groups of prospective customers could be identified in Poland (see Figures C13–4 and C13–5 for information on family incomes, purchasing power, and breakdown of expenditures).

### FIGURE C13–4

**Structure of Family Expenditures in Canada and Poland (excluding taxes)**

|  | Canada (%) | Poland* (%) |
|---|---|---|
| Food | 17.5 | 52.6 |
| Housing, household furnishings, and equipment | 24.2 | 9.6 |
| Household operation | 4.3 | 2.9 |
| Clothing | 5.3 | 11.2 |
| Transportation | 16.2 | 6.1 |
| Personal and health care | 4.5 | 3.3 |
| Education, recreation, and culture | 7.9 | 8.4 |
| Miscellaneous | 16.6 | 5.9 |
| **Total Family Expenditure** | **US $29 900** | **US $2 500**\*\* |

*Statistics cover the third quarter of 1990. Annual average would be different due to the rapid decline of real incomes throughout the year.
**The total family expenditure for Poland is based on zloty incomes from the third quarter of 1990, translated into dollar figures at an exchange rate of zl 9500/US $. This dollar figure does not represent the purchasing-power parity between average incomes of the two countries because of different price structures.

FIGURE C13 – 5

## Selected Housing Market–Related Statistics for Poland

### Income Statistics, October 1990*

| | |
|---|---|
| Average monthly income per person | zl 483 000 |
| Average monthly earnings | zl 1 083 000 |
| Social minimum per person | zl 400 000 |

Distribution of monthly
incomes per family member
(Workers' families):

| *zloty income* | *% of families* |
|---|---|
| zl 0–200 000 | 5% |
| zl 200 001–400 000 | 39% |
| zl 400 001–600 000 | 33% |
| zl 600 001–800 000 | 13% |
| above 800 000 | 10% |

### Land Utilization, 1987**

| | |
|---|---|
| Agriculture | 61.0% |
| Forests | 28.5% |
| Waters | 3.0% |
| Roads and railways | 3.5% |
| Industry and housing | 3.0% |
| Nonutilized | 1.5% |

*Current Announcements of *Glowny Urzad Statystyczny*, published in the October 1990 issues of *Rzeczpospolita*.
**Rocznik Statystyczny*, 1987.

**Low- and Middle-Income Individuals**   For all practical purposes, customers from this segment were forced out of the market in 1990. Even members of large co-operatives, despite receiving credit subsidies, could not afford to make mortgage payments amounting to more than a typical salary. The only exceptions within this category were those who received new apartments from local governments under the state subsidy program. There were some additional changes in the subsidy programs expected in 1991, but their likely effect on housing demand by this group was not clear. Some analysts predicted that, within the next 5 years, between 4 million and 6 million average income earners would create a new middle class that would generate demand for the bulk of goods and services in the country, including housing.

**High-Income Individuals**   This group included those capable of making mortgage payments at a level sub-stantially above the typical average monthly salary. Private entrepreneurs, some professionals (such as dentists, barristers, and physicians in certain specializations) and local employees of foreign companies were in this category. Statistics on the number of individuals in this group and their actual income levels were unavailable, but it was known that they were concentrated in urban areas (notably the cities of Warsaw, Poznan, Katowice, and Krakow). The number of private entrepreneurs was growing rapidly due to the liberalization of the economy. It was estimated that there were at least 500 000 private enterprises in the country. Depending on their individual incomes, customers from the high-income category might be able to purchase houses within any building category.

**Hard-Currency Earners**   This segment was specific to eastern Europe, where even low (by Western standards) incomes in hard currency were multiplied to very high values in local currencies by notoriously inflated exchange rates. The high end of this segment would be the expatriate workers of foreign businesses, diplomats, and Polish emigrants who decided to resettle in their native country. They were generally expected to be able to pay the full transaction price for single-detached houses, amounting to up to several hundred thousand dollars (US). Quality and the size of houses were their primary considerations, since they were accustomed to price levels well beyond those in even the hottest local markets, such as Warsaw. According to official sources there was the equivalent of some US $5 billion in some 5 million private bank accounts within the country. In addition, another $2 billion to $3 billion was held outside the banking system. Another indicator of the size of this market was the fact that at least 50 000 Poles were earning hard currency working on construction and service projects abroad. There were no estimates available as to the size of this market; however, the number of people in this category was growing.

## Competition

Until recently, competition in the housing construction had been virtually nonexistent. Production was concentrated in the hands of some 1500 state enterprises and more than 300 co-operatives that between them employed more than 900 000 workers and accounted for more than 70 percent of the total number of apartments built in the late 1980s. Their productivity was low due to a shortage of materials, a lack of appropriate equipment, and obsolete technology. Virtually all apartment buildings had been erected with the use of large, prefabricated-panel technology. Recently, however, some of these companies had started using different, more effective technologies, and had undergone some management changes that could improve their competitiveness.

Single-detached houses were typically built using traditional heavy materials, such as bricks and concrete blocks. This was in part due to the perception that these were durable houses ("If I am spending all my money on my own house, it should be good for my grandchildren"). Traditionally, most houses in this category were built by their owners, using the services of more than 100 000 small artisan-type private enterprises. Productivity in the single-family housing sector was particularly low. Completion of a single-detached house required six years on

average — nine times the average for countries in western Europe where similar technology was employed. The lack of financial resources and shortages of materials and equipment were the primary factors contributing to this problem.

Literally thousands of new private enterprises, foreign joint ventures, and co-operatives emerged as a result of the introduction of the new housing regulations. In addition, as a result of a decline in demand, building materials became more readily available (although expensive). New construction co-operatives were mostly engaged in the construction of multiple-family apartment houses. Since they were started principally for the purpose of providing housing for their members, they did not bid for general construction contracts. Recently, there had been an increase in the number of private companies penetrating the single-family housing market segment. Some of them were using more effective technologies, similar to those applied in Canada. The most advanced of these firms was "Drewbud," a joint venture involving domestic companies in the wood-processing industry with some foreign capital. The company offered catalogue houses provided in single-detached, duplex, and row categories in several locations across the country at an average price of $250 per square metre. The distinctive feature of Drewbud's program was that the company provided its customers with a 30-year, 15 percent mortgage[1] for the amount of the purchase price above a 20 percent down payment. This down payment was required as part of the contract to initiate construction of an individual unit. The company seemed to have been overly optimistic in its initial hope of attracting thousands of customers and was in financial trouble by the second half of 1990.

There were several foreign-based home builders in the single-family housing market as well, virtually all offering similar, wooden-frame homes. However, the nature of their experience differed widely, depending on the customer segment targeted. For example, Curtis Construction Ltd., a U.S.-based company, confined its activities to metropolitan Warsaw. It offered six types of single-detached houses built from materials imported from the United States. The company required a financial commitment for the full price of the home from the customer (US $350 per square metre) before signing the contract. Curtis ordered all materials from the United States, allowed up to two months for their delivery, then completed construction within six weeks. No data on the number of units sold by the company were available. However, indications were that the company was contemplating raising prices in the near future, which would indicate that its customer base was more than adequate. There were at least three other companies providing similar services in the Warsaw area.

Similar developments in other regions of the country stimulated a lot of initial interest from potential customers, but proved beyond their financial capabilities. Labo-Lang, another foreign company, attempted to sell up to 1000 houses a year at an average price of $250 per square metre. More than 4000 individuals initially expressed interest in purchasing these houses, but fewer than 100 were able to finance the purchase.

*Buyer Behaviour*    The housing problem was a basic fact of life for people in Poland. Most young families could not afford either to purchase or to rent a separate dwelling. A married couple typically spent some 10 years living with either the husband's or the wife's parents in substandard conditions before receiving an apartment in co-operative housing. This situation resulted in a desperate search by many people for some solution to the problem. They were ready to endure substantial sacrifices in order to achieve their goals of living independently and having a home of their own.

On the other hand, the ingrained tradition of low-cost, subsidized housing provided by local administrations made people reluctant to get involved in solving their housing problems by themselves. There was some inertia even among those who could potentially combine the resources of their families and build/purchase their own homes. There was no tradition of real estate ownership and housing was not treated as an opportunity to build one's equity base. Consequently, the real estate market was in a primordial stage of development.

In addition, cost and the problems associated with acquiring a home resulted in very low mobility of the Polish population. It could be assumed that even the best job opportunities created by local markets would not attract people with appropriate qualifications, either because of the lack of housing in the area or because of the reluctance of those who had homes to move from their established location to a new one, even if housing was provided. However, those who did not have a home of their own (mostly young, married couples) could be easily attracted to a new location by the availability of housing there.

## Sytko International Inc.

Contacts with private entrepreneurs from Poland established by Les at the Toronto conference in January allowed him to set up an itinerary for his June visit to the country. The most important piece of information he received during the conference was the name of an aspiring consultant from Torun, Mr. Porzuch, who was ready to act on his behalf in Poland. Thanks to him, Les was able to make contact with municipal leaders in the cities of Torun (150 kilometres north of Warsaw), Wloclawek (200 kilometres northwest of Warsaw), and Poznan (150 kilometres west of Warsaw). Through Porzuch, Les also made contact with other businesses, who were eager to co-operate with him. In addition, his new partner provided Les with some information on the housing market in Poland, especially on competition from other North American companies trying to establish themselves in the country.

Meetings with local businesspeople provided Les with an abundance of information on opportunities in Poland. Contrary to his expectations, he found a newly developed spirit of entrepreneurship among all the people he met. He had originally been skeptical about the ability of members of municipal governments to act in a businesslike manner, remembering his experiences with the red tape in Poland from his previous visit. Actually, he found them eager to co-operate and flexible in adjusting their policies to the requirements of business.

Les's visit convinced him that his involvement in Poland was possible and could be profitable. Promptly after returning to Canada, he began developing the organizational and legal framework for his Polish venture. He approached several people in Canada, mostly of Polish descent, who would potentially participate in his venture. His idea was that this group of 10 to 15 individuals would initially raise a total of up to US $50 000 in equity and that some of them, such as Les himself, who had experience in home building would go to Poland to run the business. He was particularly interested in the participation of a group of owners of other construction companies in Toronto, who could provide the expertise to train Polish workers in the wooden-frame technology used in Canada.

Having received some preliminary commitments from a number of these people, Les registered Sytko International Inc., a new private company, to provide an organizational framework for his venture. Les became president of the company and it was planned that all the original shareholders would form the company's Board of Directors. He thought that the diverse skills of his partners would be beneficial to the company and was still looking for some shareholders who could bring other valuable experience in addition to capital to the venture.

During a recent meeting of the participants in Sytko International, the following ventures in Poland were considered as the initial business opportunities for the company. All of these possible projects emerged from Les's June visit to the country.

*Housing Development in Torun* Les's meeting with the city mayor gave him the impression that the local government was genuinely concerned about solving the problem of acute housing shortages in the municipality. He liked the business attitude of Mr. Jaszczynski. It was clear that the possibility of quickly constructing several hundred houses, even though not for the average wage earner, had some benefits for him as well. First, local pressures for new housing would be somewhat eased. Second, the possible creation of up to 150 jobs was an important consideration during the period of rising unemployment. Third, the availability of high-quality housing was expected to attract new private entrepreneurs who could increase the number of jobs available under his jurisdiction.

The most important feature of the mayor's proposal for co-operation was that the municipality would develop land for the purpose of building 300 (largely single-detached) homes. A joint venture between the municipality and Sytko International Ltd. would be the legal framework for the deal. Logistic, legal, and technical support were additional features of Jaszczynski's proposal. As a result of a series of meetings, a letter of intent was agreed upon and signed.

Sytko International would import most of the materials. To Les's surprise, it proved cheaper to import almost all materials from Canada than to get supplies from local distributors. Besides, the quality and reliability of supplies purchased in Poland were questionable. Sytko would also provide the necessary equipment and independently contract for the construction of the homes with interested customers.

It was tentatively agreed that the land would be put at Sytko's disposal in the spring of 1991. Les estimated that he would be able to complete 25 to 50 houses in the first year. He did not consider a more extensive commitment in the first year due to his lack of experience in the Polish business environment and his uncertainty about the capabilities of the local labour force.

Initial calculations indicated that, thanks to the lower costs of labour in Poland (he assumed US $3.00 per hour as an average, including fringe benefits; this was generous compensation by Polish standards) and the almost negligible (relative to the price of the house) costs of land development, he would be able to sell houses at US $300 per square metre — the market average. His total costs for constructing a single-detached house of 100 square metres would be no more than US $24 000: about US $14 000 for imported materials and equipment, and US $10 000 for local labour, materials, and subcontracted services.

He estimated that Sytko International would have to put up US $50 000 (the equivalent of almost half a billion zlotys) to start the business. The investment was required to cover the cost of establishing an office and of purchasing basic equipment, such as a truck and hand tools. It was assumed that the subsequent financing of construction work would be from customers' down payments and the proceeds of completed sales.

Overall, the picture looked almost too good to be true. However, Les realized that there were some risks involved. First, some of the construction work had to be subcontracted. Laying foundations required heavy equipment, which was beyond the immediate capacity of Sytko International. Electrical wiring required knowledge of local standards (Poland, as did the rest of Europe, used 220V AC current). Les did not have experience in these areas and did not know whether these differences would result in increased costs. If these tasks were to be subcontracted, he was concerned about the reliability of local firms, since any errors they made could affect his credibility as a contractor.

Second, neither gas nor oil heating was widespread in Poland and Les was not sure whether coal furnaces were acceptable within the fire protection regulations in Poland. Electric heating seemed to be an option, but the cost implications for homeowners needed to be investigated before deciding on this issue.

Finally, there was the question of marketing the product. He thought that, after the next five years, Sytko might approach any of the basic customer segments except low-income individuals. However, in the short term he wanted to concentrate on the highest-income groups, with an emphasis on hard-currency earners.

*Hotel Construction in Torun and Poznan*    The municipalities of Torun and Poznan were interested in a proposal to form a joint-venture company to construct hotels in their cities. Construction of these hotels had begun during the investment boom of the 1970s but had soon been abandoned due to a lack of funds. Sytko International would be expected to arrange the necessary financing, and the municipalities of both cities were ready to form companies to run the hotels.

The proposal by the municipality of Poznan seemed to promise a substantial return on investment. Poznan was the site of a number of international and national fairs; all hotels in the city operated at virtually 100 percent occupancy all year round. The financing required to complete each of the two projects was in the range of US $1 million. The joint venture company could negotiate a loan of an undetermined amount from the local bank, as well as apply for credit from international development agencies. It was estimated that construction could be completed within one year. Potential profits were difficult to estimate at this point, but Les was aware that similar projects undertaken in Poland had provided investors with at least a 40 percent return on investment and knew that he might expect even more due to the high financial leverage.

Les felt, however, that the initial capital outlay required — estimated at more than US $200 000 — was too high for the company without additional outside equity financing. Sytko's shareholders, mostly small entrepreneurs, were able to contribute up to US $5 000 individually. To increase the company's equity base, Les would have to attract either a relatively large number of small investors or one or two larger investors. Either of these alternatives would diminish the role of Les's current partners. He was apprehensive about this approach, since the

more elaborate organizational structure required for a larger company would take away from his venture some of the entrepreneurial aspects that he personally enjoyed.

But at the same time, the hotel market in Poland was virtually untapped and a good location would guarantee the company steady, high income for at least a decade. Finally, under the current legislation, foreign investments in the hotel industry could qualify for income-tax exemption for up to six years, compared to the three years granted to foreign investments in other industries (such as the construction of single-detached homes).

*Housing Construction in Warsaw*    Based on his research and the information provided by Porzuch, Les felt that there might also be an immediate opportunity to establish his company as a custom-home builder in Warsaw, the capital of Poland. There was no commitment from the municipality of metropolitan Warsaw to co-operate, partly due to the fact that land was scarce within the immediate proximity of the city. However, the shortage of housing in the Polish capital was the most severe in the country. This shortage extended across all types of apartments and had increased prices to astronomic levels.

The influx of foreign businesses establishing branches in Poland was concentrated in the capital, since the standard services they required — such as office space, translation services, and telecommunications facilities — were more readily available here than anywhere else in Poland.

In Warsaw, Les would have to start slowly by promoting his company to prospective customers, and the company's growth there would be limited because of competition from other builders. In addition, due to the wide dispersion of building locations, the initial training of employees would be erratic and costly. But continued demand in and around Warsaw was guaranteed for the foreseeable future. Les did not consider moving into land development and tract housing as a real alternative at the start, but believed that for those that could, it would be a good way to reinvest any initial profits.

*Export Markets*    With the cheap labour available in Poland, Les felt it might be possible to export these skills to the rest of the European market. Under this alternative, Sytko International would provide initial training for workers in Poland and then, using this cheaper labour, market its products outside the country. There were opportunities in both western and eastern Europe that could be captured by the company.

Poland had just applied for association with the European Community and, although not finally approved, it had received a guarantee of automatic acceptance after free parliamentary elections had been held (scheduled for the following year). This would mean lower customs duties on material components imported from Poland to other countries in this region. In addition, some current restrictions on the movement of labour between eastern and western Europe would be waived, giving Poland's construction industry a competitive edge over its Western counterparts.

Les had not had much opportunity to evaluate the financial feasibility of such an option, but there were substantial arguments to support this idea. First, profits made from export activities as, opposed to those made in Poland, could be immediately transferred out of Poland. Prices of houses in western Europe were higher than those in Poland, a situation that could provide him with an even higher return on his investment. And, finally, there were tax incentives for exports from Poland, which would make such a venture highly profitable even after the initial three-year tax holiday. Les was particularly interested in investigating opportunities in what had formerly been East Germany. Housing shortages were not as severe there as in Poland, but with the economic recovery of the region, a substantial demand for higher-quality housing could nevertheless be anticipated. Other countries in eastern Europe could also be considered, but Les was not sure whether his prices could be attractive there. Les was aware that Canadian-style housing was not very well accepted in contrast with the more traditional housing construction in Europe and that his homes could therefore be unattractive without discount pricing.

## Final Considerations

The financial risks associated with Sytko International's entering the construction market in Poland seemed to be low and, in Les's view, there was every possible indication that the potential payoff would be enormous. Les was inclined to go after the deal with Torun, but he was afraid that Sytko's commitment to this project would tie all its resources to this local market. There was also a danger that this market segment could easily become saturated at the price level the company was contemplating.

The Warsaw market seemed to be more immune to such risks. Knowing that virtually all competitors in this area charged prices higher than those being considered by Sytko, he was confident he could gain access to that market. Moreover, Les had not investigated the possibility of approaching the governments of small municipalities within driving distance from Warsaw and offering a joint venture, similar to that negotiated in Torun. This could give him an additional competitive edge. However, in this, as well as in the Torun case, he was afraid of being dependent on a contract with a public agency for the success of his business. In some cases, he knew, business deals struck with local governments had subsequently been cancelled under mounting populist pressure from their constituencies.

Yes, his visit to Poland promised a lot of excitement. As the founder of Sytko International, Les still had a good deal of freedom in deciding on the company's strategy and shaping its corporate profile. At the same time, he now felt a burden of responsibility to the company's shareholders — who, having committed their capital and time, were relying on his judgment. This feeling made his decisions far more difficult.

## Discussion Question

1. What should Les Sytkowski do?

# CASE 14

# SPACEMAX

As part of the Entrepreneurialism course in the MBA program at McMaster University, Ashton So, Tony Valaitis, and Kirk Sabo developed a business plan for a new company. Their plan was judged to be the best submitted in the course and on April 10, 1984, they were awarded a $500 prize. The next day, over coffee in the cafeteria, the three Hamilton-area students were trying to decide whether they should pocket the prize money or use it to start a new company.

## The Company

The three students named their company "SPACEMAX," for its mission was "to provide inexpensive space-saving devices for noncommercial applications." Initially, SPACEMAX was to produce and market only one product — a portable, inexpensive, and easy-to-install locker shelf (called the "Lockermate Shelf"). The primary market for the product was students in high schools, community colleges, and universities. Secondary markets included senior elementary schools and noneducational institutions such as fitness/leisure centres, factories, hospitals, and police stations.

For the rest of 1984, their plan was to penetrate the school market in the Hamilton — Toronto area. They wanted to earn a before-tax profit of 35 percent of sales and maintain a gross margin of 55 percent. Market coverage was projected to be 3 percent and sales were calculated to be $70 000 in the first year. All these estimates were best guesses. Actual performance, they knew, could be quite different.

In future years, they felt they could geographically expand the school market while also penetrating the nonschool market. They believed that the business could expand by launching one new product each year in the space-saving device field. Further, they projected growth in sales dollars of 90 percent in 1985 and 32 percent in 1986.

The students felt they had a competitive advantage because of (1) their knowledge of and closeness to the school environment; (2) their emphasis on

SOURCE    Marvin Ryder.

personal service; and (3) low overhead costs (SPACEMAX) would subcontract the manufacture of shelf components). They recognized that the school market was highly seasonal, with more than 80 percent of sales expected to occur in September and October; thus, penetration into the nonschool market was essential to smooth out sales during the year.

## The Product

The Lockermate Shelf could be broken down into two components: (1) a single shelf board ($12'' \times 12''$); and (2) a pair of wire legs. The shelf board was made of particle board ($\frac{1}{2}''$ thick), finished with a wood veneer on one side, while the legs were made of zinc-plated wire $0.144''$ thick. (See Figure C14–1). When inserted in a locker, the Lockermate Shelf would stand approximately $12''$ high. The shelf could be collapsed into a flat unit to make packaging and shipping easier. As well, the shelf would not become a permanent part of the locker, so that the purchaser could reuse the shelf in many different situations.

Before arriving at the final design, the team of students tried 10 different prototypes. Wire legs were used with various shelf materials in seven of the designs. Thick corrugated cardboard, Coroplast, sheet metal, moulded plastic, hardwood, and some combinations of these materials were all tested and rejected. Sheet metal and moulded plastic were rejected because they were too expensive. Coroplast and the cardboard were not strong enough. Hardwood had a tendency to warp. The veneer-covered particle board was sturdy enough to take a stack of textbooks, yet cheap enough for production purposes.

Suppliers quoted a cost of $0.80 for the particle board with the holes drilled, and $0.50 for the wire legs. After assembly, shrink-wrapping and labelling would cost an additional $0.20. Cardboard boxes for shipping orders of 25 would cost $1.20. Suppliers required cash-on-delivery for all businesses with no previous credit history.

For the first year, the product would be distributed through university and community-college bookstores. Distribution to high schools would be

## F I G U R E  C 1 4 – 1

### The Lockermate Shelf

**INSTALLATION INSTRUCTIONS**

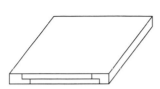

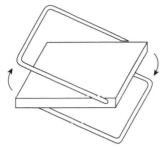

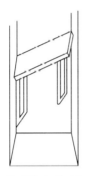

1. The LOCKERMATE
   shelf folded flat for
   convenient carrying.

2. Unfold legs.

3. Tilt shelf sideways and
   insert into locker.

4. Set shelf into bottom of
   locker and press legs
   up against side walls.

NO SCREWS, BRACKETS, or TOOLS are REQUIRED

CAUTION: DO NOT STEP ON THE LOCKERMATE SHELF ONCE INSTALLED.

---

obtained through student councils, who would sell the product as part of their fund-raising drives. As well, student-run stores and clubs in high schools could be used as alternative sales outlets. None of these outlets would require any intermediaries. Retail stores (such as Coles, Grand & Toy, K mart, etc.) would not be approached until 1985, as their purchase deadlines for "back-to-school" merchandise could not be met in 1984.

Market research had indicated that $5.00 appeared to be the upper price limit. To allow mark-ups of 50 to 55 percent, the planned selling price to the campus bookstores and student councils was to be $3.25. A recommended selling price of $4.95

would allow student councils to make a $1.70 profit per unit.

The promotion plan for community colleges and universities was somewhat different from the approach used for high schools. For the first market, campus bookstores would be contacted to identify the appropriate buyer. That person would be mailed a promotional package that would introduce the product and the company. The mailing would be followed up with a personal sales call. If the bookstore agreed to carry the shelf, SPACEMAX would provide a point-of-purchase display/dump bin unit to stack the shelves. The shelves would be sold on consignment to the bookstore to minimize financial risk. As well, shelves would be delivered to the bookstore in time for the September "rush," when lockers would be issued and bookstore traffic would be the highest.

For high schools, the process began with identifying newly elected student-council presidents. A package introducing the product, the company, and the fund-raising potential of the shelf would be mailed to that person. If possible, personal contact would be made and a presentation given. If the product was accepted, SPACEMAX would provide a point-of-purchase display for the shelves. The shelves would be sold on consignment, with free delivery and pickup (if necessary). As well, special record-keeping forms would be given to the student council to ease bookkeeping problems.

## Market and Environmental Analysis

There were approximately 1.4 million lockers in the Canadian school market (counting high schools, community colleges, and universities). The largest regional markets were Ontario (40 percent) and Quebec (24 percent), and the largest market by school type was represented by the high schools (85 percent). A breakdown of the locker market by region and type of school is shown in Figure C14–2.

The students determined that a standard locker (72″ × 18″ × 12″) was widely used in Canadian schools. The dimensions were obtained by measuring lockers in and around the McMaster University campus. The most prominent weakness of the standard locker was that it offered very limited space and usually had only one shelf, located at the top. The lack of shelving space was an even greater problem when two individuals shared the same locker. As far

as SPACEMAX could determine, no company manufactured and sold a portable shelf for use in lockers.

To help the team understand the student purchaser of a Lockermate Shelf, surveys were taken of university, community-college, and high-school students. The first two groups were surveyed using a face-to-face interview, while the high-school students completed a self-administered survey. The surveys had been administered during the first week in February, as a step in the process of preparing their award-winning business plan. For this survey "student" referred to a student using a locker. A total of 580 usable responses were obtained from the following sources: McMaster University, 83; Mohawk College, 101; St. Mary's, Lorne Park, Central, Clarkson, and Oakville secondary schools, 396. Some of the survey results are presented in Figure C14–3.

Among other things, the SPACEMAX team measured the intent to purchase the Lockermate Shelf at two price points. Students were made aware of the product (through diagrams and a verbal explanation) before being asked about their purchase intentions. Results of this part of the survey are presented in Figure C14–4.

## The SPACEMAX Team

The three students who developed the SPACEMAX business plan came from different backgrounds. Tony Valaitis was enrolled in the Co-op MBA program at McMaster. His first two work terms had been spent with Gulf Canada in its Human Resources Department. His third work term would begin on May 1, and as yet no co-op work placement had been found. Tony had graduated with a BA in geography

---

**FIGURE C14–2**

**Lockers by Location and School type[a]**

|  | Ontario | Quebec | Rest of Canada | Total |
|---|---|---|---|---|
| High Schools | 485 000 (41%) | 250 000 (21%) | 440 000 (37%) | 1 175 000 (100%) |
| Community Colleges | 40 000 (29%) | 70 000 (51%) | 26 000 (19%) | 136 000 (100%) |
| Universities | 25 000 (42%) | 14 000 (23%) | 21 000 (35%) | 60 000 (100%) |
| TOTAL | 550 000 (40%) | 334 000 (24%) | 487 000 (36%) | 1 371 000 (100%) |

[a] Market size was calculated by multiplying the number of students by a locker-to-student ratio. The ratios were determined to be 15 percent for universities, 50 percent for community colleges, and 75 percent for high schools.

FIGURE C14-3

## Selected Survey Results

| Do you share a locker? | Yes | No |
|---|---|---|
| University Students | 50% | 50% |
| Community College Students | 67% | 33% |
| High-School Students | 54% | 46% |

(60 percent of people sharing a locker were women.)

| Do you need an extra locker shelf? | | |
|---|---|---|
| University Students | 76% | 24% |
| Community College Students | 73% | 27% |
| High-School Students | 46% | 54% |

(33 percent of high-school students wanted two extra locker shelves.)

| Do you use the bottom of your locker to stack books? | | |
|---|---|---|
| University Students | 77% | 23% |
| Community College Students | 77% | 23% |
| High-School Students | 50% | 50% |

| Do you feel your locker is well organized and well kept? | | |
|---|---|---|
| University Students | 67% | 33% |
| Community College Students | 67% | 33% |
| High-School Students | 50% | 50% |

| Is having a well-organized locker important to you? | | |
|---|---|---|
| University Students | 61% | 39% |
| Community College Students | 65% | 35% |
| High-School Students | 53% | 47% |

| Are you dissatisfied with your current locker facility? | | |
|---|---|---|
| University Students | 14% | 86% |
| Community College Students | 48% | 52% |
| High-School Students | 55% | 45% |

FIGURE C14-4

## Purchase Intentions at Two Price Points

| | Would Definitely Buy | Would Probably Buy | Neutral | Would Probably Not Buy | Would Definitely Not Buy |
|---|---|---|---|---|---|
| *If the Lockermate Shelf sold for $3.00:* | | | | | |
| University Students | 48% | 19% | 11% | 7% | 15% |
| College Students | 49% | 31% | 11% | 5% | 5% |
| High-School Students | 38% | 29% | 12% | 7% | 14% |
| *If the Lockermate Shelf sold for $5.00:* | | | | | |
| University Students | 29% | 19% | 16% | 15% | 22% |
| College Students | 25% | 26% | 27% | 13% | 10% |
| High-School Students | 11% | 25% | 29% | 11% | 24% |

from McMaster in 1978 and had spent three years as the office manager for a Hamilton firm. While pursuing his BA, Tony had been a member of the varsity basketball team, and he hoped to use his last year of eligibility in the fall while completing his MBA.

Kirk Sabo was enrolled as a full-time MBA student. He had come to McMaster after completing a BBA at Wilfrid Laurier University in 1982. His work experience had been limited to summer jobs on the assembly line at the Ford Motor Company plant in Oakville and with pool-cleaning companies as crew chief. Kirk had been a member of the WLU varsity hockey team, but upon being accepted to McMaster he pursued the objective of finding a career in marketing.

Ashton So was the only married man of the three. His undergraduate degree was a BSc in chemical engineering, which he had obtained from the University of Waterloo in 1979. He had immediately gone to work for Gulf Canada, working in process engineering to improve efficiency and energy conservation at the Edmonton and Clarkson refineries. He was now a full-time MBA student.

## The Problem

The $500 that the team won for their business plan was intended to be an incentive for them to start up a new business. They could pocket the money, but they knew the professor of the course would be disappointed if they did not try to sell the Lockermate Shelf.

On the other hand, the preliminary investment would be much more than $500. Because they were students, they knew that banks would probably be wary of giving them a loan. Further, even with all their work on the business plan, they were not sure that they wanted to take a risk and begin a new venture with an untried product. There could be problems with the survey, and they had yet to do any break-even analysis. They did not know what their fixed costs would be, so in any break-even analysis some assumptions would have to be made.

They would need to make a decision soon. The lead time for one production cycle was six weeks. After exams had finished at the end of May, they would not have any shelves in stock until the middle of June. Time was already slipping by if they were to have the Lockermate Shelf in bookstores for the September rush.

## Discussion Question

1. How would you advise the team?

# CASE 15

# Porta-Broil

In April 1986, Graham Robson was trying to decide how to market his new product, Porta-Broil. Robson, a young Winnipeg entrepreneur, had purchased the right to this new method of outdoor cooking along with 8000 units of the product. The inventory was stored in a Vancouver warehouse, waiting for Robson to find a market. He needed to get Porta-Broil onto retail shelves in order to cut storage costs and recoup his initial investment.

## The People

Robson had graduated from the University of Manitoba in December 1985, with a BA. Over the preceding three years he had been involved in various entrepreneurial projects — a landscaping business, a marketing plan for costume jewellery called Twist-A-Bead, and the initial stages of a proposed health club. In the spring of 1986 he was working full-time managing a house-painting franchise, but had applied to enter the MBA program at the University of Manitoba, training that he felt would be a very good "fit" with his entrepreneurial bent.

Robson first encountered Porta-Broil while working with his older brother Grant in Vancouver. They produced *Mail-Order Marketer*, a publication that listed mail-order advertisements for a variety of products. In September 1985, the Robsons were approached by a fisherman (Jim McKellar), who had developed and tested Porta-Broil, and had arranged to have a firm manufacture it for him. However, he had no idea how to market the product, and came to *Mail-Order Marketer* for advice. The brothers were intrigued with the new product; they tried it out, liked it, and decided to purchase McKellar's entire stock of 8000 units of Porta-Broil in the

hope that they could succeed in turning a profit. Storage for these units in a Vancouver warehouse was costing them $15 per month.

## The Product

Porta-Broil was a very simple system for cooking food outdoors. It consisted of sheets of aluminum foil, in which the food was wrapped, and sheets of impregnated matting (a burlap fabric soaked in waxes) that served as fuel. The product was simple to use: the food was wrapped in foil, then wrapped in matting, which was set alight. The flame burned out in five to eight minutes, cooking the food in its own juices and providing a unique and very fresh taste. A variety of foods could be cooked this way. (See Figure C15–1 for instructions for use.)

The Robsons had arranged for Porta-Broil to be tested by several campers and fishermen; these users were enthusiastic about it. (See some of their testimonials in Figure C15–2.) A package containing six sheets of foil, six sheets of matting, and instructions was priced at $4.95 (suggested retail). The Robsons had paid $2.00 per unit for their 8000 packages. They planned to sell the packages to retailers for $2.75 each.

## Marketing Plans

Grant Robson had initially visited Vancouver outlets that sold mountain-climbing gear, but interest was minimal and the brothers felt that this was probably not the right market. After discussion with Vancouver retailers, they decided that Porta-Broil was best suited to anglers, hunters, and campers, and that Manitoba and Northwestern Ontario were the best places to offer this product.

Because the Robsons were severely limited in both time and money, they wanted to find one or more retail outlets that would buy the product from them in larger order quantities, and handle any necessary promotion. This would mean that they had only to arrange shipping from Vancouver, and while they were not sure what this would cost, they felt it would be a simple distribution system to handle.

SOURCE   This case was prepared by Morva Bowman, MBA, under the supervision of Dr. C. Dennis Anderson, as a basis for class discussion rather than to illustrate either effective or ineffective handling of an administrative situation. Copyright © 1986 by the Case Development Program, Faculty of Management, University of Manitoba. Support for the development of this case was provided by the Canadian Studies Program, Secretary of State, Ottawa; and by the Management Excellence in Small Business Program, Department of Industry, Trade and Commerce, Ottawa.

FIGURE C15–1

**Instructions for Use of Porta-Broil**

# PORTA-BROIL
## A BETTER WAY OF COOKING OUTDOORS

### THIS PACKAGE CONTAINS:

- 6 Impregnated Mattings (12″ × 9″), which act as fuel when ignited.
- 6 Sheets of Aluminum Foil (12″ × 9″), in which you wrap your food.

### GREAT FOR SUMMER OR WINTER OUTDOOR SPORTSMAN:

Light weight: can be tucked away in fisherman's tackle box, carried in a back pack, or stored away in camper or trailer for use when conventional fuels run out. Skiers, hunters, ice-fishermen will appreciate Porta-Broil, as the matting will burn in any kind of weather.

### IDEAL FOR EMERGENCY SITUATIONS:

Lost in bush — no dry wood? Take one impregnated matting and cut into strips. This will dry the wood and ignite.

### BROIL:

Fish, wieners, hamburger patties, steakettes, bacon, breakfast sausage, corn on the cob, green peppers, onions. Food broils in its own juices — a deliciously different taste.

### PREPARATION FOR BROILING:

Wrap two individual servings in one sheet of aluminum foil, airtight. Place the foil-wrapped food in the centre of one sheet of treated matting. Fold the four sides of matting over the aluminum foil and place with flap side in down position on the ground in such a manner that air will circulate around the matting. Use a couple of sticks or small stones underneath; ignite.

Made in Surrey, British Columbia, Canada.

Graham Robson approached the owner/manager of Coughlin's, a Winnipeg-based firm that is one of North America's largest distributors of camping and hiking accessories; most of Coughlin's accessory items sold for less than $2.00. The owner/manager felt that this product would be of little interest to his retail customers, and furthermore felt that the suggested retail price of $4.95 was too expensive for the end consumer.

Graham next visited Pay-Less Fishing Tackle, a large fishing equipment specialty store in Winnipeg, where the owner/manager seemed somewhat interested. He left a sample with the owner/manager, and was to check back in a week's time. Realizing that Pay-Less might not wish to buy Porta-Broil, or might take only a small part of his stock, Robson wondered what his next move should be.

## Discussion Question

**1.** How would you advise Graham Robson?

## Testimonials for Porta-Broil

I have used the product known as Porta-Broil and find that it works well. The outdoorsman will recognize the advantages of efficient, light-weight fuel.

As a Scout Leader, I believe that Porta-Broil could be of use to Scouts. A hot meal in any kind of weather is always welcome. Cubs could be introduced to outdoor foil easily and quickly with Porta-Broil.

The product seems to fit very nicely into today's theme of no-trace camping.

The idea is a good one and, when used properly, works as stated.

> Al Stevenson,
> Vancouver, B.C.

On the evening of February 22, we witnessed a demonstration of the Porta-Broil. The foods prepared were fish and wieners. It took approximately 5 minutes for the food to cook. It was then passed around for all of us to have a taste. Everyone was greatly impressed with the taste of the food, which was piping hot and cooked completely.

We are pleased to say this product does everything it states it will. And we all believe the Porta-Broil would be an asset for Boy Scouts to be associated with.

> The Ninth East Whalley Group Committee
> Vancouver, B.C.

Just a short note to let you know that we did try the sample of Porta-Broil that you gave us last weekend. It really did the trick as far as cooking the meat thoroughly and with a minimum of fuss. Going on the boat as we do, we cannot carry a lot of cooking equipment with us, and are now intending to keep a stock of your product on board.

Thank you again for giving us the opportunity of trying it.

> S.J. Pleasant,
> Surrey, B.C.

I have used the product Porta-Broil; I cooked in it when I was out fishing. It left the juices in and cooked the meat thoroughly. I was well pleased with the product and will continue to use it when I go fishing.

> M.E. Williamson
> Surrey, B.C.

We have used and are familiar with the product known as Porta-Broil, and find it to be a useful and handy product for the purposes stated. Our teenage son and his friends find it perfect for day and overnight camping and fishing trips. It is particularly suited for our often-wet climate when natural fuel is difficult to ignite.

> Shirley Simonson,
> Leslie G. Simonson,
> Surrey, B.C.

# CASE 16

# Duradent 1-2-3

Twenty-five years ago, M. L. Ringer entered the drugstore business by working in one of his father's stores when he graduated as a pharmacist. Today he manages the store, which is located on a major traffic artery in a suburban residential area of Winnipeg, and has built it into one of the most successful drugstores in Western Canada. It has provided the Ringers with a comfortable and secure livelihood. Ringer is interested in new business opportunities; however, he is cautious about becoming involved in a venture that would seriously jeopardize his existing base. He has recently been investigating a new product, Duradent 1-2-3, which seems to have significant sales potential if marketed correctly.

As a scientist, Ringer is very impressed by the technical aspects of Duradent 1-2-3, a colourless, odourless coating for dentures that allows them to adhere more naturally and efficiently. The way it works is difficult to describe, and Ringer has had mediocre success in market testing the product in his own store. With his limited experience in this type of mass marketing, he is reassessing the opportunity.

Ringer has Canadian rights to the Duradent process, which was developed in the United States. It duplicates in three simple steps a treatment that previously required elaborate equipment to apply to dentures. The process leaves a long-lasting, colourless, odourless, tasteless, and dimension-free hydrophilic (water-"loving") layer on the surface of the acrylic plastic from which most complete dentures are made. Essentially, the surface tension of moisture on the plastic is reduced, improving adherence in the way adherence (or "suction") is created when two pieces of glass are pressed together with water in between. (Because partial plates usually have clips or straps to hold them in place, Duradent is not useful in retaining them).

Some common problems experienced by wearers of one or two full plates are:

- the denture slipping laterally
- food becoming caught beneath the denture
- the denture dropping down

---

SOURCE   M.D. Beckman and Murray Kawchuk.

- odours from decaying food caught in dentures
- food sticking to exposed areas
- interference and anxiety when speaking
- embarrassment when eating
- anxiety when sneezing, laughing, and so forth

Except for lateral slippage, Duradent has helped eliminate all of these discomforts, but *only* if the dentures are well fitted (so that the suction can work).

Other products now generally used for denture retention include powders and pastes that are put into the area of contact between the denture and the gums. These relatively messy products require daily use and sometimes make users feel nauseated. Not all people use them. Generally, the poorer-fitting the denture, the more the use of such adhesives.

Instead of squeezing a paste or applying a powder onto the denture, the Duradent process requires painting the entire denture. Inside the Duradent 1-2-3 box (approximately 5×6×14 cm) are 3 distinctly labelled vials, a disposable plastic glove, 3 cotton swabs, and an instruction sheet.

The denture must be thoroughly cleaned with detergent and allowed to dry; the plastic glove prevents the skin's oils from soiling the denture. Using a cotton swab, solution #1 (Duraprime) is rubbed lightly but thoroughly over the entire denture. Using fresh swabs, the procedure is repeated with solutions #2 (Durabase) and #3 (Durabond). The denture is allowed to dry for 15 minutes. This process should take place in a well-ventilated area because the vapours from solutions 2 and 3 are similar to hydrochloric acid.

From then on the denture requires normal cleaning with water and any denture cleaner, soap, or detergent. If hard brushes and abrasive cleansers are avoided, the Duradent application will last for about 12 months.

Ringer explains that the Duradent process makes the denture "less of a foreign object to the body by increasing the hydrophilic characteristics of the acrylic plastic." This gives increased comfort to the wearer and leads Ringer to believe that Duradent can — assuming that the process is correctly performed and the dentures fit well — significantly

---

F I G U R E   C 1 6 – 1

### Radio Ads Written, Produced, and Read by M.L. Ringer

---

1. Denture wearers: There's a fabulous new denture adhesive on the market called "Duradent 1-2-3." Treat your dentures with Duradent and a micro-thin layer of moisture will coat your dentures at all times. As a result, less effort is required to hold your dentures in place. Your denture will feel more natural in your mouth, feel more secure when you eat, feel more secure when you cough, feel more secure when you laugh and when you speak. Treat your dentures with easy-to-use Duradent 1-2-3 and you'll have no need for messy powders and sticky pastes. One treatment with Duradent costs only $14.95 and lasts about a year. Duradent 1-2-3, $14.95 a kit, available only at Ringer's.

2. Denture wearers: at last there's a fabulous new colourless, odourless, tasteless, invisible denture adhesive on the market called Duradent 1-2-3. Treat your dentures with Duradent and a micro-thin layer of moisture will coat your dentures at all times. As a result, less effort is required to hold your dentures in place. Your denture will feel more natural in your mouth, feel more secure when you eat, feel more secure when you cough and sneeze, feel more secure when you laugh and when you speak. Treat your dentures with easy-to-use Duradent 1-2-3 and you'll have no need for messy powders and sticky pastes. One treatment of Duradent lasts about a year. Duradent 1-2-3, $14.95 a kit — only at Ringer's, we guarantee it!

Note: Each ad was 45 seconds long and featured only Ringer's voice without music or other introduction.

---

Source: Company records

---

improve the quality of life for denture wearers. Recently, Ringer had tested sales of Duradent from an on-the-counter display in his own drugstore. Because of his interest in the product, Ringer usually personally attended to customers who inquired about Duradent.

Over five months he used several media to promote Duradent. Mobile trailer signs, window posters, and an overhead outdoor neon sign served as advertising to passers-by. Duradent 1-2-3 was featured in a half-page newspaper advertisement and also among other weekly drugstore specials. Ringer wanted mass, knowledge-oriented advertising and, since he had some experience in developing advertising for his store, he wrote and produced two of his own radio ads (see Figure C16–1). Ringer had done many radio ads for his store, and could deliver such a commercial as well as or better than most professional radio announcers.

Ringer's promotional efforts yielded very slow sales but feedback was generally positive, though mixed. Before going further, he wants to assess the situation. Ringer sold Duradent at $14.95 a box, a price that took into consideration the quality and

longevity of the product (see Figure C16–2). Competitive powders and pastes cost approximately $2–$3 a tube, or box, with an annual cost varying greatly ($3–$20) depending on the brand used, the frequency of use, and the number of dentures. These were primarily marketed by large pharmaceutical companies on a national level.

Data on the Canadian market show that 25.9 percent of all Canadians wear dentures of some type (see Figure C16–3). Although the present growth rate is 5 percent, it is expected that long-term growth may be slowed by widespread water fluoridation and improved dental care. One type of segmentation that Ringer is considering is depicted in Figure C16–4.

However, problems in dealing with the range of prospects in this potential market might include

- prospects not entering the market in short run
- consumers failing to perceive benefits
- consumers failing to purchase the product
- consumers rejecting the product
- consumers not understanding the concept

FIGURE C16 – 2

## Duradent: Per Unit Cost Data

| | |
|---|---:|
| Sales Price | $14.95 |
| Retailer's Margin (25%) | 3.74 |
| | 11.21 |
| Wholesaler's Margin (15%) | 1.68 |
| | 9.53 |
| Materials, packaging, displays | 4.00 |
| Contribution Margin | $5.53 |

Source: Company records

FIGURE C16 – 3

## Profile of Denture Adhesive Use, Denture Wearers, and Market Share

| | Percentage of wearers | Percentage of volume of adhesives |
|---|---|---|
| Heavy users of adhesives | 20% | 60% |
| Moderate users of adhesives | 30% | 30% |
| Light users of ahesives | 50% | 10% |
| Full lower and upper plate | 47% of wearers | |
| Lower *or* upper plate | 33% | |
| Partial plate | 20% | |
| Age of wearers | | |
| 65 and over | 20% | |
| 55-64 | 20% | |
| 45-54 | 21% | |
| 35-44 | 19% | |
| under 35 | 20% | |

Source: Special report prepared for company

*MARKET SHARE:*

| | |
|---|---|
| Poli-grip | 33% |
| Fasteeth | 21% |
| Orafix | 20% |
| Corega | 12% |
| Other | 14% |

Source: Data collected by the company from trade sources

For distribution of Duradent, Ringer has considered marketing through dental clinics and dentists' offices or through a mass marketing effort. His many years of experience in the retail pharmacy industry have led Ringer to reject the first two alternatives. He feels that inadequate effort and attention would be given to his product through such channels. Before proceeding to the third alternative, though, he is entertaining the idea of test marketing Duradent in Brandon, Manitoba, a trade area of about 70 000 people. An analysis of associated costs for media coverage is presented in Figure C16–5. A properly executed campaign will cost approximately $100 000, with advertising absorbing most of the funds.

Although he favours it, this approach leaves Ringer with several concerns. First, the financial commitment will be quite large and he is unsure whether the risk is acceptable. Second, he believes that many denture wearers perceive their problems as incorrectible inconveniences that must be tolerated, a situation that leads to a seemingly different

### FIGURE C16–4

### Possible Market Segments

| | |
|---|---|
| Heavy users of adhesives | Some dissatisfaction with dentures |
| Moderate users of adhesives | Practical potential market |
| Light users of adhesives | Indifferent |
| Tried adhesives and rejected them | No dissatisfaction with dentures |

### FIGURE C16–5

### Media Rates in the Proposed Test Market

**RADIO**

| | RATES | |
|---|---|---|
| | 30 Sec. | 60 Sec. |
| AA: 6–10 AM | $23.00 | $25.00 |
| A: 10 AM–1 PM and 4–7 PM | $18.00 | $20.00 |
| B: 1–4 PM and 7–12 PM | $16.00 | $18.00 |

**TELEVISION**

| | RATES | |
|---|---|---|
| | 30 Sec. | 60 Sec. |
| AA: 5–6 PM Sun.; 6–11 PM Mon. through Sun. | $60.00 | $85.00 |
| A: 11–12 PM Sat. and Sun.; 12 PM–S/O Sat. | $50.00 | $75.00 |
| B: S/O–5 PM Sun.; 5–6 PM Mon. through Sat.; | | |
| C: S/O–5 PM Mon. through Sat.; | $45.00 | $60.00 |
| 12 PM–S/O Sun. through Fri. | $20.00 | $25.00 |

**NEWSPAPER**
Full Page....$640.64
1/2 Page....$320.32
1/4 Page....$160.16
1/8 Page....$ 80.08

Source: Report prepared for company

communication task. Finally the benefits of Dura-dent are not always perceived immediately. Sometimes a month will pass before the user begins to notice them. On the other hand, Ringer's experiences suggest that users become aware of the benefits as the treatment begins to wear off about a year later.

## Discussions Questions

1. Evaluate the steps taken by Ringer thus far.
2. Develop a marketing program that would make Duradent 1-2-3 a success.
3. Should Ringer introduce Duradent 1-2-3 into the market?

## CASE 17

# Federated Chemicals Ltd.

On May 19, 1984, an inquiry was received by the Floor Covering Division of Federated Chemicals Ltd. from a leading passenger-plane manufacturer requesting a proposal for a rubber substitute for the conventional cloth rugs used as flooring in commercial planes.

The purchasing agent for the plane manufacturer expressed discontent with the short service life of the cloth rugs then being used. He emphasized that the substitute not only should be attractive but also, and most important, would have to be fire-resistant and able to withstand spillage of food and beverages, vomiting, and normal wear experienced by a flooring material without staining permanently or sustaining other damage.

In addition, the substitute rug would have to be competitive in price. Only by possessing features warranting their consideration could the substitute induce customers to pay a higher price.

After considering the customer requirements, the technical department of the Floor Covering Division designed the "AirO Rug." The new product consists of a vinyl-coated glass fibre cemented to a sponge rubber backing material. Extended tests indicate that this new idea is the answer to the manufacturer's needs. The surface material is highly abrasion resistant and soil proof and requires very little effort to clean and maintain. The sponge backing, specially treated for fire resistance, imparts a cushioned effect to the foot much like the conventional cloth rug. A variety of colours rivals any offering of the conventional rugs, and estimated service life of the product is five years.

The Floor Covering Division is able to use a top material and sponge that are production items currently being manufactured by the Industrial Products Division of Federated Chemicals Ltd. As per company policy, material costs are transferred at the standard cost rate only; that is, no profit is included in interdivisional finished-goods transfers. The Industrial Products Division also has to maintain quality standards, replacing any material deemed unacceptable and rejected by the Floor Covering Division.

This source of supply results in the receipt of high-quality materials at a minimum cost. Then too, the raw materials do not necessitate outlays for facilities to produce them. Because the raw materials are produced in an adjacent building, incoming transportation costs are nonexistent and the lead time on materials is to be a maximum of two weeks.

## Elements of Cost

Inquiries reveal that the coated glass fibre costs $4.18 per metre in a 90 cm width, and the sponge $1.17 per metre in the same width. From the test samples, the product engineer calculates that 10 m$^2$ of AirO Rug will need 8.3 L of cement, which costs 80 cents per litre.

Using similar products and manufacturing operations as a basis for their computations, the Time Study Department estimates 1.84 direct labour hours at the rate of $7.10 per hour to construct 10 m$^2$ of rug.

The Production Department has submitted anticipated manufacturing operations costs. These monthly prorates include: supervision, $1020; inspection, $140; miscellaneous indirect labour, $84; floor-space expense, $320; and small tools and expense materials, $30. Three building tables, each costing $1320 and having a service life of five years, and a material-cutting machine with a service life of 10 years, costing $480, must be purchased before beginning the production. Selling and administrative expense are to be $4300 per month, which includes an outlay of $1150 semi-monthly for advertising AirO Rugs in *Aviation Age*, a trade magazine.

## Capacity

The building procedure for AirO Rugs is as follows:

1. Roll out sponge on table and cut to desired length.
2. With paint roller, cement the entire top area of the sponge.
3. Allow cement to tackify (dry slightly) for approximately 15 minutes.
4. Apply top material on sponge and roll with hand roller to ensure adhesion.
5. Trim edges and clean top area with cleaning solvent

While one table is being used for cementing, the other two can be used for laying the top material or final finishing. In short, three building tables are required to keep the assemblers busy and the production process flowing smoothly.

The complete production cycle to build 50 m² of rug requires an average of 3 hours and 20 minutes. Based on a 173-hour work month, the optimum capacity seems to be 2598 m² per month. Experience proves, however, that actual capacity in assembly production such as this generally turns out to be about 77 percent of optimum capacity. With this past history as a guide, actual production capacity is deemed to be 2000 m² per month.

## Cost Reduction Considerations

The requirements of the market prevent AirO Rug from being an off-the-shelf item. The colour selection offered the customers has to equal or surpass that of the competition, the cloth rug. To meet the changing demands of the industry, Federated Chemicals Ltd. specially tints the vinyl of the top material according to each customer's specification. Because the colour requirements change from time to time for each customer, top material cannot be prepared in advance. The home office of the Floor Covering Division Sales Department faxed the particulars of AirO Rug to the branch sales offices with a request to obtain other potential customers' reactions to the new product. Technical tests, which revealed a useful life of five years for the rug, were relayed in detail along with small samples to branch salespeople.

From the accumulation of responses, the home office has determined that a conservative estimate indicates a sales potential of 500 m² per month. Cloth rugs have an average life of one year, and sell for $11.50 per square metre. Installation costs are not included in the selling price of either rug, but they are estimated at $4.80 per square metre for the cloth, and $5.40 for the AirO Rug.

## Discussion Questions

1. What do you recommend as a base selling price? What would be the break-even point at this price?
2. What considerations other than cost were influential in helping you arrive at this decision?

# CASE 18

# Computron, Inc.

In July 1992 Thomas Zimmermann, manager of the European Sales Division of Computron, Inc., was trying to decide what price to submit on his bid to sell a Computron 1000X digital computer to König & Cie., A.G., Germany's largest chemical company. Were Zimmermann to follow Computron's standard pricing policy of adding a 33⅓ percent markup to factory costs and then including transportation costs and import duty, the bid he would submit would amount to $311 200. Zimmermann was afraid that a bid of this magnitude would not be low enough to win the contract for Computron.

Four other computer manufacturers had been invited by König to submit bids for the contract. Zimmermann had received information from what he considered to be a "reliable trade source" indicating that at least one of these four competitors was planning to name a price somewhere in the neighbourhood of $218 000. Computron's normal price of $311 200 would be $93 200, or approximately 43 percent higher than this price. In conversations he had had with König's vice-president in charge of purchasing, Zimmermann had been led to believe that Computron would have a chance of winning the contract only if its bid were no more than 20 percent higher than the bid of the lowest competitor.

Inasmuch as König was Computron's most important German customer, Zimmermann was particularly concerned over this contract and was wondering what strategy to employ in pricing his bid. Deadline for submission of bids was August 1, 1992.

## Background on Computron and its Products

Computron, Inc., was an American firm that had, in the winter of 1990, opened a European sales office in Paris with Zimmermann as its manager. The company's main product, both in the United States and in Europe, was the 1000X computer, a medium-sized digital computer designed specifically for process control applications.

In the mid-to late 1980s, the market for digital process control computers was growing quite rapidly. These computers were substantially different from the computers then used for data processing and engineering calculations, and were generally produced by specialized companies, not by the manufacturers of office and/or calculation-oriented digital computers nor by the companies that had produced analog process control computers, then the traditional units used for process control.

Digital computers were classed as small, medium, or large depending on their size, complexity, and cost. Small computers sold for up to $80 000; medium computers for between $80 000 and $600 000; and large computers for $1 million to $6 million.

The Computron 1000X had been designed specifically for process control applications. It was used in chemical and other process industries (oil refining, pulp and paper, food manufacture, etc.) as well as in power plants, particularly nuclear power plants.

In addition to its 1000X computer, Computron manufactured a small line of accessory equipment for process control computers. These accessories, however, constituted a relatively insignificant share of the company's overall sales volume.

During the first six months after its opening, the European sales office did only about $1.1 million worth of business. In the 1991–92 fiscal year,[1] however, sales increased sharply, with the total for the year reaching $5 million. Computron's total worldwide sales that year were roughly $44 million. Of the European countries, Germany constituted one of Computron's most important markets, contributing $1.2 million, or 24 percent of the European sales total, in 1991–92. England and Sweden were also important markets, having contributed 22 percent and 18 percent, respectively, to the 1991–92 total. The remaining 36 percent of sales was spread throughout the rest of Europe.

Computron computers sold to European customers were manufactured and assembled in the United States and shipped to Europe for installation. Because of their external manufacture these computers were subject to an import duty. The amount of this tariff varied from country to country.

SOURCE   Copyright © 1960 by L'Institut pour l'étude des Méthodes de Direction de l'Enterprise (IMEDE), Lausanne, Switzerland. Distributed by Intercollegiate Case House, Soldiers Field, Boston, MA 02163. Copied from R. Cory, *Industrial Marketing*.

The German tariff on computers of the type sold by Computron was 17.5 percent of the U.S. sales price.

Prompted primarily by a desire to reduce this importation duty, Computron was constructing a plant in Frankfurt, Germany. This plant, which would serve all of the European Common Market, was scheduled to open on September 15, 1992. Initially, it was to be used only for the assembly of 1000X computers. Assembly in Germany would lower the German importation duty from 17.5 percent to 15 percent. Ultimately, the company planned to use the plant for the fabrication of component parts as well. Computers that were completely manufactured in Germany would be entirely free of importation duty.

The new plant was to occupy 1000 m$^2$ and would employ 20–30 people in the first year. The initial yearly overhead for this plant was expected to be approximately $300 000. As of July 1992, the European sales office had no contracts on which the new plant could begin work, although it was anticipated that training of employees and the assembly and installation of a pilot model 1000X computer in the new plant could keep the plant busy for two or three months after it opened. Zimmermann was somewhat concerned about the risk that the new plant might have to sit idle after these first two or three months unless Computron could win the new König contract.

## Company Pricing Policy

Computron had always concentrated on being the quality, "blue-chip" company in its segment of the digital computer industry. The company prided itself on manufacturing what it considered to be the best all-around computer of its kind in terms of precision, dependability, flexibility, and ease of operation. Computron did not try to sell the 1000X on the basis of price. The price charged by Computron was very often higher than that being charged for competing equipment. Despite this fact, the superior quality of Computron's computers had, to date, enabled the company to compete successfully both in the United States and Europe.

The European price for the 1000X computer was normally figured as follows:

U.S. "cost"
(Includes factory cost and factory overhead)
*plus*
Markup of 33⅓ percent on "cost"
(To cover profit, research and development allowances, and selling expenses)
Transportation and installation costs
*plus*
Importation duty
Total European price

Prices calculated by this method tended to vary slightly because of the country-to-country difference in tariffs and the difference in components between specific computers.[2] In the case of the present König application, Mr. Zimmermann had calculated that the "normal" price for the 1000X computer should be $311 200. Figure C18–1 shows his calculations.

The 33⅓ percent markup on cost used by the company was designed to provide a before-tax profit margin of 15 percent, a research and development

**FIGURE C18–1**

**Calculated "Normal" Price for the 1000X Computer for König**

| | |
|---|---|
| Factory cost | $192 000 |
| 33⅓% markup on cost | 64 000 |
| U.S. list price | $256 000 |
| Import duty (15% of U.S. list price) | 38 400 |
| Transportation and installation | 16 800 |
| Total "normal" price | $311 200 |

allowance of 10 percent, and a selling and administrative expense allowance of 8 percent. The stated policy of top management was clearly against cutting this markup in order to obtain sales. Management felt that the practice of cutting prices "not only reduced profits, but also reflected unfavourably on the company's 'quality' image." Zimmermann knew that Computron's president was especially eager not to cut prices at this particular moment, inasmuch as Computron's overall profit before taxes had been only 6 percent of sales in 1991–92 compared to 17 percent in 1990–91. Consequently, the president had stated that he not only wanted to try to maintain the $33\frac{1}{3}$ percent markup on cost but in fact was eager to raise it.

Despite Computron's policy of maintaining prices, Zimmermann was aware of a few isolated instances when the markup on cost had been dropped to around 25 percent in order to obtain important orders in the United States. In fact, he was aware of one U.S. case when the markup had been cut to 20 percent. In the European market, however, Computron had never yet deviated from the policy of maintaining a $33\frac{1}{3}$ percent markup on cost.

## The Customer

König & Cie., A.G., was the largest manufacturer and processor of basic chemicals and chemical products in West Germany. It operated a number of chemical plants located throughout the country. To date it had purchased three digital computer process control systems, all from Computron. The three systems had been bought during 1991–92 and had represented $1 million worth of business for Computron. Thus König was Computron's largest German customer; it alone had constituted over 80 percent of Computron's 1991-92 sales to Germany.

Zimmermann felt that the primary reason König had purchased Computron computer systems in the past was their proven reputation for flexibility, accuracy, and overall high quality. So far, König officials seemed well pleased with the performance of their Computron computers.

Looking ahead, Zimmermann felt that König would continue to represent more potential future business than any other single German customer. He estimated that during the next year or two König would need another $1 million worth of digital computer equipment.

The computer on which König was now inviting bids was to be used in the training of operators for a new chemical plant. The training program was to last for approximately four to five years. At the end of the program the computer would either be scrapped or converted to other uses. The calculations the computer would be called on to perform were highly specialized and would require little machine flexibility. In the specifications that had been published along with the invitations to bid, König management had stated that in buying this computer König was interested primarily in dependability and a reasonable price. Machine flexibility and pinpoint accuracy were listed as being of very minor importance, inasmuch as the machine was to be used primarily for training purposes and not for on-line process control.

## Competition

In Germany, approximately nine companies were competing with Computron in the sale of medium-priced digital process control computers. Figure C18–2 shows a breakdown of sales among these companies for one year. As can be seen, four companies accounted for 80 percent of industry-wide sales in 1991–92.

Zimmermann was concerned primarily with the competition offered by the following companies:

*Ruhr Machinenfabrik, A.G.*, a very aggressive German company that was trying hard to expand its market share. Ruhr sold a medium-quality, general-purpose digital computer at a price roughly $22\frac{1}{2}$ percent lower than the price Computron charged for its 1000X computer. Of this price differential, 17.5 percent was attributable to the fact that there was no import duty on the Ruhr machine because it was manufactured entirely in Germany. Although to date Ruhr had sold only general-purpose computers, reliable trade sources indicated that the company was currently developing a special computer in an effort to win the König bid. The price Ruhr was planning to place on the special-purpose computer was reported to be in the neighbourhood of $218 000.

*Elektronische Datenverarbeitungsanlagen, A.G.*, a relatively new company that had recently developed a general-purpose computer comparable in quality to the Computron 1000X. Zimmermann felt that Elektronische Datenverarbeitungsanlagen presented a

F I G U R E   C 1 8 – 2

## 1991–1992 Market Shares for Companies Selling Medium-Priced Digital Computers to the German Market

|  | Sales | |
|---|---|---|
|  | **Dollars** | **Percent** |
| Computron, Inc. | $1 200 000 | 30.0 |
| Ruhr Machinenfabrik A.G. | 800 000 | 20.0 |
| Elektronische Datenverarbeitung-sanlagen, A.G. | 500 000 | 12.5 |
| Digitex, G.m.b.H. | 700 000 | 17.5 |
| Six other companies (combined) | 800 000 | 20.0 |
| Total | $4 000 000 | 100.0 |

real long-range threat to Computron's position as the "blue-chip" company in the industry. To get a foothold in the market, it had sold its first computer "almost at cost." Since that time, however, it had undersold Computron only by the amount of the import duty to which Computron's computers were subject.

*Digitex, G.m.b.H.* A subsidiary of an American firm, this company had complete manufacturing facilities in Germany and produced a wide line of computer equipment. The Digitex computer that competed with the Computron 1000X was of only fair quality. Digitex often engaged in price-cutting tactics and the price it charged for its computer had sometimes, in the past, been as much as 50 percent lower than that charged by Computron for the 1000X. In spite of this difference, Computron had usually been able to compete successfully against Digitex because of the technical superiority of the 1000X. Zimmermann was not overly concerned about the remaining competitors, since he did not consider them to be significant factors in Computron's segment of the computer industry.

## German Market for Medium-Priced Digital Computers

The total estimated German market for medium-priced digital process control computers of the type manufactured by Computron was currently running at about $4 million per year. Zimmermann thought that this market could be expected to increase at an annual rate of about 25 percent for the next several years. For 1992–93 he already had positive knowledge of about $1.3 million worth of specific new business. This new business was broken down as follows:

| | |
|---|---|
| König & Cie., A.G. | |
| Frankfurt plant | $ 300 000 |
| Dusseldorf plant | 250 000 |
| Mannheim plant | 150 000 |
| Central German Power Commission | 440 000 |
| Deutsche Autowerke | 160 000 |
| | $1 300 000 |

This new business noted above was in addition to the computer that König currently sought for its new experimental pilot plant. None of this already-known business was expected to materialize until late spring or early summer.

## Deadline for Bids

In view of the various facts and considerations discussed above, Zimmermann was wondering what price to bid on the König contract. Deadline for submission of bids to König was August 1, 1992. Since this was less than two weeks away, he knew he would have to reach a decision sometime during the next few days.

## Discussion Question

**1.** How would you advise Zimmermann?

# CASE 19

# Southern Cross, Pty. Ltd.

Southern Cross, Pty. Ltd. — one of Australia's leading manufacturers of surface coatings — has grown steadily since its founding in 1912. It now has factories in each of Australia's six states and employs nearly 3000 people. For readers unfamiliar with Australian geography, the country is divided into six states (Victoria, New South Wales, Queensland, South Australia, Western Australia, and Tasmania), the Northern Territory, and the Australian Capital Territory. Australia, with a population of 14.6 million, is about the same geographical size as the continental United States.

While the company has introduced several new products and developed its own chain of outlets in recent years, it is still regarded as a conservative company. Surveys show that its products are considered to be of excellent quality but the firm is not perceived as progressive compared with its major competitors.

Southern Cross offers a complete range of interior and exterior paints for domestic and commercial use. In addition, it has a wide range of stains and varnishes. The company also markets specialty lines for industrial, automotive, and marine purposes.

Southern Cross products are sold principally through hardware stores and department stores. In recent years, the firm has also let its products be sold by selected discount and chain stores. Southern Cross has also set up a network of company-owned and -operated "Southern Cross — The Beautifier" stores, which serve as both retail and trade outlets.

Southern Cross has a special sales force to run its own outlets and to sell to professional painters. Other specialist sales personnel handle the industrial, automotive, and marine markets. In addition, the company has a separate retail or direct decorative sales force in each state, with responsibility for sales to independent retail outlets.

## General Background

Michael Allen, Southern Cross's direct decorative sales manager for the state of Victoria, was alarmed when he read the latest sales figures. For the third consecutive month his branch had not made budget and he knew the head office would be expecting an explanation and a corrective-action plan. While an unfavourable economic climate explained the poor growth in demand, several smaller companies, particularly the discounters, were showing sales gains. One of these had now emerged as a major Victorian competitor via aggressive marketing and expansion of its own chain through franchising (to which it confined all its sales). Furthermore, the other major competitors were not being hurt as badly as Southern Cross. Allen began to analyze the data he had available.

## The Retail Market in Victoria

Victoria has a population of 4.1 million, or 28 percent of Australia's total population. As Figure C19–1 indicates, Victoria has a relatively small share of Australia's land area (about 3 percent). Its capital is Melbourne, with a population of 2.9 million. Only Sydney, in the state of New South Wales, is larger. An agriculturally rich state, Victoria boasts numerous towns throughout, of which the largest are Geelong (pop.147 000), Ballarat (pop. 77 500) and Bendigo (pop. 64 000).

The paint market in Victoria was undergoing a pronounced shift. During the past two years the state's market had barely grown; but the smaller paint companies, largely through aggressive discounting practices, had generally gained at the expense of the traditional major paint marketers. This change reflected not only their price discounting but also their more innovative marketing and merchandising (see Figure C19–2).

Southern Cross's sales by main product grouping's are shown in Figure C19–3. Overall the average price for paint to retailers was a little under $7 a litre, and the better margins were achieved from interior paints and strains. Flat plastics represented

SOURCE    This case was prepared by M.J.S. Collins, Principal Lecturer in Marketing at the Chisholm Institute of Technology (Australia); David L. Kurtz, the Thomas F. Gleed Chair in Business and Finance at Seattle University; and Louis E. Boone, the Ernest Cleverdon Chair of Business and Management at University of South Alabama, as a basis for class discussion. The original draft of this case was prepared for use at the Chisholm Institute of Technology. This version changes and disguises the data in order to protect the confidentiality of the company.

■ FIGURE C19–1

■ Map of Australia

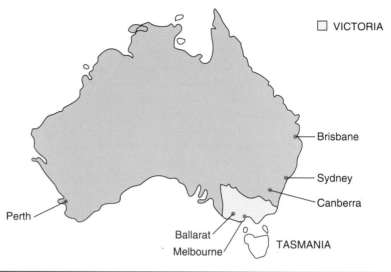

☐ VICTORIA

Brisbane

Sydney

Canberra

Perth

Ballarat

Melbourne

TASMANIA

■ FIGURE C19–2

■ The Victorian Paint Market — Millions of Litres

**Retail Paint Sales–Victoria**

|  | *1985* | *1986* | *Year to Date April 1987* |
|---|---|---|---|
| Southern Cross | 3.39 | 3.20 | 1.06 |
| Competitor A | 2.40 | 2.48 | 0.83 |
| Competitor B | 2.42 | 2.44 | 0.81 |
| Competitor C | 1.20 | 1.24 | 0.48 |
| Others | 2.93 | 3.14 | 1.09 |
|  | 12.34 | 12.50 | 4.27 |

■ FIGURE C19–3

■ Paint Sales by Product Category — Thousands of Litres

|  | 1985 | | 1986 | |
|---|---|---|---|---|
| *Product* | *Southern Cross* | *Industry* | *Southern Cross* | *Industry* |
| Interior Full Gloss | 560 | 2 140 | 585 | 2 250 |
| Exterior Full Gloss | 820 | 2 500 | 735 | 2 375 |
| Interior Semi-Gloss | 525 | 2 550 | 505 | 2 420 |
| Undercoats | 375 | 1 050 | 345 | 1 100 |
| Flat Plastics | 750 | 2 375 | 598 | 2 475 |
| Stains/Varnishes | 210 | 1 725 ⎤ | 250 | 1 875 ⎤ |
| Other | 150 | ⎦ | 182 | ⎦ |
|  | 3 390 | 12 340 | 3 200 | 12 495 |

the most cut-throat market segment. The fall in exterior paint sales reflects the reduction in weatherboard houses or their renovation with coverings that do not require painting.

Paint demand varies somewhat with economic and weather conditions and reflects certain sales peaks such as Easter. But overall sales tend to be spread evenly between quarters.

The retail market comprised all sales made through retail outlets, including trade sales as well as sales to the householder. It was estimated that industry retail sales accounted for approximately 40 percent of total paint volume and estimates divided these sales as follows:

|  | 1980 | 1986 |
|---|---|---|
| Hardware Independent Outlets (including Groups) | 45% | 41% |
| Discount Specialist Paint Stores | 10% | 11% |
| Corporate Chains and Department Stores | 20% | 22% |
| Specialist Company owned or Franchised Outlets | 15% | 18% |
| Other | 10% | 8% |
|  | 100% | 100% |

The remainder was sold directly to professional painters, commercial users, and industry.

The corporate chains or mass merchandisers and specialist outlets were gaining market share at the expense of the hardware segment. To battle this trend many hardware stores had banded together to form major buying groups. These groups were increasing in importance and aggressiveness. In particular they were promoting strongly, using cataloguing and advertising, and adopting their own private-label paint in some cases. Three major groups, accounting for some 45 percent of the independents, were co-operatives, and the fourth group was controlled by a major wholesaler that had its own field force and claimed a share of 15 percent of the total retail market. Like the corporate chains, these groups bought centrally, but the independents bought individually as well as through their groups according to the deals on offer.

The structure and function of the Direct Decorative field force is indicated in the job description below.

## Job Description — Southern Cross Decorative Sales Representative (Ballarat Territory, Victoria)

*Accountability Objective:*  Promotes and sells the Southern Cross Decorative market range to users and sellers to achieve sales forecast within expense budget.

*Dimensions:*

| | |
|---|---|
| Sales Volume | $1 165 000 annually |
| Customers | 170 000 litres annually |
| Distributor/Retailers } Painters } | 177 |
| Architects | 5 |
| Government Departments and } Local Authorities } | 8 |

*Nature and Scope of Position:*  The Direct Decorative force concentrates its activities on all Decorative sales not made through the "Southern Cross — The Beautifier" organization. Direct Decorative sales usually involve selling to the end user through the local reseller, and selling to resellers for stock purposes.

The incumbent is one of seventeen reporting to the Decorative Sales Manager. Eleven are metropolitan representatives, who service the Greater Melbourne area. Five are country representatives, of which the incumbent is one, servicing other areas of Southern and Central Victoria in a similar capacity to the metropolitan representatives except that the country representatives usually have a broader function and responsibility. The seventeenth position reporting to the Decorative Sales Manager is the Decorative Market Officer, who provides clerical and office support for the field staff.

The incumbent reports weekly to the Decorative Sales Manager on such items as calls made, mileage, cost per mile, entertainment expenses, competition activities, and the like.

The incumbent handles all customer complaints in the Ballarat territory. Complaints and problems of a minor nature or those that may require an adjustment of up to four litres of paint for repairs are handled entirely by the incumbent. Difficulties requiring an adjustment of more than that are referred to the Decorative Sales Manager for approval. For problems involving technical factors beyond the representative's technical knowledge, the Decorative Sales Manager will request technical assistance from the laboratories.

The incumbent is required to provide support for company promotions, including point-of-sale materials, merchandising, and the like. Should he or she require special assistance for a promotion, he or she must approach the Decorative Sales Manager to obtain such assistance. The representative can initiate special promotions for a territory and implement these once approval has been obtained.

The incumbent is relatively free in relation to how to sell the product, providing that the methods used are not detrimental to the company's image or policies. Product pricing is done according to a chart supplied by the firm. Prices vary according to customer classifications. The representative is not involved with the setting of prices on the chart.

An overall sales budget is set by the Decorative Sales Manager. Sales representatives set their own budget in accordance with this general plan. Before it comes into force, it must be approved by the Decorative Sales Manager, who may make alterations in consultation with the field salesperson. Once the budget is set, it remains current for 12 months. The representative cannot alter the budget.

A company vehicle is supplied to the incumbent. This is replaced after four years or 80 000 business kilometres. The representative notifies the Decorative Sales Manager and the State Accountant when the replacement time is approaching. The salesperson obtains three replacement quotes and recommends which quote should be taken.

The incumbent is required to help resellers with store and layout problems, merchandising stock levels, and the like. He or she is also expected to provide colour schemes and/or product specifica-tions for householders and others who request help. The representative keeps customer-record sheets and sales statistics as well as taking note of competitors' activities in the territory.

### Summary of Principal Tasks:

- Promotes company image to ensure ready acceptance of products.
- Maintains customer files to provide a reliable history of customers.
- Initiates and implements territorial promotions to maintain sales performance.
- Handles any problems arising from the territory, referring only the larger or more difficult problems to the Decorative Sales Manager.
- Controls the costs incurred within the territory so that the sales target may be reached within budgeted costs.
- Requests special assistance where necessary to maintain amiable customer relations.
- Reports regularly to the Decorative Sales Manager about the conditions within the territory.

## The Sales Force and Its Performance

The total sales budget set by the marketing plan for 1987 was designed to hold market share and assume an industry growth rate of approximately 4 percent. With inflation running at more than 8 percent, this represented a fall in real growth, reflecting the inroads made by nonpaint building materials, the virtually static building construction market, and the impact of more durable paints. The first four months' results for Victoria are shown in Figure C19–4.

### FIGURE C19–4

**Budget versus Actual Sales: 1987**

|  | January | February | March | April | Year to Date |
|---|---|---|---|---|---|
| Total Budget ($000) | 1 645 | 1 645 | 1 850 | 2 600 | 7 740 |
| Units (000 litres) | 240 | 240 | 270 | 380 | 1 130 |
| Actual ($000) | 1 650 | 1 489 | 1 702 | 2 353 | 7 194 |
| Units (000 litres) | 245 | 219 | 251 | 345 | 1 060 |

Brief sketches of a cross-section of the sales representatives who constitute the Victoria field force, and their respective sales performance, are shown in Figure C19–5 through C19–10, as selected by Michael Allen.

*Edwin Chandler:*  Chandler was an energetic metropolitan sales representative, aged 28, who had formerly been a junior trainee. He had been a representative for only one year, but he compensated for his lack of experience with hard work (see Figure C19–5).

*Ian Bannion:*  Bannion was a solid, conscientious representative who had worked the Bendigo territory for 14 years. Aged 51, Bannion was well known throughout the area and all his resellers spoke highly of him (see Figure C19-6).

*Colin Donaldson:*  Originally, a driver with the company, Donaldson had spent 12 years in sales, 5 of them in his current, western, more industrialized area. He was 44 years old and well liked, but his paperwork had sometimes been criticized (see Figure C19-7).

### FIGURE C19–5
### Chandler: 1987 Sales Performance

| | January | February | March | April | Year to Date |
|---|---|---|---|---|---|
| Budget A$ | 58 250 | 58 250 | 58 250 | 71 900 | A$ 246 650 |
| Units | 8 500 | 8 500 | 8 500 | 10 500 | |
| Actual A$ | 54 675 | 55 640 | 54 400 | 59 425 | A$ 224 140 |
| Units | 8 122 | 8 224 | 7 993 | 8 831 | |

### FIGURE C19–6
### Bannion: 1987 Sales Performance

| | January | February | March | April | Year to Date |
|---|---|---|---|---|---|
| Budget A$ | 58 550 | 58 900 | 58 900 | 75 350 | A$ 251 700 |
| Units | 8 550 | 8 600 | 8 600 | 11 000 | |
| Actual A$ | 62 153 | 60 035 | 60 527 | 78 775 | A$ 261 490 |
| Units | 9 014 | 8 703 | 8 911 | 11 523 | |

### FIGURE C19–7
### Donaldson: 1987 Sales Performance

| | January | February | March | April | Year to Date |
|---|---|---|---|---|---|
| Budget A$ | 68 500 | 69 850 | 69 850 | 76 750 | A$ 284 950 |
| Units | 10 000 | 10 200 | 10 200 | 11 200 | |
| Actual A$ | 56 674 | 70 219 | 61 758 | 69 388 | A$ 256 039 |
| Units | 8 398 | 10 803 | 9 486 | 10 497 | |

*Sandra Nelson:* Nelson had been promoted to representative just that year, but at 39 she showed mature judgment. She had joined Southern Cross as a junior clerk straight from school and had outstanding procedural and product knowledge. Being new at sales, she had been given one of the smaller, more remote country territories (see Figure C19–8).

*John Tarry:* Tarry was efficient and experienced. He had originally been with a competitor, but seven years previously, at the age of 34, he had joined Southern Cross as a sales representative; he had had his current metropolitan territory for four years. He

had a reputation of always doing whatever was required of him (see Figure C19–9).

*Risa Holmes:* Holmes was an astute, highly motivated sales representative with an impressive sales record. She was generally regarded as the next sales manager. She had been with Southern Cross for 15 years and was now 38 years old. She had a prime metropolitan area that had reflected excellent growth as a result of population explosion into the outer, more affluent, eastern suburbs of Melbourne. In addition, she had responsibility for one major account, which had a number of outlets in other territories but had all its sales included in this territory's results (see Figure C19–10).

**FIGURE C19–8**

**Nelson: 1987 Sales Performance**

|  | January | February | March | April | Year to Date |
|---|---|---|---|---|---|
| Budget A$ | 41 000 | 41 000 | 44 500 | 61 500 | A$ 188 000 |
| Units | 6 000 | 6 000 | 6 500 | 9 000 | |
| Actual A$ | 38 088 | 35 365 | 42 164 | 51 348 | A$ 166 965 |
| Units | 5 612 | 5 203 | 6 217 | 7 531 | |

**FIGURE C19–9**

**Tarry: 1987 Sales Performance**

|  | January | February | March | April | Year to Date |
|---|---|---|---|---|---|
| Budget A$ | 66 450 | 66 450 | 68 500 | 87 000 | A$ 288 400 |
| Units | 9 700 | 9 700 | 10 000 | 12 700 | |
| Actual A$ | 73 274 | 75 121 | 78 738 | 91 915 | A$ 319 021 |
| Units | 10 481 | 10 752 | 11 254 | 13 321 | |

**FIGURE C19–10**

**Holmes: 1987 Sales Performance**

|  | January | February | March | April | Year to Date |
|---|---|---|---|---|---|
| Budget A$ | 116 450 | 117 800 | 117 800 | 150 700 | A$ 502 750 |
| Units | 17 000 | 17 200 | 17 200 | 22 000 | |
| Actual A$ | 114 613 | 117 347 | 133 621 | 149 852 | A$ 515 433 |
| Units | 17 112 | 17 479 | 20 041 | 22 490 | |

***Compensation and Evaluation Procedures*** Sales representatives were paid on a straight salary basis. Newly appointed sales personnel were paid A$18 000 per year,[1] and after approximately three years were given a "mature" grading with a salary range of A$24,000–$27,000. A few representatives were given senior sales status, with a higher salary based on service and performance.

Each representative had a car but had to pay for all private mileage at 10 cents a mile. They were also given an advance of A$500 for expenses, and reported actual expenses on a monthly basis. Expenses in metropolitan areas were not expected to exceed A$50 per week. Car running expenses were separate from the above, which were largely used for accommodation, hospitality, and special business purposes.

From time to time, sales representatives were given the opportunity to earn additional rewards through contests. These were used to push a particular product line and generally took the form of cash based on sales over a given quota. Occasionally merchandise was given instead.

In addition to sales and budget figures, representatives were also evaluated against objectives they had set in conjunction with their sales manager. These were normally of a qualitative or descriptive nature, to reflect the way each representative intended to develop his or her territory.

## Discussion Questions

1. What actions would you implement to reverse Southern Cross's sales problem?
2. Should Southern Cross modify its compensation system?
3. What is your opinion of Southern Cross's sales organization in the state of Victoria, including the selection and recruitment policies?
4. Should the budgetary system and sales data information be changed?

# CASE 20

# Lime Light Cinema

In December 1985, after nine months of operation, the Lime Light Cinema of Burloak, Ontario, was still not generating satisfactory revenues. To attract larger audiences, head office in Montreal decided on major changes in the programming format and the pricing strategy. Bill Williams, the new manager, was faced with the responsibility for successfully implementing these changes.

## Company History

The theatre had been operated as a sex-film house under the name Cosmopolitan Cinema for 15 years. In January 1985, Celebrity Films of Montreal had purchased the business as part of an expansion plan. To reposition the theatre as a first-run art-film cinema featuring two films per evening, major renovations were undertaken in late February. In March, Celebrity Films had reopened the theatre as the New Cosmopolitan Cinema.

From the beginning, the new cinema encountered problems with image. Even though the concept had changed, association with the previous name still branded the cinema as a place to see sex films. In October, the name had been changed to Lime Light Cinema, and a new marquee was acquired. In November, the owners had fired the manager and promoted Bill Williams, who had been assistant manager for four months, to the position. Prior to becoming assistant manager, Williams had worked for five months as one of the theatre's ushers.

## Company Problems

After the name change and under Williams's new management, business had improved slightly. In January and February the average audience size had been about 60 persons per show, well below the 375-seat capacity. Attendance in December was up, to 90–100 people per show. Williams remarked, "As we will be receiving an average admittance fee of $3.40 per head, we will pretty well have to pack the place every night to break even."

In Williams's opinion, the theatre had two problems: (1) people did not know much about the theatre; and (2) people did not know much about the films being shown. "People don't know what they are getting when they go to see an art film," stated Williams.

After eight months of operation, Celebrity Films finally realized that Burloak did not have the population size or audience interest to support a first-run art-film cinema. (Cost data are outlined in Figure C20–1.)

## Recent Changes

Responding to the low attendance figures, Celebrity changed the theatre's concept again. Beginning in mid-December, Lime Light Cinema became a repertory theatre, featuring two different movies every night (one shown at 7:00 PM and the other at 9:15 PM). Features would include second-run commercial films (movies shown two to three months after their premiere), occasional premiere films, and first-run art films. Williams explained, "Most of the films shown will have been in Burloak already. People will know the films and that will make our promotion job a lot easier." The variety of films and reduced prices were key elements in the new strategy.

Lime Light would be moving (on January 1, 1986) from a straight admission fee of $3.00 for students and $4.00 for adults to a membership basis. Company management felt that the old prices were not low enough to attract enough people to come to see a film with which they were unfamiliar. Members would pay $5.00 a year to join the cinema and $1.50 per show admission fee. For nonmembers the fee per film would be $2.50. At these prices Lime Light Cinema would be offering lower prices than the other repertory theatre in town, which charged a $4.00 membership fee, and $2.50 and $3.50 for admission to members and nonmembers, respectively. Initially, Lime Light Cinema had ordered 5000 membership cards.

Williams had increased theatre revenues and profits by making changes in the candy counter operation — adding and deleting products and adjusting prices on soft drinks and popcorn. The

SOURCE    Marvin Ryder.

## FIGURE C20–1

### Theatre Cost Information

| | |
|---|---|
| Film rental per showing | $      75 |
| Estimated management salaries | $20 000 per year |
| Estimated theatre lease (building & utilities) | $  2 000 per month |
| Estimated gross margin on candy operation — 65% (0.65 of each dollar spent at the candy counter represented profit) | |
| Average staffing per night | |
| 1 cashier | |
| 1 candy counter attendant (two on Friday and Saturday nights) | } (average of 3.5 hours per person at minimum wage) |
| 2 ushers | |
| 1 doorman | |
| plus 1 projectionist (4.5 hours per night at $10.00 per hour) | |

average receipt per patron had increased from about $0.50 to $0.75. The theatre would generate a high percentage of any profits from the candy operation, so these changes were important.

## The Theatre Industry

There were eight commercial theatres and one repertory theatre in Burloak. Originally, Lime Light Cinema did not directly compete with either type of theatre. However, with the changes, they would be competing directly with the other repertory theatre in town, which was very well established. Williams expected to have some initial difficulty competing for business, but believed that there was room for two repertory theatres in Burloak.

Besides the other theatres, another source of competition was home videotape machines. By the time second-run commercial films were shown at the Lime Light Cinema, they were available on videocassettes. People could purchase or rent these cassettes for home viewing. Premiere films would not be affected by cassette sales. Art films were generally not available to the public on cassette. Only with concerted effort could some of the exotic art-film titles be located.

A wide variety of customers patronized the cinema. Williams estimated that 35 percent of his customers were students from Burloak University and Mohican College. Customers fell into one of the following categories:

1. regular moviegoers who could afford to go to commercial theatres;
2. avid movie buffs, including film students from Burloak University and Mohican College;
3. people who wanted something offbeat and different; and
4. people who were just looking for an inexpensive night out.

He believed they were marketing to everybody.

## Promoting the New Concept

Approximately $17 000 had been allocated to promotion for 1986. In the past, most of the theatre's advertising budget had been spent on newspaper space. Lime Light Cinema placed a daily ad in the *Burloak Chronicle* and an occasional ad in *The Shadow*, the university student newspaper. (See Figure C20–2 for examples.) Williams felt that radio advertising was generally too expensive, but would use it occasionally to promote premiere features. In addition, bimonthly tabloid-type program schedules were distributed to potential customers through all record stores and donut shops in the city. These schedules were provided by head office. (Information on media costs is shown in Figure C20–3.) Williams did not really know if the advertising was effective. He did know that the future promotional strategy for the repertory concept had to be success-

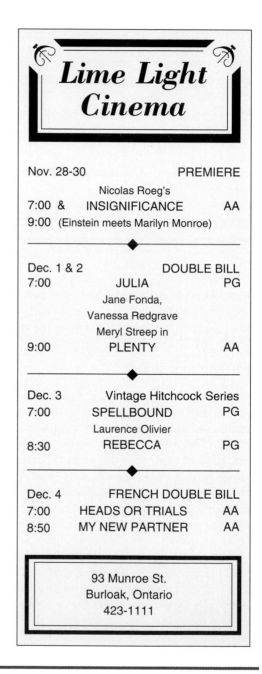

Lime Light
Cinema
Last Night – Double Bill
Jane Fonda in JULIA (PG) 7:00
Meryl Streep in PLENTY (AA) 9:00

*Lime Light Cinema*

Nov. 28-30                    PREMIERE
            Nicolas Roeg's
7:00 &    INSIGNIFICANCE        AA
9:00   (Einstein meets Marilyn Monroe)

Dec. 1 & 2              DOUBLE BILL
7:00              JULIA            PG
            Jane Fonda,
            Vanessa Redgrave
            Meryl Streep in
9:00            PLENTY            AA

Dec. 3          Vintage Hitchcock Series
7:00          SPELLBOUND          PG
            Laurence Olivier
8:30          REBECCA            PG

Dec. 4          FRENCH DOUBLE BILL
7:00          HEADS OR TRIALS      AA
8:50          MY NEW PARTNER      AA

93 Munroe St.
Burloak, Ontario
423-1111

ful or he would be out of a job. (Population information is given in Figure C20–4.)

The objective of the new promotional program was to make people aware of the repertory format and the new prices, and to sell memberships. So far, Williams had purchased a 60-line ad in the *Burloak Chronicle* to announce the opening and had arranged an interview on a CBUR-TV entertainment

## FIGURE C20-3

### Advertising Rates in Burloak

**Print**

| | Circulation | Line Rate (per column) |
|---|---|---|
| *Burloak Chronicle* | 147 448 (total paid daily) | $2.16 |
| | | $1.61 (over 10 000 lines per year) |
| *TV Facts* (Burloak edition) (free distribution) | 26 913 (weekly) | ¼ page — $105.00/week (26-week schedule) |
| *The Shadow* | 14 000 (weekly) | $0.62 |
| | | $0.48 (weekly contract) |

**Radio**

| | AAA | AA | A | B | |
|---|---|---|---|---|---|
| CABC (#1 station in Burloak area) | $55 | $43 | $35 | $28 | 60 seconds |
| | $45 | $34 | $29 | $23 | 30 seconds |

AAA — 6:00 AM to 10:00 AM weekdays    AA — 4:00 PM to 11:00 PM weekdays

A — 10:00 AM to 4:00 PM weekdays and Saturday    B — all other times

Reach plan    $35.00 per spot for 21 60-second spots consisting of 4 AAA, 6 AA, 6 A, and 5 B spots

CFBU (Burloak University station) — 60 seconds — $2.00

CFMC (Mohican College station) — 60 seconds — $1.00

## FIGURE C20-4

### Population Statistics for Burloak

| Metropolitan Burloak | |
|---|---|
| Population | 324 000* |
| Age Groups | |
| Under 14 | 72 380 |
| 15-24 | 61 920 |
| 25-34 | 51 540 |
| 35-44 | 38 045 |
| Over 44 | 84 485 |
| *Student population | |
| Burloak University | 14 500 |
| Mohican College | 4 000 |

program to talk about the new concept. He was thinking of trying to arrange a couple of radio interviews as well, but he knew more had to be done.

### Discussion Question

**1.** How would you advise Williams?

## CASE 21

# RW Packaging (A)

In May 1985, Tom Malone, MBA, a Winnipeg-based marketing consultant, was preparing for a seminar with employees of RW Packaging, a packaging and distribution firm. The president of RW Packaging, Robert Keith, had hired Tom Malone to perform a small, in-depth study of his company's position in the paint sundries market, a problem area for the firm. He hoped that both the activity of taking part in the study and the results of the study would encourage his employees to develop a more objective view of the company's strengths and weaknesses and a better appreciation of the role each employee did or could play in the company's competitive market success. Interviews with employees and major customers were now complete, and Malone had to assess the results. He wondered what implications could be drawn from the study, and how best to present these at the employees' seminar he would be conducting next week.

## The Company

RW Packaging was founded in Winnipeg in 1919 as a packager and distributor of automobile radiator antifreeze. Over the years the company had changed hands several times, and had distributed a wide range of products, from Hershey's chocolate to sporting goods.

By 1985, RW Packaging was involved with a variety of products as a packager and distributor for other firms, or as a manufacturer of in-house brands (for example, Goldex brands). Broad product segments included the following:

1. Household cleaning supplies (e.g. ammonia, bleach)
2. Automotive chemicals (windshield-washer fluid)
3. Lighting fluids (e.g., kerosene)

4. Nonprescription pharmaceuticals (e.g., castor oil, rubbing alcohol)
5. Paint sundries (e.g., linseed oil, turpentine, paint thinners)
6. Custom packaging for liquids and powders (e.g., Borax laundry products, major oil company brands of windshield-washer fluid)

Head office was located in Winnipeg, with a plant and branch sales office in Edmonton, Alberta. The company serviced markets throughout Western Canada. RW Packaging currently employed 50 people, and had annual sales of about $10 million.

Keith had produced a booklet for all employees that defined the company's mission as "To Pursue the Highest Degree of Excellence in The Packaging Field." To aid in this pursuit, the booklet defined 13 "core values" central to the organization: action; a strong corporate image; creative thinking; delegation of responsibility; growth; fair hiring policies and promotion from within; honesty, integrity, and fairness; a lean and productive staff; mistakes acceptable as part of the learning process; openness and frankness in staff relations; profitability; a profound appreciation of customers and suppliers; and, finally, maintenance of simple systems and procedures.

RW Packaging followed a "Me Too" marketing strategy. The firm was interested in markets that were already developed and showed promise of moderate growth and profitability. If the potential opportunity was a good fit with existing business, RW would enter the market, generally using a low-price position. Promotion was limited to personal selling through sales reps in each province, together with advertising rebates and volume discounts to wholesalers and retailers. RW did not engage in any promotion directed at end consumers. Wholesalers across Canada were used in distribution. In the paint sundries market, a major competitor was an eastern Ontario–based firm, Record Chemical.

## The Study

Malone's study of the paint sundries market had been aimed at helping RW employees to take an objective view of the strengths, weaknesses, and dis-

SOURCE    This case was prepared by Morva Bowman, MBA, under the supervision of Dr. C. Dennis Anderson, as a basis for class discussion rather than to illustrate either effective or ineffective handling of an administrative situation. Copyright © 1986 by the Case Development Program, Faculty of Management, University of Manitoba. Support for the development of this case was provided by the Canadian Studies Program, Secretary of State, Ottawa; and by the Management Excellence in Small Business Program, Department of Industry, Trade and Commerce, Ottawa.

FIGURE C21-1

## Person Identification Used for RW Employees' Questionnaire Responses

| Letter Code | Name | Position |
|---|---|---|
| A | Vern Downey | Purchasing Manager |
| B | Tim Bailey | |
| C | Derrick Veinot | |
| D | Daily Lennox | Marketing Support |
| E | Ken Hackett | Sales |
| F | Kelly Keith | Sales |
| G | John McIntyre | V.P. Sales/Marketing |
| H | Bob Keith | President |
| I | Michael Woolf | Operations Manager |
| J | Herb Page | V.P. Finance |
| K | B. McConnell | Q.C. Manager |
| L | Allan Smakula | Production Supervisor |

FIGURE C21-2

## Buyer Identification Used for Questionnaire Responses

| Letter Code | Name | Position |
|---|---|---|
| MC | Merchants Consolidated | Buyer |
| MW | Marshall Wells | Buyer |
| ML | McLeods | Buyer |
| D | Dominion Lumber | Buyer |
| P | Polet Lumber | Buyer |

tinctive competences of the firm relative to competitors and relative to the needs and perceptions of RW's customers. The study tied in with the "profound appreciation of customers" part of the corporate mission statement. Keith did not want to make big changes in his staff's orientation; he simply wished to encourage his employees to think in customer-oriented terms and to see that each employee (not just those in sales) had an important role to play in helping the company compete for business and accomplish the corporate mission. He also wanted employees to have a better understanding of why policies were implemented, and where improvements might be made. If the study were also to reveal information useful in planning and revising marketing strategy, this would be considered a plus.

The qualitative study consisted of questionnaires given to RW management and staff and in-depth personal interviews conducted with key paint sundries buyers.

Interviewers, working from a specially designed list of questions, gathered information on the following topics:

- Weighting of characteristics that might be offered by a supplier (quality, reputation, reliability, full product line, service, sales reps)

FIGURE C21-3

## Summary of RW Employees' Perceptions of the Importance a Paint Sundries Buyer Would Attach to Various Supplier Characteristics and the Ratings the Buyer Would Give to Record Chemical and RW Packaging

| Supplier Characteristic | Importance and Ratings | Degree of Importance to Buyer and Rating Buyer Would Give to Suppliers | | | | |
|---|---|---|---|---|---|---|
| | | *Low* 1 | 2 | 3 | 4 | *High* 5 |
| Product Quality | IMP | | J | ADGH | EFIKL | BC |
| | REC | | | ADEGHIK | FJL | |
| | RW | | | ABDGHIKL | EFJ | C |
| Company Reputation | IMP | | | BCFGHIKL | ADI | E |
| | REC | | | | | |
| | RW | | | | | |
| Price Competitiveness | IMP | | | | BE | ACDFGHIJKL |
| | REC | | | F | AEGHIJK | D |
| | RW | | L | AF | BDEGIK | OGH |
| Reliability of Service | IMP | | | GH | BFIKL | ACDEJ |
| | REC | | EIH | ADGK | F | J |
| | RW | | | GHL | ACEFIK | BDJ |
| Speed of Delivery | IMP | | | GHJKL | CDFI | ABE |
| | REC | | AEHI | GK | FJ | |
| | RW | | | G | ACEFLJKL | BDH |
| Full Product Line | IMP | HL | | AFGIK | BCDJ | E |
| | REC | | | DGI | FHK | AEJL |
| | RW | | | GK | ACDFHIJL | BE |
| After-Sales Service | IMP | GH | | FIK | ACDJL | BE |
| | REC | E | FK | ADGIJ | | |
| | RW | | | ABOGHIJ | DEFK | |
| Co-op Ad Support | IMP | | F | DEI | BCJK | AGH |
| | REC | | J | EH | G | |
| | RW | | BC | DEHJ | G | |
| Rebates | IMP | | K | CDE | ABFIJ | GH |
| | REC | | J | EH | G | |
| | RW | DF | | CEHIJ | BG | |
| In-Store Displays | IMP | GJ | BCDFK | AGI | E | L |
| | REC | F | J | EGH | | |
| | RW | DFL | ABCJ | EGI | | |
| Returns Policy | IMP | H | K | ACDFGL | IJ | BE |
| | REC | | HK | ADGJ | | |
| | RW | | | AGJ | BCFHGK | DE |
| Quality of Sales Reps | IMP | | CJ | GHI | ADIK | BEL |
| | REC | | F | AGHIJ | E | |
| | RW | | | ABGJL | CDEFHGK | |

FIGURE C21-4

## Importance a Paint Sundries Buyer Attaches to Various Supplier Characteristics and the Ratings the Buyer Gives to Record Chemical and RW Packaging

| Supplier Characteristic | Importance and Ratings | Degree of Importance to Buyer and Buyer's Rating of Suppliers | | | | |
|---|---|---|---|---|---|---|
| | | *Low* 1 | 2 | 3 | 4 | *High* 5 |
| Product Quality | IMP | | | | D | MW,MC,ML,P |
| | REC | | | | | MW |
| | RW | | | | MC,ML | MW,D,P |
| Company Reputation | IMP | | ML* | P | MW,MC,P | ML* |
| | REC | | | | | |
| | RW | | | | | |
| Price Competitiveness | IMP | | | | | MW,MC,ML,D,P |
| | REC | | | | | MW |
| | RW | | | MW,ML | MC,P | D |
| Reliability of Service | IMP | | | | | MW,MC,ML,D,P |
| | REC | | | | MW | |
| | RW | | | | MW,D,P | MC,ML |
| Speed of Delivery | IMP | | | | MC,D | MW,ML,P |
| | REC | | | | MW | |
| | RW | | | | MW,MC,D,P | ML |
| Full Product Line | IMP | | | MC | MW,ML | D,P |
| | REC | | | | | MW |
| | RW | | | | MW,MC,ML, D,P | |
| After-Sales Service | IMP | | | MC | MW,ML,D,P | |
| | REC | | | | | |
| | RW | | | MC | MW | ML |
| Co-op Ad Support | IMP | | | | MC | MW,ML,D,P |
| | REC | | | | | MW |
| | RW | MW,MC | P | ML | | |
| Rebates | IMP | | | P | MC | MW,ML,D |
| | REC | | | | | MW |
| | RW | MW,MC,ML | | | | |
| In-Store Displays | IMP | | | ML,P | MW,MC,D | |
| | REC | | | | MW | |
| | RW | ML | | MC | MW | |
| Returns Policy | IMP | | | | MW,MC,ML,D | P |
| | REC | | | MW | MW MC | |
| | RW | | | | | ML,D,P |
| Quality of Sales Reps | IMP | | | MW,ML | D | MC,P |
| | REC | | | MW | | |
| | RW | | | | MW,MC,ML | D,P |

*McLeod's buyer rates company reputation at 5 for national "pull-advertised" brands and 2 for generic, staple products.

FIGURE C21–5

## RW Employees' Perceptions of Buyers' Supplier Choice: Average Importance and Average Ratings

| Supplier Characteristic | Average Importance | Average Ratings | |
|---|---|---|---|
| | | *Record* | *RW* |
| Price Competitiveness | 4.83 | 4.00 | 3.92 |
| Reliability of Service | 4.25 | 3.00 | 4.00 |
| Speed of Delivery | 3.83 | 2.75 | 4.17 |
| Co-op Advertising $ | 3.82 | 3.00 | 2.86 |
| Rebates | 3.73 | 3.00 | 2.78 |
| Product Quality | 3.67 | 3.30 | 3.42 |
| Quality of Sales Reps | 3.67 | 3.00 | 3.58 |
| Company Reputation | 3.42 | — | |
| After-Sales Service | 3.42 | 2.44 | 3.36 |
| Returns Policy | 3.25 | 2.67 | 3.91 |
| Full Product Line | 3.17 | 4.10 | 4.00 |
| In-Store Displays | 2.44 | 2.40 | 2.00 |

FIGURE C21–6

## Summary of RW Employees' Comments on Differences Between Wholesale and Retail Accounts[*]

### Comments (paraphrased)

| Person | More Important to Retailer | Person | More Important to Wholesaler |
|---|---|---|---|
| A | Product Quality | DFK | Price |
| AIK | Package/Product Appearance | F | Local Availability of Stock |
| BD | Promotion Support | G | "Push" Effort of Supplier |
| D | Sales Reps Do Stocktaking | G | "Pull" Effort of Supplier |
| FI | Brand Name | G | Rebates |
| F | New Products Available? | GH | Advertising Funds |
| AG | Minimum Order Size | H | Front-End Money |
| ADGI | Speed of Delivery | K | Speed of Delivery |
| G | Competitive Price | F | Supplier Doesn't Sell Direct to Retailer |
| D | Service Offered by Sales Reps | | |

[*]Some people stated that there were no major differences.

- Rating of Record Chemical (competitor) on above criteria
- Rating of RW Packaging on above criteria
- Identifying the key decision-makers
- Three greatest strengths and weaknesses of Record Chemical and RW Packaging
- Rating of quality of sales calls

The results of both interviews and questionnaires had been summarized and tabulated (see Figure C21–1 through Figure C21–9).

## Discussion Question

1. Malone wanted to analyze what these summaries of employees' and buyers' perceptions implied for RW Packaging's marketing plans, and how this information could most effectively be used to inform and motivate RW employees. What would you conclude from reviewing these results?

FIGURE C21-7

**RW Employees' Perceptions of Buyers' Supplier Choice: Overall Ratings for Paint Sundries Suppliers**

| | Ratings | | | | |
|---|---|---|---|---|---|
| **Supplier** | *Excellent* | *Good* | *Satisfactory* | *Poor* | *Bad* |
| Record Chemical | L | GLJ | ADEFK | H | |
| RW Packaging | | ACDEFGIJ | BHKL | | |
| Linwo | | | K | A | |
| Howdens Brakers | | | D | | |
| Penguin | | F | | | |
| Northern Paint | | F | | | |

FIGURE C21-8

## Summary of RW Employees' Perceptions of Strengths and Weaknesses of Paint Sundries Suppliers

| Factor | Record Chemical | | RW Packaging | |
| --- | --- | --- | --- | --- |
| | *Strength* | *Weakness* | *Strength* | *Weakness* |
| Price | DHI | | CD | F |
| Price/quality ratio | | | | DH |
| Price competitiveness | AE | | | AE |
| Buying power | AGJK | | | GJK |
| Price fluctuations | | | | C |
| Product quality | | K | BCK | |
| Product selection/diversity | AE | | BEI | A |
| Production innovation | | | | H |
| Product appearance | | | | C |
| Brand names | | | G | |
| Company name/reputation | J | | FJ | |
| Company size | H | | | |
| Production facilities | I | | G | I |
| Quality of package | | | | ABIKL |
| Quality of label | | | | B |
| Product appearance | | | | C |
| Packaging machinery/cost | | | | GL |
| Factory location re: Prairies | | AEFGHJK | AGHJK | |
| Ability to supply large Eastern accounts | EGI | | | EHJK |
| Factory location re: Toronto, Vancouver | G | | | |
| Order quantities re: West buyers | | AG | G | |
| Market size served | | | | GJ |
| Reliability of supply | | I | AI | E |
| Availability | | | BD | |
| Speed of delivery/local delivery | | IK | CDEHKL | |
| Dating program | F | | | |
| Service level to customer (in Prairies) | | EIK | ACFIJ | |
| Sales reps in West (local contract) | | AEG | EH | |
| Quality of sales reps | | H | | |
| Marketing/promotion effort | L | | | CI |

## Summary of RW Employees' Opinions on the Most Important Difference Between RW and Its Major Competitors

| Person | Comment (paraphrased) |
|---|---|
| AK | Location advantage for Prairie markets |
| CE | Centrally located — 2 production and sales outlets in Prairies |
| H | RW has control over Prairies but doesn't use it |
| J | RW is not in Eastern Canada and therefore is not exposed to (successful with?) buyers in the national chains |
| L | RW has marketing and pricing disadvantages |
| B | Competitors use a stronger container with silkscreen label |
| D | Record has an edge because it is a larger, national company, with better buying power and capabilities in packaging |
| F | Competitors push harder for initial order (e.g., better dating program, attractive booking price); then it is hard for RW to get the buyer to switch |
| G | Record has a better margin mix. For example, Record can afford to reduce prices to Prairies market of a Prairie customer because Prairies are only about 25 percent of its market. If RW cut price to Prairies the cut would be on 100 percent of RW's market. RW has to broaden its market/customer base before it can be competitive on price cutting. |

# CASE 22

# RW Packaging (B)

A few days after he had conducted a seminar for the employees of RW Packaging, Tom Malone met with Robert Keith, president of RW, to discuss the seminar's outcome.

The employees had examined the results of a study Malone had conducted to discover staff perceptions of the company and its position in the paint sundries market, as well as the perceptions of some major customers. (For study results and background information on RW Packaging, see Case 21.)

A number of issues were highlighted by the study and the follow-up seminar. There was some concern over the effect of inflexible policies on pricing, minimum order quantities, promotional support, and

SOURCE    This case was prepared by Morva Bowman, MBA, under the supervision of Dr. C. Dennis Anderson, as a basis for class discussion rather than to illustrate either effective or ineffective handling of an administrative situation. Copyright © 1986 by the Case Development Program, Faculty of Management, University of Manitoba. Support for the development of this case was provided by the Canadian Studies Program, Secretary of State, Ottawa; and by the Management Excellence in Small Business Program, Department of Industry, Trade and Commerce, Ottawa.

rebates. How, people wondered, would changes in one or more of these areas — particularly pricing — affect sales and profits? Could production technology or purchasing practices lower prices without too much erosion of profit margins?

RW's lack of "brand power" — an end-customer preference for its brands — had been the topic of much discussion. What would improve this situation and provide market "pull," and what would the necessary improvements cost? And finally, while customer service was perceived as one of RW's strengths, it was felt that the firm might be vulnerable if its chief competitor, Record Chemical, moved to significantly improve its service level on the Prairies.

"It appears that this first study has generated a lot more questions than answers," said Keith. "What happens now, Tom? Do you see any clear indications for changes we should be making in our marketing mix? It looks as if we will need further research to answer some of these questions. In the light of first-round results, what kind of study would you recommend?"

# CASE 23

# RW Packaging (C)

In December 1985, Robert Keith, president of RW Packaging, evaluated the information he had obtained about the western Canadian exterior stain market. RW, a Winnipeg-based packaging and distribution firm, was considering adding an exterior stain to its product line. An informal survey had provided background material on the exterior stain market and competitors, and now Keith had to decide whether or not to proceed with an RW product entry for this market.

## Background

Although originally founded in 1919 as a packager and distributor of automobile radiator antifreeze, RW Packaging had been through several owners and a wide range of products. As of 1985, the firm did custom packaging jobs and also manufactured some household and automotive products (for example, ammonia, detergent, and windshield-washer fluid). Its paint sundries line included lacquer and paint thinners/removers, linseed oil, shellac, solvent, turpentine, wood preservatives, and an interior stain called Swedish Oil. The company employed more than 50 people and had sales of about $10 million annually. (For further background on the company, its mission, and its marketing strategy, see Case 21.)

Its Winnipeg head office and its Edmonton plant and branch office provided RW with excellent access to markets across western Canada. The company had developed a stable client base and enjoyed an excellent reputation as a well-established supplier that emphasized good service and reliable product quality. Its highly diverse product line helped spread the risk involved in any one product.

RW had generally competed on price in marketing its manufactured products, as the firm did not have the resources to compete with national brands

in heavy promotional campaigns. No advertising budget was provided, and promotional activities were limited to personal selling by sales representatives in each province, along with volume discounts to wholesalers and retailers.

The company was constantly looking for new ways to diversify its product line. If a new product required limited investment and showed promise of a satisfactory return, RW would take it on. But Keith was wary of high-risk ventures.

## RW's Stain

An exterior stain would be a logical addition to RW Packaging's paint sundries line. Thinners, linseed oil, and paint/varnish removers — all high-volume, low-margin items — were doing very well. Only Swedish Oil, the interior stain, was not a success: following a good initial reception several years earlier, sales had declined. RW staff were not sure why this had occurred.

The proposed stain would be an exterior, oil-based, penetrating stain; it would offer the consumer one-step application, deep penetration, and good weathering characteristics. Such stains are easy to formulate, require no special production equipment, and are inexpensive to produce. Olympic, Timberlok, Rez, CIL, and Benjamin Moore already manufactured this type of stain. RW was motivated to pursue the exterior stain market for two reasons: to compensate for the inexplicably poor performance of the firm's interior stain product, and to benefit from the significantly larger size of the exterior stain market.

## The Exterior Stain Market

The report Keith was reviewing included information gathered by interviewing buyers for a number of retail outlets that sold stains. The buyers felt that a reputation for high quality was very important, so manufacturers with a long history of producing quality stains, as perceived by the end user, had a significant edge. Marketing support activities offered by existing exterior stain producers included media advertising, in-store promotions, and sale price specials. These forms of consumer and trade promotions were important to most retail outlets.

SOURCE This case was prepared by Morva Bowman, MBA, under the supervision of Dr. C. Dennis Anderson, as a basis for class discussion rather than to illustrate either effective or ineffective handling of an administrative situation. Copyright © 1986 by the Case Development Program, Faculty of Management, University of Manitoba. Support for the development of this case was provided by the Canadian Studies Program, Secretary of State, Ottawa; and the Management Excellence in Small Business Program, Department of Industry, Trade and Commerce, Ottawa.

Furthermore, retailers were interested in being able to obtain a good variety of stain colours, to broaden the product line they could offer to consumers.

But most of the retailers surveyed felt that the exterior stain market was saturated; it was already being served by a large number of well-entrenched, well-financed, and long-established manufacturers. The stores purchased either from distributors or directly, through manufacturers' sales reps. The manufacturers were responsible for setting regular and sale prices throughout the distribution channel, and for extolling their stains' quality and price through media advertising and in-store promotions. Prices varied slightly (see Figure C23–1), but retailers felt that price and comparative shopping were not major factors for the end consumer for this product. (Most stain purchases were made at the store where lumber was purchased or at the outlet where the consumer regularly shopped for home improvement items). However, they suggested that brand awareness could be an important factor, as heavy advertising apparently led consumers to ask for stain products by brand/manufacturer name (e.g., Olympic, Rez, CIL).

Further research had helped Keith understand the scope of his competition and the nature of the new market. There were about 75 paint manufacturers involved in the stain industry. They were spread across Canada, with a heavy concentration in Ontario and Quebec. Olympic, which specialized in stains, was the current market leader. It had an excellent distribution system and used a tremendous pull strategy consisting of advertising, conducting in-store promotions, and offering price specials (discounting) to end users.

The stain market in Canada is seasonal, running 10 to 12 weeks — from May through July for most of western Canada, and from March to November in British Columbia (see Figure C23–2 for 1985 sales.) Water-repellent stains, which had sold well in the United States, were only just gaining acceptance in Canada. Since there were very few technical differences between the major stain brands, manufacturers relied on advertising to create a perception of difference and to develop brand insistence.

Most stains were sold through lumber retailers — both chains and independents — although specialized paint/home decorating stores such as St. Clair or Color Your World, and department stores such as Sears or K mart, sold their own house brands of stain and occasionally also sold manufacturers' brands.

## Conclusion

Keith sifted through the information that had been collected about the exterior stain market. He had to decide soon: would RW enter this market? And if so, what marketing strategy should he use, and how should he position his product entry for best results? If he chose to proceed, he would have to hurry to get the new stain on the shelves by May. Exterior

---

FIGURE C23–1

**Average Stain Prices for Four-Litre Container**

| | |
|---|---|
| CIL | $19.24 |
| Olympic | $22.20 semitransparent |
| | $22.22 solid-colour oil |
| | $24.10 weather screen |
| REZ | $16.60 |
| Benjamin Moore | $21.95 |
| Timberlok | $17.99 |
| K mart | $ 7.99 |
| Canadian Tire — Mastercraft | $24.99/17.00/10.00 |
| | best/better/good |
| Sears | $29.99 penetrating stain |
| | $33.99 weather beater |
| | $33.99 w.b. latex |

FIGURE C23-2

## Stain Sales Statistics—Western Canada, April–June, 1985 (in 000s of Litres)

| | Manitoba/ Saskatchewan | Alberta | British Columbia |
|---|---|---|---|
| Beaver Lumber | – | 2.37 | – |
| Behr Process | 6.31 | 8.03 | 8.17 |
| Benjamin Moore | 7.04 | – | – |
|   Moorwood | 7.04 | – | – |
| CIL | 4.28 | 2.19 | 4.74 |
|   Bapco | 3.42 | 2.19 | 4.74 |
| Canadian Tire | – | 3.08 | 3.11 |
|   Mastercraft | – | 3.08 | 2.24 |
|   A/O Can. Tire | – | – | 3.22 |
| Color Your World | – | – | 3.45 |
| Eaton's | 5.80 | – | – |
| Fed. Co-op/Fedco | 7.40 | 4.51 | – |
| Flecto Coatings | 7.12 | 19.44 | 11.00 |
| General Paint | – | 3.94 | 10.96 |
|   A/O General | – | 3.94 | 10.96 |
| Glidden | – | – | 2.70 |
|   Glidden | – | – | 2.70 |
| Homecare | – | 2.48 | – |
| Interlab | 6.63 | – | – |
| LePage's | – | 2.80 | 4.32 |
| Northern Paint | 4.43 | 4.08 | 5.94 |
| Olympic Stain | 5.12 | 3.99 | 4.00 |
|   Olympic | 5.12 | 3.99 | 4.00 |
| Pittsburgh | – | – | 3.87 |
|   Pittsburgh | – | – | 3.87 |
| Revelstoke | – | 3.20 | – |
| Sears | 4.37 | 4.93 | 4.04 |
|   Weatherbeater | 4.05 | 4.93 | 4.04 |
|   A/O Sears | 4.98 | – | – |
| Sherwin Williams | – | – | 8.48 |
|   Ken | – | – | 8.48 |
| St. Clair Paint | – | 3.99 | – |
|   St.Clair | – | 3.99 | – |
| Valspar | – | – | 6.97 |
| All Other | 8.38 | 2.75 | 2.71 |
| TOTAL MARKET | 5.84 | 3.75 | 4.99 |

stain seemed the next logical addition to the company's product line, but he wasn't sure whether his firm could successfully compete in the established market.

## Discussion Question

1. Would you advise Keith to go ahead or drop the project? Explain your reasoning.

# Wintec Electronics

In early 1985, Frank Williams faced a major decision: what was the next step to take in launching the new electronic spray meter control panel for agricultural crop sprayers developed by his company, Wintec Electronics Inc.? Williams founded Wintec, his own electronics design and manufacturing firm, in Winnipeg, Manitoba, in 1978. The sprayer meter control panel was Wintec's newest component-part product. It had been developed under an agreement with Can-Spray, a small agricultural marketing company. Can-Spray was supposed to buy Wintec's control panel, assemble it with other components to form a "new system" for controlling chemical mixing and flows on agricultural crop spraying equipment, and sell the new system (called Ag-Chemical Injector) to sprayer manufacturers, distributors, and/or users. However, Can-Spray had run into financial problems, and significant sales had not materialized. Wintec was faced with a frustrating situation. Williams explained: "I believe that this product has some good possibilities, but I'm not sure what the next step should be. Should I scrap the control panel and move on to something new, or should I try to buy all the rights and market it myself? Marketing is not my area of expertise, but I don't want to waste all those months of R & D if the product is a potential winner."

## Frank Williams — Entrepreneur

Williams was a professional engineer with many years' experience in electronics design. After his graduation in 1964 he had worked for 14 years in a variety of different design jobs. His experience also included marketing positions with two distributorships, and teaching electronics at Red River Community College for two years.

SOURCE    This case was prepared by Morva Bowman, MBA, under the supervision of Dr. C. Dennis Anderson, as a basis for class discussion rather than to illustrate either effective or ineffective handling of an administrative situation. Copyright (c) 1986 by the Case Development Program, Faculty of Management, University of Manitoba. Support for the development of this case was provided by the Technology Branch, Manitoba Industry, Trade and Technology; by the Management Excellence in Small Business Program, Department of Industry, Trade and Commerce, Ottawa; and by the Canadian Studies Program, Secretary of State, Ottawa.

In 1978 he started Wintec Electronics in the basement of his home. For the first two years he sold his expertise in the design and manufacturing of electronic parts, even though he had no manufacturing space. He sought contracts from manufacturers he had dealt with in the past, offering to design and build a new or improved control or part for an existing product. He sold the "product," even though he had not yet produced it. He would meet with prospective customers to determine how their needs and his abilities could fit together, and then return with a product proposal. His first customer was Versatile Farm Equipment Company, an established Winnipeg-based manufacturer of tractors and related farm implements, for whom he designed and built a new electronic turn-signal flasher to be used in various models of tractors. This initial project was successful, and the first run was followed by a larger production order. At the same time he successfully negotiated a contract with Controlled Environments Ltd. to design a prototype environmental control chamber for scientific research.

With these orders in hand, Williams was able to negotiate a lease on Advance Factory Space through the Winnipeg Industrial Technology Centre, a project of the Manitoba government's Department of Trade and Commerce. This program allows new manufacturers access to factory space with initial rent reductions, enabling their business to grow without the heavy burden that renting large amounts of space would bring. For the first six months, the company pays no rent; for the next six months, the rate is one-third the normal charge. From 12 to 18 months they pay two thirds, and after 18 months, the full rate. At the end of two years the business is expected to have grown enough to move out into regular factory space on its own, with no subsidies.

Wintec was very successful and in 1982 moved into new premises as an independent design and manufacturing firm. By 1985 the firm's annual sales volume was $2 million, and it employed a staff of 26 persons (see Figure C24–1 for a diagram of its organizational structure). The company produced 40 different products, covering three different market areas and serving five corporate customers.

About 30 percent of Wintec's work was in electronics for agricultural equipment, including dashboard control panels, sensing devices, and instrumentation electronics. Most of this production — over 80 percent — was for one agricultural equipment manufacturer, Versatile. Over the past three years the agricultural industry had not been strong and although this had been a growth area for Wintec, most of the increase had come from increased use of electronics in different types of agricultural equipment, rather than from increased sales of any particular type of machinery.

The remainder of Wintec's sales were divided this way: about 30 percent involved industrial/scientific research equipment; another 30 percent, a controller for satellite dishes; and about 10 percent, miscellaneous small jobs (see Figure C24–2). Although sales were good, they were also somewhat cyclical — most agricultural equipment components are produced during the fall and winter, to be ready for spring selling. The satellite-dish controller was also manufactured largely in the fall, to be sold as a gift item at Christmas. Production of scientific research equipment was steady, but this left excess production capacity available during the spring and summer months.

Williams was responsible for all marketing activities, and for initiating all new-product development. The development process was not formalized, but occurred in response to requests from existing customers, as a result of sales pitches Williams had made to potential buyers of Wintec's capabilities, or as a result of an individual or firm asking Wintec to do the technical development on a product idea for which the asker felt there was a market opportunity; the askers were usually prepared to do all the mark-

FIGURE C24–1

**Organization Chart for Wintec Electronics**

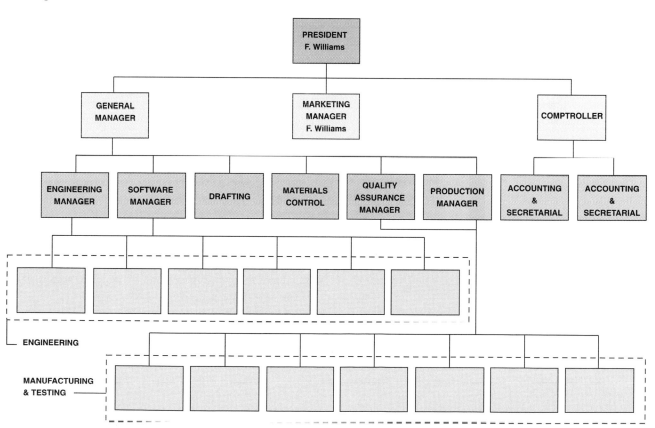

FIGURE C24-2

## Product/Market Breakdown

| Market Area | Client | Products Manufactured | Approximate Sales Volume |
|---|---|---|---|
| Agricultural | Versatile Manufacturing (agriculture OEM)* | turn-signal flashers<br>depth controls<br>transmission controls<br>warning lamp panels for dash instrumentation<br>monitor systems for grain swathers | $410 000 |
| | Can-Spray | control panel for Ag-Chemical Injector | 0 |
| | several small contracts for minor jobs — other agriculture OEM's | | $190 000 |
| Industrial/ Scientific | Controlled Environments Ltd. | environment control chamber for research | $580 000 |
| | Micro-Tool and Machine | computerized machine controls | $150 000 |
| Satellite Dishes | Sat-Scan (satellite equipment manufacturer) | 3 models of a dish controller | $600 000 |

*Original equipment manufacturer.

eting. Products were developed only when the firm had an assured customer, preferably one who made some financial commitment to the R & D process up front. There was no specific screening process — Williams decided to go or not based on his experience and personal assessment of the customers. "To compete with government-funded R & D facilities and to generate work for my production facility, R & D projects are priced at cost: Wintec's profit lies in manufacturing the finished product," he explained (see Figure C24–3).

"I'm not very aggressive in my marketing efforts," explained Williams. "I say 'no' to a lot of projects if I don't like the sound of them, and we don't follow any formal strategic planning or market segmentation outlines. It's all in my head, so far. In another year or so, if the company continues to grow like this, we'll have to hire a full-time marketing manager. I don't really have the time to give marketing the attention it deserves."

Williams identified several problem areas for the firm. "We need more customers in each of our three market areas. Right now we're vulnerable to a slowdown from one of our main customers: it could cut back almost a third of our production. In addition, like most businesses in a growth stage, we are limited by production capacity in some areas, and by cash flow. In order to compete effectively outside Winnipeg — in Canada and the U.S. — we would have to increase production efficiencies, and improve both cost and quality control."

"Our goals may not be part of a formal plan, but we do have them," continued Williams. "Just to keep up to the market and our competitors, we need to increase our volume by 30 percent per year, and I would prefer to make that 50 percent. We need to expand our product line and our marketing activities. In this business, growth is vital to keep up with the industry, and to keep good technical staff interested."

FIGURE C24-3

## FIGURE C24-3

### Selected Financial Data, Wintec Electronics

| | |
|---|---|
| Current Assets | $917 000 |
| Accounts Receivable | 360 000 |
| Fixed Assets | 149 000 |
| Current Liabilities | 700 000 |
| Bank Indebtedness | 282 000 |
| Accounts Payable | 309 000 |
| Long Term Debt | 20 000 |
| Shareholder's Equity | 338 000 |
| Sales | 2 000 000 |
| Cost of Goods Sold | |
| Material | 1 045 000 |
| Direct Labour | 320 000 |
| Production Overload | 64 000 |
| Research and Development Expense | 203 000 |
| Administrative Expense | 235 000 |
| Net Income | 133 000 |

## Development of the Ag-Chemical Injector System

The concept for a new system to handle crop sprayer chemical mixing and flow rates was originated by Can-Spray's entrepreneurial owner. The Ag-Chemical Injector was a system to control the injection of two different chemicals in agricultural sprayers. It was positioned as an "add-on" to crop sprayers produced by other manufacturers. It permitted sprayer operators to set the injection rate, thus determining the strength of the chemical mixture. It also allowed them to turn one or the other chemical on or off 'on the fly' during spraying, or to switch to just one side of the sprayer. The operator could thus do spot applications of a particular chemical where needed and, in addition, could spray half-widths along the edges of fields. The injector included a tank for concentrated chemicals, an electronic control panel, flow meters, pumps, valves, and piping; it could be readily installed on most sprayers. (see Figure C24–4 for a list of its features.) Wintec Electronics had developed and could manufacture a new control panel for the Ag-Chemical Injector. Developed under contract with Can-Spray, the marketing company that assembled and distributed the Injector,

the control panel had incurred R & D costs of $30 000, half of which was supplied by Can-Spray, the rest by Wintec. Williams had hoped to make back the investment and a profit on manufacturing the panel for Can-Spray. The panels would be sold for $425 each, and direct manufacturing costs were about $300 per unit. Production setup costs would total $75 000.

The present Ag-Chemical Injector was designed so that the choice between one or two chemicals was controlled by a remote switch mounted on the tractor. This reduced operator effort and time, since there was no need to stop the tractor and walk to the back of the sprayer tank every time spot applications or chemical choice were desired. However, controlling the flow rate of the chemicals (or "chemical calibration") had to be performed by hand, a matter of adjusting flow meters on the Ag-Chemical Injector assembly itself. Chemical flow rates were not subject to remote (from-the-tractor) control. Williams stated that a significant ($30 000 to $40 000) additional R & D investment would be required to design a system that included remote control over both functions: choice of chemical types *and* selection of chemical flow rates (chemical calibration). He had no intention, at present, of beginning work

# Universal Installation

with all the necessary fittings supplied, the Ag-Chemical Injector can be easily installed on any sprayer, old or new.

# No Wasted Chemicals

Unused chemical is not contaminated with water, and can be returned to its original container for storage and future use.

# Remote Switches

From your tractor you can apply 1 or 2 chemicals either together or individually. Spot application of selective chemicals can be done with the flick of a switch.

# Linear Flow Meters

Chemical calibration is done by the manual calibration of the flow meters. This feature allows for calibration of your chemicals separately from the water. It all adds up to more flexibility when applying agricultural chemicals.

on the next generation of the Ag-Chemical Injector system. He felt that the present design would meet with market success even though the chemical calibration or flow rate control function was not "remote."

Williams had decided to take on the project because he felt the product offered a number of distinct advantages to the farmer. Because the chemicals were mixed as needed, rather than tank-mixed, the farmer avoided wasting chemicals, and also eliminated dumping problems. Furthermore, some chemicals could not readily be tank-mixed due to problems of chemical precipitation; this equipment solved that problem, too. It was easy to install and could be sold as an add-on to any sprayer. And finally, spot applications of a particular chemical were easy with this system.

The product certainly looked good. But Can-Spray was not placing large manufacturing orders for the control panel. Due to financial difficulties, Can-Spray was proposing to postpone the whole project by at least one year. Williams, however, was concerned that the delay would allow the competition — which he described as being "hot on our heels" — to catch up. How could Wintec recoup the R & D investment it had made on the Ag-Chemical Injector? The firm did not own the rights to the panel, but if Can-Spray was no longer interested perhaps Wintec could purchase the panel. If it did so, though, Wintec would need to assemble the other system components and market the product — neither of which it was currently set up to do properly.

## The Agricultural Sprayer Market

The Manitoba Department of Agriculture estimated that of the 20 000 farmers in Manitoba, about half owned sprayers. Manitoba had about 20 percent of the Prairie provinces' total in land area and equipment investment. Most sprayers ran for 10 to 15 years, so fewer than 1000 new sprayers were sold each year in Manitoba. Chemical spraying of herbicides represented a significant investment to the farmer, who spent on average $10 000 to $12 000 per year on herbicides. For information on new spray chemicals, systems, procedures, and equipment, farmers looked to equipment dealers, agricultural chemical suppliers, and frequently to government representatives. The Department of Agriculture answered phone queries and sent out regular mailings on new-product test results to farm operators across the province. The spray chemical manufacturers and certain specialty dealers who handled chemicals, sprayer parts, and sprayers were more informed sources than were either sprayer manufacturers or broad-product-line distributors and dealers. Usually, farmers who walked into a broad-product-line farm equipment dealer or distributor would buy a general-purpose sprayer and some common add-on or replacement parts like pumps and nozzles. The farmer in that situation was unlikely to receive special-purpose parts or expert information.

There were about 15 sprayer manufacturers in Canada, with the majority located in Saskatchewan or Alberta. Three were headquartered in Manitoba (see Figures C24–5 and C24–6 for sample product information). Most of these businesses sold their sprayers through agricultural equipment distributors, who offered complete units and also frequently replaced component parts. Since there were about 200 distributors throughout the Prairie provinces, they were highly competitive. All employed company sales reps to call on dealers, and some also used direct mail to reach the approximately 110 000 interested farmers in western Canada; advertising in farm papers and promotion at major trade shows rounded out their marketing efforts. The spray chemical companies were very large, and they too were aggressive marketers, employing heavy regional promotion including massive TV advertising.

The sprayer equipment distributors sold to agricultural equipment dealers, who then resold to the farmer. There were about 350 independent dealers in Manitoba. Most were broad-line dealers; they handled large general-purpose sprayers and commonly needed replacement parts. Sprayer prices to the end user ranged from $5000 to $10 000 (for general-purpose sprayers), with both distributors and dealers taking margins of 15 to 20 percent. Some local specialty dealers handled spray chemicals, special-purpose sprayer packages, or add-on systems. These dealers were very knowledgeable about spray chemistry and technology.

Can-Spray priced the chemical injector at $1700 retail as a retrofit installation. Industry dealers and distributors considered this a reasonable price for the equipment, but had some concerns over its reliability. It had been marketed for the past two seasons in two earlier formats, but there had been a number of problems with misapplications and product breakdown — brought about, many believed, because field testing had been inadequate. As a

# MODEL TW 868 AND TW 878 SPRAYER

## TANK FEATURES
- New low-profile tank for easier filling capacity 3600 L 800 Imp. gallon Poly tank
- Large 16" filler opening enables user to reach any part of interior for cleaning
- Positive seal and vented tank lid
- Strainer on 1½" suction line, easily removed for cleaning
- Easily reached shut-off valve at tank
- 4 Jet agitators provided to give adequate mixing

## SPRAY FLOW FEATURES
- Solenoid valves let you spray left or right from tractor cab
- High-capacity 540 or 1000 RPM pump
- Valves and fittings selected to minimize flow restriction
- Quick hose release at pump
- 1" relief valve
- Pump equipped with mounting bracket for extended bearing life

## BOOM FEATURES
- Clamp on Tee-Jet Nozzles Model 17560 and 80-degree stainless steel tips
- Two headland nozzles supplied, with shut-off valves
- Easily adjusted for forward spray; constant nozzle angle incorporated

## MODEL 17560
Quick Jet Nozzle Assembly features an integral diaphragm check, providing positive feedback.

## DOUBLE NOZZLE KIT (OPTIONAL)
**#21171 Rolover Valve**
Consists of a Rolover Valve, which can accommodate two sizes of sprayer tips. NO TOOLS REQUIRED: just rotate 180 degrees and spray with alternate nozzle. No second boom required.

# FIELD SPRAYERS GRANULAR APPLICATORS AND FIELD MARKERS

## BRANDT FIELD SPRAYERS

- Tanks available in 420 Imp. Gal (500 U.S.), 620 Imp. Gal. (750 U.S.), 830 Imp. Gal. (1000 U.S.)
- Booms available in 60′ width with new unique 26′ extension kit, which can be installed in minutes
- Sprayer has a step side to make filling convenient
- 1″ aluminum spray pipes are used for uniform boom pressure at the boom
- 420 gal. and 620 gal. tanks are standard with a side fill feature
- Sprayer nozzles are always pointing down at any height, to eliminate excessive field adjustments.
- Optional — Hydraulic Boom Lift
  Optional — Chemical Fill Tank
- Optional — Hydraulic Centrifugal Pump
- Welded boom struts to reduce set up and adjustments, and to ensure consistent spray pattern

Brandt Industries Ltd., Regina    Reply Code BR-05

## BLANCHARD FIELD SPRAYERS

800 and 500 gal. models in 60 to 100′ widths. Tandem walking axle undercarriage with flotation tires. Field to transport position in minutes. 2-wheel boom stabilizers feature All Terrain Vehicle Tires or trailer-type tires. Options include double boom, mix and fill chemical system, and nozzle selection.

**AUTOMATIC SPRAYER CONTROLS:** Precision electric and electronic sprayer controls — sprayer monitors, sprayer controllers, and brilliant sprayer markers plus automatic pressure and flow adjusting valves.

Blanchard Foundry Co. Ltd., Saskatoon
Reply Code BL-03

## WILGER FIELD SPRAYERS 400 SERIES

FEATURES: 400 Imp. gal. low-profile stainless steel tank c/w special sump and agitator. Ni-Resist 1700 roller pump. Heavy-duty cart with tandem walking axles. 2″ ball hitch, adjustable for various drawbar heights. 60-80′ boom coverage. Quick jet nozzles. Booms equipped with special spring-loaded trip releases. Field to transport in minutes.
FLOW RIDE: Exclusive sprayer boom suspension system on all Wilger sprayers. Spring and shock absorber suspension virtually eliminates boom bounce for smoother, more precise spraying at higher speeds.
OPTIONS: Wilger sprayer monitor. Electric on/off boom control with remote pressure adjust. Automark dye marker and dye concentrate.

Wilger Industries Ltd., Saskatoon    Reply Code WR-03

**Boom Used in American Sprayers**

Constructed of 1¼" square tubing, this boom is flex wire rope cable supported. Spring-loaded breakaways return boom to normal spraying position after impact with objects. Mounts to category 2 or 3 hitches and folds vertically for transport. Nozzles and boom feed hoses should be ordered separately.

| Part No. | Description | Price |
|---|---|---|
| 001051 | 28′ TPH Boom 17 outlets at 20″ | $625.00 |
| 001052 | 35′ TPH Boom 21 outlets at 20″ | 798.00 |
| 001053 | 40′ TPH Boom 25 outlets at 20″ | 825.00 |
| 001054 | 47′ TPH Boom 29 outlets at 20″ | 863.00 |

result, farmers were reluctant to try again. Said one equipment distributor, "The biggest problem with this type of equipment is to convince the buyer that it will work, that it is reliable. The herbicides used are very concentrated, and one mistake can have serious long-term effects. It has to be very clearly foolproof — from both machine and operator error. This makes it an uphill marketing job. In addition, the supplier wants the distributors and dealers to be responsible for all aspects of the promotion, and frankly, I don't believe our Canadian market is big enough to make it a cost-effective proposition for a distributor or dealer. The margins on equipment usually don't allow us to engage in expensive education, promotion, and providing 'hand-holding' services to the farmer."

Several U.S. manufacturers were developing similar equipment, but distributors cautioned that the sprayer market was full of local idiosyncrasies. Sprayers were one of the pieces of farm equipment that differed drastically between Canada and the United States. Canadian farmers used a 'wet-boom' sprayer (see Figure C24–5 for an example), in which the water and chemical ran through the metal pipes forming the boom (the wide part that actually did the spraying) to the nozzles. Canadian equipment was heavy, with double axles, large tanks, and longer (80- to 100-foot) booms. By contrast, U.S. farmers used smaller, faster-moving suspended 'dry-boom' sprayers, in which the liquid ran through plastic hosing attached to a lighter, shorter boom, generally 40

to 60 feet in length (see Figure C24–7). Thus, while equipment developed for Canada could be adapted for the United States, it would require significant design changes to be saleable.

## The Environment

One factor that made the injector a viable product was the growing interest and concern among farmers, government, and the public over agricultural chemicals. Although no specific government regulation of spraying existed at this point, it remained a possibility for the future. Provincial agriculture departments had been encouraging the development of chemical injection sprayers — as opposed to sprayers using tank-mixed chemicals — for more than 15 years. Such systems, when accurately metered, prevented over- or underdosing of crops, both of which are very expensive errors (overdosing results in crop damage, while underdosing requires additional investments of money and time to respray the fields). Chemical injection sprayers also saved the farmer money by reducing wastage: unused chemicals could be saved and used later, since they had not been mixed with water. Finally, because the chemical was not mixed in the tank, the farmer no longer faced the dilemma of how to dispose of an unused portion of a tank — a dilemma all too commonly resolved by resorting to "dumping" (discarding the herbicide in a ditch). Dumping represented both a financial loss to the farmer and an environmental pollution problem.

## Conclusion

Williams reviewed his options to determine the best course for Wintec. He could try to push Can-Spray into going ahead with the marketing of the Ag-Chemical Injector system product and thus purchasing his component, but he was not optimistic about his chances for success with that approach. The development contract, unfortunately, did not include any requirement for Can-Spray to purchase a specific quantity of control panels.

If Can-Spray was no longer interested in the product, Williams might be able to buy its interest in the panel for $15 000 to $20 000. However, Can-Spray would still hold the patent on the nonpanel components of the Ag-Chemical Injector system, so Wintec would have to either design a somewhat different system around the new control panel or find another agricultural equipment manufacturer to do so. Williams wondered how either of these could be done and which of the two was the better option. Both would clearly involve considerable further investment. But would it be worth the effort to pursue either choice?

A final possibility, of course, was to write off the $15 000 investment he had made to date, and forget the product. No matter what he ultimately decided, Williams was disturbed to realize that he was vulnerable to such a substantial loss. He therefore wondered whether he should make some changes in the way he screened new-product ideas and contracted development.

## Discussion Questions

1. Suppose Williams decides to buy out Can-Spray's interest in the control panel, but is unable to find another sprayer manufacturer to work with on the project. To avoid a further loss, he might risk trying to design, manufacture, and market an entire system that would incorporate the newly developed control panel. How would you advise him to proceed?
2. Williams definitely wants to prevent such costly mistakes in the future. How could he improve his approach to screening ideas and/or to contracting for their development?

# Notes

## Chapter 1

1. Adapted from Marina Strauss, "Lawyers Emerge From Marketing Dark Ages," *Globe and Mail*, October 5, 1989.

2. Peter F. Drucker, *The Practice of Management* (New York: Harper and Row, 1954), p. 37.

3. Joseph P. Guiltinan and Gordon W. Paul, *Marketing Management* (New York: McGraw-Hill, 1982), pp. 3–4.

4. Richard P. Bagozzi, "Marketing as an Organized Behavioral System of Exchange," *Journal of Marketing* (October 1974), p. 77. Further work by Bagozzi on this subject appears in "Marketing as Exchange," *Journal of Marketing* (October 1975), pp. 32–39, and in "Marketing as Exchange: A Theory of Transactions in the Marketplace," *American Behavioral Scientist* (March–April 1978), pp. 535–536.

5. Bagozzi, "Marketing as an Organized Behavioral System," p. 77.

6. Wroe Alderson, *Marketing Behavior and Executive Action* (Homewood, IL: Irwin, 1962), p. 292.

7. T.G. Povey, "Spotting the Salesman Who Has What It Takes," *Nation's Business* (July 1972), p. 70.

8. "AMA Board Approves New Marketing Definition," *Marketing News* (March 1, 1985), p. 1.

9. Many discussions of this topic have suggested that marketing passed through a series of "eras": product, sales, and market orientations. However, Ronald A. Fullerton shows that there is little historical support for the concept of progression through various eras in his article. "How Modern is Modern Marketing?: Marketing's Evolution and the Myth of the 'Production Era,'" *Journal of Marketing*, January 1988, pp. 108–125.

10. Henceforth, the term "product" will apply to both goods and services, except as otherwise noted. The marketing principles that apply to products normally apply to services as well.

11. Theodore Levitt, *Innovations in Marketing* (New York: McGraw-Hill, 1962), p. 7.

12. The following discussion is based on Benson P. Shapiro, "What the Hell is 'Market Oriented'?" *Harvard Business Review* (November–December 1988), p. 120–122.

13. Mansour Javidan and John Rigby, "The Marketing Concept: A Cultural Perspective," *Journal of Administrative Sciences* (forthcoming).

14. Adapted from M. Kubr, ed., Management Consulting: A Guide to the Profession (Geneva: International Labour Organization, 1977).

## Chapter 2

1. Adapted from "End of The Road," *Canadian Business* (December 1989), pp. 31–32.

2. M. Dale Beckman, "What Businessmen Know About Government and Legislative Intent," *Canadian Marketer* (Fall 1973), pp. 13–17.

3. This section has been adapted and updated from a section in M. Dale Beckman and R.H. Evans, "Social Control of Business Through the Federal Department of Consumer and Corporate Affairs," adapted from D.H. Henry, *Marketing: A Canadian Perspective* (Scarborough, ON: Prentice-Hall, 1972), pp. 102–129.

4. John Kohut, "Competition Body Charges NutraSweet with Monopolizing Canadian Market," *Globe and Mail* (June 2, 1989).

5. Adapted from Drew Fagan, "Tribunal Sours Nutra-Sweet's Success, " *Globe and Mail* (October 5, 1990).

6. Consumer and Corporate Affairs, *Misleading Advertising Bulletin* (January–March 1986), p. 7.

7. James Walker and Alan D. Gray, "$1 Million Ad Fine Signal to Retailers," *Financial Times* 72:6 (July 1983), p. 14.

8. Consumer and Corporate Affairs, personal communication.

9. Consumer and Corporate Affairs, *Misleading Advertising Bulletin* (July–September 1986), p. 11.

10. Many economists argue that society is capable of

preventing future depressions through intelligent use of various economic policies. Thus, a recession is followed by a period of recovery.

11. The concept of environmental forecasting is examined in T.F. Mastri, "Environmental Forecasting," *Fairleigh Dickinson University Business Review* (Winter 1973), pp. 3–10.

12. Interesting articles related to this topic include Philip Kotler and Sidney J. Levy, "Demarketing, Yes, Demarketing," *Harvard Business Review* (November–December 1971), pp. 74–80; David W. Cravens, "Marketing Management in an Era of Shortages," *Business Horizons* (February 1974), pp. 79–85; A.B. Blankenship and John H. Holmes, "Will Shortages Bankrupt the Marketing Concept?" *MSU Business Topics* (Spring 1974), pp. 13–18; Philip Kotler, "Marketing During Periods of Shortages," *Journal of Marketing* (July 1974), pp. 20–29; Zohrab S. Demirdjian, "The Role of Marketing in an Economy of Affluence and Shortages," *Business and Society* (Spring 1975), pp. 15–21; Nessim Hanna, A.H. Kizilbash, and Albert Smart, "Marketing Strategy Under Conditions of Economic Scarcity," *Journal of Marketing* (January 1975), pp. 63–67; and Sunier C. Aggarwal, "Prepare for Continual Materials Shortages,"*Harvard Business Review* (May–June 1982), pp. 6–10.

13. David Thompson, "Rising to the Challenge," *Marketing* (May 2, 1983), p. 13.

14. Adapted from Andrew Van Velzen, "Secular Society Gave Couple Their Niche: The Wedding Business," *Globe and Mail* (August 14, 1989), p. C1.

## Chapter 3

1. Adapted from "A New Kid on the Block," *The Economist* (November 12, 1988), p. 83.

2. See Scott M. Smith and Leland L. Beik, "Market Segmentation for Fund Raisers," *Journal of the Academy of Marketing Science* (Summer 1982), pp. 208–216.

3. This section relies heavily on Harry H. Hiller, *Canadian Society: A Sociological Analysis* (Scarborough, ON: Prentice-Hall, 1976), pp. 13–37.

4. R.T. Gajda, "The Canadian Ecumene: Inhabited and Uninhabited Areas," *Geographical Bulletin* 15 (1960), p. 6.

5. T.R. Weir, "Population Changes in Canada, 1867–1967," *Canadian Geographer* 2:4 (1967), p. 198.

6. Larry H. Long, "On Measuring Geographic Mobility," *Journal of the American Statistical Association* (September 1970).

7. Kenneth Runyon, *Consumer Behavior* (Columbus, OH: Merrill, 1980), p. 35.

8. See John A. Reinecke, "The 'Older' Market: Fact or Fiction?" *Journal of Marketing* (January 1964), pp. 60–64; and Sidney Goldstein, "The Aged Segment of the Market, 1950–1960," *Journal of Marketing* (April 1968), pp. 62–68.

9. These examples are from an earlier life cycle study — see William D. Wells and George Gubar, "Life Cycle Concept in Marketing Research," *Journal of Marketing Research* (November 1966), p. 362; see also Frederick W. Derrick and Alane K. Lehfeld, "The Family Life Cycle: An Alternative Approach," *Journal of Consumer Research* (September 1980), pp. 214–217.

10. Based on Statistics Canada, *Family Income: Census Families, 1986 Census*, Catalogue No. 93-117.

11. Statistics Canada, *Changes in Income in Canada*, 1970–1980, Catalogue No. 99-941.

12. Other countries may have different expenditure patterns, however. One study of European Common Market countries revealed that housing expenditures increased as a percentage of total spending with increased income; see J. Allison Barnhill, "The Application of Engel's Laws of Personal Consumption (1857) to the European Common Market (1957–1961)," *The Marketer* (Spring 1967), pp. 17–22.

13. This section is adapted from John Chaplin, "Pigeonholes for Consumers," *Marketing* (October 16, 1989), p.28.

14. John J. Burnett,"Psychographic and Demographic Characteristics of Blood Donors," *Journal of Consumer Research* (June 1981) pp. 62–86; Mary Ann Lederhaus and Ronald J. Adams,"A Psychographic Profile of the Cosmopolitan Consumers," in *Proceedings of the Southwestern Marketing Association*, eds. Robert H. Ross, Frederic B. Kraft, and Charles H. Davis (Wichita, KS: Southwestern Marketing Assoc., 1981), pp. 142–145; and J.Paul Merenski,"Psychographics: Valid by Definition and Reliable by Technique," *Developments in Marketing Science,* ed. Venkatakrishna V. Bellur (Miami Beach: Academy of Marketing Science, 1981), pp. 161–166.

15. Daniel Yankelovich, "New Criteria for Market Segmentation," *Harvard Business Review* (March–April 1964), pp. 83–90.

16. See Russell I. Haley, "Benefit Segmentation: A Decision-Oriented Research Tool," *Journal of Marketing* (July 1968), pp. 30–35.

## Chapter 4

1. Adapted from Diane Turbide, "The Show Moves On," *Maclean's* (September 4, 1989), pp. 65–66.

2. This section is based on materials written by J.D. Forbes, University of British Columbia.

3. Fred Rothenberg, "Saturday-Night Television Isn't What It Used to Be," *Seattle Times* (July 31, 1982).

4. "Small Clothes Are Selling Big," *Business Week* (November 16, 1981), pp. 152, 156.

5. Jennifer Alter, "Toothbrush Makers' Lament: Who Notices?" *Advertising Age* (October 4, 1982), p. 66.

6. Philip Kotler and Ravi Singh, "Basic Marketing Strategy for Winning Your Marketing War," *Marketing Times* (November–December 1982), pp. 23–24 [reprinted by permission from the *Journal of Business Strategy*, Vol. 1, No. 3, Winter 1981, Copyright (c) 1981, Warren, Gorham and Lamont, Inc., 210 South St., Boston, Mass. 02111. All rights reserved.]

7. A similar analysis is suggested in Robert M. Fulmer, *The New Marketing* (New York: Macmillan, 1976), pp. 34–37; Philip Kotler, *Marketing Management* (Englewood Cliffs, NJ: Prentice-Hall, 1976), pp. 141–151; and E. Jerome McCarthy, *Basic Marketing* (Homewood, IL: Irwin, 1975), pp. 111–126.

8. A good example of this systematic approach to identifying a precise target market appears in Richard P. Carr, Jr., "Developing a New Residential Market for Carpeting: Some Mistakes and Successes," *Journal of Marketing* (July 1977), pp. 101–102.

9. "Properly Applied Psychographics Add Marketing Luster," *Marketing News* (November 12, 1982), p. 10.

## Chapter 5

1. Adapted from "Mauling the Competition," *Manitoba Business* (May 1989), p. 34.

2. Committee on Definitions, *Marketing Definitions: A Glossary of Marketing Terms* (Chicago: American Marketing Association, 1960), p. 17.

3. John A. Gonder, "Marketing Research in Canada," in *Cases and Readings in Marketing* ed. R.H. Rotenberg (Toronto: Holt, Rinehart and Winston, 1974), p. 221.

4. Bertram Schoner and Kenneth P. Uhl, *Marketing Research: Information Systems and Decision Making* (New York: Wiley, 1975), p. 199.

5. William G. Zikmund, *Exploring Marketing Research,* 4th ed. (Hinsdale, IL: Dryden Press, 1982), pp. 263–264.

6. Wide Area Telephone Service, a telephone-company service that allows a business firm to make unlimited long-distance calls for a fixed rate per region.

7. *Wall Street Journal* (June 28, 1972).

8. See Fred D. Reynolds and Deborah K. Johnson, "Validity of Focus-Group Findings," *Journal of Advertising Research* (June 1978), pp. 21–24; and Bobby J. Calder, "Focus Groups and the Nature of Qualitative Marketing Research," *Journal of Marketing Research* (August 1977), pp. 353–64.

9. This discussion follows Zikmund, *Exploring Marketing Research* pp. 450–477. Used by permission.

10. A useful article on sampling is Henry Assael and John Keon, "Nonsampling vs. Sampling Errors in Survey Research," *Journal of Marketing* (Spring 1982), pp. 114–123.

11. Donald F. Cox and Robert E. Good, "How to Build a Marketing Information System," *Harvard Business Review* (May–June 1967), p. 147.

12. "Marketing Intelligence Systems: A DEW Line for Marketing Men," *Business Management* (January 1966), p. 32.

13. "Marketing Management and the Computer," *Sales Management* (August 20, 1965), pp. 49–60: see also Leon Winer, "Putting the Computer to Work in Marketing," *Pittsburgh Business Review* (November–December 1972), pp. 1–5ff.

## Chapter 6

1. Adapted from "Chrysler Gears Up for Risky Strategy Refocussing on Car Design," *Globe and Mail* (May 18, 1989), p. B36.

2. A.J. Rowe, R.O. Mason, K.E. Dickel, and N.H. Snyder, *Strategic Management: A Methodological Approach* (Reading, MA: Addison-Wesley, 1989), p. 9.

3. Theodore Levitt, "Marketing and Corporate Purpose," in *Changing Strategies in a New Economy*, eds. Jules Backman and John A. Czepiel (Indianapolis: Bobbs-Merrill, 1977), p. 29.

4. For a more detailed discussion, see Yoram Wind and Thomas S. Robertson, "Marketing Strategy: New Directions for Theory and Research," *Journal of Marketing* (Spring 1983), pp. 12–15.

5. George S. Day and Robin Wensley, "Assessing Advantage: A Framework for Diagnosing Competitive Superiority," *Journal of Marketing* (Summer 1983), p. 82.

6. The following section is adapted from Wind and Robertson, "Marketing Strategy," pp. 16–22.

7. Oxenfeld, Alfred R. and Moore, William L., "Customer or Competitor: Which Guideline for Marketing?" *Management Review*, August 1978, pp. 43–48.

8. Robert H. Hayes and William J. Abernathy, "Managing Our Way to Economic Decline," *Harvard Business Review* (July–August 1980), pp. 67–87.

9. Benson P. Shapiro, "Getting Things Done," Harvard Business Review (September–October, 1985), p. 28.

10. The marketing mix is sometimes called the "four P's" for ease of remembering: product, price, place, promotion.

11. Adapted from George S. Day and Robin Wensley, "Assessing Advantage: A Framework for Diagnosing Competitive Superiority," *Journal of Marketing* (April 1988), p. 1.

12. Amar, Bhide, "Hustle as Strategy," *Harvard Business Review* (September-October 1986), pp. 59–65.

## Chapter 7

1. Adapted from Laura Medcalf, "Feast, Not Famine in Pet-food Marketing, *Marketing* (October 9, 1989), p. 15.

2. This definition is adapted from James F. Engel, Roger D. Blackwell and Paul W. Miniard, *Consumer Behavior*, 6th ed. (Hinsdale, IL: Dryden Press, 1990), p. 3.

3. See Albert J. Della Bitta, "Consumer Behaviour: Some Thoughts on Sheth's Evaluation of the Discipline," *Journal of the Academy of Marketing Science* (Winter 1982), pp. 5–6.

4. See Kurt Lewin, *Field Theory in Social Science* (New York: Harper and Row, 1951), p. 62: see also C. Glenn Walters, "Consumer Behavior: An Appraisal," *Journal of the Academy of Marketing Science* (Fall 1979), pp. 237–284.

5. A. H. Maslow, *Motivation and Personality* (New York: Harper and Row, 1954), pp. 370–396.

6. A.H. Maslow, *Motivation and Personality*, p.382; see also George Brooker, "The Self-Actualizing Socially Conscious Consumer," *Journal of Consumer Research* (September 1976), pp. 107–12.

7. E.E. Lawlor and J.L. Suttle, "A Causal Correlational Test of the Need Hierarchy Concept," *Organizational Behaviour and Human Performance* 3(1968), pp. 12–35. see also Jerry L. Gray and Fredrick A. Starke, *Organizational Behavior Concepts and Applications* (Columbus, OH: Merrill, 1977), pp. 27–29.

8. George Katona, *The Powerful Consumer* (New York: McGraw-Hill, 1960), p. 132; see also Engel, Blackwell, and Miniard, *Consumer Behavior*, 6th ed. pp. 490–491.

9. Burt Schorr, "The Mistakes: Many New Products Fail Despite Careful Planning, Publicity," *Wall Street Journal* (April 5, 1961), pp. 1, 22.

10. Steuart Henderson Britt, "How Weber's Law Can Be Applied to Marketing," *Business Horizons* (February 1975), pp. 21–29.

11. John Brooks, "The Little Ad That Isn't There," *Consumer Reports* (January 1958), pp. 7–10; see also Del Hawkins, "The Effects of Subliminal Stimulation on Drive Level and Brand Preference," *Journal of Marketing Research* (August 1970), pp. 322–326.

12. See James H. Myers and William H. Reynolds, *Consumer Behaviour and Marketing Management* (Boston: Houghton Mifflin, 1967), p. 14.

13. Richard P. Barthol and Michael J. Goldstein, "Psychology and the Invisible Sell," *California Management Review* (Winter 1959), p. 34.

14. One researcher reports that some overt behaviour in pathologically prone individuals can be influenced if they appeal to the appropriate unconscious wish: see Jack Saegert, "Another Look at Subliminal Perception," *Journal of Advertising Research* (February 1979), pp. 55–57.

15. David Krech, Richard S. Crutchfield, and Egerton L. Ballachey, *Individual in Society* (New York: McGraw-Hill, 1962), Chapter 2.

16. George S. Day, "Using Attitude Change Measures to Evaluate New Product Introductions," *Journal of Marketing Research* (November 1970), pp. 474–482; see also Stephen J. Miller, Michael B. Mazis, and Peter L. Wright, "The Influence of Brand Ambiguity on Brand Attitude Development," *Journal of Marketing Research* (November 1971), pp. 455–459; Frank Schuhmann, "Consumer Cognitive Systems: A Study of the Relationship Between Consumer Attitudes and Values," *Idaho Business and Economic Journal* (January 1975), pp. 1–15; and Kent B. Monroe, "The Influence of Price Differences and Brand Familiarity on Brand Preferences," *Journal of Consumer Research* (June 1976), pp. 42–49.

17. Learning is perhaps the most thoroughly researched field in psychology, and several learning theories have been developed. For a discussion of these theories, see Engel, Blackwell and Miniard, *Consumer Behavior*, 6th ed., pp. 395–431.

18. This section is based on Michael L. Rothschild and William C. Gaidis, "Behavioral Learning Theory: Its Relevance to Marketing and Promotion," *Journal of Marketing* (Spring 1981), pp. 70–78.

19. John Koten, "For Kellogg, the Hardest Part is Getting People Out of Bed," *Wall Street Journal* (May 27, 1982), p. 27.

20. "Learning How to Please the Baffling Japanese," *Fortune* (October 5, 1981), p. 122.

21. Engel, Blackwell and Miniard, *Consumer Behavior*, 6th ed., p. 63.

22. Daniel Yankelovich, "New Rules," *Seattle Times* (November 1, 1981); Excerpted from his book *New Rules: Searching for Self-Fulfillment in a World Turned Upside Down*. Copyright © 1981, Daniel Yankelovich. Distributed by Los Angeles Times Syndicate.

23. This is noted in Engel, Blackwell and Miniard, *Consumer Behavior*, 6th ed., p. 64.

24. Robert Linn, "Americans Turn Deaf Ear to Foreign Tongues," *Orlando Sentinel Star* (November 1, 1981).

25. Leon G. Schiffman and Leslie Lazar Kanuk, *Consumer*

*Behavior* (Englewood Cliffs, NJ: Prentice-Hall, 1978), p. 390.

26. Charles Winich, "Anthropology's Contributions to Marketing," *Journal of Marketing* (July 1961), p. 59.

27. Edward T. Hall, "The Silent Language in Overseas Business," *Harvard Business Review* (May–June 1960), p. 89.

28. Patricia L. Layman, "In Any Language, the Beauty Business Spells Success," *Chemical Week* (September 17, 1975), p. 26.

29. See Jean-Charles Chebat and Georges Hénault, "The Cultural Behavior of Canadian Consumers," in *Cases and Readings in Marketing*, ed R.H. Rotenberg (Toronto: Holt, Rinehart and Winston, 1974), pp. 176–180, [this material also appeared in *Revue Commerce*, September 1971]; see also M. Brisebois, "Industrial Advertising and Marketing in Quebec," *The Marketer* (Spring–Summer 1966), p. 11.

30. Gail Chaisson, "The French Market Today," *Marketing* (June 1, 1981), pp. 11, 14.

31. Eleine Saint-Jacques and Bruce Mallen, "The French Market Under the Microscope," *Marketing* (May 11, 1981), p. 10.

32. Royal Commission on Bilingualism and Biculturalism.

33. Based on Jan Morin and Michel Ostiguy, "View From the Top," *Marketing* (June 1, 1981), p. 28.

34. M. Cloutier, "Marketing in Quebec," Industrial Marketing Research Association Conference, Toronto, March 1978.

35. Del I. Hawkins, Kenneth A. Coney, and Roger J. Best, *Consumer Behavior: Implications for Marketing Strategy* (Dallas, TX: Business Publications, 1980), pp. 181–82. The quotation is adapted from S.E. Asch, "Effects of Group Pressure upon the Modification and Distortion of Judgments," in *Readings in Social Psychology*, eds. E.E. MacCoby et al. (New York: Holt, Rinehart and Winston, 1958), pp. 174–83.

36. See Danny N. Bellenger and Elizabeth C. Hirschman, "Identifying Opinion Leaders by Self-Report," in *Contemporary Marketing Thought*, eds. Barnett A. Greenberg and Danny N. Bellenger (Chicago: American Marketing Association, 1977), pp. 341–344.

37. Engel, Blackwell, and Miniard, *Consumer Behavior*, 6th ed., pp. 176–182; see also Wilson Brown, "The Family and Consumer Decision Making," *Journal of the Academy of Marketing Science* (Fall 1979), pp. 335–343.

38. "Business Shifts Its Sales Pitch for Women," U.S. *News and World Report* (July 9, 1981), p. 46; and Margaret LeRoux, "Exec Claims Most Ads to Women Miss the Mark," *Advertising Age* (May 21, 1979), p. 24.

39. George J. Szybillo, Arlene K. Sosanie, and Aaron Tenebein, "Should Children Be Seen But Not Heard?"
*Journal of Advertising Research* (December 1977), pp. 7–13.

40. Lester Rand, *The Rand Youth Poll*, 1981.

41. See J.P. Liefeld, "Problem Recognition," in *Consumer Decision-Making: An Annotated Bibliography* (Ottawa: Consumer and Corporate Affairs, 1979).

42. B.M. Campbell, "The Existence of Evoked Set and Determinants of its Magnitude in Brand Choice Behavior," in *Buyer Behavior: Theoretical and Empirical Foundations*, eds. John A. Howard and Lonnie Ostrom (New York: Knopf, 1973), pp. 243–44.

43. Engel, Blackwell, and Miniard, *Consumer Behavior*, 6th ed., p. 479.

44. For a thorough discussion of purchase location, see David L. Loudon and Albert J. Della Bitta, *Consumer Behavior: Concepts and Applications* (New York: McGraw-Hill, 1979), pp. 483–511.

45. Leon Festinger, A *Theory of Cognitive Dissonance* (Stanford CA: Stanford University Press, 1958), p. 3.

46. See Robert J. Connole, James D. Benson, and Inder P. Khera, "Cognitive Dissonance Among Innovators," *Journal of the Academy of Marketing Science* (Winter 1977), pp. 9–20; David R. Lambert, Ronald J. Dornoff, and Jerome B. Kernan, "The Industrial Buyer and the Postchoice Evaluation Process," *Journal of Marketing Research* (May 1977), pp. 246–51; and William H. Cummings and M. Venkatesan, "Cognitive Dissonance and Consumer Behavior: A Review of the Evidence," *Journal of Marketing Research* (August 1976), pp. 303–308.

47. These categories were originally suggested in John A. Howard, *Marketing Management: Analysis and Planning* (Homewood, IL: Irwin, 1963): the discussion here is based on Donald R. Lehmann, William L. Moore, and Terry Elrod, "The Development of Distinct Choice Process Segments over Time: A Stochastic Modelling Approach," *Journal of Marketing* (Spring 1982), pp. 48–50.

# Chapter 8

1. Adapted from Sandra Porteous, "Micronav Makes Three-Point Landing," *Marketing* (March 12, 1990), p. B18.

2. James D. Hlavacek, "Business Schools Need More Industrial Marketing," *Marketing News* (April 4, 1980), p. 1.

3. The 60-day figure is suggested in Bob Luke, "Purchasing Agents: Supply Sergeants to the Business World," *Detroit News* (May 20, 1979).

4. The development of the new type of pole and the problems involved in its adoption are described in Arch G. Woodside, "Marketing Anatomy of Buying

Process Can Help Improve Industrial Strategy," *Marketing News* (May 1, 1981), Section 2, p. 11.

5. These are suggested in Patrick J. Robinson, Charles W. Farris, and Yoram Wind, *Industrial Buying and Creative Marketing* (Boston: Allyn and Bacon, 1967), Chapter 1. The discussion here follows Michael D. Hutt and Thomas W. Speh, *Industrial Marketing Management* (Hinsdale, IL Dryden Press, 1981), pp. 51–55.

6. This section is based on Hutt and Speh, *Industrial Marketing Management*, pp. 80–85.

7. Buying centres are discussed in two articles in the July 1982 issue of the *Journal of Business Research*: see Gloria P. Thomas and John F. Grashof, "Impact of Internal and External Environments' Stability on the Existence of Determinant Buying Roles," pp. 159–168; and Yoram Wind and Thomas S. Robertson, "The Linking Pin Role in Organizational Buying Centers," pp. 169–184; See also Earl Naumann, Robert McWilliams, and Douglas J. Lincoln, "How Different Buying Center Members Influence Different Purchasing Phases," in *Developments in Marketing Science*, eds. Vinay Kothari et al. (Miami Beach Academy of Marketing Science, 1982), pp. 186–190.

8. Hutt and Speh, *Industrial Marketing Management*, p. 80, cite the following sources for their statistics: "Industrial Salespeople Report 4.1: Buying Influences in Average Company," *LAP Report* 1042.2 (McGraw-Hill Research, October 1977); and G. van der Most, "Purchasing Process: Researching Influences Is Basic to Marketing Plan," *Industrial Marketing* (October 1976), p. 120.

9. An interesting discussion of influences is found in Robert J. Thomas, "Correlates of Interpersonal Purchase Influence in Organizations," *Journal of Consumer Research* (September 1982), pp. 171–182. Also see Robert E. Krapfel, Jr., "An Extended Influence Model of Organizational Buyer Behavior," *Journal of Business Research* (June 1982), pp. 147–157.

10. This section is based on Manoj K. Agarwal, Philip C. Burger, and Alladi Venkatesh, "Industrial Consumer Behavior: Toward An Improved Model," in *Developments in Marketing Science*, eds. Venkatakrishna V. Bellur et al. (Miami Beach: Academy of Marketing Science, 1981), pp. 68–73.

11. These price cuts are described in Thomas F. O'Boyle, "Price Cutting Being Forced on Suppliers," *Wall Street Journal* (May 14, 1982).

12. The history and current status of reciprocal agreements are summarized in E. Robert Finney, "Reciprocity: Gone but Not Forgotten," *Journal of Marketing* (January 1978), pp. 54–59: See also William J. Kehoe and Byron D. Hewett, "Reciprocity and Reverse Reciprocity: A Literature Review and Research

Design," in *Proceedings of the Southern Marketing Association*, eds. Robert S. Franz, Robert M. Hopkins, and Al Toma (New Orleans: November 1978), pp. 481–483; and Monroe M. Bird, "Reverse Reciprocity: A New Twist to Industrial Buyers," *Atlanta Economic Review* (January–February 1976), pp. 11–13.

13. Adapted from *How to Do Business with the Department of Supply and Services* (Ottawa: Supply and Services, 1980), pp. 1–11.

14. Based on "Out of the Maze," *Sales and Marketing Management* (April 9, 1979), pp. 44–52.

## Chapter 9

1. Association of Universities and Colleges, *University Affairs* (November 1990), p. 13.

2. For a provocative discussion of this broader conception of products, see Sidney J. Levy, "Symbols for Sale," *Harvard Business Review* (July–August 1959), pp. 117–124; see also Jerome B. Kernan and Montrose S. Sommers, "Dimensions of Product Perception," *Journal of Business Research* (April 1967), pp. 94–102.

3. A good summary of the product life-cycle concept is contained in George S. Day, "The Product Life Cycle: Analysis and Applications Issues," *Journal of Marketing* (Fall 1981), pp. 60–67; Also see Gerald J. Tellis and C. Merle Crawford, "An Evolutionary Approach to Product Growth Theory," *Journal of Marketing* (Fall 1981), pp. 125–132.

4. "Videodiscs: The Expensive Race to Be First," *Business Week* (September 15, 1975), pp. 58–66.

5. Students of economics will recognize this as elasticity of demand; For a discussion of the concept of elasticity, see Edwin G. Dolan and Roy Vogt, *Basic Economics*, 3rd ed. (Toronto: Holt, Rinehart and Winston, 1988), pp. 452–459.

6. This section relies on George S. Day, "The Product Life Cycle: Analysis and Applications Issues," *Journal of Marketing* (Fall 1981), pp. 60–65.

7. Ben M. Enis, Raymond LaGrace, and Arthur E. Prell, "Extending the Product Life Cycle," *Business Horizons* (June 1977), pp. 46–56.

8. William Qualls, Richard W. Olshavsky, and Ronald E. Michaels, "Shortening the PLC: An Empirical Test", *Journal of Marketing* (Fall 1981), pp. 76–80.

9. Rolando Pilli and Victor J. Cook, "A Test of the Product Life Cycle as a Model of Sales Behavior," *Marketing Science Institute Working Paper* (November 1967), and "Validity of the Product Life Cycle," *The Journal of Business* (October 1969), pp. 385–400: this research is reviewed in William S. Sachs and George Benson, *Product Planning and Management* (Tulsa, OK: Penn Well, 1981), p. 80.

10. Fashion cycles are discussed in Raymond A. Marquardt, James C. Makens, and Robert G. Roe, *Retail Management*, 3rd ed. (Hinsdale, IL: Dryden Press, 1983), pp. 98–99; see also George B. Sproles, "Analyzing Fashion Life Cycles: Principles and Perspectives," *Journal of Marketing* (Fall 1981), pp. 116–124.

11. Stephen Grover, "Record Business Slumps as Taping and Video Games Take Away Sales," *Wall Street Journal* (February 18, 1982).

12. Enis et al., "Extending the Product Life Cycle".

13. See David R. Rink and John E. Swan, "Product Life Cycle Research: A Literature Review," *Journal of Business Research* (September 1979), pp. 219–242.

14. Bill Abrams, "Warring Toothpaste Makers Spend Millions Luring Buyers to Slightly Altered Products," *Wall Street Journal* (September 9, 1981).

15. Gail Bronson, "Baby Food It Is, but Gerber Wants Teen-Agers to Think of It as Dessert," *Wall Street Journal* (July 17, 1981).

16. Karger, "5 Ways to Find New Use: Re-Evaluate Your Old Products," p. 18.

17. Alan Freeman, "Levi Unit Tries to Give Jeans Limited Appeal," *Wall Street Journal* (August 11, 1981).

18. "Good Products Don't Die, P&G Chairman Declares," *Advertising Age* (November 1, 1976), p. 8.

19. Everett M. Rogers and F. Floyd Shoemaker, *Communication of Innovations* (New York: Free Press, 1971), pp. 135–157.

20. Walter P. Gorman III and Charles T. Moore, "The Early Diffusion of Color Television Receivers into a Fringe Market Area," *Journal of Retailing* (Fall 1968), pp. 46–56.

21. James Coleman, Elihu Katz, and Herbert Menzel, "The Diffusion of an Innovation Among Physicians," *Sociometry* (December 1957), pp. 253–270.

22. Bryce Ryan and Neal Gross, "The Diffusion of Hybrid Seed Corn in Two Iowa Communities," *Rural Sociology* (March 1943), pp. 15–24.

23. Joseph Barry Mason and Danny Bellenger, "Analyzing High-Fashion Acceptance," *Journal of Retailing* (Winter 1974), pp. 79–88.

24. See James F. Engel, Robert J. Kegerries, and Roger D. Blackwell, "Word-of-Mouth Communication by the Innovator," *Journal of Marketing* (July 1969), pp. 15–19.

25. For a discussion of characteristics of first adopters, see William E. Bell, "Consumer Innovators: A Unique Market for Newness," in *Toward Scientific Marketing*, ed. Stephen A. Greyser (Chicago: American Marketing Association, 1964), pp. 89–95; see also Louis E. Boone, "The Search for the Consumer Innovator," *Journal of Business* (April 1970), pp. 135–140; David W. Cravens,

James C. Cotham, and James R. Felix, "Identifying Innovator and Non-Innovator Firms," *Journal of Business Research* (April 1971), pp. 45–51; Lyman E. Ostland, "Identifying Early Buyers," *Journal of Advertising Research* (April 1972), pp. 29–34; Robert A. Peterson, "Diffusion and Adoption of a Consumer Durable," *Marquette Business Review* (Spring 1974), pp. 1–4; Steven A. Baumgarten, "The Innovative Communicator in the Diffusion Process," *Journal of Marketing Research* (February 1975), pp. 12–18; Laurence P. Feldman and Gary M. Armstrong, "Identifying Buyers of a Major Automobile Innovation," *Journal of Marketing* (January 1975), pp. 47–53; and Robert T. Green and Eric Langeard, "A Cross-National Comparison of Consumer Habits and Innovator Characteristics," *Journal of Marketing* (July 1975), pp. 34–41.

26. Ronald Marks and Eugene Hughes, "Profiling the Consumer Innovator," in *Evolving Marketing Thought for 1980*, eds. John H. Summey and Ronald D. Taylor (New Orleans: Southern Marketing Association, 1980), pp. 115–118; Elizabeth Hirschman, "Innovativeness, Novelty Seeking and Consumer Creativity," *Journal of Consumer Research* (December 1980), pp. 283–295; and Richard W. Olshavsky, "Time and the Rate of Adoption of Innovations," *Journal of Consumer Research* (March 1980), pp. 425–428.

27. For a more thorough discussion of the speed of the adoption process, see Everett Rogers and Floyd Shoemaker, *Communication of Innovations* (New York: Free Press, 1971), pp. 135–157.

28. See Raymond A. Bauer, "Consumer Behavior as Risk Taking," in *Dynamic Marketing for a Changing World*, ed. Robert S. Hancock (Chicago: American Marketing Association, 1960), pp. 389–398; see also James R. Bettman, "Perceived Risk and Its Components: A Model and Emphirical Test," *Journal of Marketing Research* (May 1973), pp. 184–190; Arch G. Woodside, "Informal Group Influence in Risk Taking," *Journal of Marketing Research* (May 1972), pp. 223–225; Robert D. Hisrich, Ronald J. Dornoff, and Jerome B. Kernan, "Perceived Risk in Store Selection," *Journal of Marketing Research* (November 1972), pp. 435–439; and James W. Taylor, "The Role of Risk in Consumer Behavior," *Journal of Marketing* (April 1974), pp. 54–60.

29. This discussion relies on Patrick E. Murphy and Ben M. Enis, "Classifying Products Strategically," *Journal of Marketing* (July 1986), pp. 24–42. Note that these authors argue that their classification system can be applied equally well to industrial products.

30. For an early discussion of the distinctions between homogeneous and heterogeneous shopping products, see E.J. McCarthy, *Basic Marketing* (Homewood, IL: Irwin, 1964), pp. 398–400; see also Harry A. Lipson

and John R. Darling, *Marketing Fundamentals* (New York: Wiley, 1974), pp. 244.

31. A similar classification scheme has been proposed by Leo Aspinwall, who considers five product characteristics in classifying consumer goods — *replacement rate*, *gross margin* (the difference between cost and selling price), *adjustment* (the necessary changes made in a goal to satisfy precisely the consumer's needs), *time of consumption* (the time interval during which the product provides satisfaction), and length of consumer *searching time*; see Leo V. Aspinwall, "The Characteristics of Goods Theory," in *Four Marketing Theories* (Boulder, CO: Bureau of Business Research, University of Colorado, 1961).

# Chapter 10

1. Adapted from Larry Kusch, "Firm Strikes Gold in Egg Whites," *Winnipeg Free Press* (August 27, 1990).

2. The width and depth of assortment is described in Raymond A. Marquardt, James C. Makens, and Robert G. Roe, *Retail Management*, 3rd ed. (Hinsdale, IL: Dryden Press, 1983), pp. 95–96.

3. Polaroid's product development strategies are described in "Polaroid: Turning Away from Land's One Product Strategy," *Business Week* (March 2, 1981), pp. 108–112.

4. Bill Abrams, "Despite Mixed Record, Firms Still Pushing for New Products," *Wall Street Journal* (November 12, 1981).

5. Howard Rudnitakey, "Snap Judgments Can Be Wrong," *Forbes* (April 12, 1982).

6. Abrams, "Despite Mixed Record," p. 25.

7. "The Money-Guzzling Genius of Biotechnology," *The Economist* (May 13, 1989), p. 69.

8. David S. Hopkins, *New Product Winners and Losers* (New York: Conference Board, 1980); see also "Booz Allen Looks at New Products' Role," *Wall Street Journal* (March 26, 1981).

9. Abrams, "Despite Mixed Record," p. 25.

10. This list is adapted from Roger Calantone and Robert G. Cooper, "New Product Scenarios: Prospects for Success," *Journal of Marketing* (Spring 1981), p. 49.

11. Robert G. Cooper, "The Myth of the Better Mousetrap: What Makes a New Product a Success?" *Business Quarterly* (Spring 1981), pp. 71, 72; and Robert G. Cooper, *Winning at New Products* (Toronto: Holt, Rinehart and Winston, 1986), p. 33.

12. Abrams, "Despite Mixed Record Firms Still Pushing for New Products," p. 25.

13. Reported in Ann M. Morrison, "The General Mills Brand of Manager," *Fortune* (January 12, 1981),

pp. 99–107: another interesting discussion appears in "Brand Management System Is Best, but Refinements Needed," *Marketing News* (July 9, 1982), p. 12.

14. Jacob M. Duker and Michael V. Laric, "The Product Manager: No Longer on Trial," in *The Changing Marketing Environment: New Theories and Applications*, eds. Kenneth Bernhardt et al. (Chicago: American Marketing Association, 1981), pp. 93–96; and Peter S. Howsam and G. David Hughes, "Product Management System Suffers from Insufficient Experience, Poor Communication," *Marketing News* (June 26, 1981), p. 8.

15. This discussion is based on Richard M. Hill and James D. Hlavacek, "The Venture Team: A New Concept in Marketing," *Journal of Marketing* (July 1972), pp. 44–50.

16. See D.W. Karger and Robert G. Murdick, *New-Product Venture Management* (New York: Gordon and Breach, 1972); Frederick W. Cook, "Venture Management Organizations: An Overview," in *Relevance in Marketing*, ed. Fred C. Allvine (Chicago: American Marketing Association, 1972), p. 129; and James D. Hlavacek, "Toward More Successful Venture Management," *Journal of Marketing* (October 1974), pp. 56–60; see also Dan T. Dunn, Jr., "The Rise and Fall of Ten Venture Groups," *Business Horizons* (October 1977), pp. 32–41; and William W. George, "Task Teams for Rapid Growth," *Harvard Business Review* (March–April 1977), pp. 71–80.

17. Adapted from John R. Rockwell and Marc C. Particelli, "New Product Strategy: How the Pros Do It," *Industrial Marketing* (May 1982), p. 50.

18. For an excellent treatment of the product development process, see Robert D. Hisrich and Michael P. Peters, *Marketing a New Product* (Menlo Park, CA: Benjamin Cummings Publishing, 1978); Richard T. Hise, *Product/Service Strategy* (New York: Mason/Charter Publishers, 1977); A. Edward Spitz, *Product Planning*, 2nd ed. (New York: Mason/Charter, 1977); and Chester R. Wasson, *Dynamic Competitive Strategy and Product Life Cycles* (Austin, TX: Austin Press, 1978).

19. Rockwell and Particelli, "New Product Strategy," p. 50.

20. See Eric von Hippel, "Successful Industrial Products from Customer Ideas," *Journal of Marketing* (January 1978), pp. 39–49; and James L. Ginter and W. Wayne Talarzyk, "Applying the Marketing Concept to Design New Products," *Journal of Business Research* (January 1978), pp. 51–66.

21. See William B. Locander and Richard W. Scamell, "Screening New Product Ideas: A Two-Phase Approach," *Research Management* (March 1976), pp. 14–18.

22. *Wall Street Journal* (March 26, 1974).

23. Reported in Edward Buxton, *Promise Them Anything* (New York: Stein and Day, 1972), p. 101.

24. Quoted in Mary McCabe English, "Marketers: Better than a Coin Flip," *Advertising Age* (February 9, 1981), p. S-15. Copyright 1981 by Crain Communications, Inc. Reprinted by permission.

25. Dylan Landis, "Durable Goods for a Test?" *Advertising Age* (February 9, 1981), pp. S-18, S-19.

26. Spencer Klaw, "The Soap Wars: A Strategic Analysis," *Fortune* (June 1963), pp. 122ff.

27. Committee on Definitions, *Marketing Definitions: A Glossary of Marketing Terms* (Chicago: American Marketing Association, 1960), pp. 9–10.

28. See Keith K. Cox, "Consumer Perception of Company Trademarks," *Journal of Business Research* (October 1970), pp. 128–131; and Sidney A. Diamond, "Trademark No. 1,000,000 Goes to 'Sweet 'N Low,'" *Advertising Age* (February 3, 1975), p. 39.

29. See Kenneth Uhl and Carl Block, "Some Findings Regarding Recall of Brand Marks: Descriptive Marks vs. Non-Descriptive Marks," *Journal of Business Research* (October 1969), pp. 1–10.

30. "A Worldwide Brand for Nissan," *Business Week* (August 24, 1981), p. 104.

31. See "'OFF' Row ON Again," *Marketing* (May 8, 1978), p. 1.

32. John Koten, "Mixing with Coke over Trademarks is Always a Fizzle," *Wall Street Journal* (March 9, 1978).

33. The question of brand choice is pursued in such articles as J. Morgan Jones and Fred S. Ziefryden, "An Approach for Assessing Demographic and Price Influences on Brand Purchase Behavior," *Journal of Marketing* (Winter 1982), pp. 36–46.

34. *Business Week* (February 20, 1960), p. 71.

35. Meir Statman and Tyzoon T. Tyebjee, "Trademarks, Patents, and Innovation in the Ethical Drug Industry," *Journal of Marketing* (Summer 1981), pp. 71–81.

36. Bill Abrams, "Brand Loyalty Rises Slightly, but Increase Could Be Fluke," *Wall Street Journal* (February 7, 1982),

37. Frances Phillips, "Private Label Appliances Vie with National Brands," *Financial Post* (August 13, 1983).

38. See Norman Seigle, "Generic Foods: A Further Report," *Nargus Merchandising Letter* (May 1980); Robert Dietrich, "Still Rooted in the Basics, Generics Sprout New Buds Too," *Progressive Grocer* (May 1980), p. 119; generics are also discussed in Robert H. Ross and Frederic B. Kraft, "Creating Low Consumer Product Expectations," *Journal of Business Research* (March 1983), pp. 1–9; Betsy Gelb, " 'No Name' Products: A Step Towards 'No-Name' Retailing," *Business Horizons* (June 1980), pp. 9–13; and Joseph A. Bellizzi, Harry F. Krueckelbert, and John R. Hamilton, "A Factor Analysis of National, Private, and Generic Brand Attributes," in 1981 *Proceedings of the Southwestern Marketing Association*, eds. Robert H. Ross, Frederic B. Kraft, and Charles H. Davis, pp. 208–210.

39. Private Brands Get More Public Attention," *Marketing* (August 29, 1983), p.1.

40. Frances Phillips, "New Packaging Looks are Making Some Products Winners," *Financial Post* (June 4, 1983).

41. Market Research Facts and Trends, (November–December 1989), p.1.

42. See M. Dale Beckman, "An Analysis of Food Packaging Cost: Does Packaging Cost Too Much?" in *ASAC 1978 Conference Proceedings* (London, ON: University of Western Ontario, 1978).

43. Packaging Linked to Ad's Effect," *Advertising Age* (May 3, 1982), p. 63.

44. Bill Abrams and David P. Garino, "Package Design Gains Stature as Visual Competition Grows," *Wall Street Journal* (August 6, 1981).

45. Robert Ball, "Warm Milk Wakes Up the Packaging Industry," *Fortune* (August 7, 1982), pp. 78–82.

# Chapter 11

1. Adapted from Don Bain, [Untitled article], *Manitoba Business* (April 1990), pp. 7–8.

2. The author thanks Anthony Leung for research performed and ideas presented for this chapter.

3. Edward Greenspon, "Service Industries Driving Growth, GATT Report Says," *Globe and Mail* (September 15, 1989).

4. L. Berry, "Services Marketing Is Different," in *Marketing Management and Strategy: A Reader,* eds. P. Kotler and K.K. Cox (Englewood Cliffs, NJ: Prentice-Hall, 1988), p. 278.

5. A. Rushton and D. Carson, "The Marketing of Services: Managing the Intangibles," *European Journal of Marketing* (1989), p. 31.

6. J. Bateson, "Do We Need Services Marketing?" in *Marketing Management and Strategy;* eds. Kotler and Cox, pp. 278–286.

7. Valarie A. Zeithaml, A. Parasuraman, and Leonard L. Berry, "Problems and Strategies in Services Marketing," *Journal of Marketing* (Spring, 1985), p. 33.

8. Theodore Levitt, "The Industrialization of Service," *Harvard Business Review* (September–October 1976), p. 63–74.

9. L. Berry, "Services Marketing Is Different," p. 281.

10. L. Berry, "Services Marketing Is Different," p. 281.

11. G.L. Shostack, "Breaking Free From Product Marketing," *Journal of Marketing* (April 1977), pp. 73–80.

12. L. Berry, "Services Marketing Is Different," p. 281.; and A. Rushton and D. Carson, "The Marketing of Service," p. 31.

# Chapter 12

1. Adapted from Shona McKay, "Sleeping Cheap," *Maclean's* (June 5, 1989), p. 41.

2. Adapted from David J. Schwartz, *Marketing Today*, copyright © 1981 by Harcourt Brace Jovanovich, Inc. Reprinted by permission of the publisher.

3. An alternative to the profit maximization concept is suggested in Bruce Gunn, "Profit Optimization: A Paradigm for Risk Reduction," *Akron Business and Economic Review* (Spring 1977), pp. 14–22.

4. Target rate-of-return pricing is discussed in Douglas G. Brooks, "Cost-Oriented Pricing: A Realistic Solution to a Complicated Problem," *Journal of Marketing* (April 1975), pp. 72–74.

5. Robert A. Lynn, *Price Policies and Marketing Management* (Homewood, IL: Irwin, 1967), p. 99; see also Stuart U. Rich, "Firms in Some Industries Should Use Both Target Return and Marginal Cost Pricing," *Marketing News* (June 25, 1982), Section 2, p. 11.

6. See William J. Baumol, "On the Theory of Oligopoly," *Economica* (August 1958), pp. 187–198; see also William J. Baumol, *Business Behavior, Value, and Growth* (New York: Macmillan, 1959).

7. An interesting discussion appears in Carl R. Frear and John E. Swan, "Marketing Managers' Motivation to Revise Their Market Share Goals: An Expectancy Theory Analysis," in 1981 *Southwestern Marketing Proceedings*, eds. Robert H. Ross, Frederic B. Kraft, and Charles H. Davis (Wichita, KS), pp. 13–16.

8. This section is adapted from Edwin G. Dolan, *Basic Economics*, 3rd ed. (Hinsdale, IL: Dryden Press, 1983); and Richard H. Leftwich, *The Price System and Resource Allocation* (Hinsdale, IL: Dryden Press, 1979), pp. 55–56, reprinted by permission of Holt, Rinehart and Winston.

9. For a discussion of the application of price elasticity to a consumer service, see Steven J. Skinner, Terry L. Childers, and Wesley H. Jones, "Consumer Responsiveness to Price Differentials: A Case for Insurance Industry Deregulation," *Journal of Business Research* (December 1981), pp. 381–396.

10. Experimental methods for estimating demand curves are discussed in Edgar A. Pessemier, *Experimental Methods of Analyzing Demand for Branded Consumer Goods*

(Pullman WA: Economic and Business Research, Washington State University, 1963); see also William J. Kehoe, "Demand Curve Estimation and the Small Business Managers," *Journal of Small Business Management* (July 1972), pp. 29–31.

11. Some problems of using economic models in practice are discussed in Kent B. Monroe and Albert J. Della Bitta, "Models of Pricing Decisions," *Journal of Marketing Research* (August 1978), pp. 413–428; see also Robert J. Dolan and Abel P. Jeuland, "Experience Curves and Dynamic Models: Implications for Optional Pricing Strategies," *Journal of Marketing* (Winter 1981), pp. 52–62.

12. Theodore E. Wentz, "Realism in Pricing Analysis," *Journal of Marketing* (April 1966), p. 26.

13. W. Warren Haynes, "Pricing Decisions in Small Business," *Management Research Summary* (Washington, DC: Small Business Administration, 1966), p. 1.

14. Haynes, "Pricing Decisions," p. 1.

15. Haynes, "Pricing Decisions," p.2.

16. Joel Dean, "Techniques for Pricing New Products and Services," in *Handbook of Modern Marketing*, eds. Victor P. Buell and Carl Heyel (McGraw-Hill, 1970), pp. 5–51.

17. This section has been adapted from G. David Hughes, *Marketing Management: A Planning Approach* (Menlo Park, CA: Addison-Wesley, 1978), pp. 324–326.

18. W. J. E. Crissy and R. Boewadt, "Pricing in Perspective," *Sales Management* (June 15, 1971).

# Chapter 13

1. Adapted from Adam Corelli, "The Unwaxed Reality of Those Fabulous Rebates on New Cars," *Financial Times of Canada* (March 20, 1989), p. 29.

2. Fred C. Foy, "Management's Part in Achieving Price Respectability," *Competitive Pricing* (New York: American Management Association, 1958), pp. 7–8.

3. Walter J. Primeaux, Jr., "The Effect of Consumer Knowledge and Bargaining Strength on Final Selling Price: A Case Study," *Journal of Business* (October 1970), pp. 419–426; another excellent article is James R. Krum, "Variable Pricing as a Promotional Tool," *Atlanta Economic Review* (November–December, 1977), pp. 47–50.

4. A survey technique for testing price levels above and below current levels is described in D. Frank Jones, "A Survey Technique to Measure Demand under Various Pricing Strategies," *Journal of Marketing* (July 1975), pp. 75–77.

5. An interesting study of consumer response to promotion prices is outlined in Norman D. French and

Robert A. Lynn, "Consumer Income and Response to Price Charges: A Shopping Simulation," *Journal of Retailing* (Winter 1971–72), pp. 21–23.

6. Bernie Faust, et al., "Effective Retail Pricing Policy," *Purdue Retailer* (Lafayette, IN: Agricultural Economics, 1963), p. 2.

7. Karl A. Shilliff, "Determinants of Consumer Price Sensitivity for Selected Supermarket Products: An Empirical Investigation," *Akron Business and Economic Review* (Spring 1975), pp. 26–32.

8. John F. Willenborg and Robert E. Pitts, "Perceived Situational Effects on Price Sensitivity," *Journal of Business Research* (March 1977), pp. 27–38.

9. See for example Zarrel V. Lambert, "Perceived Prices as Related to Odd and Even Price Findings," *Journal of Retailing* (Fall 1975), pp. 13–22, 78.

10. See David M. Georgoff, "Price Illusion and the Effect of Odd-Even Retail Pricing," *Southern Journal of Business* (April 1969), pp. 95–103; see also Dik W. Twedt, "Does the '9 Fixation in Retailing Really Promote Sales?" *Journal of Marketing* (October 1965), pp. 54–55; Benson P. Shapiro, "The Psychology of Pricing," *Harvard Business Review* (July–August, 1968), pp. 14–16; and David M. Georgoff, *Odd-Even Retail Price Endings: Their Effects on Value Determination, Product Perception, and Buying Propensities* (East Lansing, MI: Michigan State University, 1972).

11. Two excellent articles are Kent B. Monroe and Peter J. La Placa, "What Are the Benefits of Unit Pricing?" *Journal of Marketing* (July 1972), pp. 16–22; and Michael J. Houston, "The Effect of Unit Pricing on Choices of Brand and Size in Economic Shopping," *Journal of Marketing* (July 1972), 51–54.

12. J. Edward Russo, "The Value of Unit Price Information," *Journal of Marketing Research* (May 1977), pp. 193–201.

13. See, for instance, I. Robert Andrews and Enzo R. Valenzi, "The Relationship Between Price and Blind-Rated Quality for Margarines and Butter," *Journal of Marketing Research* (August 1970), pp. 393–395; Robert A. Peterson, "The Price-Perceived Quality Relationship: Experimental Evidence," *Journal of Marketing Research* (November 1970), pp. 525–528; David M. Gardner, "An Experimental Investigation of the Price/Quality Relationship," *Journal of Retailing* (Fall 1970), pp. 25–41; Arthur G. Bedelan, "Consumer Perception as an Indicator of Product Quality," *MSU Business Topics* (Summer 1971), pp. 59–65; and R. S. Mason, "Price and Product Quality Assessment," *European Journal of Marketing* (Spring 1974), pp. 29–41.

14. J. Douglass McConnell, "An Experimental Examination of the Price-Quality Relationship," *Journal of Business* (October 1968), pp. 439–444; see also

J. Douglass McConnell, "The Alphabet and Price as Independent Variables: A Note on the Price-Quality Question," *Journal of Business* (October 1970), pp. 448–451.

15. James H. Myers and William H. Reynolds, *Consumer Behavior and Marketing Management* (Boston: Houghton-Mifflin, 1967), p. 47.

16. See Kent B. Monroe and M. Venkatesan, "The Concepts of Price Limits and Psychophysical Measurement: A Laboratory Experiment," in ed. Phillip R. McDonald, *Marketing Involvement in Society and the Economy*, (Cincinnati: American Marketing Association, 1969) pp. 345–351.

17. *Market Spotlight* (Edmonton: Alberta Consumer and Corporate Affairs, March 1979).

18. Donald V. Harper, *Price Policy and Procedure* (New York: Harcourt Brace Jovanovich, 1966), p. 204, by permission of the author.

19. See for example Stephen Paranka, "Competitive Bidding Strategy," *Business Horizons* (June 1971), pp. 39–43; see also Richard C. Newman, "A Game Theory Approach to Competitive Bidding," *Journal of Purchasing* (February 1972), pp. 50–57; and James E. Reinmuth and Jim D. Barnes, "A Strategic Competitive Bidding Approach to Pricing Decisions for Petroleum Industry Drilling Contractors," *Journal of Marketing Research* (August 1975), pp. 362–365.

20. See Mary Louise Hatten, "Don't Get Caught with Your Prices Down: Pricing in Inflationary Times," *Business Horizons* (March–April 1982), pp. 23–28.

21. See Paul E. Dascher, "Some Transfer Pricing Standards," *Pittsburg Business Review* (November–December 1971), pp. 14–21; Thomas S. Goho, "Intracompany Pricing Strategy for International Corporations," *Business Studies* (Spring 1972), pp. 5–9; David Granick, "National Differences in the Use of Internal Transfer Prices," *California Management Review* (Summer 1975), pp. 28–40; and Peter Mailandt, "An Alternative to Transfer Pricing," *Business Horizons* (October 1975), pp. 81–86; see also interesting discussions of transfer pricing in Sylvain R. F. Plasschaert, *Transfer Pricing and Multinational Corporations* (New York: Praeger, 1979); and Roger Y. W. Tang, *Transfer Pricing Practices in the United States and Japan* (New York: Praeger, 1979).

22. M. Edgar Barret, "Case of the Tangled Transfer Price," *Harvard Business Review* (May–June 1977), p. 22.

23. See, for example, Marvin Brame, "Pricing Problems of the Water Industry: A Case Study of Northern New Castle County, Delaware," *Economic and Business Bulletin* (Spring–Summer 1971), pp. 37–42.

# Chapter 14

1. The contribution of Professor Ed Bruning to this chapter is gratefully acknowledged

2. Committee on Definitions, *Marketing Definitions: A Glossary of Marketing Terms* (Chicago: American Marketing Association, 1960), p. 10; some authors limit the definition to the route taken by the *title* to the goods, but this definition also includes agent wholesaling intermediaries who do not take title but who do serve as an important component of many channels.

3. This section is adapted by permission from Louis W. Stern and Adel I. El-Ansary, *Marketing Channels*, 3rd ed. (Englewood Cliffs, NJ: Prentice-Hall, 1989) pp. 7–12.

4. The first five functions were developed in Wroe Alderson, "Factors Governing the Development of Marketing Channels," in *Marketing Channels for Manufactured Products*, ed. Richard M. Clewitt (Homewood, IL: Irwin, 1954), pp. 5–22.

5. Wilke English, Dale M. Lewison, and M. Wayne DeLozier, "Evolution in Channel Management: What Will Be Next?" in *Proceedings of the Southwestern Marketing Association*, eds. Robert H. Ross, Frederic B. Kraft, and Charles H. Davis (Wichita, KS: 1981), pp. 78–81.

6. See Frederick E. Webster, Jr., "The Role of the Industrial Distributor in Marketing Strategy," *Journal of Marketing* (July 1976), pp. 10–16.

7. James A. White, "IBM Expands Outside Its Sales Channel," *Wall Street Journal* (October 7, 1981); industrial distributors are also discussed in James D. Hlavacek and Tommy J. McCusition, "Industrial Distributors — When, Who, and How?" *Harvard Business Review* (March–April 1983), pp. 96–101.

8. William G. Zikmund and William J. Stanton, "Recycling Solid Wastes: A Channels-of-Distribution Problem," *Journal of Marketing* (July 1971), p. 34.

9. Donald A. Fuller, "Aluminum Beverage Container Recycling in Florida: A Commentary," *Atlanta Economic Review* (January–February 1977), p. 41.

10. See Fred D. Reynolds, "An Analysis of Catalog Buying Behavior," *Journal of Marketing* (July 1974), pp. 47–51; Marvin A. Jolson, "Direct Selling: Consumer vs. Salesman," *Business Horizons* (October 1972), pp. 87–95; and Patrick Dunne, "Some Demographic Characteristics of Direct Mail Purchasers," *Baylor Business Studies* (May–July 1975), pp. 67–72.

11. Robert E. Weigand, "The Marketing Organization, Channels, and Firm Size," *Journal of Business* (April 1963), pp. 228–236.

12. Combines Investigation Act, Part IV. 1, 31.4, 1976.

13. Bert C. McCammon, Jr., "The Emergence and Growth of Contractually Integrated Channels in the American Economy," in *Marketing and Economic Development*, ed. Peter D. Bennett (Chicago: American Marketing Association, 1965), p. 496; this section is based on material in this paper, pp. 496-515.

14. See Bert C. McCammon, Jr., "Perspectives for Distribution Programming," in *Vertical Marketing Systems*, ed. Louis P. Bucklin (Glenview, IL: Scott, Foresman and Company, 1970), pp. 32–51, italics added; these are also described by William J. Hannaford, "Contractually Integrated Systems for the Marketing of Industrial Supplies," *Journal of the Academy of Marketing Science* (Fall 1974), pp. 567–581.

15. See Robert E. Weigand and Hilda C. Wasson, "Arbitration in the Marketing Channel," *Business Horizons* (October 1974), pp. 39–47; and John H. Holmes, "Leverage: A Key Factor in Marketing Channel Negotiation," *Pittsburgh Business Review* (May–June 1974), pp. 1–5.

16. See Michael Etgar, "Differences in the Use of Manufacturer Power in Conventional and Contractual Channels," *Journal of Retailing* (Winter 1978), pp. 49–62.

17. Adapted from Lawson A. W. Hunter, "Buying Groups," *Agriculture Canada: Food Market Commentary*, 5: 4, p. 15.

18. Thomas G. Marx, "Distribution Efficiency in Franchising," *MSU Business Topics* (Winter 1980), p. 5.

19. See Aaron M. Rothenberg, "A Fresh Look at Franchising," *Journal of Marketing* (July 1967), pp. 52–54; P. Ronald Stephenson and Robert G. House, "A Perspective of Franchising," *Business Horizons* (August 1971), pp. 35–42; and Jack M. Starling, "Franchising," *Business Studies* (Fall 1970), pp. 10–16.

20. See "The Finger Lickin' Fast-Food Fad," *Newsweek* (October 23, 1972), pp. 32–35; Bruce J. Walker and Michael J. Etzel, "The Internationalization of U.S. Franchise Systems: Progress and Procedures," *Journal of Marketing* (April 1973), pp. 38–46.

21. Leonard L. Berry, "Is It Time to Be Wary about Franchising?" *Arizona Business Bulletin* (October 1970), pp. 3–9; see also Donald F. Dixon, "Impact of Recent Antitrust Decisions upon Franchise Marketing," *MSU Business Topics* (Spring 1969), pp. 68–79; "A Changing Pattern for the Franchise Boom," *U.S. News and World Report* (April 24, 1972), pp. 88–89; and Shelby D. Hunt and John R. Nevin, "Full Disclosure Laws in Franchising: An Empirical Investigation," *Journal of Marketing* (April 1976), pp. 53–62.

22. Bruce Mallen, "A Theory of Retailer-Supplier Conflict, Control, and Cooperation," *Journal of Retailing* (Summer 1963), p. 26, reprinted with permission; see also F. Robert Dwyer, "Channel-Member Satisfaction: Laboratory Insights," *Journal of Retailing* (Summer 1980), pp. 45–65.

## Chapter 15

1. Adapted from Murray McNeill, "Trio Set to Fill Retailing Void," *Winnipeg Free Press* (June 2, 1989).

2. Industry Science and Technology Canada, *Wholesale Trade Industry Profile* (Ottawa, 1988), p. 7.

3. An interesting discussion of types of wholesaling appears in J. Howard Westing, "Wholesale Indifference," *The Courier* (Spring 1982), pp. 3, 8.

4. James R. Moore and Kendell A. Adams, "Functional Wholesaler Sales Trends and Analysis," in *Combined Proceedings*, ed. Edward M. Mazze (Chicago: American Marketing Association, 1976), pp. 402–405.

5. Louis P. Bucklin, *Competition and Evolution in the Distributive Trades* (Englewood Cliffs, NJ: Prentice-Hall, 1972), p. 214.

6. For a profile of the typical manufacturers' agent, see Stanley D. Sibley and Roy K. Teas, "Agent Marketing Channel Intermediaries' Perceptions of Marketing Channel Performance," in *Proceedings of the Southern Marketing Association*, eds. Robert S. Franz et al. (New Orleans: 1978), pp. 336–339.

## Chapter 16

1. Adapted from Kenneth Kidd, "Food City Tries Noise, Chaos in New Market-Style Stores," *Globe and Mail* (January 8, 1990).

2. "Canuck" *Pen Pictures of early Pioneer Life in Upper Canada*, (Toronto: Coles, 1972), pp. 80–82.

3. Gerald Albaum, Roger Best, and Del Hawkins, "Retailing Strategy for Customer Growth and New Customer Attraction," *Journal of Business Research* (March 1980), pp. 7–19; and Bert Rosenbloom, "Strategic Planning in Retailing: Prospects and Problems," *Journal of Retailing* (Spring 1980), pp. 107–120.

4. Interesting discussions include Sak Onkvisit and John J. Shaw, "Modifying the Retail Classification System for More Timely Marketing Strategies," *Journal of the Academy of Marketing Science* (Fall 1981), pp. 436–453; and Bobby C. Vaught, L.Lyn Judd, and Jack M. Starling, "The Perceived Importance of Retailing Strategies and Their Relationships to Four Indexes of Retailing Success," in *Progress in Marketing: Theory and Practice*, eds. Ronald D. Taylor, John J. Bennen, and John H. Summey (Carbondale, IL: Southern Marketing Association, 1981), pp. 25–28.

5. Frances Phillips, "Canadian Tire Finds Texas Trail a Bit Bumpy," *Financial Post* (March 26, 1983).

6. A good discussion appears in Mary Carolyn Harrison and Alvin C. Burns, "A Case for Departmentalizing Target Market Strategy in Department Stores," in *Progress in Marketing: Theory and Practice*, eds. Taylor, Bennen, and Summey, pp. 21–24.

7. Clayton Sinclair, "The New Priorities for Shopping Centres," *Financial Times of Canada* (March 21, 1983).

8. The following discussion of Reilly and Huff's work is adapted from Joseph Barry Mason and Morris Lehman Mayer, *Modern Retailing: Theory and Practice* (Plano, TX: Business Publications, 1978), pp. 486–489.

9. Huff's work is described in David Huff, "A Probabilistic Analysis of Consumer Spatial Behavior," in *Emerging Concepts in Marketing*, ed. William S. Decker (Chicago: American Marketing Association, 1972), pp. 443–461; shopping centre trade areas are also discussed in Edward Blair, "Sampling Issues in Trade Area Maps Drawn from Shopper Surveys," *Journal of Marketing* (Winter 1983), pp. 98–106.

10. Retail images are discussed in a variety of articles, for example, Pradeep K. Korgaonbar and Kamal M. El Sheshai, "Assessing Retail Competition with Multidimensional Scaling," *Business* (April–June, 1982), pp. 30–33; and Jack K. Kasulis and Robert F. Lush, "Validating the Retail Store Image Concept," *Journal of the Academy of Marketing Science* (Fall 1981), pp. 419–435.

11. This section is adapted from Louis P. Bucklin, "Retail Strategy and the Classification of Consumer Goods," *Journal of Marketing* (January 1963), pp. 50–55.

12. "Sears' Identity Crisis," *Business Week* (December 8, 1975), p. 54.

13. See Thomas J. Stanley and Murphy A. Sewell, "Predicting Supermarket Trade: Implications for Marketing Management," *Journal of Retailing* (Summer 1978), pp. 13–22; see also Danny N. Bellenger, Thomas J. Stanley, and John W. Allen, "Trends in Food Retailing," *Atlantic Economic Review* (May–June 1978), pp. 11–14.

14. See Ian Brown, "The Empire that Timothy Built," *Financial Post Magazine* (May 1978), pp. 16–47.

15. Brown, "The Empire," p. 20.

16. Superstores are discussed in Myron Gable and Ronald D. Michman, "Superstores — Revolutionizing Distribution," *Business* (March–April 1981), pp. 14–18.

17. Quoted by Mr. Knox, a Sears executive in Toronto.

18. Statistics Canada, *Vending Machine Operators*, 1988, Catalogue No. 63-213.

19. Statistics Canada, *Market Research Handbook*, 1990, Catalogue No. 63-224.

20. For a complete discussion of the "wheel-of-retailing" hypothesis, see Stanley C. Hollander, "The Wheel of Retailing," and "Retrospective Comment," in *The Great Writings in Marketing*, ed. Howard A. Thompson (Plymouth, MI: Commerce Press, 1976), pp. 358–369; see also Dillard B. Tinsley, John R. Brooks, Jr., and Michael d'Amico, "Will The Wheel Stop Turning?" *Akron Business and Economic Review* (Summer 1978), pp. 26–29.

21. "Only 10% of Consumers Interested in Shopping at Home Via 2-Way TV," *Marketing News* (May 29, 1981), pp. 1, 3.

22. Malcolm P. McNair and Eleanor G. May, "The Next Revolution of the Retailing Wheel," *Harvard Business Review* (September–October 1978), pp. 81–91; another interesting article is Larry J. Rosenberg and Elizabeth C. Hirschman, "Retailing without Stores," *Harvard Business Review* (July–August 1980), pp. 103–112.

23. Mark Evans, "An Old Tradition under Five," *Financial Post* (March 12, 1990).

## Chapter 17

1. Adapted from "Pepsi Tries for a Place at the Breakfast Table," *Globe and Mail* (September 30, 1989). Reprinted by permission of the *Associated Press*.

2. Similar communications processes are suggested in David K. Berlo, *The Process of Communications* (New York: Holt, Rinehart and Winston, 1960), pp. 23–38; and Thomas S. Robertson, *Innovative Behavior and Communication* (New York: Holt, Rinehart and Winston, 1971), p. 122; see also Claude Shannon and Warren Weaver, *The Mathematical Theory of Communication* (Urban, IL: University of Illinois Press, 1949), p. 5; and Wilbur Schramm, "The Nature of Communication Between Humans," in *The Process and Effects of Mass Communication*, rev. ed. (Urbana, IL: University of Illinois Press, 1971), pp. 3–53.

3. Wilbur Schramm, "The Nature of Communication Between Humans," pp. 3–53.

4. See William Dommermuth, "Promoting Your Product: Managing the Mix," *Business* (July–August 1980), pp. 18–21.

5. S. Watson Dunn and Arnold M. Barban, *Advertising: Its Role in Modern Marketing* (Hinsdale, IL: Dryden Press, 1982), p.7.

6. Committee on Definitions, *Marketing Definitions: A Glossary of Marketing Terms* (Chicago: American Marketing Association, 1960), p. 20, [italics added].

7. "Cost Analysis #2070," *Research Report* (New Orleans, LA: Trade Show Bureau, August 1988), p. 2.

8. Francis Phillips, "Advertisers Seek Ways to Curb the Cost of TV Ads," *Financial Post* (May 19, 1984).

9. Terrence V. O'Brien, "Psychologists Take a New Look at Today's Consumer," *Arizona Review* (August–September 1970), p. 2.

10. "Cadbury Gets Back in the Thick of the Action," *Marketing* (June 1, 1981), p. 1.

11. Lee E. Preston, *Markets and Marketing: An Orientation* (Glenview, IL: Scott, Foresman, 1970), p. 198. Copyright © 1970 by Scott, Foresman and Company. Reprinted by permission of the publisher.

12. One writer has argued that marketing communications expenditures should be included in the capital budget and treated as investments: see Joel Dean, "Does Advertising Belong in the Capital Budget?" *Journal of Marketing* (October 1966), pp. 15–21.

13. Determining the correct advertising frequency is examined in Herbert E. Krugman, "What Makes Advertising Effective?" *Harvard Business Review* (March–April 1975), pp. 96–103.

14. An excellent discussion of budgeting for marketing communications is included in S. Watson Dunn and Arnold M. Barban, *Advertising: Its Role in Modern Marketing*, 4th ed. (Hinsdale, IL: Dryden Press, 1978), pp. 266–285; see also Gary L. Lilien et al., "Industrial Advertising Effects and Budgeting Practices," *Journal of Marketing* (January 1976), pp. 16–24; William A. Staples and Robert W. Sweadlow, "A Zero Base Approach to Advertising Planning," in *Proceedings of the Southern Marketing Association*, eds. Robert S. Franz, Robert M. Hopkins, and Al Toma (New Orleans, LA: 1978), pp. 315–317; Michael Etgar and Meir Schneller, "Advertising in a Multiproduct Firm," in *Contemporary Marketing Thought*, eds. Barnett A. Greenberg and Danny N. Bellenger (Chicago: American Marketing Association, 1977), p. 527; and Joseph A. Bellizzi, A. Frank Thompson, and Lynn J. Loudenback, "Promotional Activity and the U.S. Business Cycle," in *Proceedings of the Southwestern Marketing Association*, eds. Robert C. Haring, G. Edward Kiser, and Ronnie D. Whitt (Houston, TX: 1979), pp. 27–28.

15. See J. Edward Russo, Barbara L. Metcalf, and Debra Stephens, "Identifying Misleading Advertising," *Journal of Consumer Research* (September 1981), pp. 119–131.

16. The economic effects of advertising are explored in Jean-Jacques Lambin, "What Is the Real Impact of Advertising?" *Harvard Business Review* (May–June 1975), pp. 139–147.

17. Francis X. Callahan, "Does Advertising Subsidize Information?" *Journal of Advertising Research* (August 1978), pp. 19–22.

## Chapter 18

1. Excerpted from Johanna Powell, "Mascot Maker Finds Success Is Little More Than Child's Play," *Financial Post* (September 11, 1989).

2. *A Report on Advertising Revenues in Canada* (Toronto: Maclean-Hunter Research Bureau, 1978), p. 3.

3. Francis Phillips, "Bring Back The Good Old Days," *The Financial Post 500* (Summer 1984), p. 200.

4. This section follows in part the discussion in S. Watson Dunn and Arnold Barban, *Advertising: Its Role in Modern Marketing*, 3rd ed. (Hinsdale, IL: Dryden Press, 1974), p. 5.

5. David A. Aaker and J. Gary Shansby, "Positioning Your Product," *Business Horizons* (May–June 1982), p. 62. Reprinted by permission of the publisher; see also Jack Trout and Al Ries, "Positioning: Ten Years Later," *Industrial Marketing* (July 1979), pp. 32–44.

6. See Thomas F. Garbett, "When to Advertise Your Company," *Harvard Business Review* (March–April 1982), pp. 100–106.

7. "Gulf to Tell a $3-Million Story," *Marketing* (May 25, 1981), p.1; see also G.H.G. McDougall, "Comparative Advertising in Canada: Practices and Consumer Relations," *Canadian Marketer* (1978), pp. 14–20.

8. The discussion of various advertising media is adapted from material in S. Watson Dunn and Arnold Barban, *Advertising: Its Role in Modern Marketing*, 5th ed. (Hinsdale, IL: Dryden Press, 1982), pp. 512–591.

9. The 1990 advertising volume percentages for the four major media (newspaper, television, magazines, and radio) are estimated by *Advertising Revenues in Canada* as reported by Martin Mehr, "Ad Revenues Projected to Top $10 Billion," *Marketing* (June 4, 1990).

10. Leonard Kubas, "Magazines Need It Razor Sharp," *Marketing* (April 6, 1987), p. 24.

11. Patrick Dunne, "Some Demographic Characteristics of Direct Mail Purchasers," *Baylor Business Studies* (July 1975), pp. 67–72.

12. Mailing lists are discussed in Jeffrey A. Tannenbaum, "Mailing List Brokers Sell More Than Names to Their Many Clients," *Wall Street Journal* (February 19, 1974).

13. Employment in various types of advertising organizations is explored in Jack A. Gottschalk, "Industrial Advertising Management: The Gloomy Side of the 'Glamour' Business," *Fairleigh Dickinson University Business Review* (Summer 1975), pp. 20–25.

14. An interesting discussion of the evaluation of advertising copy appears in James U. McNeal, "Advertising in the 'Age of Me,'" *Business Horizons* (August 1979), pp. 34–38.

15. William M. Carley, "Gillette Co. Struggles as Its Rivals Slice at Fat Profit Margin," *Wall Street Journal* (February 2, 1972), p. 1. Reprinted by permission.

16. Bill Abrams, "Comparative Ads Are Getting More Popular, Harder Hitting," *The Wall Street Journal* (March 11, 1982), p. 27; see also Linda E. Swayne and Thomas H. Stevenson, "The Nature and Frequency of Comparative Advertising in Industrial Print Media," in *A Spectrum of Contemporary Marketing Ideas*, eds. John H. Summey, Blaise J. Bergiel, and Carol H. Anderson

(New Orleans, LA: Southern Marketing Association, 1982), pp. 9–12.

17. This section is based on Tony Thompson, "Retail Advertisers 'Enter 20th Century,'" *Advertising Age* (October 13, 1980), p. 51.

18. This section is based on Dunn and Barban, *Advertising*, pp. 287–310; an interesting article is Carlton A. Maile, "Predicting Changes in Advertising Effectiveness," *University of Michigan Business Review* (July 1979), pp. 18–22.

19. Committee on Definitions, *Marketing Definitions: A Glossary of Marketing Terms* (Chicago: American Marketing Association, 1960), p. 20.

20. This definition is adapted from "How to Play Championship Specialty Advertising" (Chicago: Specialty Advertising Association, 1978).

21. Walter A. Gaw, *Specialty Advertising* (Chicago: Specialty Advertising Association, 1970), p. 7.

22. See David J. Reibstein and Phyllis A. Traver, "Factors Affecting Coupon Redemption Rates," *Journal of Marketing* (Fall 1982), pp. 102–113.

23. See, for example, Carl-Magnus Seipel, "Premiums: Forgotten by Theory," *Journal of Marketing* (April 1971), pp. 26–34.

24. Reported in "Sell, Sell, Sell," *Wall Street Journal* (September 14, 1971).

25. For an analysis of problems involved in identifying specific decision-makers in an industrial setting, see Thomas V. Bonoma, "Major Sales: Who *Really* Does the Buying?" *Harvard Business Review* (May–June 1982), pp. 111–119.

26. For an interesting discussion of promotional appeals, see Walter Gross, "Rational and Nonrational Appeals in Selling to Businessmen," *Georgia Business* (February 1970), pp. 1–3.

27. Quoted in James Samuel Knox, *Salesmanship and Business Efficiency* (New York: Gregg Publishing, 1922), pp. 243–244.

# Chapter 19

1. Excerpted from David Estok, "Firms Restructure for Global Market," *Financial Post* (January 9, 1989).

2. Canada, *Export Trade Month Information Kit*, October 1983.

3. Andrew Cohen, "Rising Trade Warms Kaifu's Canadian Welcome," *Financial Post* (September 4, 1989).

4. *The Age* (October 4, 1974), p. 1.

5. The Northern Telecom illustrations used in the following sections are adapted from "Mastering the International Market," *Marketing* (March 27, 1989), p. B12.

6. *Detroit News* (February 28, 1975).

7. Adapted from *Financial Post* (May 3, 1980).

8. Warren Keegan, *Global Marketing Management*, (New York: McGraw-Hill, 1989) pp. 31-33.

9. Hyman Solomon, "We Can't Afford to Be Outside Trade Walls," *Financial Post* (October 31, 1988).

10. *CandExport* (May 1, 1991), p. 3.

## Chapter 20

1. Adapted from M. Louise Ripley and George Gilbert, "The Vancouver Symphony Orchestra: Marketing," *Academy of Marketing Science News* (January 1991) p. 2.

2. Also referred to as "not-for-profit" organizations; we will use the two terms interchangeably in this chapter.

3. Philip Kotler, *Marketing for Nonprofit Organizations* (Englewood Cliffs, NJ: Prentice-Hall, 1982), p. 9.

4. These differences and others are outlined in Harvey W. Wallender, III, "Managing Not-For-Profit Enterprises," *Academy of Management Review* (January 1978), p. 26; and Cecily Cannon Selby, "Better Performance for 'Non-profits,'" *Harvard Business Review* (September–October 1978), pp. 93–95. Used by permission.

5. Kotler, *Marketing for Nonprofit Organizations*, p. 482.

6. An excellent discussion of idea marketing appears in Jagdish N. Sheth and Gary L. Frazier, "A Model of Strategy Mix Choice for Planned Social Change," *Journal of Marketing* (Winter 1982), pp. 15–26.

7. David J. Rachman and Elaine Romano, *Modern Marketing* (Hinsdale, IL: Dryden Press, 1980), p. 576; the delineation of person, idea, and organization marketing are proposed by Professors Rachman and Romano.

8. James M. Stearns, John R. Kerr, and Roger R. McGrath, "Advances of Marketing for Functional Public Policy Administration," in *Proceedings of the Southern Marketing Association*, eds. Robert S. Franz, Robert M. Hopkins, and Alfred G. Toma (Atlanta, GA: November 1979), pp. 140–143.

9. This section is based on Philip Kotler, *Marketing for Nonprofit Organizations*, 1982, pp. 306–309. Adapted by permission of Prentice-Hall, Inc., Englewood Cliffs, NJ.. See also Chris T. Allen, "Self-Perception Based Strategies for Stimulating Energy Conservation," *Journal of Consumer Research* (March 1982), pp. 381–390.

10. Michael L. Rothschild, "Marketing Communications in Nonbusiness Situations or Why It's So Hard to Sell Brotherhood Like Soap," *Journal of Marketing* (Spring 1979), pp. 11–20.

## Chapter 21

1. Adapted from William A. Brand, "Use the Right Measures to Track Marketing Performance," *Sales and Marketing Management in Canada* (February 1988), p. 33.

2. Howard Schlossberg, "Customer Satisfaction Serves and Preserves," *Marketing News* (May 28, 1990), p. 8.

3. William Brand, "Quality Is King for Marketers," *Sales and Marketing Management in Canada* (March 1989), p. 7.

4. This section is partially based on M. Skolnik, S. Lawrence, and K. Smyth, "Total Quality Management Is Substance, Not Slogan," *Marketing News* (May 28, 1990), p. 24.

5. Philip Kotler, "From Sales Obsession to Marketing Effectiveness," *Harvard Business Review* (November–December 1977), pp. 67–75. The list of definitions is reprinted with permission from p. 72. Copyright © 1977 by the President and Fellows of Harvard College; all rights reserved.

## Cases

1. Donald R. Scheen and Philip A. Sprague, "What is the Case Method?" in *The Case Method at the Harvard Business School*, ed. Malcolm P. McNair (New York: McGraw-Hill, 1954), p. 78.

2. Charles I. Gragg, "Because Wisdom Can't Be Told," in *The Case Method at the Harvard Business School*, ed. Malcolm P. McNair (New York: McGraw-Hill, 1954), pp. 2–7.

3. John T. Gullahorn, "Teaching by the Case Method," *School Review* (January 1959), pp. 448–60.

## Case 11

1. Nancy B. Finn, *The Electronic Office* (Englewood Cliffs, NJ: Prentice-Hall, 1983), p. 5.

2. WORDTECH Information Memorandum, WORDTECH Ltd., 1990.

3. Strategic Alternatives Inc., Customer Satisfaction Survey, prepared by IBM Corporation, 1990.

4. Chuck Duff and Howard Duff, "Migration Patterns," *Byte* (October 1990), pp. 223ff.

5. Brad J. Cox, "There Is a Silver Bullet," *Byte* (October 1990), pp. 209ff.

6. Yourdon, Edward, "Auld Lang Syne" in *Byte*, October, 1990, pp. 257ff.

## Case 13

1. The mortgage value was to be adjusted to the exchange rate of the zloty to the Swiss Franc. This would mean an increase in the mortgage balance every time the zloty was devalued.

## Case 18

1. Computron's fiscal year ran from July 1 to June 30.

2. Depending on the specific application in question, the components of the 1000X varied slightly, so that each machine was somewhat different from the rest.

## Case 19

1. In 1987, the Australian dollar (A$) was worth approximately 0.95 Canadian dollars.

# Glossary

**absolute advantage**  Advantage said to be held by a nation that is the sole producer of a product or that can produce a product for less than anyone else.

**accelerator principle**  The disproportionate impact that changes in consumer demand have on industrial market demand.

**accessory equipment**  Second-level capital items that are used in the production of products and services but are usually less expensive and shorter-lived than installations.

**adoption process**  A series of stages consumers go through, from learning of a new product to trying it and deciding to purchase it regularly or to reject it.

**advertising**  Paid nonpersonal communication through various media by business firms, nonprofit organizations, and individuals who are in some way identified with the advertising message and who hope to inform or persuade members of a particular audience.

**advertising agency**  A marketing specialist firm that assists the advertiser in planning and preparing its advertisements.

**agent**  A wholesaling intermediary who differs from the typical wholesaler in that the agent does not take title to the goods.

**agents and brokers**  Wholesaling intermediaries who may take possession of the products, but who do not take title to them.

**AIO statements**  Statements about activities, interests, and opinions, used in developing psychographic profiles.

**approach**  The initial contact between the salesperson and the prospective customer.

**Asch phenomenon**  The impact that groups and group norms can exhibit on individual behaviour.

**aspirational group**  A type of reference group with which individuals desire to associate.

**attitudes**  A person's enduring favourable or unfavourable evaluations, emotional feelings, or pro or con action tendencies toward some object or idea.

**auction house**  An agent wholesaling intermediary who brings buyers and sellers together in one location and allows potential buyers to inspect the merchandise before purchasing.

**average cost**  Obtained by dividing total cost by the quantity associated with this cost.

**average variable cost**  The total variable cost divided by the related quantity.

**balance of payments**  The flow of money into or out of a country.

**balance of trade**  The relationship between a country's exports and its imports.

**bids**  Price quotations from potential suppliers.

**bottom line**  The overall-profitability measure of performance.

**brand**  A name, term, sign, symbols, or design (or some combination thereof) used to identify the products of one firm and to differentiate them from competitive offerings.

**brand extension**  The decision to use a popular brand name for a new product entry in an unrelated product category.

**brand insistence**  The ultimate stage of brand loyalty; occurs when consumers will accept no alternatives and will search extensively for the product.

**brand name**  Words, letters, or symbols that make up a name used to identify and distinguish the firm's offerings from those of competitors.

**brand preference**  The second stage of brand loyalty; situation in which, based on previous experience, consumers will choose a product rather than one of its competitors — if it is available.

**brand recognition**  The first stage of brand loyalty; situation whereby a firm has developed enough publicity for a brand that its name is familiar to consumers.

**break-bulk warehouse**  One that receives consolidated shipments from a central distribution centre, and then distributes them in smaller shipments to individual customers in more limited areas.

**break-even analysis**   A means of determining the number of products or services that must be sold at a given price in order to generate sufficient revenue to cover total costs.

**broker**   A wholesaling intermediary who brings buyers and sellers together; operates in industries with a large number of small suppliers and purchasers.

**buying centre**   Everyone who participates in some fashion in an industrial buying action.

**cannibalizing**   Situation involving one product taking sales from another offering in a product line.

**capital items**   Long-lived business assets that must be depreciated over time.

**cartel**   The monopolistic organization of a group of firms.

**cash discounts**   Reductions in price that are given for prompt payment of a bill.

**cash-and-carry wholesaler**   Limited-function merchant wholesaler who performs most wholesaling functions except financing and delivery.

**catalogue retailer**   Retailer that mails catalogues to its customers and operates from a showroom displaying samples of its products.

**census**   A collection of marketing data from all possible sources.

**chain stores**   Groups of retail stores that are centrally owned and managed and that handle the same lines of products.

**closing**   The act of asking the prospect for an order.

**cluster sample**   A probability sample that is generated by randomly choosing one or more areas or population clusters and then surveying all members in the chosen cluster(s).

**cognitive dissonance**   The postpurchase anxiety that occurs when an imbalance exists among a person's cognitions (knowledge, beliefs, and attitudes).

**commission merchant**   An agent wholesaling intermediary who takes possession when the producer ships goods to a central market for sale.

**communication**   Personal selling, advertising, sales promotion, and publicity.

**comparative advantage**   Advantage said to be held by a nation that can produce a given item more efficiently than it can produce other products.

**comparative advertising**   Advertising that makes direct promotional comparisons with leading competitive brands.

**competitive bidding**   Buyers request potential suppliers to make price quotations on a proposed purchase or contract.

**competitive environment**   The interactive process that occurs in the marketplace as competing organizations seek to satisfy markets.

**component parts and materials**   Finished industrial goods that actually become part of the final product.

**concept testing**   A marketing research project that attempts to measure consumer attitudes and perceptions relevant to a new-product idea.

**consumer behaviour**   The acts of individuals in obtaining and using goods and services, including the decision processes that precede and determine these acts.

**consumer goods**   Those products and services purchased by the ultimate consumer for personal use.

**consumer innovators**   The first purchasers — those who buy a product at the beginning of its life cycle.

**containerization**   Combining several unitized loads.

**convenience products**   Products that are lowest in terms of both effort and risk.

**convenience sample**   A nonprobability sample based on the selection of readily available respondents.

**co-operative advertising**   The sharing of advertising costs between the retailer and manufacturer or wholesaler.

**corporate strategy**   The overall purpose and direction of the organization that is established in the light of the challenges and opportunities found in the environment, as well as available organizational resources.

**cost-plus pricing**   Pricing technique using base cost figure per unit to which is added a markup to cover unassigned costs and to provide a profit.

**creative selling**   Selling that involves making the buyer see the worth of the item.

**cue**   Any object existing in the environment that determines the nature of the response to a drive.

**culture**   A learned way of life including values, ideas, and attitudes that influence consumer behaviour.

**customs union**   Agreement among two or more nations that establishes a free trade area plus a uniform tariff for trade with nonmember nations.

**demand variability**   In the industrial market, the impact of derived demand on the demand for interrelated products used in producing consumer goods.

**demarketing**   The process of cutting consumer demand for a product back to a level that can reasonably be supplied by the firm.

**department store**   Large retailer that handles a variety of merchandise.

**depreciation**   The accounting concept of charging a portion of the cost of a capital item against the company's annual revenue for purposes of determining its net income.

**derived demand**   In the industrial market, demand for an industrial product that is linked to demand for a consumer good.

**devaluation**   Situation in which a nation reduces the value of its currency in relation to gold or some other currency.

**diffusion process**   The gradual or quick acceptance of new products and services by the members of a community or social system.

**direct-response wholesaler**   Limited-function merchant wholesaler who relies on catalogues rather than a sales force to contact retail, industrial, and institutional customers.

**direct-sales results test**   A test for marketing communications effectiveness that attempts to ascertain for each dollar of promotional outlay the corresponding increase in revenue.

**disassociative group**   A type of reference group, one with which an individual does not want to be identified by others.

**discount house**   Retailer that, in exchange for reduced prices, does not offer such traditional retail services as credit, sales assistance by clerks, and delivery.

**distribution**   The selection and management of marketing channels and the physical distribution of goods.

**distribution channel**   The paths goods — and title to these goods — follow from producer to consumer.

**drive**   Any strong stimulus that impels action.

**drop shipper**   Limited-function merchant wholesaler who takes orders from customers and places them with producers, who then ship directly to the customer.

**dumping**   Practice of selling products at significantly lower prices in a foreign market than in the selling nation's own domestic market.

**dynamic break-even analysis**   An approach that combines the traditional break-even analysis model with an evaluation of consumer demand.

**economic environment**   A setting of complex and dynamic business fluctuations that have historically tended to follow a three-or four-stage pattern: (1) recession, (2) depression, (3) recovery, and (4) prosperity.

**economic union**   Agreement among two or more nations that establishes a free flow not only of goods, but also of people, capital, and services among its members.

**elasticity**   A measure of responsiveness of purchasers and suppliers to changes in price.

**embargo**   A complete ban on importing a particular product.

**Engel's Laws**   As family income increases, (1) a smaller percentage goes for food, (2) the percentage spent on housing and household operations and clothing will remain constant, and (3) the percentage spent on other items will increase.

**EOQ (economic order quantity)**   A model that emphasizes a cost trade-off between inventory holding costs and order costs.

**escalator clause**   A clause allowing the seller to adjust the final price based on changes in the costs of the product's ingredients between the placement of the order and the order's completion.

**ethnocentric company**   Firm that assumes that its way of doing business in its home market is the proper way to operate, and tries to replicate this in foreign markets.

**evaluative criteria**   Features the consumer considers in making a choice among alternatives.

**evoked set**   The number of brands that a consumer actually considers in making a purchase decision.

**exchange control**   Requirement that firms gaining foreign exchange by exporting must sell their foreign exchange to the central bank or agency, and importers must buy foreign exchange from the same organization.

**exchange process**   The process by which two or more parties give something of value to one another to satisfy felt needs.

**exchange rate**   The rate at which a nation's currency can be exchanged for other currencies or gold.

**exclusive dealing**   An arrangement whereby a supplier prohibits a marketing intermediary (either a wholesaler or, more typically, a retailer) from handling competing products.

**exclusive distribution**   The granting of exclusive rights by manufacturers to a wholesaler or retailer to sell in a geographic region.

**expense items**   Products and services that are used within a short period of time.

**exploratory research**   Learning about the problem area and beginning to focus on specific areas of study by discussing the problem with informed sources within the firm (a process often called *situation analysis*) and with knowledgeable others outside the firm (the *informal investigation*).

**facilitating agency**   An agency that provides specialized assistance for regular channel members (such as producers, wholesalers, and retailers) in moving products from producer to consumer.

**fads**   Fashions with abbreviated life cycles.

**family brand**     Brand name used for several related products.

**family life cycle**     The process of family formation, development, and dissolution.

**fashions**     Currently popular products that tend to follow recurring life cycles.

**fiscal policy**     The receipts and expenditures of government.

**flexible pricing**     A variable price policy.

**F.O.B. plant pricing**     The buyer must pay all the freight charges.

**follow-up**     The postsales activities that often determine whether a person will become a repeat customer.

**franchise**     An agreement whereby dealers (franchisees) agree to meet the operating requirements of a manufacturer or other franchiser.

**free trade area**     Area (established by agreement among two or more nations) within which participants agree to free trade of goods among themselves.

**freight absorption**     The seller permits the buyer to subtract transportation expenses from the bill.

**friendship, commerce, and navigation (FCN) treaties**     Treaties that address many aspects of commercial relations with other countries; such treaties constitute international law.

**GATT**     (General Agreement on Tariffs and Trade): An international trade agreement to gradually lower tariffs.

**generic name**     A brand name over which the original owner has lost exclusive claim because all offerings in the associated class of products have become generally known by the brand name (usually that of the first or leading brand in the product class).

**generic products**     Food and household staples characterized by plain labels, little or no advertising, and no brand names.

**geocentric company**     Firm that develops a marketing mix that meets the needs of target consumers in all markets.

**Hazardous Products Act**     A major piece of legislation that consolidated previous legislation and set significant new standards for product safety; defines a hazardous product as any product that is included in a list (called a schedule) compiled by Consumer and Corporate Affairs Canada or Health and Welfare Canada.

**high-involvement products**     Products for which the purchaser is highly involved in making the purchase decision.

**house-to-house retailer**     Retailer that sells products by direct contact between the retailer–seller and the customer at the home of the customer.

**hypermarket**     Mass merchandiser that operates on a low-price, self-service basis and carries lines of soft goods, hard goods, and groceries.

**hypothesis**     A tentative explanation about the relationship between variables as a starting point for further testing.

**idea marketing**     The identification and marketing of a cause to chosen consumer segments.

**import quota**     A limit set on the amount of products that may be imported in a given category.

**individual brand**     Brand that is known by its own brand name rather than by the name of the company producing it or an umbrella name covering similar items.

**individual offerings**     Single products within a product line.

**industrial distributor**     A wholesaler who operates in the industrial goods market and typically handles small accessory equipment and operating supplies.

**industrial goods**     Those products purchased to be used, either directly or indirectly, in the production of other goods or for resale.

**industrial market**     Individuals and organizations who acquire goods and services to be used, directly or indirectly, in the production of other goods and services or to be resold.

**inflation**     A rising price level resulting in reduced purchasing power for the consumer.

**informative product advertising**     Advertising that seeks to develop demand through presenting factual information on the attributes of a product and/or service.

**installations**     Major capital assets that are used to produce products and services.

**institutional advertising**     Promoting a concept, idea, or philosophy, or the goodwill of an industry, company, or organization.

**intensive distribution**     A form of distribution that attempts to provide saturation coverage of the potential market.

**inventory adjustments**     Changes in the amounts of materials a manufacturer keeps on hand.

**joint demand**     In the industrial market, demand for an industrial product that is related to the demand for another industrial good (because the latter item is necessary for the use of the first item).

**judgment sample**     A nonprobability sample of people with a specific attribute.

**label** The part of a package that contains (1) the brand name or symbol, (2) the name and address of the manufacturer or distributor, (3) information about product composition and size, and (4) information about recommended uses of the product.

**law of retail gravitation** Principle that delineates the retail trade area of a potential site on the basis of distance between alternative locations and relative populations.

**learning** Changes in behaviour, immediate or expected, as a result of experience.

**lifestyle** The mode of living.

**limited-line store** Retailer that offers a large assortment of a single line of products or a few related lines of products.

**line extension** The development of individual offerings that appeal to different market segments but are closely related to the existing product line.

**list price** The rate normally quoted to potential buyers.

**local content laws** Laws specifying the portion of a product that must come from domestic sources.

**loss leader** Goods priced below cost to attract customers.

**low-involvement products** Products with little significance, either materially or emotionally, which a consumer may purchase first and evaluate later (while using them).

**mail-order merchandiser** Retailer that offers its customers the option of placing merchandise orders by mail, by telephone, or by visiting the mail-order desk of a retail store.

**manufacturers' agent** An independent salesperson who works for a number of manufacturers of related but noncompeting products.

**marginal cost** The change in total cost that results from producing an additional unit of output.

**markdown** A reduction in the price of an item.

**market** Requires not only people and willingness to buy, but also purchasing power and the authority to buy.

**market development strategy** Finding new markets for existing products.

**market orientation** Paying careful attention to understanding customer needs and objectives, then making the business serve the interests of the customer rather than trying to make the customer buy what the business wants to produce.

**market price** The amount that a consumer pays.

**market restriction** An arrangement whereby suppliers restrict the geographic territories for each of their distributors.

**market segmentation** Grouping people according to their similarity in one or more dimensions related to interests in a particular product category.

**market share objective** To control a specific portion of the market for the firm's product.

**marketing** The process of planning and executing the conception, pricing, promotion, and distribution of ideas, goods, and services to create exchanges that satisfy individual and organizational objectives.

**marketing channels** The steps or handling organizations that a good or service goes through from producer to consumer.

**marketing communications** All messages that inform, persuade, and influence the consumer in making a purchase decision.

**marketing communications mix** The blending of personal selling and nonpersonal selling (including advertising, sales promotion, and public relations) by marketers in an attempt to accomplish information and persuasion objectives.

**marketing concept** An organization-wide focus on providing chosen groups of customers with products that bring optimal satisfaction so as to achieve long-run profits.

**marketing ethics** The marketer's standards of conduct and moral values.

**marketing functions** Buying, selling, transporting, storing, grading, financing, risk taking, and information collection and dissemination.

**marketing information system** A designed set of procedures and methods for generating an orderly flow of pertinent information for use in making decisions, providing management with a picture of the current and future states of the market and with indications of market responses to company actions as well as to the actions of competitors.

**marketing intermediary** A business firm operating between the producer and the consumer or industrial purchaser.

**marketing mix** The blending of the four elements of marketing to satisfy chosen consumer segments.

**marketing plan** A program of activities that lead to the accomplishment of the marketing strategy.

**marketing research** The systematic gathering, recording, and analyzing of data about problems relating to the marketing of goods and services.

**marketing strategy** A strategy that focuses on developing a unique long-run competitive position in the market by assessing consumer needs and the firm's potential for gaining competitive advantage.

**markup** The amount a producer or channel member adds to cost in order to determine the selling price.

**mass merchandiser** Retailer that often stocks a wider line of products than department stores, but usually does not offer the depth of assortment in each line.

**membership group**   A type of reference group to which individuals actually belong — as with, say, a country club.

**merchandise mart**   Permanent exhibition at which manufacturers rent showcases for their product offerings.

**merchant wholesalers**   Wholesaling intermediaries who take title to the products.

**misleading advertising**   A false statement of any kind made to the public about products or services.

**missionary selling**   Selling that emphasizes selling the firm's goodwill and providing customers with technical or operational assistance; manufacturer's sales representative may help familiarize wholesalers and retailers with the firm's products and aids in-store displays and promotional planning.

**modified rebuy**   A situation in which purchasers are willing to re-evaluate their available options.

**monetary policy**   The manipulation of the money supply and market rates of interest.

**monopolistic competition**   A market structure with a large number of buyers and sellers where heterogeneity in product and/or service and (usually) geographical differentiation allow the marketer some control over price.

**monopoly**   A market structure with only one seller of a product with no close substitutes.

**motive**   An inner state that directs a person toward the goal of satisfying a felt need.

**MRO items**   Industrial supplies, so called because they can be categorized as maintenance items, repair items, or operating supplies.

**multi-offer strategy**   The attempt to satisfy several segments of the market very well with specialized products and unique marketing programs aimed at each segment.

**national brand (manufacturer's brand)**   A brand promoted and distributed by a manufacturer.

**need**   The lack of something useful.

**negotiated contract**   The terms of the contract are set through talks between the buyer and a seller.

**new task buying**   First-time or unique purchase situations that require considerable effort on the part of the decision-makers.

**nonprobability sample**   A sample chosen in an arbitrary fashion so that each member of the population does not have a representative chance of being selected.

**nonprofit organization (NPO)**   Organization whose primary objective is something other than returning a profit to its owners; also known as a *not-for-profit* organization.

**odd pricing**   A system whereby prices are set ending in numbers not commonly used for price quotations.

**oligopoly**   A market structure in which there are relatively few sellers.

**oligopsony**   A market where there are only a few buyers.

**opinion leaders**   Trend setters; individuals who are more likely to purchase new products early and to serve as information sources for others in a given group.

**order processing**   Selling at the wholesale and retail levels; involves identifying customer needs, pointing out the need to the customer, and completing the order.

**organization marketing**   Attempts to influence others to accept the goals of, receive the services of, or contribute in some way to an organization.

**penetration pricing**   An entry price for a product lower than what is believed to be the long-term price.

**perception**   The meaning that each person attributes to incoming stimuli received through the five senses.

**perceptual screen**   The filter through which messages must pass.

**person marketing**   Efforts designed to cultivate the attention, interest, and preference of a target market toward a person.

**personal selling**   A seller's promotional presentation conducted on a person-to-person basis with the buyer.

**persuasive product advertising**   Advertising that emphasizes using words and/or images to try to create an image for a product and to influence attitudes about it.

**physical distribution**   A broad range of activities concerned with efficient movement of products from the source of raw materials to the production line and, ultimately, to the consumer.

**planned shopping centre**   Group of retail stores planned, co-ordinated, and marketed as a unit to shoppers in a particular geographic trade area.

**point-of-purchase advertising**   Displays and demonstrations that seek to promote the product at a time and place closely associated with the actual decision to buy.

**political and legal climate**   The laws and interpretation of laws that require firms to operate under competitive conditions and to protect consumer rights.

**polycentric company**   Firm that assumes that every country is different and that a specific marketing approach should be developed for each separate country.

**population** or **universe**   The total group that the researcher wants to study.

**positioning**   Shaping the product and developing a marketing program in such a way that the product is perceived to be (and actually is) different from competitors' products.

**post-testing**   The assessment of advertising copy after it has been used.

**preference products**   Products that are slightly higher on the effort dimension and much higher on risk than convenience products.

**presentation**   The act of giving the sales message to a prospective customer.

**prestige objectives**   The establishment of relatively high prices in order to develop and maintain an image of quality and exclusiveness.

**pre-testing**   The assessment of an advertisement's effectiveness before it is actually used.

**price**   The exchange value of a good or service. The value of an item is what it can be exchanged for in the marketplace.

**price limits**   Limits within which product quality perception varies directly with price.

**price lining**   The practice of marketing merchandise at a limited number of prices.

**price structure**   An outline of the selling price and the various discounts offered to middlemen.

**pricing**   The methods of setting competitive, profitable, and justified prices.

**pricing policy**   A general guideline based on pricing objectives that is intended for use in specific pricing decisions.

**primary data**   Data being collected for the first time.

**private brand**   A brand promoted and distributed by a retailer or wholesaler.

**probability sample**   A sample in which every member of the population has a known chance of being selected.

**producers**   Those who transform goods and services through production into other goods and services.

**product**   A total bundle of physical, service, and symbolic characteristics designed to produce consumer want satisfaction.

**product advertising**   Nonpersonal selling of a particular good or service.

**product development strategy**   Introducing new products into identifiable or established markets.

**product diversification strategy**   The development of new products for new markets.

**product improvement strategy**   A modification in existing products.

**product life cycle**   The progression of a product through introduction, growth, maturity, and decline stages.

**product line**   A series of related products.

**product management**   Decisions about what kind of product is needed, its uses, package design, branding, trademarks, warranties, guarantees, product life cycles, and new-product development.

**product managers**   Individuals assigned one product or product line and given responsibility for determining its objectives and marketing strategies.

**product mix**   The assortment of product lines and individual offerings available from a marketer.

**product orientation**   A focus on the product itself rather than the consumer's needs.

**profit centre**   Any part of the organization to which revenue and controllable costs can be assigned, such as a department.

**profit maximization**   The point where the addition to total revenue is just balanced by an increase in total cost.

**promotional allowances**   Extra discounts offered to retailers so that they will advertise the manufacturer along with the retailer.

**promotional price**   A lower-than-normal price used as an ingredient in a firm's selling strategy.

**prospecting**   Identifying potential customers.

**psychographics**   The use of psychological attributes, lifestyles, and attitudes in determining the behavioural profiles of different consumers.

**psychological pricing**   Pricing based on the belief that certain prices or price ranges are more appealing to buyers than others.

**public relations**   A firm's effort to create favourable attention and word-of-mouth.

**public warehouse**   Independently owned storage facility.

**pulling strategy**   A promotional effort by the seller to stimulate final-user demand, which then exerts pressure on the distribution channel.

**pure competition**   A market structure where there is such a large number of buyers and sellers that no one of them has a significant influence on price.

**pushing strategy**   The promotion of the product first to the members of the marketing channel, who then participate in its promotion to the final user.

**qualifying**   Determining that the prospect is really a potential customer.

**quantity discounts**   Price reductions granted because of large purchases.

**quota sample**   A nonprobability sample that is divided so that different segments or groups are represented in the total sample.

**rack jobber**   Wholesaler who provides the racks, stocks the merchandise, prices the goods, and makes regular visits to refill the shelves.

**raw materials** Farm products (such as cattle, wool, eggs, milk, pigs, and canola) and natural products (such as coal, copper, iron ore, and lumber).

**rebates** Refunds by the seller of a portion of the purchase price.

**reciprocity** The extension of purchasing preference to suppliers who are also customers.

**reference group** A group whose value structures and standards influence a person's behaviour.

**regiocentric company** Firm that recognizes that countries with similar cultures and economic conditions can be served with a similar marketing mix.

**reinforcement** The reduction in drive that results from a proper response.

**reminder-oriented product advertising** Advertising whose goal is to reinforce previous promotional activity by keeping the product or service name in front of the public.

**research design** A series of advance decisions that, taken together, make up a master plan or model for conducting the investigation.

**response** The individual's reaction to the cues and drives.

**retail image** The consumer's perception of a store and of the shopping experience it provides.

**retail trade area analysis** Studies that assess the relative drawing power of alternative retail locations.

**retailer** A store that sells products purchased by individuals for their own use and not for resale.

**retailing** All the activities involved in the sale of goods and services to the ultimate consumer.

**revaluation** Situation in which a country adjusts the value of its currency upward.

**reverse channels** The paths goods follow from consumer to manufacturer or to marketing intermediaries.

**role** Rights and duties expected by other members of a group of the individual in a certain position in the group.

**sales branch** Manufacturer-owned facility that carries inventory and that processes orders to customers from available stock.

**sales management** Securing, maintaining, motivating, supervising, evaluating, and controlling the field sales force.

**sales maximization** The pricing philosophy analyzed by economist William J. Baumol. Baumol believes that many firms attempt to maximize sales within a profit constraint.

**sales office** Manufacturer-owned facility that does not carry stock but serves as a regional office for the firm's sales personnel.

**sales orientation** Focusing on developing a strong sales force to convince consumers to buy whatever the firm produces.

**sales promotion** Those marketing activities, other than personal selling, mass media advertising, and publicity, that stimulate consumer purchasing and dealer effectiveness.

**scrambled merchandising** The retail practice of carrying dissimilar lines to generate added sales volume.

**secondary data** Previously published matter.

**selective distribution** The selection of a small number of retailers to handle the firm's product line.

**selling agent** A wholesaling intermediary who is responsible for the total marketing program for a firm's product line.

**service** A product without physical characteristics; a bundle of performance and symbolic attributes designed to produce consumer want satisfaction.

**shaping** The process of applying a series of rewards and reinforcement so that more-complex behaviour can evolve over time.

**shopping products** Products that are usually purchased only after the consumer has compared competing products.

**simple random sample** A probability sample in which every item in the relevant universe has an equal opportunity of being selected.

**single-offer strategy** The attempt to satisfy a large or a small market with one product and a single marketing program.

**skimming pricing** A policy of selling first to consumers who are willing to pay the highest price, then reducing the price.

**social class** The relatively permanent divisions in a society into which individuals or families are categorized based on prestige and community status.

**social responsibility** The marketer's acceptance of the obligation to consider profit, consumer satisfaction, and the well-being of society as being of equal value in evaluating the performance of the firm.

**socio-cultural environment** The mosaic of societal and cultural components that are relevant to the business decisions of the organization.

**sorting** The process that alleviates discrepancies in assortment by re-allocating the outputs of various producers into assortments desired by individual purchasers.

**specialty advertising** Sales promotion medium that utilizes useful articles to carry the advertiser's name, address, and advertising message.

**specialty products** Products that are highest on both effort and risk, due to some unique characteristics that cause the buyer to prize that particular brand.

**specialty store**   Retailer that handles only part of a single line of products.

**specifications**   A description of the item or job that the buyer wishes to acquire. In the bidding process, specific descriptions of needed items for prospective bidders.

**SSWDs**   Single, separated, widowed, or divorced people.

**stagflation**   High unemployment and a rising price level at the same time.

**Standard Industrial Classification (SIC) codes**   A series of industrial classifications developed by the federal government for use in collecting detailed statistics for each industry.

**status**   Relative position in a group.

**status quo objectives**   Objectives based on the maintenance of stable prices.

**stock turnover**   The number of times the average inventory is sold annually.

**straight rebuy**   A recurring purchase decision involving an item that has performed satisfactorily and is therefore purchased again by a customer.

**subculture**   Subgroup with its own distinguishing modes of behaviour.

**subliminal perception**   A subconscious level of awareness.

**supermarket**   Large-scale, departmentalized retail store offering a large variety of food products.

**supplies**   Regular expense items necessary in the daily operation of a firm, but not part of its final product.

**supply curve**   The marginal cost curve above its intersection with the average variable cost.

**systematic sample**   A probability sample that takes every Nth item on a list, after a random start.

**target market decision analysis**   The evaluation of potential market segments.

**target return objectives**   Either short-run or long-run goals, usually stated as a percentage of sales or investment.

**tariff**   A tax levied against products imported from abroad.

**task-objective method**   A sequential approach to allocating marketing communications budgets that involves two steps: (1) define the particular goals that the firm wants the marketing communications mix to accomplish and (2) determine the amount and type of marketing communications activity required to accomplish each of these objectives.

**technological environment**   The applications of knowledge based on scientific discoveries, inventions, and innovations.

**teleshopping**   Ordering merchandise that has been displayed on home television sets or computers.

**test marketing**   Introducing a new, untried product into a particular metropolitan area and then observing its degree of success.

**tied selling**   An arrangement whereby a supplier forces a dealer who wishes to handle a product to also carry other products from the supplier or to refrain from using or distributing someone else's product.

**total quality management (TQM)**   Concept that for every customer-impinging activity, nothing less than total quality is acceptable.

**trade discounts**   Payments to channel members or buyers for performing some marketing function normally required of the manufacturer.

**trade fairs**   Periodic shows at which manufacturers in a particular industry display their wares for visiting retail and wholesale buyers.

**trade industries**   Organizations, such as retailers and wholesalers, that purchase for resale to others.

**trade-ins**   Deductions from an item's price of an amount for the customer's old item that is being replaced.

**trademark**   A brand that has been given legal protection and has been granted solely to its owner.

**transfer price**   The price for sending goods from one company profit centre to another.

**truck wholesaler**   Limited-function merchant wholesaler who markets perishable food items.

**uniform delivered price**   The same price (including transporting expenses) is quoted to all buyers.

**unit pricing**   A system whereby all prices are stated in terms of some recognized unit of measurement (such as grams and litres) or a standard numerical count.

**unitization**   Combining as many packages as possible into one load.

**Universal Product Code**   A code readable by optical scanners that can print the name of the item and the price on the cash-register receipt.

**utility**   The want-satisfying power of a product or service.

**value added**   The increase in value of input material when transformed into semi-finished or finished goods.

**variety store**   Retailer that handles an extensive range and assortment of low-priced merchandise.

**venture-team concept**   An organizational strategy for developing new products through combining the management resources of technology, capital, management, and marketing enterprise.

**vertical marketing systems**   Professionally managed and centrally programmed networks pre-engineered to achieve operating economies and maximum impact.

**warranty**    A guarantee to the buyer that the supplier will replace a defective product (or part of a product) or refund its purchase price during a specified period of time.

**Weber's Law**    The higher the initial intensity of a stimulus, the greater the amount of the change in intensity that is necessary in order for a difference to be noticed.

**wheel of retailing**    Hypothesized process of change in retailing, which suggests that new types of retailers gain a competitive foothold by offering lower prices through the reduction or elimination of services; but once established, they add more services and their prices gradually rise, so that they then become vulnerable to a new low-price retailer with minimum services — and the wheel turns.

**wholesalers**    Wholesaling intermediaries who take title to the products they handle.

**wholesaling**    The activities of persons or firms who sell to retailers, other wholesalers, and industrial users but not in significant amounts to ultimate consumers.

**wholesaling intermediaries**    Intermediaries who assume title, as well as agents and brokers who perform important wholesaling activities without taking title to the products.

**zone pricing**    The market is divided into different zones and a price is established within each.

# Photo Credits

Pg. 448, Jeff Smith/The Image Bank
Canada
Pg. 451, TV Ontario
Pg. 454, Jay Freis/The Image Bank
Canada
Pg. 458, Edmonton Journal/Canapress
Photo Service

**Chapter 17**
Pg. 470, Tonia Cowan/Canapress Photo
Service
Pg. 476, Du Pont Canada
Pg. 481, Stan Behal/Canada Wide
Feature Services Limited

Pg. 482, Cadbury Canada Marketing Inc.

**Chapter 18**
Pg. 496, Craig Robertson/Canada Wide
Feature Services Limited
Pg. 502, Du Pont Canada
Pg. 506, Shell Canada
Pg. 507, Dow Chemical Canada Inc.
Pg. 508, Ford Motor Company of Canada
Pg. 513, Johnson & Johnson Inc.

**Chapter 19**
Pg. 534, Uniphoto/Canapress Photo
Service
Pg. 537, ICI Canada Inc.

Pg. 541, Tonia Cowan/Canapress Photo
Service
Pg. 552, Industry, Science and
Technology Canada

**Chapter 20**
Pg. 560, Vancouver Symphony Orchestra
Pg. 563, Heart and Stroke Foundation
Pg. 568, Town Office, High River, Alberta

**Chapter 21**
Pg. 576, Uniphoto/Canapress Photo
Service
Pg. 581, Bell Canada

# Name and Company Index

# Subject Index

**To the Owner of This Book:**

We are interested in your reaction to *Foundations of Marketing*, fifth Canadian edition, by M. Dale Beckman, David L. Kurtz, and Louis E. Boone. With your comments, we can improve this book in future editions. Please help us by completing this questionnaire.

1. What was your reason for using this book?
   _____ university course
   _____ college course
   _____ continuing education course
   _____ personal interest
   _____ other (specify)

2. If you used this text for a program, what was the name of that program?

3. Which school do you attend?

4. Approximately how much of the book did you use?
   _____ 1/4 _____ 1/2 _____ 3/4 _____ all

5. Which chapters or sections were omitted from your course?

6. What is the best aspect of this book?

7. Is there anything that should be added?

8. Please add any comments or suggestions.

**fold here**

_____

NOTES

# NOTES

NOTES

# NOTES

NOTES

# NOTES

NOTES

NOTES

NOTES

NOTES